My 1980s & Other Essays

Wayne Koestenbaum

Farrar, Straus and Giroux
18 West 18th Street, New York 10011

Printed in the United States of America
First edition, 2013

Grateful acknowledgment is made for permission to reprint the following previously published material:

Lines from "The Changes" from *The Collected Poems of Robert Creeley: 1945–1975*, The University of California Press.

Lines from "On Rachmaninoff's Birthday." Copyright © 1964 by Frank O'Hara. Reprinted by permission of City Lights Books.

"Poem" ("I do not always understand what you say"), "Salute," and excerpts from "Poem" ("This beauty that I see"), "The Bluet," "Blizzard," "A few days," "Horse-Chestnut Trees and Roses," and "Korean mums" from *Collected Poems* by James Schuyler. Copyright © 1993 by the Estate of James Schuyler. Reprinted by permission of Farrar, Straus and Giroux, LLC.

"Poem (O sole mio, hot diggety, nix 'I wather think I can')" from *The Collected Poems of Frank O'Hara* by Frank O'Hara, edited by Donald Allen, copyright © 1971 by Maureen Granville-Smith, Administratrix of the Estate of Frank O'Hara, copyright renewed 1999 by Maureen O'Hara Granville-Smith and Donald Allen. Used by permission of Alfred A. Knopf, a division of Random House, Inc. Any third party use of this material, outside of this publication, is prohibited. Interested parties must apply directly to Random House, Inc. for permission.

Library of Congress Cataloging-in-Publication Data
Koestenbaum, Wayne.
My 1980s & other essays / Wayne Koestenbaum. — First edition.
pages cm
ISBN 978-0-374-53377-9 (pbk.)
I. Title. II. Title: My 1980s and other essays. III. Title: My nineteen eighties.

AC8.K815 2013
814'.54—dc23

2013002333

Designed by Jonathan D. Lippincott

www.fsgbooks.com
www.twitter.com/fsgbooks • www.facebook.com/fsgbooks

10 9 8 7 6 5 4 3 2

for Steven Marchetti

and

for Lisa S. Rubinstein

Contents

IV.

V.

VI.

I.

My 1980s

> Les Fleuves m'ont laissé descendre où je voulais.
>
> —Arthur Rimbaud

I met Tama Janowitz once in the 1980s. (Was it 1987?) She probably doesn't remember our encounter. She was a visiting fellow at Princeton, where I was a graduate student in English. At a university gathering, Joyce Carol Oates complimented the ostentatious way that Tama and I were dressed. Seeking system, I replied, "Tama is East Village. I'm West Village."

•

I had little to do with art in the eighties. I saw Caravaggio in Rome, and Carpaccio in Venice. I neglected the contemporary. For half the decade I lived in New York City, and yet I didn't go to a single Andy Warhol opening. Missed opportunities? My mind was elsewhere.

•

My mind was on *écriture feminine* as applied to homosexuals. I was big on the word *homosexual.* I read *Homosexualities and French Literature* (edited by George Stambolian and Elaine Marks). I read Hélène Cixous. On a train I read *Roland Barthes by Roland Barthes* (translated by Richard Howard); I looked out dirty windows onto dirty New Jersey fields. I began to take autobiography seriously as a historical practice with intellectual integrity. On an airplane I read Michel Leiris's

Manhood (translated by Richard Howard) and grooved to Leiris's mention of a "bitten buttock"; I decided to become, like Leiris, a self-ethnographer. I read André Gide's *Immoralist* (translated by Richard Howard) in Hollywood, Florida, while lying on a pool deck. I read many books translated by Richard Howard. In the eighties I read *The Fantastic* by Tzvetan Todorov (translated by Richard Howard) and meditated on the relation between fantasy and autobiography. I brought Richard Howard flowers the first time I met him (1985), in his book-lined apartment. He assured me that I was a poet.

•

I discovered the word *essentialism* in the late eighties. I should have discovered it earlier. Sex-and-gender essentialism was a dread fate. I feared that it was my condition. Essentialists believed in God and trusted the government. In the early nineties, after I stopped worrying about my essentialism, I realized that I'd never been an essentialist after all.

•

Too many of these sentences begin with the first-person-singular pronoun. Later I may jazz up the syntax, falsify it.

•

I am typing this essay on the IBM Correcting Selectric III typewriter I bought in 1981 for one thousand dollars. I borrowed the money from my older brother, a cellist. It took me several years to pay him back.

•

In the eighties I worked as a legal secretary, a paralegal, and a legal proofreader. I freelanced as a typist, $1.50 per page. I temped for Kelly Girl; one pleasurable assignment was a stint at the Girl Scouts headquarters. I taught seventh- through twelfth-grade English at a yeshiva. I tutored a man from Japan in English conversation. I didn't turn a single trick.

•

This morning I asked my boyfriend, an architect, about the 1980s. I said, "Let's make a list of salient features of our eighties." We came up with just two items: cocaine, AIDS.

•

In 1980 after Reagan was elected I began, in repulsed reaction, to read the *New York Times.* Before then, I'd never read the newspaper.

•

I remember a specific homeless woman on the Upper West Side in the 1980s. She smelled predictably of pee or shit and hung out in an ATM parlor near the Seventy-Second Street subway stop. She seemed to rule the space. Large, she epitomized. Did I ever give her money? I blamed Reagan.

•

A stranger smooched me during a "Read My Lips" kiss-in near the Jefferson Market Public Library: festive politics. 1985? I stumbled on the ceremony. Traffic stopped.

•

A cute short blond guy named Mason used to brag about sex parties; I was jealous. I didn't go to sex parties. He ended up dying of AIDS. I'm not pushing a cause-and-effect argument.

•

In 1985 I read Mario Mieli's *Homosexuality and Liberation.* I bought, but did not read, an Italian periodical, hefty and intellectually substantial, called *Sodoma: Rivista Omosessuale di Cultura.* That year, I turned to Georges Bataille for bulletins on the solar anus, for lessons on smart, principled obscenity.

•

A handsome brunet poet came to my apartment, and I dyed his hair blond. I had a crush on him. He talked a lot about Michel Foucault. The poet and I bought the dye on Sixth Avenue in the Village. In my kitchen he stripped to his undershorts, which had holes. His nipples were large and erect: impressive! I'd never seen such ready-to-go nipples. He leaned over the kitchen sink; I washed his hair and applied the dye. I kept on my undershirt during the session; I wasn't proud of my body (though in retrospect I respect its scrawiness). I continued to read Foucault throughout the eighties. Foucault never deeply moved me. I switched to Maurice Blanchot in the late nineties.

•

My boyfriend worked out downstairs. We lived above a gay gym: the Body Center, corner of Sixth and Fifteenth, now the David Barton Gym. After midnight we could hear loud music coming through our radiators: the Body Center's cleaning crew had turned up the sound system.

•

Geographical facts: during the 1980s, I lived in Cambridge, Baltimore, New York, New Haven. The important city was New York: 1984–1988. There, I worked out at the McBurney Y. I swam in its skanky, dank, tiny, cloudy, over-warm pool. I recall a not-handsome guy shaving off his body hair at the sink. Careful, I didn't once enter the Y's cramped sauna.

•

I read all of Proust in summer 1986. Proust and summer passed quickly. That same summer I reread James Schuyler's *Morning of the Poem* and experienced an AIDS-panic-related sense of life's brevity; houseguest, I sat on an Adirondack chair in Southold, Long Island. My host, hardy in the garden, was ill with AIDS. I recall wild blueberries I picked with him, and his reticence, and mine.

•

In 1986 or '87 I heard Eve Kosofsky Sedgwick give a lecture on "unknowing" in Diderot's *The Nun*. I had just read her *Between Men*. Her difficult lucidity gave my stumbling concepts one warm, fruitful context.

•

In 1984 I took a course in feminist theory with Elaine Showalter and decided to be a male feminist. I decided not to write a dissertation about John Ashbery and W. H. Auden. Instead, I wanted to write a flaming treatise. In a seminar on the Victorian novel, Showalter showed slides of Charcot's hysterics in *arcs-en-cercle* and of fin de siècle faces disfigured by syphilis. I flipped out with intellectual glee. Hysteria would be my open sesame.

•

In the eighties I was happiest when writing "syllabic" poems. Superstitiously I discovered my existence's modicum of dignity and value by counting duration in syllables, on my fingers, while I typed, on the same Selectric I am using now.

•

I saw *Taxi zum Klo* and *Diva*: two films that made a dent. I went to all the gay movies. *L'homme blessé*. On TV I saw *Brideshead Revisited* and the Patrice Chéreau production of Wagner's *Ring*. I went to Charlie Chan movies (guilty pleasure) at Theater 80 St. Marks; there, my treat was buying a blue mint from the transparent vessel on the dim-lit lobby's counter. I saw *Shoah*: only the first part. I heard Leonie Rysanek sing Elisabeth in *Tannhäuser* and Ortrud in *Lohengrin* and Kundry in *Parsifal* at the Met, and Sieglinde in *Die Walküre* in San Francisco. I heard Christa Ludwig's twenty-fifth-anniversary performance at the Met: Klytämnestra in Strauss's *Elektra,* December 20, 1984.

•

I wore a bright red Kikit baseball jacket and red espadrilles. I decided that bright blue and red—DayGlo, neon, opalescent—were passports to private revolution. I wore a paisley tux jacket and black patent-leather cowboy boots. I didn't mind looking vulgar, slutty, off-base.

•

I spent a lot of the eighties thinking about Anna Moffo, soprano—her career's ups and downs, and her timbre's uncanny compromise between vulnerability and voluptuousness. I regret not buying her Debussy song album, used, at Academy Records on West Eighteenth Street: on the soft-focus cover, she wore a summer hat. The LP era ended.

•

I focused on my sadness as if it were an object in the room, a discrete, dense entity, impervious to alteration. I never used the word *subjectivity* in the 1980s, though I was fond of *gap*, *blank page*, *masculine*, and *feminine*. I planned to call my first book of poems *Queer Street*, nineteenth-century British slang for shady circumstances, debt, bankrupty, blackmail. I found the phrase in Robert Louis Stevenson's *The Strange Case of Dr. Jekyll and Mr. Hyde*.

•

In 1980 my new boyfriend gave me a 45 rpm single (blue-labeled Chrysalis) of Blondie's "Call Me" (from *American Gigolo*). We considered it our theme song. Then I stopped listening to "popular" music. Not consciously. Not programmatically. The defection happened naturally.

•

In 1981 I made an onion-bacon-apple casserole from *The Joy of Cooking*. I served it, as a main dish, to a schizophrenic friend. A few years later she sent me a letter, dated 1975. This significant confusion of chronology meant that she had cracked up. I began methodically to cook from Marcella Hazan. I tirelessly stirred risotto in a cheap aluminum saucepan with high sides. I made a *bombe aux trois chocolats* from Julia Child: a molded dessert, for which I used a beige Tupperware bowl.

•

In 1983 I served a friend a veal roast stuffed with pancetta. We agreed that the roast tasted like human baby. We blamed the pancetta.

•

Sometime in the mid-eighties I stopped swallowing cum. I don't miss its taste.

•

The first guy I knew with AIDS died at age thirty-five. His name was Metro. I've written about this death before, and I hesitate to repeat myself. I have almost no visual memory of Metro, though I recall his precision and hypercapability; we lay on a stony beach, Long Island Sound, more rock than sand. What sand there was he dusted off his body with decisive, practiced gestures.

•

I went to Paris for the first time in the eighties: I wore blue leather gloves purchased on Christopher Street. In a rue Jacob hotel bedroom I woke up, sweat-drenched, feverish; I observed the wallpaper's mesmerizing, dull pattern, its refusal to serve as reliable augury. On the flight back from Paris I read Marianne Moore's prose and picked up pointers from its ornery mannerism.

•

Despite my best efforts, I existed in history, not as agent but as frightened, introspective observer. I began to fine-tune my sentences—a fastidiousness I learned from Moore's prose. Precise sentences were my ideals, though in practice I was slipshod and sentimental. I began to seek a balance between improvisation and revision. I revised by endlessly retyping.

•

I read Freud in the eighties. He was always describing me, my likenesses, my forebears. Anna O. became my touchstone. I decided that psychoanalysis was the hysterical child born from Freud's anus.

•

In 1981 I read Susan Sontag's *On Photography*. In 1982 I read her *Under the Sign of Saturn*. I swore allegiance to the aphorism. But I didn't read Walter Benjamin until the nineties.

•

In 1981 I published for the first time: a story, "In the White Forest," in a small periodical, *The Pale Fire Review*. In 1982 I stopped writing fiction. The last story I wrote, "Liberty Baths," autobiographically reported my San Francisco bathhouse experiences of summer 1979. A guy I met at the baths took me to his loft. A commercial photographer, he shot a whole roll of me nude, from the rear. I was insulted that he didn't photograph me frontally. I should have been grateful that he found one angle comely.

•

I spent the summer of 1983 writing fifty sonnets. My stylistic model was Auden's sequence *In Time of War*: I loved his phrase "Anxiety / Receives them like a grand hotel." I put together a manuscript called, unadventurously, "Fifty Sonnets." It never got published as a book. In one of the sonnets, I rhymed "Callas" and "callous."

•

The world was doing its best to ignore the fact that I was a writer. In search of fragile legitimacy, I obsessively submitted work to periodicals. Rejection slips arrived, sometimes with a beckoning "Thanks!" or "Sorry!" or "Send more?" I always sent more, immediately, with a treacly letter, informing the hapless editor how much the invitation to send more had meant to me.

•

I was not thinking about the world. I was not thinking about history. I was thinking about my body's small, precise, limited, hungry movement forward into a future that seemed at every instant on the verge of being shut down.

•

I didn't take the HIV test until the nineties. I spent most of the eighties worried about being HIV-positive, only discovering, in the nineties, that I was negative. My attitude in the eighties was: wait and see. Wait for symptoms. When a friend suggested I get tested, I broke off the friendship. It wasn't much of a friendship. She wanted us to write a collaborative book on Verdi's Oedipus complex. A semi-invalid, she sent me on errands to buy dollhouse furniture—her hobby.

•

I heard Leontyne Price sing a recital at the Met on March 24, 1985. I still remember the sensation of her voice in my body. I think she gave "Chi il bel sogno di Doretta" from *La Rondine* as an encore.

•

I read Jacques Derrida's *Spurs* (translated by Barbara Harlow). I wondered why he didn't use male testicles—instead of vaginas and veils—as metaphors. Invaginate, indeed! In the 1980s I made snap judgments.

•

Poems I published in the eighties, in small periodicals, but never collected into a book: "Where I Lived, and What I Lived For"; "*Carmen* in Digital for a Deaf Woman"; "Teachers of Obscure Subjects"; "The Babysitter in the Ham Radio." I published my first full-length essay in 1987: its polite subtitle was "Oblique Confession in the Early Work of John Ashbery."

•

In the eighties I wrote book reviews for the *New York Native*, a now-defunct gay newspaper. Among my subjects: James

Schuyler's *A Few Days*, John Ashbery's *April Galleons*, Sylvère Lotringer's *Overexposed: Treating Sexual Perversion in America*.

•

Does any of this information matter? I am not responsible for what matters and what doesn't matter. Offbeat definition of materialism: a worldview in which every detail matters, in which every factual statement is material.

•

I bought soft-core porn magazines—*Mandate*, *Honcho*, others—from a newsstand on Fourteenth Street. I felt guilty about my insatiably scopophilic core; culpable, it could never get its fill of images. Over the years I began to notice changes in porn bodies: the men were growing younger. Now, when I look back at those magazines (I've saved many), the men seem like old friends, guys I went to school with. Max Archer. Chad Douglas. Jesus.

•

I have always had a rather limited circle of friends; although I am superficially gregarious, most human contact makes me, eventually, uncomfortable. I didn't realize this fact in the eighties. During those years, I was intensely ill at ease.

•

I stopped using drugs (pot, cocaine) when I began to take AIDS seriously. Health suddenly mattered: I wanted always to feel tip-top, without chemical enhancement.

•

If my eighties don't match yours, chalk up the mismatch to the fact that I am profoundly out of touch with my time. I never chose to nominate myself as historical witness.

•

Notice, please, my absence of nostalgia.

•

I started dyeing my hair in 1984: reddish highlights. I stopped in 1988. I returned to nature.

•

My mission in the eighties was to develop my aestheticism. My mission in the nineties was to justify my aestheticism.

•

In 1988 I started teaching at Yale. I decided to wear bow ties. I had several: red polka-dot; blue polka-dot; amber with black triangles; neon yellow. The first semester, I taught a required core course on Chaucer, Spenser, and Donne. I also taught my first elective: a seminar decorously titled "Literature and Sexuality: Countertraditions." I was hyperconscious of authorities. In 1989, I published my first book, *Double Talk: The Erotics of Male Literary Collaboration*. When the published book first arrived in my apartment, I admired its cover—George Platt Lynes's photograph *The Second Birth of Dionysus*—but wished the book were a novel instead: same cover, different contents.

•

In New Haven, outside my apartment, 1989, I was mugged. A guy said, "Give me your wallet or I'll blow your brains out."

•

In 1989 I developed a sustaining, mood-brightening crush on the UPS man. Hundreds—thousands—of men and women in New Haven must have had a crush on that same UPS man. The first time he appeared at my doorstep with a package, I thought that a *Candid Camera* porn movie had just begun. If you want me to describe him, I will.

•

When I look back at the eighties I see myself as a small boat. It is not an important, attractive, or likable boat, but it has a prow, a sail, and a modest personality. It has no consciousness of the water it moves through. Some days it resembles Rimbaud's inebriated vessel. Other, clearer days, it is sober and undemonstrative. There are few images or adjectives we could affix to the boat; there are virtually no ways to classify it. Its only business is staying afloat. Thus the boat is amoral. It has been manufactured in a certain style. Any style contains a history. The boat is not conscious of the history shaping its movements. The boat, undramatic, passive, at best pleasant, at worst slapdash, persistently attends to the work of flotation, which takes precedence over responsible navigation. As far as the boat is concerned, it is the only vessel on the body of water. How many times must I repeat the word *boat* to convince you that in the eighties I was a small boat with a minor mission and a fear of sinking? The boat did not sink.

(2003)

Heidegger's Mistress

> We have grown very poor in threshold experiences. Falling asleep is perhaps the only such experience that remains to us. (But together with this, there is also waking up.)
>
> —Walter Benjamin

1

I'm trying to figure out why—or how—or if—I became intellectual.

One place to begin: the time my mother "pulled a knife" on my father.

The expression "pulled a knife"—is it correct?

I think a kitchen knife.

Certainly a knife from the kitchen drawer.

Probably not a steak knife.

Perhaps a bread knife.

Just a soft-edged relatively harmless butter knife.

Let's say she was making a statement.

Her performance had two direct witnesses.

One, my father. He saw her "pull the knife."

Two, my father's aunt, Alice.

Seated in a black chair, she was waiting for my father to drive her home.

My father and his aunt Alice often spoke together in German.

My mother didn't understand German.

I imagine that she "pulled the knife" as a performance directly aimed at the aunt.

The act—"pulling a knife"—had two other indirect witnesses.

My sister saw it. I saw it. We were standing in the hallway. Later we talked about the incident.

It has become, for us, a touchstone.

"The time Mom pulled a knife on Dad": that scene is a card we sometimes play; a trick we pull out of our hat; a piece of evidence.

What does it prove?

2

Did I mention that my mother was angry when she "pulled the knife"?

I don't remember whether she put it back in the drawer afterward or whether she left it on the kitchen counter.

I don't know what she was angry about.

3

I write this way not merely because I enjoy being irreverent or atopical but because when AIDS hit in the early 1980s I decided not to waste my maybe-very-short life writing what I didn't want to write or obeying rules that in the grand scheme of things (death) didn't exist. The imminence of nothingness was the only rule I would obey.

4

If you care about words you learn quite early in life that it is evil to lie.

5

I'm trying to figure out why—or how—or if—I became intellectual.

My father and I had an interesting conversation recently, when, on his world travels, he came to New York and we had dinner.

I told him I was reading Martin Heidegger.

Then my father told me the following story. Forgive me if my version contains accidental inaccuracies.

6

My father met Heidegger's mistress in Caracas, Venezuela. My father's good friend at the time, Ernst Tugendhat, introduced them.

Ernst, like my father, was a Jewish refugee: the Tugendhats had left Brno, Czechoslovakia, where they had lived in a famous house designed for them by Ludwig Mies van der Rohe.

My father's parents were uneducated, poor. The Tugendhats listened seriously and solemnly to Beethoven quartets on their record player in Caracas.

Heidegger's mistress gave Ernst Tugendhat, my father's friend, a box of Heidegger's lecture notes, which Ernst eventually translated.

Ernst and my father left Caracas in 1945 to go to Stanford. My father was seventeen. World War II had just ended.

After a period at Stanford, Tugendhat returned to Germany to study with Heidegger, and became an important analytical philosopher.

While at Stanford, my father was technically a displaced person, under custody of the United Nations. To keep his identity papers current, once a year he had to meet a Venezuelan diplomat on the streets of San Francisco and bribe this shady functionary with a few hundred dollars cash.

7

I'm trying to figure out sequence: how paragraphs connect; how generations overlap; how ideas bleed into one another. My subjects include the interdependence of fragments; the weight of incidents; subordination and insubordination; hierarchy; demonstration and denotation; shadow and palimpsest; argumentation and allusion; name-dropping and citation; causality and the aleatory; my old chestnut, overdetermination; fact and speculation; melodrama and sentimentality; time-wasting; performance and being-buried-alive; cop-out and aporia; agency and knifepoint; the beauty of detachment; misalignments; leaving projects dead and incomplete in their midst and not regretting the abandonment.

8

My father's father, Ernst—yes, the same first name as my father's friend Ernst Tugendhat—wanted my father to stay in Caracas and become a gentleman farmer, to acquire a coffee plantation. I doubt that a coffee plantation was in the offing. Forgoing agriculture, instead my father went with Ernst Tugendhat, Heideggerian, to Stanford.

I met my father's father only once. I don't remember the encounter, but I have seen a photograph of it: discontented contextless black-and-white snapshot, underexposed despite California sunshine.

9

I don't yet know the full meaning of what I am telling you. My drift concerns the romance of uncompleted projects.

10

Walter Benjamin wrote that we—moderns—are very poor in threshold experiences. We have many boundary experiences.

But we are remote from the homeland of the threshold. Perhaps only when we are falling asleep do we fully experience that lost, ungraspable, nonexistent place.

To break up a piece of writing is—I hope—to extend the threshold. When a piece of writing knows its destructibility, its frangibility, it occupies the threshold.

11

I never met my father's mother, Ilse. She died in 1940; I was born in 1958. My father often used to say that emigration from Berlin killed her; she never adjusted to Venezuela, and died of a heart condition.

My father says she was "soft." What is soft?

12

My father and his parents, uncertain whether any country would accept them, took a ship from Hamburg on January 2, 1937; they arrived in Caracas on January 18, 1937. They brought twenty-five German marks and a Leica camera.

If, magically, I found that Leica camera, and took pictures with it, what would I be photographing?

13

According to my father, his father never lost his heavy German accent.

When he arrived in Caracas, my grandfather changed the spelling of his last name: Köstenbaum turned to Koestenbaum.

I regret the transformation.

14

My father's father in Germany sold wheat to bakeries. He was a grain middleman. I am forty-four years old, and I just discovered two months ago that my father's father in Germany had been a grain middleman.

A middleman is not poor in threshold experiences.

15

My father recently told me that when I was young we had problem neighbors. The family next door had a cat that defecated in our side yard, in the gravel outside my parents' bedroom. Apparently we set a trap and then sent the cat to the pound. That incident started a feud with the neighbors. Their son broke our fence.

16

Describe Heidegger's mistress.

Explain why she moved to Venezuela.

Describe her voluptuousness, from my father's point of view.

What was she wearing when my father met her?

How fancy was her Caracas home?

List Heidegger's mistresses.

Rank them, by length of time spent with Heidegger, or by physical attractiveness (as assessed by my father, as told to me).

Find a photo of the Tugendhat house, designed by Mies van der Rohe, in Brno.

Find a photo of Carlotta, my father's father's second wife.

17

I never met Carlotta. I used to fantasize about flying to Caracas and finding her.

Once, in the mid-1960s, she telephoned our house in San Jose, California, to tell my father that his father, Ernst, had died.

Three sentences my father said to me in a recent conversation:

I'm only interested in the future.
I didn't go to my father's funeral.
I've never seen my father's grave.

18

Emotion is, at the moment, missing from this essay. I'll add emotion later. Emotion is the middleman, sometimes left invisible in the transaction.

19

How precisely can you approach the one thing it is your project to say? You certainly aren't going to let anyone else's ideas of propriety interfere. Why mask your articulations, muting their force, maintaining conventional appearances? Refuse verbal compromise.

20

On the Internet I found the Tugendhat house. It exists. It is a fact. Villa Tugendhat was constructed between 1928 and 1930 by Mies van der Rohe for Grete and Fritz Tugendhat in Brno.

21

More facts about Villa Tugendhat. The Tugendhat family left Brno for Venezuela in 1938. The Gestapo occupied Villa Tugendhat in 1939. A bomb damaged it in 1944. Red Army soldiers occupied it in April 1945. Now it is a museum.

22

Now I feel the urge to leap into an entirely different subject. Here is a story that always made a huge impression on me and that I don't entirely wish to tell.

23

My mother in 1949 or 1950 was one of only two women in a creative writing seminar at Harvard. The rest of the students were men. (Technically, she was not a Harvard student; she was a Radcliffe student.) The other young woman in the seminar was Adrienne Rich.

That story used to make me feel like literary royalty, once removed. I realize that this feeling is illegitimate and unfounded.

In 1976, when I was a freshman at Harvard, I took a creative writing seminar taught by Cynthia Rich, Adrienne's sister. I developed a crush on Cynthia. In the first short story I wrote for her seminar (the story was almost entirely autobiographical), I mentioned that my mother had been Adrienne Rich's classmate. Cynthia professed to like my story: she read it aloud to our workshop. When she came to the line that mentioned her sister, Cynthia didn't falter. Nor did she stop to say, "Adrienne Rich happens to be my sister. What a coincidence!" The allusion in the story was my private signal to Cynthia. I don't know what I was trying to communicate. She must have been irritated to see her famous sister's name dropped in a fawning student's composition.

Two years later I asked Cynthia if she would do an independent writing tutorial with me. She refused.

24

Has Adrienne Rich ever read Heidegger?

Has Ernst Tugendhat, Heideggerian, ever read Adrienne Rich?

25

On my father's bookshelf, when I was a child:

Simone de Beauvoir, *The Second Sex*.

Jean-Paul Sartre, *Saint Genet.*

On my mother's bookshelf:

Edmund Spenser, *The Faerie Queen.*

A Georges Simenon mystery, paperback, in French. I don't recall its title.

26

While writing this essay, I am reading Simone de Beauvoir's *Adieux: A Farewell to Sartre* (in translation), and Iris Murdoch's *Sartre: Romantic Rationalist.* I can take Sartre only from the woman's angle.

27

Recently my father told me that in the early 1960s he was on a panel discussion with Marianne Moore, somewhere in the Bay Area. Must now my father be my middleman to Moore? Is my connection to Moore enriched by the triangulation?

28

My mother told me that William Carlos Williams long ago came to read in San Jose, and that she didn't go to hear him. My father seemed vaguely to blame. Either he refused to drive her (she didn't yet have a license) or else he didn't encourage her to go, or help make it possible. *The time my mother didn't hear William Carlos Williams read in San Jose* is an important family story, though not as important as the story of *the time my parents heard T. S. Eliot read at Harvard.*

29

Walter Benjamin insists that *boundary* and *threshold* are not the same: "The threshold must be carefully distinguished from the boundary."

30

Fact, discovered on the Internet: a symposium was held at the University of California, San Francisco Medical Center, on January 25, 26, and 27, 1963. The symposium, in which my father took part, was called "The Potential of Woman"; it was the third annual conference in a series called "Man and Civilization." Afterward, a book was published, entitled *The Potential of Woman*. I remember seeing it on my father's shelf. I don't have a copy, and the New York Public Library's copy is missing.

I don't know what my father said about the potential of woman. At the time, I was four years old.

I wonder if my mother read his talk. I wonder what she thought of it, and what she thought, in January 1963, about the potential of woman.

31

As far as I can judge from the photo on the Villa Tugendhat website, the house seems mostly threshold. Mies van der Rohe brought outside inside. A glass wall faces the garden, as in the Eichler homes I saw, as a youth, in nearby, affluent, enviable Palo Alto.

32

In 1961, when I was three years old, my father published a translation of *The Paris Lectures* by the phenomenologist Edmund Husserl. The translation is dedicated to my mother: momentarily Husserl played middleman. When my father was doing the work of translating, I was probably one year old. A translator is a middleman. So is a one-year-old.

Here is a quotation chosen more or less at random from my father's introduction to the Husserl translation:

"The following example might clarify the point. I perceive a doorknob at this moment. The doorknob is not a diaphanous apparition but an intentional object. Part of the meaning of this particular doorknob is that it has been there for a long time, and that it will continue to be there. I make the tacit prediction that, if I touch it, the doorknob would feel hard and enable me to open the door."

Is the door a threshold or a boundary? I will call it a threshold—a zone in which to dwell, however briefly. A boundary, on the other hand, is a prohibition, a fence, not to be crossed, occupied, or trespassed upon.

My father's introduction reminds the reader that Husserl, a Jew, a teacher of Heidegger's, "was stripped of his professorship and teaching privileges by the Nazis in 1933." Husserl's papers are now, according to my father's introduction, in Louvain, Belgium, "forty thousand pages of unpublished manuscripts." (Of Louvain, Gertrude Stein writes, in *The Autobiography of Alice B. Toklas*: "Gertrude Stein desperately unhappy said to me, where is Louvain. Don't you know, I said. No, she said, nor do I care, but where is it.") As my father writes, in his introduction: "After several unsuccessful attempts to sneak the manuscripts across the Swiss border as a nun's baggage or to interest a Belgian consulate to take charge of the bulky materials, Van Breda persuaded the Belgian Embassy in Berlin to declare the suitcases containing the manuscripts as Belgian property and thus have them covered by the immunity of the diplomatic pouch."

I seek for myself the immunity of the diplomatic pouch.

I seek, for everything I write, the immunity of the diplomatic pouch.

(2005)

Advice to the Young

1

I don't like being in the position of giving advice. So, instead of occupying that unpleasant, bossy role, I will tell you about a humiliating experience that you should avoid replicating in your own life.

2

Come to think of it, I don't want to tell you about that incident.

3

My hair was almost cute when I was a college junior, but I didn't know it. My skin was smooth. All I wanted was tough-guy dermis. Now I would like to go back in time and appreciate my own former hair and skin.

4

In 1978 I tried to cruise for sex with guys in the Castro. Nineteen years old, I sat on the steps of a bank and tried to look appealing in my sailor shirt. My attempt to pan for gold came up with naught. Advice: understand your own cuteness before it is too late and you've lost it.

5

I never approached older powerful people; I thought they'd consider me presumptuous, a young twit. Now I know: oldsters like to be flattered. So why wasn't I more brave? In the restroom of the Morgan Library I met the great poet James Merrill and he complimented my peacock-blue silk jacket, and what did I say in response? Nothing. I should have followed him to the urinal. Instead I washed my hands and fled. Why didn't I try to pick him up, so I could now be telling my "I had sex with James Merrill" story?

6

Premature moral: utilize your youthful sexiness before it runs dry.

7

I stood beside a record player, listening to Bach or Berg, with a conducting student five years my senior. (I was seventeen.) I'll call him Keith; he might be dead by now. (I looked him up on the Internet. References stopped at 1991.) A mutual friend—a seventeen-year-old girl I'll call Ramona—had said, "Keith is bi." As if bisexuality were news! Ramona had seduced the conducting student. I envied the conquest. I didn't try seducing Keith myself. Perhaps I would have succeeded. At that time I was still a virgin and didn't have the slightest idea how to lure someone into bed. Keith's slim face appears to me in dreams as an echo of my own, but it was not myself I wished to seduce; I wanted Keith, though he lacked charm. Embracing him would have told me how to endure the next decade, the drunk years, the scholarly and loquacious years, when I wasted half my days talking and the other half hiding. Now I wish I had spent more time listening to contemporary music, and less time making pesto. I suppose I could have listened to contemporary music *while* making pesto. Today I like difficult, recondite works, like Luciano Berio's music for solo piano, which plays on the boom box as I write this essay.

8

I wonder what happened to Keith the conducting student and why his disappearance matters to me. I knew him only for a few days. We stood near a record player in his dorm room.

9

Keith was also a composer. I never heard any of his pieces. Illegitimate, I existed on the music school's outskirts. Keith, on the other hand, was a star.

10

I admired the fact that Keith had slept with Ramona, my charismatic friend, who had a penchant for gay men. It never occurred to me that Ramona and Keith and I together in bed might have set off sparks.

11

Keith the conducting student: I hardly remember his face. All I see is a sliver of dimness, like hibernation, and a slenderness like my own.

12

Did I say anything seductive to Keith? Did I introduce myself as a sexual being, or did I continue to wear the mask of reticence and dryness?

13

Ramona introduced me to Keith; she wore white turtlenecks, which impressed me because, unsophisticated Californian suburbanite, I had never seen preppie or ski garb. Keith's slenderness seemed (in advance of any facts) diseased; that summer I was trying to read Somerset Maugham's *Of Human Bondage*, but I never got past the third chapter.

14
Keith acted like an older brother but I didn't want to demolish or overpower him; I didn't want to outshine his accomplishments or insist he cede his territories to my chatty empire.

15
Ramona said Keith's name with a nasal, proprietary tenderness that inspired me to conquer him, though I took no steps toward that victory and, now, don't know why I call it "conquest" rather than equilateral "friendship." My personality, unfortunately, scars what it passes. And I didn't intend this essay to be a piece of self-reflection. I wanted to give advice to the new generation. I decided to tell youngsters who might not consider themselves physically attractive to give themselves the benefit of the doubt, and to realize that youth was itself an asset. I aimed to encourage novices to move ahead with romantic development, not to hold back.

16
I discovered on the Internet that Keith led a youth orchestra in the late 1980s. His charges must have looked up to slim unaggressive Keith.

17
His real name—lost friend who was never really my friend—has a secret homonymic sympathy with open western spaces, landscapes, like Death Valley, that capture the tourist. His name also is cousin to simultaneity, to the suddenness of thought when it hesitates to announce its departure.

18
I allowed myself to be bossed around when I was young. I listened to my grandfather tell me that classical musicians

ended up in the gutter. (Maybe he was right.) I wanted more sensual experience but sat in a cocoon half my own making. Must I convert this essay into a pious valedictory address?

19

I have turned literature, like every love, into a harness. The discursive situations I confront—audience, reader—hold me like a vise, and so I end up not speaking, rather than trying to begin the awful, necessary work of accommodating myself to that confinement, learning the dimensions of prison so I might transform it into a nursery.

20

Robert Schumann's *Album for the Young* begins with a "Melody" that is not exceptionally melodic, and yet it announces itself, brashly, as "Melody." On the Schirmer edition's frontispiece, my first piano teacher wrote: "Rules about the pedal: (1) Not too heavy—use sparingly. (2) Be sure that when you lift pedal, you lift *completely*, then very quickly back down again." I never properly learned how to pedal. Uncertainties over Dr. Spock basics lead me into sloughs of despond, also make sentence momentum difficult. My advice: continue along your path and refuse to accept diversions, except financial.

21

A haircutter told me in 1979 that I had fine cheekbones, perhaps a falsehood, but I was paying more for that haircut than ever before, and the unisex salon was near a tunnel bisecting the mountain on which our city rested. The tunnel marked the salon's location as a positive place for comprehending my underrated erotic bite. Be precise!

22
All I wanted was hair on my chest. Then hair arrived. Now, boys are shaving their bodies, ridding themselves of natural endowments. Should I shave mine, to return to the state of hairlessness I was eager to flee?

23
Take your intuitions seriously, even if older bossy people tell you that you are deluded and self-indulgent. The word *self-indulgent* (let's destroy it) inhibits breathing.

24
Like Ruth Crawford's "Piano Study in Mixed Accents" (1931), this essay tries to give a pointillist example of how to take seriously one's own ineluctabilities. Much about myself I can't change, even if I try. And so I try to present the flaws as starkly as possible.

25
In 1985 I wore an Eiffel Tower earring to a Greenwich Village café, and thought myself sexually adventurous, though the earring hurt my earlobe, in winter: frostbite amidst unread Francis Bacon essays and a new consciousness that my genitals could be considered poison . . .

26
Giving advice makes me melancholy: Is anyone listening? Will anyone be improved, or moved, by my admissions? Somewhere in my heart there lies, waiting to be described, the time I wanted to sleep with my art-history teacher; we rode together on a bus through an area known as the Fens because of their murkiness, wetness, inaccessibility, beauty, and connection to mythic Irish faerie lore. Darkness out the bus window did not

cast aspersions on my failed seduction of the teacher, who ended up prominent in government. His rejection of me was total, though I did not advertise my desire. Almost never have I made a direct erotic proposition; everywhere is feint and fraudulence.

27

Now I am reading about ninth, eleventh, and thirteenth chords in twentieth-century "common practice" composition (clusters, tonal centers, dissonance, restlessness): knowledge never adds up, and I remain in the dog-paddling mode I occupied twenty-five years ago, a style I should have transcended.

28

If I berate myself in public, will you, reader, reach enlightenment and recognize your superiority? Self-laceration—masochism—is a respectable rhetorical strategy.

29

How can I give advice? I am not a father. I am, however, a teacher. My favorite pedagogic trick is to give contradictory promptings that confuse the learner. For example: "Expand the last paragraph, though perhaps its failure to expand is that paragraph's secret strength."

30

Last night I dreamed a cruel former teacher with saggy jowls like an Ingres painting of a dominatrix sat outside a classroom in which my pet students were giving me a "farewell-to-pedagogy" party. One shy and unattractive kid—call him Ken—had nominated himself majordomo of the proceedings. Ken had problems at home: I had indirectly witnessed these difficulties during a parent-teacher conference, when his overweight mother insisted that I describe her son's (nonexistent) accomplishments in great detail. Ken poured me a full cup of tea, which I accepted, because it was part of the "kindness package" he was extending. I had decided to quit teaching, and this, my favorite class, a group of below-average readers and writers, was sorry to see me leave the flock, and wished to toast me. I had been the only teacher ever to diagnose their problems, to sympathize; because I was leaving the profession, they would henceforth lack guidance or support in their long journey toward unsatisfactory adulthood, a maturity I am now experiencing, regretting that I cannot correct the flaws or describe them in a fashion that might assist you. In the dream, my cruel teacher, sitting outside the classroom, called me out to join her in the hall of miscreants. There, she pointed toward a telescope, and said, "Peer through it." On the lens was a gob of sticky spit or cum; she had not placed the viscous substance on the lens, but she had not objected to its presence, and had not wiped the lens clean for my convenience. Suddenly I had access to a university phone, which it was imperative I use to communicate with my lost father, who might be proud to hear that I, too, was leaving the teaching profession, as he had done several years ago. Again I was thrilled to recognize our similitude, and wished to celebrate it, but was afraid that I had already done so, and that I would be chastised (without probation) for the repetition. Other people in the hallway—large women who resembled Bette Davis or BMW-driving realtors—recognized that my former teacher, the one who had guilt-tripped me into looking through the smudged telescope lens (at what vista? the Golden Gate Bridge?), was a mild lunatic, no longer needing institutionalization, but not to be trusted with forming young minds.

31

Why am I telling you this dream? Because I am a teacher; because I have been instructed to impart wisdom in this essay, and I feel unfit to do so; because, in order to comfort you with streamlined guidance, I must remember—revisit—images of teachers; because it is painful to do so, bothersome (I hate using the word *pain*) . . .

32

Pat, the dream teacher who mocked me in the hallway, had a husband who knew she was an inadequate legislator, but he was afraid to lead her toward reasonable classroom-management practices. I could—in the dream's logic—possibly befriend him, side with him against Pat; the husband and I might exchange bromides, and he might help me re-enter the classroom and accept the farewell party, a gift too large and importunate to dismiss. At the party's center was a piece of stale white cake, a year old; unmolested by mice or insects, the cake had kept its shape, but hardened, like a Wayne Thiebaud painting. The classroom cake was not a painting, but I was welcome to confuse it with art; there was no incentive for me to segregate *cake* from *painting of cake*; the two, image and reality, could dwell together, tea-for-two style, in a cozy cottage by the sea, unbothered by telephone or relation. I began to realize, in the dream, that I could sculpt my fate—grandiose, I considered myself a person with a destiny—and as a consequence of this new self-determination, I began to grow small, as in *Alice's Adventures in Wonderland*, until it seemed I was only a photograph of myself, a miniature pedagogue, with the jauntiness of a child on the way to kindergarten, lunchpail in hand.

33

Each year I had a new, up-to-the-minute lunchpail. TV show spin-offs, the pails had thick thermoses. (Students bought minicartons of milk for a nickel or dime at lunchhour and reserved the thermos for juice.) One morning, my thermos contained chocolate milk, but, on that special occasion, I left the lunchpail in a bus headed toward a farm, and so, when I realized the loss, the chocolate milk (growing warm and undrinkable now) seemed the epitome of unattainable treasure, a realm of objects I had forfeited through carelessness.

34

I did not remain vigilant over my possessions, and so, piecemeal, they disappeared. I collected soft-drink bottle caps, and kept them in a shoe box. The collection vanished, or was confiscated—thrown out—by a guardian. Was confiscation wise? I advise you to keep close watch over what you love.

(2002)

Anna Moffo's Funeral

1

On March 10, 2006, I heard Tchaikovsky's *Mazeppa* at the Metropolitan Opera. In the program I noticed a donor's name: Noffo. Misprint? Someone named Noffo was giving money to the Met? Midnight: I came home to the news (an acquaintance's e-mail) that Anna Moffo, my favorite singer, my nucleus, had died.

2

Anna Moffo and I never officially met. The two times I approached her for an autograph—after she sang at Baltimore's Melody Tent and after she taught a master class at New York's Merkin Concert Hall—don't count.

3

The day after Anna Moffo died, I bought a fountain pen, red, Waterman, in a blue box, white interior. This sentence is a coffin.

4

In her performance (live) of *Turandot*, costarring Franco Corelli and Birgit Nilsson, 1961, at the old Met, Anna Moffo sustains the last note of her first aria, "Signore, ascolta," longer than necessary. The glad audience reciprocates.

5

She has the habit of darkening a note, infusing it with an unrequested, honeyed dram of significance.

6

At Anna Moffo's wake, I signed the "Relatives and Friends" book, but didn't write down my address. I feared that her stepchild or cousin would send me a chiding letter: "You had no business attending Anna Moffo's wake. Wakes are for intimates."

7

Anna Moffo's last performance in an opera at the Met: March 15, 1976. Exactly thirty years later, her funeral: March 15, 2006. Who else noticed this coincidence?

8

A *Boston Globe* obituary mentions that she was nominated for a Grammy in 1972 for *Songs of Debussy*: unavailable now. (I found a pirated copy—her tone color resplendently narcotic.)

9

Anna Moffo's face seems a sugar cookie, a planet, or a pond. Her eyes, in 1972, glow with a glow I can't describe: heightened élan vital? Her dark, wide eyes pivot to their corners. Eye-swerve connotes emotional amplitude.

10

She appeared in Abel Gance's movie *Austerlitz*, impossible to locate. When I read W. G. Sebald's *Austerlitz*, I inwardly saluted Anna Moffo's earlier version.

11

Her cortège, St. Patrick's Cathedral: the front car transported flowers. The second car, containing the coffin, had a large way-back. I longed to touch the fender but didn't want funeral-home chaps to see me do it.

12

Her heavy coffin sat unsuperintended in the St. Patrick's aisle.

13

The organ pealed loudly at the end of the final processional. I didn't mind being momentarily deafened.

14

I felt befriended by the closed, compassionate coffin. I paid attention to its quiet bulk.

15

Anna Moffo debuted at the Chicago Lyric Opera in *La Bohème*: October 16, 1957. Her Rodolfo was Jussi Björling—a duo so divine it seems a mirage. He died three years later.

16

My favorite screen appearance of Anna Moffo: her German TV performance (early 1970s) of "Depuis le jour," from Gustave Charpentier's *Louise*. Her voice is not yet exhausted—its timbre still creamy. She looks like Claudine Longet, Gina Lollobrigida.

17

In Anna Moffo's duet with Elisabeth Schwarzkopf, "Canzonetta sull'aria," from *Le Nozze di Figaro*, recorded in 1959, their voices match: Anna's signature tincture of voluptuous innocence, conglobed with Elisabeth's plangent, haughty elevation.

18

Dream (April 4, 2006): I heard Anna Moffo's end-of-career *Carmen*. She turned out to be in good voice after all. And I (once more) proclaimed her greatness, though no one listened. Her clear, retrained instrument: Anna in 1979 was unbesmirched, her pitch again intact, early. I wish I'd offered timely tribute.

19

She still appears, a stalwart, in my dreams. March 18, 2008: I dreamt I found Anna Moffo on a train to Philadelphia. Quickly she disappeared, but for a moment she recognized me as her logical traveling companion.

20

One of my favorite Anna Moffo recordings is Puccini's underrated *La Rondine*, recorded in 1967. Her voice sways, foresees its limits. A beguiling liner-note photo (dimples evident) is captioned, "Miss Moffo explains a point of interpretation."

21

Outside St. Patrick's, on the sidewalk, a woman with bright lipstick (a retired singer? a garishly dressed fan?) posed for a paparazzo, who was either a hired hand, or an unpaid, self-elected witness.

(2008)

II.

Susan Sontag, Cosmophage

Susan Sontag, my prose's prime mover, ate the world. In 1963, on the subject of Sartre's *Saint Genet* (her finest ideas occasionally hinged on gay men), she wrote, "Corresponding to the primitive rite of anthropophagy, the eating of human beings, is the philosophical rite of cosmophagy, the eating of the world." Cosmophagic, Sontag gobbled up sensations, genres, concepts. She swallowed political and aesthetic movements. She devoured roles: diplomat, filmmaker, scourge, novelist, gadfly, essayist, night owl, bibliophile, cineaste . . . She tried to prove how much a human life—a writer's life—could include. Like Walter Benjamin, she was entranced by multiplicity; and, like him, she was an aphorist at heart, honing pluralities down to terse sentences not without Jamesian evasions and excesses. Again, Sontag on Sartre's *Saint Genet*: "Jerking off the universe is perhaps what all philosophy, all abstract thought is about: an intense, and not very sociable pleasure, which has to be repeated again and again." Thus in her Yeatsian tower she wrote, wrote, wrote; reiterating, she made writing's asocial motion pornographic—a subject on which she dilated in her essay "The Pornographic Imagination." Remember, she was no stranger to Robert Mapplethorpe's milieu.

•

Transference: in the early 1990s, the night before I gave a lecture on Sontag's *Illness as Metaphor*, I dreamed that she reclined, wearing a pink miniskirt, on her living room couch. I've had dozens of Sontag dreams, in which she represents intellectuality's phantasmagoria, prose's succulence, quality's fearsomeness, and aphorism's bite.

•

The first time I saw Sontag in person, she was speaking at a Samuel Beckett homage in the 1980s. Listening to her eloquent presentation, I whispered to my boyfriend, "Susan Sontag's got a crush on me." I meant the reverse: "I have a crush on Susan Sontag." Instinctive, preposterous substitution: for an instant, Sontag-besotted, I ate the world.

•

My essays would not be mine without the influence of her prose's Mercurochrome aesthetic, her stern, self-conscious, tense sentences.

•

The ends of her novels are the best parts. Closure sharpened Sontag's scalpel. The last three sentences of *The Volcano Lover*: "They thought they were civilized. They were despicable. Damn them all." The last two sentences of *Death Kit*: "Diddy has made his final chart; drawn up his last map. Diddy has perceived the inventory of the world." The last sentence of *The Benefactor*: "You may imagine me in a bare room, my feet near the stove, bundled up in many sweaters, my black hair turned grey, enjoying the waning tribulations of subjectivity and the repose of a privacy that is genuine." And here are the concluding lines of her 2001 essay "Where the Stress Falls": "Nothing new except language, the ever found. Cauterizing the torment of personal relations with hot lexical choices, jumpy punctuation, mercurial sentence rhythms. Devising more subtle, more engorged ways of knowing, of sympathizing, of keeping at bay. It's a matter of adjectives. It's where the stress falls." Dig the word *engorged*. Like Jean Rhys, Sontag kept rules and torments at bay by generating stressed prose—magnifying, through emphasis and engorgement, the opportunities for attentiveness.

•

In her first novel, *The Benefactor*, published in 1963, a year before "Notes on 'Camp,'" she wrote the following sentence: "I am a homosexual and a writer, both of whom are professionally self-regarding and self-esteeming creatures." Admittedly, this line occurs in the voice of her character Jean-Jacques. But Susan wrote the sentence, not Jean-Jacques. *I am a homosexual and a writer.* Each of her books and essays contains a similar coded declaration. Sontag "came out" in her own way, forcibly, repeatedly. Her seeming refusal of queer identity may have enraged others (e.g., Adrienne Rich's 1975 quarrel with Sontag—supposedly on the subject of Leni Riefenstahl but covertly on the subject of feminist and lesbian identification—on the letters page of the *New York Review of Books*), but in retrospect Sontag's reticence seems picturesque, contrarian, and human. And it did not preclude support for Gay Lib, even if her theory of sexuality emphasized the saturnine, not the cheerful. Listen to her praise (in a 1972 essay) of poet and social critic Paul Goodman's erotic forthrightness: "I admired his courage, which showed itself in so many ways—one of the most admirable being his honesty about his homosexuality in *Five Years*, for which he was much criticized by his straight friends in the New York intellectual world; that was six years ago, before the advent of Gay Liberation made coming out of the closet chic. I liked it when he talked about himself and when he mingled his own sad sexual desires with his desire for the polity." *Sad* sexual desires? Allow Sontag that adjective's aptness.

•

Sontag spoke up on hot-button issues (Bosnia, 9/11, racism, Vietnam) and was indiscriminately pilloried by Right and Left for her quirky, vatic pronouncements. Like her idol Antonin

Artaud, she wanted to be a creature of passion, not reason: her positions, even when logically worded, subtly dismantled sensibleness. Responsible intellectual statements weren't her forte; her temperament demanded rash, provisional utterances. In a 1975 interview, published in *Salmagundi*, she defended the intellectual's right to be partial: "People who reason in public have—and ought to exercise—options about how many and how complex are the points they want to make. And where, in what form, and to what audience they make them." After her death, only a few obituaries referred to her as a feminist. In the *Salmagundi* interview, she defended her sexual politics: "I'd like to see a few platoons of intellectuals who are also feminists doing their bit in the war against misogyny in their own way, letting the feminist implications be residual or implicit in their work, without risking being charged by their sisters with desertion. I don't like party lines. They make for intellectual monotony and bad prose." Though Sontag and Rich argued in print, they had much in common; as essayists, they knew how to be intimately magisterial, definitively tentative. And Sontag, like certain other sisters, among them Joan Didion and Avital Ronell, threw away security and pusillanimousness for the sake of daredevil phrases.

•

Sontag's credo: *Move on*. The phrase comes from her grief-ennobled, expansive essay on her friend Roland Barthes: "The aesthete's radicalism: to be multiple, to make multiple identifications; to assume fully the privilege of the personal . . . The writer's freedom that Barthes describes is, in part, flight. The writer is the deputy of his own ego—of that self in perpetual flight before what is fixed before writing, as the mind is in perpetual flight from doctrine. 'Who *speaks* is not who *writes*, and who *writes* is not who *is*.' Barthes wants to move on—that is one of the imperatives of the aesthete's sensibility." Move on, Sontag urged. Leave the field untilled. Switch projects. Change hemispheres. Make a film. Direct a play. Write a novel. Fly to Hanoi. Nonspecialist, she refused restriction, scorned the limiting identity of expert. She would rather have been considered a collector, connoisseur, sad pervert—anything but an academic.

•

Sontag achieved her customary tone of passionate detachment by refusing academic thoroughness. As a writer she was solely self-commanded, not taking editorial orders, obeying only her own momentary or abiding enthusiasms: Rainer Werner Fassbinder, Robert Walser, Marina Tsvetaeva, Bunraku, Alice James . . . So what if she stopped endorsing a certain strain of countercultural American art and experience (Jack Smith, happenings, drugs, science fiction) and turned toward sober European and Asian pleasures? She loved fragments; her finest fictions and essays use the fragment as heuristic device and as musical measurement. In this predilection, she was influenced by Benjamin and Barthes, though I imagine that these writers merely confirmed her native inclinations. And, like Benjamin and Barthes, she respected philosophy and social criticism as forms of *writing*: though she never (to my knowledge) referred to Derrida, they shared a genealogy, a set of assumptions—above all, a respect for any text's unruly, tricky self-contradictions. Sontag is usually cited for her content rather than her form or style, and yet her paragraphs and sentences bear close and admiring scrutiny as exemplars of experimental writing: avatar of *Move on*, she sought prose forms that would permit maximum drift and detour.

•

Fiction was one escape ramp; she used it to flee the punitive confines of the essay. And she used essays to flee the connect-the-dots dreariness of fiction. Her essays behave like fictions (disguised, arch, upholstered with attitudes), while her fictions behave like essays (pontificating, pedagogic, discursive).

•

At no other writer's name can I stare entranced for hours on end—only Susan Sontag's. She lived up to that fabulous appellation. No surprise that Joseph Cornell loved her. He made a collage (*The Ellipsian*, 1966) incorporating a photograph of her, and courted her, in his fashion. Attuned to synchronicity, he believed that Henriette Sontag, nineteenth-century opera diva, led to the modern Susan. The second Sontag must have savored her own iconicity, a notoriety ensured by her severe good looks and by a style of intelligence (intelligence as style) that seemed a mode of locomotion (how to get through Western Thought without stopping for traffic lights) as much as a *project*—one of her favorite words. Stardom was one project she pursued. See her 1963 essay on Alain Resnais's *Muriel*, especially this footnote: "In this film (but not in [*Last Year at*] *Marienbad*), [Delphine] Seyrig has the nourishing irrelevant panoply of mannerisms of a star, in the peculiarly cinematic sense of that word. That is to say, she doesn't simply play (or even perfectly fill) a role. She becomes an independent aesthetic object in herself. Each detail of her appearance—her greying hair, her tilted loping walk, her wide-brimmed hats and smartly dowdy suits, her gauche manner in enthusiasm and regret—is unnecessary and indelible." Here is Sontag's brief theory of stardom: ***unnecessary and indelible***. Those antithetical adjectives recall the concluding lines of Elizabeth Bishop's poem "The Bight": "All the untidy activity continues, / awful but cheerful." Another Bishop poem about placelessness gave placeless Sontag—Hollywood? Hanoi? Sarajevo? Manhattan?—the epigraph for her last collection, *Where the Stress Falls*. Sontag belongs with Bishop in that constellation of brilliant aesthetes, mostly women, whose public positions on sexual eccentricity were, shall we say, complex.

•

Adventurous as Tarzan, Sontag consecrated her life to the task of being exemplary; consciousness, for her, was a grand experiment, a spiritual vocation, like Simone Weil's. Such lives leave always a sense of the unfinished. Naturally, Benjamin's incomplete *Arcades Project* ghosts Sontag's work, not least her autobiographical short story, "Project for a Trip to China," the only thing she wrote about her longing for her dead father.

•

"Authority, idiosyncrasy, velvetiness—these are what make a star": from Sontag's *In America* (2000). I wonder what Sontag means by "velvetiness." Velvety complexion? Velvety aura? Velvety effect on beholders? Is *velvet* the zone the spectator steps into when watching a film? Is velvet the trance state of the reader who experiences identification? Does velvet—as an emotion—precede initiation into the echo chamber of *I, etcetera*, the replication booth of Sontag-admiration?

•

So far I've failed to mention cancer, AIDS, photography, atrocity—four of her major subjects. She was comfortable staring at apocalypse. She cut her critical teeth on the Six Million and the Atom Bomb. From horrors, she learned what mattered.

•

In 1968 she described Jean-Luc Godard's art as "a cinema that eats cinema." Cosmophagic, cinematophagic, bibliophagic, Sontag's literature ate literature—and ate itself. No wonder she enjoyed Bataille, Leiris, Sade, and other savants of the mind consuming itself; and no wonder she had a nose for intertextuality. She alluded to it when defending herself against silly charges of plagiarism: "There's a larger argument to be made that all of literature is a series of references and allusions."

•

Sontag was a shameless apologist for aesthetic pleasure. Accordingly, I revere her essays not only for what they say but for how they say it. The *essay*, in Sontag's hands, became perilously interesting, governed by caprice masquerading as commentary. Her capriciousness, like foppish fiction-maverick Ronald Firbank's, turned on the dime of the sentence, that unit of fidelity to the "now," to contemporaneous duration. Sentence maven, she enmeshes me still: in her prose's hands I'm a prisoner of desire, yearning for a literary art that knows no distinction between captive and captor. Such art can be sadomasochistic in its charm, its coldness, and its vulnerability.

•

She died on December 28, 2004. A few days later, I began rereading André Breton, in private tribute to Sontag, who loved French seriousness, even when it was surreal. On January 1, 2005, imitating Sontag, I saw a new print of Michelangelo Antonioni's *L'Avventura* screened at MoMA. Daily, Sontag's spirit exhorts me: *Move on! Eat the world!* In 2005 everything I do, say, read, and write will be an oblique elegy to her attainments and postures. My Susan Sontag Commemoration Project begins here.

(2005)

In Defense of Nuance

A key to the mind and body of the great Roland Barthes—whose books, though they come in pieces, can't be skimmed or summarized—is the word *laceration*, a melodramatic synonym for *wound*. Barthes wasn't a masochist. But he understood agony. He knew that subjectivity—consciousness—demanded an initiatory experience of being ravished: Cupid's dart takes aim at Saint Sebastian. "Where there is a wound, there is a subject": throughout Barthes's work, and certainly in *A Lover's Discourse* (perhaps his most aching performance), lacerations take center stage. He wasn't histrionic about woundedness; he liked lacerations because they made appearances complex, and because they banished banalities.

Barthes had one lifelong mission, a messianic thread that connects his disparate ventures into the analysis of fashions, texts, and temperaments: the fight against received wisdom, obviousness, stereotype. (And yet: he would have frowned upon the agonistic machismo of the word *fight*.) His gentle mission was to rescue nuance. What is nuance? Anything that caught Barthes's eye. Anything that aroused him. Nuance—a shimmer beyond good and evil, beyond detection, beyond system—enjoys the privileges of satiated passivity: it never combusts. Nuance offers not a substantive destination but a murmuring: "Errantry does not align—it produces iridescence: what results is the nuance. Thus I move on, to the end of the tapestry, from one nuance to the next (the nuance is the last state of a color which can be named; the nuance is the Intractable)."

Consider *A Lover's Discourse* a jar of nuances: trapped fireflies. To liberate love's subtleties, and observe their play, one must first escape the postures and mythologies, the figures of speech, that surround the pleasurable/painful state of being enamored. On a practical level, *A Lover's Discourse* is a whimsical seminar on Goethe's *Sorrows of Young Werther*, a master text that Barthes, the intoxicating exegete, dances around; on a purgative level, *A Lover's Discourse* is an attempt to get rid of "love"—its roles, its attitudes—in order to find the luster that remains when the stereotypes have been sent packing. In *Sade, Fourier, Loyola*, he succinctly described his hermeneutic method: "I listen to the message's transport, not the message." Banish the message. Preserve the exaltation that surrounds it. Investigate the perfume that the message leaves behind.

Barthes broke down perception into a contest between rival meanings—sometimes two, sometimes three. He didn't want to enter their fray. He wanted to "outplay" it—to let the wrestling match exhaust itself and produce the flower of an alternative position, a nonlocation, a floating aura without a site. In *Camera Lucida*, he called meaning's two realms the ***studium*** and the ***punctum***. The oppressive ***studium*** was the zone of the readily apparent, the sanctioned, the digestible. The heroic ***punctum*** was an accident, an insignificant coruscation, triggering a perverse chain reaction of bliss. The ***punctum*** was the detail that "pricked" him. (That's why he sought lacerations: they ripped complacent surfaces, and he preferred reality when it was ripped.) In his essay "The Third Meaning," Barthes divided visuality's kingdom into the obvious meaning and the obtuse meaning: the former tyrannized, while the latter tantalized. The obtuse meaning, soliciting the viewer's passionate attention, seemed, on the surface, trivial—a mere crease, a speck, like a trace of lipstick traveling too far outside the outline of the lip. The obtuse meaning—"obtuse" is a term of praise—gratified Barthes because it carried no allegory, no symbolism, no ideology. It unprogrammatically titillated. Barthes aimed to extract these isolated oases of pleasure, and to separate them from doctrinaire encumbrances. From all of Charles Fourier's life and work, for example, the nuances that Barthes retained were "his liking for *mirlitons* (little Parisian spice cakes), his belated sympathy for lesbians, his death among the flowerpots."

In search of spice cakes, Barthes looked away from what he called, repeatedly, *doxa*, or the repressive discourses that hamper consciousness and prevent it from being a useless, illogical thing. His mornings, afternoons, and evenings were spent avoiding *doxa*. Against its aggressions, he remained vigilant, but neutrally so, without fisticuffs. He longed for a space outside the *doxa*; this imagined space, where the battle between binaries (such as "male" and "female") has ceased to rage, he sometimes called the "neutral," and there he wanted to rest, like wounded Adonis in his garden. The theme of neutered tranquillity reached a *petite mort* in *S/Z*, which took apart Balzac's story about a castrato; basically, Barthes wanted to avoid bullying, and the big bullies in town were usefulness, gender, conjugality, nationalism, symbolism, and organized politics. "Most of my injuries come from the stereotype," he writes. One safe harbor from stereotype was the subtlety he found in human voices. And what he valued in a singer's or a writer's voice was "grain"—a keyword difficult to define: by "grain," Barthes meant the "friction" or "fringe" of contact between music and language, where the vocalizing body expresses not the message but the message's transport. The singer he found most transporting was Charles Panzéra, a now little-known French baritone who made recordings in the 1920s and 1930s (Henri Duparc, Gabriel Fauré) and who gave private voice lessons to the young Roland. Most of Barthes's love objects, erotic or not, go unnamed; Panzéra is one of the few figures to whom the writer pays undisguised homage. In the essay "Music, Voice, Language," he confesses, "I myself have a lover's relation to Panzéra's voice." (The play between the *z* in Panzéra's name and the *s* in Barthes's gives autobiographical coloration to *S/Z*, a book that anatomizes infatuation with a singer.) Panzéra, who died a year before the release of *A Lover's Discourse*, never appears in it; nor does Barthes's mother, who would die a few months after its publication. Indeed, *A Lover's Discourse* transcends any specific love relationship (platonic, pedagogic, familial, erotic) that Barthes underwent; the book describes the general experience of being in thrall to love's categories. The lover—Roland—wants to escape incarceration-within-discourse to reach the anodyne state where nuance displaces topicality, where irrelevance outshines pertinence. He achieved impertinence, though his tone is always polite, which mine can rarely be.

How do we travel between the *doxa* and the neutral, between *studium* and *punctum*, between the obvious and the obtuse? How can we switch from ordinary to sacred time? Recklessly. Don't signal. Don't make an announcement. Simply drift, or veer, into the other lane. The crucial tactic is this sliding movement, which Barthes calls "drifting": "I choose drifting." Sometimes he calls it "skidding." He wants to prevent gelling or coalescence, and to slip away without fanfare. To skid, to leak, to drift: these processes, which Barthes celebrated, had an underground affinity with cruising, a state of sexual readiness akin to readerly readiness—a willingness to pick up codes.

A Lover's Discourse, though reasonably up-front about the maleness of Barthes's ideal love objects, is by no means his sexiest book. Its language avoids libertinage and opts for a Petrarchan classicism of address—frothing but courtly. We can only marvel at the ease with which he queers amorousness without making a big stink out of sexual orientation. He treated cruising more frontally in his posthumously published *Incidents*, which describes erotic forays in Paris and North Africa. The end of "Soirées de Paris" (included in *Incidents*) might seem grim to readers who aren't partial to sexual undergrounds: "How clearly I saw that I would have to give up boys, because none of them felt any desire for me . . . Nothing will be left for me but hustlers." Don't feel sorry for Roland. A lovelorn stance—and a devotion to cruising, drifting, errancy—engendered his interpretive perspicacity, his ability to find nuance in unlikely places. Without a cruiser's mentality, Barthes couldn't have written his great books, which are bibles of how to wander away from prefab systems of desiring, and how to alight upon accidental lily pads of unmarked, transitory bliss. In a similar vein, Emily Dickinson declared herself "The Wife—without the Sign!" Barthes, though famous as a sign explicator, was half-sick of signs. He wanted the unlabeled bed, the off-site Eden. Because of this preference for the uncategorizable, Barthes omitted overt gay statements in *A Lover's Discourse*; instead, he chose a "feminized" position, or a wounded one. The book had the enormous commercial success that a more rebelliously gay book could not have enjoyed; *A Lover's Discourse* turned him into a celebrity in France, and earned him the honor of being interviewed in *Playboy*, where he laid down the law: "I refused to proffer a homosexual discourse. Not because I refuse to recognize homosexuality, not through censure, or prudence, but because a lover's discourse is not any more related to homosexuality than to heterosexuality." Of course he'd hardly be in the mood to proffer a homosexual discourse cheek by jowl with a *Playboy* centerfold.

Barthes made his living as an academic, but his path toward scholarly respectability was not straightforward. Every French intellectual of his era praised the nomadic and the fugitive, but Barthes was the most purely alien creature of them all—the one least likely to stand responsibly behind a position. It's hard to call Jacques Lacan "responsible." Yet Barthes's delicious irresponsibility exceeded the infidel Lacan's. Barthes was tangentially and influentially tied to something once called semiology or semiotics, but that's not the meat of Barthes's matter, and that's not why I've been absorbing his tumescent lessons for the last twenty-five years. I first read *A Lover's Discourse* in 1985 while riding a bumpy train from New Jersey to New York; I remember how dirty the windows were, and how my imagination quickened as I encountered the illicit words, "It follows that in any man who utters the other's absence *something feminine* is declared . . ." Lacan was comfortable invoking castration—most of cerebral France was happy to talk about castration—but only Barthes, among the men, was at ease with incarnating a site that "cannot be designated," a matte *faubourg*, without qualities; and only Barthes, among the men, was capable of writing a line as charming as "The art of the catastrophe calms me down."

Barthes never dissertates. Barthes never stops to explain. He is happy to make the lightest of allusions—a lodestone such as "Nietzsche" or "Descartes" in the margins—but to leave the reference unplumbed. Among theorists, Barthes most resembles Walter Benjamin, although Benjamin composed no great book on love. (Benjamin's erotic track record left something to be desired.) Both Barthes and Benjamin worked in aphoristic fragments and assembled the pieces according to schemes nearly aleatory; both sought maximum condensation and intensification—an essentially poetic procedure. Both wrote a variety of critical prose that asserts the right to be considered literature—enigmatic, tight, and emotionally suffused. Both had an unfashionable predilection for magical, intuitive ways of seeing; both trusted in the authority of experience, in lightning flashes of apprehension. (Neither man had a gym body.) And both had a complicated, uneasy relation with Marxism—they were fellow travelers, but their suitcases contained far too many incorrect items (including mysticism, aestheticism, nostalgia, lyricism, neutrality, and a love for collectibles and keepsakes) to pass muster with the Big Boys of the Left. Benjamin failed to achieve academic legitimacy (history played a ghastly hand in this eventuality, though temperamental idiosyncrasies also stymied his progress); Barthes, who came down with pulmonary tuberculosis as a young man, spent time in sanatoria while his peers were attending university, and it took years for him to find full academic glory. His first published essay appeared, unpropitiously, in a sanatorium student magazine, *Existences.* And it was in a sanatorium that he wrote a dry run of *A Lover's Discourse* (according to Barthes's biographer, Louis-Jean Calvet). Apparently, Barthes fell in love with another patient, Robert David, who was, disappointingly, straight; undeterred, Barthes "wrote to David every day for . . . six months, sometimes even twice a day. His letters ran to at least eight pages, often resembling small books." In small, private, pointless, disreputable books—books of nothing—begin the responsible tomes a culture later uses to interpret its dreams.

By bringing up Benjamin, I don't want to make Barthes seem weighty and apocalypse-minded; at heart he was a creator of linked miniatures, each devoted to the play of an unspecifiable, reluctant nuance. He valued nuance not because it destroys the system but because it escapes the system. As a miniaturist, Barthes resembles the composer he most admired, Robert Schumann, whose childhood-infused works were most expressive when they came disguised as eccentrically connected fragments, without an argument, safe from the classical sonata's gendered battle between first and second subject. And, like Schumann, Barthes seems a blood brother of Robert Walser, the introspective feuilletonist and novelist whom Benjamin praised but whom Barthes probably never read; Walser, like Barthes, stuffed his prose's cabinets with careless, rapid notations of ephemeral promptings. ("Careless" doesn't mean without craft; it means without pertinence.) The most uplifting and impetuous pages in *A Lover's Discourse*—the analysis of the phrase "I-love-you"—place the lover in the category where Walser found himself, among outsiders whose lives were ruled by improper allegiances to whimsies: "As proffering, *I-love-you* is on the side of expenditure. Those who seek the proffering of the word (lyric poets, liars, wanderers) are subjects of Expenditure: they spend the word, as if it were impertinent (base) that it be recovered somewhere; they are at the extreme limit of language, where language itself (and who else would do so in its place?) recognizes that it is without backing or guarantee, working without a net." Lyric poets, liars, wanderers. Carnival freaks. Cassandras. Messengers from the void. Put Georg Trakl and Franz Kafka in that tent, too, with Barthes and Walser; there, too, confine the cruiser, the sentimentalist, the amateur, and the bedwetter.

Barthes lived his entire life, or most of it, with his mother, Henriette. To the grown man who lives with his mother may be attached a certain stigma, a slur he acknowledges at the beginning of *Mourning Diary*: in response to the imagined accusation "You have never known a Woman's body!" Barthes protests, "I have known the body of my mother, sick and then dying." A pet term in his work is "*imaginaire*," which Richard Howard wisely translates as "image-repertoire"; and the maternal was the image-repertoire—mind's panoply of idées fixes—in which Barthes longed to live happily ever after. ("I want maternity *and* genitality," he proclaims in *A Lover's Discourse*.) Don't accuse him of arrested development. Henriette Barthes deserved Roland's devotion. As he would indicate in *Camera Lucida*, after her death, "It is always maintained that I should suffer more because I have spent my whole life with her; but my suffering proceeds from *who she was*; and it is because she was who she was that I lived with her." Subtly, in *A Lover's Discourse*, Barthes asserts a non-Freudian paradigm for interpreting filial piety; by invoking D. W. Winnicott, Barthes suggests that the origin of matrophilia is not the Oedipus complex but a yearning for reciprocity and recognition. To love the mother—and to declare his love: this insistence, this gesture, as much as his homosexuality, separates Barthes from customary behavior. In *A Lover's Discourse*, he lets the Tao Te Ching say it for him most explicitly: "I alone am different from other men, / For I seek to suckle at my Mother's breast." Werther chose Charlotte; Roland stayed constant to Henriette. "Ultimately, there is no Country but childhood's," Barthes wrote in "The Light of the Sud-Ouest": like Proust, Barthes found everything in the past. And for that retrospective tendency, we musn't berate him; we musn't pretend to know better about where illumination should be sought, or where a mature literature should derive its materials.

It may be imprudent to talk about illumination when confronting the work of a critic so hell-bent on demystifying ideologies; but the many references to Zen in *A Lover's Discourse*—and in *Empire of Signs* and *The Neutral*—should teach us how dearly he valued states of consciousness resembling mystical experience. To figure out whether they held water, he kept querying exaltation, emptiness, shattering—states connected not to religious belief but to heightened perception and to those judgment-suspending moments when perception halts. Barthes was not untouched by the pharmacological imagination: one of love's aims, he tells us, is "to make consciousness itself a drug." He stands firmly on the side of Charles Baudelaire, Henri Michaux, Benjamin, and other Paris-based valorizers of altered senses. And yet Barthes doesn't want hallucination. He wants an armistice from perception's systemic injuries, or the wounds produced by stereotyped sight. In the intellectual climate (skeptical, combative, variously Marxist) in which Barthes wrote *A Lover's Discourse*, it can't have been easy or unembarrassing to have switched gears and "come out" in praise (however indirect) of ecstatic experience, the territory of Christian saints, modernist aesthetes, and Buddhist monks. Barthes didn't sit around waiting for *satori*; impatiently he sought a jolt of individuating awareness (set off by a sexual/aesthetic trigger, a flash of skin between shirt and pants, a fricative consonant in a Fauré *mélodie*), juxtaposed with a skidding-away from any hope of describing the experience.

Barthes never wrote a novel, unless *A Lover's Discourse* qualifies. (It comes close.) In the last years of his life, he sometimes mentioned aspiring toward a summit he called the "novel." Maybe he actually planned to write one; maybe he merely longed for the secure embrace that the novel, as a landed genre, could offer. Anyway, he preferred the "novelistic," a headier demesne than "novel." The novelistic was the atmosphere of possibility and of detailed succor that long prose narratives bestowed—but the novelistic could grant this atmosphere without the punished trappings of story, character, and realism. He speaks of the lover's discourse as "no more than a dust of figures stirring according to an unpredictable order, like a fly buzzing in a room"; similarly, over the solid novel (a fixed locale, and he never liked immobility) floated a dust of the novelistic, and it is within this dust that Barthes sought his home. *A Lover's Discourse* displays the dust with ceremonial orderliness, each miniature chapter consecrated to a different figure, with a series of rooms, as in a railroad apartment, leading off the leitmotif's hallway. The rooms are small; some are furnished with discreetly veiled autobiographical tidbits; others, with butt-ends of philosophy and literature; others, with folk wisdom gleaned from conversations with friends, who appear under the incognito of initials. (For years, I assumed that the "S.S." repeatedly cited in Barthes's margins was Susan Sontag, though now I gather that it was the handsome Severo Sarduy, whose novels Barthes considered epitomes of the "pleasure of the text.") Throughout the book, Barthes makes spasmodic approaches to coalescence—rapid, flickering bursts of volcanic cerebration, sculpted into gnomic phrase-clusters, the interrupted clauses linked by a series of colons, colon after colon::::: an unforgiven plethora. Often he swoops into a specialized vocabulary that may be borrowed from a legitimate field (such as linguistics) but that seems free of disciplinary taint. A dust of jargon floats above the sentences; our attention is not snagged by the difficult words but is kept animated by the swift succession of colons, italics, hesitations, reiterations, refinements. Anywhere you look in Barthes you'll find these feasts of interconnected phrases that filibuster Meaning and prevent its tidy consummation: by stuttering, rising up, and then breaking off, he thwarts definitiveness. The idea dies at the end of the sentence or sometimes in the middle; he proceeds incrementally, word by word, and squeezes them fondly and a bit hysterically, as if doubting that they will do the trick. Take this passage, which I choose because of its rhythmic tics and because it describes his great love—the speaking, writing, singing voice, pregnant with its own future incapacity: "Nothing more lacerating than a voice at once beloved and exhausted: a broken, rarefied, bloodless voice, one might say, a voice from the end of the world, which will be swallowed up far away by cold depths: such a voice is *about* to vanish, as the exhausted being is *about* to die: fatigue is infinity: what never manages to end." These lacerated pangs and appoggiaturas bear kinship to the prosodies of Dickinson, Beckett, Gerard Manley Hopkins, and other exponents of living expiration, of momentum impaired by gasp and caesura. (Arnold Schoenberg's *Pierrot Lunaire*, and Anton Webern's songs, belong in that nerve-racked canon.) Recitative, not aria, is Barthes's mode: he allows language, nearly unaccompanied, to stagger, in brief outpourings, between continuo goalposts. And, although operatic recitative usually paves the way for the more liquidly emotional aria, Barthes's arias never arrive; preferring vestibule to living room, he remains in *Sprechstimme*, the threshold-lounge where words rub against music. Reading *A Lover's Discourse*, we confront a scene of carnage, the text's limbs strewn across the field; no obligation compels a reader to gather together the scattered parts of a Dionysian operation that never commits the faux pas of coherence.

The bulk of Barthes's work, including *A Lover's Discourse*, has come to English readers through the eloquent labors of Richard Howard. He is Barthes's voice-in-English; Barthes breathes, and confides to us, because Howard made it happen. Any lover's discourse is a translated affair: love, Barthes proves, is not a feeling we take raw, but a condition that passes through the mediating scrim of plots, prejudices, and assumed positions. We get love through proxies; we can't apprehend the thing itself, only the stylized miasma it stumbles through. Dust, fog, bricolage: we couldn't see without the opaque surface on which the figures play like Debussyan light on water. Howard's treatment of Barthes's surface is loving; the fact that a tender, friendly connection existed between the two men helps us imagine, as we read these translations, that an affinity is being articulated. We are not reading cold print but text warmed by direct transmission. Let one phrase serve as sign of the exactitude and aural tact of Howard's work: "*Le leurre se dépouille de son décor*," writes Barthes, and his translator replies, "The lure sheds its décor." Howard's version is transparent in its fidelity. "*Se dépouille*" becomes "sheds": the *s*, *e*, and *d* remain. We hear the ghost of Barthes's alliteration. A nuance. A retained dental.

Barthes frees nuance from its manacles. He urges us: don't subjugate nuance to the greater vehicles wherein it dwells. Many unpopular or vanguard positions have their spokespersons, tabernacles, and pilgrimage sites. Nuance, however, has too few partisans. Barthes gave me good reasons for loving nuance, but I loved nuance before I started reading Barthes: in 1974, three years before *A Lover's Discourse* was published, I decided to devote my life to nuance—a useless vow!—when an inspiring piano teacher born in the Empire of Signs showed me how hypersensitively I should observe a diminuendo in a Schumann phrase. (Disappearance itself—not the melody it enveloped—mesmerized me.) Nuance is distinct from beauty, love, or virtue. Nuance is not a direct object; it is an aura that the object surreptitiously allows. Nuance, a trace, like dust on plush, resuscitates a lost instant when someone—Schumann, Panzéra, Sarduy, the dying Henriette Barthes (née Binger), her convalescing son Roland—raptly concentrated on a stray interpretive detail. "Language is a skin: I rub my language against the other." Barthes, like any writer, wants contact. Touching his reader, Barthes achieves a melancholy euphoria only equaled by the bliss—atopical, beside the point—that he showers upon anyone willing to take him at his word.

(2010)

A Manual Approach to Mourning

in memory of Eve Kosofsky Sedgwick

I'm drafting this essay on a green Hermes 3000 manual typewriter from the 1950s. A painting student gave it to me; he found it on the street.

I imagine telling Eve about this typewriter. She would have understood how a material instrument—ink-flecked platen, jade-pale space bar—can change syntax: to looms and to Victorian textures her sentences responded, and I recognize, in her prose's rhythms, the period-specific thrill of stretched syntax, and the renunciatory satisfaction of curtailing a clause before it can exercise its right to conclude.

Although, in a self-deprecatory moment, she claimed to disregard music, I often fantasized about inviting her to my apartment for an evening "musicale." On my Steinway model M piano, I'd play a harmonically indecisive piece from Proust's era—a Fauré impromptu. She'd forgive my technical deficiencies; she'd comment on the performance's abreactive ambition (she taught me the word *abreactive*), my attempt to neutralize shame by exulting in it, my finger-labor a haptic game affiliated with her favored arts—masturbating, interpreting, containing, hugging, sitting, retreating.

Shyness, a personality trait she often asserted, justified her opulent refusal of banalities. I was less shy, and therefore more banal. Much of what I said to Eve—over a friendship, including intermittencies, spanning twenty-two years—sounded wrong: too effusive, poetic, dumb, pop, dualistic, predictable.

I'm ashamed to remember how infrequently we spoke directly about her illness. (She seemed to forgive my squeamishness, or to regard it as a species of shyness.) Instead, I'd complain about a minor ailment of my own, as if to displace emergency from her body to mine, and to suggest that we shared a pain-stricken continuum.

Conversing with Eve, I'd blurt out embarrassing declarations. At our first dinner date, I confessed that I had a soft spot for evangelists, and that when a Moonie once buttonholed me in Golden Gate Park, I'd mistaken his god-dazed eye contact for cruising. Why brag about flawed gaydar? I wanted to persuade Eve that I was bruised.

At 1989's MLA convention, I heard Eve give the electrifying talk "How to Bring Your Kids Up Gay," later published in *Tendencies*. I'll never forget the moment when she described the "effeminate boy" as "the haunting abject of gay thought itself": as if in *Last Year at Marienbad*'s many-mirrored hall, I hallucinated serried ranks of junior nellies, awaiting description and embrace. Munificently, Eve transformed sissy shame from unfortunate idiosyncrasy into golden exemplarity—to be resumed, annotated, politicized, and enshrined in art. Don't efface your abjection, she suggested; don't bury it under an avalanche of femme-annihilating intellectual styles. At Eve's flute-voiced instigation, I pledged never to disguise sissy subjectivity, never to shirk its inebriate, swishy atmosphere. And therefore both of our bodies, whose erotic inclinations I dare you to summarize, were together wrapped in a complex scene of mutual recognition. (Forgive the imprecision; around mutuality, a tense topic, I can only falter.) When she ended the talk by calling for a "strong, explicit, *erotically invested* affirmation of some people's felt desire or need that there be gay people in the immediate world," she redeemed and crystallized my eroticism at the same moment as she announced her own. Thus, whenever confronted by Eve's auratic charm, I grew physically self-conscious. (Suddenly we've wandered into Henry James's *Awkward Age*.) To say it plainly: in Eve's presence, I felt stoned on the cannabis of her smartness.

In mourning, it's difficult to be organized, or to avoid the slipshod; I can't begin, now, to honor the depth, edge, wit, melancholy, sumptuousness, and formal variety of Eve's works. Above all, her writing gave license—liberty to think, in detail, about embarrassments; permission to laminate, self-consciously. In her essay "Queer and Now," from *Tendencies*, she applauds the "flamboyance with which some critical writers—I'm one of them—like to laminate our most ambitious work." She continues: "Many people doing all kinds of work are able to take pleasure in aspects of their work; but something different happens when the pleasure is not only taken but openly displayed. I like to make that different thing happen." Her works consciously create the playground wherein others may invent and disport, unencumbered by precedent. Like Barthes, she advocated taking many-fibered pleasure in the quagmire of *what is*; and, in Eve's accounting, the *what is*—the here?—looked irrevocably queer. And therefore any queer-affirmative project, or any writing endeavor buoyed by excess, would be vulnerable to being considered *risible*, one of my favorite Eve words: "The most self-evident things, as always, are taken—as if unanswerably—to be the shaming risibility of any form of oblique or obscure expression; and the flat inadmissibility of openly queer articulation." Be complicated, she invites us; be obscure, oblique. Be odd. Especially if you can't help it. Like Henry James, be flush with innuendo, your clauses dependent, dilated, filthy, yet discreet.

Curmudgeons sometimes praised Eve's ideas but criticized

her prose's roundaboutness. The treasures of her brocaded prime were the epochal *Epistemology of the Closet* and the unfinished narrative poem, "The Warm Decembers," which appeared in *Fat Art, Thin Art* and which she embedded in "A Poem Is Being Written," an essay that links spanking and enjambment, and that forever enlarged my estimate of the rear end's profound formalism. She never feared embracing the difficult and the undraped: "Clearly for Austin, taxonomic work with particular sentences is not a rigid, Searlean reification of performativity, but rather the filthy workshop of its creation, criss-crossed with skid marks." Even in her gnarliest sentence, a reader could find a blessed phrase—"skid marks"—on which to relax, as if in the lap of an orris-root-scented Buddha.

Although unusual diction and accumulating syntax always enriched Eve's writing, in later experiments she broke through to an interrupted tempo. In *A Dialogue on Love*, by combining prose, haiku, and her psychotherapist's notes (rendered in block capitals, like James Merrill's Ouija-board transcriptions), she found a new, serenely irregular prosody. Eve's jousts with her poetic vocation (would she have called the face-offs intractably Kleinian?) were not, as she once told me, a happy story, and yet she remained, at heart, a poet, which means that she tasted words one by one and struggled to array them in shapes commensurate with their fitful emergence: "I knocked my funnybone somehow against a doorjamb—and

then I was waking
on the floor, where at first it
seemed quite natural

that people would be
saying, and with tenderness,
'Eve,' and me with my

headful of azure—
    then disorientation—
then the whole rupture

of consciousness kind
of reconstructing itself—
backward. By magic."

Enjambment—reaching toward the brim, and then exceeding it—came naturally to Eve: she liked containers, and she knew how to tease their limits.

"In every language the loveliest question / is, You can say that?" So she wrote, in a poem from *Fat Art, Thin Art.* Eve always made me feel that new possibilities for speech and embodiment were around the corner: the solution was to walk steadily and patiently until I reached the block's end and could glimpse its astonishing verso. Once, when I told her that perhaps my classroom manner was slapdash, she kindly said, "At least you're giving them a sense of the *thrilling life.*" Her day-to-day pedagogy, en passant, showered us all with a stopless cascade of thrill—open-ended horizon, prairie-wide, unparochial.

I became "me" after reading *Between Men*, and then more "me" after reading *Epistemology of the Closet.* And it continued, this tidal process of becoming "me," every time I read or encountered Eve. In no one else's eyes have I ever felt so recognized. And by "I," we mean the unfortunate mess as well as the pleased riotousness. Her written words ("For readers fond of the male body, the year 1891 makes an epoch"), and her greetings in the congenial space between our adjacent offices at school (*I like the colors you're wearing today*), lifted me from my private sump, its idiocies and fixities.

I'd say she was a Buddha, if that statement would convince you how fractal and nimble-mooded and void-attuned it felt to exist in her vicinity. From Eve in person (not merely on the page) I learned how one might hazard a life where as frequently as possible, without harming others, you acted in accord with your desires—if you could figure them out. Or maybe, following Eve's tutelage, you could throw away the compass and the chart. You could use your hands instead, and trust your fingers to discover where the action is.

(2009)

Hart Crane's Gorgeousness

1

Jacques Lacan said, in a seminar, that the signifier is stupid. Stupid, and, I'd add, gorgeous. Hart Crane's lines quiver with a weary, unsatisfied mucosity. They remind me of Robert Lowell's thick lines of steel (as in "buns of steel"). In Crane's buns/lines I love the purposeless buildup, the hefty, panting artifice. His lines want to "get off," but they can't. Facture rules Crane's poems: they are drunk with the signs of his fat hand.

2

Crane didn't "influence" me. But his desire influenced me—his wish to be a pumped-up poet, to write lines obscenely loaded with ore, after Shelley or Keats. In slightly bad taste, Crane's lines just miss being so sublime you want to jump into their Etna. Sublimity doesn't sit still long enough for him to reach it; spurned, his syntax contorts, pugilistically.

3

Reading Crane is like eating a napoleon. I'm afraid my fork will crack the structure. Sometimes I choke on the powdered sugar.

4

When I write, I'm always *not yet* a poet; I'm a striver, a yearner, hoping to crash the House of Poetry. I stand outside, like

Stella Dallas, hungering. Crane must have felt like an outsider to Poetry. He wrote high because he wanted to push his way in. Aspirational, toked-up, Crane's language articulates that forlorn position of *gazing into the future, into Poetry as futural.*

5

"Smutty wings flash out equivocations": his equivocations, always implicitly smutty, perform the arabesque (excuse this Orientalism) of perversity. Crane discovered that desire hurt, that desire was filthy, that desire never reached its object. So he manufactured excessive verses that tripped past pat signification, leaving behind a mess. Or a maze. Inside the folds, some beast is being sacrificed, its screams audible.

6

In the last forty years there has been a mistaken emphasis on clarity in the works of literature deemed to come from (and to consolidate) subcultural identities: *to be queer, you must be clear.* The point of queer poetry may also be to make murky, to distort—what Lacan called *anamorphosis.* Like Marianne Moore and Gertrude Stein, Crane cultivated inchoateness, mannerism. His aim was not to neutralize or domesticate desire but to present it as failed: desire equivocates and betrays. Crane's poetics promulgates a discourse of unhealth: its creamy presentness of sound and syllable (resonance itself seems a lifestyle) shows how ecstatic it may feel to be torn apart by the difficulties of speaking.

7

Crane will never have many adherents. He doesn't represent a cheerfully populist or communitarian platform. He offers the thorny spectacle of an erotics that is selfish, transient, contaminated by ambivalence. Without Crane, there would have been no Frank O'Hara or John Ashbery, those two great proponents of the impersonality of desire. Isn't "personism" (chumminess) just another way of being a difficult customer?

(2006)

Frank O'Hara's Excitement

1

The highest respect we can accord a work of art may be to say nothing about it. And therefore I have written virtually nothing, until now, about the poems of Frank O'Hara, though they have done more to shape my aesthetic and erotic life than any other single influence. Breaking my silence, I want to celebrate one aspect of O'Hara's work: its excited devotion to the state of excitement itself. Excitement, a quality separable from its objects and catalysts, was O'Hara's stock-in-trade; excitement seems a simple matter, although, like most visceral events (breathing, sleeping, eating, shitting), *being excited* can be broken down into a thousand parts, episodes that elude the taxonomist's grasp.

2

Frank O'Hara's poems begin with a bang. That bang—that crash of self-announcement ("I'm here!")—may be followed by some whimpers, some lists, further bangs, and then an instantaneous disappearance. The poem whose opening bang is lodged most noisily in my memory has no name; its title, in Donald Allen's edition of the *Collected Poems*, is "Poem," and therefore it has, like Keats's negatively capable poet, no identity in itself:

POEM

O sole mio, hot diggety, nix "I wather think I can"
come to see *Go into Your Dance* on TV—*HELEN*
MORGAN!? GLENDA FARRELL!? 1935!?
it reminds me of my first haircut, or an elm tree or
something!
or did I fall off my bicycle when my grandmother
came back from Florida?

you see I have always wanted things to be beautiful
and now, for a change, they are!

This poem, its conceptual organization as tidy as a sonnet or a haiku, divides its excitement into three stages. In the first stage, excitement's instigators, a blended mass, aggressively thrust themselves forward: a 1935 film, *Go into Your Dance*, and its stars, Helen Morgan and Glenda Farrell; a Neapolitan song; hot slang; aristocratic star-speak (Kay Francis saying "I rather think I can"). In the second stage, a few quick memories (haircut, elm tree, bicycle) pop up, but none of the recollections has a monopoly: all are arbitrary, delightful, interchangeable, and without the lachrymose burden of cathexis, of "caring." (The dandy, whether Oscar Wilde or Andy Warhol, must prove that he doesn't care.) In the third stage, the excited aesthete summarizes his position: victorious, he kvells, having reached his long-sought, blissed-out peak. Exclamation points and question marks, not merely icing on the cake, emphasize the emotion's possible insincerity as well as its surfeit of sincerity. O'Hara's excitement, breathlessly uttered here in long lines whose speediness announces their credo (a velocity without Futurism's militaristic seriousness), depends on the "you" who arrives in the penultimate line ("you see I have always wanted things to be beautiful").

Where did this "you" come from? The performance of excitement is aimed at the "you." The performance of excitement creates the "you." You wouldn't be there if I weren't excited about Helen Morgan and Glenda Farrell and able to say so in combustive clusters of words.

3

O'Hara's excitement, in this poem, also depends on a complicated, shifting set of historical eras. Principally what excites O'Hara is the "now"—the instant of a poem's coming into existence. And yet, this "now"—the scene of excitement's performance—relies on time-blur, a revolutionary undoing of chronology and teleology. As Walter Benjamin borrowed a superseded architectural form (Parisian arcades) and allowed it to illuminate a radical future, so O'Hara takes artifacts from 1930s culture and propels them forward (via TV's time-travel) into the 1950s, his "now," where, revivified as reruns, artifacts like *Go into Your Dance* can function not as nostalgic oases but as crystallizations of unfulfilled longings—in O'Hara's case, a childhood yearning for a world of sophistication and sexual experience encoded in "New York" and "Hollywood" and "modern art," a world of urbane immanence that comes to fruition for him in the 1950s but has meaning only because it permits reclamation of 1935. Neither 1935 nor 1960 (the year of this poem's composition) is the final resting-place of the "now": a *poetics of speed* has transformative power because it can shuttle quickly between 1935 and 1960, back and forth, and force the two instantaneities to interbreed.

4

The quick and the now: O'Hara's poems stage a devotion to the now, which resembles orgasm's erasure of past and future. I won't assert that his work demonstrates an *orgasmic poetics*, though on the basis of a poem like "You Are Gorgeous and I'm Coming" (a thirteen-line acrostic whose second half begins "With the past falling away as an acceleration of nerves"), it would be easy to claim that O'Hara wants nothing more than a cum-fest for the Proustian sake of "repeating the phrases of an old romance which is constantly renewed by the / endless originality of human loss," a sentiment I call Proustian because, like Benjamin's recycling of arcades, it uses contemporary melancholy to renew the springs of prior artifacts (*if I weren't saturnine today, I wouldn't be able to divine the revolutionary potential of the past*). The quick and the now may boil down to the venereal: "Now suddenly the fierce wind of disease and Venus," O'Hara intones with epic grandeur in "Ode to Michael Goldberg ('s Birth and Other Births)," one of his greatest poems. His *very* greatest poem is "Biotherm"; to play the canonizing game, I'll rank it with the other poetic monuments of the twentieth century, and you know exactly which monuments I mean. "Biotherm," though long, is devoted to the quick and the now: it begins "The best thing in the world   but I better be quick about it" (as if he might die before he has a chance to explain the full story). "Second Avenue," another of O'Hara's extended masterpieces, memorably shoves the "now" into cohabitation with its supposed enemy, the "past": "Candidly. The past, the sensations of the past. Now!" Isn't "Now!"—that longing for simultaneity, and for the rapturous verbalization of it—always venereal? "Second Avenue" ends with enigmatic lines spoken in an unattributed oracular voice, addressed to a "you" who might be the reader, or might be O'Hara, but is probably the I/Thou amalgam after abstraction has burned away coarse subject-object distinctions. These valedictory lines enact not only orgasm but a paralyzed immobility, a cessation in which I hear echoes of the death wish and of Valhallan/Himalayan push-pull Ab-Ex sublimity: "'You've reached the enormous summit of passion / which is immobility forging an entrail from the pure obstruction of the air.'" Why entrail? No time to answer that question. The point of a poem, or an essay, is to pose questions, not to answer them. As O'Hara put it, in the first lines of the poem "Three Airs," which celebrates simultaneity and uncertainty: "So many things in the air! soot, / elephant balls, a Chinese cloud . . ." Whenever O'Hara makes a list of items, he adores them. Otherwise, why list them? Why exclaim "Oh! kangaroos, sequins, chocolate sodas!" as he does in the first line of "Today," if you don't consider them really beautiful?

5

I'd hate to fall into the trap of saying that O'Hara is in love with the world. Yes, he's excited about things because they are beautiful—but he is also holding that excitement lightly in his hand as a mirth- and tone-bestowing practice, and he is also aware that beautiful (or faux-beautiful) things fall away from him, detach themselves, refuse his embrace. Attrition eats away at the tight bond between his "I" and the inevitably maternal world (O'Hara's object relations are in good working order, but they also fall prey to hiccups, shatterings, blackouts, and spells in solitary confinement); and he is capable of finding this attrition—or this abandonment—exciting. Excitedly another poem called "Poem" (dated November 29, 1957) begins "To be idiomatic in a vacuum, / it is a shining thing!" *Idiomatic* is just a few letters away from *idiotic*. To speak your own idiom, in a vacuum, in a pit where no one else understands your vernacular, is an exalted identity, but the vacuum exacts a price, and the price may include being considered an idiot: Emily Dickinson was idiomatic in a vacuum, and look at how long it took for her poems to come (in their unpunctuated glory) to light.

6

Quick! I need to say a few words about "On Rachmaninoff's Birthday"! And I need to make sure that I return to my main point, which is excitement. Sometimes, however, when I write, I get so excited that I can't organize my thoughts. Excitement is a pleasant sensation, though it's also nerve jangling: excitement, while writing, feels as if some exterior yet introjected force (chef? surgeon? succubus?) were taking my mind and squeezing it to extract the juice. Or excitement feels as if someone (joker? athlete? percussionist?) were treating my mind like a Nerf ball, a lightweight and low-stakes toy, and tossing it back and forth, letting it hit the walls and ceiling and vases and other people's bodies.

7

If excitement's trajectory, in "Poem" ("O sole mio, hot diggity, nix 'I wather think I can'"), broke down into three stages (explosion, memory, consolidation), the career of excitement, that jetting firework, takes a more dismal route in "On Rachmaninoff's Birthday." There are several poems entitled "On Rachmaninoff's Birthday," an occasion O'Hara was often marking, in part because he wanted to assert the seriousness of a sentimental composer-pianist like the great Russian, whose piano concerti, in particular, are touchstones of theatrically self-aware excitement. One iteration of the Rachmaninoff birthday ode, written in 1953, begins with the aforementioned bang: "Quick! a last poem before I go / off my rocker. Oh Rachmaninoff!" The poem is a sonnet, profoundly unrhymed; its emotional climax occurs in these opening lines. This shudder is stage one of O'Hara's excitement: discovery of the beloved object to which he can speedily return. The object can be addressed and saluted, but never described. He can only stand, paralyzed (gelid?) with overstimulation, at the statue's feet. Stage two is memory: he remembers "Onset,

Massachusetts," and imagines that a "fig-newton" (childhood cookie) is "playing the horn." Frontally he salutes childhood's palace of art, its Joseph Cornell–style cabinet of curiosities: "Oh my palace of oranges, / junk shop, staples, umber, basalt; / I'm a child again when I was really / miserable, a grope pizzicato." Childhood's misery has much to do with groping, or the lack therof: in "Ave Maria," O'Hara imagines a rosy if politically controversial scenario wherein a kid goes to the movies and gets picked up by an adult stranger. But no groping happens to Frank on Rachmaninoff's birthday this year. Stage three of the excitement: he seems to realize that the room is "full of smoke" and that the soup is burning. Campbell's soup, I hypothesize: the can of condensed memory, linking Warhol to O'Hara, who paid Andy no heed. When the soup burns and O'Hara beholds the return of the repressed ("So it's back," he resignedly observes), he surmises that mental sobriety (a state of Apollonian remoteness from mere excitement?) will never be possible for the "you," who has, as usual, suddenly appeared in the last line: "You'll never be mentally sober." Rachmaninoff will never be mentally sober; he'll always be an aesthetically retrograde late-Romantic drunk. O'Hara, too, will never be mentally sober; he'll always be excited, even if the excitement takes the form of *flattened perception*, a tropism toward the depressed, the merely notational, the unelevated. In the late 1950s, O'Hara deliberately forwent the semantically pyrotechnical elevations of "Second Avenue" and other earlier poems, and chose, instead, a relatively plain style (the *Lunch Poems* voice), thus enacting, in the development of his poetics, a movement from a congested and spiked excitement to a toned-down ebullience. This movement away from hyperactivity was always in the cards: in "Mayakovsky," written in 1954, he sketched the inevitable disappointment that follows soaring ("I embraced a cloud / but when I soared / it rained") and also announced a new quietness. Those quiet lines—"Now I am quietly waiting for / the catastrophe of my personality / to seem beautiful again, / and interesting, and modern"—are O'Hara's news bulletin from the distressed interstice between catastrophe's explosion and the resurrection of a new optimism. This quietness would become, in 1956, in the many-chambered poem "In Memory of My Feelings," the opening line's depiction of the quiet man (*The Quiet Man* was a 1952 John Ford film starring John Wayne), who resembles the perfect Madison Avenue cultural worker, quiet enough (sufficiently an *appreciator of others*) to sprout secret personalities on the fly. The lines are a stealth operation: "My quietness has a man in it, he is transparent / and he carries me quietly, like a gondola, through the streets. / He has several likenesses, like stars and years, like numerals. / My quietness has a number of naked selves . . ." Nakedness sometimes needs to keep quiet about itself, but nakedness is, in O'Hara's hands, always exciting. He didn't seem entirely to like Allen Ginsberg's variety of naked poetry, perhaps because it threatened to usurp Frank's own.

8

When I say "excitement," I mean sexual, aesthetic, social, political—every kind of excitement under the sun. I want to separate "excitement" in O'Hara's work from its contexts, to isolate "excitement" as an affect, a process, almost physiological. Excitement is O'Hara's contribution to the history of lyric (and anti-lyric) ardor. Imagine separating, with a centrifuge, the elements in an O'Hara poem and beholding the excitement itself: you'd see an aura of beautiful shine, a luster, resembling Rainer Maria Rilke's excitement, but dirtier; just as thing-oriented as Rilke's, but cheerier. Who, if I cried out, would hear me, among the angelic orders? Googie Withers would hear me. For years I've wanted to drop the name "Googie Withers" into an essay, and "Biotherm" gives me leave:

> it's a secret told by
> a madman in a parlor car
> signifying chuckles
> * Richard Widmark *
> * Gene Tierney *
> * Googie Withers *

9

Googie Withers, a good actress, knew that excitement comes not just from hard work. Excitement comes from being lazy and fun-loving. O'Hara worked hard, but he also took it easy. His *Collected Poems* are a manifesto of the high aesthetic rewards that accrue from a life—albeit a tragically abbreviated life—of taking easiness as the gold standard. Like Warhol's professed love of easy art (or art that was easy to make), O'Hara's love of easeful production stood in ironic contrast to the uneasy intensity that electrifies his work and complicates its every emotional posture, threading melancholy and ambivalence and the threat of self-loss into the most apparently insouciant exclamations. He revered language but also found it an insufficient reward; poetry, though worshipped, could become the enemy. He loved highfalutin stances, or loved to mock them, but he also seemed to hate metaphoricity and exclamations, which were (contradiction!) his bread and butter: "how clear the air is, how low the moon, how flat the sun, / et cetera, / just so you don't coin a phrase that changes / can be 'rung' on," he defiantly states in "Hôtel particulier," in rebellion against any poetry that espouses depth, deliberation, and metaphysical certainty. Excitement—the poem begins "How exciting it is / not to be at Port Lligat / or learning Portuguese in Bilbao so you can go to Brazil"—falls here into the "Having a Coke with You" pattern of preferring what you actually love to what you're supposed to love: *let me be excited about the objects that I choose, not the objects that cultural czars choose for me.* I'll end my brief investigation of O'Hara's excitement by quoting the loss-infused final lines of "Hôtel particulier"—"is this the hostel where the lazy and fun-loving / start up the mountain?"—and by proposing that this footloose libidinal community, to which O'Hara belongs, is capable of visionary gleams and quests, even though he wouldn't be caught dead using a phrase like "visionary gleams."

(2010)

John Ashbery's Lazy Susan

A John Ashbery poem behaves like a lazy Susan. Spin it and get whatever condiment you want, without having to say "pardon my reach."

His poems offer a model of writing-against-fatigue, a method of incorporating lethargy in the compositional act: "I'm too tired to write" and "I want to write" can coexist, sing together, in utterances equally industrious and dithering. How hard does an Ashbery poem work? Very hard. Not hard. Call it the Lazy Susan Sublime.

We classify him as a New York School poet because we want to be nice to New York, flatter the city by telling it, "John Ashbery needs you." New York is smaller than Ashbery's poetry. He belongs to no school. He went to Harvard and is praised by Harold Bloom, but John Ashbery rebuts the canon and parodies the primer mentality. His send-ups of conventional education have a Bill of Rights motivation; they burst open the multiple-choice-test grid and attract the reader who has chosen to fail every other pop quiz.

Consider each Ashbery poem an instruction manual on how to spend time fruitfully by wasting it, by growing distracted, blurry, foggy, garrulous, horny, contrapuntal. Reading Ashbery, we enter a fugue state; polysemy (Polly Seamy) overtakes us.

After Ashbery, it's impossible to use an idiom seriously. He corrupts our sincerity function, perverts it, encourages us never to mean what we say. It's banal to be transparent.

Ashbery accommodates known postures and rhetorics (lyric, pastoral, epic, "deep image," objectivist, imagist, confessional, aleatory, surreal, "Language"—and this is not a complete or trustworthy list), but every gesture of incorporation (the Ashbery poem says, "I will behave momentarily like a lyric, just because I have manners") only goes so far, and ultimately breaks down, wanders backward, loses count, decides to nap or listen to a different song, makes fun of our process of trying to understand, has a shyness spasm, grows sexually aroused, hides the "boner," turns erudite, throws a pie in the elucidator's face, wants Mother, gets big for its britches, calms down, plays cards, bemoans the weather, ends the poem, publishes it.

Ashbery's poems forgive the inner stoner. Never saying no, they extend a welcome to a theory of literature founded on altered, enhanced, narcotic ideation.

His poems do not forbid a psychoanalytic frame of reference. They are cheerful about the unconscious, abreaction, cathexis, compulsion, repression, and fetish. But they don't approach catharsis systematically. The "cure" never takes place, because no one is in the room, or too many selves are present at once, a noisy abundance of "alters." It would be foolish to assume that his poems proceed from a "self" in the dreary pre-postmodern sense, but it would also be foolish to assume that they discard identity. Verse is a selfish city. Its din is a *self* song.

Ashbery's poems avoid embarrassment. They rarely blush. To be "stupid"—to say something less than sophisticated—is to fail at wondrousness, at ambidextrousness, at precocity. He skirts the stupid, and implies, by process of elimination, that too much of contemporary literature, especially poetry, is dim-witted. His fervent aim is to escape the mud pile.

He entitles the reader to take a long pointless walk. The Ashbery poem encourages the flâneur but extends this urban practitioner's range. No longer must the flâneur assemble ennui into a philosophy, however dissolute and provisional. The Baudelairean flâneur may have been a decadent, but he was always moving into the future. John Ashbery's flâneur is an apostle of going nowhere.

(2003)

Dear Sigmund Freud,

Sorry to bother you, but I have a quick question. It concerns apples. In *The Interpretation of Dreams*, you mention "a boil at the base" of your "scrotum." The boil, you say, "had grown big as an apple." (Thanks, by the way, for pointing to your perineum, that oft-neglected limbo zone between genitals and anus.) I wonder why you compare your boil to an apple. Were you remembering Adam and Eve's apple, or Newton's apple—or William Tell's apple, balanced on his victim-son's head? In *The Psychopathology of Everyday Life*, apples appear twice. First, you write, "My daughter bit into an apple and pulled a nasty face." Second, you allude to "Schiller's William Tell," who "hesitated for a long time before shooting the apple from his son's head . . ." Did William Tell's hesitation resemble Hamlet's hesitation? What unknown avenues do your apples open? Why apples?

(2010)

Roberto Bolaño's Tone

Roberto Bolaño died (of liver failure) in 2003 at the age of fifty; he died in Spain, exiled from his birthplace, Chile. Much remains mysterious about his life. He had bad teeth. As a child he was diagnosed with dyslexia. He was arrested by Pinochet's police. He wrote at least two impossibly long novels—his last, called *2666*, is over one thousand pages—and many poems. He remains, for readers marooned in English, a relatively new discovery: I began with his two aria-novels, *By Night in Chile* and *Distant Star* (as concerned with tone as with plot, they spin out, unimpeded, in extended Whitmanic exhalations), beautifully translated by Chris Andrews, who has also rendered the newest fruit from the Bolaño vine, a collection of laconic, disaster-oriented short stories, *Last Evenings on Earth*, that pose an antidote to mainstream North American fiction's (and cinema's) tired overreliance on naive mimesis.

The tragedy of Bolaño's premature death seems a culminating or incidental detail from one of his own fictions, a demise that places him in a pantheon of the disappeared, a legion of writers not yet sufficiently appreciated, who wait patiently for revival. Indeed, the major concern of *Last Evenings on Earth*, as of *By Night in Chile* and *Distant Star*, is the fate of the disappeared writer—either the writer who has been snuffed out or kidnapped by the state, or the writer who has been forgotten, underestimated. In *Last Evenings on*

Earth, one such invisible writer "barely scrap[es] a living in the Paris gutter press"; "his manuscripts are invariably rejected." He appears in "mouldering magazines and newspapers whose mere names provoke nausea or sadness." Bolaño casts these figures as martyrs, perversely sanctified by mediocrity and anonymity; they have the dilapidated, shipwrecked beauty of Fernando Pessoa's heteronyms, or of the literary subaltern whose meandering, unhappy consciousness is the subject of Pessoa's *Book of Disquiet*. Like a John Gilbert fading with the advent of the talkies is Bolaño's mournful, sepia-tinted depiction of a poet's disappearance: "A minor poet disappears while waiting for a visa to admit him to the New World. A minor poet disappears without leaving a trace, hopelessly stranded in some town on the Côte d'Azur." Bolaño dislikes joiners, sycophants—any writer who belongs too solidly and complacently to an influential aesthetic movement, or who occupies too visible a seat in a literary firmament. (I gather that he even scorned Neruda—because of his eminence.) Like Enrique Vila-Matas's book-length essay on writerly refusal, *Bartleby & Co.*, Bolaño's stories assert that literature, as a martyr's vocation, has more to do with ignominy than with accolades. Forced into exile, Bolaño found a way to love displacement, to find philosophic comfort in dwelling's vertigo. For Bolaño, only the erased and forgotten figure glows: "The name means nothing to B. And suddenly, in the secondhand bookshop, that name, the only one that means nothing to B, lights up like a match struck in a dark room."

Bolaño's supreme accomplishment is his tone, if I may hazard such a judgment on a writer I have read only in translation. His narration, whether in his "own" voice, or filtered through the consciousness of one of his fictional avatars (B, or Arturo Belano), is unhindered by adjectives, filler, or interstitial junk;

limpid and nearly blank, sometimes with an intellectual detective fiction's antiseptic clarity, and sometimes with a sorrowful undertow, he uses, in the words of one of his personae, "a well-modulated voice, with a tone that betrays a certain sadness, a Chilean, bottom-heavy tone." Bolaño's bottom-heavy voice recalls Alberto Moravia's melancholy, genteel stiffness, as well as Peter Handke's ability to sound sane (though vacant-souled) about insane circumstances. Bolaño may have Javier Marías's noirish bonhomie and mock-joviality, but the moral weight underlying Bolaño's bottom-heaviness raises him to the level of José Saramago or W. G. Sebald, for, in Bolaño, destinies palimpsestically tremble beneath the surface of a prose whose first concern is remaining calm and reasonable, like a flight attendant on a falling plane. The horror stays offstage, as in Greek tragedy. *By Night in Chile* ends: "And then the storm of shit began." Similarly, the story "Last Evenings on Earth" concludes, "And then the fight begins." The horror will not interrupt the dinner party or puncture the narrative poise. Yet when spectactular death hits, as in Max Frisch's *Homo Faber*, Bolaño renders the horror with a curt, pointillist luminousness, as if post-traumatic, etherized depression had already descended over the narrating consciousness, now sundered from small talk. Bolaño's greatness lies in the distance between the horror of the alluded-to event and the imperturbable lucidity of his narrative tone, as if every newsreel or flashback of catastrophe could be intellectualized into fable, or turned into chill synopsis. Let two brief quotations do the work of showing how Bolaño renders ruin as the scrim over ruin and never the bloody occurrence itself: "The whirlwind of fire that would soon engulf Central America could already be glimpsed in the eyes of my friends, who spoke of death as if they were talking about a film." And: "Inside she could feel herself starting to scream, or rather, she could feel, and see, the dividing line between not-screaming and screaming. It was like opening your eyes in a cave bigger than the earth."

I am addicted to the haze that floats above Bolaño's fiction—a trance, a "certain way of expressing opinions, as if from a distance, sadly but gently"; a modest avoidance of grand statement; a sense that every divination occurs underwater, in half-light. "What color is the desert at night?" asks one character, and then rescinds the question, calls it "a stupid rhetorical question." But it won't disappear. "Somehow I felt it held the key to my future, or perhaps not so much my future as my capacity for suffering." My capacity for suffering, suggests Bolaño, is immense, though my future is foreclosed and brief. I like the blur that Bolaño creates in place of clarity: so reduced are his stories, even within their nested plots, their complexly shifting points of view, their allusions, and their autophagous tendencies, that the mere act of narration gilds disappearance, makes it bearable.

Bolaño practices an art of resistance—against punishment and police and dictatorship, yes, but also against classification and oversimplification. In one story, "Mauricio ('The Eye') Silva," the protagonist, homosexual, rescues two boys from castration in India. Torture, says Bolaño, happens. Torture happens, as in *By Night in Chile*, in the same house where literary people gather for their glittering salon. In the basement beneath Bolaño's fiction, a body is being beaten; on the floor above, where we are reading his remote, grave tales, we can imagine the screams but can't quite hear them. Are we too complacent? Are we listening carefully enough?

As Bartleby and his compatriots understood, one must leave literature to find it again; one must lower one's voice to raise it. Bolaño's work, at once baroque and attenuated, gives us the model for a literature that, Bartleby-like, flees itself, forgets its usual tasks, and achieves moral austerity through a prose that makes room for the blankness of pure attentiveness. "Is it possible to die of sadness? Yes, it is." It is possible, Bolaño implies, to write a fiction so true it dies into poetry, a prose that loses its identity or goes underground to perform another, secret service.

(2006)

Elizabeth Hardwick's Sentences

I love Elizabeth Hardwick's sentences. They're strange and wayward. They veer. They avoid the point. Sometimes they are specific, but often they grow soft-focused and evasive at the crucial moment. They fuzz out by adopting a tone at once magisterial and muffled. When I was writing a biography of Andy Warhol, I told myself, "Imitate Elizabeth Hardwick." By that advice, I meant: be authoritative but also odd.

How to explain or summarize the Hardwickian tone? It offers tenderness where another critic might offer trenchancy. Its every gesture is gloved. From her introduction to *The Susan Sontag Reader*: "Essays lie all over the land, stored up like the unused wheat of a decade ago in the silos of old magazines and modest collections. In the midst of this clumsy abundance, there are rare lovers of the form, the great lovers being some few who practice it as the romance this dedication can be." Strange syntax that second sentence has. Admire, in this opening salvo, her articles, their offer of a misleading specificity. "Essays lie all over the land . . ." Which land? Another piquant "the": "like the unused wheat of a decade ago . . ." Her use of "this"—article? adjective?—astounds: "this clumsy abundance"; "the romance this dedication can be." From her essay "Wives and Mistresses," in *Bartleby in Manhattan*: "The famous carry about with them a great weight of patriarchal baggage—the footnotes of their lives. Footnotes worry a lot. They, loved or unloved, seem to feel the winds of the future always at their back. The graves of the greatly known ones are a challenge to private history . . ." Everything here is tone, sonorous yet gracefully stumbling, a tone cemented by judicious, generous articles ("the famous," "a great weight," "the footnotes of their lives") and by weird, sudden personification, a metaphor coming alive without warning: "Footnotes worry a lot." I savor, too, the insertion of the appositive "loved or unloved" immediately after the "They" of the second sentence: "They, loved or unloved, seem to feel . . ." Divorcing "they" from "seem," she inserts "loved or unloved" like a great raw piece of beef soliciting our appetite.

In her later work, her effects grew bolder. The following, from a 1999 review of Andrew Morton's *Monica's Story*: "The shabby history of the United States in the last year can be laid at the door of three unsavory citizens. President Clinton: shallow, reckless, a blushing trimmer; Monica Lewinsky, aggressive, rouge-lipped exhibitionist; Judge Kenneth Starr, pale, obsessive Pharisee." Hardwick's art lies in the immortal, cruel epithet, the wine-dark sea of precise excoriation. Final example, from her novel-which-is-not-a-novel, *Sleepless Nights*: "Every morning the blue clock and the crocheted bedspread with its pink and blue and gray squares and diamonds." No verb. She means: "Every morning I wake up to confront the blue clock and the crocheted bedspread." But she omits the seeing, knowing "I," and she omits the verb. Every morning the blue clock gives forth the bleak yet solacing fragrance that is the Elizabeth Hardwick sentence, worth our careful study.

(2007)

Epitaph on Twenty-Third Street

Byron: "I hate tasks."

•

Quoth a plaque on Manhattan's Twenty-Third Street:

DEDICATED TO THE MEMORY OF
JAMES SCHUYLER
POET AND PULITZER PRIZE WINNING
AUTHOR OF THE MORNING OF THE POEM AMONG
OTHER WORKS, WHO LIVED AT THE CHELSEA HOTEL
FROM 1979 UNTIL HIS DEATH IN 1991
PRESENTED BY
FARRAR, STRAUS & GIROUX
JULY 1993.

On a public epitaph, words divided into centered lines, broken, resemble poetry, if only visually.

•

His *Collected Poems* (1993) dropped into the reading universe and met a familiar silence, the void that usually greets poetry, particularly if its monumentality is of the disguised, offbeat kind. The plaque substitutes for the acclaim his work deserves; makes a connection between residence and poem; asks that we, readers and pedestrians, remember where Schuyler lived and what he lived for; rebukes us for having taken his incarnation, in a hotel at once sleazy and legendary, for granted.

The *Collected Poems* communicates the pathos of a covert "Eroica": craggy masterwork of the deaf, misunderstood, unlovely shut-in. The silence surrounding Schuyler was not as immense or discouraging as the neglect encircling most dead or living poets. After all, he won a Pulitzer. He stayed in the country homes of wealthy friends. Influential figures championed him; and he used silence—the state of being ignored—as ore and material. Catatonia of an indifferent public was an atmospheric buzz against which his protected, hothouse verse could become audible to itself.

•

Stopping and starting: poetry's favorite device is the line break, which prose shuns. At the line break, the poem engages in self-regard, echo, hesitation; it eddies. A prose reader begins to fall asleep; a poetry-lover feels a rising blush. For with the line break, a poem has revealed its chant stigmata. The line break is, aesthetically, an endangered species. In the neglect surrounding poetry, hear the death of the line break; hear a culture's decreasing solicitude toward the line break's fortunes. The lost line break is a little match girl, a degraded relic. For Schuyler, it is ballast: the heart of his poetics is erratic, tender, skittering enjambment. Truism: each line break is a little death, which Schuyler faces stoically and serenely. Imagine that the verse line is a jump rope; Schuyler skips rope, pondering the break when his feet are midair. He is both light on his feet, and clumsy—a kind of oafishness which, like Charlie Chaplin's, is a high variety of grace. From "The Bluet": "Unexpected / as a tear when someone / reads a poem you wrote / for him: 'It's this line / here.' That bluet breaks / me up, tiny spring flower / late, late in dour October." The line break before "reads" reminds us of reading's oddness, reminds us that our hands are a reader's. The line break after "unexpected" warns that every line break had better deliver a surprise if it wants any supper. "It's this line / here": the fleshy finger points, saying, "Here, reader, the line breaks." "[B]reaks / me up": line's schism demolishes "me," also induces admiring aesthete tears. How late in the day I am noticing these tiny miraculous instances.

•

His lines are tight and nervous but also sometimes long and self- and universe-loving. Certainly he grew to forgive his own silence as well as his own overflow. He wrote fat poems, but also skinny poems; for the fat ones, he surmounted the line-ending's curtailment and succumbed to a physiological, shameful explosion: ". . . when my bladder flashed the message that I had to go and / I had to go *now*, not in two minutes . . ." This is how "The Morning of the Poem" ends: he remembers urine gushing forth, "piss all over Paris, not / To mention my shirt and pants, light sun tans: why couldn't it / have been the depths of winter, and me in heavy / Dark overcoat?" To write a fat, long poem, he must surrender to the memory of flood and embarrassment.

•

"What a long time since I wrote a poem" (Schuyler, in "Four Poems," dedicated to Frank O'Hara). The time between poems is always a long time, as the time of the poem is always short, or long, or concerned with the difference (negligible) between abbreviated and endless.

•

He thinks (and transcribes and dignifies) "Mme. de Sévigné / -type thoughts," and what thoughts would not yearn for such an isolate and opal pedigree? By calling them "-type thoughts" he acknowledges derivativeness, eagerness to mimic the great lady, satisfaction in being a copy. He must have loved Proust's taste for Mme. de Sévigné: I, too, adore the exiled éclat of a woman who, far from the loved one, must be satisfied with sent commonplaces.

•

Like Hart Crane, Schuyler is fond of the word *bluet*, repeats it, and therefore repossesses it. He indulges the words he loves, as he wishes each passing day would pamper him. Some typical titles: "June 30, 1974." "Dec. 28, 1974." "February 13, 1975." "August first, 1974." Each day is an eclectic collection of moods and circumstances, potentially catastrophic; toward a ruined day's end, cheerfulness sometimes breaks through. The movement of his thought owes more to the diary's or letter's amplitudes than to the poem's parsimonies. And Schuyler's politics—if he had any—found body in formalist questions. Theodor Adorno would have deplored Schuyler's gorgeous sentimentality but would have appreciated his resistance to the received and the manufactured, even if his poetic manipulations strive to look like onanism crossed with haiku. Schuyler opens up "poem" to gay air; changes the dull wallpaper; lets light fall on a neglected corner; solves the question of garbage collection—how to handle a day's waste, how to convert indolence into literature (see Willard Spiegelman's *Majestic Indolence: English Romantic Poetry and the Work of Art*). Indolence is more than a temperament. It is a religion. The indispensable poets have cultivated it. Byron: "I smoke and Stare at Mountains." Schuyler: "A nothing day full of / wild beauty . . ." Nothing days are collected poetry. Any day I read Schuyler or try to write this essay becomes a nothing day. Keats wrote: "This morning I was writing with one hand, and with the other holding to my Mouth a Nectarine . . ." A few days later, Keats will fill "To Autumn" with mythic fruit, but so much richer is the letter's inclusion of the actual, accidental, adjacent nectarine! Schuyler's poems, like Keats's letters, include the contiguous object, the nectarine in the sinister hand.

•

To include the fruit beside the blank page, the page on which one is about to write a sentence, is to be indolent enough to notice wild beauty, to stare at it, to wonder what words might begin to be useful in a description of it, but to stop several steps short of actually writing the words down.

•

Schuyler's one ostensibly political poem, about Vietnam ("May, 1972"), is a failure. He writes: "The war / must end. It goes on." He raises his voice to an unaccustomed public pitch; generally comfortable with things that "go on" (beauty, indolence, moods), he cannot enjoy war's ongoingness.

•

His poems include the perception and the moment of the perception's correction, when he discovers it to have been mistaken, wrongsighted: "Tearing and tearing / ripped-up bits of paper, / no, it's not paper / it's snow." He loves to misidentify. But on the crest of an identification (*this is a poem*) he is content to say "no" (*this is not a poem*), and stop. Hence his respect for silence: his more than merely rhetorical or perfunctory gesture of making room for catatonia, failure, and indolence within the ripped-up poem's vise. The silence he incorporates is sage *and* incompetent—the quietness of "writer's block," the dolor of deep trance. Turning away from the poem he is in the midst of writing, he stares, dumbly, at the wall.

•

His prose diaries, published by small presses, fed the poems. Framed, above my desk, is a typescript page of a Schuyler journal (Memorial Day 1988), including the following paragraph, which is a poem because it exposits and then corrects itself ("Maybe not"), and which also, because of the way Schuyler typed it, visually resembles poetry. I reproduce his exact lineation:

> Last night, after dinner in that agreeable res-
> taurant in Housatonic, where the poet brothers Gizzi
> wait table, I had a passionate desire for some-
> thing forbidden -- not what the others were having

> and I was not: a martini, wine, the kind of dessert
> called something like "Chocolate Suicide" --
> a cigarette, one lousy cigarette. Does this go
> on forever? Maybe not: right this minute, I do
> not want a cigarette.

The war goes on, but does this desire for a cigarette (a word he repeats, happily, three times) go on? Yes and no. He hovers between moving on and stopping: "go / on" is a kind of line break, lost in prose, as is "I do / not want." It's possible that Schuyler considered his prose diaries to be mildly broken into poetic lines but lacked the energy to decide about all the breaks so left the entries in prose paragraphs whose arrangement on his typed page was nonetheless fastidious. Evidently he perceived continuity between his prose and poetry, for he combined the two in his sweetly anomalous *The Home Book*, published by Z Press, which features such precious oddities as "The Infant Jesus of Prague," "The Custard Sellers," and "Shopping and Waiting," all absent from the *Collected*—which, to its credit, does include "The Fauré Ballade," defined in an epigraph as "An anthology of [prose and poetry] quotes, misquotes, and (no doubt) misremembered remarks." Stein told Hemingway that remarks are not literature. One "remark" that, *pace* Stein, Schuyler considers luminous is Thoreau's "I am a parcel of vain strivings." Acknowledgment of writing's vanity and necessary incommunicativeness underlies Chelsea Hotel and Walden Pond, twinned symbolic residences. Also in Chelsea Hotel, some years earlier: Robert Mapplethorpe, fellow gatherer, collecting tricks and flowers.

•

Schuyler's love affair with the fragment led not only to chains of miniatures but, repeatedly, to long poems that recall Keats's defense, in a letter, of the extended poem as bazaar, playground, wilderness: "Do not the Lovers of Poetry like to have a little Region to wander in where they may pick and choose, and in which the images are so numerous that many are forgotten and found new in a second Reading: which may be food for a Week's stroll in the Summer?" Of this genre—the many-acred playpen, crib, or continent; the pasture for grazing, for marveling at the freak acrobatics of an indolent poet expanding and contracting the line's bellows, creating the sine curve of remembering and forgetting—Schuyler's masterpieces are "Hymn to Life," "The Crystal Lithium," "The Morning of the Poem," and "A Few Days." I do not overstate: there are few poems I know in English (Wordsworth's *Prelude* is one) that successfully achieve this degree of openness to the grace of fact and accident, and the felicities that come only from receptivity to failure. Greatest among Schuyler's long works is "The Morning of the Poem"—because it spins into prose, or totters on the brink of it, and therefore secures a foothold in the vertigo-land called Poetry; because it amply folds in details of his life, and thereby admits Mme. de Sévigné–type thoughts into the otherwise autistic field of "poem"; because it is long as hell; because it staggers, like a good drunk; because it embodies happiness and yet is extremely eloquent about unhappiness. I repeat: if I encourage students to read and write poetry, if I write and read poetry and think about poetry while walking down the street or before falling asleep, it is at least in part because of the example set by "The Morning of the Poem," even if, when I first read it, in 1981, I took its extraordinary effects for granted, as if such extravagances as Schuyler offered were poetry's norm. Then, I assumed that there were branches full of fruit as plump as "The Morning of the Poem," ready to be plucked. Now I know how few, and how difficult to find. Happily this poem's splendors defy description. Schuyler piles up questions ("Whoever knows what a painter is thinking?") and impossibilities ("I wish / I could send you a bundle of orange lilies / To paint"). If he could send the lilies, he wouldn't need to write the poem.

•

"Hymn to Life" ends: "What are the questions you wish to ask?"—leaving us with the silence of the many, many questions the *Collected* asks of a life, that mine and other interested lives ask of his *Collected*. His long poems, in Dada mode, stun the artistic enterprise into silence ("I hate tasks," "I smoke and Stare at Mountains").

•

Silence: "Is this the moment? / No, not yet. / When is the moment? / Perhaps there is none. / Need I persist?"

•

"Sitting. Staring. Thinking blankly."

•

Against blankness, these creamy particulars: "Cazenovia Creek," "moth-wing strokes of Sviatoslov Richter's / steady fingers," "A tall cold glass of Vichy," "A brown that isn't purple, gamboge, celadon lined / with jade." These details, sonorous, could have been James Merrill's. Schuyler signs them with a self-correcting "isn't": "A brown that *isn't* purple." Why point out what brown isn't? Because he respects description's failure; he admires brown's likeness to purple and the urge to equate the two colors, but he prefers the last-minute realization that they are not identical.

•

He knows the names of flowers, forgets their names, remembers them—the drama of retrieval and amnesia that Proust brought to long prose's fore: "Pink rose of Marion, I / wish I knew your name." We congregate in literature's arbors because we want to fall asleep, and to wake from sleep with the names of flowers on our lips; we want to drift away from known words and then rediscover them.

•

His first book, *Freely Espousing*, was published in 1969, the year of Stonewall. (Frank O'Hara was already dead.) Then, after this belated debut, the poems came quickly: *The Crystal Lithium* (1972), *Hymn to Life* (1974), *The Home Book* (1977), and the great *Morning of the Poem* (1980). And then *A Few Days* (1985). The meaning of this sudden flowering is mysterious and I won't question it too closely, but I would be a clod not to mention that the 1970s was a decade of gay explosiveness, and that certainly Schuyler's poetics must have been warmed by that flame. (I almost called the flame "collective," but nothing in Schuyler's work speaks to the communal spirit—only to the communion of writer and writer, reader and reader.) An aesthetic history of the gay 1970s needs to address not only the explicit (Mapplethorpe's sexual collections) but also the arch and the adjacent (Merrill's ecstatic séance gatherings, Schuyler's temperamental potpourris).

•

Perhaps his single most memorable (or liable to be anthologized) poem: "Salute," from *Freely Espousing*. The poem concerns collecting, the failure to collect, and the desire to include failure in the poem:

> Past is past, and if one
> remembers what one meant
> to do and never did, is
> not to have thought to do
> enough? Like that gather-
> ing of one of each I
> planned, to gather one
> of each kind of clover,

> daisy, paintbrush that
> grew in that field
> the cabin stood in and
> study them one afternoon
> before they wilted. Past
> is past. I salute
> that various field.

Keats on the verge of death wrote a letter only because he feared that later he would not be able and would regret not having done so while he had the strength: "I thought I would write 'while I was in some liking' or I might become too ill to write at all and then if the desire to have written should become strong it would be a great affliction to me." Half the urge to write is the premonition that later the thought I am now having might disappear, so I had better write it down while I have the inclination, however overshadowed this desire is by indolence. Thoughts disappear. Sometimes it is fine if they vanish. Schuyler remembers an act of poetic collecting he wanted to perform, and then tells us that he never accomplished it, but of course in so telling us of his omission, he commits the lost act. Not all poems need to be written. Part of the beauty of the lyric enterprise is that one can stare at verse from across a rift of silent inaction and remark on the unwritten poems. Sometimes it *is* enough to have thought to do. The act of saluting suffices. Anyway, gatherings can't be planned; collections must be spontaneous. (If one obeys that dictum, it is impossible ever to write.) What do Jean Rhys, Robert Creeley, and James Schuyler have in common? They alter and truncate thoughts: "is / not." The line break is the cancellation stamp.

•

Imagine Schuyler committing the act of study that he postulated but never rose to. Picture the poet holding the flower, scrutinizing it. What does it mean to "study" a flower or a poem? It is particularly difficult to examine Schuyler's poems, because they are at once "studied" (mannered) and spontaneous: shiny and easy (but also, in their sleight-of-hand syntax, baffling), they deflect the interpreter's wiles. Does any meaningful segment of a nation, queer or otherwise, study Schuyler? Do we salute Schuyler? Isn't "salute" an implicitly patriotic gesture? If so, what hybrid patriotism includes Schuyler's isolated stammering, his Ponge-like quest to uncover a flower's unreproducible sine qua non? Schuyler salutes the poems he never wrote, the thoughts he never had, the lovers he never adequately cherished, and the vocation he imagines he never entirely occupied. The literature I pursue is deathbed utterance: written—and read—on a figurative border of sentience and extinction, the moment you say to yourself, "I lacked the temerity, diligence, and inspiration to pick those flowers and study them. Past is past. I salute the art I never made, the artifacts I never sufficiently appreciated." The plaque on Twenty-Third Street salutes Schuyler. In *Freely Espousing*, his apolitical book, which broaches the possibility that this alone-yet-befriended poet might espouse a creed, or (homoerotically) find a male spouse, or (like a gardener) cultivate flowers, he silently acknowledges a field whose blossoms he was too distracted, lazy, or burdened to gather. If the "field" is American poetry as a living art; if America, as Richard Howard has suggested, is no better than its poetry; then the field I salute, by extolling Schuyler, is a recklessly utopian *vers libre* approximating thought's freedom, the democracy of "a commingling sky" (the first words of his first book), of solitudes assembled in taboo congregations ("Marriages of the atmosphere / are worth celebrating"). He advocates accuracy: "the sinuous beauty of words like allergy." "[O]n the other hand I am not going to espouse any short stories in which lawn mowers clack." Thus

Schuyler's poems are at once photographically hyperreal, and *symboliste* as Pan's pipe.

•

One can enter Schuyler's creed of *freedom to espouse* through his least free poem, his divinely flat villanelle, self-consciously yet humbly titled "Poem," which I read (arbitrarily?) as an implicit address to John Ashbery, or to the aesthetic of voluptuous opacity that Ashbery was at the time espousing. Imagine Ashbery and Schuyler as two participants in a Socratic—Wildean, Yeatsian, Gidean—dialogue about words and meaning, transparency and secrecy. Here is Schuyler's half of the debate, rendered in a form, the villanelle, which traffics in paired puzzled refrains:

> I do not always understand what you say.
> Once, when you said, across, you meant along.
> What is, is by its nature, on display.
>
> Words' meanings count, aside from what they weigh:
> poetry, like music, is not just song.
> I do not always understand what you say.
>
> You would hate, when with me, to meet by day
> What at night you met and did not think wrong.
> What is, is by its nature, on display.
>
> I sense a heaviness in your light play,
> a wish to stand out, admired, from the throng.
> I do not always understand what you say.
>
> I am as shy as you. Try as we may,
> only by practice will our talks prolong.
> What is, is by its nature, on display.

We talk together in a common way.
Art, like death, is brief; life and friendship long.
I do not always understand what you say.
What is, is by its nature, on display.

Think of Elizabeth Bishop's famous "One Art" (also, significantly, a villanelle): "One Art" and "Salute" are two great postmodern statements of the poetics of the closet. Bishop wrote: "though it may look like (*Write* it!) like disaster." Simile ("like") is about to happen; self-consciousness (or writer's block) interrupts the line. Similarly, Schuyler hiccups between "what is" and "is by its nature." Is, is. Like, like. At the center of definition, exposition, or declaration, lies a stuttering repetition.

•

A prose paraphrase of Schuyler's "Poem": *I thought I was your aesthetic opposite, J.A., but actually we're allies, alongside. Sometimes I can't understand your poems. Why not "display" yourself? And yet even masks can't help but disclose. We reveal, against our will. J.A., principle of hiddenness, you permit by night what you shirk by day. Is it our "nature" to display, to flaunt? Is our "nature" natural? I love the natural world though I am a man of interiors (hotels, indolences). J.A., why do you wish to stand out, admired, from the throng of poets—to attract acclaim by virtue of your reluctance to display? Our poems are conversations with each other's. I am display, you are secrecy; my poems can't be read apart from yours, nor yours apart from mine, nor ours apart from Frank O'Hara's, who displayed everything, by night and day. We use common speech. We also follow a shared—communitarian—path. If what is, is by its nature, on display, then why bother writing poems? Won't the world display itself, without our earnest boosterism?*

•

Hearing Ashbery and Schuyler read together at the Poetry Center at New York's 92nd Street Y, in the late 1980s (the evening marked Schuyler's return, after years of no public readings), I observed separated corpuses converging, as both writers described atmospheres, cloud cover, the "changeable / silk" of sky and mood. Ashbery had never seemed more concerned with the comic, the gracile; Schuyler had never seemed more metaphysical.

•

Schuyler commonly and indolently uses the verb "to be"; he identifies. This is this. "The scars upon the day / are harsh marks of / tranquility." Do not oppose scar and happiness. Here, from "The Morning of the Poem," again, note the all-important "is": "Heart of the island beneath tall trees is all overgrown with ferns / and moss begemmed with fog and is silent." The "is" functions as a mystical aporia: where a reader wants or expects an action verb, a development, a motion, instead Schuyler delivers a fey equivalence, a swish.

•

His last long poem, "A Few Days," ends with the death of his mother: "Margaret Daisy Conner Schuyler Ridenour, / rest well, / the weary journey done." The weary journey of poem making? The weary journey of pretending that love existed where it was absent:

> And so I won't be
> there to see my Maney
> enearthed beside
> my stepfather:
> once when I was
> home a while ago
> I said I realized
> that in his way he

loved me. "He did
not," my mother said.
"Burton hated you."
The old truth-teller!

Of James the son we might say the same: truth-teller! Truth the mother tells is truth the son is unafraid to include in the poem: "Burton hated you." Some of the many truths that Schuyler told: I am lazy, I enjoy cigarettes and Guerlain's Impériale, taxi rides and lists, gifts and letters, quotations and flowers, names and fantasies, houses and boredom. I like to read but also to half-read: "Riding along in the beautiful day (there go two / blue enamel silos), half-reading about marvelous / Chamfort . . ." Reading Schuyler I'm also half-reading him: noticing inattention's radiance.

•

All the poems James Schuyler never planted: past is past. Each poem marks the place where there might also have been others, but these shadow poems live inside the ones that remain, making the *Collected* a set of epitaphs for undisplayed sentiments. Displayed poem stands in for the veiled experience, as a named rose placemarks the real rose and eventually replaces it. Schuyler loves words and therefore he often forgets and must search for them—the process of retrieval is the unfolding of the poem:

> But oh dear: I forgot the five Old China Monthly
> roses, and I always wish I'd planted Félicité
> et Perpétue—it's their names I like. And
> Climbing Lady Hillington.

And—line break—Climbing Lady Hillington is not a rose but a name. Schuyler salutes roses, but also rose books, the veritable flower buried in its epitaph, and he shows no remorse that fossil memorabilia conceal the tangible petal: "I didn't plant / a winter garden, but the book led on to his / rose books: 'The Old Shrub Roses,' 'Shrub Roses / of Today,' and the one about climbers and ramblers." Old rambler, old truth-teller!

•

Another "is," from an early poem, "Fabergé," to prove that the climactic Schuyler act is to espouse an equivalence, to correct a perception and to reclaim the beauty of the prior misapprehension: "Here, just for you, is a rose made out of a real rose and the dewdrop nestled in a rosy petal that has the delicate five-o'clock-shadow fuzz—blue—is not a tear." That was a prose sentence: studying Schuyler, one reconsiders the difference between poetry and prose, revisits the line break and asks what it hosts.

•

Words in his short lines float, stressed, atop the line's surface, bubbles or corks, sometimes bumping against one another, more buoyant than most poets' solo syllables. Now as I search through the *Collected* for an example of syllable flotation I am surprised to note that many of his feet *are* iambic ("the other dark") so what explains the not-rising not-falling weightlessness of the opening of, say, "Korean Mums":

> beside me in this garden
> are huge and daisy-like
> (why not? are not
> oxeye daisies a chrysanthemum?),
> shrubby and thick-stalked,
> the leaves pointing up
> the stems from which
> the flowers burst in
> sunbursts. I love
> this garden in all its moods . . .

His trick is parenthesis; he performs an act of metaphor (this is this, this is not this) which gets interrupted or reversed, so the simple act of identification (Korean mums are Korean mums—but this tautology climbs no ladder of definition) turns into a misidentification, a voyage away from the readily nameable. Korean mums turn daisy-like, "in" bumps into its across-the-line-break cousin "sunbursts." "Beside me": the poet writes with one hand, holds a figurative nectarine in the other hand, and admits the fruity distraction into the poem. He allows the stuttering "why not? are not?" to suffice as a line, and shoves the meatier words "oxeye daisies" and "chrysanthemum" into a separate line, thus segregating flat stammer syllables ("why not? are not") from gorgeous flower names nearly composing an iambic pentameter line: "oxeye daisies a chrysanthemum?"

•

Schuyler's poems exemplify: they are salesman samples, shop-window displays of what is possible in poetry and what is not feasible in life, or what miraculous acts quicken in the actual because he found a way to break them down into lines. Here, in "Growing Dark," simple syllables in a short line glow because metaphor or misidentification has happened—nature displaying itself but also seeming not to mean what it says. "The grass shakes. / Smoke streaks, no, / cloud strokes. / The dogs are fed." Shakes, strokes, streaks: the words sound alike but aren't; and yet the words exist in relation. They have experienced lovely nepotism. The incest of assonance. Endogamous consonance.

•

One of the only Schuyler poems in numbered parts is the great "Dining Out with Doug and Frank." I don't want to force him into "great" even though I think he deserves that designation, more often reserved for writers with occluded, unchatty vision; instead, Schuyler loves the marmoreal possibilities of the instantaneous, the slow duration of the nothing-in-particular. The poet tells us that Ashbery once asked him: "I don't think James Joyce is any good. Do you?" Schuyler remembers: "Think, what did I think! I / didn't know you were *allowed* not to like James / Joyce. The book I suppose is a masterpiece: freedom of choice / is better." (Consensual reading: consensual sex. Freedom to espouse.) Like Schuyler's simplest sentences, "Dining Out with Doug and Frank" is devoted to postponement. It begins with a gesture of turning away from the act of exposition or narration. *Soon I'll tell you about dining out with Doug and Frank, but not yet. Let me digress, first, to ephemera, queers, and soap.* "Not quite yet. First, / around the corner for a visit / to the Bella Landauer Collection / of printed ephemera: / luscious lithos and why did / Fairy Soap vanish and / Crouch and Fitzgerald survive? / Fairy Soap was once a / household word!" Rule of thumb: before the poet writes, he or she must say, "Not quite yet," and go around the corner to visit a collection that will always remain marginal (yet connected) to the poem: a realm (like Keats's nectarine) that the poem gestures toward, but that can only enter language through hesitations, detours, self-cancellations, and self-chastisements. ("*Write* it!")

•

Will Schuyler—his poems—survive only as printed ephemera? On the survival of his cakes of line-broken Fairy Soap rests the life or death of poetry. (To say it melodramatically.) In order to write poetry, one must cultivate belief in the continued life offered by the line's end. One must imagine that there are readers eager for the silence it proposes. One must turn away from a busy, beguiling, media-rich world that does not revere or notice or propose a use for our Cain mark, the line break. To read Schuyler is to envision its death, if only because his are so deft and neurasthenically self-conscious—

aware, in their delicacy, of the indifference and scorn surrounding all hypermodulated, hypernuanced sensation and utterance. The death of the line break: "Millay wrote a lovely poem about / it all. I cannot accept their / death, or any other death." Or: "Why is this poem / so long? And full of death?" One feels sorry for the line break: as if it were a dying heroine, or consumptive Keats, spitting blood in Rome. "Millay wrote a lovely poem about / it all": poems are about "it all." After the "about," what comes but an empty gesture, "it all," signifying the things that neither Edna St. Vincent Millay nor Schuyler, who accepts his Millay-like "minor" status, has the mastery to put into words?

•

Secret stoicism of Schuyler's keenly observant eye: in "The Payne Whitney Poems" he admits enough details of the context—nervous breakdown, time in mental hospitals—for the reader to gather how much is left out of the other poems, despite their apparent intimacy and casualness. (Recall the famous 1950s and 1960s poetries of breakdown, and observe Schuyler's difference; with Bishop he stands apart from the "confessional"—though what poet has *not* broken down, what poetry worthy of the name has *not* originated in an experience of breakdown, if only indirectly echoed in the line break's swan's down?) From "February 13, 1975": "Some- / one is watching morning / TV. I'm not reduced to that / yet. I wish one could press / snowflakes in a book like flowers." Pronoun is broken down: "Some- / one." One can't preserve real snowflakes in a book, and can't include, in a poem, the nectarine. Hear the sound of the ward in these lines from "What": "What's in these pills? / After lunch and I can / hardly keep my eyes / open. Oh, for someone to / talk small talk with. / Even a dog would do." Not melodramatic, not hysterical. "Talk" and "talk" monotonously cohabit one line:

"talk small talk with." The first "talk" is a verb, the second, a noun. On its measly mental-institution day, "talk" performs two separate tasks. Dreadfulness of the inner life leads him to ask, in a beautiful, if fragile, poem, "What is a / poem, anyway." Contemplate the line broken between the article "a" and the noun "poem": poems can't be so important if the word "poem" isn't allowed to embrace its petty indirect article in the selfsame line. Probe the meaning of "anyway," the throwaway word. The poem's earlier question: "And what / is that generator whose / fierce hum comes in / the window?" The generator outside the window, fiercely humming, is the force that through the sick mind drives the flower: as Dickinson would say, "*That* is poetry."

•

I slept two hours and woke up thinking, "My aesthetic health depends on describing accurately what is remarkable about James Schuyler's poetry." But I wonder if aesthetic health is an imaginary, repressive category, serving to divide unfit from able specimens. Reliable witnesses attest that Schuyler was mentally ill. But he was the picture of poetic well-being: pink and prime. Maybe my constitution depends on not describing, on letting the object of pleasure remain unexplained. Does Schuyler require the sanction of explication? Wanting, like a plaque, to announce a location on Twenty-Third Street where Schuyler, and poetry, once lived, I open (more or less at random) to the following line from the *Collected Poems*: "I pick up a loaded pen and twiddle it." How to avoid twiddling? How to explain the contiguity of poetry and twiddle, and Schuyler's deep affirmation of indecision, error, and illness?

•

An early line from Schuyler: "Then the moon goes crocus." He coldly yet exultantly notes the moment of metamorphosis:

the moon turning crocus. Crocus is a flower, not a color. I salute the long *o* of "goes" and "crocus," words to sit on. "Then the moon goes crocus" is the last line. How do you know when to end a poem? When the poem goes crocus, it's time to stop.

•

As I write these words I am living on Twenty-Third Street right next to James Schuyler's Chelsea Hotel and the plaque honoring him. From evidence in the poems, I've reconstructed that his apartment looked northward, onto Twenty-Third, while mine faces south, onto Twenty-Second. (This may be untrue.) The light in my room, when I have the energy to notice it, is not damned. I think of it as Schuyler's light. "What can one write / between the lines? Not one damn thing."

•

Schuyler light: noticed and therefore put into poems, even as it—the light—goes:

> This beauty that I see
> —the sun going down
> scours the entangled
> and lightly henna
> withies and the wind
> whips them as it
> would ship a cloud—
> is passing so swiftly
> into night.

What are withies? Willows with flexible branches. The keynote of a withy is its willingness to be whipped. Beauty enters the room, the self, the poem, only to scour the surface: to punish it. He writes "it goes, it goes." What goes? Beauty. This beauty that I see, goes. This poem is called "Poem," and it dwells in a section of *Hymn to Life* entitled "Elsewhere." Schuyler's beauty has now gone elsewhere: onto the inanimate, withy-invoking page; into the mind of a reader flexible enough to be entangled by the nearly obvious. Schuyler was "just able" to collect, into lines, what he saw:

> . . . This
> beauty that collects
> dry leaves in pools
> and pockets and goes
> freezingly, just able
> still to swiftly flow
> it goes, it goes.

So it goes, into the uncollectable. Reading Schuyler's *Collected*, one hears and admires—one loves—the "just able," the almost not able: a poetics on the verge of not emerging; a poetry on the verge of not being able to exist.

•

A more complete quotation from the Lord Byron letter excerpted at this essay's beginning: "So you and Mr. Foscolo &c. want me to undertake what you call a 'great work' an Epic poem I suppose or some such pyramid.—I'll try no such thing—I hate tasks—and then 'seven or eight years!' "

•

Writers depend on what other writers have thought but not transcribed; writers depend on between-the-lines ecstasies and fears of other writers. Rapport between a dead and living scribbler is not agon but identification, a sequence of heady questions: all I want from Schuyler's poems is that they speak, even if I can't quite identify the nature of this speaker, so profuse in what he espouses, so diffuse in what he displays. From Schuyler's "Amy Lowell Thoughts":

Draped one,
speak.
Are you a larch?

Schuyler depends on Amy Lowell having had Amy Lowell–type thoughts: inscrutable, unstudied, unsaluted. Draped poet, I want to know what you were thinking on a certain silent afternoon, a nothing day. I want to hear the gnomic thoughts that passed and dispersed before poetry, the enemy of loss, found the means to incorporate them.

•

Many, some, or a couple of his poems end with the word *goodbye.*

(1996)

III.

Privacy in the Films of Lana Turner

June 28, 1999

In *Imitation of Life*, Sandra Dee shouts to Lana Turner, "Stop acting!"

I am trying to learn how to keep my emotions private—even from the reader, whoever you are.

In the photographic series "Lana Backwards," John Waters enjoys the back of Lana Turner's head: its self-sufficient, enigmatic chignon.

Waters certainly knows that *Lana* backwards is *anal*.

I live near a historic Hudson River Valley mansion named Olana.

Frank O'Hara: "oh Lana Turner we love you get up."

Yesterday was the Gay Pride Parade—thirty-year anniversary of the Stonewall uprising. I didn't go. I've run out of gay pride.

Lana Turner has an emotionless face in *Imitation of Life*.

Though retentive, I'm not imitating Lana.

Douglas Sirk's crooked camera gives Lana no privacy: he insists that her every gesture yield its secret.

The décor grows more decadent as the story's tawdriness builds. The more Lana suffers, the richer the rooms, the pinker the walls, the larger her diamonds.

Jean Louis designed Lana's costumes. His name, in the credits, earns fancy cursive. Jean Louis has privacy because I don't know his last name.

Lana died four years ago tomorrow: June 29, 1995. I don't remember reading the obituary.

July 14, 1999 (Bastille Day)

Only holidays celebrating revolutionary freedom wake me from torpor.

Landscape was Andy Warhol's euphemism for *nude*.

I want to repeat what Andy told his *Diary* about Lana, because it reshapes the landscape she drapes around me:

> It was a busy day but I left early to catch Lana Turner at Bloomingdale's ($8). Bought one of her books ($16). Then went up to her and she said, "I don't think I want to talk to you, I've taken you out of my prayers, you said I was better when I hadn't found God, so now I pray for you—*badly*." So I think it was something I said in the Faye Dunaway interview in *Interview*, I guess she read it. And I didn't know what to do, I was a nervous wreck, I said, "Oh no, Lana, you've *got* to pray for me, please put me back in your prayers!" And I said, "Oh won't you please autograph your book to me?" And so she finally did and wrote "To a Friend" with a question mark and then "God Bless You" with another question mark. And Lana and her fairy hairdresser and I were all there with the same hair.

Note Andy's lumping Lana, fairy, and himself together—three with duplicitous hair. Note Andy's wish to enter her factitious prayers. Note his assumption that she reads *Interview*. Note *badly*. What does it mean to pray badly—to pray so incompetently that the plea backfires?

August 1, 1999

John F. Kennedy Jr.'s plane went into a "graveyard spiral." Then I got sick to my stomach and convalesced for a week, thinking about John's final thirty seconds—plunging downward into the water. No one in the press mentioned that John's stepbrother, Alexander Onassis, had also died in a tragic plane crash.

Last night I saw *Madame X*, costumes by Jean Louis. In it, Lana has privacy: she loses her identity, abandons son and husband, and pretends to drown off a yacht—but actually moves incognito to some Nordic country (Denmark?) and then to Mexico.

There, living under an alias in a hovel, she loses privacy, because Burgess Meredith, a con man, finds out her secret, barges into her room while she is showering, and offers her a Christmas bottle of absinthe. Lana has no privacy from literary echo: her desolation recalls the fictive worlds of Jane and Paul Bowles.

Nor does Lana have privacy from the viewer, who knows the Johnny Stompanato scandal (her daughter, Cheryl Crane, killed Lana's gangster lover on Good Friday 1958) and who sees the film's courtroom scene as an imitation of Lana's real life: facing trial for murder, the Lana character is defended by her son, played by Keir Dullea, who looks Martian, handsome, earnest, like someone connected to the Scopes trial, or a religious but hypersexed guy who wipes the wet counter clean with a towel at the gay bar Barracuda. Seeing Madame X confess to the judge, the tabloid-schooled viewer remembers photos of the real Lana at her daughter's trial.

The question to ask of any scene in which Lana Turner appears: is this scene taking place in a prison or in a room which Lana has liberty to leave?

I am tempted to say, *Lana is never at liberty, despite her stardom*, except this generalization seems true of any star, especially the lasting ones.

The large rooms in which Lana, pre-sin, playing wife, wears Jean Louis gowns while she ministers to her toddler, afford us scopic privacy: advantaged, we look around Lana's loneliness, scanning and surveying it, measuring its resemblance to our unfilmed solitude.

Madame X was released in 1966, the year of *Blow-Up*. And yet this Lana vehicle harks back to bygone women's pictures, such as Joan Crawford's *A Woman's Face* (1941) and Bette Davis's *Now, Voyager* (1942)—films in which a star endures exile from beauty; endures a glacial matriarch's putdowns; endures protracted, oceanic travel from one identity into another; endures love affairs with the wrong men (too old, too medical, too asexual); endures wrongful separation from her children. In women's pictures, the star's real-life travail matches the character's, and the punishing process of becoming-a-star or ceasing-to-be-a-star resembles menarche or menopause stretched to the duration of *Götterdämmerung*.

August 2, 1999

Kenneth Anger's *Hollywood Babylon* reprints the front page of the *New York Mirror*, Wednesday, April 9, 1958 (at that time I was a six-month fetus in my mother's womb): the headline is BARE LANA'S LOVE LETTERS, and beside a photo of Lana in sunglasses is a "burning letter from Lana Turner to Johnny Stompanato, knife-slain by her teen daughter": "Oh darling darling, the letter I wrote you last nite was so much in the same vein as yours I've just received—so you see we certainly are in tune . . ." Contemporary pundits may claim that only recently have celebrities lost their privacy, but Lana's career proves that the secret lives of stars have been public property for at least half a century.

From Lana's courtroom testimony, quoted by Anger:

> Everything happened so quickly that I did not even see the knife in my daughter's hand. I thought she had hit him in the stomach with her fist. Mr. Stompanato stumbled forward, turned around and fell on his back. He choked, his hands on his throat. I ran to him and lifted up his sweater. I saw the blood . . . He made a horrible noise in his throat . . .

In *Madame X*, Lana reenacts this real-life episode when she pushes Ricardo Montalban down the stairs to his death and when she shoots Burgess Meredith point-blank in the gut—both scenes reminiscent of Joan Crawford's *Mildred Pierce*, when the daughter (Ann Blyth) shoots her louche stepfather, and martyr Joan tries to soak up the blame. In life, Joan would be betrayed by her daughter Christina in the tell-all *Mommie Dearest.* Star mothers and their daughters do not, together, create the cloistered privacy of Monterchi, where Piero della Francesca's pregnant fresco greets its few-at-a-time pilgrims.

Am I indirectly telling you about my mother and my sister? I hope not.

August 3, 1999

After the death of John F. Kennedy Jr., I thought about his sister, Caroline, and was thankful that his mother wasn't alive to hear about the vanished plane.

It is difficult to get *behind* Lana's beauty—difficult to figure out where, if anywhere, it goes. Beauty, a vector, must have a direction. Where does Lana's travel? Not toward the past or the future. Her beauty, like Kim Novak's, dominates by staying put. *Madame X* proves that the 1950s lasted until

1966, if only in the form of Lana's beauty. The costumes are 1950s. The emotions are 1950s. The expectation that a woman would give up her identity to protect her son's and husband's reputations is 1950s.

The *X* in *Madame X* suggests the male chromosome, not the female. So Lana might be Madame Male, the woman who masochistically gives up her name and her life so that her son can prosper.

Where, recently, did I read that masochism had its joys? In a Lorrie Moore story about a woman who accidentally killed a baby.

August 4, 1999

I am trying to figure out what Lana's abdomen looks like. The costumes call attention to it and also disguise it. Something is up with the abdomen. I'm convinced that the abdomen is a crux of the films.

August 12, 1999

Too much time has passed since I last wrote about Lana. Since then I have become what Lana called a "Lanatic"—her lunatic fan.

I am *awaiting* Lana: as I learned by reading Maurice Blanchot's *Awaiting Oblivion*, the words *latent* and *attentive* and *await* sleep together and describe a state, mine now, of forward-moving decomposition.

After I saw Lana in *The Bad and the Beautiful* I heard about the death by cancer of Anthony Radziwill (JFK Jr.'s first cousin and best friend). I tried to imagine Lee Bouvier Canfield Radziwill Ross's grief.

Within *The Bad and the Beautiful*, Lana appears in several screen tests, filmed from the rear; we see only the back of her head, as if a frontal glimpse would scorch us.

August 20, 1999

By now I've read three books about Lana—her autobiography, *Lana: The Lady, the Legend, the Truth*; an exposé by her former escort Eric Root, *The Private Diary of My Life with Lana*; and *Lana: The Public and Private Lives of Miss Turner*, by Joe Morella and Edward Z. Epstein.

Note Lana's piquant candor:

> I'd had my appendix removed back in San Francisco, after an acute attack when I was fourteen. An incompetent surgeon had cut me open from just below the navel to near the pubic hairline, and later inserted tubes when peritonitis developed. Because of that botched operation, I had so much scar tissue that my ovaries and my colon were both affected. I suffered terribly during menstruation. My Los Angeles doctor finally had to operate to clean it up.

Here and elsewhere, Miss Turner is both diffident and exhibitionistic. She wants to conceal, but she must reveal, too, so that fans can gain access to her starry interior.

Eric Root, Lana's hairdresser, shocks us by alleging that Cheryl Crane did *not* murder Johnny Stompanato, but that Lana found the two in bed together and that she herself stabbed the mobster. Eric Root (his platinum hair in the author photo a deliberate copy of Lana's?) spills many other private details of the star's life. My favorite:

> During one of our many conversations in her twilight years, she told me that "Lex [Barker] was physically the best lover I ever had. Not simply because he was well hung, which, my darling, he was, but because he was incredible at oral sex."

> That came as no surprise to me. Throughout the many years of our relationship she'd told me many times that she preferred the oral route to conventional sex, "because," she would intimately whisper, "I was always *too tight.*"

We hear, too, about huge jugs of Chardonnay that Lana kept in her refrigerator. Booze and jewels—twinned gods—shadow her private sphere.

Judy Turner chose for herself the name Lana, but she didn't know at the time that it was Spanish for wool. Alas, *They Won't Forget*, the movie in which, playing a murdered schoolgirl, she wears the famous tight wool sweater, earning her the sobriquet "sweater girl," hasn't been released on video.

August 21, 1999

I know too much about Lana Turner: I might self-combust. I want to write a novel about the Johnny Stompanato affair, from three points of view: Lana's, Cheryl's, and Johnny's. (I have already written two novels about private matters, novels I may never publish, not only because in their present form they are poorly conceived and therefore not gripping to a reader, but because their subjects are too intimate and undisguised for public consumption.)

Harold Robbins wrote a novel based on the Stompanato murder: *Where Love Has Gone*. Snob, I don't want my projected novel to fall into the Robbins pool.

My Lana Turner novel will begin with Cheryl's story (what follows is not fact but fantasy): I will describe her sexual longings for Lana; Cheryl's horror and delight at her own developing body; marathon masturbation sessions; reveries as she stares into the mirror; stashed sweets she feeds herself; boys and girls whose bodies she craves; her car; what she thinks when she attends the *Imitation of Life* premiere on her mother's arm (only a year after the Stompanato murder); Cheryl's attitude toward Lana's chignon and toward her own imitative upswept coiffure.

Then I will turn to Johnny's story (again, not facts, merely fantasies): his bisexuality; thuggish childhood; violations he experienced as boy-victim; penchant for beating girlfriends and remorse afterward; his love for Lana's fake blonde tresses; his knowledge of her missing eyebrows, shaved in 1938 by MGM and never growing back, falsely applied every morning by vigilant Lana; his love of Lanita's breasts ("Dear Lanita," he says, and she says, in response, "I am your only Lanita, your love, your dearest Lanita"); stupor as he sunbathes, in Acapulco, beside Lana; fury because she forbids him to escort her to the Academy Awards when she is nominated for *Peyton Place* (he beats her, at home, that night, after she returns from the ceremony); his ruminations as he watches *Peyton Place*; what he hears Lana say about Joanne Woodward's performance in *The Three Faces of Eve*, for which she won the Oscar, trumping Lanita; Johnny's lust for Cheryl; curiosity about how far he can push Cheryl into the incestuous abyss; his certainty that Lana knows about his desire for Cheryl, and Cheryl's desire for him; languor as he takes a bath, water scented by a Portuguese infusion that Lanita bought for him in London, where she flew, trying to excise him from her life.

And then I will tell Lana's story, in Lana's voice—not truly her story, as Cheryl's and Johnny's stories, in my telling, are not truly theirs*: Lana's attitude toward her own stardom; Lana's ambivalence about Mildred, her loyal mother;

*Indeed, will I be able to write this book without fear of legal action by Cheryl, who is alive and well? Certainly I can't use her name without permission, which she would never grant.

Lana's love of dark men, also of blonds; Lana's curiosity about the male member, and her indifference to its shenanigans; Lana holding the knife and stabbing Johnny straight in the aorta, lucky plunge; Lana's fit of hysterical blindness as she sees Cheryl and Johnny in bed together and hears Cheryl's callous laughter; the time Lana slashes her wrists and then must cover the scars with wide bracelets (no star must seem suicidal, says MGM, and yet many of its stars were forced to that brink, Judy Garland among them, Judy once Lana's bridesmaid and neighbor); Lana's forgiveness of Marilyn Monroe's usurpation, because she knows that Marilyn has bulges and Lana has none; ritual gaze in the mirror before Lana leaves her house for a public appearance ("I must spend another two hours here, studying my face, because it is imperative I do not appear in public unless I am myself, and I have not yet adequately applied the champagne eyebrows, my hair's peach dye tiring the follicles"); Lana's devotion to the first-person pronoun; Lana's attitude toward her bra, its necessity, its normalcy, its grip on appearances, and its relation to the gaze of Douglas Sirk and the gowns of Jean Louis; devotion to Harriet, who polishes her nails; love for Carmencita, loyal maid; Lana's assumption that Carmencita is not entirely a person, but is merely an appendage, a lumpish solicitous presence holding the TV-dinner tray and the remote control; Lana's shock as she watches, at the premiere, the last seconds of *Portrait in Black*, in which her character is caught as murderer and the camera freezes an image of her face, framing her, and then, with electric-chair immediacy, reversing the portrait, turning Lana into her photographic negative, turning white Lana into black Lana, as her surrogate daughter Susan Kohner in *Imitation of Life* had secretly wished (*I want Lana to be black so I can be white, I secretly know that Lana is black and merely passing for white*); Lana's conviction that she is white and that her race is public knowledge, though also a private cognizance, like a mirror observing itself; delight in lying abed until three p.m., sleeping and waking, comfortable because she is not yet made up in Lana drag but is still Judy Turner, the failed Judy who dreams of becoming Lana; remorse as she hears Cheryl say, with disgust, "You are Lana Turner!"; certainty that in a past life she was inside Johnny's body, that the body he possesses and calls "Johnny" is hers by right; her shock when John Steele, the false name he uses for the first months of their courtship, cracks open to give birth to the violent Stompanato.

August 29, 1999

Last week I flew to San Francisco to visit my family—mother, father, stepfather, stepmother, sister, brother, brother. I asked my mother if she remembered the Stompanato murder. She said yes, but she didn't have an emotional reaction to it. It was just another scandal. Somehow I thought she would warm to the word "Stompanato," a sign of quality and difference.

If ever I imagined that my father resembled Johnny, I was wrong: my father looks like a fallen wise man from a lost Israelite tribe.

My sister, however, has Cheryl Crane's poise.

In *Portrait in Black*, Sandra Dee again plays Lana's daughter. Many blondes in the 1950s and 1960s (and thereafter) imitated Lana; and Lana knew it. She taught *temperature* to Diane Dors, Jayne Mansfield, Mamie Van Doren, Marilyn Monroe, and, eventually, Madonna.

August 30, 1999

Another intemperate gem from Lana's autobiography:

> Out of the corner of my eye I saw Cheryl make a sudden movement. Her right arm had shot out and caught John in the stomach. I thought she'd punched him.

> There was a strange little moment, locked in time, as each stood looking at the other.
>
> "Oh, my God, Cheryl," John gasped out. "What have you done?"
>
> I darted forward off the counter, afraid that John was going to punch Cheryl back. Cheryl was backing up slowly, staring at John. John took three little circling steps away from her, in slow motion. He didn't clutch his belly; he didn't cry out.

Conjure Lana's feelings as she says "John," and John's as he says "Cheryl"; picture Cheryl's humiliation. Perhaps Lana shames Cheryl by saying, "You don't want the world to know that you went to bed with my boyfriend, do you?" and so murder (justifiable homicide) seems a better rap—better to be remembered as one who defended her mother against a lover's sadistic abuse than to be remembered as a teenage tramp.

Find Cheryl Crane's autobiography, *Detour*, and devour it.

August 31, 1999

Can you figure out the difference, physically, between Kim Novak and Lana Turner? To do so, you would need to explore the metaphorical career of platinum, which is beyond my present scope.

Lana does not appear in *Vertigo*, but she almost does. *Vertigo* was released in 1958, the year of the Stompanato slaying (which Lana and Cheryl euphemistically refer to as "Good Friday" or "the paragraph"). In film after film, Lana watches a man fall down the stairs or off a roof—as if Jimmy Stewart's fear of falling in *Vertigo* reenacted (or predicted) Johnny's descent into death.

Last night, I dreamed that I embraced John Ashbery and

discovered that he had written many poems unknown to the public; in a secret, optimistic, seaside house, like Lana's Pacific Heights mansion in *Portrait in Black*, I found his munificent, endless, uncorrected drafts.

September 2, 1999

I've avoided Lana Turner for a day—too dangerous an immersion. I turn away from it as I'd shirk a hustler district I'm dying to frequent.

Yesterday, I read *A Consumer's Guide to Male Hustlers* by Joseph Itiel (a sober, levelheaded assessment of the art of procuring and vending), and I saw *By Love Possessed*—not one of Lana's best, though she wears a compelling orange bathrobe while, preparing to abandon her "cripple" husband, she packs a suitcase. Hubby (Jason Robards Jr.) had an accident, and uses a cane, which signifies, in the movie's dated parlance, impotence. (Why doesn't he go down on Lana?) Unsated, she turns to drink and jewels, and finds momentary relief in the arms of Efrem Zimbalist Jr. Susan Kohner, who tried to pass as white in *Imitation of Life*, returns, in *By Love Possessed*, as the proper white girl who wants hunk George Hamilton's love. George, predecessor of Burt Reynolds and Tom Selleck in my private brothel, plays the son of Barbara Bel Geddes (privately I call her Barbara Bell Pepper), who ghosted Kim Novak—a Lana simulacrum—in *Vertigo*.

My favorite moment in *By Love Possessed* (a snippet I replayed a dozen times): Lana's husband, self-denigrating, says, "I'm still a cripple," and she responds: "You *are* what you *are*! A strong, moody, complicated man—and you *are* a cripple . . ."

Quickly she says "and you *are* a cripple"—as if rushing to reinstate, under the guise of common sense ("and you *will* need an umbrella"), the insult she'd pretended to revoke.

I want Lana's voice to say, as the outgoing message on my answering machine: "Hello. You *are* what you *are*! A strong, moody, complicated man—and you *are* a cripple"—for I love seeing men put in their places by icy important women who might one day appreciate my mind (but never my body).

Lana has privacy in *By Love Possessed*—she spends the night with her lover in a secret playhouse. Millions of viewers see her adulterous act, but no other character in the movie witnesses it, and so Lana seems alone with her error.

September 10, 1999

Last night's Turkish delight: *Peyton Place*. In it, Lana hides her slatternly past with a prudish veneer. Daughter Diane Varsi wants to neck in the dark with a boy: mother Lana turns on the light. Lana is dolled up in a vacuum: no reason she needs to wear such phenomenal dresses, no reason her hair needs to be stretched—punishment coiffure—to breaking point in the back, as if it were Foster's Freeze vanilla, squeezed out in conical swirls.

Turn Lana around, stare at the back of her head, the part without a face, the part without expression or animation, the bun-under-duress, the public bun, the fold on the back of her coiffure, where the real hair and the fake hair meet, or where the hair tucks into itself, resembling the lock or clasp on a ten-year diary: this is the puncture point—Barthes called it a *punctum*—where the camera grows curious, instantaneous, unsure of what to do with the information. The bun is a turnover—where the mind, contemplating Lana, turns over on itself.

La Nature lies inside the artificial name Lana Turner.

A gentleman scholar recently told me, "Lana Turner's only serious film was *Imitation of Life*." Wrong. Lana Turner in *Peyton Place* exerts seriously imperious commentary on the meaning of publicity and privacy. With her star turn's assistance, we may brood about the perversity of *place*—impossible definitively to place Lana within culture's continuum of lows and highs, and impossible to place her platinum hair (the hegemonic no-color of whiteness) within the chromatic spectrum.

Who knows how she kept her hair so freakishly correct. Eventually, conveniently, she took on hairdresser Eric Root as her companion. Maintaining and coloring her hair, Mr. Root preserved her public identity's fraudulent foundation.

September 14, 1999

Some people obsessively reexamine their lives; others straightforwardly endure them. I would rather be one who endures; instead, I am an examiner.

Lana Turner and Cheryl Crane remind me of my mother and my sister battling, and of my mother and her mother battling.

Last night I saw *Where Love Has Gone*, loosely based on the Stompanato scandal. Joey Heatherton, playing delinquent daughter to Susan Hayward, has a butch pointiness to her head; the bouffant, a form of exaggeration, leans away from sense. Why is Joey Heatherton's head always pointing to the side? Why is there so much space between her hairline and her eyebrows? Why does every word she utters interrupt realism? Why does she have a boy's first name?

Susan Hayward's hair, in 1964, is big, and is certainly a wig. It prepares for the later, infamous wig she will wear as Helen Lawson in *Valley of the Dolls*. When Susan Hayward's wig and Joey Heatherton's, in the same frame, attract and repel each other, I want to shout with admiration: *How can your warfare be so perfect?*

In a photo of Lana and Cheryl together on a horse, 1959,

the "third meaning" (see Barthes's classic essay "The Third Meaning: Research Notes on Several Eisenstein Stills") is Lana's cigarette. I will never know why she is smoking while horseback riding. My definition of a star: a person around whom "third meanings" congregate, like mosquitoes.

The third meaning: the extraneous detail that captures my attention; the incidental crux that I choose to contemplate. Lana Turner is the third meaning of 1950s and 1960s star culture. Cheryl Crane is the third meaning of Lana. Joey Heatherton is the third meaning of *Where Love Has Gone*. I lean too hard on the concept of the third meaning, but I can't let go of it: it explains too much. It explains my love of inessentials and accessories, and my identification with objects that promise a definite significance but blessedly never deliver it—stars on the brink of hardening into fetishes, but never finally gaining location, and languishing, instead, as miasmic, unthematic embers.

The film's climax: we learn that Joey Heatherton, when she killed the boyfriend, had actually been trying to stab the mother. Are we therefore to believe that, in real life, Cheryl intended the knife for Lana, not for Johnny?

If I were a girl, and my mother were a movie star, might I want to kill her?

A star will kill to keep her stardom, even if she doesn't seem to be the one holding the knife. The murder implement, in *Where Love Has Gone*, is Susan Hayward's sculpting knife, which she finally uses to kill herself, after slashing the portrait of her mother, played by Bette Davis—a portrait that hangs, like Dorian Gray's, on the studio wall.

Where does the public's love go? Toward a new, young star like Joey Heatherton, who herself will turn into a legendary has-been.

Three generations of Hollywood disasters—Bette, Susan,

and Joey—must share one movie. No wonder they don't get along. Throw men into the mix—and at least one will get murdered. Stardom, a competitive psychological situation, has a built-in "murder" switch, flipped by any imbalance in fame's atmosphere.

Literature is private, and this essay is trying, modestly, to be literature. By writing circuitously, foolishly, with difficulty, I keep the meaning private.

Am I at liberty to leave Lana? Am I at liberty to unlock her significance to me, or will it remain private—incomprehensible even to the writer, who is often the last to know?

September 18, 1999

I've decided to finish this essay on my forty-first birthday, in two days.

Last night, I saw *The Postman Always Rings Twice*, often referred to as Lana's best performance. To offset the sluttishness of the character, she wears white and dies at the end. At the beginning, a sign on the restaurant lawn advertises MAN WANTED: the joint needs staff, and Lana wants a man. Her restaurateur husband gives her privacy: he tacitly approves of her affair with John Garfield, whose sweat-beaded face, in prison at the end, does not invite a goodnight kiss.

The viewer has erotic privacy, because Lana never takes off her clothes. (It's 1946.) At the beginning of the film, she resembles a boneless Jean Harlow; by the end, she resembles mature Lana, fantastically cruel and aesthetic.

During the making of *Postman*, Lana's daughter, Cheryl, was only two or three years old.

Walking this morning, solitary, I thought, "I need to reread *Walden*. I've forgotten how much I relish complete privacy." I don't like when my next-door neighbor can see me sitting on the porch, eating my pork chop and reading the autobiography of Cheryl Crane, in which she vividly describes seeing *Peyton Place* for the first time. (Heretofore, Lana had not permitted Cheryl to see any movies, least of all Lana's own.) The uncanny parallels between Lana's private life and her performance in *Peyton Place* were not lost on the melancholy girl:

> I couldn't get *Peyton Place* out of my mind. As I watched Mother act with Miss Varsi some tiny membrane snapped inside me. They were all too familiar, those icy, dangerous looks Mother gave, the imperial manner and tight-assed way of crossing a room, the way she would turn and punch a line . . . Now, for the first time, I sat engulfed by her Cinemascopic image, watching her scold a tall teenager, one whose soft-voiced manner reminded me of me. With that snap came a moment of realization: the techniques Mother used to intimidate and control me came not from a well of feeling but from her bag of actress tricks. To her, life was a movie. She did not live in reality.

Contradicting herself, however, Cheryl claims, a few pages later, that Lana's performance in *Peyton Place* wasn't acting at all, but a glimpse of Lanita-reality: "and while I resented that our private moments had been used in *Peyton Place*, I was glad she had gotten a nomination for it. Anyway, I knew why her acting was so good. It wasn't acting."

When I was a kid, I wanted a movie-star mother. Now, reading *Detour*, I feel lucky not to have had one. Listen to Cheryl: "I knew never to touch pretty Mommy, her hair, her makeup, her dress. In her commitment to seamless glamour, she kept herself in a perpetual state of camera-readiness, even at home." I misread the phrase "commitment to seamless glamour" as "commitment to seamless clamor." I grew up with clamor, not glamour.

Cheryl was molested by one of her mother's many husbands, Lex Barker, who played Tarzan. Other Hollywood households may have heard through the grapevine about the abuse, but they hid it from the press—wanting to keep private a star family's nightmare. Lana, too, wanted to keep it private: she was terrified of scandal's possibly deleterious effect on her career. She threw Barker out, but she didn't report him.

Cheryl destroys her mother's privacy by publishing *Detour*: she "outs" Lana as an unloving and inattentive mother. She "outs" herself, too, as a lesbian, although she does not detail the process by which she came to understand her desires: she simply says, defending herself against the imputation that she and Stompanato were romantically allied, "I had discovered girls and had never known a male lover who was tender. If I flirted with John at all, it was no different from the way I flirted with everyone, just like my mother did." How delicately she dispenses the phrase "I had discovered girls"! About other erotic matters she is more explicit—for example, the proportions of Johnny Stompanato's penis. Not from experience but from rumor she knows "the Academy-Award size of his phallus, which had earned him the nickname 'Oscar.'" Such candor sits oddly with her erstwhile aversion to public revelation: "When it came to my unhappy past, I had always avoided publicity."

In one photo of Cheryl, post-murder, she resembles Monica Lewinsky: poignant typecast girl with no way of telegraphing desire except through the tired visual cues of "on the make."

For a brief period at the start of Cheryl's puberty, Lana helped out. She showed Cheryl how to overcome personal awkwardness:

> She shared with me the secret of her famous walk, and I was able to copy it. You step one foot just slightly in front of the other; and then, as she advised, "Pretend there's a nickel tucked between your buttocks and you have to hold it there for dear life so it won't fall out."

Now we know what Lana was thinking when she walked. Now we know which muscles she was clenching. An unschooled viewer of *The Postman Always Rings Twice* might think her breasts were the center of the event, but now we know better. We know about the nickel. Why not a dime or a quarter? Perhaps because, in the Depression, a nickel was major money, and young Lana couldn't afford to experiment with higher sums.

Later in life I will be more organized. At the moment I am listening to William Kappel play Sergey Prokofiev, which reminds me of my father.

The slow cumulativeness of this diary's procedure defines my current relation to romanticism: distant.

This music isn't Prokofiev—it's Franz Liszt. No wonder my temperature rose.

Chromaticism edges the listener step by step toward the goal, which may be ecstasy, or it may simply be termination.

September 19, 1999

Not yet my birthday—but I want to put a temporary period to this detour.

Finally, at the end of her memoir, Cheryl recounts the moment that her mother admitted gratitude for Johnny's death: "Cheryl, have I never told you how much I appreciated what you did for me? How you saved my life?" Suddenly we understand: Cheryl was a hero! A hero, too, for bravely exploring queer bars in L.A. whilst a teen; inspired by Ann Bannon's novel *Odd Girl Out*, Cheryl discovered her kind and began to hang out at Dolores' Drive-In.

A year ago I was devouring the autobiography of Judy Garland's second daughter, Lorna Luft; I didn't understand why I was so possessed by it, and I condescended to my own fascination. Now I understand: there is no more reliable pathway into the heart of American fantasy than the recollections of classic Hollywood's disturbed yet lucid offspring.

In the 1950s, Lana's screen mannerisms began infecting her private behavior: in moments of stress, she would behave suddenly like one of her characters. Cheryl referred to these instants as the emergence of "L.T." (Lana Turner). " 'You will stand up when your mother comes to the table,' she said in her best L.T. voice," writes Cheryl.

In the past, I strove to speak with an L.T. voice. At the moment, I prefer Cheryl's voice, although it is less glamorous.

I have long wondered how people whose private lives are public knowledge experience mundane daily consciousness unfolding. What is it like to eat breakfast when millions of people know your intimate affairs? Is the experience of eating breakfast altered?

I have been listening to Charles Gounod's *Faust* while I write this entry. Flirting with damnation, I vacillate between star grandiosity (the jewel song of L.T.) and unstarlike realism, which demands shedding inflations, mannerisms, and distortions.

I see before me—an apparition—the word *putrid*, and I feel, at once, three putrefactions:

(1) a star's reputation decays;
(2) lives are ruined by nearness to stars;
(3) loss of privacy rots the soul.

Now I sound too holy!

At the moment I don't love Lana; instead, I am curious about Dolores' Drive-In, where Cheryl consorted with gay carhops. Dolores' hamburgers and milk shakes seem more real to me than Lana's hair in *Imitation of Life.*

(1999)

The Rape of Rusty

1

I used to jerk off while reading scenes from Gore Vidal's *Myra Breckinridge.*

I found it on my mother's shelf. I was ten, eleven, twelve, thirteen.

On the novel's black cover, a jubilant mannequin wore white cowboy boots, one knee raised, as if marching in place.

2

Myra Breckinridge notices—relishes—her student Rusty's body hair.

She strips him, fingers his hole, probes his prostate, rapes him with a dildo.

She performs a spontaneous, unlicensed doctor's exam on him.

The inspection is protracted, unwanted.

She arouses his nipples. She lowers his undershorts. She observes peach fuzz on his buttocks.

Eventually she opens his hole to her sadistic, cinephilic inspection.

3

Words from *Myra Breckinridge*:

"The total unveiling of the buttocks."

I beat the meat to the tune of this scene, a student's humiliation at the hands of a dildo-wielding transsexual.

I can't remember whether I brought the book into the bathroom, or read it in the living room, memorized the relevant chunks, and then retreated to our carpeted sanctum, a lavatory I could lock.

I sought the parts in *Myra* where she notices Rusty's body hair and humiliates him as if in retribution for his physical maturity.

Did I identify with shamed Rusty? Or did I identify with punitive Myra, questing for erotic information?

I don't want to pretend to stand at an objective distance from these experiences.

4

My third-grade teacher ordered a disobedient boy to pull down his pants in front of the class. She paddled his naked ass. He was crying and trembling.

Call him Robbie. Call her Mrs. Fact.

5

Myra rapes Rusty, though I never called it "rape" when I was a kid—I imagined merely that Myra was a scientist, a quester for information about how boys matured into men.

A teacher posing as a nurse, Myra wanted to discover what Rusty's body hair looked like. She wanted to touch the tufts.

I knew a Myra once. She was the mother of my friend—a prematurely gigantic kid with an unpleasantly raucous manner. This Myra was a typist, tall, blonde. I associate her with a comedic undertone and an abundance of paper clips.

6

Raquel Welch starred in *Myra Breckinridge* (the film); Mae West costarred. On my bedroom wall, I taped a poster of Raquel in *One Million Years B.C.*, and a poster of Mae in *Every Day's a Holiday*.

I performed an ordinary displacement, extracting erotic energy from Rusty (as written by Vidal) and transplanting it onto Welch and West.

I, like Welch and West, was a *W*, a Wayne.

I drank Welch's grape juice. I lived in the West.

I read Mae West's autobiography, *Goodness Had Nothing to Do with It*, largely because she appeared in *Myra*.

The movie was rated X.

A circle around the *X* was prohibition's trademark, like the ring around the copyright sign's *C*.

7

Myra Breckinridge was playing at Century 25, a bulbous theater a few blocks away from our tract house.

I begged my father to sneak me into the show, as if he had the power.

I convinced him to ask the theater manager to make an exception to the adults-only rule and to admit me, a juvenile, to *Myra Breckinridge*. The manager refused.

I didn't see the film until, at age thirty, I bought a VCR player.

The first video I rented was *Faster, Pussycat! Kill! Kill!* The second was *Myra Breckinridge*. Both films parody female sadism.

8

In memory, permanent, this image: Rusty's rear, as seen by Myra, as written by Vidal.

We watch the buttocks unfold, like plot.

Myra says, upon first beholding his genitals: "Poor Mary Ann. That's a boy's equipment."

I had a boy's equipment.

Rusty's girlfriend was named Mary Ann. So was my first girlfriend.

I met my Mary Ann in kindergarten.

By the time I first read *Myra Breckinridge*, I had already betrayed Mary Ann, rejected her, treated her unkindly—so ungenerously that her older brother, Greg, threatened to beat me up.

9

I understood what Myra wanted—to place herself in a cinematic pantheon, and to get revenge against cute hairy guys who'd snubbed her when she was a boy. She exacted retribution by sexually humiliating them—teaching them that their buttocks were erotic fodder.

10

Myra, a connoisseur, understood certain facts: "Like so many young males, he has a relatively hairless torso with heavily furred legs. Myron was the same. With age, however, the legs lose much of this adolescent growth, while the torso's pelt grows heavier."

I loved Myra's knowledgeable tone—her understanding of the consistency, amid variety, of men's secondary sexual characteristics.

She approached men's bodies as a researcher, an empirically minded pervert, a film scholar, a fan of Parker Tyler's writings.

More than once my prose has been accused of bearing a resemblance to Parker Tyler's.

11

Myra Breckinridge was my mother's book, a hardcover, shelved under *V*.

I helped alphabetize her library.

She paid me, per hour, for this service.

Fifty cents?

A good fee.

I enjoyed helping my mother classify.

Among the sorted items were D. H. Lawrence's *Lady Chatterley's Lover*, a prized source of passages describing men's furred bodies.

Escutcheon-like, hair exposed men to humiliation but gave them secret immunity from their captors.

Myra was attracted to Rusty's body hair, but she also wished to punish him for it.

12

Critics panned the movie *Myra Breckinridge.*

I read the reviews.

I remember being awestruck by the negativity of the critics.

How was it possible to hate so strongly, so self-confidently?

How was it possible to criticize Mae West from such an assured position of vantage?

I was fascinated by point of view—Myra's point of view on Rusty, the critic's point of view on the movie *Myra Breckinridge.*

This position of knowledgeability seemed an arcane and inscrutable pedigree.

13

Breck's shampoo was never far from my mind as I saw or said the word *Breckinridge.*

I knew the thick smell of Breck's, bubbly, coppery, marketable, synthetic yet agricultural, like modern poppies.

14

Rereading *Myra Breckinridge* today, I choose to interpret it as an oblique riposte to Susan Sontag's "Notes on 'Camp'" (first published four years before Vidal's novel). Myra is a scholar of camp taste, an ambulatory encyclopedia (as Warhol might have put it) of Hollywood ephemera. Significantly, Myra/Myron's psychoanalyst is named Montag. Myra, in her invincible smartness, her unplaceable eroticism, and her political ambivalence, is Sontag-like.

Sontag/Montag: S/M.

This present essay is, obviously, a montage, a manner Sontag perfected.

The second chapterette of *Myra* begins with a Sontagesque sneer against retrograde realism: "The novel being dead, there is no point to writing made-up stories. Look at the French who will not and the Americans who cannot."

Vidal dedicates *Myra* to Christopher Isherwood, in whose work the word *camp* (in its queer sense) made its first printed appearance, according to Sontag herself, who calls his sketch, in a punishing adjective, "lazy."

15

Says Myra: "Deliberately I took the Jockey shorts by the elastic waistband and pulled them slowly, slowly down, enjoying each station of his shame."

Prose divides shame into stations.

In stations, we watch Rusty's shame, or Robbie's—Robbie, whose pants were pulled down in Mrs. Fact's class, because, as I recall, he'd made the mistake of saying "hell" or "Goddamn it," a verbal infraction.

Disobedience ran in families. Two or three disobedient dynasties dominated our school—cartels of brothers who talked back.

I feared I would be Mrs. Fact's next victim. I, like Robbie, liked to talk back.

16

Our teacher had conspicuous swaying breasts and a slight mustache.

She loved her paddle.

It hung by the drinking fountain in the back of the classroom.

The paddle was inscribed with an aphorism about how punishment makes men wise.

Wisdom came also from the intercom, a broadcasting contraption, mounted on the classroom wall. This intercom—an opaque, silver monstrance—reminds me of the mask a fencer wears to protect the face.

17

Mrs. Fact divided our third-grade class into two reading groups: advanced and regular.

I belonged to the advanced reading group.

Robbie belonged to the regular.

We in the advanced group stayed after class for an extra hour of accelerated reading.

That was our gift, our prerogative—our literacy lessons took place after the rest of the students, the ordinary ones, left for home.

Robbie was a slow reader. But he'd said "hell," or "Goddamn it," so he stayed late, after the others in his middling group had departed.

Robbie stayed late to receive his punishment—the inscribed paddle—in front of the advanced students.

A step at a time, the Jockey shorts slide down. The narrative proceeds, a controlled striptease. To narrate is to participate in a tradition of sadism.

18

Mrs. Fact said to him, "Do you want to pull down your underpants here, in the classroom, or outside, where the fourth-graders can see?"

The fourth-graders were playing soccer on the lawn.

I weighed the two options. Which was more humiliating—to strip in front of the advanced reading group or in front of the soccer players?

Robbie chose to be punished indoors.

19

Robbie was wearing white underwear. I remember it as Carter's, because that was the brand I wore.

Palpitating, he pulled it down himself.

I recall his buttocks as red and pimply.

How could I see pimples from across the room?

His tears made him seem an idiot, a goat, a dog.

A slow reader.

In two years I'd be advanced enough to read *Myra Breckinridge*.

20

As Mrs. Fact paddled Robbie's buttocks, I saw his small, prepubescent, hairless penis, available for our inspection—we, the accelerated readers, gathered in a frightened circle, supposedly staring at our books, but instead riveted by the spectacle of a boy whose Carter's underwear had been pulled down; he had lowered it himself, when the teacher insisted, a pretty woman, young, recently married, formerly Miss Fancy, now Mrs. Fact.

21

I can't help replaying this scene, a remake spawning multiple remakes, *Beyond the Valley of Myra Breckinridge*, *The Return of Myra Breckinridge*, *Myra III* . . .

Replaying it, I rediscover what I call "the *eccola* effect," epitomized by the moment that Lucia di Lammermoor (in Donizetti's opera) comes onstage for her mad scene. Lucia, wearing her bloodied nightgown, holds a knife; she has just finished slaying her bridegroom, Arturo. As she enters, the chaplain Raimondo says "*Eccola!*" There she is! There is the madwoman, ready for her big number! This is her moment of glory but also her moment of humiliation because no one wants to be caught sleepwalking, no one wants to be caught onstage with soiled nightclothes.

Eccola! That might have been what the bystanders said when Oscar Wilde appeared at the train station while he was being moved from one prison to another. For a half hour in the rain, he was exposed to the mocking crowd, who spat and jeered. He considered it the most humiliating moment of his entire life.

He was being pointed out.

He was being seen.

Eccola, we say, and point.

We recognize this man at his nadir, naked, soiled, jeered at, rained upon, with a thermometer shoved up his ass, Myra's anal thermometer, Keats's "Pleasure Thermometer."

22

"It sets before me at once the gradations of Happiness even like a kind of Pleasure Thermometer . . ." John Keats, letter to John Taylor, January 30, 1818.

Happiness or humiliation.

23

Two good girls in my third-grade class saw Robbie's penis. I remember my sense of horror that the small panicked item between his legs (a slack or stiff appendage best hidden inside Carter's underwear) was being observed by girls—innocents, straight-A students, pianists. One of these good girls would later in the year perform Beethoven's "Für Elise" for our class.

24

Says Myra, of Rusty: "He leaned rigidly, all of a piece, to one side and grabbed the fallen trousers. Had he slightly squatted—the normal thing to do in his position—I might have caught a glimpse of the heart of the mystery from the rear, an unflattering angle which, paradoxically, has always excited me, possibly because it is in some way involved with my passion for 'backstage,' for observing what is magic from the unusual, privileged angle."

I, like Myra, value backstage vantage.

I appreciate the back room, the backyard, the backstreet, the back door—the prior meaning, the obscured scene, the oblique entrance to revelation.

In the back room, culture's caretakers store the junky and the obsolete, the broken and the mannered, the prose of Parker Tyler, the films of Rose Hobart, artifacts for which no profitable use has yet been found.

25

When I was in first grade, someone set my elementary school on fire.

My older brother was in third grade when the fire occurred.

He described to me the melting intercom on his classroom wall.

The heat from the fourth-grade room traveled through the wall and melted the intercom on the third-grade side.

About the liquefying intercom (like a timepiece in Salvador Dalí's painting *The Persistence of Memory*), my brother said: "That's how I knew the school was on fire. The intercom was melting."

Each classroom had an intercom, near the Seth Thomas clock and the unfinished portrait of George Washington by Gilbert Stuart.

Intercoms transmitted the voice of the principal announcing recess, the Pledge of Allegiance, assemblies, emergencies.

The intercom was a silver, speckled screen, a communicative surface, cold and heartless, neutrally releasing information, originating nothing of its own.

26

Supposedly, a local arsonist—a boy—set the elementary school on fire.

I'm not sure the authorities ever caught him.

He might have been merely a rumor.

Rumor or reality, he set several fires in the neighborhood.

The elementary school didn't burn down. It merely suffered minor charring and a melting intercom.

27

I've saved this secret, this story of Robbie's punishment, for decades. Magical possessions belong backstage, husbanded in privacy—like fondled texts, books circulated apart from customary channels of publication.

I like disseminations to take place privately, in back rooms, in grottoes, in antechambers, saunas, stalls, basements, places where one might be surprised by a foreman from the front room suddenly appearing and turning on the light to shout, "*Eccola!*"

28

The slowness of Myra's act of stripping Rusty or forcing him to undress himself, in her office, showed me that fantasies, and acts of literary production, may be slow; that analysis may be protracted; that reminiscence may crawl, not run. I took Myra's gradual rape of Rusty as a lesson in how desire proceeds incrementally through its stations and stages, never rushing to colonize its prey, but proceeding, like a fugue, layering the information a step at a time, sometimes repeating the figures, never apologizing for the repetition—for in any life, as in any invention, or any work of literature, however lofty or pedestrian, there exists a fixed set of dominating themes, and mere diligence cannot increase their number or alter their nature. Their substance, if not their sequence, remains incorrigibly the same.

29

When I returned home from school the day of Robbie's martyrdom, I told my mother what had happened. We stood in our side yard, beside the bamboo. I don't think my tale shocked her.

Of our bamboo I remember not the stalks but the thin leaves that fell compulsively and made a dry, papery sound when walked upon. The bamboo hugged the house's side wall. The leaves, which seemed happier to fall than to remain hanging on their stalks, were either brownish-yellow or greenish-yellow, an unattractive color. Our redwood fence, near the bamboo, left rust-red stains on the hands, if you were foolish enough to touch its always contagious surface.

(2006)

Cary Grant Nude

inspired by Kurt Kauper's paintings

Cary Grant Nude by the Fireplace

I never expected to see Cary Grant nude.

I'm not turned on: he's not hirsute.

His head is what we expect. I know that face! It's Cary Grant, as if on a U.S. coin or stamp. His gaze, deadened, seems steeped in formaldehyde. Hedda Hopper would approve; she liked to soul-murder stars.

In the mirror, Cary Grant's face fades into indistinguishability, as if he were mythic Daphne morphing into wood.

His right tit has begun to sag.

Someone has groomed his pubic patch, shaved his balls, powdered them with baby talc.

His long, expressive fingers appear deft as a fey banker's, an insurance executive's. I picture these hands writing Wallace Stevens's poems.

The left hand, draped over the fireplace mantel, depends from a nearly limp wrist.

His legs resemble a Carpaccio hero's, as if Cary Grant were Saint Sebastian or a courtier, a low-level warrior, more concerned with his legs than with his diplomatic mission or his bellicose duty.

A black cord has been plugged into a wall outlet. The message: *something is ready to be turned on.* Some mechanism—libido, vision—has been primed for performance.

Two rival modes of energy: the plug's electrical current,

unpictured but implied, is at odds with the boisterous fire, warming Cary Grant's legs. The fire looks fake; the plug looks real.

Surpassingly real is the reflective indigo tile on which Cary Grant stands, toes overstepping the border between mirror and wood.

His feet, the most hale part of him, seem refugees from another century, a sturdier time.

Facing me, Cary Grant evinces no shock. He expects my arrival. I am the reporter, fan, or friend who has arrived to interview him, to play squash or sleep with him, to help with household chores. I must adjust to the esoteric, perverse rules of the Cary Grant household, where naturism reigns.

The flower on the mantelpiece, in a common green vase, invites an allegorical interpretation, but the open-ended symbolism discourages investigation.

Manly fitness, of a gentle variety, is the order of the day. The wrestling scene from *Women in Love* might start at any moment. Cary Grant might begin to tussle with lover Randolph Scott. But no fluids—no sweat—will be spilled. The painting omits liquid.

Not quite. Liquid is implied by the ship on the mantelpiece's decorative white tile; by the flowers, which rest in water, unless they are artificial; and by oil paint, which has a phobic kinship to water. But the oil has dried. The categories—masculinity, sanity—have hardened.

Formally, the painting's principal members are rectangles: fireplace bricks; wedge of tile on which Cary Grant stands; sections of white mantelpiece; mirror; segment of bureau; outlet; baseboard; book spine. Cary Grant's head is itself a rectangle, as is the trim portion of abdominal infrastructure we glimpse through his skin. His tan line reveals the ghost of rectangular bathing trunks.

This rigid glut of rectangles confirms that we are deep in the heart of formalism, a state of strict controls, sameness, prudence, and restraint. Realism is itself a stricture—a requirement, met. As Cary Grant meets the viewer, so Kurt Kauper meets formalism head-on. Kauper's intimacy with realistic painting is in every way a match for our newfound intimacy with nude Cary Grant. We may not touch him. He will certainly not touch us. He is a doll for our inspection.

Even when nude, Cary Grant remains clothed in his reticence, his resistance to the vulgarities of "outing," his imperviousness to the distortions imposed by Hollywood's star-machinery. This painting pretends to be a casual nude snapshot of an actor. It poses as a spontaneous, recreational image. But its formal precision and its painterly skill remind us that we are seeing here a Cary Grant every bit as studied and mechanical as the man in the movies. Nudity, too, is a role requiring labor.

Cary Grant's penis, unerect, can't impress. His trademark face surpasses, in market value, his generic genitals.

Cary Grant Nude Walking Toward Me

Cary Grant walks toward me. His right foot arches, in process of movement. His penis is the talcum-softened one I recognize.

Cary Grant casts a sideways shadow. It falls onto his Spanish colonial mansion's tiled fountain.

He strides with a college athlete's vigor. His left hand, raised, grips an invisible tennis racket.

I want my attention to be held by nude Cary Grant, but already I take his nudity for granted; bored, I peer behind his body at the furniture in the sunny other room. Its floor catches light. A many-paned window, only partially visible, promises outdoor vistas.

I will call that back room *Cary Grant's Utopia*. He left it to stride toward me. After he gives me a hug, I will ask him to turn around (so I can see his butt) and then I will return with him to his improperly warm utopia. (We could also call it *Cary Grant's Secret*, or, for that matter, *Cary Grant's Anus*, because it is what remains behind, ungraspable, nether.) That room, like Keats's unheard melodies, is utopic because we will never enter it, just as we can never penetrate the background landscapes in Renaissance paintings of the Virgin. The more obsessively and accurately the background's details are painted, the more we are encouraged, as viewers, to flee the foreground, to turn away from the dominant narrative.

Cary Grant's nudity is the *studium*, the obvious meaning. The *punctum*—the perverse, escapist meaning—is the back room's red lamp, approximately equal in size to the glans of Cary Grant's penis.

Though the painting is shiny, its affect is matte. Cary Grant's face—his smile—radiates no interiority. A mannequin, a second-generation copy of an original "Cary Grant," this fake Cary Grant marches toward us like an apostle of an unerotic, glum faith. We are constitutionally unable to be transported by Cary Grant's greeting, his happy-go-lucky charm.

The chandelier in the utopian back room hangs from its ceiling like a spider—Emily Dickinson's or Emerson's—patiently exercising its craft, wisely spinning its centric system. The chandelier, miniaturized because of perspective's laws, is almost exactly the size of Cary Grant's head; the chandelier hangs beside his head, as if skull and light fixture were twin brothers, one stolid and the other whimsical. Indeed, the pendant lamp possesses a feyness that macho Cary Grant dares not exude. The chandelier's curves, like a French tickler's, suggest a filigreed earring that could hang from Cary Grant's right earlobe.

The objects in Cary Grant's vicinity want to assist him, to greet him. The marble sculpture below his left elbow—we see only a partial cornucopia, a Chardinesque bubble or ball—offers itself as resting point for the star's potentially weary elbow.

His skin tone reminds me of long-ago Van Heusen or Gant shirt ads—enticements to buy a mediocre, middle-of-the-road masculinity, without the fop's savor (Wilde) or the self-annihilating poet's ecstasy (Artaud).

My tone has grown severe. Nude Cary Grant brings out my seriousness, my dryness of touch, my inability to be emotional or straightforward.

The checkerboard tile floor, announcing the laws of perspective, gives us another lesson in the vanishing point. Cary Grant's nudity is the antithesis of what vanishes. His frontal nudity—his eagerness to meet us—pushes forward, out of the picture plane, into our lap. The vanishing point pushes backward, like a colossal reticence, a preverbal, previsual, amniotic stupor—the darkness of the theater before the film begins. Cary Grant's womb, his backroom utopia, is well lit. I imagine that his ass basks in the brash light of that backward room, like a sunlamp or an interrogatory flash. I can almost feel how warm this palazzo must be, to allow Cary Grant to walk around nude.

His nudity, though realistically pictured, remains our responsibility. Kurt Kauper painted Cary Grant nude, but the artwork's dynamism—the star striding toward us—impugns us as the author of this vision, insists that we have fostered or demanded his nudity.

Cary Grant's nudity is Kurt Kauper's doing, but I feel implicated, as if my desire had undressed him, as if the artist intended to render Cary Grant clothed, and my upstart X-ray spectacles unveiled the shy star.

I feel guilty for Cary Grant's nudity. It's my fault. I imposed it on him. I humiliated him, and he doesn't know it. Look at his obliviously cheerful mug. He hasn't yet figured out how ashamed of himself he should be.

Cary Grant Nude on the Daybed

Cary Grant has religious leanings. In this circular painting, which we could call a "tondo," he seems an amateur swami, a pal of Christopher Isherwood (who translated the Bhagavad Gita).

I can't see the head of Cary Grant's penis. It ends at the place where his crossed calves meet.

The line of the penis continues, however, in the cigarette, poised at the edge of a red ashtray. This ashtray has three tunnels, at its circumference, for recumbent cigarettes. These troughs ally the ashtray to Marcel Duchamp's urinal.

Three red elements in the painting combine forces. On the left, a red damask curtain reminds me of Jezebel's dress in the Bette Davis film. On the right, two red roses grow outdoors. Red curtain orients us inside; red roses lead our eye outside. Cary Grant sagely sits between the two counterposed red elements; his brilliant smile expresses mirth at having mastered the inside-outside polarity, at having risen above the push-pull battle of rose and curtain.

The daybed's fabric deserves scrutiny, its Monopoly-board rectangles a shiny, comfortless surface.

Cary Grant's body causes the bed to rumple and bend. Horizontality's reign buckles, grows distressed.

The sand, out the window, is pale as panna cotta.

The ashtray is the Cary Grant anus we cannot glimpse, the butt that his crossed ankles cover. He smiles because, though nude, he retains a final secret: his back door. He smiles because he understands the symbolic equivalence between ashtray—with its resident cigarette—and his hole.

Cary Grant's merriment lacks justification. Its groundlessness brands him a lunatic, a simpleton.

A black curved lever allows the eye to consider opening the window that will never open. That lever's black curve, almost alphabetic, or like a newly invented piece of punctuation, doesn't touch the sea's horizon line, though it almost does. That averted intersection arouses erotic expectancy. Teasingly, a small crack has been left open, an opportunity: in a more doctrinaire world, the piece of black hardware would meet the horizon edge and deprive us of that abstract, sky-blank hesitation.

Cary Grant's mood calls to mind the mystifying pundit Edward Randolph (played by actor Otto Kruger) in Douglas Sirk's *Magnificent Obsession*; Randolph is the crackpot father figure who teaches playboy Rock Hudson a more spiritual path. Cary Grant, indeed, seems a cross between Rock Hudson and that corny seer who instructs Rock in the art of altruism.

Did Cary Grant just finish skinny-dipping or screwing? Is he idling between avocations, or has he transcended action? He seems headed toward a life of permanent contemplation, his chest caved in, striated—a thorax on overdrive.

What is Cary Grant doing with his hands? Touching fingertip to fingertip, he playfully constructs a church. He assesses whether the axiom of adjacency (*objects abut each other, resist isolation*) still holds.

A gold fabric thrown over the daybed's edge contains one significant rumple or cleft, resembling the three indentations on the ashtray's lip. These minor-league clefts are important thoroughfares for fantasy. These depressions interrupt meaning, introduce noncoherence—like the place where the window's black lever almost hits the sea's horizon line, or where the intruding white window frame conceals the rose stem's upward thrust. For one beat, the rose loses track of itself, forgets its green stem. Similarly, Cary Grant's right elbow remains one telltale interstice of blankness away from touching the red damask curtain. The fact that his elbow *will never touch the curtain* means that I as viewer (or as *the one who is seduced by Cary Grant*) will never adequately grasp the painting's meanings, will never make my peace with realism. That's another reason why Cary Grant is smiling. Gloating, he knows that realism ultimately breaks down, that its complacencies are cloven.

I'll end with the painting's most important cleft: the dimple in Cary Grant's chin. The groin could be anyone's. The dimple could only be Cary Grant's. The dimple and the unseen glans echo each other: Cary Grant is smiling because he is, literally, "castrated." Kurt Kauper has lopped off the tip of Cary Grant's penis, or hidden it so effectively that only a cigarette is left to represent it.

Self-Admonishing (Self-Castrating?) Coda

Cary Grant nude—his sheen of completion, his virtuosity—chastises me, proves me incomplete, unrealistic, grasping.

Cary Grant nude reminds me of all the acts of betrayal I have ever committed.

Cary Grant nude reveals my failure to be three-dimensional.

(2005)

Brigitte Bardot Shopping in Shorts

inspired by a Karen Kilimnik drawing

BB: Thanks for drawing me in 1974.
KK: A pleasure.
BB: Being harassed by the press is no picnic.
KK: It proves you're wanted.
BB: You'd feel differently if you'd shown your breasts internationally at a too-young age.
KK: Did striptease taste like cough syrup?
BB: It felt like a sticky substance dripping down my legs.
KK: You're expert at fording your own embarrassment, and turning it into art.
BB: Wait. I'm not the most important star in your oeuvre. You've paid attention to Elizabeth Hurley—and to Lisa Steinberg, the murdered girl. Victims attract you.
KK: I like their availability to the casual gaze, to slander.
BB: The press's easy appropriation of my body was a form of trespass, but I'm too busy to sue.
KK: Busy with what?
BB: Animal rights. Reactionary causes.
KK: Had I predicted your descent into things reactionary, I'd not have drawn you shopping in shorts, a great photo from 1974 that I dreamily turned into art.
BB: Why didn't you apply color?
KK: I was feeling elemental. I wanted to capture your aggressive furtiveness, your likeness to a hunted doe.
BB: Pundits disparage me.

KK: I have detractors, too.
BB: Can we band together and find shelter from slanderers?
KK: That's impossible. We're permanently exposed.
BB: Did you picture me in shorts, rather than long pants, to signify vulnerability?
KK: I had no metaphorical intentions. I'm a literalist.
BB: You're crying now.
KK: Junk scattered in the periphery moves me to tears.
BB: Why did you invite me here?
KK: Admiration. Curiosity. Boredom. Your literalness diverts me.
BB: The longer I stay here, the more allegorical I become.
KK: I don't consider you merely a media figment.
BB: Have you seen my films?
KK: *Viva Maria! Contempt.* You're no longer famous in the U.S. You're an outsider.
BB: A pale copy of a famous person?
KK: You're almost a washout.
BB: My washout status is itself a warm enclosure, a place I find restful and rehabilitating.
KK: I was attracted to you because you were equally a washout and a star.
BB: In your drawing, I'm fleeing a crime scene.
KK: The crime of your splendor. The crime of your visibility.
BB: The crime of my readability.
KK: Readability?
BB: Must I explain? My body is so legible, there's nothing left for words to expose.
KK: You're as readable as the Ten Commandments, permanent tablets we can interpret as we choose.
BB: I'm not flexible. Unlike a law, I'm single-minded.
KK: We say monologic.
BB: Who's we?

KK: The culture industry.

BB: You're trying to borrow my estimableness to create your own self-portrait.

KK: We know, as viewers, how you move, and how you kiss, and how you despise, but we don't know much about your pet dog.

BB: Can we talk about gossip?

KK: It travels, it's unreliable, it's devalued, it hurts people, it's fatty.

BB: It clogs consciousness?

KK: It doesn't nourish us, BB, but we grow to love that lack of nourishment. The depiction of nonnourishing substances is itself a meager though sustaining diet.

BB: My image nourished you.

KK: I could suck on it, like a Popsicle.

BB: That's phallic.

KK: Not really. Popsicles disappear.

BB: People treat the phallus as if it were a fixture.

KK: It's immaterial.

BB: Like my presence in your drawing.

KK: You're trying to exit the frame.

BB: I don't belong in your mind. I'm running away.

KK: As if your prison sentence inside my fantasy life were ending.

BB: Notice that my limo driver is incompletely rendered. He's not full-figured enough to nab me.

KK: I'm curious about the difference between 1974, when you were photographed shopping in shorts, and 1985, when I made the drawing of you shopping in shorts.

BB: That eleven-year lapse of time between 1974 and 1985—it sits like a white elephant between us in the room.

KK: It sits there like a lumpy alienation factor, like rudeness or a faux pas or a bad smell.

BB: The difference between 1974 and 1985 is an iceberg that will never thaw.

KK: And so we can observe it, suck on it, like that Popsicle I mentioned earlier.

BB: It's a huge, consoling presence, cold to the touch, and damaging to the nerves.

KK: It's abstract—the difference between 1974 and 1985—but it's also palpable and repulsive, like a wrong turn a big city's administration takes.

BB: Like Nice, or Marseilles, when their governments mismanage zoning?

KK: The schism between decades is a dreary weight.

BB: Is your drawing political?

KK: You're trying to placate me by using the word *political.*

BB: Isn't gossip political? Kibbitzing about our lives, your drawing, my shopping, your ambivalence?

KK: We haven't defined *gossip.*

BB: Using the word is enough. Analysis can happen silently, between the lines.

KK: You're more famous than I.

BB: An arousing imbalance.

KK: I drew you so that I could dwell inside disparity.

BB: There you go again, with your Popsicle.

KK: Popsicle?

BB: You're always finding gaps and schisms, and treating them like luxury suites. You act as if a hole or an aporia were furnished, comfy, and enclosing—a veritable alcove.

KK: It's true. I care about plushness.

BB: And ice.

KK: Yes. I like the colder regions of thought and feeling.

BB: You're not afraid of freezing to death?

KK: I'm comfortable with long interludes of ice.

BB: And that's why you don't put more "feeling" into your work?

KK: The fish I bought at the market is safely on ice; I needn't worry about spoilage.

BB: The fish, in this case, is your "feelings"?

KK: Right. We're not afraid of rot.

BB: Now we're talking about fish. Before, we were talking about Popsicles.

KK: I must ask. What were you shopping for in that 1974 photo?

BB: The same thing I was shopping for in your 1985 drawing. The same thing I'm shopping for now.

KK: Did you find it?

BB: Not in my size.

KK: Do you plan to find it?

BB: No.

KK: Then why do you keep shopping for it?

BB: I need to keep alive the quest.

KK: That's how the slain stay busy in Valhalla.

BB: They gossip.

KK: Conversational rambles nourish.

BB: They're erotic.

KK: A slow, teasing process.

BB: You wrote "2 p.m." on the drawing. Was 2 p.m. when you finished it?

KK: I wanted to mark the moment.

BB: Now you can't remember what moment you were marking.

KK: What matters is that I marked it.

BB: With your individual mark.

KK: My mark is deliberately generic.

BB: As is mine. But, as you mentioned earlier with your

Popsicle and your interlude of ice, we find the generic to be a cozy habitat.

KK: Duly noted.

BB: I'm pooped. Let's shut off the tape recorder.

KK: If we don't like this conversation, we can start all over again, and record a new conversation on top of the old one.

BB: Traces of the first conversation might be audible through the warp and woof of the second.

KK: A palimpsest. Two overlapping conversations.

BB: Like 1974 and 1985.

KK: Two different radio stations announcing the same crime.

BB: The sameness, like your Popsicle, is consoling.

KK: Confusing, too.

BB: I'm famous for breasts, you for "hand."

KK: We live in an age that devalues the hand.

BB: Does our era devalue breasts?

KK: No. Breasts are still prized.

BB: We meant to shut off the tape recorder, but then we fell back into this trance of mutual consolation.

KK: Your presence, here, I find nebulously consoling.

BB: Roger Vadim taught me that arousal was more important than consolation.

KK: He was wrong.

BB: I'm stuck with arousal. It's my only ploy.

KK: And I am stuck with consolation.

BB: We're traveling in circles again. And we haven't defined the difference between arousal and consolation.

KK: We're not required to figure out the nature of art.

BB: I take issue with your passivity in the face of large aesthetic questions.

KK: My sloth is a pose.

BB: Like my shopping?

KK: Tell me. In that 1974 photo, were you really shopping?
BB: "Shopping" was your word. It was the term you applied to my situation.
KK: Indeed, it was the concept I imposed.
BB: We pretend to pursue the visual, but really we are creatures of the word.
KK: And yet it is visual beauty, not language, that brought you fame.
BB: We needn't divide the goods of the world into two shopping carts, *Language* and *Beauty*.
KK: So you were shopping for beauty?
BB: No. I was shopping for language. My cart was already filled with beauty.
KK: And did I give you language?
BB: No. You gave me more beauty.
KK: And that's why you came to speak to me today.
BB: To wrest some language out of you.
KK: To force me to reward you with language, after extended deprivation.
BB: Language is the Popsicle you mentioned earlier.
KK: The long interlude of ice?
BB: And beauty is the blowtorch that causes it to melt.
KK: I misspelled "Galerie" in my drawing of you. I wrote "Galere."
BB: Were you trying to repress the thought of art galleries?
KK: I wanted to cancel my loyalty to your image. I wanted to eviscerate commitments to art, to tasks, to language.
BB: Evisceration is what I'm against, when it applies to helpless animals.
KK: The evisceration I sought in this drawing was not bloody or actual. It was metaphorical.
BB: Earlier you claimed to be a literalist.
KK: Did I? I was just being figurative.

BB: I'm incredibly figurative myself.
KK: Tell me more about the blowtorch that causes language to melt.

END OF TRANSCRIPT

(2007)

A Woman Alone in Her Room

inspired by McDermott & McGough's paintings

1

A woman alone in her room is no small accomplishment. It takes, sometimes, two men to construct one woman alone in "her" room. It took MGM and Walter Wanger (producer) and Robert Wise (director) and many other men to make me, Susan Hayward, plausibly alone in my gas chamber at the end of my Oscar-winning picture (Best Actress), *I Want to Live!* (1958). The men in the viewing room—mostly men—peer through the glass to see me dying, to make sure I'm actually dead. That's the structure of an execution: men watch through glass to see me, mother, in my box, die.

2

This woman's voice, sometimes known as Susan Hayward, gives me energy, joy, fluency, speed, excitement. Her speech corrects the anomie of art. Sometimes I need numbers. That's what John Rechy called them. Numbers announce periodicity, ripple. 1911/1991. Thus we chart a blank space between two figures. This career, mine, mother's, is hard to organize. Sometimes it takes two men to keep one cock in place.

3

Against the confinement of my own stardom I speak—against the circumscription of this manufactured, copyrighted identity. I speak against the assumption that my work has an autobiographical core. I, Susan Hayward, am tired of time, tired of the insistence that our personalities have verifiable beginnings and motives. You don't know why I'm descending the stairs, and don't know whether I am Lana Turner or some unconvincing replica. The difference between *actual* Kim Novak and *fake* Kim Novak is huge and upsetting. Most of my films (I'm speaking as Kim Novak now) concern a schizoid split between doubled identities. In *Vertigo* I am likeness, rift. Any schism has a class basis: slum versus aristocracy. My doubled signature doesn't visibly appear here ("Kim Novak," by Kim Novak), but two authors are responsible for Kim Novak. Kim Novak is the creation of Kim Novak, and thus has the luxury of beholding her finished self in the looking glass of her lack. We must use the word *lack*, but not as a pejorative. Lack is what any artist of distinction wears on his/her sleeve.

4

A woman is smoking in the lower half of the painting, and she is among my aliases or stand-ins: she is waiting for *identification* to click into place, or else she is dreaming the scene taking place in the panel above, a closeup of a man and woman preparing to kiss: who is the man (we see his face) and who is the woman (we see her exposed back, with its bra strap, shockingly explicit for TV)?

5

Installation: these images have been installed in my imagination. Prewired. I came built this way. Another way to put it: in toilet-stall halation. Which makes little sense, unless you untangle the hieroglyph. I did not choose the cryptic plots—Oscar-nominated lighting effects—that structure my consciousness.

6

I tend to choose blur over clarity: clarity, like nicotine in the lungs, hurts, while blur, like a strong sleeping pill, muffles the day's traumatic residue. The difference between black-and-white and color is a monumental binary, and that is why we believe in formalism, though I as Susan Hayward am not in a position today to advance a formalist analysis—a formalist analysis would "deal with" the difference between black-and-white and color, and would also explore the function of the horizontal "zip" (fold, cleft) between the upper and lower panels. The formalist analysis that Susan Hayward is in no position today to advance would also (albeit hesitantly) broach the subject of the microdifferences between paintings from the 1960s, 1970s, 1980s, 1990s—in particular would ask what happened in the 1980s to make big painting exciting (had it ever stopped being exciting?), and would ask about the functions that photography has served in painting after 1960. (Why not include the 1950s, too? Don't exclude early Robert Rauschenberg.) This formalist analysis will not be offered today by Susan Hayward, resting before she films the climactic gas chamber scene in *I Want to Live!*, directed by Robert Wise.

7

I dreamt last night that Elizabeth Taylor had a beard and was kind. Her beard was not Old Testament; it clung to her neck's hidden, unscreened zones.

8

My women are doppelgängers, all of them: Kim Novak, Claudia Cardinale, Monica Vitti, Lana Turner. Some are ironic versions of the type (Monica Vitti is a self-aware example), and others are "natural" vacancy itself (Kim Novak and Lana

Turner are emptiness enacted as "real"). Terrible, to call a person a "vacancy"! And yet, to be vacant is an honor, not a horror. The habit of allegory depends on vacuity: the peeling-back operation of allegory (find the secret meaning of the overt symbol) always courts the danger that nothing lies behind the surface sign.

9

Remember the famous scene in Tennyson's "The Lady of Shalott," when the ensorcelled woman, prisoner of art, cracks the mirror (by moving around her room and by looking out the window to Camelot) and therefore *dies into life*, becomes an effigy floating Ophelia-like down the river. Like sped-up aging (Liz in *Giant*): quickly, belatedly, I'm undergoing the passage of time, feeling its doomed, kicky onwardness. Consistent subject: the nightmare of time travel. How to avoid it. How to stage it, control it.

10

It's impossible to tell certain legendary women apart. The same goes for topless men in erotic positions. Are these women recognizable stars, or are they dream-dashed (head-on-collision) mimeographs of some void-princess I once slept with or screened? Ditto with the men. They are all generic in their beauty, in their eligibility for orgasm causation.

11

Here are most of the films that Claudia Cardinale made in the 1960s: *South Wind*, *Il Bell'Antonio*, *Rocco and His Brothers*, *Austerlitz*, *I Delfini*, *Girl with a Suitcase*, *La Viaccia*, *The Lions Are Loose*, *Cartouche*, *Senilità*, *8 1/2*, *The Leopard*, *Bebo's Girl*, *The Pink Panther*, *Circus World*, *The Magnificent Cuckold*, *Time of Indifference*, *Sandra*, *Blindfold*, *The Lost Com-*

mand, The Professionals, The Queens, A Rose for Everyone, Don't Make Waves, Mafia, The Hell with Heroes, A Fine Pair, Once Upon a Time in the West, The Red Tent, Diary of a Telephone Operator, The Conspirators. Every word in this paragraph is history. Every word in this paragraph is core curriculum. (As Jane Eyre put it, "Reader, I cc'd him.") Claudia Cardinale is the star of this exhibit. In her capacity as carbon copy, she is the instigator.

12

I instigated the exhibit. I threw a shoe in a mirror, which shattered. The shoe I threw into the mirror, shattering it, in a film whose exact title I can't recall, is the shoe of fetishism, and also the shoe (or one of them) that M&M pictured in the painting *70,000 Dead Animals, 1928/1989*: the shoe I wield in anger is the leather shoe that animals must be murdered in order to produce: the shoe that provokes this installation is a shoe of victimization and exploitation, the shoe I protest against: I, as Claudia Cardinale, or her representative, have the right to say that your art is a protest against the domination and pillage on which modernity founds its trades and effects: no modernity is possible without the murderousness that I, with my shoe raised in protest, refuse. Once more, with feeling: these are the paintings of my refusal to comply with the abuses undergirding technological modernity.

13

Two more things you should know, and that I, as Claudia Cardinale, star of *Austerlitz*, have the authority to tell you: (1) melodrama is a financially exhausting and lucrative way to make theater out of the murder of a mother (cf. Lana Turner in *Madame X* or Susan Hayward in *I Want To Live!*); (2) according to Melanie Klein, at least in Julia Kristeva's account, matricide is (in the unconscious) the necessary precondition of symbolization. As if we could neatly divide male and female dreaming! As if we could draw a problem-free horizontal line between bottom and top!

(2008)

www.MyPornEssay.com

Like a terse sentence, porn offers the sting of declaration, of exactitude: *these events occurred.*

How do I begin the day? Pablo Casals, to renew his commitment to music, played a Bach prelude and fugue each morning. Each day after breakfast I reconsecrate my porn vows by visiting www.male4malescorts.com to read the latest hustler reviews.

An uncircumcised Russian Jew, Michael Lucas is the first and only porn star I've ever met. (His real name is not Michael Lucas.) I attended his photo shoot at Timothy Greenfield-Sanders's studio. I'd hoped Timothy would ask me to be a "fluffer" (to get the star hard), but no one begged for my services.

Detail: Michael's signature assets are large lips.

Between shots, Michael manipulated his substantial dick—mild, desultory friction to plump it up and give it the desired hang. Watching him self-fluff didn't turn me on: it seemed too nursing-home.

Posing for an informal snapshot, I put my arm around Michael and nuzzled his neck. Detail: his body makeup—bronzer—stained my white Helmut Lang corduroy jeans and my white Miu-Miu denim jacket.

(Later, at home, I washed my clothes. After two cycles, the stains disappeared.)

After the shoot, Michael Lucas and I ate lunch at Food

Bar in Chelsea. Detail: he ordered egg whites with spinach and chicken breast (the "Chelsea Boy Special"). Detail: he doused it with ketchup. A transparent eyeball, I ate my ricotta salata and asparagus.

Porn consists not merely of sex, but of what surrounds it. Porn is Michael Lucas's egg whites and ketchup. Porn is my asparagus. Porn is my American Express card. Porn is the wallpaper in an amateur porn shot on www.hunkhunter.com. Porn is the lady with smoker's hack who worked at the video store where, four years ago, I was too embarrassed to rent *Butt Munch*. Porn is the body makeup on Michael's Hermès silk shirt, which he drops off, after our lunch, at the dry cleaner's. Porn is the tired man who accepts, not just once, Michael's stained loads.

Porn is Washington Street in Boston, where I bought a porn mag (*Handyman*) in 1981. Porn is the pair of blue shoes I also bought on Washington Street. Porn is the English professor I accidentally met on the subway (Red Line) when I was en route to Washington Street to buy a porn mag and blue shoes. Porn is not the exception to photography's rule. Porn is the ceiling toward which all photographs asymptotically climb.

Walking up Eighth Avenue with Michael Lucas, I developed a theory: desirability rearranges space. A porn star's beauty gave the sunny September day a space lift, an injection of hauteur. (I like to anatomize what goes without saying.) I told Michael that walking with him was like walking with Elizabeth Taylor.

Most events in life are insufficiently sexual. Porn offers me an instant grope. Contemplating porn, I grope instantaneity; I grope seismic, sudden, present time.

Detail: after meeting Michael Lucas, I taught Robert Creeley poems to my graduate students. Creeley breaks experience down into simple words and pauses. Here is an excerpt from his poem "The Changes." Its subject is almost porn:

> People don't act
> like they act
> in real life
> in real life. They
>
> are slower
> and record the passive changes
> of atmosphere.

He might mean: ***the unseen atmosphere, like a body-in-porn, lets itself slowly be assessed and treasured.*** I didn't mention Michael Lucas to my poetry class.

After spending time with a porn star, I felt unaccountably null, empty, eclipsed. The opposite was once true. I bumped into plenitude when, as a child, I looked at Burt Reynolds's *Cosmopolitan* pinup, reprinted in *Time* or *Newsweek*, and clipped it for my private stash. I treated Burt's photo—innocuous beefcake—like porn. I hid it. I memorized it. Detail: I took Burt's photo into the bathroom as a break from math homework. Five or ten minutes of intense jerking off, and then back to algebra. Some people consider porn appalling. I consider it comforting. Perhaps I'm exaggerating. Porn, too, exaggerates. Its exaggerations approach classical epic's. The epic simile is pornographic. What is an "epic simile"? Look it up. The dictionary in which you look up "epic simile" is (momentarily) pornographic.

Annex to My Porn Essay:
Porn Dream, February 2004

In a defunct arcade
I found a rare book of film
stills—footage
cut from 1963's *Cleopatra*
starring Liz and Dick:
close-ups of anal
and vaginal penetration,
incendiary. I chalked
up the explicitness
to Liz's artistic prescience:
though typecast as fox
and harridan, all along
she'd been a closet
porn *auteur*, equal
to Artaud, who gouged
the page to prove
it posed no impediment.

(2004)

IV.

On Doodles, Drawings, Pathetic Erotic Errands, and Writing

1

If I were an artist, I would make a small drawing and hand it to you. You might thank me for the gift. Because I am a writer, not an artist, I must give you words, for which I am not usually adequately thanked.

One does not write—or draw—for the "thank you," and yet unless out there a "thank you" waits, I can't imagine bothering to produce an artifact.

Familiar, this state of *not wishing to produce*, or of wishing to produce a text that is beside the point, off-topic, unwished-for, intrusive . . .

And so if I were an artist, not a writer, I would draw something inappropriate, erratic, obscene; I would produce a drawing that signified *not wishing to produce.*

Today I wish to praise an erotics of the off-topic, the not-apropos; an erotics of the beside-the-point. Drawing is one likely repository for this erotics.

2

A preposition follows the verb *to draw*: we do not merely draw, we draw *forth*, draw *out*, draw *upon*—or else we are drawn *under*, tideswept by a paranoia we ought to have checked at the door. Not merely descriptive or documentary, drawing involves incantation, imperative, and apostrophe—*Get your ass over here! O Lord above! Dear friend, dear Mercury!*

Drawing—as practice, commodity, medium—exists inside the institution of art; drawing is a reputable province of visual production. And yet drawing likes to abandon its roost inside art and to forget where it belongs. (In this essay I will try to avoid naming specific artists, because I want to draw abstractly, to wander outside of what can be proved. The effort will doubtless fail; but that does not make it worthless.) Drawing grows disoriented, loses contact with its supervisors. Art's foremen (think *firemen*) hose down (do a *nomenclature number* on) drawing, think they know its place; and yet, drawing, that amnesiac medium, lacks the intelligence (or the ordinariness) to remain accountable to its master. Its gift for losing track, for forgetting, stems from its apparent safety: no one will say to a drawing, *What the hell are you?* A drawing can always mouth an alibi: *I am a citizen of X, I am a drawing. Do not throw me off ship.* And yet drawing does not occupy a time zone that can be accurately clocked; drawing enters the world through accident, through the garbage chute. Drawing stumbles into life as the also-ran, the warm-up, the trial. Call it "the doodle." Drawing's liability to be mere doodle allies it to the excremental (*doo-doo*) as well as to the incomplete, the incomprehensible, the noncitizen, the error, the throwaway—any entity nobly outside category, consciousness, responsibility, and marketplace.

Drawing, at its best, contains the seed of a refusal-to-be-sold. That is its kinship to unvendible fantasy, to the not verifiable.

3

Now let me depress the gas pedal and speed toward our subject—the erotic. Avoiding it, I've approached it, for *being off-topic* invokes the erotic; drawing and eroticism steer away from where the Invisible Supervisor insists they dwell. Think of Kafka's *Trial* (*Der Prozess*), where the process of coming-to-trial, of never-coming-to-trial, of being always guilty, always under supervision, resembles an aesthetic state, a "high," back-lit by paranoia. Drawing, like Kafka's antihero Josef K., exists in nomenclature's waiting room, where Elizabeth Bishop's girl-self waits for the breasty benediction of "womanhood" to be dropped upon her like an anvil.*

Is eroticism something we want to get clear about? Is clarity-about-eroticism a legal process we care to undergo, or, like Josef K., are we corrupted, doomed, marked "dead" from the start, if we grope toward knowledge?

At least a drawing will never get you arrested—unless you are its subject, and the law-employed artist aims to land you in prison. In that case, the drawing eroticizes your coming-into-focus as criminal.

4

Suddenly I feel upon me a chastising hand. It's time to be specific.

James Siena: his drawings consecrate concentration. Antonin Artaud: his drawings are skin, punctured and pictured. Chloe Piene: her drawings recall Egon Schiele, stigma leaping like hot arrows between sitter and portraitist. (When Schiele depicts himself, the duel is a soliloquy.) Tom Friedman: looking at the piece of paper he had stared at for one thousand

*Bishop, in her oft-cited poem "In the Waiting Room," notes that self becomes self only when it sees itself (misrecognizes itself) in a magazine, and thereby she reveals sight's toxicity: "I scarcely dared to look / to see what it was I was." Bishop warns us to exercise caution when looking: look both ways before crossing, or, indeed, perhaps never cross, in order to avoid looking's *horror vacui*. Recall that Bishop was an amateur painter, and that she allegedly—notoriously?—kept her erotic life apart from her poetry's thematic surface. And though Kafka cannot become a center of this essay, his account of justifiable paranoia, in *The Trial*, subpoenas any reader not yet aware that this essay, the one you are reading now, is also an erotic drawing, though of an unspecified subject.

hours, I identify with his enterprise's nothingness, its embrace of the *blank*. Louise Bourgeois: I marvel at her drawings' looseness and skimpiness, their deviation from the work ethic, even as they marshal evidence of hard daily labor. (Sleep, too, can be a task.) Martin Kippenberger: his hotel-stationery drawings summon the divinity of *temporary location*, of being momentarily housed in a waystation and forcing oneself to enjoy that posh or degraded roadstop and to use the limited tools for consciousness available there (Gideon Bible, notepad, telephone, downstairs sandwich shop). Jutta Koether: her diaristic drawings, done daily, mark art's fidelity to the diurnal, not a worshipful faithfulness—merely a truce (*Life, I'll allow you to be a daily matter, because you offer me no other option*). Andy Warhol: his drawings of nude men allude to Henri Matisse and Jean Cocteau and inscribe Andy's wish to be artistic, to transpose the moment of sordid looking (McCarthy-era covertness) into aesthetic pedigree; with miminal means, he breaks a complex body into parts—a line, a shadow, a hint of a nonexistent tint. Willem de Kooning: I savor the drawings' near-nothingness, the barely there forms, connected to scrawled note taking. Christian Holstad: like Warhol contra Rauschenberg, Holstad erases parts of a newsprint photo. I, too, once engaged in gum-eraser subterfuge, smudging out the faces of Presidents Washington and Eisenhower (and others) from my high school history textbook, and enlarging (with pencil) their lips, a practice that my queer friend and I called "subtle shading"—erasing a potentate's face and then girling it up with a Dixon Ticonderoga #2 Soft.

5

It would be easier for me to concentrate on defining the erotic if I were not plagued, at the moment, by intense toothache, the afterglow of yesterday's emergency root-canal treatment on tooth number thirty-one; it would be easier for me to concentrate on defining the erotic if I could pin down exactly what turns me on; and yet (whether because of toothache or because of a recent overdose of Internet porn) I no longer am certain which visual stimuli send me into sexual heaven; indeed, I need to find new fetishes.

Am I an erotic expert? I've publicly drawn out my libidinal fantasies on paper, in prose and poetry. "Obsessive erotomane" is how I've classified myself, if only to avoid conceptual vertigo. In the past, I drifted off-topic to explore eroticism; now, I sneak away from eroticism's falsely fixed *topos*. Wandering, I announce *errancy* as my new erotic imperative.

6

None of the Internet porn I download is drawing: all is photography, mostly self-taken. The amateur porn photo is an act of testimony, of self-attestation: *I am here, I am nude, I am obscene, I wish to make myself known to you, I wish to demonstrate my sexual being-here, I must publicly insist on my erotic nature.* An erotic drawing (or a drawing we have decided to call "erotic" because of content, context, or viewer response) also attests. But to what?

If I, as viewer, behold a drawing and define it as erotic, I am testifying that I have a chartable relation to sexuality. What's erotic about this scene-of-viewing is not strictly the beheld object but my posture of attesting.

7

Some drawings exaggerate what sex education textbooks long ago taught me to call "secondary sexual characteristics." For example: guys look hairier and more hung in drawings than in photographs.

In a notebook, warming up for this essay, I wrote the sentence, "People who don't lust after me make me ill."

8

Drawing's second-class status increases its eroticism. The more "pathetic" an erotic practice, the more I esteem it. The more "pathetic" an artistic medium, the closer it resembles my ideal sexual underground.

As Gilles Deleuze and Félix Guattari, in their book on Kafka, prophesied the existence of a "minor literature," so I point to drawing as a "minor art," an art that does not court monumentality, that consents to be degraded to diary status.

9

The discourse of neediness, of wish and lack, hamstrings me, and so I must now make a list. Among the needs met by erotic drawing (whether viewing it or making it) are

the need to use the hand;
the need to get away from it all;
the need to bury a private inscription within a public document;
the need to look at art—and at the artist's life—as a template for one's own pathetic erotic errands;
the need to sacralize pathetic erotic errands;
the need to produce and *not* produce, simultaneously;
the need to verify (or disguise) an internal fantasy by giving it visual form;
the need to draw the nonexistent into actuality;
the need to be blank;
the need to flee into abstraction;
the need to say *I have desired this*;
the need to confess antipathies;
the need to fail, to demonstrate surrender and aporia;

the need to create a throwaway and then rescue it;
the need to be unsure whether it deserves salvage;
the need to leave vital matters undecidable.

10

At this essay's reticent heart are two allusions I failed explicitly to make.

One allusion is to Roland Barthes's essay on Cy Twombly, in which the essayist admits his envy of the artist, though emulation's erotics remain unstated: "This morning, a fruitful—in any case, an agreeable—occupation; I very slowly look through a book of TW's [Twombly's] reproductions, and I frequently stop in order to attempt, quite quickly, on slips of paper, to make certain scribbles; I am not directly imitating TW (what would be the use of that?), I am imitating his *gesture*, which I, if not unconsciously, at least dreamily, infer from my reading; I am not copying the product, but the producing, I am putting myself, so to speak, *in the hand's footsteps*."* Thus Barthes makes clear his wish (and mine) to assume the body of writing's other—drawing.

A second stinted allusion is to a passage in Kafka's *Trial*. Kafka's texts were inscribed, drawn, *drilled* events (recall "In the Penal Colony," its machinic scene of writing); indeed, Kafka's paranoia, drummed up for the amusement and education of spectators, returns me to the terror at the root of any explicative task. In one strange paragraph, Kafka presents *drawing* as the ludic, likable, showstopping detour away from the onerous bureaucratic chore of *writing*; thus Kafka's parable drives home my bewildered awareness of writing's secondariness

*The purpose of quoting Barthes is not to insist that the present essay follows in Barthes's unfollowable footsteps, but to make good on another old debt, the dimensions of which are darker than I can at this moment allow, stricken as I am by a toothache that signifies normal healing but feels like the body's—the speaking mouth's—dissolution.

before drawing's priority, and underscores drawing's ability to move, with the swiftness of a sexual joke, away from writing's ponderous obligations. Writing (in Josef K.'s case, a legal petition) aims to free the slandered subject; but drawing—even a doodle, committed with a stolen pencil—upstages writing, foils it, and (if K. were lighthearted enough to accept the news) liberates it from law's literality. To degenerate from writing into drawing—to this task of erotic devolution I must next devote myself, if I wish to avoid imitating the sad fate of K.:

> But even though K. felt he could handle all this, the difficulty of composing the petition was overwhelming. At one point, about a week ago, it was only with a sense of shame that he could even contemplate having to prepare such a petition some day; that it might be difficult had not even occurred to him. He recalled how one morning, when he was inundated with work, he had suddenly shoved everything aside and taken out his notepad to have a try at drafting the general outlines of such a petition and perhaps making it available to his slow-witted lawyer, and how at that very moment the door of the head office had opened and the vice president had entered laughing heartily. That had been very embarrassing for K., even though the vice president was not, of course, laughing at the petition, of which he knew nothing, but at a stock market joke he'd just heard, ***a joke that could only be fully appreciated by means of a drawing***, which, bending over K.'s desk and taking K.'s pencil from his hand, he sketched upon the notepad intended for the petition.*

*(Emphasis mine.) Forget questions of direct influence: Artaud's self-lacerating drawings would be unthinkable without the precedent of Kafka's self-impugning prose.

I fear that this quotation, like the vice president's drawing, inappropriately avoids the obligation to describe erotic drawing's contemporary situation. But, like Kafka's vice president, I must veer—a paranoid flight from diligence—away from inscriptive systems holding me captive, however desired this duress, and must *draw my way out*: performing an intrapsychic S/M pageant, the hand escapes what it also prosecutes. The captivities of *writing* and *drawing* are not identical. Writing approaches erotics through description and rhetorical enactment; drawing approximates erotics through marks untethered to rhetoric, and thus uncontaminated by the accusations that K.'s petition chronically struggles to rebut. Need I explicitly indicate that the vice president's digressive drawing (at first I mistyped *vice* as *voice*), scribbled on his underling's embryonic petition, was doubtless dirty, and therefore unsuitable, in Kafka's pee-shy estimation, for describing in words?

(2005)

Fag Limbo

I live in "fag limbo," a useful term borrowed from artist Hernan Bas, who also employs the phrase "nouveau sissies."* My subject today is a sensibility that I will irresponsibly call "fag limbo," as if it were a neighborhood, a parking garage, a clothing boutique, a housing project, an asylum, or a treasured corner of anyone's mental library, with a drooled-over copy of Ludwig Wittgenstein's *Tractatus Logico-Philosophicus* alphabetized next to a cum-stained hardcover of David Wojnarowicz's *Memories That Smell Like Gasoline*. Fag limbo has always existed. In each generation, it takes new, vital forms.

Young skinny-armed art guys around town don't strive to muscle-build and don't announce a sexual orientation. It's gauche to ask. Only narrow-minded critics bother to delimit, to classify. I have no wish to reinstate defunct sexual catego-

*Hernan Bas writes, in the artist's statement accompanying his 2001 show, *Hernan's Merit & the Nouveau Sissies*, at the Fredric Snitzer Gallery in Miami, Florida: "My work (art) stems from understanding a new style of boy that lives in the androgynous room of 'fag limbo,' a space where everyone is worthy of suspicion. Most heterosexual boys I know exemplify this new class of boys, it is a clique that flirts with the sort of 'model' behavior typical of what is considered to be a bit sissy. They are the *nouveau sissy*, and word is finally getting out about them. This new brand of boy has the space to move at his own volition, back and forth and in and out of 'fag limbo' . . . My resulting attraction to these '*sissies*' has led to my own desire to reclaim a space in 'fag limbo.'" With thanks to Hernan Bas for his clever, elucidating coinage.

ries. I am simply responding to a homework assignment. No one has sorted, tagged, or priced the heirlooms of identity politics at sexuality's estate sale, where the prime items are disidentification, vagueness, and hovering.

Listen. A year or two ago, I wanted to make an experimental Super 8 nudie, *Why I Am Not a Painter*, based on the Frank O'Hara poem, which performs his desire to hang around attractive straight men who might sleep with him if he flatters their art. Simultaneously my nudie was to be a brief remake of *Taylor Mead's Ass*, Warhol's 1964 masterpiece. My screenplay, simple, required a three-minute close-up of a young male artist's butt. Any young male artist. Doesn't matter how cute.

I interviewed two young artists for the role.

The first demurred. He thought I was intending to make a porn flick. He said, "I don't want to be in a film whose only purpose is to get guys hard." We were drinking café con leches.

The second young artist made things complicated by talking about concept. All I wanted was intergenerational nude artmaking, a document that would posthumously stage a truce between O'Hara and Warhol through my post-Warholian gaze at a post-post-Warholian artist's ass, via 8 mm film, a pre-Warholian technology.

So I stopped talking to young artists about my nudie, and I hired a hustler instead. Two hundred dollars. He came to my apartment, took off his clothes. I filmed him with my Elmo. Through my south-facing apartment window, Chelsea afternoon light spread its bamboo fingers over his hairy buttcheeks, caught forever on black-and-white Kodak Tri-X reversal 7278 film. (I always keep a spare cartridge in the fridge, in case a good ass pays a spontaneous house call.) The guy was a theater student at the New School for Social Research. Physically he fit the role, but I'd wanted an artist, not a hustler, for my intergenerational allegory, my Pygmalion/Galatea film treatment of "Why I Am Not a Painter."

Anti-masculinist strategies (feyness, embroidery, craft, dithering, laziness, industriousness, sleeping in, hibernation, softness, sibilance, reflection, fandom, shyness, brazenness, star-fucking) characterize fag limbo. The artists I am thinking about include ________, ________, ________, ________, and ________. And there are others. Please don't pin me down. Nor do I wish to pin down the artists.* Mentioning an artist as part of a "school" is a form of hostile outing, whether or not the artist approves the appellation.

I googled the artists to figure out whether they were gay and came up with, in some cases, specific info, in most cases nothing.

Let's say that being bullied is a given of this art. Let's say that being cornered and not knowing how to defend oneself is this art's sine qua non.

Isolation tank and what you make of your isolation are the umbilici of this art.

Getting suicidally depressed and then suddenly feeling opulent gives this art its *je ne sais quoi*.

Going overboard with hobby shtick makes this art tick.

Not doing too good a job allows this art its accurate haruspication of 2004's innards.

*Some of the artists whose work informed my thinking about fag limbo, and who appear in the 2004 Whitney Biennial: David Altmejd, Hernan Bas, Christian Holstad, Terrence Koh, Virgil Marti, *assume vivid astro focus*, and Antony and the Johnsons. (There are others, too, but I hesitate to put them in fag limbo. I don't want to upset them.) However, this essay is not a description of these artists or of their work; nor do these artists form a unified school or movement. I make no assumptions about their sexualities or intentions. However, it would be disingenuous to pretend not to have been partly inspired, in writing this essay, by their work, especially the pieces selected for the 2004 Biennial.

Wallpaper and cum and Mylar and floor stickers and werewolves and snot and flat asses are a few of this art's incidentals.

Yoko Ono and Peter Max and Kurt Schwitters and Boy Scouts have met this art.

This art cares more for music than for Marx, and it understands the beauty of *do it yourself.* Nothing wrong with hiring an assistant, if you can afford it! But let's remember the virtue of handmade *Dasein*.

Don't forget that *fag* means *fatigue.*

I got into a conversation about gender with some young artists. I said that laptop computers—as visual items—contained gender codes. I also said that paintings speak gender, whether the paintings like it or not. (The young artists disagreed. Gender is passé.) I mentioned Mark Rothko. Rothko is gendered, right? Smart young people sometimes use "right?" as rhetorical interrogative. I'm acquiring this habit.

Satiation, or the experience of being historically belated, can produce envious indigestion, or it can (if the artist pursues fag limbo's Zen route) catalyze lightheartedness, an anti-erudite unencumberedness, and a refusal to "reference" in a gimmicky way. Fag limbo means taking the present moment just as it is, without the prophylaxis of peppiness (*I'm cheerful and allusive and past-oriented!*) but also without a competitive hamfistedness. Fag limbo allows the artist, and the speculator, to pursue other neighborhoods than *career*, that overvisited cemetery. To embrace limbo (*you can't pin me down*) and to embrace fagginess (*my Weltanschauung is flitty*) permit outsiderness without the doldrums and loneliness of actually being an outsider artist. Fag limbo interprets a former moment's addiction to the A-list as a spiritual disease and proposes that *flunking out of art* does not preclude virtuoso strategies. You need not renounce saturation, cornucopia, richness, skill, intensity, or texture just because you've decided to opt out of art's regular curriculum.

I'm not interested in art that wants to be successful or that imagines a brilliant career for itself. You're welcome to work hard, or to goof off, or to dream, secretly, of bigness, but don't wear that wish on your art's sleeve. Subscribing to unsuccess's tenets, I therefore value passive-aggressive art, which is sometimes a fag limbo strategy: pretending passivity, pretending not to fight for one's place at the table, this art may meanwhile house rebarbative aggressions.

If time allowed, I would now take us through a reading of Wittgenstein's *Tractatus Logico-Philosophicus*, specifically of a passage in which, pretending not to be making reference to actual autobiographical material, Wittgenstein refers to a left hand and a right hand, as if these were merely abstractions, an inessential *x* and *y*, without historical merit, without wound.* The careful reader, hearing the word ***hand***, will remember that Ludwig's brother Paul lost a hand (actually, an arm) in World War I, a loss memorialized in Maurice Ravel's *Piano Concerto for the Left Hand*. Two fags: Ravel and L. Wittgenstein. Ravel's ode to disability, and L. Wittgenstein's own inability to mourn, together create, around the space of

*Wittgenstein writes:

> The Kantian problem of the right and left hand which cannot be made to cover one another already exists in the plane, and even in one-dimensional space . . . The right and left hand are in fact completely congruent. And the fact that they cannot be made to cover one another has nothing do with it.
>
> A right-hand glove could be put on a left hand if it could be turned round in four-dimensional space.

Right and left hands—or their ***nothing-to-do-with-it*** congruencies—operate the stick shift (shtick shift?) of fag limbo's standard transmission.

the felled brother, a fag limbo in which all territorial claims, all hygienes separating music from philosophy from poetry, point toward a cross-media, intergenerational, autobiographical yet nonreferential vacuum, a zone in which real art, finally, can begin to occur; I would be able to gesture toward this zone with a more able set of maps, were there time for laborious cartography in the crowded, rushed interstice of a biennial, which places a revved-up premium on the *now* at the expense of the *then*, and which incites *thought on the run* (the only way I can think, *if* I can think). Fag limbo is, in part, this inability to think through anything but the materials right now in my room, wherever and whatever my room might be, whether bubble or cell or gallery or mausoleum or website. And were there time, within the hurried limbo of the Biennial, between the inferno of the passé and the paradiso of the *now*, I would gesture toward the liminal space (hallway? corridor?) linking the two wards in Thomas Bernhard's novelistic *Wittgenstein's Nephew*, a canal connecting the mental ward and the pulmonary ward, a passageway or arcade in which the two patients, one a mental case and the other a lung case, can tentatively meet, as if within an intergenerational compromise formation.*

The limbo between fixed, knowable sites creates a need for myth, or a space for myth's possible germination. By *myth* I simply mean the stories we invent to pass the time, *pass* not in the deathly sense (*he passed on* or *she passed on*) but in the organic, relieving sense of *pass stool*. Homosexuality was one such illuminating myth we passed, the walls of its cave detailed with drawings of Narcissus, Achilles, James Dean, Jack Smith.

*Down this passageway I do not proceed in ignorance of Marjorie Perloff's pivotal study, *Wittgenstein's Ladder: Poetic Language and the Strangeness of the Ordinary*.

More modest myths, less world-encompassing, detained us: we saw, out the corner of our eye, evidence that every artist, now and then, spins for himself or herself a cocoon of favored media and referents, a security-blanket intertext or glossary, a group of relied-upon names, colors, materials, techniques, which together form a heraldic mantle, protecting the artist against infection, indifference, bullying, comprehensibility, critics, curators, patrons, landlords, and other thruway accidents.

If there were time now—if this occasion for speech were more than a brief intervention in a space, the Biennial, too charged with meanings of its own for me to enter without risk of enchantment and paralysis—then I would lead us through a paragraph of Frantz Fanon's *Black Skin, White Masks*, where he describes fag limbo, without using the term, as a space of interracial and intergenerational envy and surveillance, wherein one man knows his authority by watching another man with another man's wife (the three men in this case are Jean-Paul Sartre, Richard Wright, and Frantz Fanon, and the one woman is Simone de Beauvoir); the fag limbo in which Fanon finds himself, without knowing or naming it, is a New York City street, within the precincts of chic, and without the defensive protection of a theory to back it up.*

*Fanon writes: "In New York, Simone de Beauvoir went for a walk with Richard Wright and was rebuked in the street by an old lady. Sartre said: Here it is the Jew, somewhere else it is the Negro. What is essential is a scapegoat." We must read this passage in concert with Fanon's earlier elliptical reference to puberty's neverendingess, where he demonstrates, through mesmerized verb tenses, that the temporal mode of fag limbo resists arrest: "During the time when I was slowly being jolted alive into puberty, I had the honor of being able to look in wonder on one of my older friends who had just come back from France and who had held a Parisian girl in his arms. I shall try to analyze this problem in a special chapter." It goes without saying that Fanon never quite arrives at that "special" chapter. Nor should we expect him ever to leap to the challenge of an unwritable analysis.

Fag limbo, in Fanon's case, involves Proust's mimetic desire (*I want that other man, I want to be that other man, I want what that other man has*) and sanctions a total absence of any overtly lubricious reference, so that we have no way of knowing whether cum-in-the-beard and cream pie are at issue.

One place to end is dream—how a culture and a psyche create floorshows. The oneiric items may be off today's menu, and yet whatever Yayoi Kusama meant when she filmed dot-making in the 1960s in Central Park (or so I recall) involved resuscitating dream-ideation, giving it mouth-to-mouth. If figurative or decorative elements reenter art under the aegis of *wish* or *fancy* (*I dreamt those shapes, I wanted those colors, I like to knit*), then art takes a salutary turn toward whimsicality as authoritarianism's antidote. I need eleven hours of sleep a night. We lack the time for a lengthy detour to Gaston Bachelard's *Poetics of Space*, which would help us understand the crucial place that dreamwork occupies in any aesthetic utilizations of the spatial. If we did not believe in space, then we could not have rooms. Without rooms, we would lack back rooms.

Dream, November 12, 2003: I French-kissed Hillary Clinton, a small woman, vulnerable, pretty, beleaguered. Was I kissing her in order to get close to Bill, or was I kissing her for the pleasure of the act itself, and for love of Hillary? How venal was my conduct? How noble? She reminded me of a foreign-language bookstore or a toy piano: she made tiny yet hard gamelan noises.

Writing about art exists, but it is a conceptual impossibility, because art has no outside: there is no space *outside* art. Writing that pretends to stand *outside* of art, looking in, also necessarily dwells *inside* art. This essay has no wish to occupy a position of superior vantage, looking down at art; nor does this essay desire to occupy a position of inferior vantage, looking up to art. Nor does this essay propose a relation of equal footing, a mutual, interactive gaze between art and writing. This essay asserts that art has swallowed it; this essay is delighted to have been digested by art. The alimentary limbo in which this essay resides, inside art's canal, is a pleasantly claustrophobic space. Limbo is writing's always-internal address within art's body; limbo is the post office box at which art's letters, written in this very typeface, always punctually arrive. Let me say it again, because I am slow today and afraid of being misinterpreted: this essay is not *about* art. This essay, bad or good or in between, is *inside* art—not because art is an honorific to be selectively bestowed but because art is the easiest, most available, most promiscuous category, the catch-all for every enacted wish, every short-circuited fantasy. Art is not a difficult achievement. It is where we already live, and it is how we identify that, indeed, we live.

(2004)

Why Art Is Always Emotional

> Frankly, the painting was not good at all. It would be impudent to maintain that it was. But, nonetheless, to me it seemed marvelous. Plain and simple as it was, it enchanted me; as a matter of fact, any sort of painting enchants me, however foolish and clumsy it is, because every painting reminds me first of diligence and industry, and second of Holland.
>
> —Robert Walser, *The Walk*

Does philosophical rumination—whether it takes the meandering form of recitative, or the straitened form of aphorism—qualify as *emotional*? Think of Nietzsche's rants and highs, or Wittgenstein's hesitant, antiseptic propositions, which sometimes, at their edges, break into moods of exaltation, curiosity, and depression.

•

Art with an obsessively worked surface, or art that is shiny and lumpy, or art that incorporates a grid, or art that is mostly monochrome, produces *aesthetic* emotion in me: tremor, flush, heart-quickening. Responding, I squint, sigh, snort, clench my molars. I jot a note on my private pad, or I comment aloud. I point. Elucidating, I play tour guide. I proclaim art's triumph over depressing circumstances. My speech grows abstract, so emotional have I become in my devotion to art's role as crutch, escape hatch, garbage chute, playmate . . . Indeed, art, no matter how lousy, reminds me that I am a person who likes to look at art and who gets emotional while thinking about it.

•

Rips, flaws, holes, punctures—signs that the artist has damaged the piece in order to make it more artful—pull my heartstrings. *Artaud was so upset and so creative that he put his cigarette out on his own drawing! Leigh Bowery was so excited and so expressive that he fastened safety pins in his fat cheeks!*

•

Any sort of art enchants me, because it allows me to make friends with curators and artists, who are often sexy, introspective, and anarchic. Art is a pimp. It procures, and, like a duenna, sits in the room while the intercourse transpires . . . Yes, I have a weakness for art that pretends to be affectless, and for anyone—harlequin, harlot, theory-head—who refuses to return my affection.

•

Apparent absence of content, in art, stimulates me: emptiness, whiteness, blueness, pinkness, and blackness license visceral expansiveness. Forms alone, colors alone, give me shivers and permit me to dwell in caffeinated ether. Abstract art subverts the sting of former embarrassments. Here's the formula: *I used to be abject, but now I'm abstract.*

•

Human contact exhausts me. I prefer art, which, regardless of its content, is a free ride to ecstasy, if you surrender to it, if you perform the requisite symbolic transpositions. (*X* equals *Y*. Thick paint equals transvalued shame. Radiant color equals conquered malaise. Deft line equals forgotten clumsiness.) Art assures me that I am bulletproof, that I am not stuck in a miserable conversation with someone who belittles me or who aims to colonize my entrails.

•

Art that deviates from precedent is, perforce, emotional, if only because it rejects the prior, the given, the laden. Rejection and refusal are always aggressive, and aggression is the motor of most emotion. Artists whose work aggressively advertises emotion: Vincent van Gogh, Nan Goldin. (Madness; blows; tears; sex; swirls; solitude.) Artists whose work aggressively avoids or disdains emotion: Donald Judd, Marcel Duchamp. And yet: I get emotional about Judd, Duchamp—about boxes, valises, peepholes, glass, shelves, parallelism. If we were to hear that Judd was a madman, or that his boyfriend beat him up, we might interpret his art as emotional.

•

Art or literature that responds to incalculable extremity—the Holocaust—may betray minimal emotion on its surface: Claude Lanzmann's documentary *Shoah* and Imre Kertész's novel *Fatelessness* probe the apparent absence of affect at trauma's core. With trauma comes psychological deadness, the catatonia of interminable interregnum.

•

Catherine Opie, in her photograph *Self-Portrait/Nursing*, depicts herself breastfeeding her child: Opie may be art history's first *inked* Mother of God, her divine body amply tattooed. Her face gives no clear signs of emotion. The baby, I presume, is feeling contentment, excitement, discombobulation. Discombobulated, certainly, am I, unaccustomed to this spectacle. Indeed, art with highly emotional content (maternity, nudity, mortality) may actually be cool, didactic, and majestically airless, while art that has no content, or buried content, or complicated and nonparaphrasable content, may contain reservoirs of tidal affect.

•

Sandra Dee died today, but I'm not emotional about her passing. I may feel moved after I read the memoir of her son,

Dodd Darin, *Dream Lovers: The Magnificent Shattered Lives of Bobby Darin and Sandra Dee.* In Douglas Sirk's film *Imitation of Life*, Sandra Dee plays emotionless Lana Turner's daughter. Brainy melodramas like Sirk's—or like Chloe Piene's *Blackmouth*, Elizabeth Peyton's *Nick (La Lunchonette, December 2002)*, and Bas Jan Ader's *I'm too sad to tell you*—distance the spectator from the theatrical emotions the works purportedly display. Sirk, milking melodrama, also took it off art's menu. Darin and his ilk (eyewitness raconteurs of stardom's toxic force field, and by stardom I mean *emotional domination*) secretly restore melodrama's ermine reign.

•

Candy Darling, on her deathbed, as photographed by Peter Hujar, makes theater of her own emergency: bittersweetly serene, she has at last become the dying Lady of the Camellias. I'd be a cad to call this moving photo "unemotional," and yet the emotion it offers is edged by ambivalence: the photo is a mausoleum for the dated attitudes it inspires in me.

•

Andreas Gursky's wide-angle photographic tableaux—often of commodities—trigger a viewer's awe: panoramas, whether from mountaintops or the moon, kick-start sublime experience, for they remix the miniature and the monumental, and shock the eye out of its complacency. In *May Day II*, Gursky represents group emotion, of which we have every reason to be suspicious. But he recuperates individual experience by permitting one eye—the camera's, the viewer's—to comprehend the entire ungraspable spectacle; reduced to one voyeur's portion, the May Day bacchanal becomes just another object to remark upon, to own, to employ as catalyst for aesthetic transport, however dressed up as politics.

•

Two trials: Martha Stewart, Michael Jackson. (I'm pro-Michael, pro-Martha, though not to excess, and not against reason. I'm anti-scapegoating.) The spectacle of crime and punishment produces mob emotion in a society—ours—incapable of passionate response to ecocide, genocide, and unjust war. I speak not as a self-righteous outsider to the contemporary predicament of dangerously unemotional deadness: like so many other dwellers in the American "now," I limit my sights to familiar, framable spectacles, and I turn away from crises too panoramic for customary consumption.

•

Chris Ofili's painting *Afro Love and Envy* hits an emotional high because it projects happiness and bright escape, and because it incorporates actual turds. Turds are objects that we might hesitate to call emotional. They have no feelings, and we who produce turds have rudimentary, disorganized attitudes toward them. And yet turds are absolutes. They materially embody human process. They are factual, or do I mean actual, like oil paint, celluloid, bones, and buildings. When inner life is so compactly extruded—turned into turd, into art, into cinema, into text—then . . . Oh, that isn't a sentence I want to finish!

(2005)

Situation Hacker

Imagine slasher films without blood; porn without nudity; the Sistine Chapel without God; the New York Stock Exchange without capital. Pretend that Hieronymus Bosch's intermeshed figures could text. Ryan Trecartin's videos depict a vertiginous world I'm barely stable enough to describe. Watching them, I face the identity-flux of Internet existence: surfing-as-dwelling. Images evaporate, bleed, spill, metamorphose, and explode. Through frenetic pacing, rapid cuts, and destabilizing overlaps between representational planes (3-D turns into 2-D and then into 5-D), Trecartin violently repositions our chakras. Digitally virtuoso, his work excites me but also causes stomach cramps. I'm somatizing. But I'm also trying to concentrate.

Walter Benjamin drew a distinction between "concentration" and "distraction." Distraction meant falling prey to false consciousness. Concentration meant rising to revolutionary art's—or history's—challenge. Occasions for concentration were fading, Benjamin feared. (Ghoulishly, one word, in German, *Konzentration*, sometimes indicates both *concentration* camp [*Konzentrationslager*] and mental concentration; the ability to concentrate, in Benjamin's 1940 Baudelaire essay, is *Konzentrationsvermögen*.) Benjamin wanted us to concentrate—a mental deliberation akin to what Michael Fried (following Diderot) has described as "absorption." (A figure, in a painting, should ignore the viewer and remain absorbed in an activity, whether reading, praying, sewing, or sleeping.) Paradox: *Trecartin's characters concentrate on distraction.* They exercise the right to honor their own skittishness—but "distraction" now wears the guise of transformation, mutability. Being distractible (ADD?) intensifies consciousness. And the intensification of consciousness (even if this intensification poses as a dilution, evaporation, or deliquescence of knowingness) is one goal of any art I stand behind.

•

Trecartin, born in Texas (a trace of drawl is a vocal leitmotif of his videos), broke into the art world with *A Family Finds Entertainment* in 2004, the year he graduated from the Rhode Island School of Design. Then, in 2006, came the seven-minute-long video *(Tommy Chat Just E-mailed Me.)*, and the feature-length *I-Be Area*, both available on YouTube and UbuWeb. In the 2009 exhibition *The Generational: Younger than Jesus*, at New York's New Museum, Trecartin unveiled installments of his epic, composed of three interconnected, modular psychodramas: *Sibling Topics (Section A)*, *K-Corea INC. K. (Section A)*, and *Re'Search Wait'S (Edit One: Re'Search Missing Corruption Budget)*. Trecartin, who writes, directs, and performs in his films, works closely with fellow RISD alum Lizzie Fitch. She, too, stars in the videos; she also collaborates on sets and costumes, and on the sculptural installations accompanying the films. (In the New Museum trilogy, Rhett LaRue is another credited collaborator; he handles the 3-D animations.) Like Andy Warhol, Jack Smith, John Waters, the Maysles brothers, and the brothers Kuchar, Trecartin capitalizes on a quarry of gifted, histrionic associates and discoveries—charismatic screen presences, including Veronica Gelbaum, Courtney Malick, Telfar Clemens, and Alison Powell. Of all the actors, Trecartin might be my favorite: his neo-brainy antics, though sui generis, have the acerbic pizzazz of Ondine, Mickey Rooney, "Little" Edie Bouvier Beale, Sacha Baron Cohen, Alex Bag, and Amy Sedaris. (Lists, lists! Can't live without them.) Trecartin's mind may be as iconoclastic as Noam Chomsky's, but his mien is as juvenile as Jackie Coogan's. Trecartin is an adorable, demented trickster, who never stops aiming twisted affect at the camera.

In sculptural works such as *The Aboutthing (in the air)* and *Now, in the Sunroom*, Trecartin and Fitch show tableaux of intertwined, evocative objects, like a dream's *disjecta membra*, or props from a trashed film studio: swimming pool, mannequins in meltdown, luggage thrown helter-skelter. The sculpture has considerable charm, ambition, and suggestiveness, but my heart is in the videos, which I'd rather see at home than in a museum or gallery, if only because the videos demand time and concentration. After several viewings, I still can't keep track of the personalities; they zap in and out, like extraterrestrial desiderata on interactive flying saucers.

I want to ride Trecartin's flying saucers, but I'm also afraid of them. His cosmos, not a tranquilizer, presents a terror-spiked forecast. Of apocalypse-as-party. Of psychological evisceration as spiritual exuberance. Of being-at-home as whirling-dervish-danceteria. All I can do is generalize about this world and point to it, with a yearning, stumped pleasure; my pointing finger is the gesture of an outsider, a tourist, gawking at a radioactive carnival I can't domesticate or quarantine. I don't want to sell or explain Trecartin. Nor do I wish to overemphasize the differences between his various works, all recently produced. I interpret them as evolving mutations of a single worldview, a visual and verbal idiom I take the risk of essentializing as "Trecartinese" (the mother tongue of Trecartinesia). What follows is a subjective survey of his idiom's idiosyncracies.

•

In Trecartin's universe, a singular personality style dominates: gregarious, theatrical, spewing. Faces are painted, often with marks suggesting wounds, bandages, plastic surgery, or racial disguise. Bodies are canvases for abstract paintings, with the subversive spirit of Yves Klein and Carolee Schneemann, and the chromatic punch of Hans Hofmann and Mary Heilmann. The stakes of Trecartin's (and Fitch's) painterly gestures are etherealization disguised as materialization: turn burdensome bodies into animated arrows, and lift the person from the doldrums of humanness by upgrading unmarked skin into brightly apotropaic abstraction.

Trecartin's world is unashamedly faggy. He digitally alters voices—pitch raised or lowered—to obscure gender. You can squeak or boom, pipe or bellow: vocal transplants occur, instantaneously. "Ethnic" talk-idioms slide the speaker outside identity categories into spiky, gratifying hipness. Conversation succumbs to monologue: everyone rants, or issues stinging declarations—diverse idiolects remixed into philosophical investigation. (A character in *I-Be Area* ventures a thought experiment that Wittgenstein could have accommodated in *Remarks on Colour*: "I think we should show him the color yellow for a year, and then the next year only the color green. And see if it makes him different or more interesting or cooler than everyone else his age. I think in high school it will give him the razor's edge.") Some players seem high, but the real drug is connectivity, morphability. Orgasm is beside the point. The kids would rather talk; their hands clutch phantom cell-phones. It's surprising that for a social world as based in visual overstimulation as Trecartin's, language retains its place as identity marker and identity transfuser: *talk* (chatter, rant, monologue) remains the plasma through which personality affirms its right to die and to live.

Players tease and set fire to one another—but nonlethally.

Here you can delete frenemies. You can cut and paste them. With digital sleight of hand, you can lobotomize or Drano them. And they reappear! Actions appear violent, but even if you've been evaporated by a sidekick's superior will, you can recolonize yourself on another atoll. (In *K-Corea INC. K* a commanding transgender character named Global Korea has the power—through incongruous cock-flash under short skirt, and through audacious stewardess-CEO-speak—to shame her fellow travelers into nonexistence.) Deleuze and Guattari described this hypersphere, but they didn't make it seem fun. Trecartin's gang blisses out on rhizomatic existence. Books are dead. Books are "cute" relics. In *Re'Search Wait'S*, one of Trecartin's characters, a "spaz" named J. J. Check, thought it would be cute to rewrite the U.S. Constitution. Every time the words *people* and *humanity* appear, he replaces them with *situations*; and every time *God* appears, he substitutes *The Internet*. J.J.'s tenancy, on screen, is temporary; he is a pit stop between other personalities—a puerile turnstile, like Linda Blair in *The Exorcist*, but with an ego purchased at the Container Store.

In Trecartin's world, there are no old people and only a few over thirty. Fathers have vanished. Goodbye to patriarchy. The moms may be several, lesbian, and kindly, but in *I-Be Area*, Trecartin himself assumes the role of a psycho mom, practical and chic as Doris Day interfacing with Lance Loud. (Is *I-Be Area* the transitional arena—of flux and play—in which "I" am "free" to "be"? Or is it the cordoned-off, always-already-under-surveillance area in which the "I" is quarantined, sequestered for observation—the "I" led on a wild-goose chase through the labyrinth of its own putative freedom?) The "mom" is a major category in Trecartin's cosmos: anyone's eligible. In this drag matriarchy, body alteration abounds, some of it recidivist, as scary as Elsa Lanchester in *Bride of*

Frankenstein. In *Sibling Topics*, one of Trecartin's gender-transitional characters proudly flashes his breast-reduction surgical scars. If you're not pregnant, you can morph your belly, anyway, to appear knocked up. All genders in Trecartinesia are created equal, but "Mom" still has an underground sway, like Erda in Wagner's *Ring*. Lacan's lingo, if summoned, could cast its complicated, pervy light on Trecartin's Mom-locus, its neo-Oedipal flora and fauna.

Don't expect old-school relics like penises or vaginas. Don't expect titillation. Pollution, pesticides, hormones, and waste-management crises have changed human anatomy: every year, the distance between a man's wiener and butthole is shrinking. Good riddance to cocksureness. Economies crash; decorators pin cash, like Mardi Gras tinsel, to circulating fans. Aspirants seize crazy new names, like household products or security codes: Pasta, Twi-Key, Sen-Teen, Adobe, Wait, Able. Parents abandon children: abandonment is the new sexy condition. Being a foundling doesn't preclude having a mom in tow. Trecartin and his muses hang out in a house, *unheimlich-gemütlich* as the homes in *Eraserhead*, *Carrie*, *Blue Velvet*, *Notorious*, and *Naked*. In Trecartin's zone, you needn't buy or rent property—just squat. Trash the place; repaint it, upload it, hit "Send." You never sleep and are never sleepy, unless your voice gets slowed down by QuickTime or some other software I don't know the name of. Slash your neck with paint. Separate your head from your body to downplay the dull genitals. Surgically mark your neck with a horizontal predella or with a pseudotracheotomy scar—as if warming up for decapitation, or posthumously recovering from it. As far as I can judge, the most conspicuous and telling body paint, in several videos, occurs on the neck. Voice is the anxiety point, and therefore the painterly—the stroke, the slash, the cut, the mark—concentrates its supposedly *retardataire* energies on the very place where orality and literacy stage their war of the worlds.

One character turns into another by discovering an alter, avatar, or replica. Personality is always transitioning: one identity devours the next in line. Spongy egos slide into one another, like transgender, transracial part-objects glomming on to embryonic epistemes. You can efficiently dis anyone. Dissing—claiming turf—happens instantly and cleanly. (In *K-Corea INC. K* the dominatrix-mogul Global Korea sends out this gnomic stinger: "Who the fuck is that baby shit-talker? That's not one of *my* condiments.") Following the ontology of *Paris Is Burning*, Trecartin sets in play a black-inflected drag system of identity manufacture and parade, complete with couture-terrorized *écoles* and slum-Situationist ateliers, or sensibility workshops run by sacerdotal "mothers" and staffed by acolyte "children" who dwell in deep danger of being branded as "unreal." Reality, in Trecartin's multiracial social bubble, derives from personality assertion; you assert eminence through bodypaint, gesture, and dialogue. And through concision. No one is tedious; players (as we learn in *Sibling Topics*) are "post-family and pre-hotel" and therefore always auditioning for Presence. Audition, or rehearsal, is a perpetually stimulated and vigilant state of being. Trecartin himself, in real life, is part of a musical group (XPPL [The Experimental People Band]); the chummy clubhouse atmosphere of his videos reminds me of *The Monkees* and *The Partridge Family*. In both situation comedies, "life" and "fiction" poached off each other. The tour bus ruled the land. The tour bus, a mobile Valhalla, pacified generational wars with a saccharine score. There's comfort to be found in occupying the niche—the area, the container, the Winnicottian holding environment—of a TV-show-length module, an infomercial, a home-schooled band. The Manson Family and the Partridge Family and *All in the Family* and the Jackson 5 and Sly and the Family Stone have found, in Trecartin's kinship corpuscles, an heir who questions the value of "family" while reupholstering it.

In Trecartin's postsexual world, everyone speaks in a hodgepodge of accents—a composite. (I say "postsexual" because there's hardly an allusion to fucking in the entire Trecartin oeuvre.) Dialects are his acrylics. Spanglish. Country and western. Hip-hop. Sotheby's. Secretarial. Subcontinental, any continent. Dallas. Instead of "yes," say "yay-us." His accents refer to class and attitude as much as to region or ethnicity. The point of an accent seems to be its potential placelessness—its telegraphic way of marking the site where recognizability gets bamboozled. Trecartin has a handsome mouthful of teeth and he puts them to good use. He paints them—green? blue? silver?—and sometimes supplements them with false teeth; he expands the mouth, which can barely contain the verbal torrent. His language shatters paradigms: in Trecartin's scripts (the lines are apparently not improvised), everyone speaks in tidbits, and these koans are a new form of poetry, laced with social critique and unclassifiable esprit. He juxtaposes lancing phrases; he sutures vernaculars. Utterances grow exciting when repeated and tidbitized, or when they are offered as propositions or dares rather than as factual statements. "Put your breasts back on." "I want a idea landfill." "I define myself as a situation hacker." "Fuck cookies." "I can't wait till the Internet declares its independence." "It reminds me of the future." "I don't know a single company that's experimental enough for me." "Am I overexisting, or am I overexisting?" "I never say 'they.' I say 'us' or 'we.'" "I love being in places that mean nothing to me." "I'm finally just an 'as if.'" "She's a toxic bisexual wearing unstable flip-flops." Occasional references to "my personal really concise pussy" leave me happy yet puzzled. (In *Re'Search Wait'S* Trecartin's character Wait, who can't cope with being gainfully employed, says, "My personal really concise pussy is creating a very inner monologue that I'm not going to share with you as I become dynamic.") "J.J., check it," the sharp-souled, diminutive performer Alison Powell squeals. (Her screen name is Roamie, and she stars in an interlude called "A Roamie Collects History Enhancements," nested in *Re'Search Wait'S*.) I've been repeating her phrase "J.J., check it" compulsively. What brave new world will interpellate me if I intone this stolen mantra? J.J. is a charming "retard." Cognitive lag or interruption is no stigma for Trecartin's personae.

Playing dress-up is philosophical boot camp. That's why Cindy Sherman's figments, whether glamorous or abject, belong with Trecartin's people. So do Nan Goldin's citizens. Like Goldin, Trecartin focuses on purgatories—depressed or zippy coteries held together by hedonistic color and the luridness of interpersonal contact revved to the breaking point. And yet Goldin's and Sherman's photographs seem comfortingly stable and monumental, like prie-dieux, when compared to Trecartin's jumpy productions—and not only because of the difference between still and moving images. I get hypomanic when I enter Trecartin's amped sphere: falling under his spell is as needling to the nerves as straddling the Scylla and Charybdis of Warhol's split-screen *Chelsea Girls*. A Trecartin quip: "Listen, don't get a boner." I'll try not to get a boner over Trecartin's evocation of the Now. Quote: "Don't look at me—look at your mother, and globalize at *her*." What does it feel like to be globalized, or to be dragged to the trash icon on the computer screen? The bubblebrain gestalt of the identity surfer turns depth psychology on its ass.

Trecartin's work might mean death to the Book, but, tonight, I don't care. I'll find a nonbookish way to drum up a conceptual shelter in his stunted avatar Wait's "personal really concise pussy." Narrative is one way: Trecartin shows that new forms of storytelling may thrive in talkative guerrilla cooperatives that eschew utopian promises, including the long-ago-dashed dream of sexual and material liberation. And yet I imagine that Trecartin's tales, like any shapeshifter's, will need to keep floating evasively through the meshes of the market, if his flipped-out personae and hacked situations want to preserve their organlessness and their concentrated delirium.

(2009)

Eric's Stubble

I live with Eric. No, I live with a photograph of Eric, taken by Paul Mpagi Sepuya (born in 1982), whose work is easy to love and difficult to theorize. I bought Eric's image at a gallery in 2007 because I felt sexual desire for what the photograph seemed to represent. Eric has conspicuous stubble; his gray-green eyes refute the stubble or establish a dialectical relation with it. Eric's eyebrows are thick, dark; his hairstyle—bangs?—recalls a Roman or Sicilian wall painting. His stubble is verdigris; his olive skin retreats into pallor, hunger, vagueness. Eric is the type of guy I tend to classify as "Levantine," which means, in my anachronistic imagination, a crypto-Jewish amalgam of Egyptian, Turkish, Greek, Italian, and a few other tinctures. We shouldn't classify guys; typology is a cruel exercise. Paul's photographs refuse to classify the men he captures, and yet the ghost of categorization (August Sander and his ilk) hovers over any photograph that isolates its human object.

•

A Sepuya backdrop is typically a blank wall, a neutral surface, gray-white, like the color Titanium Buff Deep in the Old Holland line of acrylic paints. Sepuya's monochrome backgrounds remind me of the possibility that Robert Ryman's work espouses—the hope that within so-called white there exist infinite gradations of difference and chromatic subtlety. Sepuya's uniform Titianium Buff Deep allows skin tones to register with a lyrical, alarming specificity—a specificity that blissfully evades the kinds of categorization that my earlier reference to "Levantine" tactlessly embodies.

•

Earlier, I said that I bought the photograph of Eric because I felt sexual desire for him. "Sexual desire" is a careless shorthand that Sepuya's work slowly and methodically dissects. It would be more accurate to call my desire "never-ending anticipation." Eric's image allows me to occupy an interim state that resists conclusion. The engine—desire-laden anticipation—keeps humming; ongoingness begins to serve as consolation. Sepuya's photographs specialize in soliciting this form of anticipation, of endlessly postponed coalescence. I don't mind waiting; prolongation allows me to look carefully at Eric's stubble, or at the spaces between the individual grains of embryonic hair, not yet a beard.

•

I can examine the individual blades of stubble on Eric's face because Sepuya's camera has availed itself of fastidious, intensive focus. *Sharp focus* is Sepuya's territory; focus almost floats free of its subjects and occasions, and becomes a theme in itself. Sepuya's focus lacks hyperbole. His images don't exaggerate the endowments of his sitters; the cool and nearly shadowless clarity with which we can see their faces and bodies doesn't rhyme with kindness or warmth. Focus seems, instead, an ethical issue—an Apollonian refusal to distort, to modify, to sully. Paradoxically, Sepuya's photographs are at once aloof and passionate: his sharp focus suggests disinterestedness, but the near-nudity of his subjects—or their tropism toward undress—implies sex's prelude, even if the encounter never arrives. We don't count on consummation. As artists and viewers, we depend, instead, on sex's imminence, its foreshadowings.

•

Eric is my first love. My second love, nearly eclipsing the first, is Victor. Victor has wild hair—teased into a black halo. The circle of hair, outrageously large, contrasts with his bookish—or revolutionary—eyeglasses, which recall the nerd glasses I wore in 1972. His glasses seem sweetly nebbishy, serious, unapologetic, and headed toward radical liberation. In a 2010 portrait taken in Sepuya's bedroom, Victor kneels, feet underneath buttocks, in S/M stirrups, ready for action. Glasses still on, he stares at the camera with confident yet prim expressionlessness. Victor has ostentatious stubble. To say I feel sexual desire for Victor would be a gross understatement. Wishing to forswear the phrase "sexual desire" (because of its incompleteness, its haziness, and its talent for question begging), I'll say, instead, that Victor provokes in me a hunger for narrative.

•

Looking at Sepuya's photographs of Victor, I start to spin stories and inferences. One myth concerns his hair. In this legend, which may be accurate, his hair is a Jewfro as well as an Afro. Adorably, it occupies the median position—Jewfro, Afro, seamlessly melded. Another story, perhaps also true, takes place on West Twenty-Seventh Street. I'm walking east; Victor, walking west, wears a colorful, boldly patterned suit. My suit, too, exceeds the limits of conventional taste. Victor and I lock eyes, or he intuits that I recognize him from Sepuya's photograph and that we are long-lost doppelgängers. Later, at home, I browse through Craigslist's "Missed Connections" to see if Victor has posted an ad to find me. I consider this present essay a pretext to meet Victor, to convince him of my enraptured regard.

•

What consumes me with curiosity is Victor's sly contrapposto, as if he were deliberately quoting a Renaissance or Greco-

Roman precedent. His hand, pivoting at the wrist, establishes ironic feyness as a signature of power and self-control. Opened on the folding chair is a zine, red-covered, called *FIRE!!* I won't make the mistake of asserting that my desire for Victor is this photograph's exclusive meaning. And I won't oversimplify desire; what I'm calling "desire-for-Victor" is a tangle of contradictory convictions: (1) I look like Victor; (2) I don't look like Victor; (3) I used to look like Victor; (4) no one recognized that I used to look like Victor; (5) it's too late to find Victor; (6) I need to change my life so that I can find Victor or make a career out of pursuing him; (7) I need to become a more serious artist so that I can use my desire for Victor in productive ways; (8) I need to compose a blazon for Victor; (9) I need to read more philosophy so I can grasp Victor's profundity.

•

It's not just Victor's body that I love. I worship his attitude, his audacity, his compactness. Even nude (with socks, glasses, leather stirrups), he radiates style. His body sets up a relation of concord and dissonance with the Titanium Buff Deep wall behind him. He befriends the Titanium Buff Deep; he upstages it. Against the wall's supposed neutrality, Victor's pallor registers with a legible but unclassifiable precision. What events led him to Paul's studio? Sepuya's close-grained technique effaces these stories but also opens them up for examination. I begin to imagine the friendship—the complicity, the correspondence—that underwrote this meeting, now frozen in a photograph whose power resides in the messages it can't specify.

•

I haven't spoken clearly enough about Victor's buttocks or about the hair on his chest, abdomen, and legs. That information might not interest a reader of an essay about Sepuya's photography. Or else that information might be essential. It might fall under the purview of *sharp focus*, a philosophical theme, connected to the mind's woefully finite capacity to pay unstinting attention to a single object. I pay close attention to Victor's buttocks and hair; I'd like to use Sepuya's photographs of Victor—and my relation to them—to argue for a contemplative practice of concentrating on details, radiant or unshining, that we must never take at face value but must plunge into decoding, even if the process of decipherment isolates us from consensual, commonsensical idioms.

•

Sepuya's subjects are not hunks. Distance from pulchritude constitutes their profundity. Sepuya's stylized, minimalist portraits—emotive yet even-tempered—participate in a new, anti-hunk genre of homoerotic photography, most often found in zines. *BUTT* magazine didn't begin the trend, but it is a stellar locale for this type of guy—whose look suggests several eras. Pre-clone? Post-clone? Post-post-clone? Never forget how historically specific the nude always is.

•

I reserved an hour this afternoon to write a paragraph about Daniel. My wish to write about Daniel—or the image that Sepuya calls "Daniel"—has everything to do with the hair that covers most of his chest and that leads, without a gap, to his underarms. The fact that the hair almost stops at the collarbone but continues northward testifies (in my unrepentant imagination) to Daniel's gentleness. His pallor, too, attests, within my nonlogical *imaginaire*, to a peacenik's vulnerability. He sits on a rudimentary chair but tries to squeeze most of his body onto it, more of his body than the chair can contain. I've singled him out, from among Sepuya's subjects, because Daniel's look appeals to me, but also because the photograph renders me vulnerable—more endangered than the person it portrays. Daniel, by exposing his body—and Paul, by exposing Daniel's body—have exposed *me*, have forced upon me a capitulation I often undergo when I see a male nude. I find myself inwardly surrendering to his body, especially if he is merely a photograph and not an actual presence. I surrender to Paul's photograph of Daniel because almost nothing clutters this image—no apparatus of framing, dramatic lighting, décor, only Daniel's gray socks, and a silvery chair, and a Sepuya print curling on the threshold where wall meets floor. In another photograph, Daniel raises his left arm, as if merely to ensure that the viewer can see his underarm hair, a thick vertical line, like a miniature Barnett Newman "zip." If I were paranoid, I'd say that my longing for Daniel, as I behold this photograph, attacks me: I'm its victim. However, I aggressively solicit the posture of longing. I manufacture desire for Daniel. I am legible to myself only as "the writer who feels guilty for wanting to know Daniel."

•

The word *guilty* in the previous sentence demands explanation. Why should I feel remorse for admitting that Sepuya's photograph of Daniel makes me desire its subject? (I don't mean to harp on desire. Instead, I want to emphasize anticipation, stillness, paralysis—the frozenness of waiting for Daniel to acknowledge me, a response that can never be forthcoming, although I eagerly await it.) Guilt is a consequence of trying to write about realistic photography, and of making the mistake of entering into the stories that the images suggest, rather than focusing exclusively on formal elements. Or maybe guilt is the necessary aftereffect of any attempt to do justice, in words, to pictures that excite me, even if the state toward which they impel me is shocked immobility, a quivering stasis, rather than a pleasurable satiety. Eric, Victor, Daniel: these are the men I owe to Paul. Eric, Victor, and Daniel arouse complications in my system, which is mostly linguistic—a ferryway littered with kelp, foam, myths, microbes, and other debris, some in sharp focus, some terminally blurry. Paul Mpagi Sepuya, to his credit, is never blurry, but icy clarity is not the only reason his work inflames the willing imagination.

(2012)

Cindy Sherman and Her Kind

Literature might be the wrong place to begin. Invoking words, when looking at pictures, is cheating. Yet Cindy Sherman's work has consistently sidestepped photography's silent modality and seduced viewers with murmured tales, or their trappings. First came the Hollywood B-movie stories. Later, stories from pornography and horror films. Always, characters pulled her mise-en-scène's strings—the fetishist, the pervert, the voyeur, the cineast, the necrophiliac, the mad scientist, and the department-store window dresser left alone at night with undead, plastic incubi.

The story I remembered on seeing an exhibit of Sherman's photographs (at Metro Pictures in New York in 2000) was Tennessee Williams's "The Night of the Iguana," which appeared in his 1948 collection, *One Arm*. I'm certain that Andy Warhol read the book when it was first published, and that it meant almost as much to him as Truman Capote's short fiction did. The title story, "One Arm," about a mutilated male hustler, contains a drawing of an electric chair and includes the sentence "I guess I stopped caring about what happened to me"—one possible source of Warhol's notion that *ceasing to care* was the epochal moment in an artist's life. Sherman, from the evidence of her magnificently histrionic photos, long ago ceased to care. She needn't have read *One Arm*, inasmuch as Edith Jelkes, the heroine of "Iguana," haunts all neo-Gothic portraiture; any visual or verbal fable that exhibits a character's incomplete grasp of sexual poise necessarily returns to Edith Jelkes and her kind:

> Miss Jelkes was a spinster of thirty with a wistful blond prettiness and a somewhat archaic quality of refinement. She belonged to an historical Southern family of great but now moribund vitality whose latter generations had tended to split into two antithetical types, one in which the libido was pathologically distended and another in which it would seem to be all but dried up . . . Edith Jelkes was not strictly one or the other of the two basic types, which made it all the more difficult for her to cultivate any interior poise. She had been lucky enough to channel her somewhat morbid energy into a gift for painting.

In Sherman's pseudoportraits, as in the soul of Edith Jelkes, antipodes abide: shimmer, filth; wealth, decline; extravagance, dessication; sexual success, sexual failure. Jelkes-like is the clatter of these overlapping codes, the noise of *interior poise cultivated at impossible risk*.

Perhaps I am making the mistake of caring too much about visual art's content. As Rosalind Krauss trenchantly observed in a 1993 essay: "[Sherman's doll photos] are a statement of what it means to refuse to an artist the work that he or she has done—which is always work on the signifier—and to rush headlong for the signified, the content, the constructed meaning, which one then proceeds to consume as myth." Yes, I "rush headlong" for the content. I can't help it. I'd rather behave, but against my better judgment I gobble the signified's fast food. (Paradoxically, it demands slow digestion.)

Beyond myth, I see, in Sherman's images, exhaustion's

salutary presence. Cindy Sherman is the servant of Cindy Sherman, as Jorge Luis Borges knew himself to be the drudge who wrote Borges's poems. Such servitude is psychically demanding; somewhere, eventually, the artist must express the toll and seek a tonic. In Sherman's comic pictures, I think, the cost's severity leaks out.

Noble rot rises to the surface in one of Sherman's untitled images from 2000: a woman, attempting a foxy look, must ignore her prominent and unfortunate teeth—as she has every right to do. I note her humiliated, energetic struggle against the dental burden; I note the overbite's gusto, its refusal to back down or skip town. The eyes, too, are abject; they want to transcend the tropic mouth, after seasons of ridicule. I respond to the photo by flinching, but also by laughing—not at the woman, who doesn't exist, but with delight at Sherman's virtuoso effort to simulate an extreme of failed poise.

When I asked about the photo of the woman with the unfortunate teeth, Sherman described her as a "sexy earth mama" who'd been "hot in her younger days" and was "still hot in her mind." She described another character as a "retired realtor." I heartily agreed. I said many of these women were "very realtor." Sherman reiterated that she was not "making fun of these poor characters," as some critics had intimated, and she clarified that these images depict West Coast types, to be supplemented, possibly, by a future series of East Coast types.

Sherman's work tends to segregate beauty from disgust, but there have been pronounced exceptions, like the "fashion" photographs of 1983–84, which pitted gorgeous outfits against dermatalogical derangement. The new pictures go one step further, seamlessly integrating grotesquerie and glamour; they show that abjection doesn't belong solely to the disenfranchised. Filth is equally the property of the rich.

Exposing wealth's thickness and complacency, Sherman thrusts her provocative self-misrecognition—as retaliation—into a zone, and with an aggressiveness, that may discomfit. These images do not make safe references to art, film, and fashion; they allude, dangerously, to local vanity. Specifically, they gloss the tradition of patron portraiture: might we not mistake these women for collectors of Cindy Sherman photos? Indeed, an image of a would-be blonde bombshell, whom Sherman described to Calvin Tomkins as an "ex–bit player," recalls Warhol's multiple portrait of one of his first important collectors, *Ethel Scull 36 Times*, 1963.

Class, even in its upper-ish echelons, is visually incoherent. No map can account for every eccentricity of chemise, necklace, eyebrow, lip, and hair, and Sherman's photographs playfully exploit this cacophony of signs. Cosmetic meltdown: do we call these personae elite or underdog, carnival or hodgepodge? Sherman's characters can no longer say *I know who I am and what I desire and how to excite desire in others.* As a consequence, we gleefully watch sexual poise's tectonic plates crack. And our glee comes mixed with gratitude to Sherman for generously pursuing what is often wrongly called "exhibitionism" but is surely better understood as cultural ecology—conscientiously recycling what T. S. Eliot called "the butt-ends of my days and ways." Some butt-ends. Some days.

(2000)

Diane Arbus and Humiliation

I see Diane Arbus photographs through the lens of my current idée fixe: humiliation. Looking, I ask myself the following questions (self-interrogation is itself humiliating):

Is Arbus humiliating her subjects? Is Arbus humiliated by their proximity?

Are we, viewing the pictures, humiliated?

Is humiliation contagious? Are her photos a smear campaign against public complacence?

Is she humiliating "high art" by exposing it to the contagion of deadpan freakishness?

Is urbanity humiliating? Her subjects sometimes dwell in the equivalent of SROs: is forced neighborliness—nearness to strangers—humiliating?

Does photography itself, as genre, humiliate, under the guise of enlargement and idealization? Journalism aims to humiliate, and Arbus participates in a journalistic (Weegee) and taxonomic (August Sander) tradition: expose the abject exception.

Arbus documents multiple demimondes. A group's self-constitution as demimonde (bohemian, homosexual, addict) builds a barrier reef against humiliation. In the old days, Greenwich Village and Times Square were oases where the humiliated, congregating, could scheme to take over the proper, manicured world.

Is nudity humiliating? Some of her subjects are nude, or nudists.

Is body hair humiliating? I noticed a seeming absence of depilation.

Is it humiliating to work hard? Arbus labored: the exhibit documented her arduous notetaking, her punctilious preparation. Does assiduous artistry ritually replay humiliation, aiming toward abreaction or catharsis?

Does black-and-white humiliate, using the alibi of "artiness"? Or does the black-and-white process veil an otherwise humiliatingly colorful "realness"?

Arbus's subjects sometimes seem to neglect hygiene. Is poor hygiene humiliating? Or am I humiliating myself by what I notice in Arbus's photos—body hair, nudity, stink, labor?

Is décor humiliating? Arbus's photos, portraits of misfits whose remarkableness opens the door to opprobrium, are also exposés of décor, of plush or eviscerated mise-en-scènes. Drapery and furniture upstage the portrayed freak, as porn's décor (bed, pool, wallpaper) diverts the eye from the sexual act apparently at the center.

Is smartness humiliating? (We, in the presence of Arbus's photos, may manifest shock, or else we may indulge in a protective, contrary motion of intellectualization.) Is stupefaction—the state of being stunned by her portraits—humiliating? If we are voluble in spite of the photo's demand that we be silent, we humiliate ourselves. But if we stay mute, we admit our twinship with the pictured, soiled subject.

Twinship, a seeming surplus, is humiliating; Arbus was addicted to doublings. Perhaps twinship halts the humiliation narrative: mirroring intrudes a decoy, addles the punitive eye, as Kim Novak, cloned, undoes Jimmy Stewart's immunity in *Vertigo*. Duplication, like an alias, camouflages the shady subject.

Finally, I wonder whether Arbus's disinclination for what Barthes later theorized as *the Neutral* exposes her own status as she-who-has-been-humiliated-by-significance. Her fevered pursuit of sharply exceptional characters disregards the nebulous, the subtle, the unapparent. Arbus, photographing the pathetic and the decentered, turns these figures into new, vivid centers. Dignifying them, according them significance, she shuts off a realm of accidental rustlings, an unparaphrasable territory where meaning loosens, and typecasting falters. She photographs the Jewish giant, but she neglects to photograph the dream-gray blankness in which the Jewish giant—without qualifiers, adjectives, or categories—forgets his dimensions.

(2005)

Figure

1

How frequently do you look in the mirror? Does your face please you? Are you disgusted to detect familial features? Do you worship or hate your ancestors? Do you consider your image erotic? Do you pretend that you are a star's child? If you squint, does your reflection become abstract? Is abstraction a transcendental escape from identity or a psychotic spasm of depersonalization?

2

Color-aid paper, dignified by Josef Albers in his pedagogy and in his seminal *Interaction of Color*, has the advantage of lacking soul and intentionality; like Citroëns or Edsels, the background monochromes of Glenn Ligon's 2001 self-portraits (fifty silkscreened specimens, on a range of Color-aid tints), speak with the mild-mannered tone of an apologist for big business, or with the frantic, chipper euphoria of a courtesy caller; or else these matte colors, evading revelation, merely pretend to offer assurance, regularity, and plausibility.

3

On the back of Ligon's head sits a circle produced (I presume) by a flashbulb's reflection. Abstracted, this aureole—orifice? smudge?—overtakes the image and, like the Greek rhetorical figure of prosopopoeia ("a figure of speech in which an imaginary or absent person is represented as speaking or acting"), persuades us that a journey toward meaning is under way. This bright smear on the back of the head confronts the viewer with a Cyclopean candor. One eye may more accurately hail the spectator than two eyes; one eye may offer a more flattering dose of recognition than we usually receive from strangers.

4

Andy Warhol's serial portraits, whether of shadows, socialites, or himself, propose identity as a gallantly mutating entity, wearing the mask of banality (or reticence) to shield against misinterpretation and cruel dismissal. (Better to be thought banal than to be banished or beaten.) When we see the same face again and again, each time sporting a different color, a new set of accidental striations and speckles caused by the mechanical silkscreen process, we may feel offended by the sameness or we may feel rubbed and tickled by it, nudged with a tactile incrementality (sight, too, can be haptic) toward, if not a climax, then a tsunami of hyperesthesia, like what I imagine Roman Polanski felt when he first had sex with Sharon Tate, or vice versa.

5

The V formed by the gorge of Ligon's shirt, its top buttons evidently unfastened, competes for our attention with other surface occurrences; this V vies with nose and lips and ears, with luminous splotches on the face, as well as with the backdrop's aleatory dots and spurts of ink. When I inspect gradations of cream on a Robert Ryman painting (say, *Twin* [1966]), I set up a relation of fruitless quest, of interpretive adamancy; and when I choose to lose perspective by staring at Ligon's V, I invest it with allegorical intensities, even if his V spurns my earnestness.

6

Before figuring out their final destiny, the artist might have wondered what to do with this stack of fifty self-portraits. He might have put them in a drawer and forgotten about them. He might have stigmatized them and then rescued them from his own scorn. He might have laid them out flat on a table and despaired of finding a plausible sequence. He might have doubted the rightness of framing and hanging them on a wall. He might have arrayed them in the order dictated by the Color-aid chart. He might have suspected that they reveal an embarrassing tendency, fantasy, or debt; embarrassment might hold the key to the work's forcefulness.

7

The artist's own likeness, a found object, solves the problem of deciding what to paint; the image's availability permits an artist—especially one who has consistently been a painter but has also set up a renegade's relation to that vocation—to retreat from subject matter under the guise of returning to it. The artist may yearn to be insulated from intimacy, from the viewer, from representation, from contemporary art wars, and from the joke of identity. I order a sloe gin fizz not because I want to drink it but because I remember that I am a person who tends to order a sloe gin fizz; I wear Kouros by Yves Saint Laurent not because I like its smell but because I want to be legible to others and to myself as *that person who always wears Kouros.* Ligon, by showing himself looking *like* Ligon and looking *at* Ligon, achieves the liberation of looking *like* and *at* no one.

8

Some colors are more gay than others, though all colors may, to a certain temperament, suggest a farcical polymorphousness. It's late in history to bring up "gay" as if the concept still provoked controversy, but Ligon's deadpan adoption of a color wheel inspires in me a wish to sigh, like Ruth amid her alien corn, nostalgically for my homeland of shade and nuance, my chromatic *chora* of hue, my underground of spurs and thongs and shame. If Ligon's series of figures are tenants of a revamped periodic table (Miss Helium, Miss Neon, Miss Krypton), then they speak to me of deadly experiments, of a subcultural laboratory's orgiastic trial and error. These portraits obey an austere formal logic; and yet their soldierly sameness unleashes more than an inkling of revolutionary unrest. In cabals, Ligon's figures gather, parading homogeneity; their numerousness exhibits a communitarian tendency that Walt Whitman might have called "adhesive." Whether a restive crowd, a gang of loners, a melancholy family, a *mise-en-abyme*, a reshuffled kinship system, or a toy army, this alliance evades inventory or description, especially when the heads lose individuation and disappear into the reigning monochrome. Ligon's work often plays with the dialectic of manifestation and erasure: effacement is one of his Circean signatures.

9

From Ralph Ellison, *Invisible Man*: "You wonder whether you aren't simply a phantom in other people's minds. Say, a *figure* in a nightmare which the sleeper tries with all his strength to destroy." (Emphasis mine.) The word *figure*, as if in one of Ligon's text paintings (for example, *Untitled ["I Am An Invisible Man"]* [1991]), comes with invisibility written all over it. When you see me, do you see nothing, or do you see a figure for a race, a history, a burden, a call, a crux? In Ligon's portraits, plural heads in varying degrees of visibility or opacity, of wholeness or fragmentation, articulate *figure* as the problem of *existing as a figure in another person's mind.* Looking at the portraits, I imagine that a claustral comfort sleeps within figuration's booby trap: illogically, I interpret this predicament of *being invisible within a state of heightened visibility* as a swaddled, pacified condition. Perhaps I misconstrue Ligon's representation of anonymity-within-legibility as a "holding environment," in D. W. Winnicott's terms; I mistake Ligon's tight embrace of genre (serial self-portraiture) as a fugitively secure containment. He portrays the cocooned calm of pretending to be recognizable but retaining, as secret armor and closely hugged companion, the right to be unrecognizable. I pretend to behave, to produce coherent creations, to operate within countenanced vocabularies, in order to secrete myself from your surveillance.

10

I grew up on Augusta Way, one block below Bela Drive. I imagined that Bela Drive bore a likeness to Bela Lugosi, who did not appear in *The Invisible Man*, though he starred in *Dracula*, a drama of identity-replication, contamination, and bloody diaspora. I believed that Bela Drive could not claim the authenticity or primacy of Augusta Way. In fact, my street had no firm lease on identity, on self-sureness, but borrowed its aura from Bela Drive, which reigned over all replicas and contenders. Serial reproduction—a sequence of silkscreened Color-aid self-portraits, members of a second or third generation of same-yet-different images—raises the theme of neighborliness, of adjacency. Gazing at Ligon's figures, I return to an early moment in my life, a moment of discovering the notion of *the nearby, the not-I*, and of discovering that my own location lacked solid footing and was liable to spill into abutting identities. Perhaps I might fix my self's place, seize it in a single pose, by repeating it; and thus, when I behold art that performs patient, incremental seriality or stacking, I feel the lure of a homecoming—a return to a consoling strategy, an insistence on repeatedly traversing a given terrain (the field of *I*, of *you*, of *here*, of *not-here*). My grammar school had two parallel kindergarten classes; my teacher was Mrs. Crandall, and the other group's teacher was Mrs. Hoagland. Mrs. Crandall is a figure of *the room to which I was assigned.* Mrs. Hoagland is a figure of *the room to which I was not assigned.* Being absent, in elementary school, was a sin, or at least a noticeable blip, a sign of an internal inconsistency, of a failure to appear. I recognize Glenn Ligon in these images but I also recognize his absence.

(2008)

Warhol's Interviews

1

Andy Warhol, like Blossom Dearie, was a vocal artist: he did strange things with standards. He underspoke them. A chanteuse is supposed to "sell" the song. Andy, like Blossom, stinted the standard, gave it less, in order to give (secretly) more. He sidestepped the interlocutor's assignments. Andy's idea of an I/Thou relation was a talk show; both guest and host were gods, momentarily. Momentary was the only way to be. And the space of an answer—*yes, no, maybe*—gave Warhol room enough to stretch his fairy amplitude.

2

He sang the *dumb* notes, the mute, anesthetized, autistic micropitches that ghost the public, declaimable melody. When Warhol's responses to questions sound inane, they interrogate our discourses of inanity. (See Avital Ronell's smart study, *Stupidity*.) When Warhol gives a girly answer, he insists on art's link to the tawdriest masquerades, the skankiest trannies. When Warhol praises porn, he pushes art's button; when Warhol announces that he's quitting painting, he rises to Tintoretto heights.

3

The culture police want to limit creators to one medium, one stance. Paint, but don't make films. Write essays, but don't star in soaps. Be a docent, but don't be a public indecency. Warhol spread himself thin; the interview is one more slice of bread he insisted on buttering. Space hog, he laid permanent claim to the word *interview* by publishing a magazine with that name. His own liminal behavior, whether seen or unseen, exposed the *inter* within the *view*: vision, according to Warhol, is always cut, interrupted, interposed by a wedge of thirdness. Warhol's interviews play the wedge game with indisputable mastery.

4

Like a decadent's Christ or Saint Sebastian, Warhol struck the pose of *being-stigmatized*. A journalist's hostile, unknowing questions can be acts of discursive violence. As if imitating Wilde's 1895 trial, Warhol torqued the witness stand, through irony and camp, into a tea party, and taught us how to circumvent intimidation by mesmerizing the bully.

5

Andy wanted to be left alone, and yet he paradoxically pretended to seek interpersonal encounter; into the unsafe space of the interview, he inserted not his own, vulnerable, actual body, but a replacement body, a mannequin, a dummy. *It looks like me, but it's not. I'm elsewhere. I seem to be answering your questions, but don't be fooled. Transcendentally indifferent to your groveling, literal-minded suppositions, I protect you from my barbed fury by absenting myself from the scene of polite exchange. I'm priceless: off the market. I'm only pretending to take part in art's barter system.*

6

Like Charlie Chaplin, Warhol impersonated *tramp* and *fool*: he also played *horny* and *moneygrubbing*. Those were four stock roles in the one-reel comedies that interviews, in his transmuting hands, became. Like Gertrude Stein, Warhol performed *simpleton*; direct statement—American declarativeness—suited his temperament, which was not, in the last analysis, evasive or olympian, but nakedly confrontational. *Nude* was his favorite condition: nude restaurant, nude philosophy, nude cognition, nude art, nude anything. Put *nude* in the adjectival slot, and the noun automatically gets upgraded. Andy gave nude interviews. He *denuded* interlocution—stripped it, turned it into Laurel and Hardy, or Vladimir and Estragon. Or into a spooky mirror scene, two hand puppets operated by one puppeteer. Andy's den of interlocution transparently gave onto other rooms, other scenes, other instances of revenge, equalization, and vertigo. Reading (or watching) a Warhol interview, we're never neatly *outside* it. Because Warhol isn't exactly within his body, he nudges the interviewer, too, a few millimeters away from pat embodiment. Andy's aim, in the interviews, is ambient destabilization. He unhinges everyone in the vicinity—especially those who think they know the difference between good and bad art, between worthwhile and useless behavior, and between elation and depression.

7

Warhol's affect is poised between happiness and sadness, between a speedy emptiness and a lethargic fullness. We can't pinpoint his mood, and we may, sympathetically, wish to ask: *Is Andy okay?* Do the interviews prove that he is ailing, or do they demonstrate his resilience, his at-homeness, his immunity? Interviews—like any of his screens, whether silk or silver—hardly offer unmediated revelation. They offer, instead, a cage: Warhol, playing Houdini, escapes conversation's captivity. His interviews perform a drag act of imprisonment within unsympathetic interlocution; in doing so, they paint a DayGlo exit sign that we would be well advised, as Warhol's acolytes and inheritors, to follow.

(2004)

The Inner Life of the Palette Knife

You wake up as Gregor Samsa. You discover that your body is a bug's. You incise a hole at your scrotum's base to undo the penis's stupid singularity. At odds with your body, you choose the vocation of *abstract painter* as a sane technique of reformatting flesh, cleansing it, reenvisioning its hollows and lines. Welcome to the phantasmagoria of the little-known American painter Forrest Bess (1911–77), whose works I'll use as evidence for a manifesto in praise of abstraction, retreat, attentiveness, and other private, ornery practices.

Lines, for Bess, were philosophical issues. Were lines vertical or horizontal? Did they bend or resist? These were questions as large and troubling as whether the sky is falling down or whether the earth is cracking in half. A line's behavior was a meteorological matter. Hurricane Carla devastated Bess's home in Texas; we're not wrong to imagine his paintings as weather systems, malign or beneficent. In his painting *Red Rain*, the red lines thrash downward, unevenly. Their bumpiness suggests a stance we might take toward uprightness or recumbency; when a line wavers, congeals, or hesitates, our footing in the universe shifts, and we consider this shift not a terrifying rupture but a pleasant jab of intensification.

Unrest and calm are not necessarily opposites. Bess's paintings depict the uncertain threshold between tranquillity and eruption. We could read his works as crystallizations of intense anxiety—of free fall, groundlessness—or as epitomes of restfulness, oasis. Our business is not to "read" the paintings: Bess's art asks us to experience it, wordlessly, if we can muster wordlessness. His paintings want to cast a spell on the viewer's body and temperament, to produce a sense of tranquillity at the exact moment that the peacefulness dissipates and shatters. Because the paintings are small, the shattering isn't catastrophic: we may experience it as a trembling, a wavering, as if a UFO had landed in our backyard or in the hardscrabble patch of mindscape that passes for homestead.

Texas—Bess's home—was large. Edna Ferber called it *Giant*. But Bess's body, like anyone's, was small; and its orifices were tiny, though they may have felt Pompeiian.

Despite the Vesuvian stakes of Bess's game, he never hyperbolizes. The light in this room—where I'm looking at his paintings, one by one—shines irregularly on his black paint. Sometimes the black, arrested by light, seems matte; at other instants, light causes the black paint to glisten. These modest oscillations—matte one moment, glistening the next—are not the size of Texas. You need to stand very close to the painting to see these incremental changes, nuances so minor that it seems a culpable exaggeration to call attention to them, even if these delicate effects of light and texture are Bess's major contribution to the philosophy of transgendered affect, to American abstract art, to the erotics of fear. (Like any visionary, Bess dreaded interruption: ***don't quash my trance***.)

Bess's paintings are conceptually complex, and not because of his symbols, a lexicon he helpfully laid out in a map (in a letter to Betty Parsons, whose gallery showed his work). Some literal-minded interpreters might employ this map to decode his paintings. (Red equals male. White equals female. An eye with short lines radiating around it equals a vulva. Two parallel horizontal lines equal masturbation or intercourse.) Bess's paintings record his visions—dreams, or hallucinations that appeared when he closed his eyes. If we imagine the paintings as notations (like diaries) or documents (like recordings of performances), we subordinate the paintings to their triggering circumstances. We downgrade the painting to the status of trace. In the annals of religious art and artifact, such interpretations are justified: Veronica's veil qualifies as an abstract painting, but it is also evidence.

More plausibly, we might consider Bess's hallucinations to be colorful background material—décor, rather than holy event. The painting is an end in itself; what counts is the painting, not the mishmash of delusion and conviction, of transport and agony, that led to it. And yet the hallucinations, as legends, give extra value to the painting; they elevate its status, as Van Gogh's madness enriched his art's aura.

Bess's paintings *are* his experiences, as words replace the reveries they describe. Facing a Bess painting, we occupy a loaded, numinous position: we're entering the operating theater to behold the surgery. We might feel bewilderment or joy at the intensity of his internal adventures, just as, reading Emily Dickinson's poems, we may feel not merely rapture at her language's acuity, but jealous admiration of the mental intensities that her poems record. Transport-envy: I covet Bess's elation. I want to acquire his feverishness—to learn how to live more intensely, even if these jabs of intensification are metaphorically aligned with the surgical knife making inroads into his scrotum. (I hesitate to use the word *scrotum* in an essay that is striving for a modicum of decorum, but the word appears even in a June 1982 *Texas Monthly* article about Bess. Evidently no one can discuss him without using the rather ugly word *scrotum*.)

One way of enjoying Bess's paintings is to celebrate their affinity, however oblique, to current trends in abstract art—or at least its kooky wing, where forms are neat although their placement is gravely whimsical; the forms, almost geometrical but not precisely so, couldn't sit on the canvas in any position but exactly where we find them, though we can't figure out why the artist decided on their quirkily decisive resting places. (Some names: Andrew Masullo, Amy Sillman, Thomas Nozkowski, Chris Martin, Tomma Abts, Robert Aldrich, Mary Heilmann, Monika Baer, Matt Connors.) Every time I enter a painter's studio and see a small abstraction with marks at once *crude* (a word often used to describe Bess's work) and tenderly detailed, I feel a jab of intensification. One of my pedagogical aims is to encourage writers, painters, sculptors, and performers to make work that resembles Bess's, work that is modest, grandiose, peculiar, detailed, reduced, blunt, odd, a little bit stupid, a little bit clumsy, with secret pockets of refinement, as if an Albrecht Dürer were sleeping inside a Fauve.

•

Bess's subject is time; he grants the viewer an expansive experience of duration. To receive that gift, you need to give the painting time. The painting can't communicate time unless you spend time on it. And thus his paintings engage in a complicated economic critique. They force the viewer to reevaluate what it means to spend or waste time. The viewer must become, momentarily, a dweller in Bess's Texan oasis. The viewer, who may well be urban (most paintings are seen in city museums or galleries), must give up urbanity, and, more important, must give up urban time, the clockwork of city dwelling. Bess's paintings force you to emigrate to Walden Pond: you must renounce speed, destination, and monumentality. You must become a duck or worm or pebble. And you must stop quantifying means and ends: you must waste time looking at a Bess painting, without the certainty that it will reward you with ecstasy, knowledge, or satisfaction. If you don't waste time on it, it won't reveal time's lastingness to you.

In one of my favorite Bess paintings (untitled, like most of them), composed of oil and painted foil on canvas, I lose myself—I waste time—looking at a blue foil triangle's nearness to a brown-black dot. That dot's exact placement has no clear or verbalizable meaning; I can't explain why the dot is near the triangle, though not too near. The dot belongs in the triangle's vicinity, but the two entities—dot, triangle—have no fixed relationship. In that same painting, the background is composed of black swirls or blobs. The black blobs—gesso-like?—are separate from one another but also sometimes joined or interacting. Their edges—to the extent that the blobs cluster together in a community—are at once stable and unstable; the edges ululate, but don't sing a clear melody.

To pay attention to these black blobs, or to pay attention to the blue foil triangle's nearness to a specific dot, I must pledge allegiance to abstract art's Bill of Rights, which contains, unlike the United States', only one provision: the right to look, for unstructured amounts of time, at migrant and unspecific forms, and at the relation between them, without demanding that the forms have a single meaning, and without demanding that whatever significance I ascribe to these forms be defensible, explicable, or based on any evidence but my own sensations. This right is not the same as radical indeterminacy; Bess's paintings promulgate the liberty to find determinate *but not explicable or defensible* meanings in the appearance of perhaps random and unintended shapes and in their intercourse or nonadjacency. I have the right to find supreme significance in Bess's blobs and lines, and to spend as long as I wish in a state of torpid yet ecstatic surrender to them. I'm defending the right to succumb to trance; but the state I'm praising is more precise than trance, and contains more agency. I'm also defending the right to be solitary, unpopular, and unbeheld. Bess needed solitude to make his art. Art justified his solitude, gave it dignity or purpose. Maybe half the reason someone becomes an artist—or the kind of artist that Bess became—is to experience uninterrupted solitude. The supreme craving may be for solitude, not for art. Here is how the great poet Fernando Pessoa put it, in *The Book of Disquiet*: "Art is an isolation. Every artist should seek to isolate others, to fill their souls with a desire to be alone."

•

Of all the technical effects Bess exploited, my favorites are the palette knife's traces, especially when the knife creates thin striations, like tiny panels, horizontal or vertical, not exactly linear, never equal. Some striations stick out more from the canvas. And when the striations protrude more, I care more, or am more worried on the striation's behalf. I respond to Bess's intensity of texture with either worry or delight. Even the anxiety is a form of pleasure. Indeed, I hyper-respond to Bess's palette-knife striations, their tintinnabulation, a word—*tintinnabulation*—that Edgar Allan Poe used, famously, to describe the music that wells forth from bells. It's a showy word, *tintinnabulation*, just as attention-grabbing as palette-knife striations. We hyper-respond (reader, may I include you in the coterie of hyper-responders?) to Bess's palette-knife striations; our hyper-responsiveness is Bess's gift to us. He didn't create that responsiveness, but he created a convincing theater in which it could resonate. And he created, posthumously, a social space, the coterie of Bess hyper-responders; he created a band of appreciators who could share ineffable pleasures and anxieties. These experiences of transport, keyed to painterly moments almost too small to mention, I call *jabs of intensification*—microscopic illuminations, inner shudders, tiny spurts of "oh my God!", as if a joy-bringing bubble were suddenly to open up a new hallway in my brain, or as if suddenly I were to become Keats reading Homer for the first time and standing proud on a silent peak to view the wild Pacific. But in Bess's case, the wild Pacific is merely an edge mark made by a palette knife, where yellow gets divided into adjacent, parallel mini-panels of companionate yellows.

To phrase it more emphatically: areas of monochrome, in Bess's paintings, tend to become enlivened by palette-knife marks, as if the monochrome portion were a too-calm sea that required turbulence to justify its existence. The monochrome portion—though static, steady, unwavering—paradoxically calls forth an excess of effort from Bess's hand. And we hyper-respond to Bess's effort, not because we feel sorry for him or wish to turn him into a hero, but because the juxtaposition of *effort* and *unvarying monochrome* creates in our body (or my body, at least) a turn-of-the-screw effect, a tightening or opening, as if the experience of seeing Bess's palette-knife marks were drawing out from me a conviction that life can be more interesting and complicated—more of an emergency—than I'd dreamed possible. And, paradoxically, it is precisely the *uninteresting* aspects of life—the monochromes—that Bess redeems, with his palette-knife effortfulness; by turning ordinariness or drabness into intensity (albeit a quiet intensity, undemonstrative, off-the-grid, non-urban), Bess converts somnolence into carnival.

Looking at an untitled painting of a red sky surmounting two breast-shaped hills, the sun a weak globe nearly occupying the cleavage between the hills, I notice scratch marks. I want to start a religion based on scratches, or based upon the experience of scrutinizing scratches. What would I be worshipping? Randomness: the scratch marks obey no pattern. Aggression: the scratch marks seem to stem from Bess's low-level rage—at himself, at the world, at the sky, at God. Invasion: like an Old Testament wanderer, I'll deify any voice that hits on me, any voice in the desert that rains its tablets down on me. I'll deify anything that scratches or invades me, thrusts its facture upon me. Like Antonin Artaud, Bess seems to have taken the experience of being violated—however metaphorically—as an incursion of godhead; to be raped (within the Bess/Artaud cosmology) is to receive divine visitations. And yet in Bess's case, these incursions were marks he made himself, probably with a palette knife.

•

Bess's best paintings contain heavy iconographic messages—worship me! fuck me!—but wrap these messages in imagery so elemental, so primary, so unelaborated (circle, line, wiggle, star, triangle) or in colors so unmodulated (a gray that remains gray, that heads toward the nongray but never makes much progress in that direction), that the iconography's simplicity may fill the viewer with a sense that any language's attempt to communicate is doomed to fail. In one of my favorite paintings, which contains a big yellow orb and three white stars against a black sky (the black seems composed of felt or a coat of paint that suggests a nubbly, textured fabric), I marvel at the smallness of the three stars, and I marvel at the fact that there are only three. Why not more? Why didn't Bess produce an entire constellation? The three stars seem a puny congregation; their puniness is itself inspiring—a negative theology of the outnumbered, the paltry, whereby the few can outweigh the many. Just three stars! Three stars aren't difficult to draw. And yet Bess took the liberty of performing this artistically unostentatious act, and making it the central event of his painting—almost a nonperformance, a refusal to perform, a capitulation to his own trancelike escapism. (*I want to avoid crowds.*)

I am in the habit of proposing new religions. I am not religious, but I tend to project sanctity onto my aesthetic experiences, and I have a worshipful relation to any painting that I love. I don't always worship the painting itself; but I worship the life—the path, the vocation—that the painting indicates is a possibility. Thus, in Bess's painting of a moon or sun and three stars, I worship not merely the painting itself but its gesture of rendering *only three stars*; the gesture is so simple, he could easily have decided against it. He could have decided, *I won't waste my time, or the viewer's, on a subject as jejune as three stars. I'll wait until I can successfully draw a constellation of thirty stars. Or I'll wait until I figure out how to draw a star with a more impressive set of painterly flourishes. Or I'll research art history, to figure out how my three stars fit into the avant-garde. I want to make sure that my three stars are laudable.* Bess didn't wait; he leapt directly into the painting. And now, its enigma is here before us, confronting us with a speech-defying spectacle of audacity, simplicity, recklessness, confidence, minimalism, humility, and delicacy. One of the three stars is the outsider. The other two stars hang more closely together; the third star, a loner, goes off on its own. And yet this third star thus gains the privilege of having more in common with the sun (or moon). I could write an entire essay about the poignance and humor of this third star, its noncooperativeness. In that essay, I'd probably use the word *autistic*, a word I irresponsibly use to describe a type of art that seems to celebrate our unsociable impulses, our inability to relate to one another with shared languages. Describing the position of the three stars, I'd use the word *autistic* as a perverse way of celebrating their orneriness, their isolationism, and their failure to function in an adult linguistic system.

A psychoanalytically minded critic might posit that Bess had good boundaries. Or else very bad boundaries. It depends on how we interpret the presence of clearly painted outlines. In an untitled painting from 1960, where an antenna seems to beam its distressing signals over a cowering population of piers, buildings, or stacked tablets, notice that even the huddled shapes leaning away from the antenna are clearly delineated, and that, through delineation's magic, these bodies successfully evade the antenna's attack. These clear outlines suggest that a cartoonist lurks behind the mask of a mystic, and that an illustrator's graphic consciousness bears a relation to a hermit's, a saint's, a self-flagellator's, or a sexual heretic's. I emphasize the cartoon boundaries of Bess's shapes—some of them, at least—because the edge's solidity, its thickly drawn, comfortingly legible skin, its assertion of border between object and the circumambient world, suggests a viewpoint bracingly tidy and clear. If you think that a mystic's temperament is muddy and blurry, reconsider: Bess, whether as crafty painter or as home-brew mystic, decreed that objects (and individuals), including stars, moons, mountains, and unidentified horizontal or vertical creatures, have unporous edges. *I end here; I don't bleed into the vicinity.* And yet, sometimes, as in a 1966 painting called *Untitled #2 (The Penetrated)*, a green spills onto the adjacent orange, and the orange reciprocates, lending orange to a green that had experimented with independence but then gave up and opened its body to orange's seductive suppurations.

•

In the 1930s and 1940s, before Bess arrived at the runic, abstract mode that we may call "mature," he attempted a more conventional representational style, borrowing from Van Gogh, Cézanne, and other quasi-realists closer to home. In one such work, *Still Life with Squash* (1939), the most distinctive feature is the pink wall behind the posed fruit; the pink, a monochrome, a blankness, impossible to thematize, other than by calling it a "pink wall" (and do we grant to "pink wall" the status of a major theme?), resembles the steady monochromes that populate portions of his later canvases, mostly because this pink wall refuses to be looked at quickly. An artist is defined by what he or she chooses to discard; Bess discarded Van Gogh and Cézanne but kept the pink wall, or the crackle—the distressing—on the pink wall. He retained an affinity with shapes that don't occupy three-dimensional space but that nonetheless appear to protrude, as if asking to be interpreted, caressed, or simply noticed. He remained loyal to forms and color areas that were bluntly straightforward and yet at the same time clouded over with a strange veil of distance, of déjà vu.

If I had a photographic memory, I would summon all the white (cream, ivory, light yellow) surfaces of twentieth-century paintings I've seen, and then I could compare those surfaces with the near-white background of an untitled Bess painting that especially beguiles me; I don't know how to describe the idiosyncratic crackling of its white surface, in which two black horizontal lines rest below a battalion of thirteen differently sized verticals, themselves surmounted by a bird- or heart-like white lump inside a larger black lump. I can't summon an archive of other white or near-white painting surfaces (Kasimir Malevich, Piet Mondrian, Robert Rauschenberg, Jasper Johns, Lucio Fontana, Agnes Martin, Robert Ryman, and beyond) and so I'm free from that archive, as Bess was free from it; Bess certainly had a rich internal repository of images from art history and from his own imagination, but possessing an internal reference library didn't impede his colossal freedom from influence. We don't need to compare him to anyone else; nor did he. His painting life was an adventure of disaffiliation, or nonaffiliation. He severed bonds with the prior or the contemporary, and thereby releases his viewer from bondage. When I look at this untitled painting's white field, its presentness banishes all rival ghosts. I can either face that richly monochrome field, and mine it, or I can shirk the privilege, the dare. The painting, in this case, is only 9⅛ × 12 inches, so part of the challenge is nestling up close enough to the painting to see it lucidly; I must take off my glasses so I can read the fractures and fissures and interruptions—the fine print—of its wordless surface, shorn of all symbolism, even the symbols that Bess tried to impose on it. And this intimacy with the painting, this slow possession of its surface, is at odds with the urge to generalize about family resemblances between Bess and other artists. Sometimes it's important *not* to stand back from a painting. Sometimes it's important *not* to take in the big picture. Sometimes it's important to refuse everything but what Deleuze and Guatarri call "close vision," a vision that prevents the imperial crudities of historizing. Close vision is at odds with the Haussmannization of art; with Bess as my leading example, I advocate keeping art dispersed in its little villages, and refusing to plow art down with large boulevards that oversimplify the twists of history and that prevent individual barricades of resistance from flourishing.

•

To explore issues of seduction and avoidance in Bess's work, the methods it stages of staying away from people or drawing them closer, consider *Mandala* (1967)—a reddish circle, like a gong or a moon face, its featurelessness suggesting the back of a head, a rotundity without personality. The black paint surrounding the mandala has gorgeous gouge marks that awaken in me (the urge never went to sleep) a desire to make texture my god; textures like this black paint's facture invite us forward, closer, to apprehend, nearly to touch . . . and yet the mandala's blankness declares *stay away!* A magic spell—and Bess's works were demonstrably spells, like Artaud's—may wish to attract or repel. Bess wants to bring us closer, but within guarded precincts, and with an enforced code of silence: we're not allowed to speak to the mandala. We may contemplate it, but its Buddha face expresses detachment, disinterest, a lack of regard for our specific importunings. The paintings are apotropaic devices—they intend to ward off evil. But they also ward off viewers, to the extent that a viewer is a demanding, ill-mannered, invasive interrogator, an art-history-steeped salivator over culled, harvested significances. Gorgon-faced, Bess's paintings seduce with their snaky intricacy of surface, but they need to keep secret the visions they deliver. Like forensic reports, notations from a crime scene, Bess's paintings tell us *what happened* but tell the tale in code, in whispers, with a close-grained nubbliness of surface, pocked with the edge marks of a carefully wielded palette knife, the same knife, we'd like to imagine, with which he scaled fish, leaving behind the "creamy iridescent coats of mail" that the fisherman scatters in Elizabeth Bishop's poem "At the Fishhouses." Indeed, I like to think of Bess as a version of Bishop's baptismally oriented fisherman, "an old man" whom she finds netting, "his net, in the gloaming almost invisible." (Bishop and Bess were exact contemporaries; both were born in 1911; Bess died in 1977, two years before Bishop.) Bishop's fisherman uses a "black old knife" to scrape the scales, whose sequined gleamings she calls "the principal beauty." I want to imagine Bess's palette knife as a fisherman's knife; his paintings host moving, slithering objects that he arrests, enclosing them in cameos, rendered moveless by the Medusa force of Bess's marine stare.

A painting may not be happy to remain a painting. A painting may also want to be a fish. A painting may secretly yearn to become sculpture, something fecal and three-dimensional. When Bess turned to painting, what did he give up? Did he settle for painting as a runner-up vocation, or was it his only recourse? Had Bess been a maximalist, a sculptor, or a scientist, he might have built a structure like Wilhelm Reich's orgone box. Picture an orgasmic Stonehenge in Bay City, Texas—an earthwork, like a spiral jetty, carved into the landscape, or drawn out from its bosom, to attract the euphoria-granting vibrations of extraterrestrial visitors; the smallness of Bess's paintings belies their urges for a monumentality on behalf not of his artistic ego but of the healing orgasms he wished mankind to experience, and which we, as Bess's faithful inheritors, undergo whenever we give his paintings the expenditure of time—of patient staring, of surrender—for which they bashfully beseech. (They won't bark out the request.)

Because of my own Pessoan taste for the ways in which art can blissfully isolate its practitioners and worshippers, I may have overemphasized solitude in Bess's work. In many of his paintings, indeed, there exist overpopulations, crowds, like congregated spermatozoa. Even the zigzags, in *Dedication to Van Gogh* (1946), cluster together like some crazy root system. And in *Untitled (The Void I)* from 1946–47, the intricate calligraphic forms, detailed as if in pen and ink, sit within a reversed black arch's valley, like ludic jazzed-up figures by Keith Haring, tiny graffiti hieroglyphs, cutely gathered in a bunch, as if they were carbonation's bubbles, or sediment drifting toward the bottom of the glass. By trying to convince you of Bess's mystic bent, I've stinted his comic sense, his off-kilter, snake-oil-vending taste for ceremonies-in-a-void, like a Saharan five-and-dime remake of Alla Nazimova's silent *Salomé*, but with a spartan décor—or like a shell-shocked yet carnivalesque Paul Klee who'd studied tantra. In Bess's work, I've emphasized the blank areas—the facture-laden monochromatic patches—rather than the cheerfully (or elegiacally) populated hieroglyphic crowd scenes, as in *Burning Bush*

(1953), where the vertical row of barricaded, twisting forms, whether a barbed-wire fence or a chorus line, suggests camaraderie as well as incarceration. I won't try to iron out Bess's inconsistencies by claiming that his works are always cheerful or always mournful, yet I must confess that I use his paintings as devices for taking my own mournfulness and recasting it as glee—the rapture of Joan of Arc, perhaps, or Myra Breckinridge, or any tutelary figure occupying the threshold between sexes, desires, mediums, styles . . .

I've memorized the marks of Bess's palette knife. I plan to use them as currency in a new, visionary economy, so wide-ranging and lucid, so secretive and hormonally destabilizing, that I despair of ever stumbling upon a language with which to give it voice. If Bess had taught at the Bauhaus, what would we call his course? Orgasmic Salvation 101, or My Eschatalogical Genitals, and How They Undergird a New Theory of Abstract Painting.

If my essay has a larger polemical aim, beyond the praise of Bess's paintings, that motive might be a modest bid to reaffirm abstract art's continuing relevance and strangeness. In recent years it has been fashionable to impugn Abstract Expressionist seriousness as mere grandiosity and metaphysical posturing. Bess felt that way about the Abstract Expressionists; apparently he considered their paintings artificial, mannered, inauthentic, not infused with visionary grit. And yet, for all the power and capital that has coalesced around abstract art in the last sixty years, I don't think that we've given it enough credit as a method for the mind and body to excavate its own temperatures, climaxes, opacities, and valleys; Bess's hieroglyphic semiabstractions suggest not only that he was a remarkable artist but that abstract—or near-abstract—art, hovering on the edges of codes we'll never comprehend, teaches us to pay fine-grained, undogmatic attention to the blobs and lines and curves we encounter in everyday life. Pay attention to scratches. Pay attention to the textured, importuning marks of a silent palette knife. Use Bess's paintings to understand the difficult art of human attentiveness. In a world always willing to truncate the possibilities for closely noticing what occurs, allow attentiveness to flower, however private and inscrutable its flowering, however seemingly impractical, minor, puzzling, and antisocial its procedures of self-nourishment.

(2011)

Schuyler's Colors

Why write art criticism? For love. Also, sometimes, for money. I'm sure that's one of the reasons why poet James Schuyler wrote so much of it. He was an associate editor of *ARTnews* from 1957 to 1962, and during that period he composed the bulk of his reviews (gathered in *Selected Art Writings*, edited by Simon Pettet). Although Schuyler is always associated with the New York School poets, including Frank O'Hara, John Ashbery, Barbara Guest, and Ron Padgett, his work, particularly his art criticism, makes as much sense in a variety of other contexts, from its American Renaissance precursors (Thoreau's journals, Dickinson's letters) to the French novelistic essay (Edmond Jabès, Roland Barthes, Maurice Blanchot, Georges Perec).

In writing art reviews as intensively as he did in the late fifties and early sixties, Schuyler found a way to indulge his taste for descriptive sentences that needn't be teleological, autobiographical, or narrative—sentences that could focus on an object (the artwork) but could also replace and dominate it. His art reviews were often hyperliterary, but they achieved their literariness by seeming to avoid the literary altogether. Criticism, not a parasitic genre, is governed by the same charmed tenets as poetry, as Schuyler intimates in a review of the artist Seymour Remenick: "His work had a kind of clumsiness, a telling lack of facility, a crabbed independence, like that of Thoreau: 'What care I where the off-ox treads? I plough another furrow than you see.' Those sentences scan: but Thoreau wrote them out as prose. Well, Emerson told him he wasn't a poet so he stopped writing verse. But he couldn't help it; he was an artist beyond Emerson's conceiving." So, too, was Schuyler an artist of an elusiveness beyond the pat division of labor between poetry and essay.

The aesthetic that emerges from his reviews (which resemble, in their playful syntax and their cheerful compactness, the arch squibs that Marianne Moore wrote for *The Dial*) is a devotion to *his* present moment—not because he nursed a soft-focus love for ineffable blooming Woolfian instants, but because he understood that *now*, even if ugly or abrasive, may be all we are allowed. In a review of Fairfield Porter's paintings, Schuyler states what might be taken as his own credo: "Look *now*. It will never be more fascinating." Taking pleasure in presentness involves a necessary fondness for accident and error: "It is a play of ideas, as beautiful as briefly grasping a logical sequence, or perceiving how one might come into being, a sequence of which the canceled steps, the false turns or hesitancies, are not lost, and whose consideration is found a necessary prelude to the blue, yellow and red formulations of a process which evolves toward no conclusion, but whose direction is its proof, whose offshoots—its pauses and incidentals—are its aim." That grand sentence describes a Paul Burlin painting, but it also sketches the movement of a poem or an essay, or a poem-essay like Schuyler's "The Morning of the Poem," which begins and ends with an address to his friend the painter Darragh Park and is therefore also an essay on painting. Schuyler saw, in art, a liberty that was absent from the more calcified literary circles: he found, in looking at and writing about expressionist painting, whether figurative or abstract, a pretext for focused, eye-rewarding, felicitously paced play.

Schuyler was an appreciator. Most of his reviews are favorable. He didn't bother to go into print hating something. Liking is itself an art, and a difficult one. Schuyler especially liked painting. (He may also have appreciated photography and, after his years at *ARTnews*, performance and installation, but he didn't review them.) Indeed, his tastes in art may strike some readers as tame, even conservative. Among the painters he sympathetically discussed are Porter (with whom he lived, as permanent houseguest, for many years), Alex Katz, John Button, Jackson Pollock, Robert Rauschenberg, Franz Kline, Helen Frankenthaler, Larry Rivers, Grace Hartigan, Roy Lichtenstein, Anne Dunn, Kenneth Noland, Michael Goldberg, Joe Brainard, and a host of others whose names are, to me, less familiar. The list of painters he appreciated cannot be advanced as his canon: these were simply the painters in his milieu, or else the painters whose shows *ARTnews* was in the business of covering. Schuyler didn't foresee the directions that vanguard art would take in the sixties and seventies (or beyond), but he didn't set out to be an influential critic. That he wrote about paintings, and not roses, is partly happenstance; he might have written just as eloquently and perceptively about gardening or cooking.

Unconcerned with shaping art history, Schuyler used his understated reviews to practice certain poetic effects, with rare, idiosyncratic density. He put unusual words together to short-circuit humdrum comprehension; he found new ways to describe color and to enter the life of paint; he used negation to express something present, not absent; he employed dissolves, largely through the verb *to be*, so that perceived objects metamorphose into their likenesses; like Stein, he repeated; he spread syntactic members out with deceptive evenness so that the entire sentence seems to be happening on a single plane, as in an all-over painting.

Unusual words. His exacerbated, mellifluent diction calls attention to the surfaces of his sentences. He notes a Burlin painting's "rough reds and blues on the blue-*occluded* white, *scumbled* with pink"; he enjoys an Edward Hopper painting's depiction of "tense walls, calm, fat furniture, a complex of shadows and apertures, the *unregimentable arithmetic* of the ocean"; and in an Esteban Vicente collage he notes "the sharpness of eye that values an *ooze of glue*" (emphases mine).

The coloristic life of paint. Schuyler makes theater of a painting's expressive surface, as when he describes, in a canvas by Antoni Tàpies, "a wriggle of pigment perched, like a slipped wig, on a corner of a pocked chunk," or when a woman's brown jumper in a Hilda Ward painting is "an earthy bed from which the bright tube colors flourish and curve," or when, for Lyonel Feininger, "blue light hastens into violet," and "brown is discriminated from black for the joy of making fine distinctions."

Negations that express presence. This effect he borrowed, perhaps, from Marianne Moore, with her predilection for words like *unegoistic*, *gossipless*, *unexaggeratedly denominated*, and *unpanoplied.* Such negatives provide the pleasure of an atmosphere half-there, half-gone. He notes in Ludwig Sander "a dulled *un-heavy* purple"; he finds in a Nell Blaine painting that "the *no-color* city in the soot-colored air turns out to be all color"; in Porter he seizes "a bouquet of *not-too-defined* phlox," and in Rudy Burckhardt "a silkily-stroked *unobtrusiveness*"; and he understands that "the quickening calm of swift orange, red, yellow" in a Franz Kline can be "*unharrowing* as laughter."

Dissolves that hasten metamorphosis. His most characteristic dissolves happen through the use of the verb *to be*, as in the lovely sentence describing Rauschenberg's 1958 *Talisman*: "A stain is slowed under silk." Past, present, and future perception shape one another; Schuyler cares about "things as they are in the light of what they were, of what it seemed they would become." Geography, too, plays musical chairs: a Jane Wilson painting depicts "a New York room on a brilliant winter day in Iowa." Schuyler often savors sky's waveringness: in a Jane Freilicher painting he sees that "the blue that centers one is not a river, for all its skyness," and in a Park painting, "sky as light source is everywhere adumbrated, though often scarcely in the picture, and sometimes not at all."

Repetitions. Like Gertrude Stein, Schuyler is interested in attaining or mimicking the state of still life, the somnolence of objects on tables and of bodies on chairs, and he repeats words so that the thing depicted can evaporate and then reappear, more solid because of its episode of evaporation. In a Milton Resnick picture, Schuyler appreciates "showers of petals that aren't petals." Admiring Friedel Dzubas's painterly skill, Schuyler writes, "It is conquering it that has allowed it to express itself": four forms of "it" in one sentence baffle the difference between expression and containment.

Syntactic members spread out for an all-over simultaneity. All parts of the sentence sometimes seem to be existing on the same plane, in the same instant of apprehension. In the following sentence about a Freilicher painting, the verb *is* is pivot for an equation that holds true only for the duration of the sentence and then dissipates: "An arabesque of paint is a stroke securely attached to a thin scrubbing it abuts on." The movement of a blob of paint across the screen of perception exists for the exact length of the following sentence about a Goldberg painting: "Gratuitously wandering across the surface a fat white blob tails off." A missing comma gives that sentence its poetry. Put the comma back in, and see what happens: "Gratuitously wandering across the surface, a fat white blob tails off." The comma imposes a temporal grid;

"wandering" becomes subordinate to the fat blob's static identity as a subject. Without the comma, the fat white blob is free to wander across the surface for an unmeasured stretch of time.

Despite Schuyler's connection to a heroic moment in painting, I take him, in his critical and poetic practice, to be an entirely post-heroic artist, a consciously indolent and anti-psychological observer mostly interested in the drift of static across an unpoliced surface, a movement compelling because of its apparent randomness. He was a major apostle of extraneous, minor pleasures.

(1999)

V.

Debbie Harry at the Supermarket

In the late 1990s, I stood behind Debbie Harry in line at Sloan's. We lived in the same apartment complex, a behemoth. Sloan's, the unsavory supermarket around the block, was our common ground. One summer evening, a rat crawled past my flip-flop-clad feet while I waited in the checkout line. I vowed never again to wear flip-flops while food shopping. If this essay is an allegory, I'm the rat, scurrying along interpretive thoroughfares where my filth isn't wanted.

•

In the late 1970s, I listened to Blondie with a fanaticism founded on my belief that Debbie Harry's vocal delivery would give me tips on differentiating the genuine from the fake in the apocalyptic world of romantic love, where I was a befuddled amateur, working intermittently on my heterosexuality as if it were last Sunday's crossword puzzle, a confusing grid of boxes I'd not given up trying to fill.

•

Every inflection of Harry's voice I followed, memorized, sought to explain. Why did she approach a cry or a cheer, why did she flatten a vowel or slur a consonant, why did an aluminum aura complicate a phrase? Was she angry, infatuated, indifferent—or was she turning emotionality into an amusing diversion?

•

I admired her voice's Lancelot edge, but also its indirection, its underworld willingness to grow tarnished and to sound unsentimentally street-schooled. Phrase by phrase, her voice switched sides. Momentarily, in her timbre, a metallic yet bubblegum inflection emerged—suggesting irony, wit, shininess, rage, and a fondness for things plastic and repeatable. Then, in a flash, she'd adopt a rueful, bluesy sound. She quoted mannerisms from other singers, other milieux; punk London warred with suburban New Jersey. She leapt between the borrowed and the original, the emotive and the shellacked.

•

Even her physical beauty seemed ironic; she seemed to deploy it as an analytical torch, a secret agent, dismantling the stereotypes she cheerfully traversed. In the Polaroid snapshots that Andy Warhol took of her in 1980, she gazes at him—and at the viewer—from across the moat of received wisdom, whose toxicity can't touch her; with us, she exchanges a complicit glance, as if to say, *We understand the joke that gender is, and we understand how masterfully I embody its barbed glories.* Like Edie Sedgwick (Andy's dream-double, who, in the words of a Blondie song, died young and stayed pretty), Harry seemed a cynical sylph with whom he could giddily unpack the fenced goods stuffed in gender's suitcase.

•

In Blondie's hit song "The Tide Is High," Harry claims not to be the kind of girl who easily gives up. By singing the words "I'm not the kind of girl," Harry—or her persona—admits that there exist many varieties of girl, as many as there are shades of lipstick, or verses in the Bible, or varieties of rock on the path to Lourdes. There are many kinds of girl, and Debbie has the right to pick exactly which kind she is. But she is also fated to be a specific kind—and maybe this kind of girl falls prey to dejection and wants a listener's sympathy. She loads this exclamation ("I'm not the kind of girl") with country-western grit—faked, for sophistication's sake. Listening, I inwardly volunteer to rescue Harry from her moment of simulated peril. Every time I hear "The Tide Is High," I wait for the phrase "I'm not the kind of girl." And when the phrase arrives, I experience an exaltation that brings permanent solitude as its hangover: *I imagine myself to be the ideal and only audience for understanding the emotional predicament of this woman who is too pretty to pay attention to me.* The 45 or LP or CD—or any of the new prostheses that make obsolete the original technologies that first gave me nearness to Debbie Harry—forbid her from noticing me. She can't pay attention to the listener; only the mediator—the record player—can acknowledge my presence as steadfast ear-in-waiting.

•

And so when Harry looks at the viewer, in Warhol's Polaroid, her glance negates itself; it abolishes the hope that she will ever recognize my existence. Her over-the-shoulder gaze clarifies that her contract—as divinity, as a certain "kind of girl"—forbids her from seeing me. This Polaroid, which indubitably proves her beauty (always I feel the tautological need to demonstrate that Debbie Harry is beautiful, a fact that needs no argument), offers the gift of my disenfranchisement, my ejection. The blessing she bestows on me is banishment.

•

When Debbie Harry splits up a single syllable—doubling it—I experience an internal doubling, a schism I enjoy, even if I don't understand it. In the song "I Didn't Have the Nerve To Say No," from *Plastic Letters* (my favorite album, because its audio engineers didn't cloak her timbral resources with reverb and other ungodly devices), she divides the word *no*: "I didn't have the nerve to say *no-oh.*" (This song she cowrote with Jimmy Destri, but in every Blondie number, regardless of authorship, the phrases Harry sings and the deviations she imposes on them appear to reflect her intentions.) With the doubled *o*, she injects irony and jadedness into a romantic declaration that might otherwise come across as corny. Ironic, yes: but the doubled *o* also portrays her as authentically impassioned, her consciousness overbrimming with a blinding, ambivalent pulsation.

•

I've got the ineffability blues. I feel paralyzed by my own inability to describe why I love Debbie Harry; I'm trapped, like Edgar Allan Poe's guilty narrator in "The Tell-Tale Heart," alone in a chamber with a ticker whose maniacal thumping, a time bomb's, declares, "You have twenty minutes to describe Debbie Harry's ineffable gorgeousness and irony, and if you fail, you'll be executed." If I decide *not* to explain her splendor, and to let it remain comment-free, then something in me will have perished. I will have destroyed a small creature buried in my body—the breathing embryo of *my remembered attachment to Debbie Harry's voice and image*. By explaining the attachment, I give this embryo life. If I fail to explain, I will have slaughtered some portion of my own potential.

•

The terror of being unable to explain Debbie Harry's sublimity is built into the experience of apprehending it—the terror of being stranded with the gorgeousness, either as its proprietor or as its last living witness.

•

By "gorgeousness," I mean not only her face—its echo of every blonde siren the cinema has ever known—but her singing voice's matter-of-factness, combining fatigue and rancor and nervous energy, like Jean Seberg's French in *Breathless*. A song passes quickly—four or five minutes. Once it ends, I can replay it, or I can try to communicate its pleasures to someone else, or I can decide to stop talking about the private dimensions of aesthetic experience; I can decide never again to ask, "Do Debbie Harry's voice and image submit your body to a tension that isolates you in a chamber of bliss and suffering?"

•

Susan Sontag indicates in the second volume of her diaries (posthumously published) that she places physical beauty perilously high in her value hierarchy: she has a soft spot for loveliness. So do I. Women and men with striking faces—wide cheekbones and widely spaced eyes—seem miraculously to reconfigure my watching body and to blast open my chest cavity; these faces reformat my respiration into a structure taut and airy, lightened and elevated, like Chartres cathedral, or any impossible spire that yearns upward. My breathing becomes Gothic in scope and aspiration when I see Debbie Harry's image, which exiles me to a fairy-tale topography of dungeons, primogeniture, mirrors, debasement, gold, and destitution.

•

I don't insist on small noses. I like big noses, too; a big nose authorizes its bearer to travel into that imaginary desert where the Burning Bush inextinguishably speaks. That's the story I invent to justify the delight a big nose inspires in me. But Harry's small nose, combined with her wide-apart eyes, allows me to experience an equally antediluvian and shamanistic sensation. Debbie's nose and cheekbones instigate in my nervous system what I'll call the "gulf" feeling, an illusion that I am being stretched, made inwardly ample, as if my rib cage were expanding, or as if, through identification, my own cheekbones were suddenly widening. A long Giuseppe Verdi phrase—Elisabetta in *Don Carlo* singing "*Tu che le vanità conoscesti del mondo*" ("You who knew the vanities of this world")—also sets in motion the "gulf" feeling, like a

Herculean bridge's span suddenly imported into my torso. By "gulf" I mean a body of water—the Gulf of Mexico?—but also a landlocked chasm over which the star-loving imagination can't leap, a canyon too vast for a communicable thought to cross.

•

I saw Deborah Harry perform twice in a Sarah Kane play, *Crave*, live in New York. Both times I sat in the front row. That was the era (the year 2000) when I'd begun to fear that stardom, as a device to enlarge perception and to ennoble inner transport, was eroding, and so, in an attempt to protect what I considered an endangered natural resource, I developed an eco-theory of stardom and its contemporary uses. I decided that Debbie Harry—as my test-case deity—should be given an off-Broadway theater; she would appear on its stage for one hour a night. She needn't put on a traditional show. No song, dance, script. No fancy costumes or special effects. Harry would sit in a comfortable chair onstage and receive our attention. We could ask questions, but she needn't answer. Bodyguards and bouncers would protect her. The star would simply be present; with her existence's supranormality she would bless and astound us. (Marina Abramović and other performance artists have gone far with this concept.) Picture the words *Deborah Harry* on an intimate downtown theater's marquee, advertising that the star will be in session from 8:00 until 9:00 from Monday to Friday, every night this winter, to give a master class in existence. Somewhere between a Beckett monodrama and a Warhol screen test, this impractical *Living Workshop in Star Embodiment* still seeks a backer.

•

Whenever, in the early years of this already compromised century, I'd see Deborah Harry walk along Twenty-Third Street, the block we shared, I'd marvel at her solemn, hieratic pace. She didn't trudge, march, rush, lope, stroll, or skip. In billowy pants, she led, slowly, with her hips, as if gliding through water. (Once, I remember, she wore army fatigues: couture khakis?) She explored with pilgrim curiosity the spatial zones her body passed through. Each step gestured acceptance toward the sidewalk; you may think I'm exaggerating or overinterpreting, but these memories—the sight of Debbie Harry promenading on Twenty-Third Street—are my possession, and they are not visions that will disappear, or visions whose meanings I can ignore by pretending that it makes no difference how a star's gait seemed momentous and allegorical to a primed beholder. Harry seemed at home with each step, at home with her feet and her legs as they maneuvered air and pavement. Her measured equilibrium led me to believe that she had undergone revolutions of belief and doubt, that she had passed through perils in this lifetime (if we are in the mood to believe in reincarnation, and tonight we are in the mood); she had found a peculiar restfulness, and it was her business to express this illumination to passersby on Twenty-Third Street. I elected the contemporary Deborah Harry as my neighborhood epitome of numinous attainment, achieved not by beauty or fame but by the fact that she had survived those eviscerating lures. Fame and beauty remained her possessions, but she ignored them, as she walked to Sloan's—which now is Gristedes—and waited in line to buy her daily groceries.

(2012)

A Brief History of Reinvention

History moves forward by reinventing itself. Hegel, or Marx, or both, called the process "dialectical." Some reinventions are merely cosmetic; others are revolutionary. Knowing the difference requires a discriminating eye.

To recount the checkered career of this concept, we must repeat, mercilessly, the word *reinvent.* Apologies are in order for this awkwardness.

•

Jesus reinvents Judaism. Duffy reinvents catchy naïveté.

Injections of Juvéderm reinvent the aging face. Thom Browne reinvents the male suit and, thereby, male calves. The beverage industry reinvents the movie theater as high-fructose corn syrup dump site. Deaf, Beethoven reinvents the sonata.

Carmel Snow reinvents *Harper's Bazaar.* The roulette wheel spins. John Cage reinvents silence. Talkative Isaac Mizrahi reinvents Target, and Target returns the favor. Biogenetics reinvents chicken.

Mark Spitz reinvents the bathing suit. Brooke Shields reinvents eyebrows; Richard Prince reinvents sleaze by appropriating a photo of ten-year-old Brooke, nude. The StairMaster reinvents the schlep.

England reinvents tea. Tit for tat: Bollywood reinvents Hollywood.

The word processor reinvents the typewriter. We're supposed to be thrilled. D. H. Lawrence reinvents the sexiness of soot. American Apparel reinvents men's briefs as sherbet scoops. China reinvents capitalism. Tom Cruise, exploding on *Oprah*, reinvents catharsis as "jumping the couch." Calm and collected, Marcel Duchamp's urinal reinvents the museum.

Georges Dubœuf reinvents Beaujolais. Like a ripe grape on joy's tongue, James Dean reinvents sensitivity, anticipating Heath Ledger, who reinvents James Dean. Alice Waters reinvents nearby vegetables. Thomas Alva Edison reinvents kissing.

Judy Garland reinvents herself by spawning Liza, and then Liza rejuvenates Judy: chain reaction. Jung fails to reinvent Freud; psychotropics reinvent melancholy. The Buddha reinvents sitting and breathing.

Colette—the fashion boutique, not the writer—reinvents replenishment by serving eighty different waters at Le Water Bar. José Saramago, writing the novel *Blindness*, reinvents apocalypse; on YouTube, which reinvents TV, he appears, watching the movie *Blindness*, starring Julianne Moore, who reinvents Revlon.

Nietzsche harped on Eternal Recurrence: dreck keeps happening. Freud understood the fine line between reiteration and transformation. Suffering a repetition compulsion, we aspire to reinvent trauma by replaying it. We destroyed the planet; we keep on destroying it.

Michael Jackson reinvents childhood; scandal reciprocates, reinventing Michael. Eugène Atget reinvents fin de siècle Paris by photographing it before it dies. James Joyce does the same, in words, for Dublin. Much later, Zaha Hadid sees the possibilities of squiggles, and turns them into buildings.

Money-fueled, Dubai reinvents Vegas. The Supreme Court reinvents the Constitution. Antifascist, Pablo Casals reinvents the cello.

The iPod reinvents the ear's interior. The cell-phone reinvents rudeness and renames it "communication." Martin

Luther King Jr. reinvents civil disobedience. Madonna names her 2004 world tour Re-Invention. Berlin reinvents itself after 1945. Rituals of expiation—Yom Kippur, the confessional—reinvent culpability.

•

Why ruminate on "reinvention" now? Like Mia Farrow or Angelina Jolie, we want to do good. We want to remedy crimes against humanity, to put a hex on torturers and environment wreckers. We want to stave off avian flu. DDT reinvents spring, said Rachel Carson, whose evangelism deserves repeating.

Western Europe reinvents socialism. The WPA reinvents labor. Legal abortion reinvents liberty. Didn't JFK once mention a torch? Let's get back to work.

(2008)

I Went by a Devious Route

Adoration, complicated, takes a few thousand pages to explain. Proust, describing Marcel's momentary infatuation with the Duchesse de Guermantes, who waves at him from an opera box and who nods to him, later, from her carriage, proves that idol worship is not a dead end. Sometimes, the idol smiles back. Reciprocation, however, can kill ardor.

Mirror-minded, Marcel worships the Duchesse de Guermantes, mostly because of her storied name. Voyeur, he sees her enter an opera box; her white chiffon dress dominates the eye. With a white-gloved hand, she waves at him; singled out from the anonymous crowd, he receives the individuating shower of her gaze. The next day, he starts stalking her; he follows her while she does errands around town. Unflattering detail: he notices red blotches on her face.

And then a woman in a carriage nods at him. Only after a moment does he realize that this respectful stranger is the Duchesse de Guermantes, but now her carriage has already passed, and he has failed to acknowledge her greeting. Does she secretly reciprocate his passion? Or is she irritated at his shadowing obsequiousness?

When I first read Proust, in the summer of 1986, these duchess-besotted passages reinforced my own love for upper-class mavens with imposing, stiff hairdos (Jacqueline Onassis) and for sopranos (Anna Moffo). Proust gave me leave to pursue infatuation as a calling; he legitimated fandom and made it appear poetic, not pathetic. Anatomizing adoration, subjecting it to detailed analysis, seemed, Proust's example suggested, not merely a solipsistic exercise but a high-toned quest, an act of self-ethnography. Joseph Cornell practiced it. So did Genet and Leiris. They treated their abject crushes (on stars, ballerinas, shopgirls, convicts, sailors, words) with exegetical intensity.

It's not so much that Marcel loves the duchess. He loves what she does to his mind: she rearranges perception. She is a walking piece of performance art *avant la lettre*. Her ineffability paralyzes him; she conveniently epitomizes a milieu. Marcel's extreme consciousness requires the ballast of a motionless, heraldic, feminine object. The duchess could be Vivien Leigh, or Arletty, or Catherine Deneuve, or Kim Novak in *Vertigo*, a figment one never stops searching for; the duchess is any woman you have idealized for reasons that sensible people would call silly or superficial. Proust's *In Search of Lost Time* is full of love objects, and the duchess is not the central one. And yet, in my biased estimation, Marcel's brief love for the duchess—her name, her remoteness, her station, her beauty, her nose, her pronunciation, her chiffon—stands out as the most poignant.

Once upon a time, a famous woman said to me, "Give me a call." I gave her a call. Nothing happened. She'd lost interest in me. Just as well. I can't bear nearness to fame: overmuch eminence humiliates the glare-blinded bystander. And yet when this famous woman, my Duchesse de Guermantes, said, "Give me a call," futurity opened its counterfeit gates, and, like Proust's narrator, I believed that I had stumbled upon immanence.

The duchess's thaw—suddenly acknowledging Marcel's existence—epitomizes certain sublime aesthetic experiences: recall how a difficult piece of music (Schoenberg?) eventually unlocks its latent melody and yields a thwarted warmth. Such temperature oscillations—the duchess's quick shift from indifference to interest—remind us that, when packing for a trip to the Proustian uncanny, we should bring bathing suits *and* parkas.

(2003)

Notes on Affinity

The first time I heard Brahms's D minor Piano Concerto, in 1973 or 1974, on an LP, I felt affinity for the ugliness of its opening movement's stentorian theme, and for the theme's avoidance of happiness; I understand the inability to pursue happiness, and I wanted to build a life around hiding from closure, from optimism, and from productivity. And so once again I played the LP of the first movement, to cement my affinity—but not to understand it. I wanted to know why the first theme mattered—not the second ("feminine") theme but the first ("masculine") theme, perhaps derivative of Beethoven, perhaps too luridly striving, perhaps too Promethean—or was the problem the trill, a tremolo that created dissonance and unpleasure, a tremolo that disseminated an illusion of pneumonia, of croup, of rattling phlegm in an infected pair of lungs? I wanted to step closer to that oscillating phlegm, to approach its magic circle (Grand Grimoire?), not because I'd ever say "I love it" but because it confirmed (or teased onward) some tendency of my own, a tendency I'd probably then have called satanic, anarchic, psychotic, world-destroying, family-destroying; but the opening theme was also the song of ambition, a diseased gaze away from futurity, a wish to throttle the environment, a refusal to cooperate. I call the emotion I felt upon hearing that first theme (not an emotion! rather, an awkwardness, a stirring, a hesitation, a fear, a disgust)—I call this uncertainty the birth of an affinity because the sensation brought no intellectual program in its wake, and it brought no possibility of an argument, no possibility (so I wished to believe) of ideology (as if "ideology" were a toxin I could define, circumscribe, and exile from my imagination). When the piano soloist (Rudolf Serkin) played that phrase, I felt it vicariously in my fingers; my stymied hands, lacking technique and experience, could sense an affinity with tremolos and octaves I could never execute. I label that emotion (or that stirring, that tendency, that tropism toward love) an "affinity" because the gnarly Brahms phrase was secretly my father; I can now imagine that wrecked, Olympian phrase as a difficult father with whom I might bed down, incestuously. (Or perhaps the phrase was simply vocation, father-as-vocation?) I was "called" by the phrase, but how could I invent a language (or set of actions) with which to answer the summons? Writing about this affinity, I'm thrust back to my childhood bedroom, its carpet, its curtain-filtered sunshine, its pessimism, its cramps, its *Mod Squad*, its dead flies; and I'm back, too, with my failure to imagine a location more romantic (or more estimable) than that immature phrase, whose ugliness I want now to emphasize as the aspect of its face most worthy of love.

I haven't defined *affinity* or taken a serious step toward articulating why it is a useful, attractive, or seductive category. I've said one simple thing, and I'll say it again. I call my first rendezvous with the Brahms phrase the stirring of an affinity because I can't name the object with which I felt the bond. Was Brahms the object? Was it the particular interval (minor seventh? ninth?) that the opening phrase traversed? Was my object the octave unison, two notes chiming together as one? Was my object the piano's affinity with the orchestra, an ensemble chained to the dominating, hubristic piano? Did I feel affinity with finger-wizard Rudolf Serkin, with maestro

George Szell, or with their imagined affinity? Was my object—affinity's bull's-eye—my piano teacher, a diminutive young woman who'd played that daunting concerto, a few years earlier, as soloist with a college orchestra? Did I feel affinity with this teacher, whose narcissism, and whose audacious virtuosity, I imagined as a nougat I wanted to eat? Did I feel an affinity with D minor itself, the signature of woe and of containment within that comfy category, "woe"? Was I inspired by D minor's affinity with D major, or D minor's affinity with its cousin key, F major? Did I feel mirrored by D minor's affinity for F major? And thus was my affinity triangulated, a bastard version, not safe for child consumption? Was I mesmerized by Brahms's affinity with Beethoven, or Brahms's tie to Schumann? Did I feel an affinity for Brahms's regicidal riposte, his production of an unlyrical, anti-Schumannesque phrase (heroic, stonyhearted, marmoreal, morgue-cold as the Otto Wagner church in Vienna's Steinhof hospital), a phrase more pugilistic than Schumann's wildest dreams? Did I feel affinity with a composer's envy and love for a rival? Did I feel an alien's affinity with my own fingers, their wish to commit a revolutionary, exhibitionistic folly? Did I feel an affinity with modernity or with tonality's rupture, even if tonality wasn't yet being destroyed, even if I'd be a fool to say that this opening phrase predicted Schoenberg? I call my alliance with this Brahms phrase an affinity because it fell short of love. My alliance (an undeclarable sensation I could barely notice) predicted for me a strange vocation: the phrase insinuated that my self-destructive mission would be to pursue dominant magnetisms (musical, visual, aromatic, tactile, syntactical) that in vain I'd dream of snuggling up to and conquering. Said more simply: I developed an instant crush on that phrase, and smack in the crush's central seam I understood that the infatuation was implausible, a crush I had no right to feel, a crush that would not win me friends or sympathizers; by announcing to myself that I felt affinity with that phrase, I was destroying other pacts, other possibilities of sociability, belonging, conformity, communicability. Even these sentences I'm now writing prove how damaging that affinity—or any affinity?—was; for by letting myself fall under its sway, I gave up comprehensibility. I decided: I'll side with what I can't understand in Brahms's phrase; I'll side with the possible rottenness of an object I might one day love.

(2011)

The Pump: Notes Toward a Theory of Shininess and Stupefaction

Later, in another essay, not here, I will define *shininess* and *stupefaction*, two experiences—visual, musical, emotional—that haunt me. Here, I'll reserve the terms, put a hold on them, as one puts a hold on a book at a library, a book one may have no intention of ever returning to claim.

•

I stumbled on the word *stupefaction* while reading Alexis Lykiard's translation of the Comte de Lautréamont's *Chants de Maldoror.* The word, here, refers to the sense of pleasure, however deadened and numb, that comes from not being entirely able to comprehend what one is reading: "This hybrid preface has been set out in a way which may not, perhaps, appear natural enough, in the sense that it—so to speak—surprises the reader, who does not very clearly see where he is at first being led; yet this feeling of remarkable stupefaction, from which one generally seeks to shield those who spend their time reading books or booklets, I have made every effort to produce."

•

Last night I heard for the first time Carl Maria von Weber's *Der Freischütz*, live performance, 1954 (is it plausible to still be in a state of virginity vis-à-vis *Der Freischütz*, is it possible for me never to have heard in its entirety a performance of *Der Freischütz*, and is it possible for me still to consider *Der Freischütz* a piece of late-breaking news, a cause for celebration?),

Wilhelm Furtwängler conducting, Elisabeth Grümmer as Agathe. The presence (living, gone) of her voice on my stereo in my bedroom sent me online to figure out whether she was dead, and online (is online a site of death or life?) I discovered she'd died in 1986. It may be too late to set up a cult of Elisabeth Grümmer or to excavate the meanings of her voice's purity.

•

On an Internet auction site, iGavel, I found, recently, remnants of the estate of the late opera soprano Anna Moffo, to whom I have devoted many words, in the past, and many hours of purposeless or undirected meditation, a process of perseveration that is not based in drives or instincts, but in the going-nowhere zone of *play*, non-erotic, non-climactic—a process that the psychologist D. W. Winnicott called "relaxed undirected mental inconsequence." The item that caught my eye, though I did not bid on it, was a pair of her Ferragamo pumps, on sale for a modest price. Indeed, a set of four pairs of nearly identical pumps was being offered at a starting bid of eighty dollars. What arrested me was the photo, posted on iGavel, of a pump's sole—shown to us, on the site, ostensibly to authenticate the pump's identity (Ferragamo). And yet it didn't matter that Ferragamo made the pumps. The salient fact was that Anna Moffo once wore them. Inadvertently, the photo authenticated the fact that she wore the shoes; the pump's underside was mildly stained by gravel and dirt. Call it *scuffed*. It was a pump enduring an intermediate position on the spectrum between pristinely new and worn to the bone. The pump was on its way to oblivion but someone pressed the pause button and arrested the pump in a position between use and uselessness.

The fact that I noticed dirt and scuff marks on the bottom of her pump may have symbolic meaning. We might file this fact—that I noticed the scuff marks and chose to write about them—within the *fetishism* dossier, or we might file it under *abjection*, a folder already overstuffed. We might file it under *masochism* or *sadism*. Or under *objet petit a*, Lacan's mysterious, cute concept, which I don't have the wherewithal to define. Certainly the scuff marks are an *objet petit a*, an impermissible and accidental springboard for desire, a catalyst that is at the same time desire's castoff, its dirty remnant.

The pump may seem to have a cultural location—opera, fandom, auction houses, fashion, cultural detritus, nostalgia, mourning, collecting—and yet none of these sites can explain, or explain away, the scuff marks. The fact that I noticed the scuff marks cannot be claimed by any system. That fact cannot be sold. Nor can it be placed inside or outside the concept of *artfulness*; it exists in neither zone. It is simply an experience, a fleck of dust, of outcast flotsam, that need interest no one.

•

A month or more ago the detectives who keep the nation busy thought they'd found the man who murdered the child beauty queen JonBenet Ramsey. But they got the wrong man. He turned out not to be the killer.

Before authorities discovered his innocence, newspapers printed photographs of him, and in some of those photographs, or at least one, I noticed a spot of shine on his forehead. Perhaps it was sweat, or the stigmata of a fatty diet. It might have been the unflattering reflection of press flashbulbs. I remember thinking, when I saw this photograph, that my attentiveness to the shine on his forehead was not part of the story's allegorical and legal trappings; the forehead's shine was a decision I had made, a private instant of curatorial whimsy. I had singled out this shine, and was not going to do anything with it. It would undergo no transformation into art; I would not mention it to anyone. I would not even read the newspaper article that accompanied the photo. I would file the shine in the dossier tentatively called *reprieve from certainty*. I would file the shine under *ellipsis*, *vacancy*, *random stains*, *scuff marks of no particular value or meaning*. I would file it here, and leave its interpretation up to you.

(2007)

VI.

Play-Doh Fun Factory Poetics

That is the way memory serves us, details return ill assorted, pell mell, in confusion.

—Ezra Pound, *Gaudier-Brzeska* (1916)

My poetics—anal, alimentary, abstract—resembles a Play-Doh Fun Factory.

I practice what Foucault called, in reference to the history of sexuality, "the care of the self." I trim, slash, shape; I perform askesis. But my material is not "self." It's words: Play-Doh.

Last night I dreamt my mother showed me her vagina: an offering.

Each new paragraph interrupts the previous. Paragraphs have the privilege of parataxis.

In 1913, Ezra Pound demanded: "Direct treatment of the 'thing,' whether subjective or objective."

Without my sexual compulsions, my penis would sit inert in my pants and endure a dull, nonmonumental existence. Without my sexual compulsions, I would have no poetics.

In a brand-new poem, I wrote: "Play-Doh Factory, / I loved your poop / ambience, extruded quadri- / laterals vast yet squat."

As a youngster, I liked the smell of Play-Doh, an odor of chalk and vanilla, enriched by cardamom and pavement.

Play-Doh smelled like the Pentateuch, or the golem, or a Robert Ryman painting—abstract, blank, complex, eerie, bumpy.

Difficult to remember whether it was more fun to push the Play-Doh out the factory's chute or to lop off the Play-Doh after it had been extruded and formed. Maybe the greatest pleasure lay in choosing the shape—the filter—through which the Play-Doh would be forced.

Today, on the piano, I warmed up with a Brahms exercise ("broken arpeggio figuration in contrary motion with repeated notes") and an etude from Carl Czerny's *Art of Finger Dexterity*: "Changing the Fingers in Rapid Playing." Then I worked on Isaac Albéniz's naive, forgotten Sonata no. 3. I love the fact that it is forgotten.

Each book, poem, or paragraph I produce is a physical machine, generated by hand movements. I like to put my fingers to work. I value diligence, facture, momentum.

I write to experience inner folds. Call them psychological and spiritual contortions; or call them abject, self-debasing, self-enlarging contractions. José Saramago (in *The Gospel According to Jesus Christ*) describes such a contraction: "In self-abasement his soul shrinks into itself like a tunic folded three times, surrendering his defenceless body to the mercy of the mothers of Bethlehem . . ." When I write, my soul shrinks into itself like a tunic folded three times.

I write longhand in a diary, for no reader, nearly every day. I have done so for thirty-three years. My diary, the longest book I've ever written, is a lifelong experiment in accretion—a scroll, remote from audience, coherence, or plan.

In my diary, on Sunday, November 8, 2009, I wrote: "Dream: I tried (energetically) to explain to my mother the gay scene in Berlin. I mentioned *Taxi zum Klo*. All this conversation was occasioned by a foreign film (French: Agnès Varda or her ilk?). My mother stood in the Augusta Way garage, by the front step. She momentarily concealed herself behind a curtain. Neighbors had three scrawny trees. The neighbors either praised or disapproved of our property's shrubbery. They were working their land, we were working ours." If this dream finds its way into a poem, I'll probably use the words *Agnès Varda* and *Taxi zum Klo*, and maybe the neighbors' disapproval of our property's shrubbery. I like the musical affinity between the words *property* and *shrubbery*. And I could use the phrase *scrawny trees*, and the pathetic scene of trying (with futile zeal) to describe to my mother the gay scene in Berlin, my father's birthplace.

These days, for first drafts of poems, I use a manual typewriter and colored construction paper—red, orange, yellow, beige, purple. I type quickly, without forethought, usually in quatrains. Each quatrain is a box, an arbitrary module, a friendly lump, of an accommodating size. Later, I scavenge clumps of language from these construction-paper improvisations and turn these clumps into poems—reassembled, like Frankenstein's monster, from pilfered parts.

Recently I found my first diary—from 1968. I was nine years old. Here are a few entries. "Thursday January 29. I get in a play which Brad made. I have the 4th biggest part! I am going to record it with a movie camera." "Monday March 18. I find my long lost library card. And it was right in front of me. We have the play today." "Wednesday March 20. Today I film it! It is very fun to film a movie. I have to memorize a poem." "Saturday June 29. A fat girl babysits today. Mommy and Daddy go to *The Odd Couple*. It's their anniversary." Why did I say "fat girl," but not give her a name? Already I was interested in shameful singularity, in abject exemplarity. Here's another entry: "Wednesday June 5: Robert Kennedy was shot. Not dead yet. He won the primaries. No [Cub Scout] den meeting."

A paragraph is a container for sentences—like a shadow box, a bureau drawer, a coffin, a laundry hamper, a diaper hamper, a time capsule. I put as many sentences in the box as will fit. Sometimes I keep the box relatively empty. I shake the box and let the sentences fall into different positions.

I write for solitude's sake, not for companionship or communication. My writing may seem chatty but its aims are inexpressive and abstract.

I write to wallow—to feel a soaring upward and then a crash downward. Adjective or noun or verb or adverb can be anagnorisis and peripeteia happening simultaneously. Diction should hurt. I like to twist a word into its dirty groove.

I like em dashes, parentheses, ellipses, semicolons, colons, line breaks—any form of stoppage or interruption. A short utterance, or an interrupted one, is a gasp rather than a statement. Short sentences—words conspicuously crammed together or omitted—remind me of a finger pointing, either to indicate or to condemn.

I write inside a bleak, turgid morass; I peer out from the muck, sometimes with clarity, forgiveness, or curiosity, but sometimes with recursive distaste for the self-made muck I'm peering through.

I wrote my undergraduate thesis on the relation between "word" and "thing" in the early poetry and prose of Ezra Pound. The core of the thesis was a chapter on his *Cathay* poems: "What is the use of talking, and there is no end of talking . . ." My epigraph came from Emerson's *Journal*: "In good writing, words must become one with things." I palpate a word's thingness with my eyes, mouth, and fingers.

Between words, I seek sonic similarities. I like chunky words, chunky adjacencies—monads crammed together, without a gap. My favorite Pound line: "Quick eyes gone under earth's lid." A death line. Chunky words, or strongly stressed words ("Quick eyes gone"), each vowel a different pitch and mouth shape, are mausoleums: the emphatic, chunky concentration of stresses is at once an elegiac sigh and a violent mimesis of war's murderousness.

A William Wordsworth line that kills me begins with a trochee: "Breathless with adoration." "The holy time is quiet as a Nun / Breathless with adoration." I love the chasm between "Nun" and "Breathless." The stoppage. And then the reemergence, with "Breathless," into activity. But a sliver of silence has intruded between "Nun" and "Breathless." A simple effect. But it kills me. He breaks the line because he wants to slay me, and I want to be slain: we participate together in this funeral rite.

I teeter between graphomania and a laconic thwartedness—the drive toward excess is not estranged from the drive toward death.

For prose, my rule is: revise nine times. Stations of the cross: the ritual practice of nine drafts is itself a temporal event—the construction of a tomb but also a paring-away, a self-shedding.

I stare hard at each sentence, nine times, to find the fat. Always nine times.

When I write, I feel spasms of self-disgust. I try to do something productive with the self-disgust: make it bloom. Extract a nugget from it, a calcified chunk.

Swimming is part of my poetics. As a child, I feared water; through practice, I overcame terror. I know only two strokes: crawl and breaststroke. I alternate strokes: one lap breast, one lap crawl, one lap breast, one lap crawl. Back and forth, breast, crawl, breast, crawl. Without variation. These repetitive movements pare away at consciousness, empty it of specificities.

Schmutz and its removal are part of my poetics. Too much schmutz in my language. A trench coat has a stained collar. A pink shirt has ruined sleeves. A fuchsia shirt is too blowsy. A favorite black shirt is now gray. A pair of boots has chipped toes. My boyfriend rips up underwear and socks when it's time for them to die.

I cook dinner every night. I spend as much time preparing food as I spend writing. (At the greenmarket today, I bought parsley, arugula, romaine, Russian potatoes, broccoli rabe, cauliflower, carrots, celery, radishes, yellow cherry tomatoes.) Cooking, swimming, piano playing, and writing are dumb bodily necessities, exercises of Play-Doh Fun Factoryesque mechanicity.

Play-Doh, apparently nontoxic, is made from flour, salt, water, boric acid, silicone oil, and other substances.

Last night I dreamt that I was a graduate student again, taking a seminar in modern poetry: this week we were reading George Oppen, but I needed to skip class because there were fatal errors in my health insurance eligibility form.

I love Oppen. I once stole his *Selected Poems* from a bookstore in San Francisco. I also stole Anaïs Nin's *House of Incest* and Yukio Mishima's *Confessions of a Mask*. But the best theft was Oppen. I read him while standing on a San Francisco bus. The bus swayed: I concentrated on his line breaks, their abruptness and probity. On a different bus, I read Robert Creeley's poems—purchased, not stolen. I loved Creeley's omissions, his bluntness. I appreciated how much he discarded, and the interrupted lumpiness of what remained.

My mother's father grew up on the Lower East Side and from that fertile nothingness he spurred himself to get a PhD in English literature from NYU but no college would hire a Jew so instead he taught English and disciplined the boys at Brooklyn's Abraham Lincoln High School. Hypercritical, he sent me vocabulary lists, so I could study for the SAT. From him I got my taste for words like *rodomontade*.

In grammar school, I hated wearing hard shoes—stiff leather. I only wanted to wear soft shoes—Keds sneakers. Poems are soft shoes. Prose is a hard shoe.

Once my mother caught me wearing sneakers to school. Out the kitchen window she saw me cross the street in forbidden footwear. She called me back to the house and wrote a note to the teacher. I'll reconstruct it: "Wayne is late to school today because he refused to wear the shoes that give his feet the proper support." My parents worried that my feet would grow deformed. Because our family doctor said that going barefoot would lead to disease, my mother's repeated exclamation—a household mantra—was "I step on bare feet." Five strong-stressed monosyllables. Not unlike Pound's "Quick eyes gone under earth's lid." The girls across our street were pigeon-toed. My mother said, "Gail and Sharon are pigeon-toed because they go barefoot outside."

Pound wanted "words that hover above and cling close to the things they mean."

I grew up among orchards. Gradually, during my childhood, developers cut down the trees and built tract houses and shopping malls. I remember driving by the remaining orchards and enjoying the instant when the trees line up—when the eye can make of the arbor a parallel, uninterrupted arcade. In our backyard we had a peach tree, but I remember not the fruit but the galvanized steel bucket in which we put the fruit after it was picked. When my fingers touched the schmutzy bucket, I felt neurasthenic shivers of horror.

Play-Doh smells like oranges mixed with ashes. When the Play-Doh canister's lid closes, it locks the substance in a dark cavern. Rilke, in *The Notebooks of Malte Laurids Brigge*, described the relationship of lids to jars. The jar longs for its lid, desires the tight fit of closure and containment. Rilke: "Let us agree on one point: the lid of a can—or let us say, of a can that is in good condition, whose edge curves in the same way as its own—a lid like this should have no other wish than to find itself on top of its can . . ." Emily Dickinson knew about lids: "If ever the lid gets off my head / And lets the brain away . . ." I should summarize. My subject is lids—earth's lid, mind's lid, Play-Doh's lid, the I's lid, what holds the "I" in place. Autobiography is not a defunct practice. Please don't prematurely put the lid on its fragrant complexities.

I didn't own a Play-Doh Fun Factory. I encountered the toy at the house of a friend—a freckled, redheaded Mormon, whose penis was the first uncircumcised specimen I'd ever seen. I wondered why he had a deformed flap hanging from the end of his wienie. His tract-house street was infinitesimally fancier than mine. No one could accuse my street of being opulent.

Sentences are Play-Doh constructions, shaped, chosen, extruded, timed, enjoyed, rejected. Sentences—or lines, or word groups—are pushed out, through a filter, or attachment, which controls the shape into which the sentence's dough will be formed. I am a sentence factory.

I look coldly upon my sentences. I expect them to please. If they don't, I'm disgusted. I wish I could describe more luxuriantly the varieties of disgust I feel when I appraise my sentences and try to figure out which words should live and which should die.

Because I'm rereading Giorgio Agamben's *Remnants of Auschwitz* (which acknowledges the impossibility of testimony), I'm moved to tell you the following story. My father's cousin Wolfgang survived Auschwitz, though Wolfgang's parents were gassed upon arrival. I wasn't nice to Wolfgang. That's part of my poetics—not being nice (not being a mensch) to Wolfgang and not being nice to his wife, Luisa, who also survived Auschwitz, I wasn't nice to her, either, I wasn't a mensch, and that is part of my poetics, not being nice to survivors of death camps, my permanent culpability and rottenness is part of my poetics, an integral part. I could go into detail about my not being nice to survivors; going into detail would be part of my poetics. (I wrote this final paragraph while eating chocolate cake at a hotel restaurant.)

(2009)

Assignments

Write a Jean Rhys imitation. Include five examples of understatement. Include one hyperbole. Include one sin. Structure the piece not as a narrative but as a definition or a lesson.

•

Write seven paragraphs of self-praise. Use no adverbs, or few.

•

Write a history of your neighbors. In the middle, ask questions of an artwork, and intrude a bodily urge as a way to interrupt or cut open the prose.

•

Make a list of abandoned writing projects. Say why you abandoned them.

•

Make a list of media you gave up (e.g., watercolors). Say why.

•

Describe five unlikely locations for the erotic.

•

Discuss a specific prescription drug's relation to politics.

•

Write about a crime. Use repetition. End the first paragraph with a surprise.

•

Make a list of worries. Interview a famous person. Combine the two.

•

Imitate David Antin.

•

Discuss a shopping quandary.

•

Deflation: write about a "scene" that's supposed to be exciting but actually isn't.

•

Quote a line from a novel or a poem. Selfishly manipulate and misuse the quote.

•

Follow Gertrude Stein's directions: "Dismantle a prevailing shawl or pleasure."

•

From memory, describe a scene from a movie you haven't watched in years. Then, see the movie again, and write a second description of the scene.

•

Respond to one passage from Fernando Pessoa's work but don't mention his name. Include one dream, one movie title, one embarrassment, one scientific term, one capital city, one real name, one fictitious name, your birth date.

•

Use anaphora to write a portrait of someone you know very well, too well.

•

Write ten blurbs. For ten different books. In the manner of Marianne Moore.

•

Write ten blurbs. For the same book. In the manner of Marianne Moore.

•

Write about a color without mentioning its name. Include a sentence you enjoyed or hated from Wittgenstein's *Remarks on Colour*.

•

Interpret a Lorine Niedecker poem. Go as far as possible into the absurd.

•

Write about the occult.

•

Write about utterly rejecting your influences and your environment.

•

Write about a town, not here, where you wouldn't mind living.

•

Write about a witch or warlock you know. Use as many street names as possible. Include names of businesses.

•

Write about disorientation. Include twenty words you've never used before. Among them should be at least three verbs.

•

Write a rebuttal to a Laura Riding poem. Structure your piece as a curt dialogue—stichomythia.

•

Write an application letter for a job. Make the letter a covert defense of a literary movement.

(2007)

The Desire to Write

The Desire to Write About *Blue Nude*

Writing, alas, is never nude. Grammar clothes me with adjectives, prepositional phrases, and dependent clauses—a costume I didn't choose, a costume that clashes with my native inclinations, which respect no division between the body's secret holes and that bleak fringe of futurity where Henri Matisse, in *Blue Nude* (1907), might have wished to point, if paintings can point, if paintings can embody a wish to plunge forward.

The Desire to Write About *Young Sailor*

I could exorcise my love for this Matisse painting by writing about the patch of unadulterated blue, a triangle, that represents the receding plane of the sailor's chair. Because this blue patch echoes the blue sky, mimicry modifies our ability to read the chair as a surface; instead, the seat becomes the brightest horizon we'll ever receive an invitation to traverse and to destroy. I don't want to write about the young sailor's crotch; my desire to write about Matisse's colors exceeds my waning wish to describe his evocation, in black and green, of (according to an exhibition catalog) "a young fisherman he had met in Collieure." Trying to pronounce *Collieure*, I pucker: an agreeable astringency.

The Desire to Write About *Woman with a Hat*

Language's impoverishment contradicts the voluptuous blue, green, orange, yellow, and purple that Matisse employs to render a woman whose hat is twice as big as her face. The green beside her head is a detail I seize to avoid being inundated by a bewildering superfluity of colors; I cling to this green as to an island, a hermit's cell, like the rock cleft where Willa Cather's heroine Thea Kronborg, in *The Song of the Lark*, hides. I want to hide in Matisse's combustible, multiform colors—especially the curvy hat's preposterous blue. Am I espousing an aesthetics of the curve and of the swerve? Yes, but I'm also trying to be straightforward. I'd rather paint than write; now, with an unaccustomed sobriety of tone, I'm trying to contemplate why I might want to write about *Woman with a Hat*, and what I might say about *Woman with a Hat* were I to begin the unmanageable project of writing about it.

The Desire to Write About *Boy Leading a Horse*

The desire to write about Picasso's *Boy Leading a Horse* is accompanied by—and nearly drowned by—a contrary desire: the desire *not* to write about *Boy Leading a Horse.* This entropic tendency, the desire *not* to write about *Boy Leading a Horse*, a desire I'm afraid to encourage, itself depends on a desire even more obscure—the desire to *be* the boy leading a horse, or to be that boy's companion, his mirror image, his compatriot in the art of being nude. His feet grip the ground with a firmness equaling the firm black outlines surrounding boy and horse. These outlines, meaty and obtuse, give more satisfaction than any emotion we might attribute to the boy, a troubled cipher; the emphatic outlines, as if carved in wood, speak of the artist's pleasure. I want the pleasure of the line-making hand more than I want the pleasure experienced by the boy leading a horse, or the pleasure of trying to approach that nude boy with these emphatic yet nebulous words.

The Desire to Write About *Boy with Butterfly Net*

"I am an exhibitionist," I said to myself, while walking home from the doctor's office after my yearly physical—an appointment, this year, marked by an episode of unintended tumescence, mine, while my kindly general practitioner, a gay man my age, with hazel-colored wavy hair and hazel-colored eyes, palpated my testicles. In response to my arousal, he said, "You've been blessed," and I'm still not certain, five hours later, exactly what he meant. Any painter is an exhibitionist; so is any model, even if underage. Children are the least remunerated exhibitionists in the history of Western painting; Matisse and his model, Allan Stein (subject of a novel by Matthew Stadler), shared, according to the exhibition catalog, a "mutual affection," though the only aspects of this mutuality that the painting captures are the mutuality of blue and green, the mutuality of red and brown, and the mutuality of realistic portraiture and its thrilling demise.

The Desire to Write About *Self-Portrait*

When I look at Picasso's *Self-Portrait* (1906), or at a reproduction of it, my right index finger wiggles. My fingertip, in air or on my right thigh, traces the outline of Picasso's face—especially the left eyebrow's exaggerated semicircle and the oversized nose, whose comic magnitude makes Pablo seem a simpleton, a vaudevillian clown (Fatty Arbuckle, Buster Keaton, Jackie Gleason) we'd mock and reject. Alternately, the rotund nose, in conjunction with the Oedipally effaced eye, makes Pablo seem like sexy Gérard Depardieu in Bernardo Bertolucci's *1900.* My right index finger, connected to an inner eye that wishes to prove the act of looking to be always covertly haptic, doesn't know how to navigate the faint crosshatchings beneath the gray background. These crosshatchings might be the voice of the raw canvas itself, whose grain outsings the gray oil paint, either because Picasso applied only a thin layer, or because the canvas's élan vital, its honeycomb signature, overpowered his efforts to silence it. I want to write about this self-portrait because of its small size—a mere 10½ × 7¾ inches. Its modest—infantile?—dimensions match the tidy boxiness of a paragraph, the container in which the desire to write compels me to dwell; I enjoy a paragraph's outer edge, that moment when a sentence decides to terminate its journey.

The Desire to Write About *Woman with Bangs*

The desire to write about Picasso's *Woman with Bangs* may echo my desire to lift this depicted woman from her depression. (A painting can't be depressed; this woman is only an effect of blue oil paint applied in 1902.) Because both the background and the woman are shades of complicated blue, the totality of blueness suffusing this scene allows no exit—no chance for a joke, a candy bar, a trip to the Laundromat. My desire to write about the blue woman's gloom (and thereby to reinforce it) is a diseased enterprise; I can't alleviate an imagined woman's desperation by writing complicated sentences, or by presuming that the color blue—when it swamps background and foreground, without distinguishing between woman and wall—is a logical dumping ground for my hothouse empathy. This woman's heavy-lidded eyes imply a roof of bone, a skull I'm eager, when I finish this paragraph, to ignore, so I can pay attention to the yellow-eyed beans boiling on my stove.

The Desire to Write About *Landscape: Broom*

The looseness with which Matisse applied oil paint to his pencil sketch, in *Landscape: Broom* (1906), a miniaturized venture into the louche and the smudged, inspires in me a wish to practice, in my own life, an analogous looseness—whether a looseness of morals (I will allow myself a variety of unsanctioned sexual escapades, and I'll vow not to berate myself afterward) or a looseness of writerly technique, whereby I launch into the sentence's open field without a plan, accompanied only by a wish to intensify my experience of random greens, violets, and pinks. My desire to write about this looseness—Matisse's combination of chromatic opulence and austere omission—is a desire to participate in a practice of attentiveness that doesn't shut down, out of prudence or shyness, when writing begins. Attentiveness intensifies as the sentence progresses; the writing session, whether fifteen minutes or two hours, affords a plein air openness to mental stimulation. I write to multiply occasions for stimulation and to magnify my power to experience pleasure. The pinkish-orange center of Matisse's composition contains white horizontal brushstrokes, which seem to be moving left to right, as if striving to approach a blue semicircle that is itself yearning to approach a tree where small black and green strokes—animals, shrubs, or flowers—huddle. The purples and the oranges (especially the orange tree trunks) stimulate my body (I inhale more deeply, as if gasping); I don't want to brag about my hypersusceptibility to purple and to orange, but I didn't survive the twentieth century to lie to you about my clandestine relationship to color.

The Desire to Write About *Interior with Aubergines*

Writing about Matisse's *Interior with Aubergines* (1911) seems the antithesis of the stupor incarnated by the five-petaled blue flowers that Matisse has plastered (with distemper) over floor and wall equally, in a room whose mood of reverie and escapism is Moroccan by proxy—the patterned, imageless universe of the Alhambra. Does the term *all-over* describe the Abstract Expressionist version of this Alhambran impulse, which, appropriated by Matisse, authorizes stasis and meandering as two sides of one ethereal coin? Matisse's blue flowers, courtesy of Novalis, repeat. Their mandate to erase depth perception in favor of an entranced flatness allows me to become that giddy flatness by writing about it; writing about the proliferating, block-print-like flowers, I side with them. I ingest the flowers, and take on their no-nonsense wish to totalize, to level distinctions, to bliss out. I've lied; depth exists in this painting, but these mini-tableaux of depth are framed vistas that resemble flat panels. By writing about *Interior with Aubergines*, I want to legalize my own blue-flowered interior—my word-cave, the brainy hollow behind my eyes, where jasmine petals in my childhood house's front yard are still unpicked and fragrant. Those flowers, in 1962, weren't jasmine; of unknown genus, they embodied the numberless, the oppressively uncommunicative.

The Desire to Write About *Red Madras Headdress*

Last night, I dreamt that I was scheduled to give a piano recital, whose pièce de résistance would be Franz Schubert's final sonata. In the dream, I hadn't mastered the sonata, and so, with relief, I canceled the recital, even though my brother had already inscribed it in his calendar, a notebook he considered sacred, not subject to the indignity of last-minute cancellations. In my fingers, as I informed my brother of the cancellation, I could feel the melancholy opening theme of the sonata's first movement, a melody I realized I would never play in public; in my fingers, I could feel the injury I was inflicting on my family by canceling a concert that, though negligible, had become our only nourishment. Later in the dream, a large clump of orange-yellow wax fell out of my left ear; the wax was the color of the chair on which the woman in Matisse's *Red Madras Headdress* (1907) sits—a yellow reminiscent of banana, papaya, summer squash, and Sauternes. In the dream, I bragged to everyone about my ear's waxen trophy, this honeyed evidence of auditory prowess. Like Odysseus, I was now prepared to endure the song of the sirens; tied to the dream's mast, I no longer needed a waxen encumbrance to shield me from a lethal melody.

The Desire to Write About *André Derain*

Matisse's 1905 portrait of André Derain attracts me because thick paint slashes form a coercive band around the subject's neck, and because equally thick paint slashes provide Derain with a breastplate. On his chest, green-blue slashes crawl up to the yellow lines above, but remain dwarfed, humbled by yellow. The green-blue lines yearn to be something other than blue; they seem doomed to lose their marine identity in an undifferentiated whiteness, a whiteness that illustrates a desire to be obliterated, a whiteness that confesses a temptation not to announce a theme but merely to indicate the presence of a brush, knife, or fingertip. The fingertip exerts steady pressure, pushing the paint, in channels, runnels, or ruts, into the ready canvas, a canvas that, like the bedroom wall of my childhood tract house, had no personality of its own, but passively received projections. A blue-green line bisects Derain's neck, travels up the beard's periphery onto the mustache, ascends the rim of hair above the brow (half-hidden by red beret), and then soars up to the empyrean unspecificity (Percy Bysshe Shelley would have called it the "intense inane") above Derain's head. Into the creamy, naive blue background, Derain's mustache seems to tumble; a mustache always means a drunken loss of control. The art of painting, for Matisse, in 1905, implied a Faustian exuberance I long to imitate in my body language, as if a satyr-like tendency within my rib cage could emulate Matisse's aggressive brushwork, its taffy-like gusto, its suggestion of pressing, smashing, denting, pushing—the eye thus inciting the hand to take on, by transference, the neediness (or pushiness?) of a painterly facture that paradoxically signifies madness and a decisive intellect. Today at lunch a young poet told me that he had wordless sex recently with a financier—wordless except for one sentence, when the financier said, abruptly, "I'm ready to come." My young poet friend, like me, is a cross between a cocktease and a professional lubricator of interlocutory atmospheres: we specialize in keeping conversations running. His beard and mustache are thick and tangible, like oil paint pressed into grooves. Portraiture, as a genre, alternates between modesty and boastfulness. A portrait is always boasting about its resemblance—or its lack of resemblance—to its subject. A portrait is always modest about its status as merely a portrait—a genre with limits. However, Gertrude Stein, in her word-portraits, was rarely modest; boastfulness is intrinsic to aesthetic innovation. You can't make it new without bragging.

The Desire to Write About *La Rue des Bois*

If I want to insert narrative into a description of Picasso's *La Rue des Bois* (1908), purchased by Gertrude and Leo Stein, I'd need to anthropomorphize. The trees are easy to anthropomorphize; they come in pairs—two sets of bony twins, tall as Franz Liszt or Abe Lincoln, but without virtuosity or eloquence, and substituting for flashiness a puritanical leaflessness. The leaves, when they finally arrive, are few but chunky, almost qualifying as bushes, lampshades, or balloons. My heart, however, is not in the leaves; my heart is in the green, its monochromatic domination of the field. The green's decision to wipe out dissent (to silence the rebuttals of red or blue) reminds me of any decision to stick to one color, one action, one book, one body, one house, one desire; any monotheistic fidelity puts to rest the brain's traffic and simplifies the horizon, even if such radical simplicity (I choose green, and only green), like all abstentions, takes discipline. Two nights ago I dreamt that a literary critic I no longer love was flossing his teeth in my bathroom; this critic (I'll call him Leo Stein), naked from the waist down, was semierect, not because flossing was an aphrodisiac, but because he didn't belong in my bathroom, and intruding on a former rival's property can be a turn-on. If I were to declare an erotic allegiance to any element in Picasso's *La Rue des Bois*, I'd choose the green horizon curve that cuts, like a sickle or a bent bow, across two thin trees; this curve ignores the two trees it cuts, but also nonviolently includes them in its sinuous embrace. If there weren't curves in this proudly vertical painting, with its upright trees, I'd feel abandoned; curves offer me a surge of liberty. In my dream, Leo Stein's penis curved—perhaps because he was only half-hard. His penis, unable to make up its mind, chose to curve instead of aiming its missive at a single addressee. And his undershirt, in the dream, billowed outward, like a maternity shift.

The Desire to Write About *The Acrobats*

I sat in the sex room, a waiting room. I'm often sitting in this underfurnished, underlit room, a space (heated, windowless, cramped) devoted to the religion of the under: undercover, underground, underwear, underarm, under erasure. Into this undemonstrative room, a room without connotations, another man entered. He had, so far, no name; I'll call him Francis Picabia, the artist whose painting, *The Acrobats* (1935), I'm looking at while I write this account. Picabia, whom Gertrude Stein admired and encouraged, walked into the sex room and sat a few feet away from me on a white horizontal platform.

He crossed his legs to conceal his penis, which I had little desire to see. I prefer the area surrounding the genitals—the penumbra of inferences and speculations tripped into motion by the presence (real or imagined) of a penis. With dispassionate scrupulousness, Picabia rubbed his thighs, as if to verify their palpability, or to wipe off scum. Then he uncrossed his legs and put his hands over his crotch, to shield me from a display I might find appalling or disappointing. His modesty wounded me; as retaliation or compensation, I wriggled out of my tight blue uniform, as a clumsy Salome might execute her final dance, and turned to face Picabia, to give him my nudity's veined ultimatum. Picabia, whether to avoid my advance, or to show more of himself, stood up from the white platform and turned around. On his right buttock, a large brown mole, not disfiguring, was uncannily beautiful and individuating, much like (if you'll forgive the sacrilege) the late Elizabeth Taylor's beauty mark, a flaw that highlighted the presence, below, of famous breasts. If my stranger's name weren't temporarily Picabia, I'd say that his buttocks were Rubenesque; in this context, it might be more appropriate to say that his buttocks had the dark gravity—the heft, the humor, the consoling solidity—of Gertrude Stein's body, clothed in eccentric, Buddhist/Maoist garb, in photographs by Cecil Beaton, Man Ray, and others apotheosizers of the surreality that animates a fashionable body. I placed my hands on Picabia's buttocks, to judge their worth—and he moved toward me, until his buttocks were level with my mouth. Paradoxically, by capitulating to my desire, he was punishing me. His buttocks, their cooperativeness, wordlessly aimed invective at me, and I became a nullity, a receptacle for his contempt. Picabia's buttocks smelled of vetiver; when he finally turned around, I noticed that his crotch and its complicated vicinity smelled of lavender mixed with turpentine, the oil painter's companion.

The Desire to Write About *The Green Line*

A green line bisects the face of Matisse's wife, in a painting Henri made in 1905, and so we call the painting *The Green Line*; the line's unreasonable presence overshadows the woman it besmirches. Or does the line have nothing to do with the woman? Should we leave her out of it? Before I felt the desire to write about *The Green Line*, I felt an overwhelming desire to write about a 1922 Man Ray photograph of Alice B. Toklas entering the atelier she shared with Gertrude Stein: Alice hovers in the doorway, maybe entering, or maybe standing frozen, commanded by Man Ray to strike a characteristic pose; I felt a desire to write about Alice's threshold status, her occupation of an ambiguous point between arrival and departure, but I felt a stab of remorse when I realized that Toklas reminded me of a friend whose husband had died a decade ago of heart disease. Though I was not responsible for this man's death, and though I would be doing no damage to his widow by writing about Alice entering the atelier, nonetheless their resemblance chastened me and made the prospect of writing about the Man Ray photograph seem an act of premeditated violence; to write honestly about this photograph, I would need to write about the widow, and to write honestly about the widow, I would need to describe the outline of Toklas's breasts beneath her dress, a smock that modestly veiled her body but allowed the breasts to declare their existence with an unembarrassed directness that corresponded to the steady, large grace of Gertrude Stein seated (in that same photograph) at her desk. Stein's blouse, tucked into her skirt, bunched in the back; this bunched place, a site of pressure and crowding, underlined Stein's physical amplitude, her regal comfort on her writing throne, a seat she occupied in a suspended present she would have called a *continuous* present. Permissive, unbroken, the time of writing (and the time of reading) didn't stop at the gate to pay a subservient toll but stretched into the past and future with a lazy (and secretly splenetic?) unfetteredness. If I were to write honestly about Stein's body and about her writing process, and if I were to write honestly about the visible implication of Toklas's breasts within her floral dress, then I would also need to describe the body of my friend whose husband died a decade ago of heart disease, and I would be trespassing on her body by mentioning it; to write about her body, I'd need to describe my torpor, as if I were drowsing in a Florida room whose jalousies admitted a variegated light, like the operating theater in *Suddenly, Last Summer*, or the ward where Tennessee Williams's sister, Rose, received a lobotomy. Afternoon torpor, redolent of jalousies and lobotomies, overtook me when I considered writing about Toklas entering a room suffused with a fine dust; and so I decided to write instead about Matisse's portrait of his wife, a portrait subtitled *The Green Line*. By defecting from Toklas, and hiding behind *The Green Line*, I felt cowardly—guilty of shirking my vocation's duties and cowering behind abstraction (the green line) as a way to avoid the hard work of describing ambivalence, destructiveness, guilt, and fatigue. The green line attracted me because it permitted a face to say two things at the same time. The green line permitted one half of the subject's face to be burdened (or heightened) by flesh-pink brushstrokes, wedges of conspicuous paint that offered a pressured statement, a demand, an exhibition; the other side of the face, yellow and flat, unenhanced by thick paint or emphatic brushwork, nonetheless borrowed enough green to cloak the eye socket. Thus the face's downtrodden side flourished, albeit in a mephitic, doomed fashion, a dignity composed of too much green. Matisse's abundant green signifies a luxury that, for a writer, can only be approximated by the silence that follows an act of composition: the ordeal of sequential language, word following word, has been surmounted, and now the complicated respite of green, an indescribable green, can begin.

The Desire to Write About *Strolling Player and Child*

Last night I dreamt that my father killed himself, but first he divided his property and explained to me the division. I would receive one portion; my siblings would also receive one portion each. (My father's fortune, in the dream, was divided into "portions," each symbolized by a medicinal lozenge—a cough drop.) My stepmother would receive merely one portion. My mother (my father's ex-wife), however, received three portions, although they'd been divorced for nearly thirty years. I hoped that the news of this inheritance would cheer her up and remind her of my father's noble sentimentality, a trait he shared with Goethe's Werther; perhaps the inheritance—three portions!—would revise her pessimistic narrative of their marriage and its final shattering. I looked forward to using my father's suicide as a ploy to wrest sympathy from my friends, who, in the dream, had grown angry with my unreliability; now they would understand my neurasthenia's paternal origin, and they might forgive my selfishness. The night before I dreamt about my father's suicide, I dreamt that my lover fell off a superhighway's entrance ramp. When I saw him lean over its edge, I restrained myself from criticizing his imprudence; I scold him too frequently. And then he fell over the edge. Looking down, I saw a small figure plummeting faster than I have ever seen any object fall. From a distance, he looked like a minnow or a dandelion. The instant he fell into the water, I forced myself to wake up; my own body felt bruised, a woundedness antithetical to the blue and orange pastels in Picasso's *Strolling Player and Child* (1905). The boy-child's blue costume—like pajamas—is essentially the same blue as the backdrop (wall, sky?); against that background he stands, his shoulders touched, with a companionable or paternal watchfulness, by the tall Pierrot, dressed in an orange whose docility equals the softness of the boy's blue apparel and of the blue atmosphere dispersed behind him. Who exactly are the boy and his clown-protector? They might be brothers, or father and son, or merely coworkers, belonging to a motley troupe, itinerant players granted license in sexual and sartorial actions. By writing about *Strolling Player and Child*, I try to join a guild of orange- and blue-appareled wanderers, writers, artists, loners, fantasizers. I don't understand color theory, but my eye tells me that orange moves forward, and blue moves backward. The boy's blue atmosphere—a domineering shroud—exceeds the puissance of the older player's orange; the boy's blueness proposes that moods and fantasies overtake the categories in which we try to keep them contained. I'm afraid of this writing session ending; without the fountain pen in my hand, and Picasso's blue boy and orange man, in reproduction, in front of me, I'd lack blood and skin. I'm the one ending this paragraph, but I feel as if the paragraph were ending me, choosing me as the victim of its violent wish to terminate anything blue, abundant, and flowering. I often feel like the victim of my own elation; excitement overtakes me when I write (though lethargy, too, tampers with my onward motion), but excitement then becomes my persecutor, a figure holding a whip and urging me to walk forward, even when my body aches. Excitement, my persecutor, gives me the illusion that I inhabit two bodies at once—the small blue body of my raptness and motility, and the large, slender, punitive, orange body of my caretaker, whose calves are muscular from hard labor, whose eyes are narrow and judgmental, and whose hands grip my shoulders with a tightness I earlier called companionable but now I will call coercive. The caretaker's grip is no more coercive than syntax, my blue master, with its adjectival arms, its participial thighs, its orange litanies. Last night I dreamt that I flunked math and couldn't graduate from high school. I argued about my grade with the math teacher, who doubled as art teacher; his face, lightly bearded, seemed irrevocably lodged in the Gay Liberation movement of the early 1970s, as interpreted by Vincent van Gogh and André Derain. The point of writing—of my writing, at least—is to travel forward under the guise of traveling backward.

(2011)

Acknowledgments

I thank my agent, PJ Mark, for his spectacular energy, his intellectual avidity, and his sublimely dapper effectiveness; I thank my virtuoso editor, Sean McDonald, for his structural acumen, his capacious sensibility, and his generous-souled complicity with essayistic wanderings; I thank, too, everyone at FSG, especially Jonathan Galassi, Jeff Seroy, Stephen Weil, and Emily Bell. Seth Stewart kindly helped check last-minute details. Maggie Nelson showed me new vistas. Bruce Hainley kept my imagination alive.

Many writers, editors, curators, and artists prompted me to write the essays in this book; for their encouragement, inspiration, and advice, I wish to thank André Aciman, Hanna Andrews, Jack Bankowsky, Eric Banks, Nicholas Baume, Amy Cappellazzo, John D'Agata, Marion Duvert, Timothy Greenfield-Sanders, Tim Griffin, Kenneth Goldsmith, David Haglund, James L. Harmon, Stephen Hartman, Stuart Horodner, Kurt Kauper, Michelle Kuo, Herbert Leibowitz, Glenn Ligon, Nathan Lump, M Mark, Nancy K. Miller, Shamim M. Momin, Michael Montlack, Molly Peacock, Tim Peterson, Paul Mpagi Sepuya, Ingrid Schaffner, Adam Sheffer, Debra Singer, Matthew Stadler, Guy Walter, David Weiss, Dominic Willsdon, and Patricia Yaeger.

—

I offer grateful tribute to the editors and publishers of the following periodicals and books, in which these essays, sometimes in different versions, first appeared:

American Poet: "Frank O'Hara's Excitement"
Artforum: "My 1980s," "Susan Sontag, Cosmophage," "Schuyler's Colors," "Situation Hacker," "Cindy Sherman and Her Kind"
The Best American Essays 2004 (Houghton Mifflin, 2004), ed. Louis Menand: "My 1980s"
Bookforum: "Roberto Bolaño's Tone," "Hart Crane's Gorgeousness"
Contemporary Erotic Drawing (The Aldrich Contemporary Art Museum, 2005), ed. Stuart Horodner, Sara Kellner, Harry Philbrick: "On Doodles, Drawings, Pathetic Erotic Errands, and Writing"
Getting Emotional (Institute of Contemporary Art, Boston, 2005), ed. Nicholas Baume: "Why Art Is Always Emotional"
Glenn Ligon: Figure (Yvon Lambert, 2008): "Figure"
Guilt and Pleasure: "Heidegger's Mistress"
I'll Be Your Mirror: The Selected Andy Warhol Interviews, 1962–1987 (Carroll & Graf, 2004), ed. Kenneth Goldsmith: "Warhol's Interviews"
Kurt Kauper: Paintings 2001–2007 (Deitch Projects, 2007): "Cary Grant Nude"
McDermott & McGough: Because of Him (Cheim and Read, 2008): "A Woman Alone in Her Room"
Mississippi Review: "John Ashbery's Lazy Susan"
Modern Painters: "Brigitte Bardot Shopping in Shorts"
My Diva: 65 Gay Men on the Women Who Inspire Them (University of Wisconsin Press, 2009), ed. Michael Montlack: "Anna Moffo's Funeral"

"My painting is tomorrow's painting. Watch and see.": Forrest Bess (Christie's, 2012): "The Inner Life of the Palette Knife"

Parnassus: Poetry in Review: "Epitaph on Twenty-Third Street"

Paul Mpagi Sepuya: Studio Work (D.A.P., 2012): "Eric's Stubble"

PEN America: "Dear Sigmund Freud"

PEN America (blog): "Elizabeth Hardwick's Sentences"

PMLA: "A Manual Approach to Mourning"

The Private I: Privacy in a Public World (Graywolf Press, 2001), ed. Molly Peacock: "Privacy in the Films of Lana Turner"

The Proust Project (Farrar, Straus and Giroux, 2004), ed. André Aciman: "I Went by a Devious Route"

Salmagundi: "Play-Doh Fun Factory Poetics"

Seneca Review: "Assignments"

Studies in Gender and Sexuality: "Diane Arbus and Humiliation"

T (*The New York Times Style Magazine)*: "A Brief History of Reinvention"

Take My Advice (Simon and Schuster, 2002), ed. James L. Harmon: "Advice to the Young"

Timothy Greenfield-Sanders: *XXX: 30 Porn Star Portraits* (Bullfinch Press, 2004): "www.MyPornEssay.com"

Truth in Nonfiction: Essays (University of Iowa Press, 2008), ed. David Lazar: "The Rape of Rusty"

"The Desire to Write" was presented at the San Francisco Museum of Modern Art in 2011, and published on the museum's website.

"Fag Limbo" was first published in the Whitney

Museum of American Art's 2004 Biennial Exhibition catalog.
"In Defense of Nuance" was first published as the introduction to the 2010 reissued edition of Roland Barthes's *A Lover's Discourse* (Hill and Wang).
"Notes on Affinity" was first published on the website *La Clé des Langues*, in conjunction with the Villa Gillet, Lyon, France, 2011.
"The Rape of Rusty" was first published as a chapbook by Matthew Stadler for the Back Room, Portland, Oregon, 2006.

PRAISE FOR JODI ELLEN MALPAS

"A brave, cutting-edge romance . . . This is a worthwhile read."
~Library Journal on *The Forbidden*

"Unpredictable and addictive."
~Booklist on *The Forbidden*

"The Forbidden proves that Jodi Ellen Malpas is not only one of the romance genre's most talented authors, but also one of the bravest. In this raw and honest portrayal of forbidden love, Jodi delivers a sexy and passionate love story with characters to root for. The Forbidden is easily my favorite read of 2017!"
~Shelly Bell, author of *At His Mercy*, on *The Forbidden*

"The Forbidden is a gut-wrenching tale full of passion, angst, and heart! Not to be missed!"
~HarlequinJunkie.com on *The Forbidden*

"Every kiss, every sexy scene, every word between this pair owned a piece of my soul. I could read this book a hundred times and still react as if it was the first time. The Protector is a top 2016 fave for me."
~Audrey Carlan, #1 bestselling author
of *The Calendar Girl series* on *The Protector*

"4.5 stars. Top Pick. Readers will love this book from the very beginning! The characters are so real and flawed that fans feel as if they're alongside them. Malpas' writing is also spot-on with emotions."
~RT Book Reviews on *The Protector*

"With This Man took this already epic love story to a whole new, unthinkable height of brilliance."

~Gi's Spot Reviews on *With This Man*

"Super steamy and emotionally intense."

~The Library Journal on *With This Man*

"Jodi Ellen Malpas delivers a new heart-wrenching, addicting read."

~RT Book Reviews on *With This Man*

"We really don't have enough words nor accolades for this book! It had everything and MORE with added ghosts from the past as well as a surprising suspense. But mostly, it was about a love that proves it can conquer anything and everything placed in its way. A beautiful addition to one of our favourite series!"

~TotallyBooked Blog on *With This Man*

The CONTROVERSIAL PRINCESS

ALSO BY JODI ELLEN MALPAS

The This Man Series

This Man

Beneath This Man

This Man Confessed

With This Man

All I Am—Drew's Story (A This Man Novella)

The One Night Series

One Night—Promised

One Night—Denied

One Night—Unveiled

Standalone novels

The Protector

The Forbidden

The CONTROVERSIAL PRINCESS

JODI ELLEN MALPAS

First published in 2018 by Jodi Ellen Malpas Ltd
ISBN 978–0-9967818–2-4

Cover design by:
Hang Le

Edited by:
Marion Archer

Proofread by:
Karen Lawson

Interior Design & Formatting by:
Christine Borgford, Type A Formatting

For my Zoe.

If there is an example of a loyal,
devoted, perfect assistant, then she is it.

Thank you for everything. xxx

1

I STARE AT myself in the large, elaborate mirror while my long, dark hair is tugged and teased into place at the nape of my neck by my personal stylist, Jenny. She ensures I always resemble the enviable, beautiful princess I'm supposed to be. I look like my mother—dark hair, dark eyes, olive skin. My looks are the only thing I inherited from the Spanish princess, who is now the Queen Consort of England. Her doting, dutiful, compliant nature escaped me, much to the disappointment and frustration of King Alfred of England. Her husband. My father.

My old man is a stickler for tradition, values, and rules. Antiquated rules, and frankly, unreasonable rules. The modern age apparently bypasses kings and queens.

My black satin pencil dress is as noncompliant as my nature—tight and backless—my heels as high as my long legs can carry, and my lips painted disgracefully red. My look will certainly raise the bushy eyebrows of the King, and, as usual, I couldn't care less.

I close my eyes, losing the sight of my scandalous self, while Jenny spritzes my loose updo with hairspray. "You could smile, you know," she muses, tweaking the loose strands framing my face. "It

is your birthday, after all."

I open my eyes and pick up where I left off, staring into the dark, empty gaze reflecting back at me in the mirror. I'm thirty years old today. I'm supposed to be married by now to some blue-blooded member of the aristocratic world, someone like Haydon Sampson. The son of David Sampson, the King's lifelong friend and one of his trusty advisors, is my father's choice of husband for me. It's a shame Haydon is not *my* choice. I will not marry him. Ever. "Tell me what I have to smile about."

"Not everyone gets a garden party thrown at the palace in honor of their birthday."

I move my gaze to Jenny. "You think today is all about me?"

Ignoring my question, she picks up my clutch and places a lipstick and a few other makeup items inside. Jenny has been primping and preening me for royal life for as long as I can remember. She knows how I feel about Claringdon Palace, garden parties, and rubbing shoulders with royalty and aristocracy. "Try to have fun."

I look past Jenny when Kim, my private secretary, enters my suite. She looks as formal as ever, her short body encased in a stiff grey trouser suit, her red hair held off her face with a clip secured low on her nape. I disregard her raised brow when she takes in my choice of party wear. "Your car's waiting."

"Thank you." I breathe in some courage to face the afternoon ahead, and accept my clutch from Jenny. "My phone?"

"In the side pocket."

I nod my thanks and wander out of my suite, Kim on my tail. "How long do I have to endure this afternoon?" I ask as we round the huge gallery landing of my home at Kellington Palace, one of many official royal residences in central London. It's elaborate and sparkling, everything a royal palace should be. I take in the walls as I go, portraits of my ancestors filling every available space, all dressed respectfully, all intimidating. One day, I will hang beside them, undoubtedly looking as royal as they do. Except my portrait

will be smoke and mirrors. A lie.

"You mean how long do you have to endure your own birthday party?" Kim asks, amused. "I'd say you're there for the duration."

I grimace. "Wonderful."

"About Friday night," she says.

"What about Friday night?"

"Your little indiscretion with a certain banker."

I smile, remembering the indiscretion well. Gerry Rush, president of Britain's largest bank. He may be mid-forties, but the man is distinguished and delicious. "What about that indiscretion?" I look at Kim as we come to a stop at the top of the grand staircase, not liking the form of her tight, straight lips. "He's married."

"No, he's separated," I say, remembering the article published a few weeks ago in one of the tabloids.

Kim holds out a newspaper, and I look down to see an image of Gerry Rush with a woman on his arm. His wife. "When was that taken?"

"Thursday. Seems they reconciled."

My hand meets my chest, my face dampening from the cold sweat breaking out. "Oh my goodness," I breathe. "The dirty rat. He never said."

Kim is quick to dab my cheeks down with a soft handkerchief, soaking up the beads. "Of course he didn't."

"Does the press know about us?" If they do, then my father does, and that will be a headache of epic proportions that I really could do without. And it would have been even before I knew the lying cheat was making amends with Mrs. Rush.

"Felix took care of it."

I deflate a little, silently thanking the head of communications at Kellington Palace. He won't be happy with me either. No one ever is. "So there was something to take care of?"

"A few pictures."

"How did they get them?"

"They must have followed you from the Royal Opera House." Kim purses her lips. "I mean, really, Adeline. Separate cars going from the same venue to the same hotel?"

"It was his idea."

"And I bet your arm took some severe twisting." She reaches into her bag and pulls something out. "There's this in *Woman*. Far more respectful, don't you think?" Kim presents me with the magazine, where I'm gracing the cover. I take in the picture of me getting out of a car outside the Royal Opera House, being shielded by Damon, my driver and head of security. The headline reads: *"To be blessed with beauty, style, and a royal title. What is it really like to be Princess Adeline? Let us tell you!"* I roll my eyes and flip to the double-page spread, where they detail my life—all inaccurate. Carefree? Exciting? Fulfilled? I snap it shut and hand it to Kim, taking the stairs to the entrance hall. "My gown looked fabulous, so they got that much right."

"I bet it looked fabulous on Gerry Rush's hotel room floor, too."

"Funny," I quip, taking the last step and hitting the mosaic-tiled floor, nodding at Damon, who is waiting by the door. He nods back, his usual sharp acknowledgment. His customary black suit has been replaced with a navy one. "Going somewhere special?" I ask seriously, prompting a discreet smile from his worn-in face.

"Happy birthday, ma'am." His deep, baritone voice does what it always does. Soothes me. Relaxes me. Damon has been my driver and head of personal protection for ten years and is a permanent fixture in my life. It's a good job I'm quite fond of him, otherwise I might resent him and his intrusion on my life.

"Thank you, Damon. How is your lovely wife?"

"Very well. Thank you for asking, ma'am."

"Wonderful to hear. Now, let's get this afternoon out of the way, shall we?"

"It might not be that bad, you know," Kim says as she stuffs the magazine into her bag, and I laugh, because of all people, she

knows. She just knows. I straighten my shoulders and head for the door, looking down to make sure my chest isn't showing . . . too much. Damon pulls the door open and stands back, letting me pass. "Thank you, Damon," I say, coming to a stop at the top of the steps when I see someone blocking my path to the open door of my car.

"Happy Birthday, Addy." Eddie grins at me, a bunch of white roses held under his chin.

"Eddie!" I virtually throw myself at my brother. "You scoundrel. You never said you were coming home."

Catching me on a laugh, he swirls me around on the steps of Kellington Palace. "Don't get too excited." He places me on my feet and gives my dress a mild disapproving look. "I haven't bought you a gift."

"I don't care," I declare, looking at Damon. "Did you know?" My driver shrugs, his hand still resting on the door handle. I turn to Kim. "Did you?"

"He might have called last week." She starts tapping at the screen of her mobile, leaving me to get back to my beloved Eddie, the youngest of my two elder brothers. My savior. The only one who understands me. He's adorned in his military uniform, his green beret sitting perfectly on his gorgeous head. Part of me envies him serving our country, a daft notion, I realize, but at least he gets to escape this circus for nine months at a time when he's on tour.

"So let's party," Eddie quips, throwing his bag and my flowers by the door. Olive, a member of our household staff, swoops them up before they've barely come to rest.

"At the palace?" I grumble, utterly unimpressed by his enthusiasm.

"Drink plenty of champagne and smile. I'm here. It's bound to be more fun." His hazel eyes gleam mischievously, and that *will* be his present to me. Some fun.

My birthday just improved tremendously. I can always count on Eddie. I watch as Kim, who I share with Eddie when he's home,

as well as Kellington Palace and all other staff members, rolls her eyes in mild dread. I grin. She'll be jumping straight on the phone to Felix as soon as we're in the car. Poor Felix is kept busy enough when I'm home alone. With Eddie back, he'll be run off his Italian loafers trying to keep our royal reputations perfect.

"We had better be going before the King sends his minions to track us down." I link arms with Eddie and walk to the pristine Mercedes.

"I believe Davenport has already called, ma'am," Damon says as he holds the door open for us.

"Now there's a surprise," Eddie breathes, giving Damon a friendly smack of his suited shoulder. "Is that stick still stuck up his arse?"

I laugh. Major Davenport, the King's private secretary, is old school, just like the King. I'm a thorn in his side, Eddie more of an itch, whereas our elder brother, Prince John, is the saint of the King's three offspring. The arse-licker. The Heir Apparent, and the perfect prince with it.

"I believe it is, sir," Damon replies dryly as we both get into the car. I smile my thanks as he shuts the door. I might hate my royal existence, but I love my staff. Unlike my father's entourage of personal aides, advisors, and servants, mine aren't stuffy, old-fashioned, uptight, pompous windbags. It's a mild relief in my suppressed world, especially given my apparent flaws. I smile and cuddle into my brother's side, so relieved he's home to lift my spirits.

Happy birthday to me.

2

AS WE APPROACH the gates of Claringdon Palace, the street is awash with crowds of the British public and the Metropolitan Police lining the railings that hold them back. Camera flashes are constant, the press out in force. Damon slows the car to a crawl, and I hear the chants of my name, calls of birthday wishes.

"They love you," Eddie says softly, like a reminder that at least someone in this world admires me, because my family—present company excluded—certainly doesn't.

"They love you equally," I reply, smiling across the car at him. But while the youngest of my brothers has the public's affection like me, he has our family's fondness, too. Unlike me. He has a purpose in the military, is making use of himself. "Stop the car, Damon."

"Ma'am?" His eyes jump to the mirror, unsure.

"Stop the car," I repeat. "I'd like to have a walkabout."

"But it's not scheduled, ma'am."

I just about refrain from rolling my eyes. "It's my birthday. All these people are here hoping to catch a glimpse, and I don't want to disappoint them."

Eddie remains quiet, knowing I'm going to do what I'm going

the Marines, I have had no such distraction from trouble.

"And the birthday girl." The King moves in on me, his suited body decorated with a sash displaying his many medals of honor.

"Father," I breathe, ignoring his less-than discreet disapproving look at my attire. I bow a little before he embraces me in a hug. "You are late," he says quietly in my ear. "And what of this nonsense walkabout?"

I peek across the room, seeing Sir Don, the King's chief advisor and Lord Chamberlain. He takes his job very seriously, informing the King of . . . everything. "News sure does travel fast around here," I say under my breath, noticing Sir Don watching me with predictable disapproval in his eyes. "Maybe, Your Majesty, an impromptu walkabout from yourself every now and then might go down well with the public."

"Do not test me today, Adeline."

I brush off the King's scorn and paint on my smile, ready to face the guests invited to celebrate my thirtieth. It's all rather marvelous, but I've been here for twenty minutes and still haven't had even a whiff of champagne.

We're all assembled around my father and mother, in the usual, neat fashion, just inside the opposing French doors that lead to the topiary-filled gardens, where fountains trickle peaceful water at every turn, and the lawns look artfully painted, not a blade of grass out of place. The whole palace is perfect, just like the Royal Family.

Breathing in, I widen my smile and straighten my shoulders as the doors are opened and the crowds, many of whom I will not know, all clap and smile in greeting. Father and Mother both roll their wrists, slowly waving, as we stand at the entrance, a united front, letting everyone here receive the honor of marveling at us for a few minutes.

At the first sign of movement from my father, I break away and swipe a glass of champagne from the closest tray. "Fed up already?" Eddie asks, pulling his green beret off and smoothing down his dark

blond hair. I'm the only one of the three of us who inherited our mother's Spanish looks. John took Father's fair hair and blue eyes, and Eddie fell somewhere between the King and Queen Consort, his hair dark blond, his eyes hazel.

"It is a farce, really, is it not?" I sip my champagne as I watch our family break off in various directions, being accosted by guests, who are all simply *dying* to shower the royals with compliments and praise. I laugh to myself. They're all monarchists, the best of the best when it comes to licking royal arse. There won't be any anti-royalists here. Oh no. We keep those bastards well away. Though I'm secretly smug that they are not so anti-royal when it comes to me.

I point my champagne across the lawn, where my gay uncle is showing a united front with his wife while chatting to guests. "The King's brother is as gay as the day is long," I muse to Eddie. "His marriage is fake and loveless." Moving my pointed glass to Aunt Victoria and Uncle Phillip, who are laughing and smiling, I rest my weight on my hip. "Aunt Victoria and Uncle Phillip, the wonderful Duke and Duchess of Sussex, can hardly bear to even look at each other, let alone talk. And then there is our wonderful brother, the perfect Prince John and his perfect wife, Princess Helen, who have all the ingredients of being the perfect successors to Father and Mother, except for one thing."

"What's that?" Eddie asks, truly interested.

"They have been married for eight years and still no heir."

Eddie laughs. "Do you think our perfect brother is shooting blanks?"

"Not so perfect," I muse, motioning a footman over and swapping my empty glass for a full one.

"Impossible. Like every other royal couple, they had fertility tests before they married. Maybe they're just not compatible."

"What's not compatible?" Matilda joins us, and the three of us, the most normal three of the entire family, stand and sip champagne.

"John and Helen," I say over the rim of my glass. "The heir has

not yet got *himself* an heir."

"Adeline thinks he's shooting blanks," Eddie adds as he looks across to our brother, who's looking super official in a mess jacket, trousers, cummerbund, and black bow tie.

"Adeline is wrong," Matilda counters, pulling both Eddie's and my attention her way. She grins. "I heard Mummy talking with the King. Seems you will have a niece or nephew very soon."

"She's pregnant?" I ask, my champagne flute lowering from my mouth. Matilda nods. "Nice of them to share the news. When were they planning on telling us?" Just as I say those very words, my father calls for the attention of everyone in the garden, and I know it's not to wish me a happy birthday.

"Now?" Eddie quips, grinning at me.

"First *you* steal all the attention, and now this?" I scowl playfully as Eddie wraps an arm around my shoulders and kisses my temple. "When can we have some real fun?"

"Patience, little princess," he soothes me. "Duty first."

We listen as the King makes an award-worthy speech, expressing his gratitude for such a wonderful family to support him in his reign as King of England, the same old mumbo-jumbo, before he delivers the exciting news of a new addition to the Monarchy. John's wife circles her stomach with her palm, smiling at my brother. She is power-hungry, always has been. This will thrill her, being impregnated with what will be the second in line to the throne, meaning Eddie and I have slipped down the line of succession. Well, damn.

"That throne is getting further from your reach, brother dearest," I whisper in Eddie's ear, making Matilda laugh hysterically, followed quickly by my brother. "What?" I ask innocently, pouting. "You don't want to be king some day?"

"About as much as you want to be queen." He chuckles to himself and puts his green beret back on as he wanders across the lawn to join our mother.

"You two are terrible." Matilda knocks my shoulder with hers as

someone catches my eye. Someone I actually *do* recognize, though what he's doing here is a mystery. "Is that Josh Jameson?" I ask Matilda, nodding discreetly through the crowds.

"You mean the actor? The hot American actor?" Her neck cranes to see, and then there is a small gasp from my cousin. "Oh, golly, yes. What is he doing here?"

"I have not the faintest idea," I say quietly, taking a few small steps to the right to get a better view. I breathe in controlled, but exhale a little shakily. By gosh, he's even more striking in the flesh. One is a little speechless. Twinkly blue eyes that harbor mischief and pure sex, permanently roughed-up brown hair, and scruff to match. He's perfectly rugged and dangerously handsome. Josh Jameson. I sigh, smiling to myself, enjoying my new delightful view. He was recently voted the World's Sexiest Man Alive and has an Oscar under his belt to boot. He is the perfect male specimen, every woman's fantasy. A Hollywood poster boy. A bloody *god*. But to me, he is prohibited. The World's Sexist Man Alive is off limits. Typical. I pout to myself as I continue to admire his fine form, silently damning my royal bones to hell and back. But then he looks in my direction and our eyes meet. I quickly turn away from him, a little taken aback by the blaze in his stare. *What is he doing here?*

"It's the London premiere of his new movie soon," Matilda muses, popping a canapé in her mouth. "I read it in a magazine."

"But why is he here? At my birthday party?"

She ignores my question, her eyes widening somewhat. "Oh, gosh. Adeline, he's coming over."

"He is?" I feel my body straighten out, all the stressed muscles unkinking. "Why ever would he do that?" Josh Jameson's face and body is splashed on millions of billboards and magazines across the world, his playboy reputation renowned, and now he is here? In the flesh? In a suit, looking all handsome and ruggedly distinguished? At my birthday garden party?

A slow, lazy smile stretches my red lips through my increasing

fluster. Josh Jameson.

My, oh my.

"Your Highness." The rough American accent takes my simmering blood and directs it to my epicenter. And I don't mean my heart, though it is certainly thrumming. The thrill is electrifying. *Your Highness.* Never before have those words turned me on. I always feel the inclination to shove them back down the throat of whoever has spoken them to me. Not today. I turn slowly and cock my head in question, suggesting he should prompt me on his name. Of course, I know exactly who he is, yet a deep desire in me does not want to let on that I am privy to his identity.

"Josh Jameson." He smiles, all bright and dazzling, with a hint of cheek, but it is one hundred percent knowing. Who doesn't know who this man is?

I don't try to conceal my demure grin. "What a pleasure, Mr. Jameson. Please, there is no need for formalities. You may call me Adeline." I'm lying. There is *every* need for formalities, as expressed in Matilda's shocked look when I catch her eye. But the truth is, I want to hear him say my name. Softly. In that gorgeous, rough American drawl.

"Adeline," he muses delicately, taking my charging blood to boiling point. I am far from disappointed. On the love of the King, holy *bloody* hell. "Happy birthday."

I inhale deeply, allowing my eyes the pleasure of journeying his long, svelte body to his feet. His three-piece screams bespoke, and his shoes are without doubt handmade. But he looks effortlessly well turned out, the pale pink hanky poking out of his breast pocket not neatly folded, but more stuffed inside as if it could have been a last-minute addition to his attire. He does perfectly roughed-up so well, a mix of neat in his clothes and messy on his face. Goodness, he is edible.

A nudge in my elbow knocks me out of my silent admiring, and I turn to find Matilda staring at me with too many questions in her

eyes. I quickly gather myself and shoot my gaze up, immediately finding Josh Jameson regarding me closely, no doubt relishing the scrutiny he's under. Clearing my throat, I raise my glass to my cousin. "Mr. Jameson, this is Her Royal Highness the Duchess of Kent."

"Pleasure, Mr. Jameson," Matilda purrs. "You may call me Matilda." Her sarcasm has me peeking out the corner of my eye to her.

"The pleasure is all mine." Josh smiles, another knowing smile. It is almost too much.

"So how did you come to be at my birthday celebrations?" I ask flippantly, trying not to express too much interest.

"My father met the King during his time in the military many years ago."

"But you are American."

"No shit," he retorts quickly, reining in a cheeky smile. I'm both outraged and in awe. "You Brits and us Yanks are allies, ma'am."

"I know that." I roll my eyes dramatically, buzzing with something wild and electric. He cursed at me. It's unheard of to use such vulgar language in the presence of a royal.

"My father is now a senator." He points across to the King, who is talking to a rather round man in a black tux. "He was in town, and the King thought we might like to join him and his wonderful family today."

"How lovely," I muse. "So you are gatecrashing, for a lack of a better term?"

"Well"—he shrugs—"no man in his right mind would turn down the opportunity to meet the beautiful and illustrious Princess Adeline of England. And I must say, Your Highness, your pictures do you no justice."

I force my eyes not to widen, gathering myself. "Touché." My murmured reply is loaded with lust and suggestion. I toast the air, smiling around my pout. "I hope you are having a splendid time."

"Oh, I am. And you?"

"Things are looking up." I take a measured sip of my champagne, mesmerized by the sparkle in Josh's blue eyes.

On a smile, he looks around the grounds. "I've often thought how alike we are."

"Oh? How so?"

"You seem very passionate."

"I do?"

"Yes." His smile is now suggestive. "As am I."

"Interesting."

"And you seem to know what you want."

"Indeed."

"I like to have fun."

"As do I, Mr. Jameson. As . . . do . . . I."

"So we're a match made in heaven."

I laugh lightly, feeling Matilda's despair as she endures this outrageous flirting match. I plan on winning. "In your dreams, Mr. Jameson."

"Or maybe, Your Highness, in yours." Josh flashes another one of those dashing smiles, and I'm ashamed to admit it, but I am struggling to maintain my composure. So I do what is best and free myself from the suffocating intensity of Mr. Jameson's presence before I make a fool of myself and start dribbling. "Excuse me." Putting one foot in front of the other is far more difficult than it should be. "Delightful to meet you, Mr. Jameson." I silently scorn myself for such a poor choice of word as I walk away. Delightful?

"Wasn't it just?" he muses, his body turning as I pass him. A quick glimpse back has our eyes meeting again, his face almost cocky.

Bugger it. I curse myself all the way over to my mother.

"Are you flustered, Adeline?" Matilda asks, giving me another nudge in my side as she flanks me.

I sniff and straighten my posture. "Whatever are you talking about?"

My pathetic question has her chuckling discreetly. "I never

thought I'd see the day."

"You haven't." I smile brightly when Mother opens her arms to me.

"Adeline, darling, how are you enjoying your celebrations?" Her Spanish accent is nearly lost completely now, masked by the plums that have been forced into her mouth since she agreed to marry my father. Something that hasn't been completely masked is her love of my flair and vitality. She *should* love it, since I inherited it from her, but naturally, she can't openly approve. Although I can see from her small smile that she secretly likes my choice of dress for today's event.

"Wonderful, Mother." I tap each of my cheeks with hers and glance over my shoulder. Josh Jameson catches my eye again and winks. He bloody winks at me. The nerve. Who winks at a member of the Royal Family? I raise my nose and turn away from him, outraged again by his behavior. And hot. So very hot. "A new baby. So wonderful." I collar John and Helen from a nearby group, apologizing for stealing them. "Congratulations." I hug them both like I really mean it, because I do. They're not my favorite people in the world, all holier-than-thou and respectfully proper, but more attention on them in the future means less on me. Hopefully.

Helen, with her perfect lipsticked lips, smiles a fake smile, ever cold and disapproving. "Sorry for stealing the limelight on your birthday."

"No, you are not." I laugh, waving off her apology. Neither John nor Helen pretend to be offended, and instead allow themselves to be pulled away by more guests, without so much as a happy birthday to me.

"This is torture in its best form," I say to Matilda, resting my weight on one hip and sipping my champagne with a lack of anything else to do, while Prince John and Princess Helen lap up the fervent attention and congratulations. Not that I'm slighted by the lack of well-wishes coming my way, more irritated that, as

traditional in this godforsaken family, the future of the Monarchy takes precedence over *everything*.

I sigh and look down at my empty crystal flute, but the glass in my light hold is removed and replaced with a full one before I can see to it myself. I lift my gaze and find Josh Jameson standing before me.

"Miss me?" I ask cheekily, raising my glass to him, playing it cool.

"Maybe, Your Highness."

"Please, not so formal."

"It doesn't seem right to address you so personally, since you're third in line to the British throne."

I laugh softly, and something in his blue eyes changes. There's a hint of amber washing over the aqua, making them appear greener. I watch as Matilda wanders away to join her parents, a definite subtle shake of her head as she goes. It is a shake to suggest she is aware that I'm in a rebellious mood, and she wants no part of it. I'm always in a rebellious mood. Now that mood is being fueled by this dishy American man and the constant rush of pleasure he encourages. Josh Jameson is not a suitable man for me to date, to see, to screw, to even kiss. Which makes me want to do all those things all the more. Temptation to defy the rules is almost too much to resist.

He's staring at me, his striking face perfect. Here before me stands a man who has made my blood hot just by looking at me. I have to glance away for a moment and blink. "Don't let my position in the line of succession intimidate you," I say, braving returning my eyes to his. I bring my flute of champagne to my mouth as I maintain our stares over the rim. I sip. I swallow. Slowly.

"Intimidate me?" he questions, interested.

"Yes."

"Why would I feel intimidated?"

"Well." I laugh, as if he needs to ask. "My eldest brother is the Heir Apparent. My other brother, Eddie, is a backup heir to the Heir Apparent. I am a backup for the backup, but neither Eddie nor I will

be required. The heir's wife is pregnant, therefore with every baby born to my siblings, I fall further down the line of succession." *Or fall further from grace*, I add to myself. Both apply. "I am really not as important as they would have everyone believe."

"I'm not intimidated," Mr. Jameson says quite frankly. "Not at all."

His words surprise me, though I maintain my composure. Just. Never has a man had the audacity to say such things to me. Most men tiptoe around my royal status, eager to please. And never has a man had my blood pulse with excitement. I've had lovers, many in fact. But this man? He's igniting something in me far too easily. I'm almost tempted to move away from the challenge. *But where's the fun in that?* "I am a challenge for you," I say, just as frankly. If he can be upfront, I don't see why I cannot be, also.

He smiles, accepting a glass of champagne for himself when one of the footmen offers the tray. Mr. Jameson waits for us to be alone before he levels me with a serious expression. "Don't pretend I would represent anything more than a challenge to you, Your Highness."

Those words flick thrillingly up my spine again, forcing me to readjust my stance. "I don't believe I did, Mr. Jameson."

His head cocks. "Interesting."

Mine mirrors his. "Indeed."

And together we smile, now both of us knowingly. This is all rather disgraceful, but this is the most fun I've had in a very long time.

"So like I said," he goes on, "we're uncannily alike. But you're way out of my league, Your Highness."

I wish he would stop addressing me so formally. It's distracting me from keeping my stone front in place. "Says who?"

"Everyone, I expect." He flashes me a challenging expression. He definitely shouldn't look at me like that. He's goading me, and I rarely need much provoking, least of all from such a divine, handsome creature such as him. "But I've never been one to play

by the rules," he adds quietly.

"Me either."

He grins down at me. "Off with my head."

"Which head?" I ask around my own smile, thoroughly enjoying our light banter.

His grin transforms into a genuine smile, and it is out of this world. Although I'm certain he's hiding a little shock at my brashness. Shocked is good. "So it's true what they say?" he asks, his expression taking on an edge of intrigue.

"What do they say?" I gaze around the grounds casually, spotting my father looking over, his tall, embellished body making him look like the sovereign he truly is. I smile and raise my glass to him, and he does the same, though considerably less smiley, and his observant gaze is passing between Josh Jameson and me. My father is looking at Mr. Jameson like he looks at all men who may be showing interest in the princess. With disapproval, and like he is mentally plotting their disappearance from my life.

"Rumor has it that Adeline Lockhart is the unruliest royal that's ever lived," Josh says, winning back my attention. "And after spending just a few minutes with you, I know the rumors are true."

"You have absolutely no idea." My tongue slips into my cheek of its own accord while he mulls over my suggestion. "I have two vices, Mr. Jameson."

"And what are they?" he asks. "No, wait. I think I know one of them." Staring deeply into my eyes, he studies me, his lips puckering in a cute pout. "One *must* be hot American men."

"Quite," I reply honestly and quickly, pulling a satisfied smirk from him. "So how is Hollywood?"

"Oh, so you do know who I am?" he asks, his smile turning cocky. "My, my, Your Highness. If you're going to feign ignorance, you need to at least keep up the act."

I could kick myself, but instead I roll my eyes. "Well?"

"Tiring," he answers candidly. My imagination spins into

overdrive. Tiring. I bet. I've seen the endless women draped off his finely tuned body.

"Because of all the women throwing themselves at your feet?"

"Jealous?"

I sigh. "No, more sympathetic."

"Why would that be?"

"Well, you are clearly unviable for most women, with your fame, inflated ego, and good looks."

"Am I unviable for you?"

I just manage to withhold my surprise at his continued straightforwardness. "I'm quite sure the King would not approve."

"But since I'm not one for following rules, and you, Your Highness, seem less than compliant, perhaps I could tempt you to join me for dinner while I'm in London."

Dinner? I want something, and it isn't dinner. "You want to have dinner with me? Why?"

"I think you and I will get along."

"You think?"

"I *know*."

I stall for far too long, increasingly mesmerized by the conceited rogue. "It's very kind of you to offer, but I'm afraid I must decline." I dig my feet in. I'm being stubborn, playing the game. Making him chase.

"Why?"

"Well, you see, Mr. Jameson, my private secretary keeps my diary. That diary is presented to the King on a weekly basis so he is kept abreast of my royal engagements and everything else I may or may *not* be doing. If I somehow manage to hide the entry in my diary that will enlighten him of my dinner plans with a renowned Hollywood actor, the journalists who shadow me will ensure he knows. And the rest of the world, for that matter."

His eyebrow cocks, interested. "Would it be such a bad thing if we were seen together?"

"It would be a frightfully terrible thing, Mr. Jameson. The Princess of England cannot be seen to be cavorting with a Hollywood sex symbol."

"Who said anything about cavorting?"

"I notice you have not challenged my portrayal of you."

"Why would I? You are one hundred percent right, and even if you weren't, I'm not likely to tell a member of the Royal Family they're wrong."

"Why me?" I ask, cutting off all the other games and getting to the point.

"Maybe I want to violate a princess."

I laugh, probably a little too loudly. "I assure you, Mr. Jameson, I need no violating."

"Oh, I have no doubt." His hand meets the curve of my arse over my dress, and I go tense, scanning our surroundings for watchful eyes. "But you've never been violated by me. So, what do you say, Your Highness?"

His confidence does things to me that have never been done before. By *any* man. "Are you trying to get me into trouble, Mr. Jameson?" I need no help there. Just ask my private secretary and the head of communications at Kellington Palace. Actually, don't ask. It's best not to know.

Pulling his touch from my backside, he takes my hand and kisses the back through a smile. "Most definitely."

I don't know why I pout, like I could be pondering whether or not to dance to his tune. I'm going to let this man violate me, and I'm going to love every second of it. A glimpse of a picture of Josh Jameson could make my thighs tighten. Being in his presence, hearing his smooth accent, feeling him caress my bottom like it's something to be worshipped, has me burning where I stand. *I'm a princess*, I mentally tell myself. Why I now feel the need to remind myself of that little matter, I haven't the faintest idea. It is never usually an issue. But while Josh Jameson is Hollywood royalty and

most women on earth would jump him at the first flash of his disarming smile, I am *actual* royalty. I am a royal princess and jumping a man in public would be highly frowned upon, and will definitely land me in hot water with the King. But what I do in private, away from these self-important idiots, is my own business. "I have a terrible habit of getting myself into trouble," I tell him candidly.

"Want to get into trouble with me?" He steps back and lightly rests his hands in his pockets, waiting for my answer, smiling an adorable, irresistible smile as he does.

"That's an offer one could never refuse." I smile, too. I can only hope that it's as enticing as his. *Well, happy birthday to me.* "What did you have in mind?"

"I have a gift for you."

"You? Naked? With a bow covering . . ." I drop my eyes to his groin, chewing the inside of my lip. "Actually, no bow."

He laughs, rich and deep. "You are like nothing I've ever encountered before, Your Highness."

"Neither are you," I admit, tingles licking up my spine.

"Is there anywhere private around the palace?" he asks, gazing around the grounds. "So I can give you my gift."

"There is a maze of conifer trees at the most southern point of the grounds." I look away, smiling at the many people smiling at me. "Meet me there in half an hour."

His grin is wicked, and I just know his body and talents will be, too. Having a quick scan around us, he moves in toward me and slaps my arse. I jolt, despite it being a light rap. "Just warming up my palm," he whispers in my ear. He's lucky no security personnel are directly behind him. Said palm would be cuffed quite quickly. My body rolls deliciously, my insides furling. But I'm struggling to identify whether it's with anticipation or nerves. It's anticipation. It has to be. I don't get nervous around men.

"Look forward to it," I reply, strong and even.

"Me, too." Jameson looks past me when someone catches his

attention. "I'm wanted."

"Don't waste too much energy on talking now, will you?"

He laughs a little, landing me with eyes full of intentions that stimulate me. Half an hour might be too long to wait. "My energy levels won't be an issue, Your Highness. But your tolerance levels may well be." A cheeky wink is flipped, and my mouth drops open, astounded, but I'm mostly bubbling with exhilaration. My teeth nibble the edge of my glass as he saunters off across the lawn.

"You are a frightful flirt, Adeline Lockhart," Matilda says, joining me, her eyes stuck on the exact same thing mine are: Josh Jameson's delightful backside.

I tilt my head, thoughtful. I plan on digging my fingernails into that arse very soon. "I'm having fun at my birthday party." I turn toward her and raise my glass. "Happy birthday to me." I sip, very ladylike, but my mind is currently bloody filthy, and my lacy knickers are drenched with desire.

"The King will skin you alive."

"If he finds out. Which he will not." I cast my eyes across the lawn, nearly yawning when I spot someone heading toward us. "Oh, bugger, here comes Haydon."

"I don't know why you refuse to date him, Adeline," Matilda says, painting on a smile to match mine. "He's handsome, with very good prospects, and most importantly, your father approves."

"My father's approval in men is not something I seek, Matilda. Haydon Sampson is not for me."

"No man is for you."

"Oh, I don't know about that." I catch Mr. Jameson's eye and raise my glass on a reserved smile.

"Adeline," Matilda gasps, and my smile widens. "He most certainly is not for you. The backlash would be catastrophic."

Catastrophic? I was thinking orgasmic. "Oh, stop being such a bore." She's supposed to be in my corner. "Haydon," I chime, seeming thrilled to see him. If only Matilda really understood my

plight, she would not see the man in front of me as a suitable match.

He takes my hand and gives it a customary kiss, bowing as he does, before moving in for a kiss on my cheek. "You look absolutely sublime, Adeline."

I force my sigh back. I wasn't going for sublime. I was going for sultry. And one man here certainly saw that. Haydon is sweet, terribly sweet, but he does not make my heart flutter. We have known each other for so long, since children, and I was there for him when his mother sadly passed a few years ago. But as a friend. Just a friend. "You're too kind."

"Happy birthday, my darling." His term of endearment grates on me somewhat. I hate the way he talks to me like we've been married for years, like I belong to him. The King may say so, as well as Haydon's father.

I, however, do not.

"Thank you." I act as graciously as I can muster, which is so very hard. This poor man refuses to give up hope, the backing and encouragement of our fathers keeping him annoyingly optimistic.

"Here, let me hold your purse." Haydon takes it from my grasp before I can protest. "Can I get you anything? A drink? Something to eat?"

"I'm fine, Haydon." I strain another smile, once again catching the eye of Josh Jameson, who is looking over with interest as Haydon fusses over me. Josh extends his arm and looks down at the watch decorating his wrist, and then back up at me as he taps the face.

I breathe in, being attacked by tingles of the most wonderful kind, cocking my head in silent acknowledgment. He then starts clenching and unclenching his fist, smiling a devilish smile. Good Lord, the man is sex on legs. I clear my throat and return my attention to Haydon, ready to thank him for coming, but I'm stopped in my tracks by a small, leather box held out to me in the center of his palm. Unconsciously, I step back, wary. The box is small. Like engagement ring size small, and though it might sound preposterous,

given that I haven't even kissed him *or* agreed to go on a date with him, I would not put a proposal past Haydon. I bet my father put him up to this. After all, I'm thirty today. My eligibility lessens with every year that passes and each year I refuse to play royal ball.

"I hope you love it," Haydon says, hopeful and smiley. I feel so sorry for him. He has been hanging on forever for me to finally see supposed sense. To me, the King and Haydon's father are plain cruel, making him endure rejection for all these years. He is a wonderful man, he really is, and there are queues of women out there who would eagerly seize a ring from him and prance down the aisle to declare their undying love before God. But I am not one of them. I wasn't when I was sixteen, and I'm even less so now. And deep down, I know Haydon knows that. I've told him in the nicest possible way on a few occasions over the years, have even tried to encourage him to date the women who have shown an interest. He's too blindsided.

"Haydon, I—"

"It's not what you think it is." He cuts me off quickly but shyly. "Though . . . one day . . ."

I smile and graciously accept the box, despite my instincts telling me not to build up his hopes. I am aware that our fathers are watching. I don't want to cause a scene, or embarrass him. Opening it up, I am confronted with an antique ring. I look at him, confused.

"It's a friendship ring. One I hope will eventually be replaced with a ring that represents my love."

I shrink, feeling the walls of suppression closing me in from all directions. Forcing myself not to scowl at Matilda when she sighs dreamily drains what remaining energy I have left, leaving me with no fight to stop Haydon from removing the ring from the box and sliding it onto the middle finger of my left hand. I can barely look at the ring without showing my displeasure, and Haydon does not deserve that kind of disrespect. Oh, Haydon. He hears me, but he doesn't listen to me. Other voices are louder than mine. I take a

moment to find the poise expected of me and raise my eyes toward the many people watching. And, of course, my father's face is awash with satisfaction. I could happily slap it off. "It really is beautiful," I murmur, searching out a footman for more champagne. "Thank you, Haydon."

"Always welcome." He snaps the box shut and slips it into his jacket pocket as I reach for another flute of my savior. It has never escaped my notice that my father's footmen are always lingering close by with the goods to save them the constant back and forth delivery of my medicine of choice.

"And now time for His Majesty to make a fuss of you," Haydon says, making my glass pause midway to my red lips. Make a fuss of me? Or berate me? I look across to the King, seeing Major Davenport talking closely in my father's ear. The King nods sharply, and then focuses his full attention on me, motioning for me to go to him, which, of course, I do. Because he is the King.

"Happy birthday, Adeline," my father says sincerely, swooping his arm out toward the path that leads to the front courtyard.

I gasp, my palm meeting the black satin that's half concealing my chest. "Father?" I question, watching as Sabina, the royal stable manager, walks a black stallion through the crowds of people.

"He's a champion," Father declares proudly, guiding me to the beautiful beast. "He comes from one of the most dominant sire lines in thoroughbred history."

"He's beautiful." I run my palm down the glossy coat of his neck as he stands, still and obedient. "And he's mine?"

"All yours, my darling girl."

To say I am overwhelmed would be the biggest understatement in royal history. I've always kept horses; they're my only true passion, but the King has always deemed it inappropriate for me to dabble in the world of racing. And this is a racehorse. What on earth has changed? "And I can race him?" I ask tentatively.

"When he's ready, you can race him. He will need vigorous

training to get him to champion level." The King gives my birthday present a solid smack on his neck. "We'll have your racing colors officiated as soon as you decide what they should be."

"I don't know what to say." This is a monumental gesture by my father. "What is he called?"

"Spearmint, after his great, great, great, *great* grandfather."

I scan the stallion, estimating him to stand maybe sixteen hands high, and he has a white sock on his right foreleg. "Hello, Spearmint." I stroke his nose, and he snorts and shakes his head. The crowd bursts into rapturous laughter, applauding Spearmint's hello to me. I smile, overcome with happiness.

"Let us get him back to the stables," my father says, as Sabina, who also happens to be Haydon's grandmother, smiles at me. She's a wonderful woman, her passion for horses equal to mine. She has taken care of the royal horses for years. "Look after him," I tell her pointlessly. Of course she will. "I'll come by soon to see him."

"Enjoy the rest of your birthday, Your Highness," Sabina orders softly, taking Spearmint's reins. She kisses my cheek sweetly and leads my new horse away, his hooves clicking the granite pathway as he goes. I watch until I can no longer see his well-groomed tail swishing as he rounds the corner, back to the front courtyard.

"You lucky thing," Uncle Stephen says as he joins me. "A thoroughbred gifted by the King is not to be sniffed at."

"I know." I turn into my uncle, who prefers to devote most of his time to painting rather than the equestrian side of royal life.

"I see something else that is not to be sniffed at." Stephen flicks his head past me, and I look over my shoulder to find Josh Jameson studying me so very closely. He taps the face of his watch again, reminding me that I have an unofficial engagement I am now late for.

I blink and sink my teeth into my bottom lip as I return my attention to Uncle Stephen. "Do you know who he is?" I ask as nonchalantly as I can.

"Who doesn't?" He brings his face close to mine, a wicked

twinkle in his eyes behind his spectacles. "If you can't behave, be disgraceful," he whispers.

My small gasp is fake, and Uncle Stephan knows it. "I really don't know what you are talking about."

"Dear niece, remember who you are trying to fool." He kisses my cheek. "If you will not be disgraceful with him, then I most certainly will."

"You are terrible."

"Don't tell anyone." He meanders off to join his wife, and I stand alone, thinking for a few moments. My brashness toward Josh Jameson is forgotten as I ponder my intentions. Why I am now questioning them is beyond me, yet I am. He is not like any other man I have known, and not only because he's more famous than God. I watch him casually break away from the group of people he's talking to, take a bottle of champagne from the table nearby, as well as two glasses, and head for the arch that will take him to the path toward the far side of Claringdon Palace. Just before he disappears from view, he looks over his shoulder and flicks his head in gesture for me to get a move on. It's a demand. I don't bow to demands. But, and I'm confused as to why, my feet come to life of their own volition, adrenalin starting to course through my veins. I walk, feeling unstable and shaky, something that is alien to me, too. How does he elicit such reactions from me *and* so very easily? It's so very intriguing. He's confident, cocky, and unfazed by my royal status. It is rather refreshing.

I scan the scatterings of people as I fall away from the activity, seeing my father taking charge of a game of croquet and my mother entertaining a group of ladies by the string quartet. Everyone seems distracted from my silent escape. Then I spot Eddie, who is talking to Haydon. I come to a stop beside the statue of a plump angel that's peeing water through his rather unimpressive penis. Haydon's back is to me, though my brother is facing my direction, and his eyes are dividing their attention between Haydon and me. Did Eddie

see Josh Jameson wander this way a moment ago? I press my lips together and hold my breath as Haydon makes to turn toward me, maybe wondering what has Eddie's split attention. But my brother takes his arm and laughs, pointing toward the King who has just declared croquet war on Haydon's father. They start walking to the grass playing court, volunteering their skills, and Eddie looks back at me, shaking his head so very mildly. He knows how I feel about Haydon Sampson, and though he doesn't entirely condone many of my activities, he understands why I don't want to be married to a man who I have no feelings for beyond friendship. I mouth my *thank you* and back up, passing through the arch that will take me to something both scandalous and illicit.

And hopefully something wonderful.

3

THE WHOLE WALK to the far end of the grounds is spent jumping between sureness and reluctance, my steps faltering one too many times for my liking. My self-assuredness has never been dented by a man, and I'm uncertain as to whether I love or loathe the notion.

When I reach the maze of conifers, I stop and have a stern word with myself, telling my nerves to pull themselves together and welcome this unexpected birthday gift. Weaving the maze, I momentarily wonder if Josh found his way to the center, or if he is lost somewhere amid the trees, finding dead ends or taking wrong turns that will disorientate him. The thought makes me smile. When I was a child, this maze felt colossal, and I spent hours running the labyrinth of paths trying to navigate my way to the middle. Now, I know exactly what route I need to take in order to get me there the quickest.

I breach the final opening and see the statue of my grandfather, my father's father, King Harold of England. He's tall, imposing, made of solid marble, and his face is stern. He *was* stern, high-handed and strict with his children, as well as his grandchildren.

A summons to his office meant trouble and was cause to tremble. Which I often did as a child. His robe, the Pallium Regale, is long and lavish, the scepter held lightly in his hand, Saint Edward's Crown perched on his large head. The entire statue is intimidating.

But there is Josh Jameson standing before it, leaning casually back against my late grandfather's shins with a bottle of champagne in his hands, his legs crossed at the ankles, a smile on his face.

This is an entirely different level of intimidating.

"Your Highness." He casually pushes himself off the solid homage to one of the greatest kings to rule England and slowly wanders toward me, each step measured and confident. "How are you enjoying your birthday?"

"It's been . . . unexpectedly pleasant."

He reaches me and starts circling my static form, heightening my awareness when he comes to a stop behind me. Not wanting to give him the upper hand, I slowly turn to face him, bringing us chest to chest. He obviously finds my move amusing, a tiny, nearly undetectable curve tugging the corner of his lips.

"About that gift," I whisper, taking one step back, if only so he doesn't feel my deep inhales pushing into his chest.

"Oh, the gift." He starts to round me again, and I move with him, keeping us facing each other, circling. Stalking each other. Our gazes are glued, chemistry sizzling between us. Good God, I've never felt anything like it. It is obvious that he, like me, doesn't want to be the first to give in to it. "I think you'll love my gift," he whispers.

"You are a very self-assured man." I come to a stop, leaving Josh to move in behind me. I shut my eyes, feeling his mouth close to the bare nape of my neck.

"And you are a very self-assured woman," he says quietly, and then tactically blows a cool stream of air across my flesh. My body locks, my breath held as I try to find my ever-present poise. Where the hell has it gone now, when I'm confident that I need it the most? "I like it," he claims. "A lot." I'm forced to open my eyes when I

feel the chilly sensation of something smooth resting on my lips. A flute of champagne is held over my shoulder, Josh's mouth now touching my pulsing neck. I shudder, unable to stop it.

He nips my throat, and, God help me, I moan, feeling him smile against my skin. "Drink," he commands, tipping the flute at my lips. My mouth is bone dry, so the cool liquid is welcome. I swallow, sweeping my tongue across my bottom lip to catch a trickle. "Good?" He presses his front into my back.

"The champagne, or the feel of your arousal against my backside?"

He answers by dropping the champagne and glasses to the grass and slipping an arm around my waist, splaying his palm across my tummy to hold me still, so when he thrusts his hips forward, I am trapped, at the mercy of his solid manhood pressing into me. "I know *that* feels good." Biting my earlobe, he drags it through his teeth until it pops free. My legs give a little, sending my body limp against his. "Just like I know *this* will feel good." His hand cups me over my dress.

"Fucking hell," I say on a rush of breath.

Josh chuckles. "Is it wrong that hearing you cuss in your proper English accent turns me on?"

"It should probably shock you more than turn you on," I admit, laying my hand over his between my thighs, ignoring my mind's demand to put pressure there, to make him rub and stimulate me further.

"It doesn't shock me." Kissing my neck, he turns me in his arms and lifts my chin until I'm looking into his eyes. They're lustrous and lush, almost lazy. "Kneel." His demand is sharp and serious.

"Excuse me?" I choke, somewhere between amusement and shock.

"I said, kneel." He drops my chin and takes a backward step, leveling me with an expressionless face. No, wait. His face is not expressionless at all. There's challenge hiding somewhere there.

"You are aware that you have just demanded the Princess of England to kneel?"

"I am." He sighs heavily, raising his eyebrows at me. "And yet she's still standing." Pulling that pale pink hanky from his breast pocket, he flaps it out. "I won't ask again."

I drop to my knees at his feet with no further prompt, shocking myself, but clearly not Josh. And though I can see he is satisfied, he doesn't demonstrate it, but rather circles me, straddling my legs behind me. His palm rests on my throat and tips my head back until I can see him looming above me. "Open your mouth."

I swallow and do as I am bid. I'm like a puppet, bowing to his demands, kissing my strong will goodbye. His eyes travel every inch of my face, settling on my lips, and he bends at the waist, closing the distance between our mouths quickly. His lips hit mine with force, and he pushes his tongue inside my mouth and circles firmly, giving me just a teasing taste of him. And then he pulls away before I can gather myself to respond. I cry out for my loss, panting, seeing my scarlet lipstick smeared all over his mouth. I don't ask for more. Somehow, I know I won't get it. Not now, when he's drawing the material of his silk hanky through his deft fingers before me, smoothing it, pulling it taut. He's going to gag me. That expensive handkerchief is going in my mouth. I flick my eyes to his, my neck craned back to keep his upside-down face in view. A small smile ghosts his lips as he brings the material down, filling my mouth with it. And I do nothing to stop him. I remain on my knees, a man I've known barely an hour doing with me as he pleases.

What the hell are you doing, Adeline?

I stare ahead, feeling his fingertips brushing my shoulders, eliciting goosebumps. I've never had goosebumps before. I've never felt my stomach cartwheel like this, or my heart thrum without the help of exhaustion. Josh Jameson isn't approaching me like the delicate princess, pampering and fussing over me. It's a new feeling to me, one of liberation.

At that very second, my dress is yanked up past my waist and a wicked slice of pain rips through me, his palm connecting brutally with my backside. I can't scream—my gag won't allow it—but I do fall forward onto all fours to steady myself. He's kneeling behind me quickly, his hand tugging my knickers aside and his fingers slipping straight through my wetness and plunging deep. I choke on nothing, my eyes wide and shocked.

The heat of my burning bottom spreads through my bloodstream and sets me alight, my eyes blinking repeatedly as Josh pummels me with three fingers unforgivingly. I feel my climax building within seconds, defying my need to be disgusted by his treatment of me, my body moving back and forth as his spare hand strokes down my spine.

And when I reach the summit, the point of release, he pulls out and leaves my building orgasm to flutter away.

I whimper, the sensation of him smoothing his palm over my burning arse telling me to brace myself. My frantic mind reels, torn between depraved delight and fear. Not because of his brutal kiss, or his brutal palm, or his ability to control my pleasure so easily. But because I want more, and I have never wanted more from a man in my life. Adeline Lockhart does not ever want more from a man. She takes what she wants, knowing he won't be around for long. She's the one in control. She is the one calling the shots. She's the one men bow to. *What am I doing?*

I reach for the gag and pull it from my mouth, my breathing out of control. "No," I pant, struggling to my feet and throwing Josh's pink hanky to the grass. I wipe my mouth with the back of my hand, smudging my lipstick even more than Josh has with his blazing kiss.

"No?" He slowly gets to his feet. He's surprised, and he can't hide it.

"No." I pull my dress down as I turn and walk away. "It was a pleasure, Mr. Jameson." I don't look back. I do not ever want to

lay eyes on him again. I don't take too kindly to men who try to overpower me, men like my father and eldest brother, no matter in what capacity that is—suppressing me or dominating me. I will not be controlled, and I'm furious with myself for even remotely enjoying it.

Remotely?

I enjoyed it too much. My blood heated too much. I *wanted* to bend to his will, and that is a monumental achievement on Josh Jameson's part. I should hate him for it. Yet I don't. Frighteningly, I want more. And I will never be allowed to have more. That is why I always maintain the control with men. That is why I call the shots. Because I know it won't be long before the King finds out about my flavor of the month and rids them from my life. I never get attached; there's little point when I know the longevity of my relationships is non-existent. My feigned annoyance swiftly turns into panic.

"Adeline!"

I ignore him shouting after me and navigate my way out of the maze with ease, hurrying back to my party, my usually cool persona flustered terribly.

Matilda is the first to spot me, her face a picture of horror. "Oh my gosh, Adeline."

"What?"

"Your lipstick is everywhere."

I wipe my cheek, seeing the evidence of my red lipstick smudged all over my fingertips. "Oh, blast."

"Here, you left your bag with Haydon.' Matilda passes my purse, her lips straight.

"Have fun?" Eddie asks sarcastically, joining us. "If you insist on misbehaving, Adeline, you could at least hide the bloody evidence." He focuses on my lipstick-smeared face.

I make a mad dash for the washroom, leaving behind a bemused Eddie and Matilda. Fun? No, it was not fun.

Skirting past plenty of people who look like they would like to stop and talk, I don't indulge any of them, hoping my hand over my mouth will maybe communicate that I am going to vomit, rather than the fact that I am hiding the evidence of an American man's heavenly mouth all over mine.

Slamming the door shut behind me, I go to the mirror. "Bloody hell," I breathe, grabbing a washcloth and running it under the tap. I look as flustered as I feel, and the burning flesh of my bottom is a good indication that one cheek of my arse is as red as the lipstick smeared disgracefully all over my face. Pulling up my dress, I turn and get my raw rear in view, gasping when I see the glowing imprint of a large palm. "The nerve," I whisper, wincing when I apply the cool washcloth across my skin.

There's a knock at the door. "One minute," I call, rushing to make myself more presentable, smoothing out my dress and reapplying my lipstick carefully, blotting away the redness on my chin and cheeks with some loose powder. Once I have made the best of myself, which is not brilliant without Jenny around to work her magic, I straighten my shoulders, slap a smile on my face, and open the door. "I do apologize for taking so—" My smile plummets, and I'm shoved back inside the washroom by Josh bloody Jameson. "Do you mind?" I blurt, outraged.

He slams the door, locks it, and pushes his back against the wood. I guess that means I'm not going anywhere. "Tell me why you refused me," he growls.

"I beg your pardon?"

"You played it all cocky, laid your cards on the table, made it perfectly clear what you wanted, and then you bottled it. I want to know why."

"It may have escaped your notice, Mr. Jameson, but I do not have to justify myself to anyone, least of all *you*. Now, if you will excuse me." I fix him with a resolute glare, ignoring the returning influx of pleasurable feelings sweeping through my bloodstream.

He's even more handsome, even harder to resist when he's angry. His jaw pulsing, his eyes narrowed, his nostrils flaring. Knowing I'm the reason for this fluster in Josh Jameson turns me on, and I really do not want it to.

"When you provoke my cock into something resembling stone, Your Highness," he breathes, "you most definitely need to justify yourself."

I recoil at his continued frankness. "Your inability to control . . ." I fade off, glancing at his groin. He's still hard, and I nibble the inside of my cheek, undeniably delighted. "Your inability to control yourself is not my concern."

He laughs and rearranges himself. "You're mistaken, ma'am."

"I am?" I tilt my head, interested. "I seem to recall you mentioning something about *not* telling a royal when they are wrong."

"I've changed my mind. You're wrong." His scowl is not playful. It's serious, and I know I should be wary of it. I *am* wary. Very wary. Which is why I back up. Just two steps, not that it gains me space for long. Josh Jameson soon closes the extended distance I've put between us. "You're scared."

"Of what?" I laugh.

He, however, does not laugh. "Me."

"I assure you, I am not scared of you." I glance away and silently curse myself for it.

"Liar."

"That's absurd. Why ever would I fear you?"

"Because I whipped that fine ass of yours, and you, Your Highness, fuckin' loved it. You loved me owning you in that maze, you loved me ruling you, and you *hate* that you loved it. That's the problem here."

My jaw tightens. "You're wrong." I can see that my refusal to concede is increasing his aggravation. It's delightful to witness this renowned sex symbol look rejection in the eye. It pushes my revived fortitude to new heights, because, right now, I have the power. It's

familiar ground to me, and I am once again thriving, regardless of the miniscule detail that he is one hundred percent right. "You are keeping me from my birthday celebrations, Mr. Jameson. Would you mind?" I step forward, and his scowl deepens. More thrills lick my skin.

"Yes, I would mind." He remains blocking my path to the door. "I'm not moving until you admit it."

"Oh," I laugh. "Have I injured your ego?"

His face screws up. "Fuck me, you're infuriating."

I smile, sly and seductively, feeling power trickling through my veins. "So I'm told. What are you going to do, spank me again?" I pass him, feeling like myself once more, until he seizes my wrist and yanks me to a stop. I keep my eyes on my escape, my arm heating under his touch, and my bottom tingling as a reminder of who really does have the power here.

"Whether I spank you again depends on whether you continue with the insubordination. You're being a very naughty girl, Your Highness." He slowly turns challenging eyes down to me and burns a hole in my profile with the concentration of his stare.

"I'm always a naughty girl." I meet his eyes briefly before dropping my gaze to his lips. "Defiant, some might say. Untamable and unruly. No man has, or ever will, succeed in controlling me."

"Then the wrong men have tried. I don't fail." He drops my wrist and moves away. "You'll submit to me eventually. Until then, Your Highness, game on." Josh takes the door and swings it open, sweeping his arm out in gesture for me to lead the way.

"There will be no game," I mutter, my vocal cords tight from the constant swallows of restraint.

"There already is." He follows me out of the washroom and falls into stride beside me, buttoning up his suit jacket. "And, for the record, I'm currently winning."

"Losing is the new winning? How very modern of you." He's right. There is a game, and I need to find the will not to enjoy

playing, because I know beyond question that I cannot win.

I break out in a sweat when Haydon's father, David, appears as we make our way through the grand foyer of the palace toward the rear grounds. "Ah, Mr. Sampson," I chime, high and nervous. "Have you met Mr. Jameson?"

"I don't believe I have." David offers Josh his hand. "Nice to make your acquaintance, Mr. Jameson."

"Likewise," Josh replies, his accent heavy. And thrilling.

"I was just showing Mr. Jameson the gallery of Lockharts," I explain to David when he gives Josh a dubious look.

"In the library?" Haydon's father looks a little confused as he drops Jameson's hand. "But that's on the other side of the palace."

"We detoured," I explain. "Mr. Jameson hasn't had the privilege of a guided tour before now."

"I'm sure one of the household staff would have been happy to give Mr. Jameson a tour, save you missing out on your celebrations and guests." By *guests*, he means his son, Haydon.

"More personal." I smile tightly.

David matches my smile. "I guess there's nothing like a royal tour led by a royal."

"I particularly enjoyed the maze." Josh smiles, and I choke a little.

"Oh, the maze. Her Royal Highness and my son used to romp in there for hours when they were children." David heads toward the washrooms, leaving me with a rare agape mouth.

"Romp?" Josh asks, turning his penetrating, twinkling eyes onto me.

"You particularly enjoyed the maze?"

I'm blinded by his smile. "As did you."

I roll my eyes and walk toward the garden. "If it pleases you, Mr. Jameson."

"Oh, it does, Your Highness."

"Will you please stop addressing me in that manner?"

"No."

I toss a scowl back at him, picking up my speed as Major Davenport appears, as if by magic, blocking my escape to the garden. "The King has requested an audience," he declares on a sniff, his stoic expression pointed over my shoulder. To Josh? Bugger it. Was my father's private secretary spying again?

"An audience?" I sigh. "I am his daughter, not the Prime Minister or a member of the Privy Bloody Council."

Major Davenport's straight face turns to me. "In your own good time, ma'am," he says, ignoring my insolence as he walks toward the stairs that lead to my father's regal office.

I just want to enjoy my party. Is that too much to ask? I solidify when I feel a hard torso meet my back. "If the King wants to pass out punishments, I'll happily volunteer my palm." Josh juts his hips forward and catches my sore bottom with his still-solid arousal. "Just sayin'."

"You are incorrigible." I break away and head for my father's office, hoping my walk appears stable when on the inside I am infuriatingly rickety. And it is all Josh Jameson's fault. And it will also be his fault if my father is privy to my reckless shenanigans in the maze.

Major Davenport is waiting for me with the door held open. I walk in and find Sir Don in a chair opposite my father's desk and my father looking at the portrait of himself at his coronation that hangs above the stone fireplace. He has a brandy in his grasp and a cigar in his mouth. "Father," I say, pulling him from admiring himself. "You wanted to see me?"

"Ah, Adeline." Holding his half-smoked cigar out, a footman takes it and places the brown, putrid-smelling stick on a freestanding ashtray. "Take a seat."

I'm reluctant, even more so when I turn to see my mother enter the office. I know she sees my growing despondency, because she gives me that peaceful smile, the one she gives me when she thinks I should hear my father out. My beautiful mother glides gracefully

across the carpet, the pleated skirt of her gown floating behind her. She sits on the velvet chesterfield, and Davenport shuts the door with him on the wrong side of it.

"That'll be all, Major Davenport." My mother is the only person who can dismiss him, aside from the King. But despite the Queen Consort's order, Davenport still looks to my father for confirmation. The King nods, as does Davenport in response, before he silently leaves me alone with my parents and Sir Don.

Okay, I think to myself. *What is it going to be?* A reprimand on the shot *Woman* got of me outside the Royal Opera House? I cannot help that. Maybe Sir Don has advised the King of my indiscretion with Gerry Rush on that boring evening. Well, boring until I made it to the banker's hotel room. I wince when I remember the image Kim showed me of Rush and his wife. Communications have handled it. I can't be here because of that. So perhaps I am about to be lectured on—

"It's time you marry," the King says in his usual inflexible tone. "You're thirty now, Adeline. You've had your fun."

I balk. *Fun?* Is that what he calls it? Well, I'm not done having *fun*. Maybe never will be. "I'm quite aware of my age, Father." I sit up straight in the oversized, gilded chair, feeling my mother's despairing eyes on me, and Sir Don's condemnation. I flick Mother a glance and see her mildly shake her head, silently pleading for me to bow to the King's demands. Never. I refuse to fall victim to an arranged royal marriage. They're all a farce in one form or another. Not one married member of the monarchy is genuinely in love. There was no love at first sight or sizzling chemistry, because, Lord have mercy on our souls, we don't screw out of pleasure or because the chemistry is too potent to resist. No. We screw to produce heirs, to keep the royal bloodline strong and the country appeased. I don't want to get married, not now, maybe never. I don't want children, either. I would never thrust this life on a child. No one deserves this kind of suppression.

The King sighs, looking at my mother for support. He won't get it from his queen, but I will not gain her defense either. She knows her position. Mother will remain quiet, overseeing the debate, sitting pretty. So my father looks to Sir Don, and I find my contemptuous eyes finding him, too. Sir Don is another story. A descendent of the greatest lord chamberlain this country has ever seen, his desire to make it into the history books with his grandfather is really quite sad. His life has been dedicated to advising the Sovereign. To maintaining this country's greatest asset, the Royal Family. To help hide the many scandals and secrets. To support the monarchy.

My father nods firmly, taking direction from Sir Don. "Haydon Sampson—"

"Is a lovely man, Father, but he is not my cup of tea."

"No, your cup of tea is a gentleman from a certain persuasion." His bushy brows meet in the middle, his chin dropping to his chest. "Like married bankers."

Oh, bugger. How? Then I laugh under my breath. Do I even need to ask myself that? I turn a filthy look Sir Don's way. That's how.

"Felix may have kept the incident out of the newspapers, Adeline," my father says, "but there is not much you can keep from me."

That's not true at all. I've had many encounters with men that my father has never caught wind of. Thank God for Felix and the communications team at Kellington Palace.

Father narrows displeased eyes on me, and Sir Don chooses now to step in with his thoughts. And we all know what they will be. "I'm sure you do not need me to tell you that the scandal arising from this would cast an unsightly shadow on the Monarchy."

"No, I do not, so why are you telling me?"

"Have you no scruples, Adeline?" Father asks. I am not given the chance to defend myself, not that I have a defense. "You will marry Haydon Sampson. That is not a request." His voice gets louder until he finishes on a boom.

I grind my teeth. "Edward is older than I am. Why is he not receiving such devotion to finding him a *suitable* wife?"

"Your brother has been busy fighting for our country." He's losing the plot rapidly, now standing over his desk in that imposing way that makes most people tremble when they are on the receiving end on his tirades. "He's been making himself useful."

"Oh, I see." I stand abruptly, unable to maintain my calm composure. "So the only use I have to you and the monarchy is to marry and reproduce? To make appearances on request and mimic the words of royal advisors when I'm allowed to actually talk?"

"Adeline," Mother breathes, making a rare intervention. "Darling, your father only wants what is best for you."

"No, he doesn't. He wants what is best for the monarchy. It's ridiculous. Do you think the public is not aware of the sham marriages within this family? Open your eyes, Father."

His fist lands on his red box, the box that's delivered daily with important papers for him to sign, information to read, news to know. "My eyes are very much open. I am the King, dear daughter, and, like it or not, my word is final."

His word? Or the words of the small army of men who advise him? The army led by Sir Don. "Exile me. I don't care. I will not marry Haydon Sampson to keep up royal appearances."

"You will do what I say!"

I take myself across to my mother and kiss her cheek lightly, feeling her despair. Then I turn to my father, whose face is now red with rage, and to Sir Don, who maintains a respectful silence, though I expect his thoughts are damning me to hell. "Thank you for a wonderful afternoon and for my lovely birthday gift." I walk out, hearing Mother trying to placate her husband as he rants on about disobedience and my audacity to question his authority.

I pass Major Davenport as I leave, and I make sure he sees my glower. Although the man is impenetrable, probably necessary after nearly thirty years serving the King, and fifteen years prior to that

serving my equally demanding grandfather.

"What's ruffled your feathers?" Eddie catches me at the bottom of the stairs, and I spew out my grievances in one fell swoop, informing my brother that I would rather live as a pauper than marry Haydon Sampson. Perhaps I should join the military so my life has more *approved* purpose.

"Please," I beg, grabbing my brother's hands and squeezing. "Let's go back to Kellington and get outrageously drunk. Today has been utterly tiresome. I need a stiff drink."

"And something else stiff? Or have you already had a bit of that?"

"No, I have not, but I'm beginning to wish I'd taken him up on his shameful offer."

"You turned him down?" Eddie's shock is clear. "Josh Jameson?"

"And what of it?"

Snuggling my hand into the crook of his arm, Eddie starts to walk me out, nodding for a footman to fill my other hand with some champagne. Maybe I should stop drinking. My head is starting to feel a little woozy. "Not that I'm encouraging such scandalous behavior," Eddie says. "I'm just surprised you turned down guaranteed fun."

Fun? I inwardly scoff. Well, it was until I realized I was genuinely enjoying Josh Jameson's idea of fun. "So when do we get to party properly?"

Eddie chuckles and gets his phone from his pocket. "I'll send out an informal, impromptu invitation and let you know."

"Oh, goody." I kiss his cheek. Eddie sending out an "informal, impromptu invitation" is the best party invitation one could receive. And I am the special guest. I accost a footman and ask him to let Damon know I'll be ready in half an hour. I've done my royal bit for today. Or maybe forever.

4

I SPEND THE next day bored out of my poor mind, flicking through endless correspondence and letters that have made it through security and onto my desk. I read the words before me, though they don't sink in, my mind far from focused. My head is not in my office. It's in that blasted maze, and the wall of memories are too high for anything else to gain access to my head.

I curse under my breath and slam the papers down, giving up on trying to absorb any information. Getting up from my chair, I wander to the elaborately dressed window and gaze out across the well-kept grounds. The walls are beautiful, old, and made of rumbled stone, but high and impenetrable. The walls of my prison. What is Josh Jameson doing now, out there in the free world? Dinner somewhere? Maybe a spot of sport in a good old British pub? I'm being naïve. He is insanely famous. There are no pints of beer waiting on any bar tops for him.

Hearing my office door open, I look over my shoulder to find Eddie dressed in his military uniform. "Been to the barracks?" I ask, turning to face him. He nods, taking in my form thoughtfully. Frowning, I look at my black skinny jeans and cropped tee. My

feet are bare, my hair piled high, my makeup minimum. "What?" I had nothing to do today except sit in my office. I'm hardly going to have Jenny glam me up for such a mundane task.

"You will do," he declares, collecting me from the window.

"What are you doing?" My eyes are covered by Eddie's palms as he walks me out of my office, and I laugh, taking tentative steps through the palace.

"Straight ahead," he orders, shuffling along behind me.

"Did you get me a surprise?"

"My birthday gift. Keep walking." He steers me to the right, toward the ostentatious dining room that seats fifty comfortably around a table, but never gets used. I can hear muffled music and people. Lots of them. Eddie stops me, his hands still covering my eyes, and I hear the tall double doors open, the music becoming louder, but the chatter quieting down. "Happy birthday, little sis," he says, removing his palms, revealing the room, splitting at the seams with . . .

"Oh my," I breathe, my delighted eyes taking in the scene before me as I wander in. A grin slowly forms on my face. "Now this is what I call a party." I snag a bottle of Belvedere off the table, as well as a bottle of Fever Tree tonic—a glass is not necessary—and I throw myself into the crowd of soldiers, the bottles raised above my head.

"They have their warnings," Eddie calls after me, as the men all cheer my arrival.

That is all good and well, but I don't recall getting *my* warning. "Well, hello, gents." I slam the two bottles down on the highly polished dining room table, which is already cluttered with various bottles of alcohol and mixers. I spot Matilda across the room with our friends from boarding school, including Felicity. They raise their bottles of alcohol, eyeing the crowd of sex-starved soldiers. "Let's have some fun." I take the pins from my hair and shake out my long, dark waves, just in time for a man—a handsome man—to pick me up and lift me onto the huge table.

I smile at him as he passes me my bottles. "Thank you, kind sir."

"Center stage for the princess." Collecting his bottle of Jack Daniels, he hollers across the room for someone to turn up the music.

"Adeline." My private secretary appears at the foot of the table, pushing a man off her when he tries to get her dancing.

"Oh, Kim," I sigh, crouching down a little. "I've had a monotonous day. You're not going to try and spoil my fun, are you? I will behave, I promise."

Her skeptical look is justified. "Just keep it contained to this room, okay?"

"Okay." I nod obediently.

"Damon will be outside if you need him."

I look up and see my head of security by the double doors, delegating positions and posts to three of his team. He has done this before. If anyone gets too excitable, he'll be quick to eject them. Damon catches my eye and gives me a thumbs up, his way of asking me if I am okay. I return his thumbs up and mouth my *thank you*. He's so unruffled; he never makes a big deal of anything, just gets on with his job. I return my attention to Kim. "Time for you to go home."

She looks around at the rowdiness building and nods her agreement. "See you in the morning."

"Not too early." I rise and swing around, summoning Matilda and Felicity to join me. "Come on," I call, hearing Duke Dumont's *The Giver* blast from the speakers. "Woo hoo." I swig from my personal bottle of vodka, and wash it down with a bit of tonic as I spin on the spot, hell-bent on making my belated birthday party one to remember.

"Adeline, you are wild," Matilda sings, getting up on the table.

I laugh when she grabs me and spins me on the spot. "Are you going to have fun?" I ask my uptight cousin. She rarely lets her hair down, unquestionably bound by the restraints the Royals impose.

"You have enough fun for *all* the family." She bends and snags a bottle of Hendricks. "But your place is the *only* place I can let go. Bring on the drinks," she sings. "And the men."

Felicity throws her arms in the air, shouts a declaration of love for me, then proceeds to strut down the length of long table, giving sultry eyes to every man lining the room. The whistles follow her all the way. I smirk, being thrown back to our boarding school days when we used to sneak out of the window of our dorms and over the wall that kept us contained. Those nights spent getting outrageously drunk in the local village pub with the boy soldiers from the army barracks nearby were some of the best nights of my life. I was anonymous and free.

Taking the Belvedere to my lips, I chug down a healthy amount, cast the Fever Tree aside, throw one arm in the air, and get to having some bloody fun.

HALF A BOTTLE later, my party is rocking and the dining table is carrying the weight of a dozen people, all flinging themselves around, bottles in hand. I laugh, feeling light and free, out of breath but thriving, as I yank one of Eddie's army friends toward me and start dancing with him. He looks a bit cautious at first, but alcohol soon takes over and douses his delicate approach to me. He spins me away from him, his bottle of whisky extending over my shoulder in front of me. He brings it to my lips for me to take a mouthful as he grinds into my arse in time to *Lost Frequencies*. Some liquid spills down my chin and T-shirt, but wiping myself clean is not top of his priority list, and instead, he shoves me out and grabs my hand, twirling me around on a laugh. "Come on, girl." He throws our hands up, smiling, and it is now that I register it's the guy who lifted me up to the table when the party started. His blond hair is hidden under his green beret, his camouflage jacket gone, leaving him now in just a khaki, *tight* T-shirt and combats.

"Giles," he declares, taking my hand to his mouth and landing it with an over-the-top kiss.

"Hello, Giles," I purr, letting him pull me into his chest.

"Hello, Princess." He grins, sliding his hand onto my bottom. "May I kiss you?"

Don't ask, just do! I push my lips to his, tasting whisky and cigarettes, and he moans as we sway and kiss, drunk and a little clumsy.

"Hey!" Eddie's yell is fierce, and I break away from Giles, ready to argue my case and defend Giles from my brother's wrath. I mean, come on! Eddie set this up. Am I expected to look and not touch? I locate my brother, but when I find him, his attention is not on me, and neither is it on Giles. It's on another soldier, a younger lad, who has his mobile phone pointing in my direction. I just catch the flash of the camera before Eddie practically rugby tackles him to the Oriental rug, snatching the mobile from his grasp.

"Bloody hell." I take my fingers to my mouth and belt out an ear-piercing whistle. Damon bursts through the doors a second later, searching me out. When he finds me, I point to Eddie, who is now holding the click-happy perpetrator down while he scrolls through the pictures on his phone.

Eddie curses, grabbing the young soldier by the scruff of his neck and pulling him to his feet. "There's an unwritten rule when in the company of a royal, lad. You do not take pictures."

"Sorry, I didn't know." He holds up his hands in defense.

Eddie snarls and thrusts him into Damon's waiting grasp. "Time for you to go home."

Damon manhandles him out of the room, looking back at the mobile phone in Eddie's grasp. "You going to take care of that?"

"Done." My brother drops it to the wooden floor by the door and stamps on it with his army boot.

"Nice touch," Damon quips, pushing the kid out of the door.

"Okay, the show is over." Eddie grabs a nearby bottle of tequila and strides over to me. "Open up."

I smile and lie down on my back, hanging my head off the edge of the table. Then I open my mouth and Eddie tips the bottle, filling my cheeks with tequila until I hold my hand up for him to stop. I wince as I swallow. "Where's the lemon?" I shudder.

Eddie laughs. "Don't be a wimp. Next."

Giles drops to his back and follows my lead, and as soon as he is done, the next person takes their position, until the whole length of table is lined with horizontal bodies, mouths wide open to take their hit. Eddie roams up and down, a continuous flow of tequila streaming into the waiting mouths until the bottle is empty and he casts it aside on a loud whoop.

As I wobble my way back up to standing with the help of Giles, I spy Damon at the door brushing his hands off, his way of telling me the problem has been dealt with. I nod on a hiccup when he gives me our sign. I'm fine. Thumbs up.

"Sure?" he mouths, taking the handle of the door, ready to close our noisy rabble back inside the room.

"Sure." I search out my vodka and gingerly bend to retrieve it, lifting it to my lips as I raise my body back upright. Although the clear, cool liquid doesn't make it into my mouth, instead spilling down my front before my lips meet the rim. My eyes pop out of my head at the sight of a man standing next to Damon by the double doors. *What the hell?*

Damon once again gives me a thumbs up, but this time he follows up with a thumbs down.

Yes or no? Yes or no? Yes or no?

I don't know.

Josh Jameson remains still, watching me closely while I stall answering Damon. Today his long, lean legs are covered in some well-fitting stonewash jeans, his prime torso covered in a black T-shirt. Oh . . . my . . . goodness. My thumb hovers in no man's land, straddling between thumbs up and thumbs down. The dangerous surge of energy powering through my alcohol-drenched veins

should serve as a warning, should force my thumb downward to tell Damon that Jameson is not welcome. Yet when I peek down, I see my thumb pointing toward the ceiling, and when I cast my eyes back to Josh, he's smiling discreetly at me where I stand on the table, his gaze hooded. Then he subtly starts rubbing his palm against his jean-clad thigh. He's warming it up. The energy powering through me sparks and crackles, and my lungs drain as I lift the vodka to my lips.

My stare follows Josh to the Sonos player, where he fiddles between that and his phone for a few moments. Then he cranks up the volume to max, turning toward me. I scowl at him when the track registers in my warped mind. Oh, he thinks he is hilarious. Yeah Yeah Yeahs *"Heads Will Roll"* bursts from the speakers, and the party goes wild, everyone roaring their delight at Josh's choice. Everyone except me. *Off with his head*, indeed. I watch him make a beeline for me, nothing but pure intent and determination written all over his aggravatingly handsome face.

"Who invited you?" I ask when his thighs meet the edge of the table before me, his neck craned back so he can look up at me standing over him.

"Prince Eddie." He's smug, and when I shoot a disgusted look Eddie's way, my brother shrugs, looking cautious. Like he's regretting it. "Thought you'd be pleased to see me."

I huff and swivel, dancing my way to the other end of the table, finding Matilda and engaging in some outrageous dance moves with her.

"How did he get in?" my cousin asks, dancing but looking to the other end of the dining room.

"Eddie invited him, apparently."

"Why?"

"I don't know. It's not like I need help to get me sent to The Tower, is it?"

"What happened with the guy and the phone? What if he got

pictures, Adeline?" Matilda's panic is sobering her up too fast for my liking.

"Calm down. Damon and Eddie took care of it. The phone has been destroyed."

"But—"

"It's fixed," I assure her assertively, putting pressure on the base of her bottle to lift it to her mouth. "Drink and enjoy."

I'm suddenly hauled back by an arm around my waist, and I gasp, my eyes wide. "Where were we?" Giles's lusty voice in my ear does nothing for me now, and I know it's because another man is in the room hunting me.

"Not now." I shrug him off and throw myself into Matilda, swapping positions so I am out of Giles's reach, dancing at a safe distance from him. My gaze catches Josh's as I spin on the spot, taking mild pleasure from the flash of *dis*pleasure that blazes his features, making them dark for a brief moment.

"Off with your head," Matilda sings, throwing her head back on a laugh. "I love it."

I smile, strained, remembering the words Josh spoke to me yesterday, the ripple of naughty pleasure that coursed through me too fast to stop. It makes me uncomfortable. I need air, the room suddenly suffocating me.

"I need a cigarette," I tell Matilda, slipping down from the table, unable to remain under the fixed glare of Josh Jameson any longer. My cousin doesn't miss me for long, soon distracted by Giles, who is over his loss of me and onto the next willing female. I slide out of the room by the doors at the other end, scooping up a half-empty bottle of Belvedere on my way. I wander through the empty lounge to the foyer to let Damon know I'm heading out for a sneaky cigarette.

"Hey," I call, grabbing his attention. My head of security frowns at me as he pushes his back from the doorframe and strides toward me, his worn-in face questioning. "Got any smokes?" I ask on a

sickly sweet smile.

He rolls his eyes. "I quit."

"Liar." I help myself to his inside pocket when he makes it to me, finding a pack of Marlboro Lights. "Lighter?"

"You quit, too."

"Don't nag me, Damon," I moan, walking with him to the French doors through the library. "Father always has a cigar hanging out of his mouth."

"Kings smoking Cubans is customary." He opens the door and lets me pass, but not before taking my vodka and setting it on a cabinet.

"Maybe I'm establishing my own customs." I smile as I slip a cigarette between my lips and offer Damon the open packet.

On a shake of his head, he pulls one free before popping them back into his pocket and lighting mine then his. I draw in a long drag and let a plume of smoke spill on a satisfied exhale. "Oh, that is so good."

"Princesses shouldn't smoke, ma'am." Damon takes his own hit of nicotine. "Mind you, they also shouldn't throw wild parties, get steaming drunk, and screw bankers and actors."

"I have not screwed the actor," I correct him. "Just for the record."

"Yet," he adds cheekily.

I narrow my eyes playfully on him. "And I won't be." Of that, I am certain. "You should head off, anyway. I'll be fine for the rest of the evening."

"If it's all the same to you, ma'am, I think I'll stay."

"Isn't Mandy waiting for you?" Damon's wife is as lovely as her husband, so laid-back, she is virtually horizontal.

"We have date night tomorrow night." He smiles, almost shyly. "Because you have no plans for tomorrow evening, right? So I don't need to be here. Correct?"

"Right. And what does one do on date night?" I raise my chin and

bring my cigarette to my mouth again, as Damon shifts awkwardly on his black shiny shoes.

"That, ma'am"—he reaches forward with his spare hand and taps the end of my nose—"is top secret."

"But I'm marvelously good at keeping secrets."

"No, Felix and the PR team are marvelously good at keeping secrets *for* you."

I pout, with no argument coming to me. Damon is right. They are wizards at keeping things contained and away from the press, but not so much from my father. Not that I'm ashamed of myself, but the earache from the hierarchy is utterly boring. To them, I am an out-of-control headache. Regardless, spending a night with a man would not be deemed disgraceful and newsworthy if I were a regular thirty-year-old woman. But I am not. The self-reminder makes my face screw up.

"Oh, okay, keep your secret." I sniff, marveling in the calming powers of the nicotine as I take another draw, as well as the calming powers of my beloved Damon. I'm so lucky to have him. "It's frightfully chilly this evening."

"Would you like my jacket, ma'am?" Damon holds his cigarette between his lips and starts to pull off his suit coat.

I reach for him and rest my hand on his arm, stopping him. "No, but thank you."

"Glad to have Prince Eddie home?"

"Delighted. I do so miss him when he is gone."

"Like the terrible two are back together," Damon quips, taking my smoked cigarette from me and stubbing it out in a nearby marble plant pot. "I'm sure Felix is as delighted as you are."

"Oh"—I wave a dismissive hand at him—"Felix relishes the challenges I present him with."

"What, like fixing things?"

"Well, yes. After all, he's so good at it." I grin wickedly.

"You've given him a lot of practice, Your Highness." His arm

slips across my shoulders and he leads me to the doors. "Because you are very good at misbehaving."

"Fun is prohibited when you are a royal, Damon. You know that."

"Not for you, though."

"Never."

"But tell me one thing, ma'am, if you don't mind me asking." He stops us and looks down at me, clearly pensive.

"What, Damon? Anything." My staff is not like the King's stuffy aides, in particular Sir Don and Major Davenport, who have a permanent stick up their bottoms. My staff is more laid-back, but that is not to say they do their job any less effectively. All of them are so great, and I would fight tooth and nail if my father ever tried to replace them. But I am particularly fond of Damon. I don't know how old he is exactly, but he's been with me for ten years now, after retiring from MI6 due to an injury sustained during a secret mission. I guess he's nearing fifty, maybe a smidgen older.

"Are you truly happy, ma'am?"

Damon's question gives me pause, too long of a pause for me to pass off with a laugh, though I do try. "Of course I'm happy."

He nods sharply, though I sense he's not convinced. "Then that's the most important thing."

"Yes, you are right. I mean, it's not like I will ever be required for anything more than keeping up royal appearances. What I do in private is my own business. I'm never going to be Queen." I shudder at the mere thought. "It's oppressive enough being a backup to the backup heir, and it is entirely unfair that I am expected to live a life of suffocation because I happened to be born to the King of England. So, if it is all the same to my father, I will be having some fun. You understand what I'm saying, don't you, Damon?"

He rolls his eyes. "You don't need to explain yourself to me. I understand, ma'am."

"Good. Now then, let me get back to my belated birthday celebrations."

"As you wish."

We both turn, but neither of us go anywhere, because someone is blocking the entrance into the library.

"Josh," I breathe.

5

"YOUR HIGHNESS." HIS straight lips do not sit well. Not well at all. I fold on the inside, grabbing at air, unable to fathom why he looks so annoyed, and more significantly, why I am bothered by it.

"Ma'am?" Damon questions, looking at me.

"I will be fine, thank you, Damon." I give him a forced smile that most definitely does not have him fooled. He leaves me, nevertheless, closing the French doors behind him and taking up position inside.

"Can I help you?" I ask, trying to convince my mind to level out. That is not going to happen while I'm staring at him, only two feet away, so I turn on my bare feet and take the steps to the granite pathway that weaves through the botanical gardens.

"It's a cold night," Josh muses, tailing me.

"Then perhaps you should go back inside. Or better still, go home."

"Anyone would think you're trying to get rid of me."

"I am." I take a right when the path forks, wandering slowly as I study the white gravel in the beds that edge the pathway. The small stones sparkle with the help of tiny spotlights embedded

between the plants, illuminating the neatly trimmed display. "You shouldn't have come."

"It'd be rude to decline an invitation from a prince."

"It is rude to spank a princess, but that didn't hold you back, did it, Mr. Jameson?"

"The princess was begging for it. Flirting. Goading." He takes a deep breath and sighs dramatically. "But it would seem she couldn't handle me."

I slow to a stop and scowl at the open space before me. "I wasn't begging for it." I lie. "And I most definitely could handle you."

Josh's front meets my back, his mouth at my ear. Sparks ignite the simmering flames within me, my eyes closing, my breathing becoming short, my body refusing to break the contact. "Your Highness, do you feel like you've met your match?"

Yes. Yes, I do, and it is freaking me the hell out. Josh Jameson strips me of my trusty sass with one smoldering look. "You realize they will chase you out of the country if they get a sniff of your interest in me." It has happened before when my father has found out about some of the men who I've kept company with, and it will happen again and again until I relent to my father's demands and marry Haydon Sampson.

"Then I'll work hard to make sure they get no *sniff*."

"The King has a way of finding out things."

"I don't think you're scared of the King, Adeline." His tongue meets my ear and licks slowly up the shell, spiking wild activity in every nerve I possess. "I think you're scared of me."

My body softens, leaning back into him. "I'm not scared of you."

"Liar," he whispers. I shiver, and it has nothing to do with the cold air. "Want to let me prove your powers of resistance are worthless?"

"You can't."

"You know I will." His arm slips around my waist and hauls me back into him, the side of his face against mine. "Let's have some

fun, Adeline."

My mind spins for a moment. But *only* for a moment. I turn in his arms without thought or question, and lift my eyes to his. "That is all it will be." Or *can* be. He will simply be a pawn in my mission to defy all the rules. I won't get attached, because I *can't* get attached. I don't *want* to get attached. "Fun."

His lips meet mine softly, carefully, and we fall into a delicate kiss, a kiss that rebels against my intention. "Game on." And with a smack of my recovering arse, I am reminded that Josh Jameson's kind of fun may leave its mark on my skin. I can live with that. Just as long as I don't let him leave his mark anywhere else. Like on my heart. I almost laugh at the thought. A stupid thought.

A light cough interrupts us, and I glance to my left to find Damon a few feet away. "Apologies, ma'am, but you have a visitor."

"Who?" I ask, not liking Damon's uneasy disposition. It's a disposition I've grown to recognize acutely. Someone is here who I don't want to see.

Damon's eyes flick to Josh momentarily. "Mr. Sampson, ma'am."

"Haydon?"

"Oh," Josh breathes, a sarcastic edge apparent as he releases me. "This should be amusing."

I take his remark as a clear indicator that he is up to speed on all things Haydon Sampson. "How so?"

Josh takes my hand and lifts, pointing at my birthday present from Haydon. "I know you appreciated *my* birthday gift a lot more."

I raise my brows, interested. "Oh, really?"

"Really." Turning me toward Damon, he swats my bottom to send me on my way. "Get rid of him."

"I can't just—"

His palm covers my mouth from behind, and I stare at Damon, eyes wide, while Josh pushes his mouth to my cheek. "Would you rather I did?" I shake my head. "The party's over. His party, anyway. Ours, Your Highness, is just beginning." Releasing me, I virtually

stagger toward an interested Damon, caught in a state of awe and trepidation.

"Ma'am." Damon nods as I pass him.

"Do not say a word." I exhale, breaching the entrance into the palace.

"Wouldn't dream of it." Damon picks up pace beside me. "Although it's quite a bemusing sight, seeing you do what you're told for once."

I glare at him, not in the least bit amused. "I am not . . ." I trail off when Damon's eyebrows pinch, challenging me to try and talk my way out of it. I sigh, relenting. "Where is Haydon?"

"In the foyer, ma'am. I thought it best to keep him away from the . . . action." He nods in the direction of the dining room, where I expect things are even messier now than when I escaped.

"Thank you, Damon." Goodness, Haydon would keel over with shock if he saw what was happening in there, *or* in the garden. "What is he doing here, anyway?"

"A bedtime kiss?" Damon quips.

"Funny ha ha."

"With all due respect, ma'am." He takes my arm and pulls me to a stop, just before we round the corner to the foyer. He looks back toward the garden.

"I know what I'm doing," I say before he can lecture me.

Damon laughs lightly. "Do you?"

"Of course."

"I don't think you do."

"Why?"

His hand flexes on my arm. "You're still shaking. A man has never made you shake before."

"It's cold," I say automatically, claiming back my arm.

"You've also never done what a man has told you before. And I've never seen this sparkle in your eyes, either. I can't figure out if it's mischief, or something else. Something more."

I blink, as if I can dull down this so-called sparkle. I'm struck rather dumb, surprised by Damon's observations, and especially surprised he has voiced them to me. I scamper through many replies, many counters to put his mind at rest. And maybe mine, too. But though my words of reassurance gather and form satisfactory sentences in my mind, none of them are prepared to be spoken. "Is that all?" I mutter, looking away.

"That's all, ma'am." Damon links his hands behind his back and steps away, giving me space. "Here if you need me."

"Thank you." I find Haydon pacing the foyer when I make it there. "Whatever are you doing here, Haydon?"

He breathes out and comes to me, and I brace myself for his kiss. But he stops before he gets his hands on me, looking me up and down. "Are you okay?"

"Yes, I'm fine."

"You look . . . off." At that moment, a huge crash comes from the dining room, followed by loud cheers. Haydon glances across the lobby. "What was that?"

"Eddie is entertaining a few friends. I was just going to bed."

"Oh, I see." Haydon mumbles, as more bangs and crashes ring out. I wince with each and every one of them. "Sounds . . . rowdy."

"It is, which is why I am retiring to my room." *Take the hint!* "Why are you here, Haydon?"

"Dinner," he says, his attention constantly flicking between the dining room doors and me. "I wanted to take you to dinner tomorrow evening. An extended birthday treat, if you will."

I study him for a few moments, his disposition twitchy, his attention split. He could have called and asked me to dinner. Is he checking up on me? "You have already treated me enough." I am not going to dinner with Haydon Sampson. It will potentially give the press pictures and cause to speculate. My father and his minions will delight in it all too much. They might even be the ones to tip off the paps.

"Is that your way of saying no?"

"It is my way of saying you have already treated me enough," I clarify. "Besides, Damon is off tomorrow evening, and I have resided myself to a much-needed evening beside the fire."

"Then another day, perhaps?"

"Perhaps," I agree easily, if only to move things along. To get him out of here before any drunk men fall out of the dining room and Haydon snitches to the King, or, worse, Josh Jameson makes an—

"There you are." Josh's voice has my shoulders shooting up to my earlobes on a flinch of dread. I watch, stunned into stillness, as Haydon turns to seek out the source of the rough accent. Oh, goodness me. Josh strides toward us, confident, his blue eyes focused solely on me, as if Haydon is not here, as if he isn't looking at Josh in worried interest. "I've been looking for you." Josh's arm lands around my bare shoulders, his lips on my cheek.

Well . . . damn.

I soak up his attention, helpless, as he makes a banquet of my flaming face. The bloody rogue. Damon coughs, and I shoot my gaze to him, finding him trying very hard to conceal an amused smirk. I narrow my eyes on my head of security and shrug off Josh.

"Josh Jameson," Haydon says, clearly taken aback by Josh's brash behavior.

"And you are?" Josh, full of feigned politeness, offers his hand to Haydon, who doesn't entertain his invitation to make his acquaintance.

Instead, he just looks at Josh's extended offering before turning questioning eyes my way. "I didn't realize you had company."

"I don't have company." I move away from Jameson, feeling irritation growing. "Mr. Jameson is Eddie's guest." That is technically true. "Like I said, I was just retiring to my suite." I move toward the stairs, eager to remove myself from the thick atmosphere. "Good evening, gentlemen." I take the steps fast, hearing a few mutters from Haydon before the doors of Kellington close behind him.

When I reach the top of the grand staircase, I turn to find Josh standing at the bottom, Damon a few steps behind him. "That was not necessary," I grate, my jaw tight with frustration. His Tarzan move may have landed me in very hot water with the King. I don't need any more lectures on appropriateness, and who to be appropriate with.

"Did you want him to stay?" Josh asks seriously.

"No, but that is not the point."

"Would you like *me* to stay?"

I withdraw, my mouth snapping shut. I don't know, is the truth. "Yes." The answer comes from nowhere, something taking over my questioning mind, and I reach for my lips as if I have said something sinful. Josh smiles, victorious, and turns to Damon, offering his hand. "I've got it from here, buddy."

Buddy? I'm stunned further when Damon accepts Josh's hand and shakes on a nod. "Watch her, Mr. Jameson. Like your life depends on it."

"Because it does?" Josh asks, smiling.

Damon returns his smile. "I don't want to hurt you. I love your movies."

My mouth falls open and Josh laughs. "Understood."

Damon gives me his customary nod, straight-faced and sharp, before moving away, leaving me alone with Josh bloody Jameson.

"Let the games begin," he muses, slowly pivoting back toward me. I don't want to, but I start fidgeting with anticipation, my blood alight with thrilling forbiddance.

"Maybe I don't want to play."

"You don't get to play." Josh tells me with an authority I wouldn't dream of challenging. It's a revelation, one that I am mad at myself for liking entirely too much. "You, Your Highness, will obey." He stalks up the carpeted steps slowly, making sure I have ample time to try to regulate my ragged, shallow breaths. Ample time that is useless to me. All the time in the world wouldn't help. I'm virtually

panting by the time he is one step below me, his face perfectly level with mine. Brushing his palm across the material of my T-shirt, onto my stomach, and over my hip toward my bum, he tilts his head, as if thoughtful. "I'm the one who gets to play." *Slap!* I jerk forward, my palms shooting to his torso to support me. The feel of solid, sculpted muscle beneath registers quickly, and my palms start moving across his delectable chest. "I get to play with you. With this." His gaze plummets down my body. "And I'm quite possessive of my play things."

Oh, bloody hell. "I'm a play thing?" I should feel repulsed. I don't. I'm simply turned on.

"You are, and I have a feeling you might become my favorite toy." He bends and catches me behind the thighs, lifting me over his shoulder.

I pull in air quickly, nearly choking on it. "What on earth are you doing? Put me down." A man has never dared to throw me over his shoulder in such a caveman way.

"No. Which way?"

"Left at the end of the corridor," I answer without so much as a millisecond's hesitation, quickly accepting that I'm desperate to be his play thing. His favorite toy, because I know without question I have found mine. I get a lick of pleasure bolt through me. It's unnerving. But it is far more exhilarating than that. This scandalous bastard deserves at least some of my time, if only because he has achieved what no other man has ever achieved before. He has made me want. *Really* want. He has made me desire something because I really want it for myself, not to be disobedient and defy the rules. It both surprises me and scares me.

He carries me like I weigh nothing. "Here?" he asks, approaching the double doors that lead into my suite.

"There." I mentally hurry him along.

He lets us in, makes a quick scan around, and moves straight across the thick, luxurious cream carpet to the bedroom on the far

side. "Nice pad," he quips, throwing me onto the four-poster bed.

I land with a gentle thud. "You must be used to nice pads." I lie still, burning his clothes off with my eyes.

"I'm used to luxury, not palaces."

"Comes with the job," I murmur, and he smiles, a smile that could blow my knickers off. And then he walks away, casually strolling around my room, looking at photos, gliding his finger across the wood of my dresser, picking up and toying with pieces of jewelry. What is he doing?

"Has a man ever been in here?" he asks, gently setting down a sixteenth century broach that has been passed down to me through my mother's Spanish royal heritage.

It's only now I realize I haven't ever invited a man into my private quarters. I haven't done *this* before. Mind you, Josh Jameson didn't exactly ask to come in. "No."

He sits on the edge of the antique dresser, folding his arms over his chest. "So I'm the first?"

"And the last," I retort softly, casting my eyes around my space that's packed with historical pieces of art, treasures, and family heirlooms. My suite is so very old-fashioned and extravagant for a thirty-year-old *single* woman, but again, it comes with the job.

"I like the sound of that," Josh says, kicking one ankle over the other, relaxing back, getting himself comfortable.

I realize my error quickly. "I didn't mean—"

"Are you gonna rain on my parade?"

"Are you going to fuck me?" I ask, losing both my patience and will to remain on the bed. Lord, if I have to have a man in my suite, he could at least hurry himself along and make it worth my while.

"Come get me." He remains where he is. A ruggedly handsome, suave, if cocky, Oscar-winning Hollywood actor . . . on one of the Princess of England's historical dressers.

Pushing myself to the edge of the bed, I slowly get to my feet and take one step forward. I'm not too shy to take what I want.

And I want him more than I'll ever openly admit. I wrestle with my mind momentarily, wondering why. The men I bed are off limits, apparently. But you don't get any more off limits than Josh Jameson. Is that why he thrills me? The forbidden, as it were. Yes, that must be it. Because I refuse to let myself believe it is anything else. I take another step, and ano—

"Stop where you are."

I'm stunned to a halt, not only by his sharp order, but by his palm held up.

"Take off your clothes, Your Highness."

I balk mildly. "You want me to strip?"

"You're bright, aren't you?"

I scowl at him as I pull my T-shirt over my head, toss it aside, and unzip the fly of my jeans. I wriggle them down my legs before stepping out and kicking them away. I take the greatest pleasure from his pupils dilating and his nostrils flaring.

"Bra and panties."

"I'm sorry, I don't wear panties." I leave my underwear exactly where it is, relishing in his frown. "I'm British. I wear knickers."

His smile is so bloody beautiful. "Please, ma'am, will you remove your *knickers*?"

"I will." I smile sweetly and push them down my thighs slowly, watching his lazy gaze follow them to the floor.

"That's a line I never imagined I'd say," he muses quietly, moving his stare to the juncture of my thighs, before continuing to my breasts. "The bra."

"Yes, sir."

"Sir? You learn fast."

"I'll call you *sir*, and you can call me *Your Highness*?" I free myself of my bra and drop it to the floor. "Anyone would think you are feeling inferior. *Sir*."

"On the contrary, *Your Highness*, I am feeling very fuckin' powerful right now. Get on your knees."

I smile and slowly lower to my knees, no question, no argument. Nothing. The weightless feeling is new and thrilling, and most of all, it feels cathartic.

"All fours."

"Are you going to spank my arse again?" I rest some weight on my palms and look up at him.

"Crawl to me."

My coolness wavers for a split second, but hopefully not long enough for him to notice. He is simply trying to get a rise out of me. He wants the princess to object, to tell him she is better than crawling to a man on demand. Maybe she is. Yet she has an overwhelming craving to give Josh Jameson exactly what he wants, and he wants the princess to crawl to him. So I do. Slowly. Relishing in the sight of something growing beyond the fly of his jeans, and in the satisfaction on his face.

"Does this turn you on, sir?" I purr, steadily placing one palm in front of the other, leisurely making my way to him.

"You have no fuckin' idea." He crouches as I approach and takes my chin, holding me in place firmly as he pushes his lips to mine. "You are one sexy fuckin' woman, Adeline Lockhart."

I smile around his lips, feeling a sense of accomplishment. "I was beginning to think you were immune to my spell."

He laughs a little, breaking the contact of our mouths, and he stares so deeply into my eyes, I'm sure he sees right through my false bravado. "I wish I was immune to your spell, 'cause I have a feeling you're gonna curse me for life, woman." One more hard kiss before he grabs me and hauls me up, directing my thighs around his waist. I grip him tightly and smash my mouth to his, feeling power surge into me. I've got him. Hook, line, and sinker, I've got him.

But then he tosses me on my bed, and before I can gather my bearings, he's flipped me onto my front and trapped me on the mattress with his hard physique. "Remember this?" he asks, dropping something to the pillow beside my head. The pink handkerchief

he gagged me with yesterday is in my line of sight, laughing at me.

"Fuck," I exhale, feeling Josh's hands move to my wrists and take a secure hold.

"Say that again." He bites my earlobe, and I buck beneath him. "Say it."

"Fuck," I yell.

He stuffs the handkerchief into my mouth and flips me over, getting his face up close to mine. "Pink hanky has a friend." Josh pulls his belt from his jeans and wraps it around his fist. "I'm thinking helpless will suit you well."

I shake my head and Josh nods his, taking the black leather to my wrists and expertly wrapping it around before using the buckle to secure the ends. I jiggle my arms out of instinct. He did that far too swiftly and coolly to be a first time. I am his toy for tonight and tonight only. He's had plenty more before me, of course he has, and there will plenty more to come.

"Now," he muses, skating his gleaming blues down my naked form. "What am I going to do with you?" Reaching for my nipple, he tweaks it viciously, making me jerk under his harsh touch on a muffled yelp. He cocks his head, enjoying the fact that I am at his mercy. And, Lord, give me strength, so am I. My body is singing with need, every inch of my skin flaming under the power of his stare. "I think I'll fuck you." He walks his fingers across my stomach, down to the narrow strip of hair marking my entrance. I stiffen, working to breathe through my nose as best I can. "With my fingers first." Brushing over my pulsing lips, he toys with me teasingly, and I whimper my despair, closing my eyes in search of some strength to carry me through. "And then with my cock."

I groan, tossing my head from side to side as he plunges a finger inside of me. Everything in me constricts, gripping him harshly. I am so turned on. More turned on than I have ever been, my heart thumping with want, my body blazing with need. I have never felt so utterly consumed by a man, and I am certain it is doing me no

favors in the long-term. Though the long-term is hard to think about in this moment, when I am being lavished and worshipped by this American god.

My useless wrists wriggle within the leather bounds, burning my flesh, the licks of pain delicious on my skin. Suddenly, my jaw is grabbed, and my eyes fly open, finding his face close as he slowly, so painfully slowly, pulls his finger free from inside me. Staring at me with too much satisfaction, he re-enters me with force, pushing me up the bed. I cry out, the sound muffled. Oh God, my blood is on fire as it races through my veins with only one end point possible. I can't scream, can't grab him. Josh's constant smirk tells me he likes that. I try to close my legs to stem the intense beat in my clit and get nowhere, his knee forcing them apart again, his eyebrow hitching in warning. "What is it, Your Highness?" he whispers, low and smooth, doing nothing to cool down the burn in my body. "Feeling helpless?" Releasing my jaw, he pulls free of my dripping channel and grabs both of my wrists, yanking them up to the bedframe. I moan, unsure if it's in protest or excitement, when he unbuckles the belt and refastens it around one of the gold posts, leaving my arms restrained above my head. Oh, the irony. A royal princess sleeps in this bed, the most famous princess in the world.

And now she is tied to it.

Helpless.

But loving it.

Sitting up, Josh straddles my stomach, placing his palms over my aching, heavy breasts. I breathe in as he molds, squeezes, and pinches my nipples, before lowering his mouth and licking across one of the bullets, sending a sharp flash of pleasure straight down between my thighs. My eyes roll, my face trying to hide in the crook of my extended arm. Jesus, his tongue, his mouth . . . his potency. He makes a feast of me, dividing his attention between my boobs equally, playing and fondling, licking and biting. I am out of my mind with want, moaning with every flash of pain, every

part of me vibrating. "That good?" he asks, sucking my flesh into his mouth and rolling his tongue. My groans are broken, and then I jolt upward when he sinks his teeth in, clamping down hard and pulling until my nipple pops free. *Fuck!* I curse like a sailor in my head but breathe through the stab of pain. His laughing eyes both anger and delight me. "Time for me to get naked," he declares, taking the hem of his T-shirt. "You ready?" I don't know. Am I ready? Josh pulls the black material over his head, and the sight of his cut torso blurs my vision, every perfect bit of it calling for me to caress it, kiss it, lick it.

No. No, I definitely am not ready. He stands on the bed, his legs straddling my hips, and pops the button of his fly. I swallow on a hard gulp, my eyes crossing. I get a glimpse of some hair, short and neatly trimmed. No underwear? More swallows. Then he drags his jeans down, revealing inch after perfect inch of his assets. I sigh, relaxing a little, totally overcome by his long, smooth hardness. Every woman on the planet has seen this man's body, but how many have seen his impressive manhood? Kicking his jeans off, he takes his position, straddling my waist again, and takes a firm, possessive hold of his dick at the root. My mouth is watering behind the stupid pink hanky gagging me, my hands struggling in the restraints of his belt. And when he starts to massage himself, breathing in deeply, I lose my mind completely, no longer in awe of him, but hating him for being so bloody cruel. I close my eyes, refusing to indulge in the sight.

"Open your eyes, Princess," he orders through low pants. I shake my head, pleading silently for him to stop with the torture. "Open." A nipple is squished savagely, and I buck hopelessly, barely moving him an inch, his solid body restraining me as effectively as his belt. My eyes spring open, wide and wild, falling straight to his fist pumping his erection. I whimper pathetically, but I can't move my gaze, watching as beads of his pleasure gather at the tip and his fist increases in pace. His stomach, solid and chiseled, tenses and

relaxes, causing a ripple effect up his torso. This is hell and heaven. His spare hand lands on my breast as he works himself, squeezing, his jaw tightening. He's on his way to climax, his body rolling, his gaze glazed. I couldn't close my eyes if I wanted to, the sight of him pleasuring himself now holding me rapt. His head drops back, his throat pulled taut, and he starts to mumble a jumble of incoherent words to the ceiling. Then on a yell, he moves forward on his knees, releasing his cock, and rests it between my boobs, clamping it between them by pushing my swollen mounds of flesh together. He starts to thrust his hips, both of us looking down at his cock sliding back and forth between by breasts. His quiet curse signifies his ending, followed by the flow of white liquid that shoots from the tip of his pulsing dick, spurting up my neck, some landing on my chin and around my mouth. My tongue fights behind the cloth in my mouth, desperate to taste him. But it's trapped, so I'm forced to settle for the vision of Josh Jameson, the object of millions of women's fantasies, sweating and heaving his way through his release as he straddles me. This is the best belated birthday present ever, despite a lack of release for me. This. This sight. This feeling.

"Wow," he breathes, his cheeks blowing out. Releasing himself, he shuffles down a little and drops to his forearms, suspending himself above me, his face close to mine. His smile is otherworldly. Pulling the hanky from my mouth, he uses it to wipe me up before tossing it aside and resting his mouth on mine, not kissing or licking or biting. Just touching. "I feel honored."

"Why?" I ask, thinking it is me who is the lucky one here, which is a claim I never thought I'd make, given the lack of my own orgasm.

"I just came all over the Princess of England. How many men can claim that?"

"None," I answer truthfully, clearly delighting him. "Except you. That must please you."

Beaming at me, he pushes his lips to mine. "It did, but not nearly

as much as watching you come apart."

"Are you finally going to fuck me?"

Josh laughs a little, like he's privy to something that might shove my brashness clean away. "In time, Princess." He reaches for my bedside table drawer.

"What are you doing?" I ask, a little panicked. "That drawer is private."

He ignores me and pulls it opens, revealing the contents. "Well, what have we here?" He reaches in and pulls out my vibrator, and I close my eyes, not embarrassed, but more nervous. Especially when I hear the buzz kick in.

"That is mine," I say as firmly as I can, with no hope that he will listen to me.

"How often do you pleasure yourself, Your Highness?" he asks, placing the tip on a nipple and swirling it slowly around. I groan, stretching out my body as best I can with him pinning me down. "Once a month? Once a week?" He trails it down to my tummy and drags it from side to side. "Once a day?"

"Josh, please."

"What, Adeline? What do you want?" He scoots down my thighs, exposing my pussy, though my legs remain closed, and I am quietly grateful. Until he moves off me and spreads them. "Tell me."

I pull at my bonds pointlessly. "Make me come."

"With this?" He drops the buzzing silicone to the patch of hair framing me, and I choke on an inhale, fearing the condition I'll be in if he moves south just a fraction. And the bastard knows it.

"Josh." I level my wild eyes on his flawless face, pushing as much warning through the lust of my gaze as I can. He simply smiles and slides my vibrator between my legs, the pulsations catching my clit. I jolt like I could have had a million volts of electricity surge through me. "No." Sweat instantly beads on my forehead and trickles down my temples. He removes the device and chuckles.

"What's it worth?" he asks seriously. "If I bury my cock inside

you and fuck you to orgasm, what will I get in return?"

Just the thought of his cock gracing my pussy tips me over the edge. "Anything," I say desperately. Any caution I should have has been obliterated by my desperation. "Anything you want."

"I want you." Another teasing touch of the vibrating tip on my clit sends pleasure ripping through me, but just as quickly, he pulls it away, leaving me a panting, despairing mess.

"You have me," I pant, yanking on my restraints to demonstrate.

"I mean *again*. And maybe again after that."

I still, pleasure draining from me quickly, being replaced with caution. "What?"

He smiles a small smile. "You're flighty."

"Where have you heard that?" I ask, unreasonably indignant. I'm flighty because there's no point getting attached.

He shrugs. "Rumors."

"I've told you, rumors are rumors."

"And I'm quickly figuring out that all rumors I've heard about Princess Adeline of England are true."

"And your point is what?"

"I don't have a point."

"Then what is the bloody point?" I'm getting wound up, but not in a sexual way. I'm agitated. So what if I am flighty? What does it matter to Josh Jameson? I'm not necessarily flighty through choice. The King catches wind of me seeing someone and takes the necessary steps to halt it going further, whether it be blackmail or something else. I never ask, because I never want to see them again, anyway. I don't get attached. And there is *my* point. From the moment Josh Jameson and I started sparring with words and chemistry, I knew I could quite easily get a little addicted to his disregard for who I am, his playfulness, his wickedness, and his ego. He is like nothing I've dealt with in the past. He's not tiptoeing around me, treating me like a lady, bowing to me. He's doing the exact opposite, and it is quite possibly the worst thing he *could* do.

Because I like it. I like *him*. I like the fact that he's keeping me in my place with his palm and a few leather bounds. I like the feeling of abandon when he takes charge. I'm always so hell-bent on being defiant and strong-willed; it's a relief to hand the control over to someone who I actually want to have it. And all this is worrying. Very worrying, because when the King finds out, there will be no playing anymore. There will be no more Josh Jameson. It will be game over.

Josh studies me for a few quiet moments, the vibrator still buzzing in his hand. "The point is," he whispers, dropping a gentle kiss on my lips. "I want you to agree to play with me again."

"You call this playing?" I half laugh, despite very much enjoying myself.

"Don't pretend you're not having an amazing time." He teases my clit with the tip of my vibrator again, and I stiffen everywhere as a result, gritting my teeth. "I'll admit," he goes on, "at first you were a challenge."

I roll my eyes to myself. I already knew that. "Lucky me."

"But now," He gets his face close to mine, and I breathe in, waiting for what might come next. Now, what? "Now I'm thinking nailing it won't be enough." He smiles when I balk. "So, will you play with me again, Your Highness?"

Nailing *it*? The nerve. "Make me come."

He pulls back, refocusing his attention further down my body. "I decide when your orgasms come. Not you." One more tease of my clitoris increases my body temperature, as I lift my hips to try and seize the looming climax. But he pulls it away, a cocky eyebrow raised. "Say yes."

"Before you make me come?"

"Yes."

"No." I slam my head back. "I'm not bargaining for an org . . . ohh." My body locks up when the vibrator pushes firmly into my clit, pushing my simmering blood quickly back to boiling point.

My hips flex against the pressure, savoring the sweet sensations.

"Agree," he whispers in my ear, licking the sensitive spot beneath my lobe. "Agree to play with me again."

"You sound desperate."

"I am. I want you and me to be a rumor, Your Highness."

"Okay," I breathe, lost in ecstasy, vulnerable to his every demand. Right now, with pleasure drenching me, I would agree to anything. "Kiss me."

His lips touch mine as he works me with the vibrator, my arms locked at the elbow. "Talk to me," Josh demands. "Tell me how it feels."

"Good." I roll my tongue through his mouth, savoring the hint of Scotch mixed with his scent. "So good."

Biting my bottom lip harshly, I get a hint of the coppery taste of blood as he maneuvers quickly, pulling the vibrator away and replacing it with his mouth. Licking, sucking, biting, kissing. I'm done for. I tumble into an abyss of unspeakable pleasure, feeling totally weightless, my body trembling deliciously as the most satisfying orgasm rips through me. "Oh . . . my . . . God." I arch my back, my arms going rigid against my restraints as Josh feasts on me, his whole mouth encasing me and sucking me dry.

"Hmm," he mumbles in appreciation. His fingers claw into the flesh of my thighs until my body liquefies and goes lax beneath him. I keep my eyes closed, breathing shallow and low, willing my heartbeats back to a steady rhythm.

"Jesus," I exhale, so unbelievably sated and relaxed.

"Royal pussy tastes as fine as I imagined." Josh's voice is husky as he pecks light kisses on my sensitive button of nerves, before moving his mouth to my thighs, and then working his way up my navel to my breasts, flicking his tongue across each nipple. "Fuckin' delicious," he declares, and I smile as his tongue makes it to mine and he wipes his lips across my mouth. Lifting his face, I catch the evidence of my release smeared around his lips, his tongue sweeping

across them to clean up the remnants. Oh Jesus, I have never seen anything so erotic. "And now I'm keen to find out if your cunt around my cock will feel as good as I've imagined."

His mouth is vulgar, yet just like that, I'm swimming with want all over again, my orgasm barely leaving my body, another building. "So you're going to fuck me now?"

His grin is wicked. "Beg, Your Highness."

"Please," I whisper, caution completely and utterly thrown to the wind, my inner slave breaking free willingly. It's alien territory but at the same time, so very natural. Especially when the gratification in his gaze at those words is almost blinding. "Please, sir, I beg you. Play with me. Lick me, bend me." I lick my lips seductively. "Fuck me."

"Oh, shit, Adeline Lockhart." His lazy eyes scan my face, a small frown marring his perfect brow. "I have a very addictive nature, and that's bad news for you."

"Why?"

"Because addiction means wanting constant access to the hit you need." He kisses each corner of my mouth. "And constant access isn't the kind of thing a man can depend on when he's addicted to one of the most protected women in the world."

I catch his lips and coax his mouth open, lapping my tongue softly across his. "So it is bad news for you, yes?"

"I don't think I've ever been in so much trouble." He deepens our kiss, his body sliding across mine briefly before he rises to his knees, smiling at his growing cock. "Cross your hands at your wrists," he orders, which I do immediately, just in time for him to flip me onto my knees. "Hold tight, Your Highness." I grip the gold bar of my headboard hard, grunting when his palm connects with my right cheek, reigniting the blaze across my skin. I don't shout, don't curse, and I don't even jolt. In fact, I smile sadistically, focusing on the warmth that follows the sting and my body's need to turn that sting into pleasure. My hair is gathered into his fist and tugged back viciously, and I still smile. With his body bent over mine, he

brings his mouth to my ear. "Was that a smile?"

"What of it?"

"I love your cockiness." He curls my hair around his hand and yanks until my head is forced back and I'm confronted with his face. "I need my belt."

"Too bad it's being used to restrain your prey."

"Then I'll have to find another."

I wonder what for, but I don't voice it. Because deep down, I already know. Squaring unaffected, sure eyes on him, I speak, just as certain and strong. "Bottom drawer of the chest in my dressing room."

His smile is a blend of awe and approval, and he kisses me hard, fisting my hair tightly as he does. "Don't move," he orders as he gets off the bed and paces to my dressing room.

"Because where the hell can I go?" I say quietly, knowing I'm about to be thrashed, and wondering where the hell my objection is. I'm on my knees, hands tied, arse exposed, and I have never been so relaxed in my entire life. *What is wrong with me?*

Or maybe I should be asking what is right with me? *Him*. He is what's right here. Josh bloody Jameson, actor extraordinaire, who is currently rummaging through my drawers to find a belt in order to whip my arse. I shake my head at myself and then still when I hear the crack of leather.

"Nice belt," Josh says quietly, prompting me to look over my shoulder. He's threading the leather between his hands, slowly and purposefully, that wicked grin on his face again. It doesn't take a genius to figure out that Josh Jameson is a kinky bastard. Hankies, slaps, belts, and restraints. Why I am so eager to play with him is not something I'm prepared to analyze right now. I'm too wound up. Too desperate for him to bend me to his will, to beg, to make me melt away under his expert touch. To make me forget I'm a product of the most privileged family in the world, and this kind of behavior should be well off the agenda.

Another sharp crack jolts me from my reasoning, and I zoom in on the belt again, now dangling by his naked thigh. He stalks slowly forward, eyes rooted to my bare bottom, his face full of gratitude. "When I'm done with you, Your Highness, you're going to be questioning who your true king is."

I inhale sharply, not just at his words and that he's most probably right, but at what he's holding in his other hand. My maternal grandmother's tiara, a beautiful piece bequeathed to me—her only granddaughter—by the late Spanish queen. It's personal to me, and though it was argued that the treasure should be locked away with the rest of the family jewels, my mother insisted that as a Spanish treasure, it was a gift for me to admire, to wear, to cherish. It is one of the only battles she has won with the King. The antique, diamond-encrusted headpiece weighs a ton, and is so very uncomfortable. But it's stunning, and it screams royalty. And it's even more special because my mother fought for it. For me. What's Josh doing with it?

He must catch the question in my eyes. "It's beautiful." He comes to a stop by the bed.

"It was the Queen of Spain's."

"It's heavy."

"Which is why I rarely wear it, except for the occasional royal engagement in Spain."

"That's a shame. Something so beautiful shouldn't be hidden away." He reaches forward and places the embellished tiara on my head.

I close my eyes, aware of what happens next. "Get on with it, Josh."

"Are you telling me what to do?" The leather of the belt snaps threateningly.

My flinch is mild. "No."

"Good. As long as you know where you stand."

"I'm not standing," I retort, unable to stop the words before

they fall from my mouth.

"One," he shouts as I'm thrashed with the belt, my backside bursting into raging flames. But just as quickly, the tip of his finger draws a line up my center, transforming that pain into pleasure of the most desperate kind.

"Too hard?"

I bite down on my lip, taking oxygen into my lungs, breathing through the pain. "Not enough."

I can almost hear his smile. And a second later, another thrash of the belt. "Two."

I pant, squeezing my eyes closed as his whole palm strokes at my entrance.

"Fuck me, Adeline. I don't think I've ever seen such a superb vision. You, restrained, a crown upon your head, and your ass glowing."

I can only imagine what I must look like. The Princess of England on her knees, bound by leather, being whipped by leather, a priceless family heirloom perched on her head, with a famous Hollywood actor delivering the blows. It's a mind-bender, for sure. But good God, I feel too uninhibited to devote any time to examining it further than that. He is a hedonistic man. I am a willing woman. That is it.

I space out, struggling to keep my head up with the weight of the tiara weighing it down, my palms sweating and slipping around the gold bar that I'm clinging to, causing me to slip a few times, the bonds cutting into my skin. Yet the pain is only a blip on the pleasure sweeping through me, Josh's fingers tickling the edges of my dripping pussy, teasing me, torturing me. I vaguely hear him count through five lashes, three to my arse, and then one to the top of each thigh. They sting terribly—my flesh throbbing—but it doesn't even dent the passion surging through my veins. I am on the brink.

I hear the ripping of a foil packet, and then a firm hand on my waist holds me in place as he walks on his knees toward my waiting

arse, the head of his cock sliding straight past my lips and hitting me deep. "Have mercy," Josh chokes, stilling, sending me dizzy with the depth he has achieved from one perfect stroke. I pant, fighting for air, my mind twisting. He reaches for my hair and yanks back, eliciting a small cry from me. "Ready to let go?"

"Ready," I confirm, *desperate* to let go. Or let go even more. I'm already in a sex-induced daze. It's laughable really, because we haven't even had sex yet.

"God, I'm so ready." He withdraws and pounds forward brutally, and the pace is set from there. Fast. Hard. No mercy, no holding back. Our bodies slap together as loudly as the leather did, the force of his body smashing into mine making me unstable on my knees. I lose my grip of the bar, forcing Josh to release my hair and manipulate my hands back into place. "You tell me if it's too much."

"No." I accept his ruthless pounding, silently begging him for more.

Because with each violent drive, I'm being taken further and further away from my reality.

My stomach begins to furl, my mind spinning faster, the blood racing quicker. "Josh," I breathe, warning him.

"Not yet, baby," he spits urgently. "Don't you dare let go yet."

I groan, tinkering on the edge of explosion, losing my fight. "Josh, I can't hold it."

His strokes become more measured, more timed and accurate. "There's no such thing as can't." He slaps my sore arse, but it doesn't serve as a warning; it is more of a trigger, making my mission to cling to my release harder. And I think the bastard knows that. "Hold it," he growls, squeezing my breast.

"You are not helping."

"No?" He pinches my nipple, sending a shot of pain straight to my pussy, the sensation mixing with the unrelenting burn.

"Oh God!"

"Hold it."

"Josh!"

"Don't disappoint me, Adeline." He rams into me, grunting with every hit. "You can do it."

I zone out, closing my eyes and breathing through the torture. Because—and it is a revelation—I don't want to disappoint him. His strokes are beautifully consistent now, albeit still brutal. I feel completely out of my body, entirely at his mercy, and my challenge has lessened under his expectation. Then I hear the words, "Let go, baby," and I tumble, spiraling into my release on his command, my skin tingling fiercely as my inner walls are massaged through my climax by Josh's throbbing cock.

He moans, his pace reducing until his movements stop and he's held within my warmth, our heaving bodies rolling as we both gasp for air. I would collapse if it wasn't for the belt and Josh holding me in place.

I feel his hands move to mine, unfastening the buckle quickly until my wrists slide free. I don't have the chance to fall to the mattress. Josh catches me and turns me in his arms, bringing me to my back and our sweaty chests together. My arms are stiff, my wrists sore, and my arse burning. But none of it takes away from the serenity I feel in this moment.

"Thanks for playing," he mumbles against my wet cheek, biting it. I feel him smile around his mouthful of my flesh.

"Have you not marked me enough without putting teeth marks in my face, too?"

"Be quiet and give me a hug."

I laugh, utterly amused. "You have thrashed me to within an inch of my life, and now you want a hug for it?"

"Are you questioning me again?"

"No." I reach around his shoulders and hug him, smiling into the crook of his neck. "It was fun."

"Wasn't it." Lifting up, he blows a wisp of hair from my face and pushes my grandmother's tiara to the side of the bed. "Let me

get you a drink. Water?"

I frown around my smile, intrigued by his offer to wait on me. "I have staff who can fetch drinks if you would like one."

"Of course. How could I forget? But surely you don't want them to see me." He plants a solid peck on my mouth and gets off the bed. "Besides, I'd like to get you a drink."

"If you must. There are glasses and bottled water on the cabinet through there." I roll over, wincing at the instant pull of every muscle I have, some of which I didn't know I had. "Hurry up, now."

Josh grabs his jeans and tugs them up his perfectly sculptured thighs, grinning. "Yes, ma'am." He disappears out of my bedroom, and I'm unable to stop the satisfied smile from forming. I have never felt this before. So . . . sated. So looked after. Yet I was anything but, really.

I look at my wrists, where red welts are developing before my eyes, and I shift, flinching at the soreness rubbing on the covers. He *really* doesn't give a stuff about my status. "Bloody hell," I mutter, struggling to sit up. I have an official engagement in two days, opening a new art gallery that's been set up by a charity that I'm a patron of. It looks like long sleeves will be in order.

I'm distracted from inspecting my injuries when Josh rushes back into the room, no water in sight. "You forget something?" I ask.

"Your boyfriend's back."

"What?"

Josh makes quick work of snatching up his shoes, T-shirt, and belt, before darting into the bathroom, just as Haydon marches into my room. I quickly grab my covers and pull them up my body. "Haydon, what on earth do you think you are doing?"

He scans the room, before his eyes land on me. "I was just checking if you are all right."

What the hell? Annoyance replaces the amazing weightless feeling I had, which only serves to piss me off more. He's not checking if I am all right. He's checking if I am alone. "I'm fine, Haydon. Now,

if you don't mind, I was trying to get to sleep."

His face screams regret, and I don't feel in the least bit guilty that he is onto me, even if he thinks he has made a massive mistake. *How dare he?* How dare he barge into my suite unannounced like this? Where's Damon? "I thought you left?"

"My car won't start. Damon's taking a look at it."

So he used Damon's distraction to sneak up here? "I suggest you leave right this minute before I call Damon and have you escorted off the grounds."

"Adeline, I'm—

"I don't want to hear it." I flip myself onto my side and snuggle down, dismissing him. "Please leave." I wait until the door closes before I look over my shoulder, checking he has gone. Then I cast my eyes across to my bathroom. Josh appears in the doorway, but he isn't grinning in satisfaction like I would have expected. He looks pensive, and for the first time since he sprinted away to hide, I wonder why. He was more or less marking his territory in the foyer earlier when Haydon showed up. "Why did you hide?"

He pouts his lush lips, seeming to think really hard about it. "I don't know," he admits, making his way back to me. I eye him suspiciously, moving over when he nudges me to give him room. He lies next to me in his jeans, his bare back against the headboard. "All part of the game, right?"

"Right," I agree slowly, a little injured for reasons I'm not willing to look into. We're playing. Just playing.

"So, are you gonna marry him, then?"

I snort, patting down the covers around my body. "Did it sound like I want to marry him?"

"Do you have a choice?"

"Yes," I reply adamantly. "Despite what my father thinks."

"But your father is the King of England, Adeline," Josh cruelly and unnecessarily reminds me. "No one gets away with saying no to him."

"What can he do?" I ask. "Send me into exile? To the Tower of London to rot? Behead me?" Any iota of peace, any serenity I found, has been completely chased away with the reminder of who my father is and what my obligations are.

Josh crosses his ankles, his long jean-clad legs stretched to full length on my bed. I have to admit, he looks good on my bed, all roughed up and relaxed. "You sound resentful." He looks at me, a little thoughtful. "Is life as a royal that bad?"

I shrug a lot more nonchalantly than I feel. "It is if you refuse to abide by the rules. I guess it wouldn't be so bad if I bowed to every order and expectation."

"So why don't you? For an easy life?"

"Easy doesn't make me happy. It would be settling for second best. I don't want to settle for anything."

He holds my eyes, and I see compassion in their blue depths. "Then don't," he says quietly, taking my hand and toying with my fingers.

"I don't plan to."

"I'm glad to hear that."

"Why?"

"Because I'm not a second-best kinda guy." Tracing one of the red blemishes around my wrist, he stares at it, leaving silence lingering that I try to use to figure out the meaning of his statement. And in this moment of quiet, I sense a kindred spirit in Josh. He lives a life before the focus of many lenses too, has little to no privacy, and quite possibly feels as suppressed as I do. But before I can think more about that, he shakes his head, as if shaking himself from some unwanted thoughts. "So, when are we playing again?" He smirks that devilish smirk and rolls onto his side, settling his hand neatly on my stomach.

I stall, and even though it's because I'm wondering if playing again would be a good idea, I don't express my reservations. "I'm a busy woman."

"Then make yourself *un*busy," he orders, with no hint of amusement.

I laugh anyway. "I am in demand, Mr. Jameson. Representing the Monarchy and behaving for the cameras, remember?"

"Behaving? Oh, behave." Josh chuckles and shifts quickly, pinning my wrists above my head and crowding my body with his. His nose touches mine, his brow furrowing. "You're only allowed to misbehave with me in future."

Creases invade my forehead. Is he telling me no other men are allowed? "I don't do exclusive," I say. "You know that."

"The rules have changed."

"What rules?"

"The rules of this game we're playing." He subtly pushes his groin into mine, failing to hold back his victorious smile when I breathe in and hold it. Bloody hell, there goes my body temperature again, through the flipping roof.

"I thought the game was finished."

"The game only finishes when I say it finishes." Landing his lips on mine, he kisses me deeply, backing up his confident words with a confident kiss. And as I lose myself in it completely, I wonder if Josh hiding in the bathroom was because he understands that if anyone catches wind of our encounter, this game really will be over. And the game only finishes when Josh says it finishes, therefore no one can know about us. Which *should* be fine by me, since a massive part of me wants to play his game. But another part of me, a part I am finding too easy to ignore, is wondering if I should get out before I become too swept up in it. "Aren't you a little too busy also?" I ask around his mouth. "Films to make, billboards to grace, women to send dizzy?"

He smiles against my lips and pulls away. "Are you trying to get rid of me, Your Highness?"

"I'm simply reminding you of who you are." When does he imagine we are going to play this game of his?

"Don't you worry that pretty little princess head of yours." He kisses my forehead delicately. "All you have to do is as you're told."

"You are outrageous. Haven't you figured out yet that I don't like being told what to do?"

Taking my cheeks in his palms, he scans me for a few thoughtful seconds, allowing me the pleasure of viewing his lovely face so close. His jaw is perfectly peppered, his eyes perfectly sparkly, and his hair perfectly fucked. Josh Jameson is perfect. "And haven't you figured out, Your Highness"—he languidly brings his eyes to mine, his pupils dilated, drawing out the blue and green completely—"that you did very well being told what to do when it was *me* telling you?" He watches as my eyes expand in silent realization, and he nods mildly. "It was easy then, wasn't it, Princess?"

He's right. So easy. "Yes."

"Why do you think that is?" he drawls, his accent enhanced.

"I have no bloody idea," I admit, and he smiles, white and blinding, clearly relishing my confusion.

A chime of a mobile phone sounds, and Josh looks around my suite. "That's my cell."

"Then you had better answer it."

"There you go again, trying to get rid of me." He bites my nose and jumps off the bed, answering. "Yeah, I'll be there in a minute." Josh looks at me and pulls a face to suggest he's cringing. "Just getting a tour of the royal"—he stalls and skates his gaze down my half-exposed naked body—"palace." He finishes on a grin. "Awesome." He hangs up and slips his feet into his shoes. "My driver's waiting." Making his way over as he feeds his belt through the loops of his jeans, he dips and kisses me more sweetly than I would have liked him to. Although, apparently, my body is absolutely fine with his affection, my arms twitching with the force it's taking me to keep them by my side and not cradle his wide shoulders. He needs to leave so I can have a little meltdown and reflect on his claim. Reflect on the fact that I bowed to him without question or

hesitance. Without hardly thinking. That is not me. I shouldn't let it be with Josh. "It's been a pleasure, ma'am." He nibbles on my bottom lip. "I'll call you."

"How?"

He takes his phone and hands it to me. "Because you're going to give me your number."

Like a programmed robot, I punch my number into his phone and hand it back to him.

His smile is victorious as he lands a hard kiss on my cheek. "Sweet dreams, Princess." He strides out while I wonder what the hell I was thinking giving him my number. Am I mad? I laugh. Yes, quite possibly. Then I ridicule myself for my stupidity, forcing myself not to take any pleasure from the vision of Josh's solid, defined back as he leaves. I don't admire him. I don't analyze every detail, every feeling, every height of pleasure I just experienced.

I shouldn't think of Josh Jameson ever again, because despite him doing everything he could to make me feel less precious, he actually made me feel more precious. Treasured. And that is dangerous territory to venture into, for no other reason than I know I cannot sustain a long relationship with Josh Jameson. He'll be taken away from me faster than he caught my attention in the first place.

6

OF COURSE, MY sleep is restless, and I wake too many times with a startle, echoes of our cries of pleasure and visions of our tangled bodies invading my slumber. By dawn, I am utterly exhausted, aching, and as I stare at my reflection in the full-length mirror in the dressing area of my suite, I'm horrified by what I see. Bruises, welts, and red, tender skin. I'm disturbed I let him do this to me. And, worse, I loved every minute, almost goaded him, pushed him on. What on earth? Shame engulfs me. It is a misplaced emotion, and I really have no idea what I should do with it.

"Your Highness?" Kim's voice drifts into my suite, and I urgently scan the room for something to cover my naked, marked body. Oh my goodness, I cannot let anyone see me like this.

I spot my robe lying across the back of my velvet couch and quickly snatch it up, throwing it over my shoulders. "In here."

"As ordered, not too early." She stops at the door and runs eyes up and down my body, settling on my wrists. "What the hell happened to you?" she screeches incredulously, pointing at my arms.

I look down and cringe when I see the angry marks, not even remotely concealed by the sleeves of my robe. Because my robe

has three-quarter length sleeves. Bugger. I take my arms behind my back and scan the floor at my bare feet. "It's nothing."

"Nothing?" Kim marches over to me and seizes my arms from their hiding place, gasping when she gets the full visual force of the welts. "Oh my God."

I reclaim my sore limbs and head for the bathroom, pulling my hair into a ponytail as I go. "I'll be going to the stables." I tell her, my curt tone making sure she dares not interrogate me further. "Please ask Damon to have the car ready in an hour." I shut the door behind me, just catching sight of Kim's dropped jaw.

Letting my back fall against the wood, I sigh, inspecting my wounds. Christ, I look like I've been brutally beaten. Not that I need to remind myself of the state of my arse, I lift my robe and turn toward the mirror over the vanity unit, staring at the lash marks across my bottom and upper thighs. They seem to be getting fiercer. Maybe riding isn't such a good idea.

"Adeline?" Kim calls through the door. "Your phone is ringing."

"Take a message," I reply, flipping the shower on and letting my robe fall to my feet. I make sure the setting is cool, flinching at the mere thought of hot water on my sore skin. I hear Kim greet my caller as I walk into the shower stall, but a knock on the door stops me from reaching the spray. "Yes?"

"I believe you'll want to take this," Kim says, almost dryly.

"Who is it?"

"Josh Jameson."

My eyes bug at the closed door. *I gave him my number!* I fumble for my robe and sling it on, yanking the door open to find Kim with high, interested eyebrows. Her red hair—as usual, pulled back—ensures every disapproving line on her face is visible. "The actor?" she hisses, thrusting my mobile at me.

I snatch it and push it into my chest to muffle what he will hear. "Yes, the actor," I answer indignantly. "What of it?"

"Did he do that to you?" She motions a limp hand up and down

my body.

"Of course not," I snap, looking down at my phone, wondering why on earth I gave him my number. I certainly don't want to talk to him. So in a moment of impulse, I disconnect the call.

"Who gave Mr. Jameson your number and why would he be calling you?"

I cringe on the inside. "I don't know, probably Eddie. Mr. Jameson attended the garden party at the palace by invitation of the King. His father is an American senator. Knows my father." My phone rings again, and my jaw clenches as I reject the call.

"So, again, why is he calling you?"

"I don't know." My shortness doesn't affect Kim in the slightest.

"Do I need to call a meeting with Felix?" she asks, going into fixing mode without even knowing what needs to be fixed. Goodness, she would disintegrate with panic. I'm halfway there myself.

"No, you do not." It's my body that needs fixing, and Felix can't help with that. And maybe my willpower, too. "Now, can I please take a shower in peace?"

"Sure. Jenny's on her way up to do your hair."

"Send her home. I'm only going to the stables, and I have no arrangements for this evening."

"As you wish." Kim nods in feigned obedience, her eyes constantly falling to my wrists. "I'll see you downstairs, *Princess* Adeline." She's being sarcastic, placing emphasis on my title as if it is a joke that I am royalty. I guess it is.

"Very well." I shut the door and look at the screen of my phone where a voicemail is waiting for me. Perhaps it's stupid of me, but I click and raise my phone to my ear. His deep voice sinks into me like I could be a sponge, reviving every wonderful feeling I felt with him.

"Your Highness, I hope you slept well and woke feeling as satisfied as I am." I scoff, tempted to delete his message before listening to any more. But I don't. Of course I don't. Damn me. Satisfied? More like really *dis*satisfied. I listen on. "I'm ready for round two

of our game. Call me."

He may well be ready for round two, but my body definitely isn't. Call him? "I will do no such thing," I say to my phone, deleting his message and holding it to my chest, thoughtful. I'm far from dissatisfied, and I'm a fool for trying to convince myself otherwise. "The brash, American idiot," I mutter.

AFTER I'VE SHOWERED and am ready, I stand on the threshold of the dining room, gazing at the mess. Olive is on her hands and knees scrubbing at the antique rug, and various other household staff members are collecting up endless empty liquor bottles.

"Have fun?" Felix appears across the other side of the vast room, his journal resting on his forearm, his phone on top of it. The shine of his polished Italian loafers would probably blind me if my vision wasn't so foggy from lack of sleep.

"I sense disapproval," I breathe, going to my bag to reject the fifth call since I got out of the shower.

"Your senses serve you well, ma'am." He sweeps an arm around the room, as if I could have missed the condition of the stately room. "And we have bodies, too."

I look under the table where he's pointing, seeing three men, all in army uniforms, sprawled out on the rug, unconscious. "Oh dear," I muse, noting one of the stray bodies is the Prince himself. I scowl at his comatose form, making a mental note of his condition to hold it against him in future if he chooses to berate me on my inappropriate behavior.

"I have some calls to make," Felix says, strutting toward the corridor of offices. "I trust I have no clearing up to do." He looks over his shoulder at me, eyebrows high. "No calls from editors to prep for?"

"We were on our best behavior."

"Looks like it." Felix sniffs, taking one more despairing glance

around the dining room before he disappears toward his office.

I wander over and poke Eddie's thigh with the toe of my riding boot. "Wake up, sleepy head."

He groans and blinks his eyes open, frowning when he catches sight of the underside of the table floating over his face. "What happened?" he croaks, struggling to pull himself up to his elbows.

"I would take an educated guess and say that you passed out, brother dearest."

"Wow, that was wild," he mumbles as he sits up, smacking his head on the table on a load thwack. "Shit."

I laugh as Eddie rubs at his head and falls back to the rug. "I'm spending the day at the stables so I'll see you later."

"Oh, Spearmint. I forgot about your new man."

I smile, proud as punch. "I'm certain it's father's way of bribing me. Why would he finally relent to my desire to dip a toe in the racing world when it has always been strictly for the males?"

"We both know the answer to that question." Eddie gets onto his hands and knees and crawls from beneath the table, and I'm attacked by an onslaught of flashbacks. Me. Crawling to Josh. His wicked smile. His wicked touch. "Adeline?"

I jump, immediately looking to my wrists where they're safely concealed under the sleeves of my black roll-neck sweater. "Sorry, I was daydreaming." I turn and make a hasty getaway before my brother can quiz me about last night.

"Wait right there, Addy," he orders, and I stop, scowling at my escape route. I hear his army boots treading the rug. "Where did you disappear to last night?"

I paint on a smile and turn to him. "I was rather sleepy, so I retired to my suite."

One of his hazel eyes narrows, his lips twisting in contemplation. "It's rather uncanny that a certain American disappeared around the same time as you, isn't it?"

"I have no idea what you are insinuating, but I am offended."

Eddie, quite rightly, scoffs. "You are not talking to Father now, little princess."

"I'm not talking to anyone." I march out, relieved to see Damon waiting for me by the car. "Thank you." I slide into the back and let him shut the door, and though I know Eddie can't see me through the blacked-out windows, I can see him, and he looks miffed. It is all his damn fault, anyway. Had he not invited Josh Jameson to my party, I would not currently be shifting in my seat trying to get comfortable on my sore bottom, and I also would not be at war in my mind, which is running riot trying to surmise exactly what that flutter in my tummy is every time I think of Josh. I mean, really? What has gotten into me? I should be repulsed by his treatment of me. Not fantasizing about enduring his kink all over again.

"Nice evening, ma'am?" Damon asks as he pulls out of the gates of the palace.

I glance up to the rearview mirror, finding my driver's eyes on the road, where they should be, I suppose. It doesn't stop the blush creeping into my cheeks, though. "Wonderful, thank you, Damon."

His eyes flick to me, a definite knowing twinkle in them. "Glad to hear it, ma'am." He's saying something without really saying anything.

"You love his movies?" I mimic Damon's words to Josh last night, cocking my head in mockery. "Really, Damon?"

His big shoulders shrug under his suit jacket. "The man has talent."

Especially in his hands. "You have no idea," I breathe.

"Pardon, ma'am?"

"Nothing." I settle in my seat and focus on planning my day ahead in a vain attempt to stop my mind from wandering elsewhere.

AS DAMON ROLLS to a stop on the cobbles of the stable courtyard, I spot my mother riding in from the fields with Aunt Victoria. My father's sister is a massive fifth in line to the throne, much to her

displeasure. The woman is aloof and frosty, and speaks with three plums in her mouth as opposed to the customary one.

Damon opens the car door for me. "I assume you'll be here for a while?"

"Yes, at least a few hours."

"I'm to collect Prince Edward and drive him to the barracks. Shouldn't be longer than an hour."

"No problem. See you soon, Damon."

"Adeline, darling," Mother croons as Aunt Victoria nods her acknowledgment of me.

"Mother." I smile as their stallions trot toward me.

Aunt Victoria is the first to dismount, sliding off her horse with the grace expected of the Duchess of Sussex. "Good morning, Adeline," she says with no warmth. "Did you enjoy your birthday celebrations?"

I smile to myself, reflecting on last night when the *real* party began, the dancing and the disgraceful rate at which we poured alcohol into our mouths. I would love nothing more than to bring Aunt Victoria's snootiness down a notch or ten by telling her that her precious Matilda had a fabulous time, but I would never do that to my cousin. "The garden party was wonderful," I exclaim, with a pathetic amount of enthusiasm. My faux excitement doesn't escape my mother's notice, her lips straightening in displeasure. Lord Almighty, I can only imagine the family's disgust if they saw the shenanigans of Kellington Palace last night. But I definitely cannot imagine their abhorrence if they were privy to what I got up to in the privacy of my suite with a certain tall, handsome, American actor. It is off the disgrace scales, like nothing heard of before from a royal. I grin on the inside, and then kick myself for it. Because I, too, should be repulsed. "Must dash," I blurt, kicking my feet into action before I can let any flashbacks take hold.

"But, darling," Mother calls. "Are you not joining us for afternoon tea?"

I cringe, running through all the things I would rather do. "I

was not aware that there was an afternoon tea in the schedule," I say, pivoting to find my mother shaking her head in dismay as she slips off her horse.

"My secretary called Kim. We're celebrating your brother's wonderful news with the ladies. Did she not mention it?"

It's utterly ridiculous for my mother's private secretary to call *my* private secretary. Why can't my mother simply call me? "She didn't." I can think of nothing worse than enduring my sister-in-law for the afternoon, especially now she's carrying the second in line to the throne. I would not be surprised if an army of close protection officers tail her every waking moment. And every sleeping moment, for that matter. And on top of enduring Princess Helen for an afternoon tea, every other female member of the Royal Family, too? All in one room, sipping tea and picking delicately at cute cakes and sandwiches? I would rather be whipped with a riding crop. I flinch at my stray, inappropriate thought, my eyes falling to the riding crop in my mother's hand. And my body heats. And my heart speeds up. And a throb starts a cruel beat between my thighs. "I have made plans to spend the day here getting to know Spearmint. Sabina has kindly set some time aside for me, and I really don't want to cancel. I know she is busy, and her time is precious."

Aunt Victoria rolls her eyes slowly and dramatically, fully intending for me to catch it. "Priorities askew as normal," she mutters, walking her horse on to the south stable block.

I barely restrain my scowl at her back, and Mother doesn't breathe a word in my defense. I'm not sure why I continually let it bother me that she never fights in my corner. She knows as well as I do that the women in my family, all but Matilda, see me as rebellious and insolent, just because I have not allowed myself to be marched down the aisle and handed over to a man of the King's choosing. Because, of course, they're all living in wedded bliss. It hacks me off. They are a bunch of frauds. The whole bloody family is an institution of frauds. "I will be sure to send my love and a gift to

John and Helen," I assure my mother, making a mental note to ask Kim to order some elaborate baby gift for my brother and his wife.

Mother sighs, and I make tracks to the north stables before I can be forced into showing my face at their afternoon tea. I send a quick text to Kim as I walk, asking her to source a gift, and then drop Matilda a quick message wishing her luck this afternoon. Her response is immediate.

You're not coming? How do you always wriggle your way out of these things? And where did you disappear to last night?

I stall for a beat, breathing in.

I was tired. Enjoy the afternoon tea!

As I round the corner, I slip my phone into my suede tote and look up, spotting Sabina hunched against the giant trailer that stores the manure collected from the fields. I'm about to call for her, but someone appears from behind the wagon. The King. I skid to an abrupt halt and hide myself from view. Avoiding my father is at the top of my priority list, especially after our little *meeting* on my birthday.

I watch as he rests his hand on Sabina's arm, a gesture of comfort as she wipes at her cheek. She's upset, clearly, but why? Sabina and her husband, Haydon's grandparents, have been managing the royal stables for as long as I can remember. Sabina's a gentle soul, unassuming and open-minded, and despite her son being relentlessly supportive of my father's attempts to marry me off to her grandson, Sabina has never pushed the matter with me. It has only made me appreciate her more.

"If there is anything I can do," my father says, smiling sadly at Sabina. It's a rare display of compassion and comfort. "Please, just ask. You've been so loyal and committed to my family for many years. Maybe you should go home."

Sabina removes her arm from the King's touch, leaving his hand

falling to his side. "Thank you, Your Majesty. But I would rather keep myself busy."

My father nods his understanding, pulling on his tweed coat before settling his flat-cap atop his head. "You have always been a fighter." He motions for one of his footman to come to him, accepting his shotgun and checking the chamber.

"I have," Sabina says quietly, taking a tissue from the pocket of her Barbour jacket and wiping her nose. I'm sure I detect a flash of resentment as she utters her agreement. "One needs to be in this world, Your Majesty."

"One does," my father agrees easily, almost automatically.

I watch as Sabina stares at my father, who is now distracted, inspecting his gun. Yes, that's resentment, easily detectable on Sabina's face, whose features are normally so soft and serene. I've never seen this hardness in her expression before.

"Princess Adeline."

I jump and swing around, finding a stoic Davenport looming behind me. I breathe out and roll my eyes. "You don't have to creep up on me, Major," I mutter.

"No creeping, ma'am. Perhaps you were too engrossed to hear my approach." He passes me, and I follow him to my father, aware that my cover is blown. Damn it. The King's right-hand man never misses a bloody thing, which is undoubtedly why he carries one of the longest records of royal service. He could have retired three years ago, but he has devoted his life to serving the Sovereign. He'll probably outlive my father, too. I'm told the Major has never taken a sick day in his career, not when serving my father, and not when serving my grandfather either. His commitment is unquestionable, yet I often wonder how lonely he is when he is off duty, albeit rarely. The miserable old goat has never married, and he has no children. Not that I could imagine the cold, stony stickler ever being loving toward a woman and kids. In fact, I can't imagine the Major being anything less than stiff and impassive with *anyone*.

"Your Majesty," Davenport says as he approaches my father. "The Prime Minister has requested an audience."

"He has? Outside of our usual weekly meet? Whatever for?" My father's interest in the man who runs the country is, as always, lacking. Not that I'm included in affairs of a political nature, but one thing I do know is that my father believes it's preposterous that in these modern times, the Sovereign has no say over who runs his country for him.

My father continues to faff with his shotgun while Davenport mentions the Chancellor of the Exchequer and something about this year's budget. "Shall I confirm four thirty, Your Majesty?"

"Yes, yes. I should have popped a few birds by three." He points his gun to the sky and mock shoots a real pigeon. "Get the clays loaded."

"Sir." Davenport nods and leaves to relay the King's orders to whoever's controlling the trap for Father's shooting session.

"Adeline." The King finally notices my presence, turning his pot belly toward me and pulling a cigar from the inside of his tweed jacket. A footman is under his nose with a lighter before the fat, brown stick makes it to his mouth. "I didn't see you on the schedule to ride today."

"Last-minute plan," I answer, glancing at my phone when it rings. It's him again. "Sabina said she is free to spend a few hours with Spearmint and me." I slip my phone into my pocket as Father sucks on the end of his cigar. "But if it is a bad time, Sabina, I understand."

"No, no." She waves off my concern as Father and Davenport head off to the Land Rover, and I sag a little, glad I avoided another earache about Haydon and my obligation to marry him. "Let's go see that fine beast of yours," Sabina says. "I haven't had a chance to saddle him up just yet."

"No problem. I would actually like to do it myself." The more time I kill, the better. I will muck out his stables too, and even plough the field for horse shit if I must. Anything to keep me busy.

"Are you okay, Sabina?"

"I'm fine." She smiles and links arms with me, and we start to wander to the north stable block. "It's Colin. He was admitted into the hospital last night with a suspected heart attack."

"Oh my goodness," I gasp. Sabina's husband, like Sabina, is so active, his racehorse training skills making sure of it. A heart attack? I suddenly feel rotten, not only for Sabina, who I'm so fond of, but for Haydon, too. I was so short with him last night. Did he know his grandfather was unwell when I dismissed him from my suite? "Sabina, you shouldn't be here. Please, I can see to things myself."

"Like I said to His Majesty, distraction is better. Besides, Colin's sleeping mostly. I'm of no use fussing over him when there are an army of nurses to do that. In fact, he dismissed me himself."

"Does David know? And Haydon?"

The mention of her grandson and son brightens her smile. "David escorted me to the hospital late last night. We didn't want to worry Haydon unnecessarily so delayed advising him of his grandfather's condition until this morning."

"And how is his condition?"

"He's stable. Tough as old boots, my husband." She chuckles a little. "Anyway, enough of that. How did you enjoy your birthday?"

"It was lovely, thank you."

Sabina glances at my hand, and then back to me, a semblance of a knowing smile gracing her lips. "You're not wearing Haydon's ring."

I, too, look at my hand. "Oh, I didn't want to damage it while riding." I scan my mind for the last time I saw it. In the bathroom. I took it off to shower this morning and forgot to put it back on.

"Understandable," Sabina muses, "that you would forget to put it back on, since it doesn't hold the sentiment that Haydon would hope."

I flame red and glance away from her knowing eyes. "That's not the case," I murmur pitifully.

Sabina stops and turns me into her, taking me by the tops of my arms. There's no escape, and strangely, I don't want to. I am so fond of Haydon's grandmother, hold her in high regard, and only a small reason for that is because she doesn't push me toward her grandson like everyone else does. "Adeline, you know my thoughts on the King and my David's persistence in trying to bring you and Haydon together. You can't manufacture love."

I sag a little, so relieved to hear her say that. "They won't listen to me, Sabina. I adore Haydon, I do. We grew up together, but—"

"You don't need to explain yourself to me, Adeline." She laughs. "Lord, you'd eat my grandson alive."

I laugh too, because she's right. I can't promise if my father and Haydon's father ever succeeded in wrestling me down the aisle, I would not take out my bitterness and resentment on Haydon. He doesn't deserve that. He deserves someone who will love him truly and deeply. That someone is not me. "How can I make them see?"

"You can't." Sabina starts walking again. "No one can challenge the Monarchy when it comes to their public image. The smokescreen is too thick to penetrate." There is that hard edge to her features again, and I frown. I know she's right, but why do I sense there is a personal tinge to that statement? "I'm speaking hypothetically, of course."

"Of course," I reply quietly, falling into thought, desperate to ask if there is something specific she is referring to. But one thing I know is that asking questions will get you nowhere with the royals and their close aides.

We enter the block, and I spot Spearmint in the second stable. "There he is." His beauty wipes all questions from my mind. I slide the bolt across and coax him back as I enter. "God, you are so handsome."

"His grandsire won countless races," Sabina says, looking over her shoulder when someone approaches. "Doctor Goodridge," she murmurs, her face noticeably dropping.

The old man nods, his face somewhat solemn. "Your Highness."

I smile my hello. "You go," I say to Sabina, not wanting to keep her. Doctor Goodridge obviously wants to talk about her husband, and I feel somewhat grateful that he's on hand to care for Colin Sampson. The old doctor has served as the King's private physician for decades, serving my grandfather before that. He's way past retirement, but like most people who serve the Royals, he doesn't seem to want to break free. I run a palm down Spearmint's muscled neck. "I can see to Spearmint myself."

"You sure you don't want me to saddle him up?"

"No, I'll do it. I should get to know him."

"Thank you, ma'am." Sabina gives my arm a soft pat. "Go easy on him. He's been out cantering already this morning."

"We'll do no more than an hour."

"Okay. And then we need to discuss his routine. If you want to run him in the mornings, that's fine. Just give me notice so I don't send him out before you arrive. He'll need a rest day, too."

"That's fine. I can ride Stan if Spearmint needs to rest."

"Call if you need anything." Sabina heads off with Dr. Goodridge, leaving me and Spearmint to get to know each other.

"So then, Spearmint. What is your guilty pleasure?" I pull my fingers though his silky mane, laughing when he snorts. I reach into my pocket and pull out a sugar lump. "You look like a sugar kind of guy to me." Spearmint chomps down the cube, giving me a chance to inspect his teeth. They are about as perfect as a horse's teeth could be. "Let's get you saddled up, boy. Back in a moment." I let myself out of the stable, but before I head for the tack room, I wander down to the far end of the block to see Stan, my pride and joy. "Stan," I sing as I approach his stable, smiling when I hear his hooves clip-clop across the concrete floor. His grey speckled head pokes out, and, I swear, the big burly beast smiles. "Hey, boy." I make a huge fuss of him to be sure he doesn't feel left out, and I don't just give him the one sugar lump. I indulge him with two. "I'll

be back later. We'll go for a hack, what do you say?"

My friend nuzzles at my pocket in search of more treats, making me laugh. "You only want me for my sugar lumps." I slip him one more and then head for the tack room, scanning the rows of bridle hooks and saddle pegs, spotting Spearmint's name on the very end. I heave his giant saddle up and grab his tack, heading back to the stable. Every time I come here, Stan is always ready for me to jump on and trot off. I had forgotten how much I've missed saddling up.

I'm in my element as I get Spearmint ready for our first outing together, my hands working fast and expertly. He fights me a little as I slip the bit into his mouth, flinging his head in protest, but a stern word and firm handle soon has him complying. After a quick check that the leg reins are even and his girth belt not too tight, I lead him out to the courtyard.

"Fine beast you have there, Your Highness," Burt calls from the piles of hay, his fork breaking up the bales. The old farmer has supplied the stables stock of horse feed and bedding for decades, rumbling down the lane in his tractor twice a day.

"Thanks, Burt." I put on my riding hat and fasten it before working my hands into my leather gloves. Then I slip my left foot into the stirrup and grab the pommel, hauling myself into the saddle. "Easy, boy," I soothe when Spearmint shifts on his hooves.

I try to get comfortable in the seat, wincing and hissing as I do. Holy good Lord. Riding after a night with Josh Jameson is a terrible idea. My backside and thighs hurt in places they've never hurt before. But I persevere, and on a few more winces and grimaces, I click Spearmint on, walking to the training arena. His stride is different to what I'm used to after years of riding Stan, but my body soon falls into his rhythm and as soon as we are in the large square enclosure, I work him up to a trot and do a few laps, feeling him just as much as he needs to feel me. "I think you and I are going to get on just fine, Spearmint." He rides like a dream, gracefully and confidently, as if there is no weight upon his back, as if he is wild

and free. It's exactly how I feel every time I ride Stan through the fields, and though my horse is different and our cantering space is limited to the safety of the royal land, it is still the best feeling. My mind clears and I focus on being at one with Spearmint, taking him through the motions, getting to know him. I feel no discord, no need to defy. I'm alive, more myself. This is what freedom feels like for me. I won't allow any negative thoughts to intrude on this moment, because this is where my heart feels full. This is where my heart knows peace. This is where I can imagine my life beyond the constraints of my royal life. Where I may pursue dreams and live a life I choose. Where I can be myself and not what I am expected to be.

This is the real me.

7

AN HOUR HAS passed before I realize it, and Spearmint has worked up a good sweat. "I think that is enough exercise for you today, boy. Sabina will be scolding me." I slow him to a steady walk, shifting myself in the saddle on a hiss of discomfort. "And my backside can't take much more friction," I tell him as we head back to the stables, stopping at the water trough where I swing my leg over his saddle and jump down.

"He looked good," Sabina calls across the courtyard, her arms full of tack.

"He did beautifully." I assure her as she nears. "Is everything okay, Sabina? With Colin, I mean."

"Yes. Doctor Goodridge was giving me an update." She gives me one of her famous soft smiles and carries on her way.

I let Spearmint get his fill of water before I lead him to his stable and strip him down. Slipping his saddle over the stable door, I pull off his cloth and spend some time brushing him. I need to do this more often. It's so therapeutic. I reluctantly finish on his mane, stopping before I brush him until he disappears. "You'll do," I say, smacking him lightly on his muscled rump.

"Is it my turn for a rubdown?"

I swing around and find Josh with his forearms resting on Spearmint's saddle where it hangs over the half-height stable door. "Oh bloody hell," I mumble, not nearly as quietly as intended. My relaxed, serene state quickly changes to tense and shaky, and my bucking heart does not assist in helping me fix that. Josh's grin is almost angelic, contradicting the devilish intentions in his eyes. And just like that, I am ambushed, not only by countless flashbacks, but by a formidable desire I really don't want to feel.

Shit.

Shit, shit, shit.

"How did you get in here?" I ask, taking my brush back to Spearmint, ignoring the fact that his skin is probably numb from being groomed so much already.

"Why are you ignoring my calls?"

"Maybe because I don't want to speak with you. Again, what are you doing here?"

"The King offered my dad the use of one of his horses."

His rough accent drips over me in the most infuriatingly pleasing way. "That was very kind of him."

"I thought so, too."

I hear the bolt of the stable door slide. *Oh no.* My hand falters in its sweeping motion across Spearmint's coat. "You shouldn't come in here." It is way too cozy already.

Of course, he completely ignores me. "You don't sound happy to see me."

"I'm not."

"Why?"

I breathe in and force myself to face him, except now I have the full length of him, and the sight, in addition to his stunning face, is all too lovely. His cream chinos are a perfect fit, and with his shirt hanging out, he looks all relaxed and yummy. And his hair . . .

I drag myself back from the brink of pathetic and level Josh with

a cool expression. "I am rather busy."

"Is that an answer to my question? Because if so, I won't get in your way."

"You are already in my way," I retort as he steps forward and I step back. He stops and smiles, and then takes one more step forward. Instinctively, I move back. My only escape is around the back of Spearmint, and being behind a horse should be avoided at all costs. And it seems now the cost is my dignity, because if I remain here a moment longer, there is a huge chance I may grab Josh Jameson and tackle him to the hay. I can't seem to control myself around this man. It's dangerous. Possibly more dangerous than escaping him around the back of Spearmint. *Damn it!*

"You won't even know I'm here." He pulls an imaginary zip across his mouth.

"Not likely," I mutter to myself, facing my fear and walking forward. I stop before him when he doesn't move, cocking my head and fighting back the want consuming me. I knew this would happen. I just *knew* I would wind up wanting him again. It doesn't make much sense to me. "Excuse me," I say politely.

Josh steps back, opening up my path, and I make quick work of collecting Spearmint's tack before escaping the stable. The huge horse isn't the only thing taking up all the space. It is also the thick chemistry, and it's overpowering. I scuttle to the tack room, holding everything in my arms tightly to avoid revealing my trembles. Christ, why him? Why does his mere presence have my heart racing like a pathetic little school girl with a crush?

"You look fuckin' awesome in your riding gear, by the way," Josh says casually.

I dump the saddle on the saddle horse with far less care than I should, and loop the tack over a hook hanging from the ceiling. "Thank you." I wander over to the sink and fill it with warm water.

"Want some help?" Josh appears next to me, brushing my arm with his, forcing me to put some space between our close bodies.

"You want to help me clean tack?" I ask, amused, grabbing a sponge and plunging it into the water. I squeeze it out and make my way to the saddle horse, Josh on my tail.

"Yes, I want to help."

I start to wipe over the leather, my eyes dancing between the saddle and Josh, who is roaming the room with his hands buried in his chino pockets, casually looking around. "What do you know about horses and their care?" I ask.

"Nothing," he admits, turning his eyes onto me. They're bright blue today. I could melt under that gaze. Quite easily. "But you can teach me."

I laugh, looking away from him before I *do* actually melt, and concentrate on cleaning Spearmint's saddle. "You want me to teach you about horses?"

"Yes. Seems fair, since I gave you a few lessons last night."

My working hands pause, and I look at him. *Don't ask!* "Lessons?"

His smile is smug and victorious. "In submission, Your Highness."

"Excuse me?" I choke.

"You heard."

"I think I heard."

"Oh, you heard." He meanders over to me, placing himself on the other side of the saddle horse. There is a huge wooden stand between us, but it still feels like he could be touching me, and my skin erupts in tingles. He smiles, like he is aware of my condition. "The notoriously headstrong Princess of England is submissive," Josh whispers. "Who would've thought?"

"I am not submissive," I argue weakly, remembering how I succumbed to his every demand, how I took everything he dished out to me, and how I willed him on, begged for it.

Loved it.

The sense of freedom, the weightlessness, the relief of surrendering control. Of not having to think, just do. Of being at someone's mercy, and most significantly, wanting to be. The whole

time I was lost in Josh Jameson, bending to his will, I didn't feel the stifling containment of my everyday existence. I was free. I want to feel free again.

I swallow and glance down, disturbed by my revelation. I have never once considered submitting power to a man in the bedroom. Why would I when I fight so hard to keep it in my life? But I guess, now I am enlightened, I should ask myself if it is built into me, or whether my apparent subservient nature is reserved only for Josh Jameson. "What do you want to know about horses?" I ask quietly, my mind sprinting.

"Everything you can tell me." He fondles with the bridle hanging from the ceiling hook, and I just know he is imagining tying me up with it, maybe even whipping my arse with it. I swallow and shift in my stance, feeling my tight jodhpurs rubbing at my sensitive bottom. "What's this?" he asks.

"That is a brow band."

"And this?"

"A throat lash."

Josh's eyes widen, and I hear the thrash of my belt connecting with my upper thigh. "Lash," he whispers.

I make a hasty getaway from his suggestive gaze, tossing my sponge in the sink, grabbing the pot of saddle soap, and swiping a clean sponge around the inside of the container. "Anything else?" I rub at the leather of the saddle like a madwoman.

"What's this?" he asks, fingering a metal piece of the tack.

"A bit. It goes in the horse's mouth."

"What are you doing there?"

"Oiling the leather."

"With?"

"Glycerin."

"Oh," he says, drawing out the word on a long exhale as he swipes a fingertip across the seat of the saddle. "Like lubricant, right?"

I stop and inhale, straightening and facing his cheeky smile. He's adorable in the most annoying fashion. "Yes, like lubricant."

"Wow. Throat lashes, mouth bits, lubricants." He gazes around the tack room languidly, before dropping those starry eyes onto me. "A sexy princess, too. I think I might like it around here."

I breathe out on a laugh, astounded by his front. "You are a cocky American arsehole, Josh Jameson."

He's around the saddle horse in a flash, seizing me and pinning me against the nearest wall. I don't get a moment to gather my bearings, or to warn him off. Not that I want to. His hard body is flush with mine—touching everywhere—and it feels amazing.

Nose to nose with me, lips almost touching, he breathes in my face. "Actually, I'm a cocky American *ass*hole. But whatever. To-may-to, to-mah-to."

My smile is unstoppable, and so is the want flooding me.

"Kiss me, Your Highness," he whispers, and that's all it takes. One order, and I am his. I push my lips to his and drop the sponge in my hand so I can hold his shoulders. Soft lips roam mine, a soft tongue swirls through my mouth, and his body softens against me, molding to my every curve, fitting perfectly. He smiles around my mouth—happy he has me—and nibbles gently on my bottom lip. It is worlds away from the command he had over me last night, but commanding nonetheless. And the sense of freedom that sweeps through my body with the pleasure indicates I really am in trouble here. His soft touch caresses my cheek as his eyes wander across my face. "How's your ass?" he asks, sliding a palm down to my bottom and stroking gently. "Sore?"

"Yes."

"Regret it?"

"No."

He grins and smacks me lightly on my bottom. "Me neither."

"You hardly suffered." I laugh, pushing him off my body to free myself. We're at the stables. Anyone could walk right in at

any second.

"I assure you, I suffered."

"How?"

"When I left," he answers candidly, and I shoot him a surprised look. His shoulders shrug under his shirt, his smile shy and boyish. "Don't make a big deal of it."

"I didn't say a word."

"You didn't have to."

"You didn't want to leave?"

"It was the last thing I wanted to do, actually."

I don't know what to do with that information. Or even know what to say, and I think Josh must sense that because he jumps in with a quick subject change. "So, you gonna teach me how to ride, or what?"

"Yes," I answer without thought, because—and maybe I should be worried about this—I want to spend more time with him. *More time when he is not whipping me into submission, that is.*

Josh smiles, a knowing smile, one that I mirror on a shake of my head. What has this man got me doing? "We'll call it our first date," he declares, clapping his hands and rubbing them together. "Where do we start?"

"We need to saddle up."

His rubbing hands cease to rub, his eyebrow hitching in interest. "I like the sound of that."

"Of course you do." I laugh, fetching Stan's saddle.

"Stan?" Josh questions, looking at his name above the wooden peg. "What about Spearmint?"

"He's in training. He has already been over exercised today." I dump Stan's saddle in Josh's arms and grab his bridle. "And I don't know him well enough to trust him with a beginner. Stan's reliable. I know him best after riding him for the past seven years."

"Lucky Stan," Josh quips, following me back through the stables. "What do I have to do to earn those privileges?"

"What, me riding you every day?" I ask over my shoulder, laughing when Josh moves the saddle down over his groin area, giving me a warning look. The thrilling feeling of knowing I can have the same effect on him as he does on me satisfies me deeply. "Okay?" I ask.

His jaw tenses from his clenched teeth. "Ever got the feeling you might regret something?"

I laugh on the inside, hysterical laughter, because there is a potentially huge regret following me. "As a matter of fact, yes." I offload Stan's bridle and relieve Josh of the saddle. "You need to change."

Josh looks down his front. "What's wrong with this?"

"Those trousers don't look like they have much stretch."

He bends at the knees until they pull taut. "Sure they have."

"Suit yourself." I continue saddling Stan, quick and efficient after years of practice.

"What's that you're doing?" Josh asks, making me smile. He's like an inquisitive child.

"Making sure Stan's girth strap is not too tight." I slip two fingers between the leather and his ribs. "Always two fingers."

"Two fingers? This gets better."

"You are incorrigible." I chuckle, nodding to the stable door for Josh to open, which he does speedily on a charming smile.

"Your Highness."

"Thank you," I say as I pass him, tugging Stan's side reins until he clip-clops after me. "*Sir.*"

"Adeline." My name is a warning, delivered slow and clearly, and I secretly smile, playing Josh Jameson's game with way too much ease. "If you're lucky"—Josh falls into stride beside me, dipping to get his mouth close to my ear—"for letting me ride your horse, I might let you ride me later."

"Very lucky me," I whisper back, every nerve ending in my body sizzling electrifyingly. I am struggling so badly to repel the effect he has on me. His game is too easy to play, too much fun, and the sense of abandon is all too addictive. I pull Stan to a stop where

the hats are stored, grabbing mine from the hook before selecting a suitable one for Josh. "I'm really not sure if we have a hat that'll fit your big head," I say seriously, scanning the rows.

He grabs me around the waist and sinks his face into my neck, mauling me, making me shriek with a mixture of shock and undeniable enjoyment. "Very funny."

I smile like mad, turning my face to his, being blinded by the sparkle that greets me. Eyes locked, breaths suddenly strained, we stare at each other, my smile slowly falling away. *It's a game, Adeline. Josh plays games.* But my thoughts wobble when Josh starts to lower his mouth to mine, and suddenly, the only thought running rampant in my mind is how amazing it is going to feel with his lips on mine again, to taste him, savor him. His flesh has barely brushed mine when a loud clatter sounds, snapping me from my carelessness. I withdraw and scan our surroundings for peeking eyes. We're alone.

Goodness, how stupid of me. But Josh makes being stupid easy. Almost . . . right. Grabbing a hat, I hand it to him, but he doesn't take it. "This looks like it will fit."

"I want you to put it on," he declares quietly, closing the distance I've put between us.

I try not to let his request faze me, handing him my own hat to hold so I can follow his request. He takes it and dips a fraction, allowing me to rest the hat on his head. "Lift your chin," I order softly, having to bat down my admiration when his throat stretches, presenting me with the challenge of not licking his taut, stubbled skin. My fingers work fast adjusting the straps, that wretched tremble returning and making my task trickier than it should be. My eyes jump up to his, finding him watching me closely.

"Concentrate," he commands on a small smile. "It'll hurt like a motherfucker if you pinch my skin in that clip."

"Please, do not tempt me," I warn, pursing my lips playfully. It will be a small price for him to pay for the torture he put me through last night. And I don't mean the pain.

"Does it suit me?" he asks.

"Very much so."

"How come your hat has a fancy red cover with a gold emblem, and mine's plain, boring black?"

"Because I am a princess." I step back and take my hat from his hands, putting it on. "The emblem is the British Monarchy's coat of arms. The cloth is a silk."

"Silk, leather . . ."

I grin and reclaim Stan's reins. "Come on."

"Yes, ma'am."

I lead Stan on, bringing him to a stop by the giant mounting block, while Josh tails me, faffing with the strap under his chin, constantly stretching his neck, as if realizing my battle not to stare. Or touch. Or lick. "Climb up," I order, shaking my thoughts away.

"Onto that?" he asks, eyeing the huge lump of concrete.

"Yes."

"I see something better I'd like to climb," he mumbles, going around the back of Stan.

It is terribly hard, especially after that almost smoldering kiss, but I disregard his cheeky wit. "Always give a horse a wide berth if you are behind them."

Josh moves away speedily, eyeballing Stan with caution. "He's a big dude, isn't he?" He plods up the steps to the top of the mounting block.

"Seventeen hands."

"You're enjoying all this talking in code, aren't you?"

"Not at all. Slip your foot into the stirrup," I say, pointing to it.

"I know what that is."

"Then do it."

"Are you telling me what to do?"

"Yes, and I'm enjoying it. Don't spoil my fun and do as you are told." I smile a sweet smile. "Please, sir."

His eyes narrow to warning slits, and I can literally see him

mentally plotting his revenge. A revenge I will no doubt enjoy. Slipping the toe of his shoe into the stirrup, he searches for somewhere to hold.

"Here." I take his left hand and place it on the pommel. "Use that to pull yourself up and throw your leg over the saddle."

Josh does it with surprising grace. "Okay?" he asks.

"Okay. Just keep hold of the pommel." I walk Stan a few steps away from the block so I can access both sides.

"Pommel?"

"Yes, and there is no sexual spin you can put on that." I flip him a small smirk.

"Oh, I don't know. Let me think about that one."

I find myself laughing again. He's just too cheeky for his own good. And handsome. And talented. "Drop your legs."

"What?" Josh gives me surprised look. It is so totally false.

"Take your feet out of the stirrups and drop your legs. Your knees are too high. I need to adjust the stirrup leathers."

Josh follows my order, and I push his leg back so I can flip the saddle flap. "Are you trying to spread my legs, Your Highness?"

I smile as I work, unbuckling the leathers to release them a few notches before taking his foot and placing it back in the stirrup. "Better?"

"Much."

"Good." I walk around to the other side and match it, and then stand at the front of Stan to make sure Josh's legs are even. "Perfect." Claiming the reins, I look up. "Ready?"

Josh smiles down at me. "Are you?"

I prepare to fire some smart counter, I'm not sure what, just something that will shut him up, but I am interrupted mid-thought when I hear the clip-clop of hooves from behind. I turn and find Senator Jameson leading Bob, one of our resident horses, out to the field by his reins.

"Hey, y'all," he croons, his strong southern accent drawling, and

so very different to Josh's smooth, almost dulcet tone.

"Pops." Josh definitely sighs through his greeting.

"Good morning, Senator Jameson," I say politely.

"Your Highness." He bows his head. "What a pleasure. I didn't get the opportunity to speak with you at your garden party." He eyes his son atop Stan with interest, and I look to Josh to find he is no longer looking cocky, and his lips are firmly shut.

"Heading out for a hack?" I ask Senator Jameson, wondering what has made Josh so quiet all of a sudden.

"Yes." Josh's father mounts Bob and gets himself comfortably and expertly into position. "I don't ride nearly as much as I want to these days."

All that's missing from him is his cowboy hat, but then, as if by magic, it appears from a saddlebag and he pops it on his head. "Back to my roots on the ranch." He winks, nodding to his son. "What's my lovely boy roped you into?"

Roped? I flick Josh a nervous look, and, of course, he's now sporting a devilish smirk. "A few riding lessons," I reply.

"Lessons?" Senator Jameson belly laughs, looking at Josh with a shake of his head. "You ass."

I frown and look at Josh, getting a sheepish disposition in return. And then it hits me. "You bugger," I exclaim, smacking his leg. "You know perfectly well how to ride a horse."

"Thanks, Pops," Josh mutters, flipping off Stan in a swift, acrobatic move. "I thought you were already out in the fields."

"On my way now, son." He directs a warning glare Josh's way before he clicks Bob on. "Have fun."

I turn my narrowed eyes onto Josh. "You fraud."

He laughs through a shrug. "I can't help it. I like playing with you."

"Lesson over," I declare indignantly, marching on my way with Stan in tow.

"Hey, hey, hey." Josh claims my arm and pulls me to a stop. "I'm

not finished playing yet."

"Well, I am."

"C'mon, Adeline. Stop being so stuffy. Let's ride together." He lowers his chin when I deepen my scowl. "On Stan, I mean, of course."

When he says ride *together*, I sense he does not mean him on one horse, me on another. I'm just about to declare it impossible for us to ride double due to Stan's size, but, of course, I can't now that I know Josh has an expansive equestrian knowledge. Any horse enthusiast would look at Stan's sturdy frame and know he will carry both of us with ease. "I don't think so."

"I do." He starts to unfasten Stan's saddle, his motions quick and confident.

"You are surely not suggesting that we ride bareback?"

Josh bursts out laughing, and I cringe, wanting to grab the words and stuff them back into my stupid mouth. I know what is coming as he continues to strip Stan of his saddle, chuckling his way through his task. "I hope one day we can." All this horse business is making being around Josh Jameson even harder. "You offering to take care of birth control?"

I balk at him. I honestly don't think I have ever met such an arrogant male in my life. "You are assuming there will be another encounter."

"Oh, I *know* there'll be another encounter." He unhooks Stan's side reins from the D-rings and pulls his saddle off, pushing it into my hands. "We're going for a romantic ride together, Your Highness. Go get a pillion saddle."

I pout. Romantic? I would say it'd be impossible for Josh Jameson to be romantic, but I remember him cuddling into me last night after he had screwed me mindless, and I remember him wanting to fetch me water. Silly, but still. It was nice. And then I remember everything that came before that small window of affection. The dominance. The control he took with such ease. How much I loved

surrendering to him. My heart flutters and those flutters work their way down to my tummy. "I think I'll pass," I say, stepping back. Josh Jameson is about as far from grace as I could fall. And, worse, I want to fall. Or throw myself off the edge. It is obscene for me to think that way, because I know it will result in an agonizing crash to the ground. I like him. Way too much for a princess to like a man like him. Because I will never be able to have him.

"What are you afraid of, Adeline?" Josh asks, his features softening. "Having *real* fun instead of the manufactured *fun* you claim maintains your free will?"

"I have fun," I counter quietly. Unconvincingly.

He huffs a little bout of amusement, and then breathes in deeply, reaching for my cheek and stroking down my skin with the pad of his thumb. I close my eyes and relish his gentle touch, forgetting everything in that moment except for him. "I'm in London for a week. I like hangin' out with you. Let's make the most of it, yeah?"

I'm having the most fun that I've had in . . . forever. With someone I rather enjoy spending time with. What harm can a week do? "Yeah," I breathe easily.

"Go get the pillion saddle," he orders again, this time gently.

I back away and do what comes instinctively to me where Josh is concerned: what I'm told. Trekking to the stables, I hand Stan's saddle to one of the stable girls and request a pillion one instead, then spend the few minutes it takes her to deliver it trying not to think about the potential deeper trouble I'm about to get myself into. A week. We are just *hangin' out*, as he says.

"Would you like me to saddle him up, ma'am?" the girl asks when she returns.

"No need," I say, getting on my way.

When I make it back to the courtyard, Josh is chatting to Stan. He looks up when I approach, taking the saddle and putting it on. "Stan and I are best friends," Josh declares.

"He already has a best friend." I frown at my beloved horse as

I take a sugar lump from my gilet pocket and hold it out for him.

"Oh, playing dirty, are we?"

"Dirty is *your* way of playing, Josh."

Slipping his foot into the stirrup, he swings himself into the saddle and holds his hand out to me. "Side-saddle, my lady?"

"No," I laugh, placing my hand in his.

"You like to straddle?"

"A horse, yes. You want me in front or at the back?"

His eyes gleam. "After last night, I think I'll try the front." He pulls me up as I giggle like a silly little girl, once again wondering how he does this to me. The butterflies. The smiles. The lightness that could easily be weighted back down if I think too hard about what on earth I'm doing. So I'll simply not think about it.

I come to rest in the saddle and hiss at the unrelenting soreness of my backside.

"Still hurting?" he whispers in my ear.

"Very much."

He laughs, a light laugh full of satisfaction, as I take a hold of the pommel, feeling Josh's chest pushed flush with my back. I gulp involuntarily, straightening my spine as he reaches past me and takes the reins. I can hear him breathing, as well as feel it. "Don't move too much," he warns. "There's no more room in this saddle for any guests." His hips push into my lower back, and I look to the sky for help. "Ready?"

That's the operative question, isn't it? "Ready," I reply, and he kicks Stan on, heading toward the lane that will take us to the bridle path. Stan falls into an easy, meandering pace, and I start to relax into Josh's chest, content with him taking the reins, so to speak. Besides, he does it so well. In all areas of our involvement, it seems. The atmosphere is easy and comfortable. It's refreshing not having a man fussing and so keen to strike up boring conversation in an attempt to keep my attention.

"Is that your car?" Josh asks.

I look up as it rounds the corner onto the lane. "Yes." I had completely forgotten about Damon, and I had also completely let it slip my mind that I'm not supposed to leave the stables without him. I can only blame the present distraction. "He should be accompanying me."

"This will be even more romantic than I planned," Josh quips as Damon slows to a crawl. I see his window slide down as he approaches us, and I smile when his thumb appears out of the window, hovering between up and down. "Is that some sort of code thing you guys have going on?" Josh asks, bemused.

I smile and give my head of security a thumbs up as he passes. "Do you have your phone?" Damon asks, and I tap my pocket. "Don't pass the boundary," he orders, with all the threat he means. "You have half an hour."

"Thanks, Damon." I smile and he nods, rumbling up the lane toward the stables.

"I get a thumbs up?" Josh murmurs in my ear, causing all kinds of funny sensations to spring into various parts of my body. "Does that mean I get to keep my head?"

"Yes." I laugh as he steers Stan onto the bridle path.

He sighs, inching forward in the saddle a little more, as if he doesn't feel close enough. "Then why do I worry that I'm already losing it?"

I smile at the endless space before us. "What, you? The irresistible Hollywood heartthrob? Behave. With the amount of women throwing themselves at your feet, I bet you are losing your mind weekly."

He drops a light kiss on my cheek. "I'm a single guy. I date."

"A lot of women."

"I get bored easily."

My lips purse. That right there is another reason to rein myself in. "I must remember that," I reply quietly.

"I don't think I could ever get bored of you, darlin'." I don't

want that statement to warm me. Yet it does. "And that's bad news."

"Why?"

"Because you are quite literally the only woman in the world that I can't have."

"One week. Fun." I force the words over the worry clogging my throat. Josh doesn't reply, and my thoughts become further warped with what he might be thinking.

We walk for a while, the silence easy, the fresh air luscious and refreshing. The sky is a tie-dye of powder blue and fluffy white, the sun drifting in and out of the clouds. The springtime breeze licks my cheeks as we amble along in a blissful haze, the only sound that of nature. The English countryside cannot be rivaled—the various shades of green, from subtle to vivid, canopying the path we're taking down the side of a field. A tractor rumbles in the distance, cows graze, and birds swoop the sky as free as I'm feeling right now. Every so often, a bunny darts across the path, and a couple of times Josh has to calm Stan when he is startled by one of the speedy little creatures.

"Whoa." Josh pulls on the reins when a swan waddles out of a nearby clearing and stops slap bang in the middle of our path.

"Just hold him still," I tell Josh, as Stan starts to tread on the spot. "There is a lake through these bushes." The swan starts to hiss, warning us back.

"Nasty little fucker," Josh mutters. "If we were back home, I'd have my shotgun. Boom. Bye-bye, Mr. Swan."

"You can't kill it." I laugh.

"Why not?"

"Because it belongs to the King."

"He has a pet swan?"

I shake my head, thoroughly amused by his ignorance. "The King owns every unmarked mute swan in UK open waters."

"He does? Fuck, that must keep him busy." He nudges me in the back with a light thrust of his hips, and I laugh. He does it so easily.

Makes me laugh, just as easily as he makes me a wanton mess. "So what do we do?" he asks.

"About the swan?"

"No, about this." Another thrust.

"Will you stop?" I swat his hand in front of me, and squeal when he sinks his teeth into my neck.

"Having fun?" he asks around a mouthful of my flesh. "I mean *real* fun?"

"I am." I push the side of my face into him. "You can walk on now," I say as the swan relents and waddles out of our way.

"We should probably turn back before they send out a search party for you."

I sag, disappointed. He is right, of course. We have been gone for twenty minutes, and it will take another twenty to make it back. I'm already going to be late. "No, keep going," I say, not wanting our time to be up just yet. "I'll text Damon."

"I'm not going to argue with you." He kicks Stan on while I tap out a quick message to Damon, telling him that I'm fine and we'll be another half hour.

"Your father's accent is different to yours," I muse, clicking send and slipping my mobile back into the pocket of my gilet.

"I'm a southern boy, darlin'," Josh drawls, his accent now as thick as the senator's. "Born and raised, but fifteen years bouncing between New York and LA diluted it. I grew up on my father's ranch in Alabama."

"So you're a true cowboy?" I smile, imagining Josh in boots and a Stetson. It is a ridiculously hot mental image indeed.

"Until I was eighteen. Rodeos, mountain trekking, you name it. Two hundred acres of unspoiled beauty."

"Sounds wonderful."

He breathes in, not that I hear it, more feel it from the expansion of his chest against my back. "It wasn't really all that awesome." He pauses for a few long seconds, and I look back to him. He smiles,

but it goes nowhere near his starry eyes.

"Are you okay?"

"Yeah, I'm fine." He returns his attention forward, prompting me to do the same, though I do it reluctantly, wondering what is playing on his mind. "It's weird how so much space can be suffocating."

"I know how that feels," I agree, casting my eyes across the vast beautiful land before us. Feeling damned and blessed is so conflicting.

"My hometown was in the middle of nowhere. Population 1341."

"That's tiny. How did you meet people?"

"I didn't. Everyone knew everyone or was related to you in one way or another."

"So how did you get into acting?"

"Anyone would think you want to get to know me," he muses teasingly. "Isn't that off limits for you?"

"Everything about you is off limits. Yet here I am on a romantic horse ride in the English countryside with you."

I feel him smile against my cheek as he moves the reins into one hand, his spare now pulling up the sleeve of my jumper. "Quite a contrast to last night, huh?"

I look down and see him fingering the red welts glowing around my wrists. "Quite."

"Do they hurt?"

"Not as much as my bottom." I say as he lifts my hand and gently kisses my reddened flesh, heating the dying burn. "Have you always been so . . ." Drifting off, I ponder the right word.

"Kinky?" he finishes.

"Or brutal." I shudder for effect, earning myself another bite of my neck.

"You loved it."

I really can't oppose him. "So have you always been kinky?"

"Not really. I guess my tastes developed as I did. My first time was a very clumsy affair."

"Who was your first time with?" I ask, smiling to myself.

"I'll tell you, but remember I told you I was from a small town, okay?"

I frown. "Okay."

"My third cousin." I feel him juddering behind me. "Nice, huh?"

"That's not so bad. My great grandparents were *first* cousins."

"They were? That's kinda . . . wrong."

I shrug. "It wasn't unusual. It kept the royal bloodline strong."

"Rather than diluting it with vulgar American commoners such as me?" He dips and rests his chin on my shoulder, and I peek out the corner of my eye on a grin.

"You are not vulgar."

"Why, thank you, Your Highness. Does that mean you like me?"

"You're all right, I suppose." I return my attention forward, smiling like crazy on the inside when he flexes his hips into my bottom. "So tell me about your acting."

"I left Alabama when I was eighteen. I caught a part in a low-budget series. In fairness, no one held out much hope for the network taking it from the pilot episode." He laughs. "I look back and cringe my ass off. It was a pile of trash, but they bought it. Six years and six seasons later, total hit."

"What was it called?"

"The Wanderer. I was a bounty hunter in the late eighteen hundreds. My horse and I roamed the West and wreaked havoc on the vigilantes. And the women." I hear the smile in his tone and turn my face into him, finding a smile, too. He shrugs. "I was quite good on a horse."

"And on a woman."

"A pro," he replies, biting my nose. "Tell me about you."

"Me?" I ask abruptly, turning away from him. "Doesn't the world know everything there is to know about me?"

"I'm not talking about Princess Adeline of England that the papers talk about. I'm talking about the real you."

"That is the real me."

"What, the style icon? The headstrong royal who doesn't believe in marriage?"

"I do believe in marriage. Just marriage to someone I love. Not someone unsuitable for me but suitable for my family."

"Is Haydon Sampson unsuitable?"

"Grossly," I mutter.

"Not according to the British Monarchy."

"What do they know?" I ask, resentment tingeing my words. "Half the marriages in my family are loveless. Arranged to strengthen the crown."

"You want to be loved for who you really are, not who your family wants you to be."

His words come from leftfield, startling me a little. "Is that a statement or a question?"

He doesn't hesitate. "A statement."

"That's very observant of you."

"You don't need to be observant to realize that."

"How come no one else has, then?"

"Because you've not let them close enough." He pulls Stan to a stop and takes the reins in one hand, using the other to slip around my waist and pull me back into his warmth. I go with ease, no resistance at all, despite not liking our direction of conversation. Nuzzling into my face so I am forced to turn into him, Josh looks so deeply into my eyes, I fear he may have found my bitter soul. "The question is, have I got the real Adeline?"

I don't realize my hand is over his on my stomach until he laces our fingers and constricts, and I don't realize I am holding my breath until I release it on my answer. "I don't know who the real Adeline is anymore."

He doesn't say anything in return, he just kisses me, tilting his lips onto mine and gently working them in a delicate, dreamy dance of tongues. "I don't think you've ever really known," he murmurs,

and I know he is right. I haven't. And I'm not in a position to figure it all out at this moment in time, when I'm lost in his deep, meaningful kiss. I'm not sure which side of Josh I like the most. The domineering, controlling, brutal lover. Or the gentle, soft, and giving gent. I'll take both. Both sides of him ease me, settle me in one form or another. I hum my contentment and fall deeper and deeper and deeper. "You taste fine, Your Highness."

I'm floating away, but I am cruelly yanked from my dreamy moment by the sound of a roaring engine, and I pull away, all too breathless, blinking back the stars from my vision until I see a Land Rover racing across the field in the distance. I'm about to curse whoever is at the wheel, knowing if they come much closer at that speed, Stan will get distressed, and with two of us in the saddle he'll be harder to control. But then the vehicle slows, and the blurry form of the driver becomes Damon. I have seen Damon mad only once in the time he has served me. It was *not* a sight I relished. And it isn't now. He looks fuming.

"Damon?" I question when he gets out of the Land Rover, his shiny leather shoes sinking into the soft muddy ground. He looks down and breathes in, his jaw tight.

"Your Highness." He addresses me properly but tightly. "We agreed half an hour."

"But I texted you," I argue, getting my phone and pulling up my messages to prove it. "Oh." I stare at the red icon telling me the message failed to send. "I must have lost network." I hold up my phone to Damon and give him an apologetic smile. "Sorry." At that moment, with my phone held high, obviously catching a few bars of service, Damon's phone dings and mine notifies me of a dozen missed calls.

He shakes his head. "I believe it's time to get back, ma'am." He sounds calmer than he's clearly feeling. "Kim is on her way to the stables and wishes to see you urgently."

"She couldn't have waited for me to get back to Kellington?"

"Apparently not, ma'am. I believe Felix has accompanied her."

Felix? Stupidly, I wrack my mind for another Felix who works for the household. Any Felix. Any Felix other than the head of communications at Kellington. The fixer.

Damon clears his throat, obviously seeing the questions and worry in my expression. "Something about a bank, ma'am."

I recoil without thought, and Josh catches it, tightening his grip of me. A bank? Or a *banker*? "Oh . . . umm . . . yes." I nod decisively. "Then I suppose I ought to get back."

Shit, shit, shit.

There is only one reason Felix would make a trip to the mucky stables, where his fine threads and Italian loafers are at risk of being polluted by horse manure. There is a crisis that needs fixing. With a banker.

Damon motions to the Land Rover. "I suspect they'll have arrived by now. May I suggest Your Highness drives back with me?" He looks past me to Josh, communicating silently everything he means. I have to agree. I trust Kim wholeheartedly, but I won't hear the end of it from her *or* Felix if they catch me riding back into the stables with Josh Jameson wrapped around me. Especially after Kim caught sight of my blemished wrists this morning *and* answered my phone to him.

I look at Josh, who has remained respectfully quiet, but I can see the questions in his eyes. "Do you mind?"

"Sure thing." He drops a chaste peck on my lips and helps me down from Stan. "He hasn't had a good run yet. I'll ride him back."

"Thank you."

Josh makes no big deal of it and turns Stan, before kicking him into a trot, and quickly breaking into a full-on canter. And I stand there, watching in awe as he rides away like the pro he is, his strong legs keeping his body out of the saddle with ease.

"Ma'am?" Damon nudges me from my daydream and I sigh, wandering to the Land Rover as I remove my hat.

"I'm sorry, Damon." I know he'll have been on the edge of losing it while I was enjoying my trot through the countryside. I like romantic Josh.

"All is well, ma'am. Let's not make a big deal of it."

I laugh on the inside, but I choose not to mention the epic speed at which he appeared over the horizon of the field, like he could have been in pursuit of my kidnapper. I know he was probably sweating while he couldn't get hold of me. If the King found out Damon had allowed me out in the fields alone, his job would be on the line. The fact that I wasn't alone would not make a teeny tiny bit of difference. In fact, the matter would be a whole lot worse.

I'M FULL OF dread when Damon pulls up at the stables, especially when I see Kim and Felix step out of a shiny Mercedes, both looking stiff and stony. "I'm in trouble," I mumble, unclipping my belt.

"I'll take care of this." Damon takes my hat from my lap.

"Can't you take care of them?" I ask, giving him pleading eyes. "Please?"

He laughs softly, the fine lines around his eyes deepening, and then his face is deadly serious. "No." His answer is abrupt and flat as he gets out of the Land Rover.

"Great." I wouldn't usually wait for Damon to open the car door for me when here, but it buys me a few more seconds to mount my defense. "Thanks." Stepping out, I straighten my shoulders, all confident . . . but I still have no words in my defense.

"Your Highness." Felix nods as I approach, as formal as ever, grimacing at a small mark on his Italian loafers.

"Felix." I greet him before nodding at Kim, tilting my head in question. I get discreetly widening eyes in return, but she doesn't say a thing. I sigh. "Whatever could be so urgent that you needed to come to the stables? I was rather enjoying a long overdue hack."

Felix clears his throat. "There's a matter of concern, ma'am."

"There is?" I ask, bracing myself.

"About Gerry Rush, ma'am."

The banker. "What about him?" I try to sound nonchalant, but my stomach sinks and I swallow, betraying my forced front. I was assured those pictures were intercepted; I don't know how and I tend not to ask.

"Mr. Rush has been trying to make contact with you, ma'am."

"Pardon?"

"He would like to see you."

Needless to say, that isn't going to happen. "Whatever for?"

"It would seem he's been bewitched, ma'am."

I laugh. "After one night?"

"Yes."

"That's utterly ridiculous."

They look at each other out of the corner of their eyes, as if it is *I* who is the ridiculous one. "Ma'am," Felix pushes on, "we have blocked his attempts to reach you, of course. But it seems he won't heed our warning. Mr. Rush is married, as you know." Felix cocks a sarcastic eyebrow. I don't appreciate it, and my deep breath of impatience tells him so. "It goes without saying that we need to contain this. Rest assured, there won't be an issue if we handle it swiftly and diligently."

"Handle it swiftly and diligently, then," I retort, far shorter than I should. They are only trying to avoid me getting caught in a potential scandal. "Thank you. Both of you." I unbutton my gilet, feeling a little hot, and shrug it off before pulling my hair from its ponytail. But my motions slow as it occurs to me to wonder, again, why they're here at the stables telling me all this.

"There is one other small matter, ma'am," Felix goes on before I get the opportunity to ask.

"What?" I sound as cautious as I feel.

"We need to discuss *how* we're handling this situation."

"We do?" That's not normal. The communications team do what

they do, and I'm rarely consulted in the methods they adopt to clean up my mess, whether I want them cleaning up that mess or not.

"Yes, ma'am. It appears Mr. Rush has been enjoying some extracurricular activity." Something in the way that Felix speaks tells me that I am not the extracurricular activity he's referring to.

"But not from me?"

Felix hands me a file, and I open it to find some photographs. "What is this?" I ask, flicking through, trying to make something out in the darkened shots.

Kim reaches forward and takes a photo, turning it the right way up. I still at the sight of what is all of a sudden a perfectly clear image. Too clear. "That, ma'am, is Gerry Rush in the throes of passion."

Yes, isn't it just. His face is strained, his body rigid, as he holds on to a woman's hips who's bent over a chair. My heart jumps too many beats as I pull the picture closer, trying to make out the woman's face.

"It's a prostitute, ma'am," Kim tells me matter-of-factly, and I look at her, unable to be relieved that it isn't me. She steps back, as if nervous.

"What?" I drop the file, retracting my hands to my chest. "A hooker? When was this?" I suddenly want a shower.

"A few weeks ago, ma'am. We thought you should know in case—"

"In case what? I choose to see him again?" I laugh, thinking these two should know me better. "I can assure you, that is not going to happen." I look at the pictures on a grimace as Kim gathers them up. "Not after I saw the picture of him with his wife, and *especially* not now."

"Just needed to be sure," Kim says, tucking them away.

I don't understand. Gerry Rush is a respected man, with kids and a gleaming reputation. If he doesn't back off and stop trying to reach me, I just know *those* pictures will make it onto the desk of some editor at some tabloid in London. He will be ruined. Where's

his sense? Then again, he took me back to his hotel room and has been trying to contact me. Clearly he has no sense. I know better than to ask how Felix got hold of those photographs. That won't be information I will be privileged with. A hooker?

My lip curls. "Do whatever it takes to get rid of him," I order, swinging around and marching away, shuddering as I go. The dirty, rotten womanizer. *A hooker.* So much for clean-cut image. He wants to see me? Bewitched? The nerve.

My thoughts trail off and my pace slows as I catch sight of Stan trotting up the lane with Josh, both of them a little out of breath. All agitation eating me alive melts away at the sight of Josh's smile when he spots me. When he slows to a walk, I give him wide eyes, discreetly flicking my head in an indication that he should be wary of the people in close proximity.

"Your Highness," he greets me rather formally, yet those words and his accent, in his *voice*, still caress my tingling skin.

"Mr. Jameson." I nod as he passes, heading straight for the stable block.

I let Felix and Kim pull away before I wander in after Josh to help him strip Stan down of his saddlery. He is nearly done by the time I make it to him. "He's worked up a good sweat," I say as I take a brush to Stan's coat.

"He's had an awesome time, haven't ya, boy?" Josh lightly smacks his neck. "Are you okay? You look . . . stressed."

"I'm fine."

"So your people were here for their health, were they? Because they didn't look like the riding type."

"Small matter now dealt with."

"A matter like you and I could be?" he asks casually, clearly reading between the lines and getting the gist of my *small matter*.

Shame eats me from the inside out, remorse and guilt, too. Why do I care what Josh thinks of my exploits? He is hardly Mr. Straight-laced himself, dating woman after woman and getting

bored. Besides, it's not like I knew Gerry Rush and his wife were trying to reconcile, or that he dabbled in hookers. I shudder at the thought again. "It was a family matter," I lie, if hesitantly, earning a quick flick of Josh's eyes to mine. I look away, feeling my cheeks heat with guilt. "Did you enjoy your hack?"

"I did. Thanks for lending me your horse." He smiles, looping Stan's tack over his shoulder.

"Anytime." I shrug nonchalantly, although I don't feel very nonchalant. Not at all. Damn it, I like him. Josh Jameson brings a smile to my face, calm into my world. Few people in my orbit elicit such reactions. Inside, I wish he could turn up at the stables every morning and make each day wonderful.

His phone rings and he pulls it out. He definitely deflates a little. "Yeah?" He starts to pace the stables, scuffing his boots as he goes, kicking up the hay. "Sure. Give me five." He cuts the call and holds up his phone. "My driver's here." He looks at his watch and laughs a little. "Early."

I force back my disappointment. "It was nice to see you."

He seems amused as he returns his eyes to me. "*Nice* to see me?"

I shrug. "Well, it was."

"Nice?" He paces forward, and I step back until I collide with a pile of hay and tumble to my back on a yelp. Josh is on me like a wolf, pinning me down by my wrists above my head. "Nice?" he asks again, pushing a lock of hair from my face with his nose. I try to catch my breath, loving the hardness of his physique pushing me into the softness of the hay. Before I can even think to find another word to replace the one that clearly displeases him, he attacks my mouth with a profound, familiar force, exploring deeply with his tongue. I wonder whether his suspicions regarding my *matter* has him all green-eyed and he's marking his territory. I have a sneaky suspicion I'm right.

His power and passion steal my breath, and I don't get it back once he has ripped his lips from mine. "Nice," he pants, rolling his

groin into me.

My back arches, pushing my breasts into his chest. "I'd give you another word," I breathe, "but I'm rather blank at the moment."

"Let's see if we can wake up that mind, then," he muses, securing both of my wrists in one grasp and reaching for the hem of my roll-neck sweater. As soon as his skin skims mine, my mind *does* wake up, providing me with many words, most of them ones of a pleading nature.

"Josh." I'm unsure whether I'm begging him to stop, or encouraging him on. Anyone could catch us.

My sweater is yanked up, my bra down, and he's on my breasts in the blink of an eye, swirling that god-loving tongue around and around, wide and firm. Then his teeth sink into my hard nipple and I buck, tinkering on that dangerous edge between pleasure and pain. He hums, he moans, he growls. "Shit, you are so fucking delicious."

"Your Highness." Damon's voice calling me doesn't penetrate the haze of pleasure holding me captive, doesn't have me darting up in a panic or fighting Josh off me. I'm lost.

"Fuckin' hell," Josh mumbles around my flesh, kissing the tip of my nipple before pulling the cups of my bra into place and my sweater down. "Playtime is over."

I pout, falling into instant mourning for my loss.

"Ma'am?" Damon sounds slightly concerned, and without Josh's tongue distracting me, I suddenly appreciate how close he is.

"Quick, up you get." Josh hauls me up from the hay and brushes me down before turning me by the shoulders and pushing me toward the stable door. "I'll hang back."

I gather myself and straighten my shoulders, aware of the many people floating around the stables. For a moment there, I completely forgot myself. I need to find some control.

I steal one last glimpse of Josh as I leave, wishing I could bottle the smile he gives me and store it forever. I'm desperate to ask him when I'll see him again, but my pride, as well as a sliver of sensibility,

won't allow it. "See you."

"See you," he mimics, his smile now thoughtful.

I round the corner, working hard to wipe the permanent grin from my face and the goosebumps from my tingling skin.

"There you are," Damon mutters, clearly fed up with my disappearing acts today. "Time to get back."

"Back to my prison? Oh joy."

He gives me a funny look, stopping me in my tracks to the car.

"What?"

"Nothing." Damon takes up his professional pose, the one where he stands with his joined hands behind his back and his chin lifted slightly.

"Then why are you looking at me like that?"

"Have fun in the stables?"

"I don't know what you're talking about." I head to the car, pushing a blush back from my cheeks.

"Ma'am?"

"Yes?"

"You have hay in your hair," he says, opening the door for me.

I reach up and brush at my free locks, the blush now unavoidable. "Damn it," I curse, catching Damon's wry smile.

"Fun?" he asks again.

"Oh, behave," I breathe, slipping into the back seat, not at all worried. I don't only trust Damon with my life, I trust him with my secrets. And Josh Jameson is one gigantic secret.

As we pull out of the stables, I see a Range Rover heading toward us, every window blacked out. I fall back in my seat and twiddle my fingers in my lap, trying not to let my mind venture to silly places. Places I am not allowed to be, and usually would have no interest in staying. But Josh is broaching my walls. And I cannot allow him that level access to my heart. Because it could easily be broken when he's wrenched away.

8

THE NEXT DAY at the stables is not nearly as wonderful. I saddle up Spearmint, distracted, I ride him, distracted, and I clean his tack, distracted. The whole time I'm there, I hope for a surprise visitor. He doesn't come, and I leave the royal stables feeling despondent.

As we pull up at Kellington, my phone rings and my eyes roll. "Mother," I say as I step out of my car, thanking Damon with a nod. My coat is pulled from my shoulders by Olive as I stand in the entrance hall and listen to my mother deliver a point-by-point rundown of the afternoon tea at Claringdon Palace, held in honor of Helen. "Sorry I missed it," I lie, handing Olive my bag on a smile. The prime examples of English ladies all in one room is my idea of hell—all swooning over pretty little cakes, Earl Grey tea being sipped through pursed lips from fancy china, and over-the-top fussing of my over-indulgent sister-in-law. No thank you.

"I hear you spent rather a long time at the stables with that new horse of yours," Mother says very casually, and I tense a little, stalling on any reply. She heard? From whom? "I had tea with Sabina yesterday evening."

My tense body softens, relieved. "Just getting to know him." I

roll my eyes at Damon when he smirks a little, clearly grasping the direction of conversation.

"She said he shows smashing potential."

"He does."

"Now, onto another matter. I wanted to speak with you before Kim brings it up."

"What's that?" I ask, just as Kim appears from the corridor that leads to my staff offices. She has her bulging diary in her arms and a pen in her mouth as she talks on her mobile.

"Your father has been requested to unveil a new monument in his honor in Madrid."

I sag, knowing what is coming. "That's lovely." This tribute has been in the making for years, Spain's display of union with England through the marriage of my mother to the King.

"Rather unfair that my husband gets paid homage in my motherland, and I get nothing, don't you think?" She chuckles, and I smile, knowing she could not care less. "Anyway, where was I? Oh, yes. He's unable to attend the unveiling as it collides with an existing royal engagement. Spain can't change the date due to a public holiday, and your father can't withdraw from his commitment. So it has been decided that you should represent him."

I groan under my breath, wandering through to the lounge with Kim following me. "What about you, Mother?"

"I will be with your father in the British Virgin Islands."

"And John?" I fall to the couch and give Kim eyes to suggest she should help me out. She shrugs, because when my staff receive instructions from the top, they obey.

"He's scaling back his royal duties, what with Helen's condition," Mother says.

Condition? She's pregnant, for goodness sake. "Eddie?" I put forward my last card, with no hope of it being played.

"Adeline, darling, Edward has been serving the country for months. It would be unfair for us to expect him to fulfil royal

engagements so soon after his return."

And then there's me, with nothing better to do than smile, look pretty, and gush about my family to all who will listen. I have one use. Obey when ordered. "When is it?"

"Kim has the details."

I scowl at Kim for no other reason than I need someone to note my displeasure. "I'll be sure to talk to her."

"Good evening, dear."

"Good evening, Mother." I hang up and hang my head. "So I am going to Madrid."

"It's one week, Adeline. Look at it as a holiday."

"A holiday?" I laugh as Olive slides a tray of tea onto the table before me. "Thank you, Olive. I'll serve," I say, sitting forward and pouring myself a cup, as well as Kim. I push it across the table to her. "You and I both know there will be no chance of a holiday. Besides," I grumble, "royals are only allowed to sun themselves in England, which, of course, limits their exposure to the sun a great deal. When am I to leave?"

"Next month. I'll collate your itinerary." Kim makes a few notes in her diary. "The gallery opening this Friday."

"What about it?"

"Your outfit."

"I haven't thought about it."

"No need to. Victoria Beckham's people are sending over her new collection."

I smile. Well, that's made Friday more appealing. "Fabulous. When are they arriving?"

"Tomorrow morning."

"Great." I clap my hands, my mood lifting. "Is that all?"

"For now." She stands and gathers her things. "You're in residence this evening?"

"Why are you asking it as a question when you control my diary?" I flick her a sardonic grin.

"Just checking that you're not planning on going rogue on me."

"Damon is off this evening, so if I do want to go rogue, I will have to grow wings and fly myself out of here. Besides, where is there to go?" I grab my phone and call my cousin. "Matilda," I sing when she answers.

"I'm not talking to you."

I pout, feeling only marginally guilty for leaving her to endure the delightful afternoon tea without me. "Will you talk to a bottle of Moët?"

"I may be swayed."

"Good. This evening we are drinking Moët and perusing the glossies." As I declare our plans to Matilda, a pile of this week's glossies land on the table in front of me, courtesy of Kim. "Be here by seven?"

"And how do you propose I get there?" she asks. "Unlike yourself, one does not get the luxury of a personal driver. The King's private duchy doesn't stretch that far, or rather he won't let it. So I have to share my driver with the rest of the family, and Mother and Father are out this evening at a charity gala."

"Oh. How inconvenient."

"Rather," she mutters.

"Then I will have Damon collect you. From Farringdon Hall?"

"Marvelous."

"One problem."

"What's that?"

"He's technically off duty this evening, so he won't be able to drive you home."

"Don't worry. I'll grab a cab." She snorts a burst of laughter, as do I, because no royal gets a cab. Well, that's not technically true. I did it once. I smile at the memory, remembering the last time Selfridges was closed to the public for me to shop. I saw freedom through the glass-bolted doors as I waited for my staff to collect my many purchases, and it was too much to resist. I wandered out

into the night-time air, hailed a cab, and I let the lovely cockney man drive me home. He was constantly peeking in the rearview mirror, a frown embedded into his crabby forehead. He would shake his flat-capped head every now and then, and I would smile, because he was clearly wondering if it was a joke. It wasn't. Neither was the fact that I had no cash when we arrived home. The paps had a field day, and the kickback from Claringdon Palace was ridiculously over the top. The King was livid. Damon was livid. The public, however, loved it. And I rather enjoyed my little jaunt around London in a black cab. I'd never been in one before. Just for a little while that night, I was like any other regular person. Free. My stifling existence was forgotten in that perfect hour when I saw London through new eyes while safe in the back of the cab.

"I'll have Olive get one of the guest suites prepared," I say, wandering through Kellington in search of Damon. "See you soon." I hang up and eventually find him in the kitchen, sitting at the huge island that dominates the middle of the room. My cook, Dolly, is faffing over him, as she always does, and Olive is clearing a tray. Both nod and greet me formally before getting back to their tasks, and Damon stands.

"Ma'am?"

"Damon, would it be terribly inconvenient for you to collect the Duchess of Kent from Farringdon Hall before you leave?"

"Not an inconvenience at all, ma'am."

"Thank you, Damon. Olive, will you make sure the Albert Suite is ready, please? My cousin will be staying this evening."

"Yes, ma'am."

"Thank you."

"Girls' night in?" Damon settles back on his stool. "I hear The Graham Miles Live Show has a great lineup tonight."

My forehead crinkles as Damon goes back to his tea, like he hasn't said something so bizarre. Graham Miles? I don't think I've ever watched his chat show in my life. "He does?"

"Yes. Some popular Hollywood actor."

"Josh Jameson," Olive squeals, before quickly slapping her hand over her mouth. "Sorry, ma'am."

I'd tell her not to be silly, but I am at a loss for words. He's on the Graham Miles Live Show? I suddenly have the urge to go out this evening, because resisting not putting the television on is going to be hellish. Damn.

Olive scuttles off as Dolly shakes her head and Damon smiles into his cup.

"Will you be eating, ma'am?" Dolly asks. "I have all the ingredients for my famous chicken soup in the pantry."

I shake my head, mentally planning the night ahead. I hope those glossies are loaded with juicy gossip that will keep Matilda and me busy all night. "That's very kind of you, Dolly, but Matilda and I will probably just pick." I wander over to her perfectly organized pantry and open the door, peeking inside. "Do we have things to pick?"

"There are tortillas, ma'am. And I have some freshly made salsa in the fridge."

Oh, Dolly's salsa is delicious. "Perfect. Thank you, Dolly." I head off to my suite to get into something a little more comfortable. Something loose. Something that isn't going to rub in all the places where I'm *still* sore.

THAT SOMETHING IS an oversized T-shirt and some shorts, minus the knickers beneath. Matilda and I are slumped on the couch, sipping Moët, picking at tortillas, and flicking the pages of the magazines. I am being perfectly distracted by the latest in the celebrity world—the divorces, the scandal, the analyzing of famous women's weight gain/loss. "Oh, really?" I sigh as I turn the page and come face-to-face with someone familiar. Me. "This picture is old news."

Matilda leans over and laughs. "You look annoyed."

"I was." I don't indulge in the article that will undoubtedly be divulging inaccurate details of my *perfect* life. "I was leaving the spring/summer launch of Stella McCartney's new collection. There was an after-party. I wanted to go."

"Oh."

I curl my lip and continue to flick the pages, now a little roughly, still feeling bitter that the King *conveniently* summoned me just as the champagne was served. Thinking of which . . ."Another bottle?"

Matilda raises her glass in acknowledgement, and I toss the magazine aside, jumping up from the couch. "Back in a minute." I dart to the kitchen and pull open the door of the fridge dedicated to Moët, smiling as I take a bottle from one of the racks. The empty kitchen is blissfully quiet, a rare occurrence around here. Of course, there's staff floating around somewhere—there's *always* staff floating around somewhere, but the evenings are less suffocating.

Popping the cork, I make my way back to the lounge, my pace gradually slowing when I hear a familiar voice. A familiar voice that is not Matilda and is not any of the palace staff. I come to a confused stop as I cross the foyer, looking around me for where it might be coming from, not seeing a speck of life. My buzzing skin tells me whose voice that is, even if my brain is a little slow in catching up. *Josh?* And then raucous laughter erupts, and I quickly follow the sound, finding Matilda standing in front of the television with a remote control in her hand. The colossal 64-inch screen is filled with Josh, and the number to the left, currently rising, tells me Matilda is turning up the volume, like I need him to be louder. My heart squeezes at the sight of him, preened to perfection, his three-piece suit pristine as he sits relaxed on a couch, one ankle tossed over his knee. The crowd, mostly women, are going potty as he dazzles them with a rather shy smile, and Graham Miles swoons along with them, gesturing his hands to Josh, like *look who's here!* So Josh Jameson is not *technically* in the lounge, but he may as well be. My body is having its usual riot of reactions when presented with him.

"Adeline," Matilda shrieks. "Oh my God. Adeline, quick."

"I'm here," I mumble, transfixed by the television. Or transfixed by *him*. My God, he looks heavenly.

"It's him."

"Turn it off." I force my gaze away before I melt at the sight of him, frantically searching out my champagne flute and dashing over to refill it.

"What?" Matilda looks at me like I might have grown ten heads and breathed fire on her.

"Turn it off," I repeat, sinking my whole glass.

"Wh—"

"Matilda, please." More champagne gets thrown into my flute.

"Okay, okay." She points the remote control at the television, just as the crowd settles and Graham Miles crosses one leg over the other.

"I think they like you," he says, deadpan. "I have no idea why."

More laughter breaks out, and Josh blushes the most adorable blush. "Wait," I blurt abruptly, winning back Matilda's attention. "No, turn it off." I flap a hand at the screen and she looks at me in exasperation, dropping the remote control to her side.

"Off or on?"

"Off."

She re-points.

"No, on."

"Adeline, seriously?"

I lower to the couch, back to being mesmerized by the divine creature gracing the screen. "Sorry," I mumble as she joins me. I don't need to be looking at her to know she is frowning at me.

"Whatever has gotten into you?"

"Him," I say without thinking, feeling her stunned expression rooted to my profile. "Literally," I add.

"Oh my gosh."

"Shh!" I slap her thigh, trying to listen to the television. Matilda grabs the champagne and joins me in downing one glass after the

other, sitting forward on the couch, as if it is not loud enough for us to hear even if we were on the other side of the palace.

"So," Graham relaxes back, all casual, as if he doesn't have the world's most handsome man within touching distance. I wish I could be so cool in Josh Jameson's company. "Josh Jameson, you're here in London promoting your new film, The Underground." An applause breaks out as a promotional image pops up on the screen behind Josh. My eyes burn as I absorb the image of him in all his glory, a gorgeous woman cuddled into his side, though he is not embracing her hug. "I assume from this picture it is not about trains," Graham quips dryly.

Josh laughs a full-on belly laugh, craning his head back to see the image. "No. No trains."

"Tell us about it. Because it's based on a true story, right?"

"Right. I play Austin Tate, a troubled man in sixties New York. He had severe autism."

"So despite you in all your body-beautiful glory throughout the film, and, ladies"—Graham turns to his audience—"it's *very* glorious." He fans his dreamy face and returns his attention back to Josh. "There's a really poignant story here."

"Sure." Josh shuffles on the couch. "Like many people who have autism, Austin struggled to recognize and understand other people's emotions, but on a *really* extreme level. He literally showed no one any mercy, would hide in the library most days researching the behavior of *'normal'* human beings, and nearly killed himself in the gym most nights. It was like a stress alleviator for him. He interacted with no one. Until he met Wendy." Josh goes on, detailing the character's background, the research he did for the role, and the training to get his body in tip-top shape. "Six hours in the gym a day, man." He flexes his bicep, which is clear through his suit, causing another stir in the audience. "And eggs. If I never see another egg in my life . . ." He shudders.

"Well, I think we all agree the discipline paid off." Graham

coughs and smirks at the camera cheekily. They chat some more, and then a trailer for the movie is shown, like my torture couldn't get any worse. Josh, in glasses. And then naked, a full-on nude from behind. The crowd go potty, as do my insides. "Goodness gracious," Matilda breathes, blindly smacking at my thigh repeatedly.

"So what have you been up to in London?" Graham goes on once the crowd has piped down and he's shared the details of the release date. "Do you like it here?"

"I love England," Josh gushes. "The food, the people."

"A little birdie told me you've been keeping company with the Royal Family, no less."

I feel all the blood drain from my face as Matilda starts to smack me again, engrossed as much as I am by the interview. How the hell does he know that? Josh fidgets on the couch, obviously trying to play it cool. "You mean the garden party?"

"Not just *any* garden party, but Princess Adeline's thirtieth birthday garden party at Claringdon Palace. How did you wangle that?"

Josh visibly relaxes, and I grab oxygen to fill my shrunken lungs. "Wangle?"

Graham laughs. "Wangle. Like pull it off."

"Oh." Josh reaches for his water and takes a sip. "You British have some weird terminology."

"Oh, you've been getting familiar with our weird terminology? Give us some words. What have you learned?"

"You call chips *crisps*." His attempt to sound British has Graham falling back in heaps of laughter. "And panties are *knickers*?"

My eyes widen as Graham shoots up straight in his chair. "Seen any knickers while in London?"

"Sadly, no." Josh brushes off Graham's cheeky question with a wave of his hand.

"I'm sure we can arrange something." He looks to the audience, and the women all shout their willingness. "Me first," Graham tsks, rolling his eyes and returning his attention back to Josh. "Where

were we? All this talk of knickers . . ."

"The palace."

"Ah, the palace. So what did you do? Scale the walls, tunnel underground?"

Josh smiles and places his water on the table. "My father's here on political business. He and His Majesty King Alfred met during their military days and kept in touch. I was my father's plus-one."

"You know, I was invited," Graham muses.

"Then why didn't you go?"

"I'm protesting."

"Why?" Josh asks, genuinely interested.

"The King missed me off his honors list *again*." He sighs, exasperated.

"Oh, that sucks."

"Will you put in a word for me?" Graham asks seriously.

Josh chuckles, the sound out of this world. "No sweat."

"Great. I'll invite you to the celebratory party once I receive my knighthood. Now, you're voted the world's hottest man. You have an Oscar, for Christ's sake. You probably have more money than God and a body that rivals a gladiator. And I've never met you before today, but I think you're quite charming."

"Thanks." Josh laughs.

"So your love life?" Graham drops that bombshell and sits back, waiting.

"What about it?" Josh's laugh turns nervous.

"It causes constant speculation in the press, Josh. The pictures with her, and then her, and then her."

"You're straight to the point, aren't you?" Josh rearranges himself on the couch, and I feel myself go stiff as a board. I know Matilda senses it because she glances at me. I keep my eyes on the television, my grasp squeezing around my glass. Josh gets bored easily. I must remember that.

"Anyone special?" Graham prompts again.

I swear, Josh looks straight down the camera, and I sit back, my eyes on his. "There's no one special," he tells the world, dragging his gaze back to his host. I don't know how to interpret that. Was he telling me there is no one special, or was he telling me *I'm* no one special? I don't know, and I hate, hate, hate that I need to. "Turn it off." I grab the remote from Matilda's hand before she has a chance to obey my abrupt order, and aim it at the screen, pressing the on/off button with a firm fingertip. The screen dies, leaving silence. Not for long, though.

"Tell me everything." Matilda turns to me, and I feel myself fold.

But I need to tell someone. Someone I can trust, and who isn't my driver. Not that I actually tell Damon. The poor man has no choice but to know since he is practically my shadow. I feel like I'm going out of my mind. "When he showed up at my private party, we somehow found our way to my suite." My eyes are pointed to my lap, but a quick glimpse up confirms Matilda's open mouth.

"You said you were tired. You went to bed."

"I did go to bed. With him." I shrug lamely. "And yesterday, he showed up at the stables."

"You like him."

I laugh, no counter coming to me, diving into the sanctuary of my champagne. "You know me. I don't get attached. There's no point."

"You're falling for him." Her claim comes from nowhere, and I stare at her, flummoxed.

"That is utterly ridiculous. I hardly know him."

"You're falling for him."

"Will you stop saying that?" I reach for the Moët and abandon my glass in favor of the whole bottle.

"Adeline, I know full well that you make a point of not getting attached to the men you . . ." She fades off, trying to find an appropriate word while I wait.

"Screw?" I prompt.

"Share company with."

"This is why you make a much more suitable princess than I do." I toast her etiquette and slurp from the bottle.

"My point is, you don't get attached because we all know what will happen if you do. Men you see are disposed of."

"I've never met a man I'd *want* to get attached to," I mumble round the rim of the bottle.

"That's because you make a point not to. But you were not anticipating Josh Jameson, were you? And now it's driving you bonkers, because you're falling for him and you most definitely cannot have him." Matilda laughs, and then stops just as quickly, shaking her head in dread. "Jesus, the King would go potty."

"Thank you for the reminder of my reality."

"Welcome. So, what are you going to do?"

"Nothing." I grab a magazine and casually scan the page, pretending my mind isn't racing and my heart isn't booming. "And I am not falling for him," I tell her. "Just having a bit of fun, since it is seriously lacking around here. He leaves next week."

"Well, you don't need me to tell you that you're on dangerous ground." She slumps back and kicks her feet onto the table.

No, I do not, but this doesn't feel like the usual dangerous ground I dance on. I'm not being defiant for the sake of it, to prove some kind of personal point to myself—I am my own person and cannot be told what to do and who I see. I'm dancing on this particularly dangerous ground because I really, really want to. It defies logic. I know once knowledge of my involvement with Josh Jameson is discovered by Claringdon Palace, steps will be taken to make sure he stays away. And for once, it bothers me what the King and his minions might do. Why? Because I care for him? I reach up and rub at my chest, not liking the mild ache developing. Do I care for him? I hardly know him. No, I *like* him. He's fun. I grin to myself, getting a vivid and graphic playback of our time in my suite, belts, hankies, tiaras, and all. And then my grin fades when I remember

our ride yesterday. He is a multi-dimensional man, and I like it all. He's the most fun I've had in a long time, maybe ever, and it is *real* fun. Just like Josh said, it isn't manufactured. I'm not pretending with him. I'm not fooling myself.

I look at the screen of the blank television and see his eyes boring into me when he told the world there is no one special. And I ask myself again, was he talking to me? And what the bloody hell did it mean? I groan to myself, dropping my head back. I'm obsessing. I'm jealous—jealous of every woman who has come before me. Every woman on his arm in the endless press shots. Every woman he's worked with. None of those women would have to skulk around. Hide. But, then again, I doubt they have to worry about any of that, anyway, if Josh gets bored easily. Is he bored of me? Already?

Olive wanders in with a tray, and I sit up, catching sight of a plate covered by a metal dome. "Thank you, Olive, but I told Dolly we didn't want supper," I say as she rests the tray on the table in front of the couch.

"Dolly didn't prepare it, ma'am."

"Then who did?"

"It wasn't prepared. It was delivered."

"What?" I look up at Olive. Delivered to Kellington Palace?

"Security checked the package, ma'am. They weren't going to let it through, but Damon cleared it before he left." She wanders off. "I'll be back to collect the plates shortly, and then I'll be off for the evening."

"What is it?" Matilda asks, just as my phone rings.

"I don't know." I answer my phone, reaching for the handle of the dome covering my plate. "Hello?"

"Evening." His rough voice sends bolts of pleasure straight to my nerves. The dome clangs back down to the plate.

"Evening." I sit back, my mystery delivery forgotten. Matilda smacks my hand, and I look at her, nodding, telling her that yes, it is who she thinks it is. Her expression is between excitement and

dread. A little bit like how I am feeling. "How are you?"

He laughs under his breath, smooth like the best whisky, full and bodied. "I've just been grilled on live TV. I'm fine now I have a drink in my hand."

I don't say a thing. He'll know I've been watching. "Sounds lovely."

"Ever eaten a burger?"

"I'm sorry?"

"A burger. Ever eaten one?"

"Why would you call me to ask that?"

"I bet you eat à la carte every evening, don't you? No bad cheeseburgers for the princess."

I bristle. "Of course I've eaten a burger."

"You've not eaten a burger until you've eaten my favorite dirty cheeseburger. Hope you're hungry."

I shoot forward and pull the lid off the plate, finding a huge, dripping cheeseburger speared by a skewer dressed in pickles. There's an American flag on top.

"Oh wow, that looks scrummy." Matilda dives forward and snags a few chips.

"You sent me your favorite burger?" I ask mindlessly to the plate. I can't believe it.

"Are you shaking at the sight of it?" Josh asks. "I mean, all that badness on one plate."

I realize he's talking about a cheeseburger, but there is an erotic edge to everything he's saying to me, and it's making me hot and bothered. "I don't think I've had a cheeseburger this bad before." I get up and walk away from Matilda, letting her pick at the chips.

"Every girl needs something bad for them now and then, Your Highness."

"Are you telling me you are bad for me?" I cut straight to the chase, though I know the answer. Of course he's bad for me. He's not royal, for a start.

"I think we're bad for each other."

"I think you're right. So why send me the burger? What is it, the last supper or something?

"I really enjoyed yesterday." He goes off course completely, and I close my eyes, sensing this is his way of saying goodbye. The message through the camera was meant for me. I'm no one special. He's bored. The burger is a peace offering. Now he's telling me he enjoyed yesterday, and I just know there is a "but" on the way. Really, though, he's doing us both a favor. I can't blame him, because sex is sex, and he can snap his fingers and have any woman he chooses without the tiresome task of sneaking around and risk facing the wrath of the British Monarchy. How can I not understand that? At least he has the decency to call me and explain. But I'll save him the trouble.

"It was good while it lasted," I say, cutting the call before Josh can spill the words I do not want to hear, no matter how much I tell myself it is for the best. It should end before I can get too attached. And I need to be the one to end it, because that way I am in control. Why my heart feels like it's sinking is a mystery. It's also bloody annoying. But, and I hate to admit it, he is right. We are bad for each other. This is for the best, letting go before there's anything really to hold on to. Done. Dusted. "Damn it," I yell, throwing my phone onto one of the couches.

"Not falling for him?" Matilda asks casually, shoving a chip into her stupid mouth.

I close my eyes and work hard on bringing myself back down to earth after my short time floating on clouds.

You're a princess first, Adeline. A woman second.

Heart be damned.

9

I DIDN'T EAT the burger; my stomach wouldn't tolerate it, not because my royal tummy is not accustomed to such food choices, but because I felt physically sick. Matilda, however, scoffed it down in a few greedy bites and assured me that it really was the most delicious burger she'd ever eaten, if a little cold after going through security checks. Not that she has tried many burgers, either.

I went to bed and tossed and turned for most of the night, every blemish on my body pulsing as a constant reminder of him.

By the time morning arrived, I was going out of my mind, so when Kim turned up with a rack of dresses courtesy of *VB* for me to try on, it was a welcomed distraction. But I couldn't very well strip down and expose my battered body to them, so after seeing Jenny and Kim out of my suite, I made sure I tried each of the ten dresses twice. I walked around my suite in each and tried on a dozen different pairs of shoes with every single one. I was determined to make my task last most of the day so I could eat my supper before killing the rest of the evening in my office, going over official correspondence and letters that have been screened before making it to my desk.

By five o'clock, I was happy I'd achieved my goal, though Kim and Jenny looked thoroughly bewildered by my mess as they gathered up the dresses and matched the scattered shoes around my suite, boxing them and putting them in my dressing room.

Dolly serves my supper at six, and the table's set for two. "Who's eating with me?" I ask Olive as she sets down a beautifully dressed plate of poached salmon before pouring me some lightly sparkling water.

"Prince Edward, ma'am. He will be joining you shortly." Olive disappears out of the dining room, just as Eddie wanders through the doors at the other end. I smile at the sight of him, relieved I won't be alone with my thoughts throughout supper. He wanders the length of the huge dining table to me, his finely tuned body dressed casually in some dark jeans and a Vivian Westwood shirt.

"Evening, little sister." He kisses my cheek and settles in the chair opposite me, two meters of shiny wood between us.

"Evening." I wait for Olive to deliver Eddie's supper before collecting my silverware and cutting into the salmon, the flesh falling away with little help from my knife. As I stare at the plate, the pink fish morphs into a juicy big cheeseburger, topped with pickles and oozing cheese. My mouth waters, my mind wanders. It's bad for me. I should make better choices.

"Adeline?"

I look up to find Eddie watching me across the table, his silverware in his hands ready to eat. "Sorry, I was daydreaming."

He cuts into a potato slowly as I take my first mouthful of my supper. "What did you do today?" he asks.

"Tried on dresses," I answer. "I'm opening a gallery on Friday evening for a charity I'm patron of."

"You look thrilled about it."

I realize my enthusiasm is lacking, so I try to rectify it. "It's a great charity." I fail, feeling deflated.

Eddie places his silverware down and takes his water, resting

back in his chair. "Come on, tell me."

I sigh and drop my knife and fork, my stomach churning too much to eat. "I don't know how much longer I can do this. It's okay for you. You go off on tour, serving our country. You have a purpose. I don't. Well, I do, but being married to a man I have no feelings for, producing a few babies, and being the dutiful wife is not appealing to me."

Eddie gives me that sympathetic look, the one that reminds me there is no way out of my life. I don't own myself, the Royal Family owns me. Their expectations, their traditions, their duties. "The public loves you."

"The public loves the polished, free-spirited princess who apparently won't settle down until she is ready. They wouldn't love the whore who sleeps with inappropriate men."

"Adeline, less of the whore-talk. What has possibly brought all this on? You are usually so content with yourself."

"That's just it, isn't it, Eddie? I'm none of those people. Not the whore, not the polished princess, and—"

"You are the princess the people love. The free-spirited young woman. We all know your bad decisions are based purely on that rebellion in you. You don't need to be wild to make a stand. It just earns you a headache from the top."

"That's rather rich coming from you," I scoff, picking up my fork and poking at my salmon. "You party harder than me."

"I drink. I have mate-time."

"Oh, yes, I forget that a bit of boisterous behavior from the Prince Soldier is perfectly acceptable around here. Besides, no matter how uncertain I am about myself, I'm certain I will never want to marry Haydon Sampson, and that alone labels me a rebel, without any of the other stuff."

"Stuff?"

"Men. Drink. Parties." Oh, how I wish I had planned a gathering for this evening. Anything to take my mind off my plight. Instead,

I must blend into an extravagant dining room meant for a banquet and reflect on everything that is wrong with my life. So much for distraction with the help of Eddie. "Anyway. Enough of me and my woes. What have you planned while you are off duty?"

"The gallery opening Friday evening."

"What about it?"

"I'll accompany you."

I sit up straight in my chair. "You will? Oh, Eddie, I would love that."

"Me, too." He resumes his dinner, and my appetite returns. "I'll be at the Royal Marines Association in the morning, meeting the families of fallen soldiers. I should be back in plenty of time."

"Do you enjoy things like that?" I ask, spearing a piece of asparagus and nibbling the end. "It must be dreadfully depressing."

"It's sad, of course. But it's important to make sure the families know their loss hasn't been in vain. They have a massive support network available for them. Not that it can ever compensate, but . . . well"—he shrugs—"they're heroes."

I return to my food, a small, sad smile on my lips. Here's me wailing about the constraints of my life. At least I have a life. "Did you know that Father met Senator Jameson when he served in the military?" For the life of me, I don't know where that question came from.

"I did." Eddie gives me a curious smile across the table that I battle not to react to. "Why do you ask?"

My eyes plummet to my plate. "Just wondered."

"Just wondered," he muses.

I drop my silverware and breathe out. I can't contain it. "Why did you invite Josh Jameson to my party?"

"And there we have the problem." Eddie follows my lead and rids his hands of his cutlery, too. "Is this why you are moody?"

"I am not moody."

"What happened between you two?"

"Nothing." I gather my napkin from my lap and place it by the side of my plate, forcing a meek smile.

Eddie's high eyebrows virtually merge with his hairline. "Nothing?"

"Nothing."

"He's gotten under your skin."

I snort at the mere suggestion. "No man gets under my skin. There would be little point allowing them to, since the King would ensure they were dug out with a blunt knife rather speedily."

"So you're not playing with something you cannot have, you *want* something you cannot have." He laughs, and the sound, along with his statement, is torture. "That's a whole new ballgame, Addy."

I stand up, ready to put an end to this preposterous conversation and my brother's outlandish insinuations. "You are so far off the mark, Edward."

His laughter increases. "You only call me Edward when you're on the defense."

"Good evening, brother." I march away from him, outraged, hearing him sigh to himself as I go.

"Adeline?"

"What?" I bark, swinging around at the door.

His face is serious. I don't like it, not one tiny bit. "Let go before they make you."

I inhale sharply, in a staring deadlock with my beloved brother, no counter coming to me. "I'll be in my office." I turn and walk away on trembling legs, and when I make it to my office, I drop to my chair like a brick, my body heavy, my heart heavier. Everything is heavy. *Don't think, don't think, don't think.* I pull my box of correspondence forward and start flicking through the papers. The itinerary for my trip to Madrid, the finely tuned plans for Friday evening's opening, the request for an appearance at a local women's shelter. I drop them all, unable to engage my brain. With my head in my hands, I slump over my desk and fall deeper into despair. Josh

Jameson was like a red flag to a bull. The ultimate no-go zone. It was only supposed to be a bit of fun. And I can see for Josh, it was exactly that. The morning after our *game*, he called nonstop until he finally tracked me down at the stables. Last night I thanked him for our fun and called it a day before he did. I've not heard from him since. *I don't think I could ever get bored of you, darlin'.* It was a good line. But it was just a line. What was I thinking? What was I hoping for?

I push the questions away quickly. What does it matter? It is done with now.

10

"READY, MA'AM?" DAMON asks as I take the stairs to him, ready for a morning at the stables, followed by an afternoon at the stables. A long, *long* time at the stables until it is time to get ready for this evening's engagement.

"Why did you let the cheeseburger through security?" I ask, eyeing him unhappily. Damon wasn't here yesterday so this is my first opportunity to ask. Let's see what he has to say.

He shrugs. "It looked pretty spectacular as far as cheeseburgers go. And I know there was no risk of Mr. Jameson lacing it with poison."

I laugh under my breath as I slip my arms through the sleeves of my Barbour jacket when Olive holds it up, and then accept my bag. "Thank you, Olive."

I drop into the back seat and pull out my phone. There's a missed call from Josh. And a voicemail. So much for not trying to contact me. On a thump of my heart, I clear the screen of both and wind down my window when I see Kim coming down the steps. "Everything okay?" I ask.

"I can't get hold of Sabina to let her know you're on your way."

Kim dials again and takes the phone to her ear, huffing her displeasure when she gets Sabina's voicemail greeting again. "I've left a message. Hopefully she'll get it before you arrive."

"I don't mind saddling up Stan myself."

"You might have to." Kim passes me a sheet of paper. "The schedule for this evening. You're due to arrive at eight, so we'll have to leave here at seven-thirty, at the latest. Jenny will be here at four to do your hair and makeup."

Four? I have seven hours to kill. "Please let Dolly know I'll have lunch at the stables."

"Okay. Your dress is ready. Did you decide on shoes?"

I ponder again which ones to opt for. "I don't know," I admit. "The dress needs a stiletto. My Jimmy Choos are perfect, but they're black. The dress is screaming for red."

Kim rolls her eyes at my less than subtle hint. "I'll find them in red."

I smile gratefully. "I love you."

Her expression is as sarcastic as it could be. "You couldn't have told me this when you tried the dress on?" she moans, dialing someone, no doubt that one special person who can get anything anytime.

"See you at four." I close the window and Damon starts driving, but instead of doing a left as he exits the gates, he turns right. I lean forward in my seat. "The stables, Damon."

He looks at me through the rearview mirror, his eyes apologetic. "Major Davenport called, ma'am. The King wants to see you."

I groan, going lax in my seat. I have only just left Kellington and my day is already on the slide. This doesn't bode well. The only reason for my father to have Davenport call Damon is because come hell or high water, my driver will get me to Claringdon Palace as demanded. Unlike me, Damon can't refuse. It's more than his job is worth. "Why have I been summoned?"

"I don't ask, I do." Damon keeps his focus on the road, and I look out of the window, trying to stir up the fortitude and strength

I need to endure another browbeating about Haydon. Or will it be regarding the banker?

~

I'M SURPRISED DAVENPORT isn't awaiting my arrival at the entrance to Claringdon, as one would usually expect. Instead, the Master of the Household, Sid, is there, patiently standing tall. Damon opens the door for me, and I look at him, my bottom glued to the leather beneath it. He offers a small smile meant to reassure me. It doesn't work.

"Ma'am," he prompts subtly.

"Thank you, Damon." I sigh, grudgingly pulling myself from the car. Breathing in some strength, I put one riding boot in front of the other and make my way up the grand steps to the palace's entrance. "Good morning, Sid," I greet as I pass him, entering the giant, bustling foyer of my parents' home. Staff crisscross the highly polished marble floor before me, all precisely turned out in their royal uniforms. I must see two dozen staff members in the space of only a minute, but that is but a speck on the five-hundred strong workforce we have, some of who reside at the palace in one of the ninety staff bedrooms. Their life is to serve the Royal Family in one fashion or another.

"Your Highness," Sid says as he joins my side. "This way."

I fall into step behind him, performing an eye-roll of epic proportions. This way? Like I don't know the route to my father's office? "How are you, Sid?"

"Very good, ma'am." That is all I get, as always, nothing to lead a conversation. "His Majesty is expecting you," he says as we take the stairs up to the massive gallery landing.

"I would assume so, since he summoned me," I mutter, nodding at one of the housekeepers who stops and bows her head as I pass, a pile of freshly laundered sheets resting across her arms. "Is my mother in residence?" I ask as we cross the space to the far right.

"Yes, ma'am. Having breakfast, if I'm not mistaken." Sid reaches my father's office, and I hear voices from beyond. Loud voices. Annoyed voices. My heart sinks as Sid opens the door. "Her Royal Highness Princess Adeline of England," he announces.

I walk in to find my father pacing and Davenport standing by the fireplace, his tall frame as stiff as normal. The stick that's constantly stuck up his arse is growing, making him seem taller and more intimidating every time I encounter him. When my father looks at me, I see angry lines distorting his round face. I don't just bow my head out of respect and duty, I bow it to escape the furious glare burning me on the spot. "Your Majesty," I murmur, seeing David Sampson out the corner of my eye sitting in one of the smoking chairs opposite my father's grand antique desk. I only just manage to keep my curious frown at bay. What's Haydon's father doing here? My worry only grows when I spot Sir Don, too. Oh, great. He's called in *all* the reinforcements.

"Sit down, Adeline," the King orders, getting my feet moving to the chair next to David. As I near, I see he also looks awfully mad. I am outnumbered four to one.

"Is everything okay?" I ask, resting my hands in my lap. No one speaks, creating an uncomfortable silence. But before I can break it and push this along, get it over with, whatever *it* is, my father picks up something out of the red box that's delivered to his office each morning. That box contains official papers on all matters of which the Sovereign needs to be consulted on, or simply advised on. So when a tabloid newspaper lands in front of me, folded, I'm somewhat confused. But then I spy the bottom half of a picture gracing the front page. I recognize those jean-clad legs. My sinking heart charges back up my throat and chokes me. Oh no. Those are my legs, and there is also a pair of man's legs covered in combat trousers. I recognize what I can see of the background, too. The dining room at Kellington.

Unable to move and fold the paper out to confirm my fears,

David takes the liberty of helping me out, reaching forward and flattening out the tabloid. The picture in all its awful glory is revealed. I wince, taking in the full image through squinting eyes, like it can lessen the impact of the shot. Oh God, there is me atop the dining table, a bottle of Belvedere in one hand, a man in the other. Our mouths are stuck firmly together. The headline reads . . .

WILD PARTIES, NEAT VODKA, AND ORGIES.
THE LIFE OF A PRINCESS WHEN THE CAMERAS ARE OFF.

I swallow and move away from the paper, unwilling to read on. I don't have to, because I know one of these four men will enlighten me on the contents. Keeping my eyes downcast, I wait for the hurricane that is my father's temper. "You are an aberration, Adeline," he shouts. "A disgrace to the Royal Family!"

I flinch at his harshness, but I don't bother mounting my defense. There's little point. The journalist who printed this will have embellished the truth. A source close to me who doesn't want to be named will have been quoted to confirm the headlines. It doesn't matter that the close source is either made up, not close to me at all, or simply lying. People believe what they read, and in that article, I'm painted as an alcoholic, sex-mad, out-of-control princess. It will all be massively exaggerated. *How did this happen?* I saw Eddie stamp all over that mobile phone, and the idiot who it belonged to was ejected from the palace without it.

"We are constantly fighting back against the republicans." The King launches into what I know will be a damning rant. "You are not helping matters."

I catch David and Sir Don shaking their heads out of the corner of my eye. It takes everything in me and more not to retaliate.

"And how do you think Haydon will feel?" Father rants on. "The boy is waiting patiently for you to see sense, and you are carrying on like you are not promised to him."

My jaw might crack from the force of my bite, my veins heating. "I am not promised to anyone," I say calmly, defying the tornado of anger swirling in my gut.

"Wrong," Father says simply, slamming his hands into the wood of his desk and leaning across threateningly. "I will not stand for this any longer. You will behave like the princess you are and fulfil your obligation's as the King's daughter, do you hear me?"

I close my eyes and inhale slowly, trying to reason with the anger dominating me. Don't argue. Don't retaliate. It will get me nowhere. But I also won't agree to this madness. So I remain quiet where I sit. Father snatches the paper up and tosses it aside, huffing and puffing, getting more and more stressed by the minute. He will give himself a heart attack one of these days. "Davenport, get me a drink," he orders, not even looking at the Major. I should feel sorry for him, constantly being barked at by the King, but he chose this life. Being the King's private secretary isn't as glamourous as it should be, at least not for Davenport.

"Am I excused?" I ask, rising to my feet, ignoring the disdainful looks pointed my way by all four men. I don't appreciate it, but one thing I am managing to be grateful for is the fact that it is not my encounters with Josh Jameson that are cause for such anarchy. The soldier in that shot with me will be dealt with in one way or another. One kiss with the princess and he'll be thrown out of the British army and have all sorts of skeletons crawling out of the closet, some possibly real, some undoubtedly fabricated. He will be labeled a fraudster, anything to discredit him and shine me in the best possible light. He will have spiked my drink, tricked me, or maybe something worse. And as for the snake who took the picture, I dread to think of the repercussions he'll face.

"One more thing." Father drops to his chair and collects a cigar from the shiny teak box by his phone. Snipping the end off with his cigar cutter, he lights up before dragging in a huge hit and letting it billow from his mouth as he relaxes back in his chair. "Colin

Sampson passed away last night." He says it so casually, like he hasn't just advised me that Sabina has lost her husband, David his father, and Haydon his grandfather.

"What?" I look to David, expecting to find sadness at the mention of his father's death, but all I see is an indifferent expression, nothing there. "David, I'm so sorry. How is Sabina?"

He looks at me, stoic. "Grief stricken."

I'm so sad for her. "And Haydon?"

His blankness doesn't waver. "Do you care?"

"Of course I care," I splutter, deeply offended. I may not love the man or want to dance down the aisle into his arms, but I care deeply for him.

"Then maybe you could demonstrate that by comforting him through this difficult time."

Well . . . ouch. David's father has just passed away, and he's monopolizing this as a way to push me toward his son? "I will be sure to call Haydon immediately. And your mother."

David huffs, dismissing me by looking away. "Maybe your compassion and support will redeem you with my son after the disgrace you've brought upon this family."

This family? He talks like he's already a direct member of *this* family. "Good day." I strain a smile and get on my way before I lose all resistance and ping-pong around the King's office in an inappropriate outburst.

"We will talk again once you have had time to think about your actions," Father calls, short and clipped.

My hand squeezes the solid gold knob on the door. "Why are you doing this?" I grate.

He ignores me, turning to Davenport to accept his drink, completely dismissing me. Picking up some papers from his red box, he scans a few and drops them again. "How much of this do I actually have to read? I'd like to go shooting."

"Sir." Davenport approaches the red box and pulls out a file,

opening it up. "These require your signature."

I leave my father signing correspondence, of which he has no idea what it is about, and put myself on the other side of the door, bubbling with resentment. Not just for myself, but for Sabina and her family. Colin served my family for years and my father's dismissed his death so callously. You would think by now I'd have mastered the art of keeping my cool, would have learned to keep the façade of serenity in place. But today? I've been attacked for something that should never have made the news. Four obnoxious men cast their judgement, and I feel completely muzzled. They believe my reputation will only be restored if I marry Haydon. *If he'll have me now.* Insufferable. My heart feels squeezed, and I once again think how awful it must be for those of my family in loveless marriages. I will never be allowed to be with a man outside of this smothering world. I've never fully actualized the cost. *My heart.* Now, I'm truly worried for my future. And like an omen or something, my mobile sings with a call from Josh. I reject it and spend a few moments staring at the huge portrait of my grandfather on the opposite wall, the previous King of England, his noble nose held high, his stout body embellished in red velvet. Like my father, his successor, he was hell-bent on shining the family in the best light and building the support through the monarchists, no matter the cost of his family's happiness. We're here to serve. It's that simple.

"Your Highness?"

I blink myself out of my thoughts and find Dr. Goodridge approaching. "Oh good, you're here," I mutter, pushing my back off the door. "His Majesty could do with some Valium."

Sid's lips purse and Dr. Goodridge frowns as I pass them, making my way to my car. I dial Kim as I go. "I've just seen it," she says when she answers. "Felix is in meltdown."

"How did we not know about this?"

"The editor of The National is a fully-fledged republican. Shouts about it at any given opportunity. He's one we can't control."

"Well, he has certainly shouted about it," I mutter. "I've just left my father's office. My name is mud."

"We've had calls from *Hello*, the BBC, and ITV in the past half hour, all trying to secure interviews with you to put your side of the story to the nation."

"There is no bloody story. I kissed a man while having a few vodkas, for crying out loud."

"Well, the King has vetoed them all, so it's a moot point."

"Are they preparing a press release?"

"Yes. Something along the lines of them being disappointed that an editor who notoriously has a vendetta against the royals would make an innocent birthday celebration into something sordid."

I laugh out loud. Sordid? Oh, they have no idea. But the party before the sordid stuff really was innocent. "I bet the press is having a field day."

"Well, you're trending on Twitter again. And, frankly, most are singing your praises. Even some republicans are shouting loud about you being the most human of the royals. Don't beat yourself up too much about it."

I huff sardonically, but appreciate her trying to help me see the positives. "It's not some of the public's incorrect opinion of me that bothers me so much. It's the fact that whoever printed that headline has made my life ten times worse with the King. I'll be locked in the tower soon."

"I'm pretty sure social media will launch a petition to have you freed."

I smile. "Did you find the Jimmy Choos in red?"

"They've been delivered."

"Thanks, Kim. I'm heading to the stables. I'll be back by four in time for Jenny. Sabina's husband passed away in the night. I need to send her some flowers and a card as soon as possible so she knows I'm thinking of her."

"Oh dear. That would explain why I can't get hold of her. I'll

sort it." Kim hangs up and Damon comes into view. I can tell by his face he knew all along why the King had summoned me. "Traitor," I mumble as I reach him.

"You still have your head," he retorts on a small smile. "The kid had Dropbox synced to his phone, so Prince Edward may have destroyed the device, but the picture had already made its way into cyber space. Sorry about that."

"You weren't to know."

Damon nods past me, indicating for me to look, and I see Sid coming down the steps. "Ma'am, Her Royal Highness Queen Catherine has requested you join her for breakfast."

I don't mean to deflate, but I do anyway. I want to leave this stifling pile of bricks, yet I can't bring myself to refuse my mother when I know she's dining alone, like she does most mornings. "I'll wait for you here," Damon says as I reverse my steps and let Sid escort me to the dining room that puts Kellington's to shame.

"Adeline." Mother reaches her hand out to me. "Thank you for coming."

"You don't need to thank me," I say, dipping to kiss her cheek as I take her hand. "I was already here."

She squeezes my hand before motioning to the chair beside her. "Sit."

I do as I'm told and let one of the staff pour my tea. Mother seems as serene as ever, her olive skin glowing, her hair in a neat bun at her nape. I would question whether she is aware of the goings on in the newspaper, but it's The National. The whole bloody world knows. "Mother," I sigh, ready to air my grievances, if only to get them off my chest. I know nothing can be done about them, but, as they say, a problem shared . . .

"My title symbolizes status, darling. Do not mistake it for power." Mother peeks up at me as she trails a pretty silver teaspoon over the rim of her china cup. "I will be staying out of the way of your father today."

"They have blown it out of proportion."

"Of course they have. That is what the press does." She brings her teacup to her lips and sips. "Our relationship with the media is a fragile bond, darling. We must not put a strain on it. We feed them morsels to pacify them. We don't give them a banquet to feast on."

Taking my knife, I smear a small bit of butter across my toast and nibble on the edge, talking myself down. There is nothing I can say or do to make them see reason, because there is no reason to be had. We are royals. We comply with tradition and expectation.

"We were discussing baby names." Mother places her cup down gently and starts to fiddle with the pearls around her delicate neck.

I laugh a little. "Discussing? Why?" We all know what that child will be called if it is a boy, and we also know what it will be called if it is a girl. I am named after my father's mother, and my two preceding names are that of my mother and maternal grandmother. Adeline Catherine Luisa Lockhart. Therefore, should John and Helen's baby be a boy, it will be named after his grandfather, Alfred, with John and Harold preceding. A girl will be Catherine Helen Elizabeth. Everyone knows that, even the public. Why are we wasting time discussing it?

Mother gives me a tired look but says no more on the matter. We finish our breakfast chit-chatting about my engagement at the gallery this evening, Mother taking an interest in my dress as usual. One thing my mother and I have in common, as well as our Spanish looks, is our passion for lovely clothes. Although poor mother is more restricted than I am when it comes to breaking the rules of royal attire, her neat frame always hidden in the expected formal skirt suit and matching headpiece or hat.

We say our goodbyes with the usual formal kiss, and I finally head toward the stables. I spend the afternoon bonding with Spearmint, the absence of Sabina acute. I hope she's okay. I hate to think of Sabina lost in grief. I finally pluck up the courage to call Haydon while riding Stan down the bridal path, Damon trailing me

in the Land Rover. "I am so sorry to hear about your grandfather," I say with true sympathy. He was a good man. "How is Sabina?"

"You know my grandmother. As strong as those horses she trains every day. I had to stop her from going to the stables this morning."

I smile. "And you? How are you, Haydon?"

"I'd be better if my damn father would show his face. He left an hour after Granddad passed, and we haven't seen him since."

It's at this point it occurs to me that Haydon clearly hasn't seen the papers yet. Should I tell him? I bite my lip, contemplating my best move. I'm sure telling Haydon that his father has been at the palace all morning dealing with a silly crisis would not be a move well played. Nothing should take priority over his duty to be with his mother and son. "Was he okay?" I ask tentatively.

"Not really."

Silence falls. There's really not much I can say to that. "Haydon, listen, there is a story in the paper today. I need you to—"

"I've seen it."

I pull Stan to a gradual stop. "Oh. I see."

"We all know the papers dress things up."

I frown at thin air, caught off guard. "Yes, they do," I reply, sounding unsure. So that's it, then? "Please do let me know if there is anything I can do to help."

"Thank you, Adeline. I will." Haydon hangs up, and I slowly spin my phone in my hand, a little confused by that conversation. He turned up at Kellington the night of my party, and I know he was checking up on me. He may not have found Josh Jameson in my suite whipping me with a belt, but he knew something was going on, and the papers have confirmed it, even if they're reporting a morsel of a story and detailing the wrong man. Princess Adeline kissing a soldier is nothing compared to Princess Adeline tied up and being thrashed by Hollywood actor extraordinaire Josh Jameson. Haydon's happy to let the kiss slide?

"Heading back, ma'am?" Damon asks, pulling up next to me,

his bent arm resting out of the open window.

"Yes, I believe I've had enough for today." I turn Stan and give him a kick, letting him canter back to the stables. The feel of the wind in my hair would usually have me smiling, but today I can't appreciate it. Something just feels . . . off.

11

IT DOESN'T MATTER that each time I'm standing here, I'm wearing a different dress. Or my shoes are different. Or my hair and makeup have changed. I still only see a hollow woman. I wince as Jenny pulls and sweeps the front of my hair over my ear, pinning it in place securely before spraying my low chignon with lashings of hairspray.

"Lips?" she asks, looking at my red Jimmy Choos.

"Red." I know I should go for something more subtle and girlie, more acceptable for a royal engagement. But the defiance in me refuses to mismatch my lips from my shoes to please the Monarchy. It's red. The shoes are red. Slutty, scandalous red. I open my mouth as Jenny lines my lips and fills them in with the perfect red to match my shoes. Standing back from the mirror, I take in my form. The welts on my wrists are faded now, hardly noticeable, although still detectable if you look very closely. "I'll do." I accept my red clutch and let Jenny put the finishing touches on my makeup. "Thank you."

Kim appears at my suite's door. "Time to go, ma'am."

"I'm coming." Air. Lots of air. I pull it into my lungs and leave, Kim flanking me. "Walk me through it."

"You'll be greeted by the gallery owner, as well as his staff. You will be introduced, you can say a few words to each of them, if you wish, and then you'll unveil the plaque and declare the gallery open. Have you prepared any words of your own?"

"A few," I tell her, taking the balustrade as we reach the stairs. "But what else am I required to say?"

"I gave you a prepared speech this morning. You were going to weave your own words throughout."

I wrack my mind and find no recollection of that conversation. I shrug my apology and Kim sighs as she hands me a sheet of paper. "Here."

"Thank you. Is there alcohol?"

"You may have one glass."

"You are so generous, Kim." I could do with a bottle. Or ten.

"We're expecting gossip paps amid the press." Kim flicks me a look as her steps match mine down the stairs. "Security will keep them as far away as possible, but questions will be called, given the recent headlines. Ignore them. The formal greetings were due to be outside the gallery, but we need to get you inside ASAP, so we have changed the plans."

"Very good." I smile at Damon when he nods and opens the car door for me.

"You look beautiful, ma'am."

"That's very kind of you, Damon." I slide into the back seat and look up at him on a small smile. "But it's all rather a waste with no one to appreciate it."

His eyebrows rise slowly, as if he doesn't agree. "If you say so." The door shuts, Damon puts himself behind the wheel, and Kim drops into the passenger seat. She goes straight to her mobile, checking ahead of our arrival that everything is in place. I look behind to see a car tailing us, as well as one up front.

The door opens and Eddie slips in beside me, brushing through his dark blond hair with his hands. He looks dashingly handsome

in his tux. "Evening," he says, leaning over to give me a kiss on the cheek. Taking my hand, he squeezes, his way of telling me we are good. "How was Father this morning?" he asks.

"Oh, you know about that?" I sniff, returning his squeeze. "Your name wasn't even mentioned during my royal dressing down."

"I wasn't the one caught eating a man alive."

"You eating a man alive?" I laugh softly. "Now that would be real cause for a media frenzy."

"We'll leave the men eating men alive to Uncle Stephan." Eddie grins, and I smile, then focus on adding my own words to the manufactured speech.

~

OH GOD, THE street outside the building is swarming with press, cameras flashing, railings holding people back. Kim curses under her breath. "Bloody hell." She unclips her seat belt and turns in her seat to face us. "Damon will walk you in, okay?"

"No walkabout?" I quip, counting endless press, as well as members of the public who have come to steal a glimpse of me.

Damon holds his earpiece as he reels off instructions to his men, scanning the vicinity. "Set?" he asks. "Good." When he looks back at me, I give him a thumbs up and take a deep breath. He nods and exits, followed swiftly by Kim. A few seconds later, my door is opening and flashes are blinding me. "Fast but steady, ma'am," Damon orders, placing his hand on my lower back. "And remember to smile."

"Like you need to remind me?" I paint on my smile when the crowds erupt, letting Damon guide me into the gallery.

"Princess Adeline. Princess Adeline," they shout. I wave to the sea of people being held back by railings, the press also being pushed back by the Metropolitan Police. Looking over my shoulder, I see Eddie emerging from the car, immediately flanked by security. The excitable crowd moves up a level at the unexpected appearance of

Prince Edward. "Marry me," one girl calls. "I love you," another screams.

I laugh, being ushered into the gallery where a line of people awaits me. "Okay?" Damon asks, checking on Eddie.

"Yes, thank you." I compose myself and slip my clutch under my arm as he takes a step back and falls into his silent but oh-so-very-present pose, his fingers resting on his ear to listen for the all clear.

Kim joins me, looking way too flustered. "Ready?"

I nod and perfect my smile as Kim walks me forward and announces me to the first person standing in the perfectly straight line, a short, rather round man, who I recognize as the CEO of the charity. Kim motions to him. "Your Highness, this is Gary Perkins, founder of High Spirits."

"Your Highness." He bows his head and takes my hand when I offer it. "Thank you so much for joining us on this special evening."

"It is my pleasure," I reply, claiming my hand back as he straightens and looks at me. I can see the nerves on his face, like most people I am introduced to on formal occasions such as this, so I quickly work on putting him at ease. One thing I have learned over the years of royal engagements is to make them laugh. It relaxes them in an instant, and therefore relaxes me, too. I lean forward, like I am going to tell him a secret. "I hope you don't mind, but my brother was at a loose end this evening. I told him you wouldn't mind if he gatecrashed your party."

As planned, Gary bursts into a deep belly laugh, the nerves disappearing in an instant. "Not at all, ma'am."

"Oh good. He's usually well behaved." More laughter. "Although, probably wise to keep him away from that champagne fountain."

"Thank you for the advice, ma'am. And I must thank you for being such a wonderful patron for the charity."

"Very welcome." I smile, guilt niggling the corners of my conscience. I am a patron for over one hundred charities, and truth be told, I am only told what I need to know regarding the operations of

them. But the point of having a known face as a patron is exposure. The tweets, the messages of support, and the media articles are not my words. They're the words of my advisors. The speech-writers. "Can I just say, the work you do for the young adults is tremendous. Really tremendous."

"It's such a passion of mine, ma'am. Creativeness, art, and expression. It's all such wonderful therapy, and as you can see"—he motions around the gallery, and my eyes follow, seeing the walls adorned with canvases, and the floor scattered with stands displaying sculptures—"the results truly speak volumes."

"They really do," I agree. "Well done for giving these vulnerable people such a valuable opportunity."

He nods and motions down the line. "May I introduce you to the key members of our team, ma'am?"

"Certainly." I scan the line and quickly gauge the length. It's going to be a long haul. But that champagne fountain is waiting at the other end.

"May I introduce Professor Lennington," Gary starts, motioning to the lady first in line. She curtseys, her mane of frizzy locks falling forward, her glasses slipping to the end of her nose. She quickly rectifies her out-of-place spectacles and takes my hand. "She is a very talented painter." Gary goes on as Professor Lennington's hand trembles in mine.

I place my other hand over it, applying a little pressure. "I hope your hand in steadier with a brush in its grasp," I say lightly.

She laughs. "Your Highness, such an honor to have you here."

"Professor Lennington has donated her time and invaluable knowledge to the project. We couldn't have done it without her." Gary smiles proudly.

"How wonderfully generous of you." I release her hand.

"It's been an amazing experience seeing these young adults expressing themselves so ingeniously."

"Maybe Edward and I should explore the possibilities of

expressing ourselves in such a way." I look back to my brother who grins cheekily, offering his hand to Professor Lennington.

"I'm terribly clumsy with my hands," Eddie says softly.

More laughter breaks out, and my brother gives me a discreet wink.

Over the next hour, we're introduced to the entire line of twenty people, and then a dozen more before a glass of champagne is placed in my hand. I'm still not done, though I do get to sip while I am given a guided tour of the gallery, being shown endless paintings and sculptures while hearing the story of the artists, from young, homeless people, to people with learning difficulties. Listening to so many inspiring stories has the smile on my face fixed naturally.

When my tour is complete, Kim checks in with me quietly. "Can I get you anything?" she asks.

I shake my head as Eddie slopes off, collecting another glass from the fountain and settling in for a conversation with some of the charity's representatives while I continue the pleasantries with Gary, listening to him explain how the project works, with the artists receiving a percentage of all sales to encourage their newfound hobby. I'm about to declare my intention to purchase one of the stone sculptures, a beautifully simple naked woman, when a raucous cheer erupts from the street outside, the crowds clearly still holding fort. I look across to Damon, whose hand instantly moves to his earpiece, listening carefully. He nods and catches my frown, but assures me with a mild shake of his head.

"Time to say a few words," Kim says, motioning me to a nearby wall that has a small pair of red velvet curtains concealing what will be a sparkling engraved plaque. I move into position and face the gathered people, waiting for it to quieten down.

Then I clear my throat. "Thank you." I smile, scanning the crowd, making sure I address everyone before me. "I am so very thrilled to be here today to . . ." My words get lost amid a tidal wave of shock when my scanning eyes fall upon something that

I'm unprepared for. Or some*one*.

My breath lost, I stare at Josh Jameson standing at the back, his head literally head and shoulders above everyone. His face is straight, his blue eyes watching me. My blood sparks. My heart misses too many beats. Two suited men flank either side of him, standing tall and ominous. A cough jolts me from my stunned state, and I swallow, looking away from him. My mind is blank. Where am I? What am I supposed to be doing? Everyone is staring at me, and when Eddie frowns and looks back, I see recognition on his face as I try to focus on fixing my shakes. "I am so very proud," I start again, breathing through my words, "to be a patron for High Spirits Charity." I keep my eyes well away from the back of the room. *What is he doing here?* "Their work is truly inspiring." I force a smile, my body arrested by shock, fear . . . *heat*. The words I memorized in the car have escaped me. Gone completely. Taking hold of the silver chain beside the curtains with a shaky hand, I fast-forward through all of my forgotten words. "I am delighted to declare the High Spirits Gallery now open." I pull the chain, and the curtains slide across, revealing a silver plaque engraved with my name and today's date. Applause breaks out, and Damon is quickly by my side.

"Everything okay, ma'am?"

"What is he doing here?" I ask through gritted teeth, my panic rising when I see Josh breaking through the crowds, leaving a sea of frowning people in his wake.

"Your guess is as good as mine, ma'am," Damon says. "And my guess is pretty good."

I flip him an incredulous look. He's doing a terrible job of concealing his smile. "Funny ha ha," I mutter indignantly.

"Am I the only one who knows of your numerous meetings with Mr. Jameson?" Damon asks out the corner of his mouth.

"Matilda does. But only you and her, and let's please keep it that way."

"Of course."

Josh saunters over, his gait confident and smooth, his face wickedly handsome. He's all smart casual in a suit, opened collared shirt, no tie. Damn his gorgeousness. "Your Highness," he purrs, bowing his head only a very little. That accent, the way he says the words I hate. It reduces me to a pool of want every time. It's like a shot of adrenalin that wakes up my entire body.

I'm aware that everyone in the room is looking this way, to the Hollywood actor and the Princess conversing. What is he playing at? I offer my hand and plaster on my smile, though it takes everything out of me. I've been captured off guard. I'm unprepared. "Mr. Jameson, what a pleasure to meet you." My vocal chords tremble.

His smile is knowing as he kisses the back of my hand. "Always," he whispers, and my tummy tightens as I feel his hot, wet tongue meet my skin.

I snatch my hand back and fight my eyes not to widen, looking to Gary, who looks a little shell-shocked by the appearance of Josh Jameson in his gallery. The media attention he has already will be amazing for his project. Now, it will be extraordinary.

Scanning my surroundings, I see clusters of people talking between themselves, though their attention is never far away from Josh and me. Kim eyes me curiously, and Damon steps back, giving us space that I really don't want. Not now. Not here. I don't search out Eddie. I don't need to see him to know he'll be keeping a close eye.

I turn and wander over to the nearby sculpture of a naked woman, the one I was planning on purchasing. It is minimal, only the outline of her long, willowy body detectable. As I knew he would, Josh joins me and also feigns admiring the art.

"You've been ignoring my calls."

"Correct."

"Why?"

"*There is no one special.*" I repeat the words he spoke in the interview without thought, and quickly close my eyes, full of regret. I have seen him only a few times. Of course I am no one special.

"You wanted me to declare to the world that I'm seeing you?"

"No, because you are not." I brush him off with my strongest voice, however weak I feel inside. "You realize pictures of us will be splattered all over the media tomorrow," I say quietly, disturbed by this stupid stunt of his.

"I'm buying art. Nothing unusual. Besides, I arrived separately so there will be no pictures of us together."

"Josh Jameson showing up to a gallery opening unannounced isn't unusual?" I laugh at his stupidity. "The media will be going wild."

"Talking of the media . . ."

My eyes start to burn from staring at the same spot on the sculpture, where Josh's hand is now resting. That hand. That wicked, talented hand. *Talking of the media.* I don't say a word, leaving Josh to press on.

"So the night I fucked you blind, you had another man's lips on yours before mine?"

I swallow and blink slowly. "What of it?"

"*What of it?*" He laughs, running his hand across the hips of the woman. "For a start, if I had known, I would have whipped that beautiful ass of yours a lot fuckin' harder."

I inhale, shocked, and scan the vicinity for prying eyes and ears. We are safe, but still. I clear my throat and search for calm. "I think it's time you looked around the gallery that you're apparently rather interested in."

"There's only one thing in this gallery that I'm interested in."

My mind reels. He's changed his tune. A flash of satisfaction darts through me, but I am quick to rein it in, reminding myself of why Josh and I are never going to happen. My life. His boredom levels. "Well, that *one thing* is not interested in you."

"Why are you denying me?"

"If I don't, then they will." My thoughts tumble from my mouth, and I feel his eyes on my profile as I mentally run through every

reason why I need to keep myself away from Josh Jameson. There are too many, not least the fact that I get that wonderful feeling of freedom and relief whenever I'm with him. Like now. There's an army of people and press outside, crowds of people behind us, yet I hear none of them. I see none of them. I sense nothing except Josh. It's wonderfully therapeutic, like nothing I have felt before. It's also something I must not get used to.

A loud cough startles me back to the here and now, where Josh is standing next to me caressing a sculpture of a naked woman.

His hand pauses, his leather shoes bringing him a step closer to me. "You're imagining me doing this to you, aren't you?"

"Yes," I breathe the word out mindlessly. Instinctively. I look at him as he looks down at me, his face expressionless. "But it can't happen again." I turn and walk away, being immediately collared by a smiley man.

"Your Highness." He performs the customary greeting. "Enjoying the champagne?"

"I'm sorry, you are?" I ask, seeing Damon moving in quickly.

"Not quite a whole bottle of Belvedere, though, eh?"

I frown, looking at my glass, confused. It is then I spot his camera bag resting on his hip. My heart jumps.

"How many men did you share a bed with, ma'am? Two? Three? We heard it was three. Can you confirm that?"

"Excuse me?" I cough, astounded by his rudeness.

"We were told there was cocaine, too. Care to comment?" He moves in, his phone in his hand.

"I was enjoying my thirtieth birthday. There were no drugs, and there was no sex."

"And the man in the picture. He's your lover, right? What about Haydon Sampson? Is a proposal from him definitely off the cards?"

"Enough." Kim is by my side in a second as Damon seizes the journalist, who struggles boldly, continuing to shout his incriminating questions.

"Oh!" I stagger forward when I'm jolted during the scuffle, my palms coming up to save me.

"I've got you." Josh catches me, righting me with ease, and I look into eyes full of concern, tinged at the corners by rage.

"I'm okay," I murmur, dropping my eyes. "Thank you."

He doesn't let go of me, watching on as Damon manhandles the journalist out of the gallery, taking his phone as he does. "No comment, ma'am," Kim hisses. "Always no bloody comment."

I breathe back my nerves, unable to stop my shakes. "I can't believe that."

"Everything cool?" Josh asks, letting me gently break away from him.

"Yes, everything is *cool*," Kim retorts, turning into me. "What did he say? What did *you* say?"

"Nothing. He was just trying to put words in my mouth."

"Damn republicans." Kim scans the gallery. "Time to go. Where's Damon gone, for God's sake?"

"I'll walk her out," Josh interjects.

Kim's disgusted face tells everyone what she thinks of that idea. "I don't need any fuel adding to the fire, thanks," she says as Damon strides back through the crowds, his hand held to his ear. "We're leaving," Kim informs him.

Josh moves into me quickly, his hand wrapping around my wrist, his mouth dropping to my ear. "See me again," he whispers. "Tell me you'll see me again."

"I . . . I can't."

"Yes, you can."

"No, I—" I'm pulled abruptly from Josh's hold by Damon. He says nothing as he places his hand in the small of my back, lightly pushing me onward. I look over my shoulder as I'm directed to the exit, finding Josh not far behind, his jaw tight. Kim's trying to convince him to hold back, and the other guests are starting to recognize him, people moving in from every direction to crowd

him as he tries to bump his way through. His eyes never leave mine.

"Pay attention, Adeline," Damon orders as we make it onto the street, and I'm forced to rip my stare from Josh's. The car door is held open for me by one of Damon's men, his watchful eyes scanning the area. I slide into the seat and quickly move across when I see Eddie being led to the car by another one of Damon's team. He falls in beside me and is immediately on my case. But not about what should be being addressed here.

"You and Jameson," he says accusingly as the door is shut behind him, closing off the flashes of a million cameras.

I sit back in my seat and look directly forward at the back of Damon's head. "There is no me and Jameson."

"Then what the hell is he doing here?"

"Buying art, I expect." The car pulls off quickly once Kim's in the passenger seat.

"Addy, I know what I saw just then. This is bad news." His hand goes to his forehead and rubs. "They'll never allow it."

"There is nothing to allow," I grate, my frustration building. I know my brother is only trying to protect me from the inevitable strong-arm of the royal household. And protect Josh too, really. He has so much to lose. Being discredited by the British Royal—

"I hope so," Eddie mutters as I fish through my purse for my mobile when it chimes. I discreetly turn the screen away from Eddie when I see who has sent me a message.

Either tell Damon to pull over, or I'll stop your car in the middle of Oxford Circus.

Your call, Your Highness.

I look out the back window on a skip of a few heartbeats, scanning the darkness. I can only see headlights.

"Yes," Damon says to one of his men through his earpiece, looking up at his rearview mirror. "Run a check on the plate."

"What's going on?" Eddie shoots forward in his seat, worried.

"Unknown vehicle following," Damon informs him, cool as can be, clipped and to the point.

Eddie immediately looks out of the back window too, and I begin to sweat as I reread Josh's message. The unknown vehicle. It's him. I know it's him. At that very second, Damon's eyes catch mine in the mirror, and I sense that someone's confirmed who is in the unidentified car. I force a smile, and he shakes his head, returning his attention to the road. "For fuck's sake," he mutters. He rarely swears, so to hear him do so now, I know he's exasperated. And rightly so. Josh needs to pull back before this blows up.

"What?" Eddie asks, his attention divided between the back of Damon's head and the back window. "What is it?"

"A fan," Damon quips.

"Keep driving," I order, but a red light flashes up ahead and Damon starts to slow the car. "No, keep driving."

"Ma'am, we're on Oxford Circus. You want me to run someone down?"

I slowly turn back and look out of the window. I find Damon's men exiting the car behind, blocking someone from coming to the car. What is he doing? I quickly ring him, and he's just as quick to answer. "Josh, are you out of your mind?"

"Yeah, I am." There's a few scuffles and a few curses, and I see Josh's own security wrestling with mine. "Get the fuck off me," Josh yells.

"Oh my God," I breathe.

Eddie laughs, a short sharp laugh that's loaded with sarcasm. "Nothing to tell," he mimics in a silly female voice.

I put my hand on the door to get out, but Eddie dives across the car and stops me. "What are you doing?"

"I'm going to sort this out."

"Adeline, don't be stupid. We're in the middle of Oxford Circus, for Christ's sake. He's causing enough of a scene already. Add you

to the mix and all kinds of shit will hit the fan."

I throw myself back in the seat and grudgingly admit he's right, though not out loud. "Get me home," I order shortly, before I dive out of this car and give onlookers the show of the year. Maybe even the decade. Josh Jameson, my drug of choice, is a few meters behind trying to get to me, and there is nothing I can, or *should*, do about it. I feel like I'm going cold turkey. Being starved of something I so desperately want. Or, more disturbingly, something I desperately need.

BY THE TIME I make it to my suite, ignoring everyone who tries to talk to me for the rest of the journey, I've had numerous missed calls from Josh. But I wanted privacy to speak to him.

I shake my head at Olive as she goes to follow me into my bedroom after I darted past her at the entrance, where she was waiting to take my coat. I shut the door, kick off my shoes, and accept the next call from him.

"Josh." I drop to the couch in my room and wait with bated breath for what he has to say.

"You drive me insane," he informs me frankly.

"This has to stop."

"No."

"Yes. You leave London next week, anyway."

"This isn't stopping. You don't want it to. I don't want it to. I'll admit, Adeline, at first you were a great fuckin' challenge, no matter how attracted to you I was. But now . . ." He drifts off, and I defiantly force down my hope. *Now? Now, what?* I shouldn't ask.

I push the tips of my fingers into my temple in despair. "They will—"

"I don't give a fuck about them," he spits angrily. "I didn't think you did, either."

"I usually don't."

"Then tell me, why now?"

The truth is my only option. "Because I think I would care if they took you away from me."

There's a long pause down the line, one that seems to stretch for an eternity. He finally speaks. "You *think* you will care?"

I close my eyes and reach up to massage my chest. This is all too much. I'm drowning and flying, and it is hurting my mind. "I know I'll care."

"We'll be discreet."

My eyes spring open in shock. "What? Like trying to storm my car on Oxford Circus? Like turning up at an art gallery that I'm opening?"

"Like I said, you drive me insane. And in case it's escaped your notice, you are the Princess of fuckin' England, Adeline. A man has to think outside the box if he's going to get to see you."

I laugh, despite myself. "And you are Josh Jameson. Don't you see how much this *can't* work?"

"No. I only see you. It would seem you have become a bit of an Achilles heel, Your Highness."

My heart flutters as I get up and start to pace my room, my head in bedlam. "Josh, I . . ."

"Do you want to see me?"

I come to a stop and squeeze my eyes shut, my mind vehemently demanding I say no. "Yes." My heart wins easily.

Josh breathes out. "Jesus, Adeline. I can't even begin to explain how into you I am. I want to tie you up and whip that fine ass of yours to kingdom come."

"Josh—"

"Don't try to fool me that you don't love the sense of freedom you get from me restraining you, of letting me have all control over you."

He's right. I go into my bathroom and put myself in front of the mirror while I work my way out of my dress, turning to see

the fading evidence of Josh's heavy hand on my backside. The marks will be gone soon. "Why do you like that?" I ask. "Why do you like whipping me?"

He's silent for a few moments, contemplating his answer. "You need it."

Again, he's right. I zoned out and strangely found peace in my crazy world. He knows what he does for me.

"Have dinner with me," Josh suggests, gentle and pleading.

I can't help the small disbelieving laugh that escapes me. "Where?" I ask. "It's not like I can wander into a local restaurant and order the daily special." Grabbing my robe, I slip it on.

"At my hotel. I'm at The Dorchester in the Harlequin Suite. It'll be private, I promise. Tomorrow night. Say yes."

"Yes." It's an easy yes. Probably the easiest agreement I've ever given. I can't say no to him, and what is more, I don't want to.

"Have Damon bring you to the staff entrance at the rear at eight o'clock. I'll have my security team meet you there."

Wandering into my bedroom, I perch on the edge of my bed. "Okay."

"Adeline?" he murmurs softly, waiting for my acknowledgement.

"Yes?"

"I look forward to it."

I smile, looking at my lap shyly, butterflies exploding in my tummy at the thought of being alone with him. "Warming up your palm?"

"I'll be gentle with you."

"Maybe I don't want you to be gentle with me."

"You're a very bad girl, you know that?"

I hum, thinking it is he who has unearthed this particularly bad side of me. *Or is it bad at all?* Maybe it's the best thing that could happen to me. Or maybe the worst. It hurts too much to think the latter, so I'll try my hardest not to and focus on savoring the company of my ultimate vice while I can. "Good night," I whisper.

"Sweet dreams, Your Highness."

"Sweet dreams, my American Boy."

He chuckles lightly and hangs up, and somehow my heart rests. It's as though *his* call, *his* assurances, of being with *him*, calms me. I can finally breathe again. He wants me to be with him.

I can't even begin to explain how into you I am.

Don't try to fool me that you don't love the sense of freedom you get from me restraining you, of letting me have all control over you.

He's only known me for a tiny moment of my life, yet he *knows* me. How is that possible?

Our conversation whirls around in my mind for the rest of the evening and well into the night.

Why do you like that? Why do you like whipping me?

You need it.

I do.

I also *need* him.

12

THE NEXT DAY, I keep myself busy at the stables doing everything the stable girls would usually see to. I muck out, clean saddles, and even tidy up the tack room. I'm lost in all things horses, as well as my thoughts, for most of the day, and when I'm on my way back to the car, I see Sabina for the first time since I found out about Colin.

I pull off my gloves as I divert toward the hay barn. "Won't be a moment, Damon," I call to him by the car, breaking into a jog. As I approach the stable doors, I hear a raised voice and slow to a cautious walk. The voice isn't only raised, but it's angry too, and it isn't Sabina's voice. It's David's.

"I cannot believe all this time," he yells.

I make it to the door and peek around the corner, seeing Sabina holding his upper arms, trying to placate him. "David, please. You must calm down."

He shrugs his mother off and stomps his way to the other end of the barn. "Were you ever going to tell me?" He swings around, and I pull back quickly to avoid being seen. "I should have known."

"Some secrets should never be told," Sabina replies, rather

meekly. "You should be mourning your father's death with me. Helping me arrange his funeral."

David scoffs, loud and coldly. My mind races, my curiosity piqued more than is safe in my world.

"I'm busy," David spits heartlessly, and I frown, almost cynically. He's busy all right, interfering with me and my life. I hear David's footsteps hitting the concrete, getting louder. He's leaving the stable. I quickly dash toward the car, ignoring Damon's questioning face when I make it there. I'm just dropping into the back seat when David appears through the door, Sabina following quickly after him, though they're not speaking now. Not when they're in earshot of others.

"You okay, ma'am?" Damon asks, winning my attention.

"Yes, I'm fine." I look at the back of his headrest. "Home, please, Damon," I say when he is in the driver's seat, my mind refusing to slow down.

What is going on?

MY MIND HASN'T slowed much by the time Damon pulls into the gates at Kellington. Olive greets me at the door and takes my coat. "Will you be joining Prince Edward for supper, ma'am?"

I let her pull my coat from my shoulders. "Not this evening, Olive. Please let Dolly know I'm eating out."

The flash of surprise that flickers across Olive's face makes me smile on the inside. It's warranted. Whenever do I "eat out", especially at such short notice? "As you wish, ma'am." She scuttles off, and I turn to find Damon looking at me for answers. Oh, of course. I haven't told Damon of my plans yet. In actual fact, I haven't told anyone. The less people who know the better, but since Damon needs to accompany me for obvious reasons, I can't very well keep it from him. I smile nervously, and he rolls his eyes.

"Where am I taking you?" he asks.

"To The Dorchester. Eight o'clock."

"Am I to assume no one else knows?"

I nod.

"And you will be seeing Mr. Jameson, yes?"

I nod again.

"I need notice for things like this, ma'am." He pulls his phone from his pocket and dials. "Men to have in place, checks to carry out."

"I'm sorry, Damon, it slipped my mind." It didn't. I've thought of little else but my date with Josh tonight. I was just nervous, is all.

I can see quite clearly that Damon desperately wants to give me advice, which he knows I'll dislike very much.

I smile meekly. "Make it as low-key as possible, okay?"

"Low-key?" Damon almost laughs. "Adeline, need I remind you of who you are?"

"No," I grumble. "No one need do that. I am simply requesting that I don't have half of MI6 on our tail. Just get me in the back door of the hotel, and that will be that."

"That will be that," Damon repeats on a disbelieving shake of his head, as if I'm naïve. I know he thinks I am. Shooing me away, he starts planning, and I leave him to it, turning to head for my suite and ready myself.

But my path is blocked by Eddie. My laid-back brother doesn't look too laid-back right now, and the many reasons why I've avoided him today are now before me in the form of a face lined with an expectant expression. "You're seeing him, aren't you?"

I'm not getting into this conversation, especially with too many listening ears around. I walk past him and take the stairs, ignoring the sound of his boots following me. "I'm afraid I won't be joining you for supper."

"I got that message loud and clear, Addy. Please, listen to me."

"I'm not listening," I insist, rounding the gallery landing and scanning the space for staff. "My mind is made up. I am having

dinner with him."

"Father will not allow it, Adeline. You know that."

"Father does not know, and he won't." I stop and turn to face Eddie when I reach the entrance of my suite. "Will he?" I ask, cocking my head in question. "Only you and Damon know, so my secret should be safe."

"He finds things out, no matter how hard you try to keep them from him. I won't breathe a word, but that doesn't mean anything, and you know it."

I grit my teeth and push my way into the suite, refusing to accept that he is right. I've never worked as hard as I plan on working to keep my meetings with Josh from the King. He won't find out. I shut the door, but Eddie walks straight in, clearly not ready to give up trying to talk me out of it. I realize he's only trying to save my hurt. That's his only motive here, but I can't help resenting him for it, anyway.

"Adeline." He gives me beseeching eyes. "I just—"

"No, Eddie." I hold up my hand. "This conversation is not going to happen so don't waste your breath." Hurrying to my bathroom, I lock the door behind me to ensure he can't storm in. Then I start getting myself ready for my evening with Josh. My stomach twists and turns, a mixture of nerves and excitement. And just like that, my reality is forgotten as Josh reclaims his place at the forefront of my mind.

I DON'T KNOW if Damon purposely took notice of my request for low-key because I requested it, or because it's safer, but we travel in a two-car convoy as opposed to the usual three. I don't ask. Besides, my stomach is swirling with more nerves now, less excitement, and it's becoming increasingly tricky to focus on anything but the night ahead.

When Damon pulls up at the rear of the hotel and cuts the

engine, he signals for his man to go and do whatever he has to do before Damon allows me out of the car. They communicate via their earpieces, talking, confirming, debating, though the one end of the conversation I can hear from Damon really isn't sinking in. I'm too busy being nervous and giving myself a mental pep talk.

"Ready?" he asks, letting himself out before I have the chance to answer. It's a very good question, though I'm aware I've taken Damon's enquiry out of context. My body is ready, oh so very ready, but my heart is not so sure. The door is opened and I get out as Damon continually scopes the area with watchful eyes. I slip my shades on, despite the sun having left the sky some time ago, and flip the hood of my long silk mac over my head. I don't move before Damon collects me by placing his palm in its customary place in the small of my back. I have never considered before now how such a light touch can feel so utterly safe. He walks me through the corridors in the bowels of the hotel, one man up front checking the way, two men behind following on. We reach a service elevator and find two suited men, as stern as they are large. Josh's security.

One steps forward, presenting his hand to Damon. "Well, I'll be damned," he says on a smile. "Damon, my man. Good to see you."

"Bates," Damon greets, showing a rare smile when he is on the job.

"You know each other?" I question, glancing between the two men.

"Bates and I served in MI6 together," Damon says. "It must have been, what—"

"Fifteen years," Bates clarifies. "Fifteen long-arse years." He smacks the call button on the service elevator. "Going up, ma'am?" he asks with a cheeky twinkle in his eye.

For the life of me, I don't know why, but I blush. "Yes, please."

"Your chariot awaits." He motions into the lift and Damon laughs softly, prompting a chuckle from me. We hustle into the giant elevator, though it doesn't feel so big with these six meaty

men filling it. I'm flanked at every angle, totally concealed in the middle. The ride to the top is rickety and long, giving me more time to get myself worked up. I try to breathe some calm into my lungs, try to steady my sprinting heartbeat. It's no use. I have never been so nervous before. I'm not silly enough to ask myself why I am a wreck. I've already figured out that much.

For the first time in my life, I really, *really* like a man. And therefore, I'm anxious.

The doors open and Josh's men lead the way, Damon by my side, and the rest of my close security a few steps behind. A door opens, and I instinctively lower my head when someone exits a room. Damon moves in closer to me, Josh's men slow, and the men behind speed up, all of them closing me in, making it as difficult as possible for the bystander to see me. They disperse a little when we're out of the danger zone, and we come to a stop at a door. A card is inserted into the reader, the door is opened, and I am ushered inside. Quickly removing my coat and glasses, I pat down my loose hair and turn to a nearby mirror, checking I look presentable and not crumpled. The Herve Leger off-the-shoulder gold bandage dress couldn't possibly crease during the car ride here; there's no spare or loose material to crease. My dark hair is fanning my bare shoulders, and my lips are nude. I feel lovely, and I chose this dress thinking Josh would very much approve, yet now, strangely, I'm doubting my choice. Nerves. It's the nerves.

A cough has me startling and pivoting quickly, making my hair whip my face before coming to settle over one shoulder. "Holy fuckin' shit." Josh makes no bones about his pleasure, standing beyond all the men who accompanied me up here. His gaze takes its greedy time lazily dragging down my frame, before wandering back up, eventually arriving at my face. I'm relieved that he made as much effort as I did, with his well-worked physique dressed splendidly in a Wentworth-grey three-piece suit. I smile when I see his pink hanky stuffed in the breast pocket. His hair doesn't look like

it's fully dried from his shower, and he hasn't shaved. Oh, gosh, he looks unimaginably gorgeous, and tonight it is all for me.

"Thanks, guys," Josh says, nodding to his men and shaking Damon's hand. "I've got it from here."

Damon casts a look over to me—a wary look. I don't know what to say. Damon won't go far, and I can't expect him to stand in the corridor all evening, though I know he would without question.

Josh must see my conflict, as well as Damon's uncertainty, because he is quick to reassure us. "There's a room through there." He motions to a door. "Play cards, chill out."

I give Damon a thumbs up, happy he has somewhere comfortable to wait for me. "I will be fine."

"I'll look after her," Josh slips in.

Damon laughs abruptly, holding his hands up as he backs away. "Too much information, my friend."

And there go my cheeks again, bursting into flames. I can't look at any of the men as they shift into the other room, Damon's old friend from MI6 throwing his arm around Damon's shoulders as they go, insisting on hearing everything that's happened in his life since they last saw each other. Fifteen years' worth? That could take a while.

"Let me," Josh says, taking my coat from my hands. Then he stares at me, looking so content with what is before him. I can't deny that I'm happy by the notion. No man has looked at me like this before, completely and unapologetically admiring me. Admiring me for being me. Not Princess Adeline. Just me.

He's still admiring me a few seconds later, and I start to fidget. "What?" I ask, snapping him out of his reverie.

His gaze meets mine. "You look stunning. Fuckin' beautiful."

"Thank you," I say quietly.

"I had planned on wooing you over dinner, but now . . ." He shakes his head to himself.

"Now what?"

"Well, now you're standing here with that fuckin' dress defining every curve I love, and I'm suddenly not too keen on the idea of dining you." He tosses my coat on a nearby chair. "Come here."

I step forward, and he seizes me with one easy arm curled around my back. Landing me with a hard, chaste kiss, he lifts me from my feet and carries me through the suite. "So we're not eating?" I ask, smiling like a crazy woman against his lips.

"Oh, I'm eating, for sure." He bites at my neck, and I squeal through a laugh, feeling my tight dress ride up my thighs. When we get into the lavish bedroom, Josh stops and looks up at me. My laughter fades as I stare into his serious eyes. "I'm fuckin' starving," he says quietly. "Starving for you, Adeline." I smile a small smile, nodding a tiny bit, knowing he understands I feel the same about him. "And I'm worried," he goes on, kissing my lips gently. "Because no matter how much I gorge on you, I don't think the hunger will ever be curbed."

I swallow, flicking my eyes briefly past him. "There will be no need for curbing if this fling gets out."

"Fling?" Josh asks, tugging my face back to his. "Is that what this is?"

"It's all it can be, right?" Finishing a statement with a question is never wise. It shows your uncertainty, your need for confirmation, your need to stop doubting what you think you know.

"Right," Josh breathes, searching my eyes. The pain that cuts through my chest is unfamiliar. And I positively hate it.

"So let's play." I force the words out and fist his damp hair in my hands. "Sir."

His growl is possessive. His expression hard. I'm dropped to my feet and the zip of my dress found with ease. Although he doesn't yank it down like I expect. He inches it open slowly, breathing in my ear as he does. The side of my face nestles into him, electricity bolting through every nerve. Closing my eyes, I raise my hands and place them on his shoulders, my senses heightened by the sound

of his light breath in my ear. His lips meet the hollow beneath my lobe, and he kisses his way down my neck, my head dropping back to give him full access to the column of my throat. I space out, lost, my body alive and hypersensitive.

"Josh," I whisper, gliding my hands down the sleeves of his suit jacket.

"I'm here," is all he says, finding my lips and kissing me deeply, but only very briefly. My dress hits the floor, and he steps back, visibly struggling to move away. His breathing is rapid, his body rippling, his eyes heavy. Passion and sex personified is before me, ready to take me into the clouds where I'm light and carefree. I step out of my dress and kick off my shoes, bringing my eyes level with his Adam's apple, which is rolling under his stubble from constant swallows. His gaze drinks in my lacy underwear as he strips his body of his clothes, my impatience growing with every inch of his skin revealed. His clothes drop to the floor one by one. I lick my lips, mentally roaming his flesh with my tongue. Every single inch of him. His body—his hard, beautiful, perfect body, is enough to reduce me to tears. I wait for my instructions, my impatience growing, the magnetism of his presence tempting me to claim him.

And when his eyes meet mine, I lose the will to maintain the space between our bodies, and shoot forward, throwing myself into his arms. Our bodies crash together, as well as our lips, and the passion flares. I'm hauled closer to him, my legs curling around his waist, my hold of him solid as our tongues dance, swirl, and plunge over and over. He tastes divine, feels divine.

He is my heaven.

Our desperation is making our union crazed and chaotic. "Fuckin' hell, Adeline," he mumbles between tangled tongues. "Fuckin', *fuckin'* hell." We fall to the bed and roll until I'm pinned beneath him. He growls, frustrated, as he yanks his mouth from mine and thrusts my arms up over my head. My chest pulses, my gasps for breath loud. "Where are your manners, Your Highness?"

he pants as he straddles my waist, a small smile playing at the corners of his mouth. "You need to ask nicely if you want something."

"Please," I gasp, unabashed. There is nothing I wouldn't do. Beg or steal, I would do it for him. "Take me to the clouds."

His discreet smile fades as he stares down at me, his mind seeming to whirl at those words. "The clouds," Josh murmurs, flexing his hold of my wrists. "Like heaven."

"Better," I confirm, lifting my head to capture his lips. He doesn't deny my demand for his mouth, falling straight into my kiss on a moan, releasing my wrists to allow me to hold him.

"I'm dripping," he tells me, rubbing his groin into my thigh. "Aching." He pulls me up from the bed and carries me across the room with urgency, lowering me to a nearby dresser. With one swift yank, my knickers are ripped from my body and tossed aside, and the cups of my bra tugged down, my boobs spilling out. His mouth is on my chest a second later, his fingers slipping between my lips to test my readiness. "I'm not the only one."

He's not. Goodness, I am completely drenched and pulsing. "Fuck me," I demand. "Hard. Like you own me." Words are coming without thought, need hijacking me. "Do it, Josh." My legs snake around his hips and tense, tugging him closer.

"Like I own you?" he questions, pushing his fingers deep on a brutal drive. I cry out, my head falling back. "I owned you the second you dropped to your knees for me, Your Highness." His fingers pull free, and he levels himself up, pounding forward on a roar. The penetration robs my lungs of air, my mind spacing out.

"Josh!" I yell, grappling at his damp back to find my grip, my face falling into his neck.

"Not hard enough?" he questions, withdrawing and slamming forward again. "Not feeling owned yet?"

My teeth sink into his shoulder, my body at his mercy. The brutal bite doesn't faze him, but his fingers dig deeper into my backside, propelling me back and forth onto his cock. His thrusts are unforgiving, the loud smashing of our sweaty bodies filling the room.

I force my head up and recline until my back meets the wall, my fingers interlaced at his nape, my arms straight. His face. It's tight, harsh, and dripping wet, his hair a fucked-up mess. The veins in his neck are ballooning, his tight jaw set to crack. His chest rolling, his biceps swelling. It is the most beautiful, erotic vision I've ever seen.

With every smash into me, I cry out. With every roll of his hips, I moan. My heart is pounding. My skin buzzing. My whole being vibrating. It's sensory overload, the sounds, the feeling, the sight. I'm dancing on the edge of explosion, fighting back the climax simply to extend this moment.

"You're going to come with me," he grunts, never losing his rhythm, not even for a second. My laced fingers slip, forcing my hands to the surface of the dresser to keep me upright.

"Jesus, Josh." I'm losing it.

"Ready?"

"Yes."

My confirmation has his pace increasing further, the shouts louder, the pleasure unimaginable. I hold my breath, my eyes locked on Josh as he watches me reach the pinnacle of pleasure. I can't hold back any longer. I throw my head back and release my breath, screaming to the ceiling as my orgasm rips through me mercilessly. I'm tackled from every angle by the intensity of it, my body shattering. I hear Josh's yell through the ringing in my ears, his fingers clawing brutally into my arse as he rocks his hips, spilling everything he has into me.

"Oh my God," I pant to the ceiling, as Josh's face falls forward, meeting my shoulder. I peel my palms off the wood of the dresser and settle them on his back, heaving like I've sprinted a marathon. Josh's weight resting on me holds me pinned to the wall, my head resting back. I'm exhausted.

"Owned," he heaves, turning his mouth into my neck and biting lightly.

I smile, smoothing my hand into his hair and combing through the wet strands. "Fine by me," I reply quietly, letting my heavy lids

fall closed. I wouldn't mind if we remained exactly here for the rest of the night, connected so intimately. Josh has other ideas though, and pulls away, his softening cock slipping out on a wince from both of us. He glances down at his groin, as do I. "That's bareback done, I guess."

I laugh, unable to feel remorseful for our lack of protection. Our craving for each other got in the way.

Josh chuckles with me and helps me down from the dresser, grabbing a tissue from the nearby box and cleaning me. "Would you think less of me if I told you I feel no remorse?" He takes my cheeks in his palms and holds my face, looking deeply into my eyes.

"I don't feel remorseful, either." I shrug. God, if he never wears protection again, that's fine by me. That was . . . unreal. "I take the contraceptive pill."

He smiles and presses his lips to mine. "I got all dressed up for you."

I inwardly swoon but outwardly grin. "I prefer you without clothes."

"What a coincidence. I feel the same about you." He moves back and has a little inspection, smiling at the cups of my bra still pulled down. I roll my eyes and reach to sort them out, but my hands are seized. "Just take it off."

"What about wooing me over dinner?"

"I don't think there's any need for wooing now, do you?" He points to the dresser on a hitched brow, and I grin like a loon.

"Suppose not." I unhook my bra and let it fall to the floor.

Josh matches my grin and slips his arms around my shoulders, pulling me in and walking me to the bathroom. "I'd offer you a shower, but I'm quite liking the smell of me all over you." He takes a white fluffy robe from a hook and holds it open for me. I catch sight of myself in the mirror as I turn to feed my arms through the sleeves.

"Gosh, I look—"

"Deliciously fucked," he finishes for me, reaching around my front and securing the tie. "Let's keep you that way." A light kiss is placed on my cheek. "It suits you." I don't know about that. All my makeup has been rubbed away, and my hair is a frightful mess. Taking a robe for himself, he puts it on and I pout at the lost vision of his nakedness. "Come." My hand is seized in his, and I'm led through to the main suite.

We pass a beautifully laid table for two. "That was a waste," I say as Josh pushes me onto one of the couches.

"Not half as wasteful as passing up the opportunity to fuck you." He falls to the couch at the other end and picks up the phone on the side table. "Yeah, hi. Guest Services, please. Yeah, sure." He looks at me. "They're transferring me."

I laugh. Crazy American Boy. "I need the bathroom," I tell him, getting up and hurrying back through the bedroom. Closing the door behind me, I use the toilet, but no sooner have I released the muscles of my bladder, Josh walks right on in, with no knock or call of warning. "Josh," I yell, unable to stop the flow, leaving me no choice but to remain where I am—sitting on the bloody toilet having a pee in front of Josh Jameson. I close my eyes, like if I can't see him, then he can't see me.

He starts laughing, and I open one eye, so mortified, though Josh clearly is quite unperturbed. "You look cute sitting on the toilet." He rests his back against the doorframe and gets comfortable.

"Some privacy, please?" I ask, my bladder now empty.

"What's the big deal?" He nods at the toilet roll. "We've skipped through first, second, and third base, and I nearly hit a home run the very first time we met. I think this is the next natural progression, don't you?"

I snatch the toilet roll and shuffle the robe to conceal me while I do the unthinkable; wipe myself. In front of Josh Jameson. His grin is slap-worthy, my embarrassment making me squirm. "The natural progression?" I ask. "So what comes after peeing in front of you?"

"Oh, you know, moving into my condo, marrying me, popping out a few ankle-biters."

I shoot up from the seat, my eyes round in shock. "What?"

"I'm kidding." He laughs, holding his hands up in defense.

I breathe out, flushing the chain and wandering to the sink. I wash and dry my hands. "That was not funny."

He mirrors my playful scowl as I move toward him, yelping when he grabs me and suspends me back in his arms. "You're right. I need to fuck your ass before we think about moving in together." He swallows my incredulous gasp when he kisses me, smiling around my lips, and despite my shock, I laugh too, because Josh Jameson has that effect on me.

He returns me to vertical and pushes my hair over my shoulder, studying me for a few moments. "Tell me. What are your dreams, Adeline?"

"Freedom," I answer honestly and quickly, and Josh smiles.

Leading me to the bed, we lie down, him on his side, me on mine, facing each other. "And if you had that freedom, what would you do with it?"

"Oh my God, everything," I say, just imagining how different my life could be. "I'd go back to university and study something I actually want to study."

"Like?"

"Fashion, textiles, art, ancient history." I mirror his smile. "My subjects were chosen for me." When he cocks an eyebrow, I go on. "British history, so that's basically my ancestors. Geography, maths, English. More or less everything that would make me the intelligent, well-spoken princess they wanted me to be, and nearly nothing that would help me realize my dreams."

"Intelligent?" he asks, and I smack his arm, making him chuckle. "What's the dream, then?"

I shrug. I've never dedicated too much time to thinking specifically about it. What was the point? "Anything I want," I say.

"Maybe design clothes, maybe open a store, or maybe I'll travel the ancient world."

"Sounds perfect to me."

Sounds perfect. It is. But it's out of reach. "Tell me what you would do if you didn't act."

"I'd run a ranch," he answers without hesitation, rolling onto his back. He's clearly thought a *lot* about it. "I never got to appreciate the wonder of space and peace before I moved away from Alabama. Now it's more appealing than ever." He turns his head and drops his eyes back to mine. And I see it. The same kind of suffocation I feel. "So one day, I'll have my ranch and you can design your clothes. I'll travel the world with you. I might even loan you one of my stables to use as a store."

I grin, as does Josh. "Okay," I agree easily. How is it possible for this man to not only understand my dreams, but validate them as well? This is the sort of man I've dreamt of. Someone who sees and hears me.

"Good." Leaning over, he kisses the tip of my nose. "Now, food's on the way. We'll have a carpet picnic, what do ya say?"

"I've never had a carpet picnic before."

"Say what?" He looks horrified. "Never?"

My shoulders jump up on a little shrug. "It's all fine dining, posh china, and solid silver cutlery at a table that's so shiny you can see your face in it."

"Then tonight we fix that." He pulls me up and walks us through to the lounge. "Get all the cushions on the floor." He pulls a throw off the back of a chair and wafts it into the air while I pull all the cushions from the couch. I watch as Josh gets on his hands and knees and starts pulling at the corners of the blanket, straightening it out and placing cushions.

I have a permanent smile on my face, fascinated by his deep concentration. "You are doing a tremendously good job," I say, clearing my face of my smile when his motions falter and he looks up at

me. One of his eyes narrows, and in a lightning move, he snatches my wrist and yanks me down to the floor. I cry in surprise, being rolled to my back until I'm once again pinned against something by his body. Not that I'm complaining. Would never dream of it. I blow a tickling hair from my nose and grin at him.

"You're making fun of me." He dips and bites the end of my nose.

"Not at all." I chuckle, squirming beneath him while he makes a meal of my face.

"Too good for a carpet picnic, are you? You want a throne?"

"Definitely not," I blurt. "Unless your face will be my throne."

Josh pulls back speedily on a little choke, his eyes bulging. I press my lips together as he stares at me in shock, like *how could such a vulgar thing have fallen from the lips of a princess?* "I think I just fell in love with you."

It's my turn to choke. "Blimey, you fall easily, don't you?"

"Actually, I don't fall at all."

"No?"

He shakes his head. "Baby, I'll be your throne any day of the week."

"Honored."

"It is me who's honored. It's not every day a real-life princess tells you she wants to sit on your face."

Laughter erupts from deep within me, my eyes clenching shut, my head thrown back. My position and lack of control gives Josh the perfect opportunity to ravish my throat. And he does, growling dramatically, squirming above me . . . rubbing me.

"Oh . . ." I sigh, my laughter settling. My hands go to the back of his head and guide him to my lips. "You taste so good." I bite at his lips, kissing from one side to the other. Nothing could rival the taste of him—not caviar, not the finest champagne—nothing. I hum and fall into a dreamy kiss.

But a knock at the door ruins my moment and Josh lifts his head,

looking toward the entrance, just as Bates exits the room where they're gathered. He's followed swiftly by Damon, who overtakes Bates to the door. I cough and pull my robe over my exposed thigh, hiding my rosy cheeks in the crook of Josh's neck.

"At least you're not naked," Josh whispers, pulling a smile through my embarrassment. "Or sitting on your throne."

I'm off again, laughing like I've never laughed before as Josh jumps up and leaves me to rearrange my robe and prop myself against the couch. He strides toward the door where Damon is looking through the peephole.

"You order room service?" Damon asks as Josh reaches him.

"Sure did." He gets his wallet and pulls out a note, but Damon doesn't move from the doorway and instead holds his hand out for the tip.

"I'll sort it. You're hardly presentable, are you?" He flicks his head at Josh's robe on a sarcastic smile.

"Thanks." Josh backs up, leaving Damon to accept the food and tip the waiter, but he doesn't open the door until Josh is back with me in the lounge, and he doesn't let the hotel employee into the room when he does eventually open it. Instead, he hands over the tip and helps himself to the trolley, wheeling it into the room and slamming the door behind him. "Dinner's served," he says as he nears.

Josh chuckles, and I flip a small, embarrassed smile to my head of protection. God love him, the things he'll endure for me. "Hey," Josh says. "If you're hungry, go ahead and order something. Just put it on the room."

"I don't eat past nine." Damon casts his eyes over to me on the floor. I smile. And when Damon struggles to maintain his straight face, an indulgent and rarely seen grin threatening, I know he recognizes how happy I am. I'm so happy right now. It's crazy, but I won't question it. I refuse to question it. Because to question it would be to ruin it.

Damon leaves us, and Josh sets our feast on the floor, pours champagne, and passes me silverware. "Is it solid silver?" I ask, tapping the fork on the back of my hand. "I can only eat with solid silver." Josh smiles at the bucket as he nestles the champagne in the rocks of ice. "So, what are we having?" I look at the two plates, wondering what's beneath the silver domes.

"This." He takes the lids off both plates, and I grin hard, reaching forward to pull the American flag off the top on the burger and popping one of the pickles in my mouth. I chew and swallow, accepting the plate when it's handed to me. I study the beast of a cheeseburger with all the caution it deserves, wondering how on earth I'm going to eat it without spilling sauce down my chin. Not very ladylike at all. And not a good look in front of a man I really like. I probably won't be able to get my hands around it. It's a monster. I glance at the silverware in my hand and then across to Josh, finding a face-splitting grin.

"Don't hold back for me." He picks up his burger and sinks his teeth in, spilling sauce everywhere. "Yum," he says around his mouthful.

I shrug and dive in. Bugger it. My mouth is watering. I take a huge bite and sigh, closing my eyes in pleasure and kissing goodbye to the years and years of etiquette and decorum that's been drummed into me "Oh," I mumble. "That's so good." I chuckle as I catch a drop of sauce from dropping off my chin.

"That's my girl." Josh passes me a glass of champagne while praising my lack of manners. "Wash it down with that."

"A dirty cheeseburger and Dom Pérignon?" I toast the air and take a sip. "Perfect."

"Only the best for my girl," he replies, so casually, without even looking at me, his attention on the greasy, dripping burger in his hand. My chewing slows. Those words. *My girl.* He said them so easily, and they sounded *so* right. I smile on the inside, though it's tinged with a little sadness. "Okay?" he asks, pausing with the

demolition of his burger.

I nod, fighting away the dejection with all I have. "Yeah."

We each make our way through the deliciousness, my moans of pleasure constant. It is so bloody good, and Josh seems to be taking immense satisfaction in my obvious enjoyment, his smile fixed around his chews. He reaches over more than once to wipe sauce off various parts of my face, and each time he licks his finger clean. I'm in my element. It's so refreshing to let go in so many ways—sex, food, laughter. This is me. I can't imagine the face of any man in my current life if I were to dribble burger sauce down my chin and chomp through it like I hadn't eaten for a year. But Josh is not fazed at all, and I am past caring about what I must look like, my hands dripping, my tummy bloated from fullness.

"That was so yummy." I drop the small piece of bread left in my grasp and fall back against the couch, fit to burst. I've never been so full.

I watch as he clears the plates and sets them on the trolley before settling beside me. Handing me my champagne, he chinks the edge with his and raises his glass. "To being bad."

I'll drink to that, though I know he's not referring to the million calories we have both just gobbled down in the space of minutes. "To being bad," I whisper, wondering what of this is really so bad? Me and Josh. Him and me. A princess and a sex symbol. The Monarchy will deem it bad. Some press will deem it bad. Half of the British population might deem it bad. But why? Because of tradition? Because of the rules? Because of strong blood? Appearances. Suitability. Who says we're not suitable? Where in royal English history was it decided that a royal couldn't be with someone they love?

My lips purse on the rim of my glass.

Someone they love?

"Adeline?"

I startle. "Yes?

Josh smiles through a faint frown. "What are you thinking?" He

shuffles down until he's lying on the floor on his side, facing me. He pats the floor in front of him, encouraging me to do the same.

I, too, shift down until I'm mirroring him. His hair has dried now, and it's all floppy and flat, the color lighter with a lack of product or water darkening it. It makes his blue eyes seem greener, his skin more olive. "I was thinking that I'm having a really lovely evening." It's not entirely a lie. That thought is what prompted the subsequent more unappealing thoughts, but I don't want to tarnish the lightness of our time.

"Me, too." He takes my hand and brings it to his lips, kissing the back lightly. "Now, are you going to tell me what you were *really* thinking?"

My gaze drifts from his, willing him not to ruin it. On the one hand, I love how he's understood me so well so quickly. On the other, like now, I don't. "That's what I was really thinking," I counter quietly.

"I don't believe you." Returning my hand to my personal space, he moves back a foot or so, giving me more. "I have some questions."

My instant stillness must speak volumes. "What questions?"

"And in return I'll answer anything you'd like to know."

"Anything?" I ask, testing the waters, now more focused on what I'd like to know about Josh rather than what Josh would like to know about me.

He nods, smiling through it. "Anything," he utters quietly. I sense his amusement is because he knows what my first question will be.

So I go right on ahead and ask. "Why did you spank me the first time we met?"

"Who said you get to ask first?" he counters, tilting his head in question.

My face bunches in displeasure. "Have you not heard the term *ladies first?*"

"Oh, yeah, I've heard it. And I'm a firm believer in it." He raises

his glass and takes a sip. "When I'm in the company of ladies."

I recoil, completely affronted. "I *am* a lady."

"I'm jerking around with you, Adeline. Stop being so stuffy."

I'm offended. As a royal, I don't think I'm *stuffy* at all. I certainly don't have *too* many plums stuffed in my mouth. "I am not stuffy."

"Maybe less stuffy now you've had some American cock inside you." He grabs his crotch and thrusts into his own palm, grinning a wicked grin. "Want some more?"

I very nearly spit out a resounding *yes,* my body flaming as a result of his crude mouth, but I pull up before I dive on him and eat him alive, realizing what he's doing. "You scoundrel." I reach across and slap his hip. "You can't distract me that easily. Tell me."

"Tell you what?"

"Why you thrashed my arse?"

"Why'd you love me doing it?"

"Wait, that is not what we agreed." I shake my head in demonstration, not prepared to let him turn this on me, though it clues me in on his direction of questioning once it's his turn to ask. "You suggested the game. Now play."

"Fine, you win." He huffs and refills his glass, and I watch him as he takes a long time to reposition himself and take more than half the glass in separate sips. He's still showing signs of amusement. "Honestly, your self-assuredness bugged the shit out of me." The shock of his words means my champagne makes a swift exit from my mouth. "I'm not used to women being so cocky. I wanted to pull you down a peg or two."

"What?" I splutter, leaving my chin dripping with the good stuff as I stare at Josh's handsome face. He laughs and reaches forward to clean me up, while I continue to gape at him, my mind not giving me the first idea of what I should say next. He wanted to punish me for being . . . *me*? Doesn't he realize that my bravado and front was all an act that day? A shield? "So you whipped my arse to stroke your bruised ego?"

Taking my hip, he tugs me forward until our fronts are touching and our faces are close. "Pretty much. Control is something I strive for in all elements of my life but rarely get. My life, my career. It feels like a runaway train most of the time. Pressure sucks."

I laugh lightly, completely understanding him. "But you are in full control when it comes to women." Do I have no filter with this man? He's obliterated my walls.

"Yes." His nose touches mine. "Until I met you."

"So you brought me down a peg or two."

"I did. But you know what?"

His question gives me pause, and I assess his serious face as he searches my eyes. Dare I ask? "What?"

"With you, I don't enjoy the control so much. It's not about me having the power over you."

I frown. "I'm not sure I understand."

"With you, I realized quickly you weren't accepting everything I threw at you because you wanted to please me. You accepted it because you needed it, and that flung my attraction toward you into fuckin' orbit." He takes his hand to my nape and pulls me onto his mouth, grazing his lips over mine. "With me, you do what your body and heart tells you, not what your warped mind is screaming. You love kissing goodbye to the power you battle to maintain every day of your life. You love letting me rule you. And that, Your Highness, turns me on more than anything."

"In a nutshell," I murmur, fully acknowledging his claim. And maybe because I'm falling for him. And because no man—no one, really—has taken the time to see me. Understand me. I swallow and look away from him, growing increasingly fearful for myself.

Josh jolts me until I look at him again. "I want us, Adeline. I love being your freedom. I *want* to be your freedom."

"But you're not my freedom, are you? Not truly. Not when we're having to hide in a hotel room to spend time with each other."

"You want the whole world to see me tanning your ass?" He

cocks a cheeky eyebrow, casting light on the dismal conversation.

I shake my head no, but truly, this isn't about our sexual relationship. This is about me being able to step out on the arm of a man I choose. A man I know is good for me. More than anything, I know this man is good for me. I want to yell from the rooftops that we are dating . . . or whatever this is. I want to hold his hand in public so they know he is mine. But it's horribly out of my reach. My despondency eats at the corners of my contentment, and to let it take hold would be to let my royal life win. It takes all my might, but I force back the depressing thoughts and grab onto some fortitude. Tonight has been wonderful. I'm not ruining it now. I don't want to talk about how we can't have each other. "Tell me about your childhood," I say in an attempt to steer my thoughts to more appealing things. "I want to know everything there is to know about you."

"My childhood?"

"Yes, your mum, your dad."

Suddenly very awkward, Josh pulls away and takes another drink, and my curiosity goes into overdrive.

"The senator isn't my biological father." Josh swallows and looks past me, and I'm once again struck silent. "My real father was an alcoholic. A bully. A womanizer. A criminal." He looks at me and smiles, raising his glass. "He was a nasty bastard. Cheers to that." Then he downs the lot and breathes out, dropping his head back and looking at the ceiling.

"I'm so sorry." I curse myself the moment I apologize, because I get the feeling Josh doesn't want that.

"Don't be sorry. Mom should have left him."

"She didn't?"

"She didn't need to in the end. He was driving home from the bar in his truck one night and ran someone down. He was wasted. Killed the woman, a mother of three children under five." Josh shudders, and I find my hand over my mouth, stunned. "He was

sent down for manslaughter, and you know what?" He looks at me, his face a little twisted from his inner turmoil. "It was probably the happiest day of my damned life, and the guilt I have for feeling that way when three little girls lost their mom tears me up if I think too much about it. So I don't." He nods decisively, swaps his glass for the bottle, and knocks it back. I feel rotten for bringing it up now. "It was only when my father was locked up that Mom felt safe." He smiles fondly. "Then she met the senator and he made her so incredibly happy, treated her like she deserved, and took me in under his wing. I wasn't the easiest kid, but he didn't give up on me, and I'll never forget that."

I reach over and take his hand, threading my fingers through his. I sensed Senator Jameson was a good man. He radiates warmth toward Josh. "That's really admirable."

"He's a good man. Said I needed something to express myself, and he was right. Acting came so naturally, and he set me up with contacts in New York. The rest is history."

"A good history." I smile, encouraging one from Josh.

"I didn't turn out too bad, I suppose. I'm sitting here with a member of the Royal fuckin' Family, after all. Cheers to me."

I laugh a little, moving a little closer to him. There's been no mention of Josh's mother in present tense. I'm almost too afraid to ask. "Your mum?"

"Died five years after she escaped my dad. Just two years after she married the senator. Cancer. Fuckin' cruel, right?"

I squeeze his hand, making a point not to say how sorry I am. He knows. "Right."

Turning his face to me, he smiles. "I've never told anyone that before."

A sense of privilege overwhelms me. So does a need to bring us back to the here and now. I push myself up and crawl onto him, pressing into his shoulders to force him to his back. "Therapy is over, Mr. Jameson. At least, the talking part is." I drop my mouth to his

and tease his lips as I unfasten my robe and pull it open.

He skates his palms onto my arse and helps me forward until my entrance is lined perfectly with his mouth. "Your throne awaits, Your Highness." He blows cool air across my sensitive flesh, and my body folds with pleasure.

I groan and my hands meet the side of the couch to hold me up. I slowly release the muscles in my thighs and lower myself onto his waiting tongue. I'm immediately engulfed in ecstasy, and my head is immediately tossed back. "Oh . . . God, yes."

Light flicks skim the tip of my buzzing clit, constant and consistent, working me into a fevered mess of a woman. His palms land on my breasts with a slap, molding and squeezing viciously. Light flicks turn into little nibbles. Little nibbles turn into long lashes of his tongue. Long lashes turn into firm circles. He is feasting on my flesh like a madman, and he's quickly turning me into a madwoman as he does. He moans in gratification, and then he swathes me entirely with his mouth, indulging in my most private place as if he could be kissing me passionately on the mouth. My hips start to grind, and my world starts to spin in a haze of hedonism. I'm ablaze, lost in this rapturous ecstasy. My head drops as I cry out, finding Josh's eyes wide and staring at me as I reach breaking point. And when he locks his mouth over me and sucks, I fly over the edge of restraint and burst, seeing stars as I come all over his mouth. He sucks it all out of me until I'm a limp, breathless wreck atop of him, gasping for air. "Oh, God," I exhale, damp with sweat.

Shifting a little, Josh manages to move me back so the apex of my thighs is at the very top of his chest, meaning he has a perfect view of my pulsing flesh. He stares down, smiling, running his palms up and down my hips as he admires my quaking core. "Sweet Jesus."

I manage a small laugh through my exhaustion, loving the enhanced southern twang that shows through his lusty accent with those two words. "My American boy sounds sated."

Maneuvering my useless body until I'm lying down, he tucks

me into his side. An affectionate kiss is placed in my hair, and I relax into his body, feeling serene and happy. So, so happy. And suddenly so tired. My eyes are instantly heavy, yet a small part of my brain keeps thinking that I should be repaying the favor. But he's content because I'm sated. I've never known such a selfless lover.

"It's the premiere of The Underground tomorrow night," Josh says quietly. "I'd love you to come."

I laugh as hard as my exhausted body will allow. "Good God, it would be a frenzy."

"I know," he says, relenting easily. "But the thought is nice, huh?"

"Yeah," I sigh, too tired to let dejection edge its way into my tranquil state. "Really nice." My eyes give up on me and close, and I drift off in his arms, hoping my dreams will take me to the premiere of his movie and let me relish being on his arm for all to see.

13

"RISE AND SHINE, sleeping beauty."

My blinks come rapidly as the words wrestle their way into my mind, my body stretching out, my skin rubbing against the smooth, silky sheets. The blurry vision of someone sitting on the edge of the bed leaning over me slowly becomes clear.

Josh.

I inhale on a smile rolling from my back to face him. "Good morning," I sigh. He's wrapped in a towel, his hair wet, his chest so close it's dizzying.

"Isn't it just." His smile is bright enough to knock me unconscious again. "You looked so peaceful. I couldn't bring myself to wake you."

Where I am, who I'm with, and the memory of me dozing off in Josh's arms all hit me at once. I quickly sit up, panic superseding my tranquility. "Damon!"

"Hey, cool it."

"Oh God, the poor man will be walking dead this morning."

"He wouldn't leave and he wouldn't wake you up, either. I carried you to bed and you didn't even stir." He grins. "But you clung

onto me tightly."

I roll my eyes, falling back to the pillow as I hide my own grin. "He's a stubborn old sod."

"No, he's protective of you." Josh tilts his head, raising a serious brow. "As he should be. You're lucky to have him."

I frown. "I don't need you to tell me that." Damon is a blessing in my suppressed life. I'm grateful for him every day, but Josh's light scorn is making me wonder if Damon knows how much I appreciate him. I don't know, so I make it a point to tell him just as soon as I find him. "I need to go before Kellington Palace files a missing person's report." I scan the floor as I shuffle down the bed. "Where's my dress?"

"Hanging in the closet." Josh gets up and wanders to the wardrobe, pulling my dress out. "Can't have a princess walking the walk of shame in a creased dress, can we?"

I narrow my eyes on his grinning face, taking my naked body over to him and swiping my dress from his hand. "Why do I sense that you're thrilled at the thought of me walking the walk of shame?"

"Because you're walking the walk of shame from *my* hotel room. That's why." Casually and lazily, he pulls the towel from his hips and pouts. "Or you don't have to walk anywhere."

My hungry gaze plummets down his chest and meets his groin, and I fall into an admiring daydream, mentally mustering a plan to keep me here. I run through a few plausible explanations for being missing in action so I can hide here all day with Josh and let him maintain this wonderful state of serenity, but before I can voice any of my ideas, the door to the bedroom bursts open.

I startle and swing around, forgetting that I'm naked, therefore giving our unannounced visitor a full-frontal. I stare into a pair of stunned eyes, the eyes of a girl with a pile of clean sheets in her hand. Her stare jumps from me to Josh, back and forth, her forehead gradually furrowing in confusion. Oh, bloody hell. I can

see the penny slowly dropping, the girl from housekeeping slowly grasping what she is faced with. Or *who* she is faced with. I quickly come to my senses and hold my dress against my front, and then grab Josh's towel when he shows no signs of trying to cover himself, shoving it in his chest.

And then an excited scream rings out and the girl descends quickly into a meltdown. "Oh my God!" The sheets drop from her hands and she covers her mouth. I close my eyes in despair. I can't blame her for her reaction. The woman is faced with two of the most famous people in the world. Her star-struck state won't allow her to wonder why we are both here in the same hotel room together, but I have no doubt it soon will. This is awful. How did she get in here?

As I think that, Josh's security fall through the door, and Josh must suddenly comprehend the potential problem we're faced with because he springs to life.

Flicking his head to one of his men, he makes quick work of refastening his towel around his hips.

"Oh my God," the maid shrieks again. "Oh my God, oh my God, oh my God!"

"Come on, love." She's gently ushered from the room by the friendly smiles of Josh's security before one of the men looks back at our less-than-decent forms with apologetic eyes.

As soon as the door closes, panic finds me, and I have my very own little meltdown.

That's it. My time in Josh's heaven is over. Poof! Gone.

"This is a disaster." I start pacing the room, at the same time fighting my way into my underwear.

I'm halted in my frantic actions when Josh appears in front of me, taking the tops of my arms and holding me still. "Stop panicking."

"I'm not panicking," I screech, less than calmly, managing to fasten my bra. I step into my dress and get it to my waist. "She'll be dashing to the office of the nearest national newspaper and

tomorrow it will be front-page news. You and me. Naked. In a room at The Dorchester." I run out of breath as a result of my screeching episode, but quickly pull in more air, not quite done yet.

Josh's hand lands over my mouth, his eyes like saucers. "Will you calm down?"

I snatch his hand away. "Calm down? This is the worst thing that could happen."

Stunned eyes quickly transform into . . . what is that? Anger? "The worst thing?" His jaw goes stiff. "What, ashamed to be associated with a lowly actor?"

Is he trying to be funny? "Don't be so ridiculous." I step away, holding my dress to my front with my arms to stop it from dropping to the floor. "It's just . . ." My eyes plummet.

"Just what?"

"It's just . . ." What can I say?

"What? Goddamn it, Adeline. What?"

I burst, my frustration and helplessness pouring out of me unstoppably. "When they find out, they'll find a way to stop me from seeing you again," I yell, making Josh recoil warily, though I can't be sure if it is because of my shouting, or *what* I'm shouting. I breathe in deeply to calm myself down. "And *that* will be the worst thing that could happen," I say calmly, keeping my gaze low, wishing I would think before I speak. But I've dived in now. May as well see it through to the end. So I take the plunge. Feet first, in I go. "I like you." I frown to myself, the words so alien. "That's not happened before, me liking a man so much. It's a very lovely feeling, but equally terrifying."

There's silence, a long, painful, awkward silence, and it's not long before I'm regretting being so loose-lipped. I'm such a foolish idiot. He's the epitome of Hollywood, for goodness sake. And the most desired man on earth. He is free to cavort with any woman he pleases. Me? My love life is hampered by things out of my control, and now, more than ever, I hate everything about my existence. I

might just be a score for him. A challenge. An accomplishment. A private one, since no one will ever know about it, but an accomplishment nevertheless.

I clear my throat of the silly lump that has formed, collecting my clutch from the bedside. "I'll be going now."

I don't make it two paces toward the door before he's blocking my path. "Wait."

"No, really, I must go." I skirt past him and pull the door open.

It's slammed shut by Josh with me on the wrong side of it, and I suck in air when he pushes me front forward into the wood with the length of his body. "Someone's forgotten the rules of our game." His accent is rough again, low and serious.

"This isn't a game, Josh." I'm not sure when it turned into something more than that, but it has. For me, anyway.

"It's a game, Your Highness," he breathes in my ear. I swallow, my eyes darting across the wood before me. "And now *you* are winning." His teeth nibble at my lobe, and then his tongue traces the shell of my ear. Before I can control myself, I've lent back against his chest, the magnetic pull too much to stop. "By a long fuckin' shot, Adeline. You may have already won, in fact."

"What?"

He turns me around and brushes his palms over my hair, holding my head. "I like you." Unlike me, Josh's eyes remain glued to mine as he speaks his confession. "A lot. A *real* lot."

My stomach lunges, that statement turning it in circles. "You do?"

"I can't believe you're asking me that. The Princess of fuckin' England. The expert seductress. You're asking me if I really like you?"

I ignore his statements and question. I'm not interested in those. Only one thing matters to me. "You do?" I want confirmation. *Need* confirmation. Anything to tell me that this hasn't been my imagination. That he's felt it as deeply as I have. That I am not alone in these crazy feelings.

He smiles and drags the pad of his thumb across my bottom lip. "You have completely and utterly blinded me to anything else but you, woman. That good enough for you?"

I press my lips firmly together, stupidly not wanting him to see how happy that makes me.

"You can wipe that shit-eating grin off your face." He laughs.

Seems I lost my battle. My smile is way too big to conceal. But it quickly falls when I remember why we're having this conversation. "The maid." Now I'm even more anxious. Now I'm even more determined to keep what we have under wraps, since we appear to be on the same page in liking each other *a real lot*.

"If we're going to date, we can't hide it forever."

I laugh. "Oh, yes we can." I get my hands behind my back and fasten the zip of my dress as high as my arms can reach, until Josh sees my struggle and turns me away, taking over.

"You're not talking sense." His tone is admonishing. "It'll be impossible."

"I'm talking perfect sense," I assure him, positively dreading the thought of the hierarchy finding out.

He drops a light kiss on my shoulder through a sigh, displaying a little exasperation. "Maybe we should talk about this once we've dealt with the maid."

"Maybe that is a very good idea." I turn to face him as he pulls some jeans up his legs and a T-shirt over his head.

"I've never dated a woman who needs more security than me." His lovely forehead wrinkles on a frown. "It's . . . weird."

I scoff. "I'm erring more on the side of annoying, actually, but if *weird* fits." I brush my dress down and flick my hair over my shoulders. "God, I must look frightful." Josh chuckles, and I stare at him in dismay. "Whatever's tickled you?"

"You, Your Highness." He collects my hand and leads me out of the room. "Your British lingo and posh accent."

"Well, it's how I speak."

"And I love it."

We find Josh's men in the small room where they congregated last night, all huddled and talking quietly. But no Damon. "Excuse me," I interrupt, breaking up their close circle. "Where is Damon?"

"Here." His gruff voice comes from behind, and I pivot to see him entering the suite. "What's going on?" he asks, taking in the scene.

Bates steps forward. "One of the hotel staff walked in on Princess Adeline and Mr. Jameson."

Damon's instantly alert. And mad. So very mad. "How was that allowed to happen?"

"I had a call about a fan trying to get to Mr. Jameson's suite. I left to deal with it." Bates looks to the other two members of his team. "I thought I left them in good hands."

Both men cower back a few paces, even more so when Damon lands his deadly glare on them. "I hope you have other career prospects," he grates, turning his eyes to Bates. "I'll have an NDA sent to you. Get them to sign it before you fire them."

I step forward, cautious. "Damon—" I snap my mouth shut when he turns his hard stare on me, effectively shutting me up. He gets his phone from his pocket, and I know it's in readiness to call Felix. "Don't the hotel staff know the protocol for high-profile guests?"

"The maid is new to the staff," Bates says. "Seems she didn't get the memo. I'm taking it up with management."

"Good."

I let go of Josh's hand and sit down, giving Damon worried eyes. "Where were you?" I ask. It's so unlike him to leave his post.

He holds up his mobile, his jaw tight. I can see he's angry with himself. "Major Davenport. Apparently, the King would like to breakfast with his daughter at Kellington this morning. He's there. And you are not."

"Oh."

Damon turns his eyes back to Bates. "I thought these guys were

MI6 trained."

"They are. They can use their newfound free time to go back into training."

My mobile rings from my purse, and Eddie's name fills my screen. I feel rotten for rejecting his call, but I need to debrief with Damon and find out what he has said before I speak to anyone.

"I don't think we need to worry about the maid," Bates assures us, going back to our original problem. Damon looks less than assured, and I don't feel it. "She was more worried about losing her job. She won't talk."

"I don't know about you guys,"—Damon waves his phone in their direction—"but we don't operate on *don't thinks*. Get her back here once we've gone and get her signature on an NDA." He starts dialing, and I shoot up, placing my hand on his phone to stop him from calling Felix.

"Let us not be too hasty," I say, glancing at Josh. "Maybe involving Felix would be a little presumptuous?" I'm trying to think sensibly amid my worry. The more people in the royal household that know, the more likely the King will find out. Felix ultimately answers to my father. Not me.

"We'll talk in the car. Where's your coat?"

"Here." Josh collects my mac from the chair and helps me into it. "Call me, yeah?"

I nod. "Have fun at the premiere."

"I'll try." A sweet, delicate kiss is pressed against my cheek, and I catch Damon's eye as Josh pulls back. His expression tells me he knows beyond doubt that I am in deep. He's worried for me, and that just makes the reality of this more unsettling.

I'm led to the car flanked by both Josh's and my men, and I only breathe again once I'm safely in the back. Now I can register the pale complexions and tired eyes of Damon and his men, I feel rather awful about it. "I'm sorry for keeping you up all night."

"We slept in shifts. It's not a problem." He brushes my concern

aside as easy as that.

"I'm grateful. I want you to know that."

He looks at me in the mirror. "I know that."

"Good. I'm glad." I smile and cherish the one he gives me in return. "Now, what am I to say to the King?" I bite my lip, aware that I sound desperate, maybe because I am.

"I told Davenport you had an early start at the stables. It's all I could think of. So long as we can get you to your suite undetected, you should be fine, ma'am."

"You are a genius, Damon. Thank you."

"All in a day's work." His eyes flick up to the mirror. "Apparently."

I inwardly laugh and settle back in my seat, looking out the window. "I think I would like to have a bumming day today," I declare. "So you can take the day off, if you'd like. I'll see you tomorrow morning."

"As you wish, ma'am."

"I do wish." I wish for so much more too, and now I know Josh *likes me a real lot*, I cannot help but wish harder. And dread more. Considerations need to be made for what happens next. I would like to think I can go to my father and tell him that I've met a really wonderful man, one I know he'd love for me to date. But my father isn't only my father. He's the King of England, too. Our family's first marriage is to the throne, not our spouse, and rarely our heart. Happiness is only an illusion.

MY EYES ARE rooted on the entrance of Kellington as we pull up to the gates, watchful for the people I hope to avoid. My father being the first and foremost. "Do we know if the King is still here?" I ask Damon, but no sooner have I uttered my question, I see his Bentley. "Drat." I look at my seated form on a sigh. What are the chances of me getting to my suite without being spotted by him or one of his minions? Not likely. "I hardly look like I have been

to the stables."

"Nothing a bit of forward thinking can't solve." Damon gets out, and I spot Olive rushing down the steps of Kellington, her arms full of my riding clothes, her eyes constantly looking back to see if she's been spotted.

"Oh, Damon, you are too good to me." The back door opens and Olive passes over the goods on a small, nervous smile. "Olive, thank you. Thank you very much."

"Ma'am." She nods and scuttles off. The door is closed again and Damon stands with his back to it while I fight and wrestle around on the back seat to change, constantly peeking up to check the coast is clear. Not that I need to. I'm just pulling my riding boots on when there's a warning tap at the window.

I look up and see Davenport coming down the steps toward the car. My heartbeat accelerates. I stuff my Herve Ledger dress under the driver's seat, along with my shoes, and quickly pull my hair into a ponytail. Then I paint on my smile and tap the window for Damon to open. "Major," I say as he approaches, aware of the suspicious look being cast up and down my form.

"Your Highness," he says tightly, quickly changing his direction to join me as I walk into Kellington Palace.

"To what do I owe this pleasure?" I ask, pulling off the gloves that I've just urgently tugged on. I hand them to Olive on a small smile.

"Rather early at the stables this morning, ma'am," he replies, avoiding my question. I turn a happy face onto him, quietly smug that he thought he'd catch me out.

"Seemed a shame to waste such a beautiful morning." I turn toward the dining room, knowing that's where I'll find my father. Damn it. It was such a wonderful night, and now I'm back to my wretched reality.

As I enter the dining room, I find not only my father, but Eddie and John, too. My eldest brother looks at me in his usual high-browed way, and my youngest brother looks at me in his usual wary

way. He'll want an explanation for my whereabouts last night. Lying to him isn't an option, what with him also residing at Kellington. I nod graciously to my father when he looks up from his coffee, but he doesn't acknowledge my greeting, turning his attention to Major Davenport. "Have you reached David Sampson?"

"Not yet, sir."

"Let me know the moment you do. Wherever could he be, for crying out loud?"

"I will be sure to advise you the moment he is located." Davenport backs out of the room, and father points his attention to me.

"Is there a problem?" I ask, remembering the last time I saw David *and* the circumstances.

"The wanderer returns," Father quips, ignoring my question. Of course he ignores it. I have no place in business talk.

"I've been to the stables." I take a seat while a coffee is poured for me. "Spearmint is coming on in leaps and bounds, Father. You will be delighted with his progress." John laughs under his breath, prompting me to look across the table at him. "How is Helen?" I ask sweetly.

"The first trimester is taking its toll. She's being monitored carefully."

I inwardly roll my eyes. "I expect so. A pregnant woman in her late thirties is classed as a high-risk pregnancy." I lift my cup and saucer and sip some coffee, catching Eddie's eye. He's shaking his head at me in dismay, but I can't help my snide quips where John is concerned. I would say he is above his station, but being the Heir Apparent, the only higher station is our father. The King. That being said, if he didn't treat me with such contempt all the time, then maybe I wouldn't retaliate. Not for the first time, I dread the prospect of John being King and Helen Queen Consort. Both will thrive on the power and throw their weight around with the family, probably more than my father does. It will be a lower form of hell

than I am already in.

"That's enough, Adeline," Father says, getting up from the table. Oh good. He's leaving. "It would have been lovely to dine with all three of my children this morning, but alas, one wasn't in residence when I arrived."

"Ever the disappointment," I say on a sigh. "If I had known you were gracing me with your presence this morning, I would have known to be here." I'm not bloody psychic, and this is all very out of the norm, anyway. Father never joins us at Kellington for breakfast. If he wants to eat with his children, we are summoned to Claringdon with at least twenty-four hours' notice. And what on earth is John doing here, too? He's not stepped foot in my residence for . . . I can't even remember.

"In future, we'll be sure to work around your hectic schedule," John says flatly, taking his napkin from his lap and laying it on the table as he rises. The acid lacing his words grate on every nerve I have, the ulterior meaning crystal clear.

"Yes, it's awfully demanding sitting around looking pretty," I snipe, unable to hold it back. I give him a sweet smile and flick my hair over my shoulder.

John rests his palms on the table and leans forward, his lip curling. "Get married and make yourself useful."

"John," Eddie snaps, shooting up from the table. "Don't speak to her like that."

I'm eternally grateful for Eddie's intervention, but it will have entirely no effect. "Well," John huffs, "we all work hard while she flounces around without a care in the world, doing as she damn well pleases and leaving a mess in her wake for everyone else to clear up."

"I've never asked for my messes to be cleared up." I stand too, matching John's threatening pose. "I wouldn't care if my messes were left messy. Who cares who knows if I had a date with a banker? Who cares if I shared company with a lawyer from Shoosmiths? Let the world know."

"A date?" John laughs. "Shared company? Is that what you call opening your legs for any man who crosses your path?"

"For Christ's sake," Eddie breathes, anger clear in his expression.

I feel my blood begin to boil, and it doesn't cool when I look at my father and find his eyes on me, interested in my potential comeback to John's accusation. "I do not open my legs for any man who crosses my path," I seethe. "And I would love to *date* like a normal person and not sneak around, but I am not permitted to do that, because I am a member of this God-forsaken family."

"Enough," Father roars, all his anger directed at me and me alone. As I would have expected, of course. "I will not hear you speak with such disregard for the Monarchy."

I turn toward the King, feeling my nostrils flare with rage, and I once again comprehend how impossible my life is. He listened to my brother talk to me like I'm a whore. He shouldn't tolerate that. I want to scream at him, tell him where I really was last night, and who I was with. But that would be cutting off my nose to spite my face. So I do the only thing there is to do. I curtsey to the King and leave the room, my eyes brimming with tears as I go. My vision may be foggy, but I see the bleakness of Damon's expression as I pass him in the foyer. He heard it all. Everyone in Kellington heard. I rush up the stairs, keeping my head low to avoid the eyes of any staff, and fall into my suite, slamming the door behind me. And I do something that I haven't done for years.

I cry.

I hide my face in my palms and sob like a baby, feeling so hopeless and distraught. I could easily run away. Disappear to somewhere they'll never find me. Be anonymous and free. It's a wonderful notion, if completely unrealistic. No matter where I go in this world, I will always be recognized.

And they will always find me.

14

"THAT'S HARDLY A nutritious meal," Dolly says to me where I'm slumped over the center island, nursing a glass of Merlot and picking at green olives. "Why don't you let me cook you supper before I head home?"

I sigh, looking at the olive held between my fingers. "I'm not hungry." Popping it in my mouth, I chew and wash it down with another slug of red as Olive wanders into the kitchen with a tray and sets it next to the sink. "Thank you for what you did earlier, Olive." The poor girl was obviously uncomfortable hustling my clothes out of Kellington just to keep me out of trouble.

"Welcome, ma'am."

"What's this?" Dolly asks, pulling off her apron.

"Oh, nothing." I flap a dismissive hand and reach for the bottle to top up my glass. Dolly will nag poor Olive something rotten if she knows she was an accomplice in my misdemeanors. Tipping the bottle, I frown when nothing comes out.

"Another?" Olive asks, pulling my attention to her. She already has a bottle in her hand before I can confirm my need for more.

"Thank you." I push forward the empty and let her top me up so

I can continue to drown my sorrows. "Here, have an olive, Olive." I chuckle to myself like an idiot, and Dolly sighs in despair. Olive is far too polite to berate me. Regardless, I can tell she has heard that pathetic joke more than once. "Sorry." I shrug and dive back into my wine.

"That's me done for the evening," Dolly declares, dusting off her hands. "I'll see you bright and early in the morning."

"Goodbye, Dolly." I watch her leave and notice the only things left littering the spick and span kitchen is my wine and the dish of olives. Oh, and me.

"I should be going now, too." Olive follows Dolly, and I smile as much as I can muster. She stops at the door, holding it open. "Forgive me, ma'am. I realize it isn't my place to ask, but are you okay?"

My smile now is genuine. She is the sweetest thing. "Never apologize for being concerned for someone, Olive," I gently scold her. "I'm fine." My reassurance isn't fooling anyone. "Just silly family politics."

She nods, thoughtful for a few moments before she speaks again. "I would like you to know I admire you greatly. I think you're very brave for standing up for what you believe in."

If it would be appropriate, I would cuddle her, even if she is wrong. I am not brave at all. I'm a coward. If I were brave, I'd say to hell with it, step out with Josh, and let the world see. Let my father see; let the whole wretched family see. But I'm terrified of the consequences. Of losing Josh. No more floating on air. No more losing myself in him. My father and his army of advisors will make sure of it. They'll also ruin him. I can't let that happen. I offer her a small smile, hoping to reassure her. I don't know if I succeed. "I believe in letting your heart guide you. But my heart is caged, and will only be released under conditions."

"Then I hope he breaks it free for you." She quietly goes, and I stare at the empty doorway for a long while after she's gone. Sweet Olive is smarter than she lets on.

I turn back to my wine, losing myself in my thoughts. Tears pinch the back of my eyes. Maddeningly, I feel like I'm letting myself down by sitting here being all melancholy. But frankly, each time I tackle this institution with an argument, I feel wiped out. Despondent. Maybe I even question the whole bloody point. I will never win. Maybe a battle, but never the war.

I startle a little when my phone starts vibrating, and my heart jumps when I see it is Josh. And then I'm frowning, because isn't he supposed to be at his premiere this evening? "Hello?"

"Hey, my girl."

My bouncing heart mellows at the sound of his voice, everything in my world balanced and perfect again. "Hey, my American boy." I rest my elbow on the marble of the island and prop my chin on my hand, all dreamy and content. "Correct me if I am wrong, but aren't you supposed to be somewhere special this evening?"

"Yes, I am. Are you near a TV?"

"No, I'm in the kitchen. Why do you ask?"

"Find one and turn it on. Be quick. I look like a jerk standing here on my cell."

Utterly intrigued, I swipe up my wine and rush to the nearest lounge. I find the remote control and quickly turn on the television.

"You found a TV in that palace of yours yet?" he asks.

"Yes."

"Put *E! News* on."

I fumble with the button and eventually source the channel. "Oh, it's you," I sing when Josh comes on the screen, not directly as such, but there in the background on the red carpet outside the Odeon on Leicester Square, surrounded by his people. He's talking on his mobile. To me. "Is it live?" I ask, lowering to the table between the sofa and the television.

"How many fingers am I holding up?" He gives the camera the peace sign, and I laugh.

"Two."

"Affirmative." He smiles brightly as the presenter, a glamourous woman in a killer red dress, talks and constantly looks back to Josh, maybe to see if he's finished on his call so she can collar him for a few questions.

"You look very handsome," I say, drinking in the pure exquisiteness of him in his tux, his hair a stark contrast to the sexed-up mess I left this morning.

"Thank you, Your Highness," he says as someone appears by his side and whispers in his ear. I don't hear her down the line, because his hand is covering the phone. He nods to her, holding up one finger.

"Who's that?" I ask.

"My publicist. I'm wanted by the networks lining the carpet."

"I think that woman in the red dress is waiting to snare you, too," I say, seeing her look back again, telling the viewers she will be talking with Josh Jameson any moment. I envy her.

"I know. Better go. Wish you were here."

"That may be so, but I would bet the crown jewels on the fact that every woman in the world is glad I am not."

He laughs, and I get the full pleasure of the sound down the line and the sight on my huge television screen. "I'll call you tomorrow." Hanging up, I watch as the presenter moves in and Josh accommodates her, his publicist keeping a few meters distance.

"And we have the man of the hour, Josh Jameson, people," the presenter gushes, smiling a toothy, red-lipped smile. "You look radiant."

Radiant? I roll my eyes. Women look radiant. Not men. "Thanks." Josh finds that statement rather odd too, judging by his half-smile half-frown.

"Anything to do with the lady on the end of the line?" She purses her lips and shoves the mic under Josh's nose.

"Sorry about that." He thumbs over his shoulder. "One of the frat boys from college put an emergency call in. He wants me to

get your number for him."

The presenter flames red but quickly gathers herself, and I applaud Josh for his clever diversion from her probing. I can only imagine the amount of media training he has had to deal with inappropriate questions. "Come on," she coos. "Don't play games with me. I heard her talk. It was a woman, wasn't it?"

"Didn't your mom teach you it's rude to eavesdrop?"

"Yes, but then I became a journalist." She shrugs, unashamed. "Are you dating, Josh?"

Josh's publicist steps forward, ready to intervene, but Josh stops her. "It's early days."

My heart virtually stops in my chest. The excitement from the presenter is electric, virtually reaching me through the television. I can't blame her. She just got herself an unexpected exclusive. I'm stunned, part ecstatic, part panicked. He's told the world he's dating someone, and now the world will be desperate to know who. It's hard to be mad with him when I'm feeling so utterly chuffed.

"Too early to bring her along to the premiere of your new film?" the presenter pushes.

He chuckles, glancing away. "This is all a bit below her, to be honest."

I gape at the screen, just as Josh flicks his eyes to the camera that is panning in on him. The rascal. Below me? It is not below me. I grab my phone and text him exactly that, clicking *send*.

"Below her?" she coughs. "Red carpets, world premieres, and you on her arm is below her?"

Josh grins as he glances down, and I figure very quickly that he's just caught sight of my text. "Are we going to discuss the film?" he asks. "Isn't that why we're here?" His publicist steps in and ushers him away toward the next waiting mic before the presenter can get on to why they're really there, but she doesn't care. She unexpectedly scooped the story of the night. Maybe even the year. I know in my heart of hearts that Josh just made a very silly move, tossing

the media morsels of information on a relationship and woman in his life, aware that they will want the whole three-course meal. But I cannot stop the deep thrill and insane contentment of knowing that *that* woman is me. I don't pay much attention to the part of my brain that wants me to focus on his stupidity. I'm more inclined to side with the part that's wondering if he's making a point. Being brave. Setting the standard. Maybe I should be brave, too. It's easy to think it. Not so easy to do. My stomach revolts against the wine I've poured into it, at the thought of what Josh could endure should he end up at the mercy of my father and his aides. Gerry Rush and his hookup with a hooker is a prime example. Yet if Josh has no skeletons in his closet, what could they possibly do? I laugh to myself. Everyone has skeletons in their closet. Josh is Hollywood. He will definitely have skeletons in his closet, and if he doesn't, I know someone will put them there.

I turn the television off and make my way to my suite, mulling over the notion of being brave. Of standing up to the people who keep me caged. I wash, brush my teeth, and crawl into bed.

My thought process has me tossing and turning for a few hours, sleep evading me. Nothing has ever consumed my mind so much, and the lack of an answer for my problem is positively maddening.

I'm about to give up on sleep and find something to read when the darkness of my suite is suddenly illuminated by the glow of my phone. I roll over to take it from the nightstand.

Awake?

Every thought polluting my head is forgotten in an instant as I stare at his simple question. I tap out a quick *yes* and then wait for a response, tummy whirling, face splitting. I don't get a message in return; I get a call. "Hello?" The sound of music in the background is deafening, as well as the cheers and shouting. I'm forced to pull my phone away from my ear.

"Hello?" Josh shouts. "Adeline? Hello?"

"I'm here. I can barely hear you."

"Hold up. I'm looking for somewhere quiet." The music continues to pump as I wait patiently for Josh to find somewhere quiet. "Still there?" he shouts.

"Still here." I laugh.

"Fuck, this place is like a fuckin' maze."

"Where are you?"

"After-party. Wait, I think I've found somewhere." The ear-splitting sound suddenly dulls to a muffled fuzz. "That's better. Can you hear me?"

"Yes." His voice sounds more gravelly than usual, no doubt from shouting to be heard. "Where are you?"

"I don't know," he says. "I can't see a thing."

"Then turn on the light," I chuckle, imagining him feeling around in the darkness for a switch.

"I'm good. I can hear your voice. It's the only light I need."

I melt. Positively melt into a girlie puddle on my pillow. "Have you had a nice evening?"

"Great. You?"

"Oh, you know. Rocking and rolling in my suite all alone," I joke, now happy I struggled to find sleep, else I could have missed his call.

"Come see me."

I laugh at his ridiculous demand. "And how would you propose that happen?"

"Fuck." His curse is sharp and full of frustration. "I can't stand this."

My contentment waivers for a moment. "That was a rather silly thing you said to the presenter earlier."

"You want me to feel remorseful? Because I'm not."

"They will want to know who is apparently *below* the glitz and glamour of a world premiere."

"Let them wonder." He brushes off my concern with ease, and I let him. "I'm due to fly back to the States in a few days."

Tenseness fills me. Already? Where has the time gone? "I see." My heart sinks. It's daft, really. I knew he was here for business, but still.

"I've changed my plans."

I scan the darkness before me. "You have?"

"Well, I'm due on set in New Zealand in two weeks to start a new movie. I'd only be going back to LA to relax and repack. I can relax here, and London has malls. I'll buy new clothes. Makes sense for me to fly from here."

I press my lips together to stop an excited squeal from slipping free. "Sounds sensible."

"I thought so, too. So, I mean, if you're free, so am I."

My grin splits my face. "I'll check my diary."

"Ouch."

I laugh. "I'm only kidding. Didn't you know I'm only here to keep up appearances. That's my sole purpose."

"No, your sole purpose is to keep this smile on my face."

"Josh Jameson, you are really on form this evening. Have you been drinking?"

"I've had something far more addictive than alcohol," he says softly, making me all warm and lovely inside.

"You have? What's that then?"

"Her name is Adeline Catherine Luisa Lockhart."

I cannot remove this smile from my face. "I've heard you *'like her a real lot'*." I try to imitate his American accent. I do a frightfully terrible job, but it makes him laugh nevertheless, and the sound only makes my contentment grow.

"Yeah, I do. I'll show her just how much when I see her next."

I stop myself from asking when that might be. It's not like I can simply pop out to see him, or he me. If I allowed it, that thought might dampen my mood, but for now he's on the other end of the phone, and I can hear his voice. "Look forward to it."

"You should. So when do you make my change in plans

worthwhile?" he asks frankly.

"Tomorrow?"

"I would love nothing more, but I'm scheduled for back-to-back interviews all day. Sucks, huh? What about the next day?"

"I have to attend a polo match. It's the Cartier King's Cup. A big deal in the polo world." Since Matilda and I sip champagne and sun ourselves for most of the day, it's one of the few annual events I don't mind attending. The King and the other men are too busy swinging mallets and egos around the field to bother me. But now . . .

"Polo, eh?"

"Yes, the sport of kings, don't you know?"

"Do you play?"

"God, no. The polo field is a man's playground. But I must show my face."

"So the next day, then?"

Three days away? God, that feel like centuries. "Okay."

"Call me, yeah?"

"I will. Enjoy the rest of your party." I click *End Call* and roll onto my side. He called me from his super important premiere. Twice. He wanted me to be there. I smile to myself. I like the Josh Jameson who likes Adeline Lockhart *a real lot.*

15

JENNY IS FAFFING and fiddling with my ponytail in the back of the car, while Kim gives me the rundown from the passenger seat of everyone attending this year's Cartier Cup game. Basically, everyone who is anyone. I hiss as Jenny tugs a little too hard. "Sorry, just need to tuck this lock in somewhere."

"Just leave it." I moan tiredly. I'm casual but smart today, in a cream Zimmermann embroidered-silk georgette dress matched nicely with silver strappy flat sandals. All-day comfort, and perfect for the spring sunshine.

"The photographers are out in force," Kim says.

"Can't have me looking anything less than perfect then, can we?" I quip, putting my tassel satchel over my head and across my body, making Jenny tut when I knock her hand as she fights to secure that loose, defiant piece of hair. "It's fine." I peek into the rearview mirror. There is not a hair out of place, my ponytail immaculate and smooth. She's being picky.

Stepping out when Damon opens the door, I'm immediately aware of the photographers in the distance, happily snapping away to catch the Royals jollying it up in a good old-fashioned royal tradition.

As I scan the crowds, I take in the sea of elaborate hats and champagne flutes in every hand. I start across the grass with Damon in tow, spotting every single member of my family except the one I actually want. Matilda. My mother waves me over, standing in a group with my snarky sister-in-law and Matilda's parents. Where is she?

"I'm glad you are finally here." Matilda swoops in from behind me.

"There you are."

She passes me a glass. "Have you seen the new guy?"

"What new guy?" I look toward the field where she points, but only see the polo ponies saddled up and ready to play.

"There. Look. On the other side of the field with John and Eddie."

I spot my brothers talking to a man, but his face is hardly distinguishable beneath the guard of his hat. His body looks quite fine beneath his tight trousers and top, though. "Who is it?"

"Some Argentine polo whizz. Santiago something or other."

"Santiago Garcia?" I try to focus harder, past the bars of his guard. It's no use. Anyone could be under that riding hat.

"That's the one. Did you know he plays off a six-goal handicap? And he is insanely good-looking."

"I've heard." I tip my glass to my lips as Matilda gazes across the field. "Do you think he would fall into the approved category of men?" I ask, not that I am interested. While this polo player extraordinaire is apparently insanely good-looking, he isn't Josh. But asking is what I would usually do.

"I don't know. His father is apparently a diplomat, and his grandmother a descendant of the Spanish royals."

"Great, so I'm related to him somewhere down the line."

"Never stopped the royals before," Matilda quips.

"He's all yours." I chink her glass in congratulations, quietly pleased with myself for appearing my usual self. Truth be told,

if Josh was not in my life and consuming all my thinking space, I would probably have some fun with Mr. Polo Whizz over there.

"You heard from Mr. Hollywood?" Matilda turns into me, though her eyes are keeping a keen eye on Santiago.

"No." I brush off her question casually, appearing unfazed and unaffected at the mention of him, despite how exhilarated I feel. "In hindsight, he was all power no precision." I've never told such a barefaced lie in my entire life, and Damon's cough from behind me confirms it. I cast a brief look over my shoulder, ready to scowl at him, but he is too busy scanning the surroundings.

Matilda giggles through her mouthful of champagne, struggling to swallow. "How disappointing."

I hum my agreement, spotting Felix hurrying toward me. "Oh, bore. What is he doing here?" His beige suit is immaculate, his hair combed with precision to the side. "Will you be divot stomping with us in between chukkas, Felix?" I ask when he joins us.

"Your Highness." Felix nods in greeting. "I think I'll leave that to the lords and ladies of this fine land." He looks at his shoes, no doubt dreading the thought of his signature loafers getting smeared with dirt.

"Suit yourself." I give Matilda a flick of my head, indicating we should follow our sense of smell to the champagne tent without delay. "We will be on our w—" Champagne is forgotten, and my need to escape my head of communications is halted when my eyes, now wide, spot Senator Jameson across the field, all geared up and ready to swing his mallet. Oh my goodness. If he is here, then . . .

My silent pondering stops right there as Josh appears from behind Senator Jameson's horse. "Oh no." Mixed feelings swirl through me—delight, excitement . . . disappointment. How on God's green earth am I going to keep my eyes off him, let alone my hands? Darn it. He knew I was coming here. He probably knew he was, too.

"You okay?" Felix asks, looking back to whatever has my attention.

"Perfectly fine, thank you," I squeak, slipping my shades on. Even if the sun is swallowed up by clouds at any point during the afternoon, these sunglasses will be staying firmly on my face to conceal the direction of my stare. Matilda has just caught sight of Josh, too. Her tongue-in-cheek expression and sarcastic raised eyebrow tells me she has put two and two together.

"Oh, Josh Jameson," Felix breathes, shaking his head in . . . what is that? Condemnation?

"What does that mean?" I can't stop myself from asking.

"I'm surprised he dare show his face in public."

What? I look across to Josh, where he is deep in conversation with Senator Jameson. "Why?"

"Well, this." Felix magically produces a printed email from nowhere and pretty much shoves it under my nose. "Tomorrow's front-page news. It's shocking."

My eyes can't focus fast enough, and Matilda is quickly on my shoulder, gasping at what is looking back at us. My heart skips a few too many beats as I absorb the words.

SUITE TRASHED. JAMESON OVERDOSES ON WOMEN, DRINK, AND DRUGS IN AN ALL-NIGHT WILD PARTY.

The pictures below show various rooms in a suite, a suite I recognize . . . because I've been in it. It is completely smashed to pieces. In the main area, there are glasses on the floor, chairs broken, empty bottles of liquor scattered everywhere. In the bedroom, the sheets are tossed all over the floor, the mirror is shattered, and the dresser he screwed me on is face down. I zoom in, seeing various pairs of knickers scattered on the carpet.

What?

I step back, away from the bold letters of the proposed headlines and the damaging images of Josh's suite. My eyes refuse to drop to the article, worried that what I'll read might pale me further and

give me away. He didn't sound very intoxicated when he called me from the after-party, but then again, it was only eleven o'clock. The night was young. *Why? How could he?* My shaking hand passes the email back to Felix. "Where did you get this?" I breathe, my lungs squeezed dry of oxygen.

Felix looks kind of smug as he slips the paper back between the pages of his diary. "Ma'am, it is my job to keep myself abreast of breaking stories. Contacts, contacts, contacts."

"He is despicable. How dare he show his face here?" I murmur, catching Matilda's pursed lips. I ignore her grave expression and point my empty glass to the tent where more of my savior can be found. "Shall we?"

She just nods, as Felix answers his phone. "Yes? What? Darn it," he spits down the line, looking back toward the club's entrance. "I don't care what it takes, do not let him in. I'll be there in a jiffy." He hangs up. "Must dash."

I watch as he runs off, thankful for whatever emergency has removed him from my increasingly sweaty form before he notices something untoward. Matilda is still here, though. Staring at me. "You okay?" she asks.

"Yes. Why wouldn't I be?" I start across the grass, my stinging eyes straying to where I saw Josh. He's gone, but that doesn't make me feel even remotely better. He's here somewhere, and I don't know where. How could he? After that wonderful night we shared, the words, the understanding, how could he do this to me? I swallow lump after lump, fighting to keep myself together. At least I don't have to be concerned about keeping my hands to myself anymore. Ignoring the deceitful bastard should be easy as pie now.

I purposely dodge every member of my family, choosing my route carefully to the tent so I can avoid engaging with any of them. "Let's get squiffy," I declare, arming Matilda and myself with two fresh glasses of champagne.

"You know, you could seduce the Argentine and get him out

of your system."

"There is nothing in my system that needs to be removed," I assure her, my damn traitorous heart bleeding for something I didn't really have in the first place. I down my fizz and claim another. "But still, he has some front showing his face at a royal event after what he's been up to." My discontent starts to bubble into anger. Of all people, I know the press embellish things for entertainment and shock value, but I also know that there is no smoke without fire. You would think he'd be trying to avoid me, but here he is, bold as shiny brass at a royal gathering. If things were hopeless for us before, now . . . well, now it will be impossible. "He should be ashamed of himself," I spit, throwing back another glass. "Women? Drugs? Vandalism? What a fool. I mean, who does that? Who behaves so deplorably?" I catch Damon at the entrance of the tent, watching me, his face stoic, though I can see the concern in his eyes. I sigh and look away, feeling utterly humiliated, despite the limited people who know of Josh's and my rendezvouses. "I need a cigarette," I declare, marching over to Damon and holding out my hand. "Don't say a word. Please, just give me a cigarette."

"I wasn't about to say a thing, ma'am." He reaches into his inside pocket and slips his packet and lighter into my bag where it rests on my hip. "Want to be alone?"

"Please."

"Around the back of the tent. Stay close to the ice buckets. It's out of view."

"Thank you, Damon." I'm aware Matilda is hot on my heels after my silly little rant, wanting to nail me down and squeeze all of my sins out of me, but Damon intercepts her. I need to be on my own for a few moments to calm down and talk some sense into myself.

Locating the ice buckets, I sit on a champagne crate next to them and light a cigarette, pulling in the longest draw. "You are a first-class idiot, Adeline," I say on an exhaled plume of smoke. I let my guard crumble for the first time in my life and look what happens.

I'm hurting in places I never thought I could hurt. I've been strung along, and I feel utterly humiliated. And angry. So very, *very* angry. And I'm angry for being angry. I shouldn't care.

A cough sounds from behind me. It's an over-the-top cough, a cough to suggest that my little vice is killing someone in close proximity. I'm about to turn around and tell whoever is invading my quiet time to find somewhere else to choke, but they speak before I can send them on their way.

"You told me you had given up." Haydon rounds me, and I look at him looming over me, feeling like a naughty child caught misbehaving. "Now, now, Adeline, you know it is bad for you." He reaches down and plucks the half-smoked cigarette from my fingers, looking at it in disgust.

"Maybe I like things that are bad for me, Haydon," I mutter indignantly as I push myself up off the champagne crate and collect a whole bottle, working the foil. "Are you not playing today?" He's wearing linen trousers and a dress shirt, no polo kit in sight.

"I thought it bad taste given my grandfather's passing."

"Oh, Haydon. Yes, of course. I'm so sorry for being so insensitive." Now I feel terrible for him. *Shit.*

"We have a special guest playing. I volunteered to sit out."

"Oh, the Argentine." I pop the cork and catch the overflow with my mouth. Maybe I will devote a little attention to Mr. Garcia, if Matilda hasn't pounced already, which I highly doubt. The woman dilly-dallies somewhat awful when it comes to men. "I hear he is a bit of a polo whizz." I hold the bottle up on a smirk before tipping it to my mouth and swigging as much as I can before having to come up for air.

"Whatever has gotten into you, Adeline?" Haydon asks, obviously disgusted by my behavior.

I huff on a sarcastic laugh. "An American," I whisper under my breath, tipping the bottle to my mouth again, somewhat determined to wash away my hurt with alcohol.

"Pardon?"

"Nothing," I sigh, forcing my face into something resembling a smile. "I'm sorry. I'm not feeling myself today." That is entirely untrue. I haven't been myself since I first set eyes on Josh Jameson.

"Oh, are you unwell? Would you like me to call Dr. Goodridge?" Now Haydon looks genuinely concerned, and I brace myself for the fuss I'm about to endure. His palm lands on my forehead, his eyes scanning my face. "You do feel a little hot."

That would be my blood burning with rage. I take his hand and pull it away. "I'll be fine." Time to change the subject. "How is Sabina?" I ask, letting my true concern for his grandmother show. I know she lost her husband, but she hasn't been herself lately, and those conversations I overheard are leading me to believe there is more to it.

Haydon's soft expression adopts a sharp edge. "She would be better if my father would display a little grief and sensitivity."

The spite in his tone, as well as his words, makes me recall David's lack of reaction when I heard the news in my father's office. Having just lost his father, you would think the trivial issues of my antics would not be top of his priority list, yet there he was, joining in on the Adeline Slamming Party. "Maybe he is in denial." It's the only explanation I can think of. "People express their grief in very different ways." But then again, I also remember the strong words he and his mother were having when I saw them at the stables.

"Well, I wouldn't know how he's displaying his guilt right now because we haven't seen him for days."

"Oh, where is he?"

"We don't know."

I reflect on the other morning and my brief breakfast with John, Eddie, and my father. Davenport couldn't get hold of David. "I'm sure he has taken a timeout," I suggest, though he doesn't seem concerned, more irritated.

"That's what I've told Grandmother."

My hand reaches for his arm in an instinctive display of comfort and gives it a little rub. "Probably just trying to come to terms with it."

Haydon nods, a flicker of something passing through his eyes that I know I am not mistaking as hope. His hand rests on mine. His illusion that my display of compassion is anything more has me pulling away. "Have a lovely afternoon, Haydon," I say, turning on my sandals and heading back to the crowds.

"We'll stomp some divots together," he calls, the hope in his tone matching that of what I saw in his eyes.

I force a smile over my shoulder. "Sure." What can I say? No? That would be cruel when he's having family troubles. Yet it is also cruel to give him hope when there is none. Not for Haydon and me, anyway. And now not for Josh and me, either. The resentment that has been missing for the past few minutes while being distracted by Haydon returns full force, the images of a trashed suite at The Dorchester spinning like a camera reel through my mind. And the word *women* punches at my nerves repeatedly. There were several pairs of lacy knickers on that bedroom floor.

I look at the bottle of champagne in my grasp, seeing it as my only form of escape from the agonizing let-down. Yet I wonder what I expected from him. A fairy-tale romance? The man warned me that he gets bored easily. I laugh curtly and swig from the bottle as I round the corner, but it's swiped from my curled lip.

Damon tosses it in a nearby bin. "Don't show yourself up on his account," he says quietly, not looking at me. "Head high before that fucking crown falls off." He's speaking hypothetically, of course, but I appreciate the meaning and the gesture.

He's right, as usual. I don't need Josh to help me fall from grace. According to my father's condescending aides, I plummeted from my pedestal long ago. "Thank you, Damon."

"Don't thank me, ma'am. Just do as I damn well say."

I smile as I nudge him in the shoulder, feeling like I hit a brick

wall. He doesn't budge, but his lip quirks at one corner. "Am I allowed to drink at all?"

"In moderation. You've had a whole bottle in the thirty minutes since you arrived, so may I suggest orange juice for a while?"

"You may." Only a few seconds with my level-headed bodyguard is making me see sense. "Damon?"

"Yes, ma'am."

"I don't know what I would do without you."

"Very good, ma'am," he says, simple as that.

"I'll be off to get some orange juice."

"I'll be here if you need me." He widens his stance and gets comfortable, ready for a long day of watching polo. Or watching me.

Collecting an orange juice, I go to find Matilda and curse her to death in my head when I locate her with every direct female member of my family, all gathered in a cozy little circle. God, they're *all* here. I'm welcomed into the group by the usual glares of condemnation from the lovely Helen, as well as Matilda's mother, my delightful Aunt Victoria. But my mother, as always, regards me with warm eyes full of love, oblivious to the other's display of disdain for me. Or ignoring it. As much as I wish she had more backbone and would openly support me, I'm glad her indifference isn't because of disgust.

"Orange juice?" Helen questions, shocked by the non-alcoholic drink gracing my hand. "Did you get ill?" She chuckles, Aunt Victoria joining in. Matilda smirks at me, and Mother remains in her usual state of Switzerland, ever the placid one.

"Ha ha," I screech, folding at the belly in an over-the-top bout of feigned laughter. "Yar yar, very good, yar?" Both Helen and Aunt Victoria pipe down quickly, shocked, and Mother astounds me with a mild smirk. Matilda, however, dares not express a hint of amusement and risk the sting of her mother's tail, though I can see my cousin has a fight on her hands to stop her face splitting with a smile. I sniff and sip my orange juice. "John said it is *you* who has

been ill, in fact," I say, indicating to Helen's stomach. "Morning sickness sounds utterly miserable."

Aunt Victoria coos her sympathy. "I suffered terribly with Matilda."

"I did with John and Adeline," Mother says, looking off into the distance, a little glazed. "But I breezed right through it with Edward." I look to where Mother is staring, finding her looking fondly at Eddie.

"It's frightfully inconvenient," Helen grumbles, circling her tummy. "How is one supposed to get on with everyday life?"

Everyday life? She hardly does a thing. "I'm sure one will find a way," Uncle Stephen's wife, the mousey Sarah, says, which surprises me. She never speaks up in social situations. "I'm sure the blessing of a baby supersedes the temporary inconvenience of nausea." She smiles, and it is sincere. The poor woman is married to a secretly gay man, and there's nothing she can do about it. She has no children, and at forty-six, she isn't likely to now, especially with Uncle Stephen, not only because he's gay. He's eight years her senior, so his clock is ticking faster than Sarah's. She would probably do anything to go back in time and know what she knows now. I can guarantee she wouldn't marry Uncle Stephen, if she even had a choice. Not because he's a horrible man. He's not. He's wonderful; he just isn't supposed to be married to a woman. I smile sadly at Sarah, reaching for her arm and touching it gently. She returns my small gesture, patting the back of my hand.

"I can't think past how ghastly I feel at the moment," Helen scoffs, her attention on Sarah. "Not that I could expect *you* to relate."

I gawk at my sister-in-law in disbelief, and Sarah squeezes my hand lightly as if to reassure me that it's nothing. It is *not* nothing. Helen is an insensitive, snotty, self-important cow. I've never thought her maternal. This baby is simply to secure the throne for John's line.

"Oh, the match is starting," Mother declares, taking my arm and leading me away, purposely stopping me from saying anything

to upset the apple cart. She links arms with me and leans in, whispering, "Morning sickness really is dreadful. Maybe one day you will see for yourself."

I roll my eyes at her less-than subtle hint. "How does it feel to have a self-important, entitled bitch for a daughter-in-law?" I ask sardonically.

"That is no way for a princess to talk." She gives me a light nudge in my shoulder. "Helen's emotions are all askew," Mother says quietly, as if Helen isn't always an insensitive arsehole. "Let us go easy on her."

"Yes, because God forbid we upset her when she is carrying the King's first grandchild and heir."

"Now, now, Adeline. You'll make yourself ill with all that bitterness."

"It's not bitterness, Mother. It's principle." We approach the field, where the players are now on horseback, waiting for the umpire to start the first chukka. "I'm merely pointing out that she should be a little more sensitive."

"Okay, darling." Mother releases my arm and joins the rest of the crowd in clapping the players onto the field. "What a wonderful day for it."

And that signals the end of our conversation. I exhale dramatically and look at my orange juice despondently, before casting my eyes back to Damon. He taps the face of his watch, meaning I have not had sufficient time on the non-alcoholic beverages just yet. His gesture doesn't only prompt me to think about the lack of champagne in my grasp and when I might get it. It also makes me think of the day at the palace for my thirtieth, when Josh Jameson was tapping the face of *his* watch, reminding me of my appointment with him in the maze. The skin of my bottom heats with the thought, and I glance around the crowds, searching for him. There is no sign.

"Really, are you ill?" Matilda whispers in my ear, completely serious as she joins me on the field side.

"No, I'm thoroughly irritated." The words are out before I can stop them.

"Dare I ask why?"

"No."

"Thought not." The game begins, and Eddie launches the ball with spectacular precision to John, but as John swings, a player from the opposing team hooks his mallet and Eddie shouts his frustration at our older brother for losing possession. I smile at Eddie's competitiveness, and smile harder when John snarls at our brother. Eddie is a superstar player, and would have gone professional had he not chosen to serve in the military. John, however, is average, and he positively hates the fact that his younger brother is better at something than he is.

"Poor show, John," I call, delighting in the glare I receive. "Gee up, boy."

"Adeline, behave," Mother says, scolding me, closing her eyes to gather patience. "Why can't my children all get along?"

"I love my brothers, Mother," I assure her, kissing her cheek sweetly. I'm not lying. I love them both. I just don't *like* John. "It's simply silly sibling rivalry."

"Adeline, look." Matilda jars my shoulder roughly, nearly knocking me onto the field. "It's him."

"Who?" I ask stupidly. The appearance of only one man would warrant such physical contact to alert me. So I ask, "Where?" instead.

"Over there." Matilda points her champagne glass across the field, and I spot him in an instant, staring at me. I divert my gaze immediately, heart racing. Was he smiling at me? Smiling like he was pleased to see me, like I would have no clue about a damning and explosive story that will be dropped like a bomb tomorrow? Of him indulging in women, drink, and drugs? I shake my head, muddled. "I think I need a drink," I say to myself, taking the opportunity of the cheering crowd as a result of a goal to break away.

I weave through the people in my way, nodding and smiling as best I can to everyone who greets me. "Okay, ma'am?" Damon asks from close behind, tailing me.

"I don't know." My eyes are on my feet now, my painted smile fading. I don't have the strength or inclination to force it back into place. I peek up to gauge the distance to the tent.

And collide with someone.

I'm caught from behind by Damon, and in front by Josh.

"Hey, are you avoiding me?" Josh asks, looking genuinely perplexed.

I have no words for him, only a blank stare. "Ma'am?" Damon asks, still holding on to me, as is Josh in front of me. I'm sandwiched between both of them, relying on them to hold me up.

I quickly engage the muscles in my legs and wriggle my way free from between them. "Excuse me," I murmur, scuttling away while scanning the vicinity for anyone who might have caught that awkward moment.

"Whoa, wait a minute there," Josh says on a laugh. It's nervous and laced with confusion. He catches my wrist and pulls me to a stop, and I swing around, finding Damon within touching distance. "What's going on?" Josh asks him, keeping a firm hold of me.

Rather than answering Josh, Damon looks to me, his thumb hovering in no man's land.

"Thumb down," I grate.

"No," Josh seethes. "You do *not* get to give me a fuckin' thumbs down, woman. Not without me knowing why." He turns back toward Damon. "Thumbs up. Turn the goddam thumb up."

"Down," I counter, barely able to talk through my panic.

Josh looks on the verge of explosion. "Up!"

Damon glares at us like he wants to tear our heads off, then motions around us, as if to remind us that we're in full public view. "Move it somewhere private, perhaps, ma'am?" He levels me with a serious stare. "*If* you want to talk." He's asking me, and I hate that

he has to. Because he must see how conflicted I feel. He must see the hurt. And my lack of an answer gives him his.

I suppose that must be why he doesn't stop Josh when he growls and yanks me across the way toward the portable toilets. Toilets? Okay, so they are the most unrivaled portable toilets in existence, the poshest out there, but still. It's a toilet. And small.

"Nice night at the after-party?" I spit, being dragged along behind Josh.

"Yes, and I spoke to you, remember? What the fuck has changed since then?"

"Sex, drugs, and rock and roll," I retort, trying to win my wrist back. I lose.

Josh drags me up the steps to the toilets, shoves me into one of the luxury cubicles, and slams the door. There is roughly two feet between our chests with our backs pressed to opposite sides of the box. Very cozy. *If* I was talking to him, which, of course, I am not.

"What the fuck are you talking about?" he barks.

I divert my stare from his angry blue eyes, but with limited space comes limited options. I resort to focusing on his shiny tan shoes, a safe bet. Until they move, telling me he has taken the one and only step available to bring him closer.

I can't breathe with him so near, can't think. "Your wild party at The Dorchester. That's what I am talking about. The women you entertained, the fact that the place was trashed."

"What?"

His ignorance ramps up my anger, and I brave facing him. I immediately regret it. His handsome face is like a sucker punch to my gut, reminding me of one of the things I love about Josh Jameson. Just one. The attraction. And with the vision of the face that has scrambled my entire existence comes every other amazing thing about him, all things I love. His way with me, his lack of veneration for my title, his softness mixed with his hardness, his ability to take me to faraway places where only we exist. My eyes begin to burn

with the onset of an emotion I have no idea how to deal with.

Josh must see the glaze wash over my eyes, because he frowns, withdrawing a little. "Talk to me, Adeline."

"The head of communications at Kellington advised me of a story that is running in tomorrow's paper."

Josh's body locks up, and he reverses his step, his back meeting the opposite wall. "What story?"

"The one of you getting drunk, entertaining women, *plural*, and trashing your hotel suite."

His mouth drops open, and he looks to the door of the cubicle, his forehead a roadmap of creases. "I didn't trash my hotel room."

It's hardly surprising I don't focus on his denial, but only on his lack of reference to the women. So, he can say lovely things to me, build my hopes up, tell me it will all work out, but he has no qualms about fucking other women while he waits. I'm a fool. I'm done. Through. "I saw the pictures, Josh. And you may have forgotten, but I've been inside that suite so can verify the photographs' authenticity. Do not treat me like I'm stupid." I go to leave, getting nowhere, his hand like a vice on my forearm. I glare at him with all the disgust I feel. "I only have to shout and Damon will be in here within a second."

"Then fuckin' shout," he snaps, goading me, shoving his spare hand in his pocket and pulling out his phone.

So I do. "Damon!" The door to the lavatory is open within a heartbeat, Damon brooding on the steps before me, taking in the scene. "Get me out of here, please," I all but sob, yanking my arm free and rushing past my head of security.

"Adeline," Josh yells after me, but I don't slow my pace, dashing to the field to immerse myself in the crowds where I know Josh can't corner me. I cast my eyes back as I round the corner, seeing Damon placating Josh, allowing me to escape. I need to go home. Get away from here, and that is exactly what I intend to do when Damon comes back.

"You are acting weird today." Matilda looks at me with a heavy frown when I land by her side, all flustered and still drink-less. So I help myself to hers. "Dive in," she quips. "What's going on? Did you talk to him?"

"Why would I talk to him? What he does is not my concern."

She snorts, thoroughly amused by my pathetic attempts to feign coolness, yet her apparent disbelief doesn't encourage me to spill the beans. Besides, there is technically nothing to spill now. "You slept with him, Adeline."

Except that, which my cousin already knows because I was daft enough to tell her. "I have slept with men before. What is your point?"

"No point." She shrugs nonchalantly. "Except that you are absolutely smitten with this one. Probably best he has turned out to be a moron. It's not like it could have gone anywhere." Cocking her head at me in interest, she claims back her champagne. "Cheers." I stare at her as she returns her attention to the field, paralyzed by my conflicting feelings.

She's dead right, of course. This is the best thing that could have happened. Or it would be, if I wasn't so head over heels.

"Santiago Garcia is a god on horseback, by the way." Matilda pouts, and I slowly turn my attention to the field. "Bravo!" Matilda yells, as the god on horseback swings his mallet, connecting perfectly with the ball and sending it straight toward Eddie. My brother swiftly finishes it off, landing it in the goal in time for the end of the second chukka. Eddie rides across to Santiago, who pulls off his hat, revealing his stunning looks to all as he shakes Eddie's hand.

"Did I hear your heart just flutter?" I tease. "Or was it your thighs vibrating?"

"Adeline." Matilda scolds me, though she is still smiling toward the Argentine.

"I know," I say quietly, glancing around me. "I'm a disgrace."

"Yes, you are."

The crowds disperse for the small interval, most venturing toward the champagne tent to replenish. I remain where I am, scanning the area, wondering where Damon is. I'm itching to escape.

He appears, as if responding to my thoughts, and paces over. "Ma'am, a word, please?"

"Thumbs down," I say, just in case he needs reminding.

"I'm aware of your wishes."

"Good."

"But I must insist you accompany me to the car." Damon places his hand on my back and moves me along.

"Why do we have to go to the car?" I ask, my legs working fast to keep up with his long strides.

"Kim would like a word. Something about a bank."

I nearly crack my neck when I snap my head up to look at him. Gerry Rush? Has he not disappeared into the black hole full of hookers where he belongs? "So much for a lovely day at a royal polo match," I mumble to myself.

"Quite, ma'am." Damon opens the door to the back of my car while I brace myself for whatever I'll be challenged by now. Maybe I should relent to my father's wishes and marry Haydon, because I'm suddenly so very tired of the constant discord in my life. Could I learn to be content? Could I pretend like the rest of my family?

I slip into the back and the door slams quickly after, barely giving me enough time to settle in my seat.

"Now you will listen to me," Josh says from beside me.

I suck in an incredulous breath and immediately reach for the door to let myself out, but I hear the mechanics of the locks kick in before my searching hand finds the handle. *What the hell?* I yank at the lever nevertheless, and despite it having no effect, I repeatedly pull, cursing Damon for his underhanded stunt. "Thumbs down," I shout through the window to his back.

"No thumbs down," Josh replies calmly. "You will listen to what I have to say."

"I'm not interested." I give up on my bid for freedom and slam my back into the seat. "He will lose his job over this."

"No, he won't. You love him too much." Josh's hand lands on my bare knee, and I immediately push it off.

"Don't touch me."

"As it belongs to me, I will touch it when I want." His statement is deadly serious, his hand back on my knee, his flesh fused to mine. Heat courses through every vein, muscle, and nerve. How can I be so hypersensitive to his touch? How can I react this way when I'm so angry and disgusted? The thoughts are twisting my head.

"I do not belong to you." I spit the words out with pure venom.

"Wrong," he states simply, reaching for my jaw with his spare hand and forcing me to look at him. Amber flashes in his blue eyes back up his potent anger. "You became mine the second you dropped to your knees for me, Your Highness."

I defiantly tug my jaw from his grasp. "And you became an arsehole the second I saw evidence of your little *party*."

He exhales through his nose, clenching his teeth. "Oh, that."

Oh, that? The man has a nerve. "Yes, that."

"You mean this?" He collects his phone from his inside pocket and drops it onto my lap.

I look down and see an image on the screen. An image I have already seen. I grab his mobile and toss it onto the seat between us. "Well, thank you for refreshing my memory on what a massive arsehole you are." I take the handle of the door again and pull in vain.

"Read it." His phone lands back on my lap. "Now."

"Fuck you," I spit.

"You know, for a princess, your mouth is vulgar sometimes."

Releasing the handle, I turn my body fully into him, leaning close. "Fuck. You," I breathe, restraining my hand, which is dying to slap his face.

"And I love it," he growls, grabbing my neck and yanking me forward.

Gone.

Our mouths smash together—fuse together—and our tongues connect like they've never been apart. And I'm back floating on air in that amazing place he takes me to like I never left. I'm in my own seat one second, on his lap the next. It's a messy kiss, one of tangled tongues, smashing teeth, and constant cries and groans. It's an angry kiss. There is no effort on my part to stop myself being swallowed whole by him. I don't fight his fingers from crawling up my inside thigh and slipping past the seam of my knickers. Even mad and confused, I'm wet for him.

Then my mind's eye quickly reminds me of his hotel suite. The knickers. The women. It's a stark reminder of why I'm here in the back of the car with Josh, sparring with words. "No," I gasp, prying myself away from him, short of breath. I fall back into my seat. "You are a liar and a cheat."

His head drops back, his own breathing as labored as mine. "I don't appreciate being accused of shit I haven't done, Adeline."

"I'm not accusing you. I have the evidence."

Snatching up his phone that was knocked to the floor during my lapse of restraint, he shoves it into my chest. "No, what you have is a pile of fabricated trash, *Your Highness*. Read the fuckin' date. Tell me when they claim I threw this wild party and fucked endless women."

I recoil, searching his angry eyes.

"Read. It," he grates, taking my hand and placing the phone there.

I look down, wincing at the headline and the images, quickly working my way to the main article. I'm forced to endure too many graphic details before I reach the bit I've been demanded to find. Bewilderment comes on strong. They are not claiming all these defiling activities happened the night of the after-party at all. They state quite clearly that this so-called wild party and orgy went down the night before the after-party. My hand quickly covers my

mouth and I shoot my eyes to Josh. He's looking at me expectantly, his eyebrows raised.

"But I was with you in your suite," I exclaim, looking at all the images of Josh's trashed room. "I was with you all night."

"Yes, you were." He takes his phone back. "I didn't leave the after-party until four in the morning. When we got back to my suite, it had been ransacked, though I can assure you there were no panties on the bedroom floor. We assumed a robbery or a deranged fan and called the police. But nothing was stolen, not even a pair of my boxers or a bottle of cologne. It didn't make sense." He shakes his head, his jaw so tight. "Now it makes perfect fuckin' sense."

It does? "How?" I'm utterly confused. Yes, newspapers decorate stories, but completely fabricate them?

"They can't claim all this happened on the night of the after-party because everyone knows I was at another venue until dawn. There are pictures in every fuckin' magazine." Josh looks at me gravely, his palm on his nape, massaging. "It seems someone's out to discredit me, Your Highness. Why'd you think that is?"

I can't help my recoil. "You think this has something to do with me?"

"Who else?"

"But no one knows," I whisper as I search my frantic mind for another plausible explanation. I come up blank.

He's right.

Who else could it be? Who else would want to tarnish Josh's reputation? Just because I have had no indication that my father and his army know, doesn't mean that they don't. I come over a bit claustrophobic, my mind reeling. This is everything I dreaded. This is every reason why I should have stayed away from him. They will destroy him before they allow me to be involved with him. I swallow down the pain running riot through me, staring at the back of the driver's seat. "You should leave me alone." It physically pains me to say it. Hurts like nothing else has hurt me before. I can't risk his

reputation and career being sabotaged by the bastards that advise the King. I care too much for him. "They will ruin you."

"Never." Josh reaches across the back seat and manhandles me back onto his lap, pushing my bent legs to either side of his hips. I don't fight him. "Do you hear me?" My face is cupped in his palms, his blue eyes daring me to deny him. "Never." Bringing his nose close to mine, his soft gaze flutters across my face, taking it all in carefully, as if he could be photographing each and every piece of me to memory. A small smile ghosts his lips. "We were made for each other, Adeline. I'll be damned if royal blood and fame get in the way of that."

I feel overcome. "Really?"

"Damn straight. I own that beautiful royal ass of yours."

Never has anything sounded so amazingly right. "Really?" I ask again, at a loss for any other words.

"Really." Pushing his lips to mine, he growls as he kisses me, sealing his authority over me. And I let him. But just as quickly, I'm breaking his kiss, unwanted worry and fear plaguing me. This is bad, and the news breaking tomorrow is all the proof we need that it is all so very hopeless. Josh doesn't know what he's up against. No one does, really. "Josh, there's nothing we can do to stop them."

"I won't let you believe that."

"But I already do."

"Then you are not the woman I thought you were."

I drop my heavy head. "That isn't fair." My voice is thick with emotion and bleakness. "You can't confirm you were in your suite, because they will check all the CCTV footage and see me."

"Aren't you prepared to fight for it? To fight for happiness? To fight for *me*?" he asks, prompting me to peek at him. "Because I'm ready to fight for you, Adeline. I'm already armored up and set for battle, and I'm pretty fuckin' determined to win. Because the prize is you."

His valor is admirable, if wasted. "But at what cost, Josh? Your

career, your rep—" A hand is sealed across my mouth, silencing me.

"I don't care." He sounds so adamant. "As long as the cost isn't you."

I stare at him, trying so hard to comprehend what this means. I would like to think that it means a permanent place floating on air with him, but, first and foremost, I know it means war. A war between my family and me. A war between Josh and my family. Quite literally. But to keep him? To keep the feeling of freedom? It sounds crazy since he has claimed he owns me. But the fact of the matter is, I am free when Josh owns me. Free from the constraints of my life. Free from the suffocation and suppression. The way he whisks me away to that special place is enough to keep me going. His faith in me. His friendship. His belief in *us*. He will fuel me with the fight I need.

"Just tell me you're in with me." He's pleading. He doesn't need to.

In with him? I'm so far in, I'm drowning. Drowning in him, and I can think of nothing better. Everything worth having in life is worth fighting for. The pain I feel just thinking about Josh being absent from my world, no matter if it's me walking away before the carnage breaks, or him being taken away when it does, is unbearable.

"There is only one right answer to my question," he whispers. "And there will only be one winner in this war. It won't be them."

"I'm in." I exhale, feeling like my commitment to this battle lifts the burden of wanting him so badly. "I'm in, I'm in, I'm in." I fall forward and sink into his chest, needing him all over me.

"Correct answer." His lips vibrate against my neck, and I close my eyes, falling deeper, trying not to think about what is at stake. My fear isn't for the strength I'll need or the anguish I'll experience on this journey. My fear is for possibly coming out the other side of it without Josh. The agony of not having him touching me again, or speaking to me in his dreamy American accent, of surrendering to him with a simple demand or look. Of laughing and joking with

him. Of letting him relieve the pressure from my shoulders. Of letting him take charge over me and welcoming the relief of it. I can't sacrifice any of it, not for anything or anyone, and especially not for a throne. I'm in. I don't care if I never find my way out, as long as Josh is in with me.

"You know, Your Highness," he says into my skin, kissing me between every other word, "this spell you have me under is fuckin' strong."

I make no attempt to move out of his embrace. "I don't have you under a spell."

"Don't argue with me."

"Okay." I smile. "Whatever you say."

"You're a fast learner."

While it's lovely being here all cuddled on his lap being playful, I'll soon be missed. I sigh deeply. "I should go before my absence is noted. What are you going to do about the article?"

"You're not the only one with a wizard to deal with the press," Josh assures me. "My reputation will still be intact tomorrow."

Grudgingly, I place my hands on his warm chest and push myself away, and he grudgingly lets me, albeit on a murmur of protest. "I really don't understand how this has happened." There has been nothing to suggest the King knows of my connection with Josh. Not one thing. Or . . . wait. His surprise visit to Kellington for breakfast? But nothing was said about Josh. God, I feel like my head could pop. "I'm certain no one knows. Only Damon, Kim, and Matilda, and I trust them with my life. And Eddie would never betray me like that, no matter how worried he is for me."

"That's four people, plus both teams of security we have tailing our asses every step we take."

I shake my head, confident that none of my staff would divulge my private life to anyone. "It doesn't make any sense. If my father knew, I would be summoned to the palace and warned."

"Let's tread carefully until we decide what to do, yeah?"

I nod, agreeing, because agreeing is all I can do. Josh taps the window, helping me across to my own seat. "I'll hang back until the coast is clear." He taps his cheek in silent order, and I lean over to drop a kiss where indicated. "Enjoy the rest of your day."

"I will."

"And for the record"—his face takes on an edge of repulsion—"that Haydon dude is cruising for a bruising."

"He's misguided," I sigh in his defense. "It's not his fault. Plus, he is dealing with some family problems. Don't be too harsh."

Damon pulls the door open, and I hop out, brushing down my dress. "A bank?" I question him dryly. "You horror."

"You forget, ma'am, I was in Mr. Jameson's suite that night, too. He deserved his chance to explain. The man's been shafted."

"But by whom? Nothing has been mentioned from the top about Josh."

"I'm aware of that," Damon muses, clearly as mystified as me as we wander toward the field.

"I don't know what to do." My fingers twiddle with the tassels on my bag.

"For now, you smile." He nudges me in the shoulder and my smile pops onto my face as if by magic. "Oh, and you should know, Felix really was looking for you. I told him you were MIA."

"Seems plausible," I say on a light laugh. "What did he want?"

"The call he got earlier was security on the gate. Gerry Rush was trying to get into the club."

That magic smile drops away like a rock. "What?" I can't take any more. *What the hell is wrong with him?* He's married, for God's sake.

Damon's eyebrows are scarily high. "Mr. Rush was demanding to see you. He soon departed, mind you, when Felix waved a few photographs under his nose."

I feel myself shrink. But there we have it. Threats come first, then action should warnings not be heeded. My family's army of advisors can't possibly be responsible for the wreck that was Josh's

suite. It's not how they operate. After being summoned to the palace, Josh would have received a polite *stay away*. It's of no consequence that Josh would never take notice of a threat, nor would I obey my father's demand. The point is, neither of those things happened. They would never jump straight into fixing a problem that may not need that much fixing. This is hurting my head.

"Just be careful, ma'am," Damon offers gently, nodding past me to give me the heads-up that we soon won't be alone.

Matilda joins us, falling into stride beside me as Damon drops back. "I'm not even going to ask," she says snootily. "I'm offended by your lack of trust in me."

The game is now over, the riders all dismounted and shaking hands. "He was set up. It was Josh's room, but he wasn't there when it was trashed." I keep my eyes set on the field before me. "It happened while he was at an after-party. But the night they're *claiming* it was done, I was with him all night. He's been set up." I peek out the corner of my eye to gauge her reaction.

My cousin is looking at me like I could be a unicorn pissing rainbows. "What?" she chokes, a little too loudly for my liking.

"Keep it down." I link arms with her and start walking around the outskirts of the field, out of earshot of everyone.

"I don't know what question to ask first," she admits. "Wait, yes I do. You spent *all* night in Josh Jameson's suite?"

"Yes." I can't help the smile that creeps up on me, my mind giving me a lovely replay of that night. And just now, back in the car when he laid it all out for me. He leads, I follow. It seems so natural.

"And you're not falling for him?" Her glare dares me to deny it.

"I've fallen so hard I'm black and blue." I laugh on the inside at the irony of that statement. My body has never been in such a terrible state, yet my heart has never been in a better state. As for my head, I haven't the first idea how to deal with the state of that.

"Oh my goodness, Adeline."

"I do not need you to tell me what a mess I am in, Matilda. Please."

"No, you don't. You have photographs of Josh's hotel suite to tell you that."

"That's just it. I don't think the wonderful institution that is our family is responsible. Only you, Eddie, Kim, and Damon know, and I trust you all wholeheartedly. Besides, they would never steamroll in and tackle a problem so brutally, not without the mundane warnings first."

"Who else would want to paint Josh in such a terrible light?"

"I don't know." We come to a stop on the opposite side of the field, and I scan the crowds, my eyes falling on my father, who is flanked on all sides by close protection. "The King would never be able to hold back on berating me if he knew I had been keeping company with Josh Jameson, and he sure as hell wouldn't allow Josh here today."

"True," Matilda agrees, lowering to the grass.

I join her, picking at the blades, observing the people waiting in line to lick my father's boots.

"There's your lover." My cousin jars my forearm with a flick of her elbow.

I look to where she's discreetly indicating and follow Josh's path until he reaches Senator Jameson, who greets him with a firm slap to the shoulder before walking him over to my father. I watch, rapt. Matilda is quickly holding my arm tightly, equally as interested, and maybe nervous, too. My mind only bends more when the King gives Josh a friendly smile, taking his hand and shaking it firmly. I witness only civility in my father's countenance. Then they're laughing, all three of them, sealing my conclusion.

"His Majesty seems to like him," Matilda says. "Maybe you are worrying over nothing."

"Oh, Matilda, you say some stupid things, but . . . really?"

"Okay. It was a silly suggestion." She turns into me, crossing her legs and pulling her dress over her knees. "Now, I want to know everything."

I laugh. She really doesn't. "Like what?" Where would I start?

The whipping? The commands? The romantic ride on horseback through the countryside? The tiara upon my head when he fucked me? Or drifting off to sleep in his arms? I sigh dreamily like a lovesick teenager, all of my woes forgotten.

"Like everything, Adeline." She looks across the field toward Josh, where he is still conversing with the King and the senator. "He has gorgeous eyes."

"He has gorgeous *everything*," I admit, getting a flurry of mental images flicker through my mind, every picture a piece of Josh's anatomy—his biceps, his insanely tight stomach, his thick thighs, his hard pecs, his . . .

"He doesn't look like his father."

I don't divulge what I know. It's not my place. "I think he must look like his mother. She passed away."

"That's sad."

"It is." Smiling fondly at Josh across the way, I can't help but feel a little proud of him for everything he's achieved. Yet his success still won't be good enough for my father. "Oh, look." I point to the left of us, where the Argentine is wandering over with his horse, his hat dangling by the thigh of his tight trousers. His appearance gives me the perfect opportunity to change the subject. "That's a bulge and a half."

"You are disgraceful." Matilda sniffs, coming over all fidgety. "I wouldn't know. I have not looked."

"Then do so, because it is *delightful*." I yelp through a chuckle when she elbows me in the side. "He's heading this way," I inform her around a grin. "And he has his eyes on you."

"Oh my goodness, what do I say? What do I *do*?"

"Relax," I laugh, helping her to her feet. "Ask him about his beast. And I mean his horse, not his bulge."

"Adeline!"

My grin widens as Santiago makes it to us, nodding politely. "Ladies," he purrs, his accent thick and rough and sexy. I can literally

feel my cousin crumbling under the pleasure of it.

I quickly kick off the introductions before Matilda screws it up. "Mr. Garcia, what a pleasure to meet you." I offer my hand.

"Your Highness, the pleasure is mine."

I smile and claim my hand back. "This is Her Royal Highness the Duchess of Kent. But you may call her Matilda."

"Matilda." Santiago flashes my cousin a mouthful of perfectly pearly white teeth, and, I swear, a twinkle sparks in his eye. The man is gorgeous, no doubt, but he is a little too pretty for my taste.

When Matilda fails to offer her hand to him, he takes the liberty of collecting it himself, placing a lingering kiss on the back. She stares at the back of his head, frozen, until I jar her from her inertness with a poke to the arm. She darts a panicked look at me.

Ask about his beast, I mouth, backing away on a smirk. She rolls her eyes, her chest expanding.

"That's a fine beast you have there," she says, and I chuckle as I leave them to it, making a mental note to call her later. I want every juicy detail. Well, perhaps not about his beast.

I watch Josh with fascination as I wander toward the hub of things. He's laughing along with my father, and Eddie has joined the group, too. Senator Jameson is congratulating him on a game well played. I'm curious of what the King could possibly be talking about with a Hollywood actor, but I know not to muscle in on man-talk, not without an invitation, so I head toward the tent. Besides, I can't be certain I could hold it together with Josh so near in front of an audience.

"Adeline." My father's booming voice cuts my journey short.

I cringe at the entrance to the tent, contemplating, just for a second, pretending not to hear. That would be very unwise of me. So I paint on that smile and pivot, finding all four men looking at me. Eddie is the only one without a smile. I don't like it. *Be cool. Be cool. Be cool.* "Father," I sing, making my way to him, accepting his warm welcome. It's quite a novelty after the last few times I've

seen him, when he has ranted and raved at me.

"I don't believe you have been formally introduced to the Senator and his son."

Christ. My smile falters, but I quickly remedy it. "I don't believe I have."

Eddie clears his throat, and Josh flicks a curious look his way. I was right to avoid this cozy little group. How awful. "Oh, she has," Senator Jameson pipes in. "At the garden party."

Oh God. I'm as stiff as a board, frantically searching my mind for my next words. I have just blatantly lied to the King. Why would I do such a thing if I have nothing to hide? But he saw me talking to Josh. Is it possible he doesn't remember? I don't know, but I need to play it down. "Oh, of course." I smile at Josh who is looking at his dad like he wants to rip his head off. "Forgive me."

"You're forgiven," Josh says coolly, slipping his hands into his pockets. "Your Highness."

Heat blazes my skin, damn him.

The King laughs, loud and rumbling. "Josh here makes movies. He's quite an accomplished actor."

"How delightful." I smile tightly, trying to keep my composure. Just the simple fact that my father doesn't know of Josh's fame speaks volumes. Hollywood royalty isn't on his radar, so I'm not surprised he thinks it won't be on mine either. But it is. Like a huge, bright screaming beacon. I analyze my father's disposition. He's relaxed, smiling, and he is far from wary of the American before him. In fact, I would go as far as to say he is rather impressed by him. Maybe even likes him.

"And you are a very accomplished shooter, I hear?" Josh relieves me of his burning eyes, giving the King his full attention.

"Years of practice on the clays, my boy."

"I used to shoot. Haven't for years, mind you, but I used to enjoy a hunt from time to time."

"What did you hunt?" the King asks, interested.

"Elk, deer, moose. If it moved in the woods, it was mine."

Father is more than impressed now. "I hunted elk once in Arizona. Thrilling. You must join me one day. I like a bit of competition, and no one around here provides that."

Did my father just invite Josh out for the day? I stare at Josh, astonished, who gladly accepts the King's offer, because no one, no matter who you are, declines the King. I'm not quite sure what I'm witnessing. Silly thoughts start to bounce around in my head, visions of my father aiming for a clay and turning the gun onto Josh at the last second. *Bang!* I flinch on the spot, my mind now having the King tossing Josh's body in a nearby ditch. Christ, what's going on in my head? Or maybe the King really will approve of Josh and give us his blessing. Now, I'm inwardly laughing, because that is, without question, the silliest thought I have ever had. Even more silly than the idea of the King having Josh killed off.

I'm gratefully distracted from my crazy thought process when Davenport appears by my father's side, whispering into his ear. The King's expression goes from delight to dismay in a heartbeat. "Very well." He moves away, addressing the group. "Duty calls, I'm afraid."

Everyone nods at the King's departure, and I use it to break away myself. "Excuse me, gentlemen." I nod, turning away before I make eye contact with Eddie, the senator, and especially Josh. I'm ready to go home and process everything that has happened today. It might take me a while. And plenty of champagne, since I've been denied too much today. Whatever is going on?

16

THE NEXT DAY after I've spent most of it at the stables, we collect Eddie from the barracks on the way back to Kellington. I've managed to avoid him since yesterday's polo match, but now . . .

The atmosphere in the car is painful. I make idol chit-chat, none of which he indulges in. He mostly looks out of the window, lost in thought. And I positively hate the fact that his thoughts are undeniably centered on me and my predicament. Because that is exactly what it is. A dilemma. Me being smitten with a man, the perfect man for me, is a problem. I can't even appreciate that Eddie is worried about me. I'm too worried for myself. The first thing I did this morning was check the online news for anything related to Josh and a trashed hotel suite. My heart pounded as I worked my way through every publication. I found nothing. My heartbeats calmed, but only a little. I'm still anxious.

A few times on our ride back to Kellington, after I've tried to engage Eddie in conversation and he has blocked me dead in my tracks, I look to Damon in the rearview mirror, as if seeking help. My head of security just shrugs his big shoulders, leaving me pondering alone. I don't know what to say to my brother, and I am not

sure it would make even a bit of difference to his opinion if I did. So in the end, I close my mouth and endure the wretched silence.

When we pull into the grounds of Kellington, I'm like a rocket out of the car, darting up the steps to the entrance in a rush to get myself to my suite so I can be alone and away from the lingering silence of the car.

"Your Highness." Olive's hands are held out in front of her ready to take my bag, but letting her help me would stall my escape. So I whizz past, catching her stunned look in my haste. "But, ma'am, your supper," she calls to my back.

"I'm not hungry, but thank you, Olive." I take the stairs two at a time.

"But Dolly has cooked your favorite, ma'am."

King prawn linguine? My steps stutter to a stop on the stairs, my shoulders dropping in defeat. "She has?" I squeak, cringing at the plush carpet runner on the stairs before me. Dolly only ever makes me my favorite dish when she's pulling no punches. She knows it's the only meal that will get me to the table, no matter how much I try to convince her I'm not hungry. It is the dish she uses as a weapon, to force me to eat when I don't want to. It is also a dish that she will be grumpy about should I decline to eat it, since it takes up so much of her time and steers her well clear of her usual, traditional meals. "I'll take it in my room." I try to bargain my way out of it, not wanting to upset Dolly, but at the same time wondering why today she has pulled out the big guns.

"But His Royal Highness Prince Edward has requested the table be laid, ma'am." Olive, God bless her soul, sounds nervous at delivering this news. She should be. So it's Eddie who's pulling out the big guns? He wants me to eat with him. Why? So he can talk to me? We just had alone time in the car together, and he didn't murmur a word.

I slowly turn, full of dread, finding my brother standing behind Olive, observing my stalled fleeing form on the stairs. His face is the

most serious that I have ever seen. "Dinner awaits," he says flatly, gesturing to the dining room.

I suppress my sigh and take the stairs back down to the foyer, letting Olive take my bag and scarf. But not before I retrieve my mobile phone. The quick dip of my hand into my bag isn't missed by Eddie. "Thank you." I smile a small smile at Olive, who wastes no time removing herself from the thick atmosphere. I envy her. There is no escape for me. I look at my brother, who gives me nothing but a straight face. I want to tell him he looks less handsome when he doesn't smile, that his boyish features look twenty years older. But that would be in spite. The flat look on his lovely face is indicating where dinner's conversation will go, so I roll my shoulders back and make my way into the dining room, determined to see this through. I will tell him exactly what is happening, if that is what he wants. I have not been holding back because I don't trust him. I simply don't want someone raining on my already flooded parade.

"Looks very nice," I say to the perfectly laid table, taking my seat and letting one of the footmen drape the 500 thread count napkin across my lap. "Thank you." I smile at him as he backs away, and rest my elbows on the table, something I'd never dream of doing if dining with the King. I also wouldn't dream of lifting my silverware before the King began his meal, but since the King isn't here, I grab my knife and fork and dive into my creamy pasta as soon as it lands on the table in front of me, if only to distract myself from Eddie, who is staring at me across the table, not bothering with his supper. I feel my irritation build with every silent second that passes, to the point I resort to clenching my silverware in my grasp and breathing in deeply, looking at my brother with an expectant look. Like, yes, just say what you want to say.

And he does. Bringing his balled fist to his mouth, he clears his throat and squares me with a level look. "Enough of the games. What's going on?"

I match Eddie's stark look, fumbling for the right words and

the best way to say them. I don't know whether it's his reproachful expression or my muddled state, but the only words I can find are those of a negative nature, and it's a challenge to hold them back. I want to scream at him to let me be, to let me figure this out on my own. I don't need to hear what I am faced with. I know fine well. "I'm seeing him," I mutter, annoyingly casting my eyes away as I confirm what he knows. What I wanted to do was look him square in the eye with confidence and conviction. Why can't I do that? Why can't I push forward with determination? It takes two seconds to reach my conclusion, and with that conclusion comes a reminder of the fear that accompanies the path I've chosen. I've fallen for Josh. I care about what happens to him. It matters to me if he's tarnished in any way. That amplifies my fear, because it all leaves me vulnerable.

Eddie laughs, and it is the most condescending laugh I have ever heard.

Ignoring it, I battle forward. "I try to feel free every day," I begin, keeping my voice calm and even, determined not to lose my temper with the brother I love so much. "I—"

Eddie laughs harder, bringing my intended plea to an abrupt halt. "You are a Lockhart, Adeline. The word *free* doesn't come with the job."

"What if I don't want this job?" I grate, stabbing at a prawn with my fork, just for something to take out my frustration on. I'm not going to eat it. I have no appetite. I'm just here to show some willingness.

"You don't get a choice." Eddie leans across the table, and for the first time in forever, I see my father in him. Not because he looks like him, he looks *nothing* like him, but because he sounds like him. And I resent him for it. "This is your life, Adeline, and it is mine. I've gotten used to it. You should, too. Enough of the games. You've played them for long enough. Forget about him. Forget about your silly little fling. Move on and do what Adeline Lockhart does best."

"What do I do best?" I question. "Come on, what do I do best, Edward? Keep up appearances? Dance to the tune of the King and his minions?"

"Really? Like you do any of those things."

"You're right. I don't. What I try to do is feel free. *Try*. That's the key word here. I force it. Do things I tell myself will make me feel better about the restraints I live with. The rebelling, the behavior; it's all my way of trying to hold on to my free will." I take a deep breath, seeing I now have Eddie's full attention, and I plan on keeping it. No interruptions. No more batting me down with a reminder of our obligations. That's it, now. He asked, so he shall get. I drop my silverware and stand, resting my palms on the table. "With Josh, I don't need to try. I don't even have to think about it. It's effortless. Natural. I'm not lying to myself. He makes me feel good about *me*. He knows *me* without even really knowing me. He sees me. Not the painted princess. He sees *me*. The woman. The desire. The need to have a man tell me that this is how it's going to be, but he's telling me that because he knows what I want. What I need. Not what my country needs. Not what the King needs. Not what the bloody monarchy needs. Me. It's about *me*. So if that is bad, if you can't deal with that, you are more than welcome to go join the army of power-hungry bastards who will try to stop us from being together." I catch my breath, if only to make sure my next promise is as level as every other word I have spoken. "I will take you down as hard as I plan on taking them down. With no mercy. No guilt. No looking back. This is about me being a better person, a more useful person, because I have what I so desperately need in my life to function. *Him*. Josh." I manage to note through my declaration that Eddie's eyes are wide and startled. "I would rather sacrifice my entire existence as a royal than be without him. I'm useless without him. I *have* been useless without him. For the first time in my life, I feel valued. I have a purpose beyond answering correspondence and keeping up appearances. I want to do the

things with my life that I never dreamt I would be able to do. He is a blessing to me, and I will not let you or anyone else try to make him out to be anything else." Throwing my napkin on the table, I walk away, so damn proud of myself for getting all those words out without so much as a stutter or a crack in my voice. There. I think I made myself clear.

Olive moves swiftly from my path as she enters with a tray, and when my phone rings in my hand and Josh's name appears, I be as bold as one can be, answering and greeting him by his name, just so Eddie knows exactly who I'm talking to. Call it blunt. Call it brazen. I don't care. "Josh," I breathe, taking the stairs steadily.

"You sound out of breath. Everything okay?"

"Not really. I just had a horrible argument with my brother."

"Oh? About . . ."

"Us."

"I won't ask what he said. I caught the way he was glaring at me yesterday at the polo match. Are you all right?"

"No." I make it to my bedroom and shut myself inside, collapsing to the couch. "Eddie is my favorite of them all. I hate fighting with him." Leaning down, I start to pull off my riding boots. "And the worst thing is, what I just faced will be nothing compared to what is to come." All the fortitude Josh filled me with yesterday wanes, and I flop back on the couch on a heavy sigh.

"Maybe I can help out."

I would laugh, but that would be condescending, so I settle for an eye-roll instead. "And how do you propose you will help?"

"I'm going shooting with the King and my dad tomorrow."

I'm sitting up straight all of a sudden. "Tomorrow? When was that arranged?"

"Just before I left the match. Some tall, lanky old dude told me where to be and when."

"Davenport," I tell him. "Looks like his face would crack if he smiled?"

"That's him. Who shit in his coffee?"

I chuckle. "He has one expression. Has since I've known him." I get up and wander into the dressing room, getting myself out of my jodhpurs with one hand. "He served my grandfather before my father. He is a piece of the royal furniture, and I'm pretty sure he hates me."

"Why do you say that?"

"Just the way he looks at me. Like I'm a thorn in his side." I pull my phone away to get my jumper over my head and drop it to the floor. As I'm wandering out, intending on heading for the bathroom, my eye catches my grandmother's Spanish tiara. I nibble my lip, smiling to myself. "Guess what I'm looking at?" I lift the heavy piece and turn it in my hand.

"If you say you're naked and standing in front of the mirror, there will be serious consequences."

"I have my underwear on, and the mirror before me is hanging over my dresser, so I can only see the top half."

"That's still not fair play. Wait. Your dresser?"

"Uh-huh." I grin, looking to my reflection. My eyes are sparkling nearly as much as the encrusted headpiece in my hand.

"Put it on your head," he orders. I pull my ponytail free, letting my hair tumble over my shoulders, and then rest the heavy weight atop of my head. "Take a picture and send it to me."

I don't even think to question him. Pulling my camera up, I pout and snap a quick selfie before attaching it to a text and sending it on. "Done. Did it come through?"

"Oh Jesus," Josh breathes.

"Is that a yes?"

"That's my new screensaver."

"Don't be ridiculous." I laugh, lifting the heavy weight from my head and placing it down. "People will see. How would you explain it?"

He grunts, annoyed. "Where are you?"

"Just about to take a shower."

"Adeline!"

"Well, I am." I laugh, entering the bathroom and grabbing a towel.

"Come see me."

"I can't." I sigh, pouting as I flick the shower on. "Damon's going home soon. I'm going nowhere tonight."

"Then I'll come to you."

"Yes, you do that. Wear your invisibility cloak and all will be fine, I'm sure."

"Damn it, Adeline, why'd you have to be so fuckin' important?" He sounds utterly exasperated, and I have to admit, so am I. Although he's a fine one to talk.

"You are hardly a nobody yourself, Mr. Jameson," I point out. "I did tell you this would be impossible."

"God, I need to see you. Tomorrow I'm going to blindside the King so much, he'll be begging me to date his daughter. And if that fails, I'll put my gun to his head until he agrees."

I snort down the line. "I hope you're ready to fail." I stare at myself in the mirror, thinking how desperate I am to see him, too. So desperate. How could I make that happen? I gaze into my eyes, an outlandish idea coming to me. "I could sneak out," I mumble, more to myself than to Josh.

"What?"

"Of the palace," I explain. "I could sneak out of the palace."

"Wanna borrow my invisibility cloak?"

I look at my phone quickly, registering that I have roughly thirty minutes until Damon clocks off. I need to be quick. "I'll be there in an hour." I hang up and shove my hair in a messy knot before I dive in the shower. I haven't the luxury of time to wash and dry my mane. I fly over my body with soapy hands and quickly wash it off. A quick check of the time tells me I'm down to twenty-five minutes. Christ, it will take me ten minutes to get myself to the

garages, possibly longer if I have to crawl combat-style through the palace to avoid being seen. My heart starts pumping fast with adrenalin and excitement.

As I'm rubbing in some face cream, my phone rings, and I peek down to see Josh flashing up on my screen. "I haven't got time to speak," I say to myself, letting it ring off. I spritz, and then dart into my dressing room, grabbing some black skinny jeans and a black lightweight jumper, throwing them on quickly. I finish with a black scarf looped round my neck a few times, and I release my hair, letting the messy waves do as they damn well please. I hope Josh appreciates au naturel. I have not a scrap of makeup on, and I don't care. I'm too desperate to see him, and my window of opportunity will close any minute.

Throwing my bag over my shoulder, I grab the first pair of comfortable shoes I can lay my hands on. My Uggs. It's the wrong time of year, but I shrug and pull them on, then I dip into the bottom drawer of my dresser, knowing it was in here the last time I saw it. "Come on, where are you?" I ask, as I rummage through the contents. I smile when I lay my hands on it. Taking myself to the mirror, I slip the New York Yankees baseball cap on. "Perfect." If I keep my head down, I should be good.

As I'm rounding the gallery landing, my phone rings again, reminding me to turn the sound off. I can't answer and risk being heard, so I let it ring off again. The next second, I get a text.

You're shitting me, right? Sneak out?

I ignore him, not willing to let him talk me out of it, and make my way through the palace, choosing a less than efficient route through endless connecting rooms, but a route that will ensure the chances of me being seen are minimal. My only stumbling block comes when I have to pass the kitchen in order to get to the garage. With all the other external doors fitted with active sensor alarms, it is my only way. I hear Damon and Dolly chatting in the kitchen

as I creep down the corridor, the exit into the small courtyard that leads to the garage block in sight. I'm as quiet as a mouse, tiptoeing with my shoulder close to the wall. A quick peek around the corner tells me Damon has his back to me and Dolly is rifling through a cupboard. I'm clear, but just as I am about to shoot across the doorway, Olive strolls into the kitchen, and I jump back, sticking myself to the wall.

"That's me for the evening," she declares.

"I'll be off, too," Damon says, and I hear the feet of his stool scrape the tile floor.

Damn it! It's now or never. I hold my breath and practically dive across the doorway, and then run to the door on light feet, praying I don't hear the signs of anyone coming after me. I only start breathing again once I have made it into the courtyard, shutting the door quietly behind me. Then I run toward the garage like my life depends on it.

Scrambling for Damon's car keys in the cabinet, I click his car open and replace them before getting in the back of his car and wedging myself in the space behind the driver's seat. I'm squished completely, but my time mentally moaning about my uncomfortable form is limited to seconds, because the heavy footsteps of someone approaching the car makes me still. My phone, however, doesn't get the memo to be quiet and vibrates in my hand, illuminating the car with the light from the screen. "Bugger," I curse quietly, fumbling in my confined space to get my phone in sight.

Answer your phone!

Josh rings again, and I apologize to him in my head as I turn it off quickly and try to settle in for the ride. My knees are virtually in my mouth, my body scrunched and bent in the most awkward way. A contortionist I am not. The door opens, and I hold my breath once again as Damon drops into the seat and starts the car. All is well . . . until he decides he is too close to the wheel and presses

the button that slides the chair back. *Oh God!* My shoulders meet my earlobes, and I scrunch my eyes closed, waiting for the crack of bones.

For a moment, I question my sanity. Then I remind myself of what is waiting for me at the end of what is going to be a journey that is the furthest from first class travel I could find. Mentally willing Damon to drive, I force myself into complete stillness, aware I'm so wedged into the back of his seat, he will feel even the slightest move I try to make. This is hell. Pure hell. But Josh is heaven, and if I need to go through hell to reach my heaven, then so be it.

Damon pulls out of the garage and crawls along for a few moments before slowing again when I assume he reaches the gate. He lets the window down. "Have a good evening," he says, low and gruff.

"You too, Damon," the gateman replies, and I hear the gates starting to creak open.

The car picks up speed, and my misery gets some light relief when Damon turns on the stereo and starts singing along to . . . *Take That*? I have to hold my breath to stop myself from laughing out loud. Oh my, how will I ever refrain from teasing him about this? My big, bruising Damon belting out the lyrics to *Never Forget* is high up there on my list of most entertaining moments. Not because he's good. He's not. He's terrible. My ears are bleeding, but his gusto and the effort he is putting into his rendition is priceless. I suppress my snort of amusement, wincing constantly. The man is tone deaf.

It already feels like the longest—and loudest—journey ever, and I know I have a way to go. From memory, Damon lives in Lambeth, all the way on the other side of the river. The Dorchester is a mere mile away from Kellington, on the other side of Hyde Park. I'm going miles out of my way, but it's the *only* way to escape the palace.

After ten minutes, I'm covering my ears. I assumed *Take That* was on the radio. I was wrong. Damon has the greatest hits album wired through his iPhone, and he knows every single word to every

blasted track.

It is a relief when his phone rings and interrupts him. "Hey darling," he answers, all chirpy.

"Hey, you on your way home yet?" his wife, Mandy, asks.

"Just left the palace."

"Good day?"

"Always interesting." He takes a corner a bit too sharply. "Everything okay?"

"Yes. Dinner's nearly ready. Will you stop and pick up some wine?"

Yes! Stop and pick up some wine. Right around here would be super.

"Sure," Damon says. "Red?"

"We have steak, so that will be perfect."

"Steak?" The interest in his voice makes me smile. "Steak's my favorite."

"I know it is," Mandy teases. "And if you eat it all up like a good boy, I have something special for dessert."

My eyes bug, and I blush, despite no one being able to see me. I'm sure the car picks up speed.

"I'll be quick."

She laughs. "But don't kill yourself being quick, okay? I want my husband home in one piece. Save your speed skills for when Princess Adeline needs them."

"Got it."

Listening to my bodyguard chatting with his wife, just like a normal married couple, makes my heart swell. I want that. Normal. Talking about what's for dinner and what wine we might have with it.

"I'm just coming up to Sainsbury's. See you when I get home." Damon pulls to a stop. "And Mandy?"

"Yes?"

"Be naked when I get there."

I die where I'm balled up, covering my twisted face as best I can

with my limited movement. This journey has been more painful than I ever imagined, and not only because my arms and legs are bent at the most insane angles. When Damon gets out of the car and slams the door, clearly in a hurry, I release all the air I have been holding, breathing properly for the first time in fifteen minutes. He's in a rush. It won't be long before he's heading back out of the store with his bottle of red to race home to his wife.

Peeking up out of the window, I see the entrance to the store and Damon disappearing into it. "Thank goodness," I sigh, wrestling my way up from the floor of the car. Pulling the door handle, I practically fall into a pile onto the pavement. I can't appreciate the sense of freedom, nor can I relish the stretch of my muscles. No. I get none of those luxuries, because the alarm of Damon's car starts screaming at me. I stiffen and look left and right, seeing plenty of people, yet none of them particularly bothered by the shrill sound of the nearby car alarm. I skulk away, pulling the peak of my cap down, at the same time trying to gauge where I am. It's only at this point in my thirty-year existence that I appreciate how isolated I have been. I've lived in this city for three decades, yet I haven't the first idea of where I am. I recognize nothing.

I resort to finding a sign to gain my bearings. Chelsea Bridge. It's only my mental map of London that can offer me my route and how long it might take me. It's at least a forty-minute walk. That doesn't bother me so much. It's the vigilance I'll need to maintain that worries me more. The thought makes me lower my head, while trying to look up for signs of a black cab. I spot one and wave my arm, but it sails by. And then another does, and then one stops but some rude person dives in before I make it off the curb. I sigh and start a brisk walk toward the end of the road, my shoulders huddled high, my head bowed. I don't make eye contact with anyone, dare not look up higher than the slabs before me. I'm jostled on the pavement by the crowds, and with each step I take, my nerves become more frayed. I feel so small out here, alone in

the world, so utterly vulnerable.

My breathing is labored half an hour into my walk, and it has nothing to do with the brisk pace I have maintained. A harsh bump of my shoulder nearly spins me on the spot, and a suited man curses me for getting in his way. "Look where you're going," he yells. I mutter an apology, my chin nearly touching my chest to avoid what I know will be an angry glare.

I collide with another pedestrian, my body ricocheting back a few feet. "Watch it!"

The thuds of my heart are becoming heavier, my anxiety growing. I'm out of my depth. I reach for my phone and realize I haven't switched it back on. My shaking hands fumble to bring it to life as I'm knocked out of the path of a young woman.

"Pay attention," she barks as my phone crashes to the ground. The back of my mobile cracks and the screen shatters as it jumps around my feet. I gasp and lower to gather it up, my crouching body obstructing the pavement. I'm kicked by someone passing, and someone trips up my arm as I reach to snatch up my phone.

"I'm sorry," I murmur, being cursed at from every direction, the annoyed voices all morphing into one beastly scorn. I need to call Josh. I need someone to come find me. I'm becoming more and more panicked. The irony doesn't escape me. Here's me, always fighting the constraint, and now I have freedom—actual freedom—and I'm terrified. What if someone recognizes me? What if a photographer snaps a photo of me? I rise and hurry on my way, at the same time trying to turn on my phone, praying it's not broken. My fumbling hands refuse to stop trembling, and when my phone comes to life, all that greets me is a green, fuzzy screen. I swallow, feeling tears burning the back of my eyes, and break into a jog, desperate to escape the chaotic streets of London.

17

BY THE TIME I make it to the hotel, I'm shaking no less, but my racing heart slows to a safer pace with the relief that washes over me. I hurry toward the entrance, but my Uggs pull me to a stop when my mind registers the crowd of people blocking my way. Some have cameras. Some have phones. Some are screaming Josh's name. My steadying heartbeat rockets again. There's no way through, not without being seen. I back away, quickly turning before any of them look in this direction, and hurry around the side of the building.

More people, dozens of them, are crowding the pavement with more cameras. I stutter to a stop, panic racking me again. *What was I thinking?* That I could just wander on into a hotel and ask reception to call up to Josh's suite? I suddenly feel so very foolish, my anxious eyes darting, searching for a way through all the people. There isn't one.

Without checking for traffic, I rush across the road toward a doorway, searching for cover. I hear tires skid, and then the angry sounds of a car horn blaring. My body freezes, my legs failing, leaving me standing in the middle of the road with the bonnet of a car virtually touching my knees. "You stupid woman," the driver

yells out of the window, smacking his horn a few more times. I look up through the windscreen, startled, and just as quickly shoot my eyes back down again, forcing my muscles to engage and remove me from the road before the driver registers who he just nearly run over. Falling into a doorway, I will my hands to stop shaking, swallowing repeatedly to stop myself from crumbling under the pressure.

"Please work, please work, please work," I chant, turning my phone off and on again, waiting for some signs of life. The cracked screen illuminates, flashing green again. I can't see a damn thing past the fuzz, only the edges of a few icons. "No," I sob, sagging against the dirty brick wall inside the doorway.

And that's where I remain for a good five minutes wondering what I do now. How could I have been so stupid? I truly have no idea how to navigate the real world. My education was based on my need for knowledge as a royal in a world protected by status and power, not my need for knowledge as a real person in the real world. Because I'm not a *real* person. I'm not supposed to be in the real world.

I look left and right, my despair building. And then my mobile rings in my hand, and I shoot my eyes to the distorted screen. There's no prompt to answer, and I can't even see who is calling me. I wildly punch at the area I know the answer icon to be. And then I hear him.

"Adeline? Adeline, are you there?"

"Josh!" I'm way beyond the ability to control sounding so freaked out.

"Adeline, for fuck's sake. Where the hell are you?" If it's possible, he sounds even more panicked than me.

"I'm outside. I can't get through the crowds. There are too many paparazzi and fans."

"Where's Damon?"

I flinch, shouting at myself for being so irrational. "I'm alone."

"Jesus, woman," he all but breathes, and I hear the sounds of his footsteps in the background. "She's outside," he says, his voice muffled, like he is covering the phone with his hand. "Where outside? Tell me exactly where you are."

"I don't know." I can feel my voice cracking, the situation getting too much. "At the side of the hotel. I can't see a street name." I scan the side of the hotel opposite, desperately searching for a sign to tell me where I am.

"Adeline, listen to me," Josh says calmly, though I know he's anything but. "When you were at the front of the hotel, which direction did you head, left or right?"

It's a straight-forward question. An easy question, but it takes my brain a stupid amount of time to recall.

"Adeline."

"Right."

"Don't move." The sound of a door slamming in the background pierces my eardrums.

"There's press everywhere." My eyes dart left to right constantly, terrified that any one of them will see me huddled in the doorway at any moment. "What's going on?"

"They've been camping there since I came back from an interview. Just stay where you are." His breathing becomes a bit labored. He's running. "Just keep talking to me, okay?"

"Okay."

"Christ, Adeline, what were you thinking?"

"I just wanted to see you."

"How did you get here?"

I'm cringing again, aware that I am about to get a thorough telling off. "Damon's car."

"So where is he?"

More cringing. "He didn't know I was in his car."

There's silence, like Josh is trying to comprehend what I just confessed. "You hid in his car?"

"It was the only way I could get out of the palace without being seen."

"Fuckin' hell, Adeline. Do you know how stupid that is?" Another door slams, and the background noise is suddenly deafening.

"Now I do," I admit. "I'm sorry."

"You fuckin' will be. Look to your right across the road. The hotel garage entrance."

I glance up, not sure what I'm expecting to find, maybe one of his security team, but instead I see Josh, being followed not too closely by two of the huge men who protect him, though today they're not in suits, but casual jeans and T-shirts. I exhale down the line, unable to appreciate the risk he's taking. I'm too relieved he's here.

Watching as he takes a wide berth around the crowds, I register his sweats and a zip-up hoodie, and he has a baseball cap pulled low on his head too, the hood of his sweater pulled over it. He looks up, his phone to his ear, as he strides toward me. He's tense, shoulders high, an effort to conceal his identity as best he can. "Can you see my face?" he asks down the line.

"Yes."

"Good. Then you can see how fuckin' mad I am with you."

I shrink. "I'm sorry," I say again, feeling so very remorseful. All this risk, to both of us, because I had a silly harebrained plan, a plan that has backfired on me in the most spectacular way. I'm an idiot. "The last twenty-four hours have been horrible. Polo yesterday, Eddie today. I just needed to see you," I whisper.

"Well, now you can." He reaches me and drops his phone to his side, looking up from under the peak of his cap as he pulls back the hood.

His face, no matter how cut it is with anger, sets off my emotions, and my lip wobbles uncontrollably. "It was a good idea at the time." My voice breaks and the burn at the back of my eyes wins, turning into tears. There is no point holding them back now. The alleviation of anxiety is too much. So I cry. In the dirty doorway

on a London street, tears stream down my cheeks. Because I didn't look a big enough wreck already.

Josh sighs, reaching for my nape and tugging me into his welcoming warmth. "This doesn't mean I'm not still mad with you," he whispers, enveloping me in his arms. I cling to him, my body softening in his arms. Strangely, this is enough. His hug. Genuine affection, something I ordinarily live without. It should feel foreign to me—being engulfed in someone's solid arms—but instead it calms me. I never knew what I'd been missing until now. Contact. Warmth over lust in a man's touch. Everything is so much better.

"I don't care what mood you're in as long as you're here." I mean it, too. He could rant and rave at me for all I care. I would still be thankful I'm with him. My nose burrows into his neck and breathes him into me.

"Josh, we need to get moving," Bates says, forcing Josh to break away. "Before you draw attention."

At that exact moment, the sound of a shrill female screaming Josh's name seems to bring the whole of London to a stop. "It's him. Over there!"

"Fuck." Josh quickly unzips his hoodie and shrugs it off. "Put this on." He forces my arms into the sleeves and pulls the hood up over my cap. "Keep your head down, do you hear me?"

"What about you?"

"Head down, Adeline," he whisper-hisses, rearranging the hood so it is nearly touching my lips. "They've seen me already. We need to make sure they don't see you." I let my head drop, feeling Josh's arm curl around my shoulders, pulling me in. My whole body bunches forward, making myself as small as possible. "Walk." His command is curt, and his body turns into mine as he guides me across the road, shielding me from the crowds as much as he can.

"Straight ahead," one of his men says, his boots only a few feet in front of mine.

"We can't let them see her, Bates," Josh warns, pulling me in

tighter, like he expects someone to try and pry me from his arms at any minute.

"Just keep her close. We'll get you through."

There are suddenly many more shoes in my downcast view as I'm huddled along, questions being fired relentlessly.

"Josh, who's under the hoodie?"

"Is this the new girlfriend?"

"How are you finding London?"

"Can we get a smile, Josh?"

"Let us see who's under the hood."

My fear amplifies, and my head jars back, a result of someone behind yanking at the hood. "Get your fuckin' hands off her," Josh yells, shoving them away.

"So it's a *her*, huh? Come on, Josh. Relieve everyone's curiosity and give us a name."

Josh's pace increases, as does mine, flashes going off everywhere. A camera appears in my downcast vision, and I turn my face into my arm to try and hide. "Back off!" Josh smacks the camera away, and it crashes to the ground at my feet. "All of you, back the fuck off."

I close my eyes briefly, my remorse returning tenfold. This will be tomorrow's news. *What have I done?* Looks like I didn't need my father to ruin this for us. I've done it myself. I've never been this stupidly irrational.

We break into a jog once free of the crowds, making it into the garage relatively unscathed. "Are you okay?" Josh asks, following his two men. I just nod, completely bewildered by the whole episode. Is this what it's like for him all the time? This chaos? My encounters with the press and fans are generally calm situations, their respect high. That out there was crazy.

Josh waits until we are in the service elevator, the same elevator I used the last time I was here, before he slowly pushes my hood back, bringing me into the light. He examines my face as I stare at him with wide, stunned eyes. I have never experienced anything

like it. That was unbelievable.

I'm not looking at Josh's men, but I don't need to see them to know they are displaying immense displeasure. I've caused a circus. My lips press together to try and stop another wobble of my lip.

"Well," Josh starts, his face serious. "That was—"

"Horrible." He must think I'm a brainless idiot, and he would be right. "I'm so sorry. I didn't know there would be press—"

His finger lands on my lip, hushing me. "I tried to call to tell you."

"I dropped my phone, and it broke, and then I panicked because people were bumping into me, and I was worried I'd be recognized. I didn't mean to cause such madness."

"It's always madness."

"But I fueled it."

He softly smiles, his palm smoothing down my cheek. "Could you imagine if they knew who was hidden under that hoodie and cap?"

"Don't." I shudder, it all becoming very real. The madness our relationship will cause, on so many levels of our lives.

"You look gorgeous, by the way."

"What?" I look down my disheveled form to the Uggs gracing my feet. I'm wearing no makeup, and my hair is flattened under the cap. "They probably wouldn't have recognized me even if they did get a peek."

Josh moves in for a kiss, but the peaks of our caps clash, jarring both our heads. I laugh on a flinch, as does Josh, who then swipes off both of our caps and takes my lips, swallowing down my chuckle. Our kiss is fragmented and clumsy, both of us smiling too hard to seal our mouths. "I'm glad you're here," he tells me, wiping away all the stress.

Then our kiss finds a smooth rhythm, our tongues lapping lazily on hums of contentment. Until a cough interrupts us. I pull away quickly, feeling a blush color my cheeks. It's so easy to forget

my surroundings when Josh possesses me so completely. "Sorry," I mutter, my head now low for other reasons. The two men move to the side to open our path when the doors slide open, and Josh takes my hand, leading the way. We pass the door to his suite, and I frown.

"They're still clearing up the mess someone kindly made," he says as we reach another room. "I'm in here." He opens the door and ushers me into an equally lavish suite. "So since you've put me through hell tonight, how do you intend on making it up to me?"

He's been through hell? *What about me?* I had a meltdown in the middle of a busy London street, just so I could snatch a moment with him. "How would you like me to make it up to you?"

Kicking his trainers off and tossing our caps onto a table, a devious smirk forms on his face. My trauma is forgotten with the hint of suggestion flickering in his eyes. Without a word, he strolls casually forward, the temperature of my body rising with each step that brings him closer to me. Josh Jameson is a god. He's perfection on every level, all wrapped up in a body that's built for sinful things. He's built to be worshipped, and he's built to be worshipped by me. Just me. And I want to so badly worship him.

Stopping before me, he sizes me up, taking in every piece of my bedraggled form. Maybe I should be conscious that I look such a wreck. Maybe I should be wishing I was standing here before him in a killer dress, my hair and makeup as perfect as they always are. But I'm not. Josh sees past the painted woman. He sees deep into my soul, past the forced exterior. He sees *me*. He knows *me*. He also knows what I want. *Him*. I want him with every fiber of my being, desperately so. I'm willing to walk through fire, and eventually, that is exactly what I'll have to do. But not now. Now we are locked away safely, away from the prying eyes of the world. Nothing else exists, except him, me, and the electricity sizzling between our wanting bodies. My heart pumps erratically in my chest while I wait for him to tell me what he wants. Not that I need to hear it. His body is speaking to me all by itself. But I want him to say it. I

want to hear the words that will tell me he is as hooked on these feelings as I am. That he's becoming as addicted and obsessed as me. And I wait. And wait.

"Fuck, you're divine," he murmurs, his eyes greedy, still roaming up and down. When they finally reach my face, my lips have parted and my breathing is shallow. I refrain from touching, from taking him, because this is his move to make. And he suddenly makes it. On a growl worthy of a lion, he seizes me and tosses me over his shoulder with little effort, stalking toward the bedroom, a man on a mission. Fire blazes inside me and every stressful minute of my quest across London to make it to him is certified worthwhile.

I sail through the air when he launches me from his arms, landing on the bed on a gasp of delight. His T-shirt is virtually ripped over his head, his sweats kicked off just as aggressively. And then he's naked, and it's my turn to be greedy in my observing. That body. It's on thousands of billboards across the world, plastered in endless magazines, but nothing, and I mean *nothing*, compares to the vision of him in the flesh and blood. Nothing. "Oh my . . ." I breathe, mentally licking every single glorious piece of him, my fingers mentally tracing the waves of his hard stomach.

Stepping forward, he takes an Ugg in each hand and pulls them off, casting them aside. I'm stripped down, his hands working slowly as I watch him focus on his task, my skin hypersensitive to every brush of his fingers on my flesh. I'm laid out before him like a sacrificial lamb, and it's apt in its symbolism. Because for him I would sacrifice everything.

As my bra is drawn lazily away from my aching breasts, he dips and kisses each nipple in turn, and my body curves upward in response, spiking a faint smile to ghost his lips. And once my knickers are pulled down my legs, he pushes my thighs apart, spreading me open, and that faint smile vanishes, his expression serious as he stares at the juncture of my thighs. "There are so many things I want to do to this beautiful body." His voice is thick and husky.

"Then do them." I'll take anything from him. Let him do anything to me.

"I wasn't asking for your permission." His fingertip rests lightly on my clit, and I feel my pulse pushing into it consistently. My hands ball, fisting the sheets at my sides. "I will do with you as I please, and you will beg me to do it." Collecting a belt from the nearby dresser, he pulls the leather through his fingers, regarding me closely as I comprehend exactly what he means. "I need to loosen us up."

My eyes light up, as does his. "How so?" I know exactly how so.

He snaps the leather together, one eyebrow hitched. "Off the bed."

I edge to the end of the bed and find my feet. "And now?"

"Turn around and give me that fine ass."

I turn, bending over the bed and jutting my bottom out in invitation. Closing my eyes, I fill my lungs, already feeling that weightless sensation take over me. *Thwack!* I grunt and jolt forward, the biting sting of the leather chasing away every solemn thought, peace replacing it. *Thwack!* My eyes roll behind my closed lids, my body rolling, too. The burn spreads and penetrates me to my bones. *Thwack*! I cry out, the sound desperate and hungry. *Thwack!* They're getting harder, each strike more powerful than the last. My flesh is on fire. His breathing is heavy behind me, each lash delivered on a shout of victory. *Thwack!* This one connects with the backs of my thighs, spanning both, and sends me to my knees, my body pooling the end of the bed. Part of me wants to scream *enough!* But a bigger part of me wants him to go on, to thrash me until I'm weightless.

There's a long pause, and I open my eyes, feeling drowsy. Josh straddles my collapsed body and grabs my hair, pulling my head off the bed. "Who is your king, Your Highness?"

"You are," I breathe, no hesitation or thought, staring at him looming over me, exuding power.

"Damn straight I am." Bending, he kisses me hard, a kiss of ownership and possession, one that cements his claim. "Up." He

lifts me, turns me, and pushes me to my back, dropping the belt and shoving my thighs wide. "Soaking," he mumbles, full of appraisal as his head lowers. I hold my breath, bracing myself for the heat of his mouth over my throbbing, wet flesh. The stroke of his tongue is firm and long, dipping inside of me before lashing straight up the center.

I cry out, tossing my head back, my body locking up, as if tensing can protect me from the blessed torture of his mouth. His long lick doesn't stop when he reaches the strip of hair that frames me, and instead continues up to my belly button, Josh crawling up the bed, following his tongue as it travels on, up between my breasts, to my chest, onto my chin, and then into my mouth. His cock finds where it wants to be, falling into place and slipping inside of me, deep and high with one precise thrust of his hips on a grunt into my mouth.

The powerful plunge steals my breath, and I don't care if I never get it back, because this, right now, is perfect. If it were my last moment in this life, it would send me out in a blaze of glory.

My nails sink into his back, my teeth into his neck, and my legs curl and grip his hips with an unthinkable strength. I feel so overcome by our connection—by our closeness—that tears spring into my eyes. I can't stop them.

"I feel the same," he whispers, stilling, buried as deep as could be inside of me. "I feel it. All of it." Breaking away, his flesh dragging through my bite, he gazes at me, and I am certain through my clouded vision that he has water in his eyes, too. "You've fallen in love with me."

A ragged sob ignores my fight to hold it back, wanting to be out there, heard. I pointlessly close my eyes and sink my face into the crook of his neck, but I'm not blessed with my sanctuary for long. He withdraws and plunges forward again, nuzzling me from my hiding place as he hits me accurately, pushing me up the bed a little.

"Look at me." His demand is clipped and rough, his body stilling again. I let my eyes peel open and face my weakness. He is

my weakness. My American boy. Yet he is a formidable strength in me, too. His gaze, twinkling and alive, holds me in place. "You love me." He states it as the fact it is, and I nod, clamping down on my bottom lip. My acknowledgment makes him smile as his cock throbs against my internal walls and his eyes, the very essence of him, take on a brilliant sparkle. "Say it."

I don't have to think twice. "I love you," I whisper, laying myself bare before him.

"And I love you." His reply is quiet, yet the loudest thing I've ever heard. "I think I loved you the moment you yielded to my command to kneel."

"Because I did what I was told?" I question, my heart bursting with joy.

His big shoulders hitch a little from a half shrug, his gaze leaving mine, just for a second. "Many women do what I tell them." He dips and circles his nose with mine. "But only you made the whole world disappear when you did." His mouth presses to mine. "Only you made me insane with want. Your face, your body. Only you have monopolized every thought in my head. Your wickedly smart mouth. Your fiery temper. The fact you've let me dismantle your high, protective walls." He laps his tongue through my mouth slowly and softly. "Only you have made me wish more than anything that I could be a real fuckin' prince so I could serve you and support you. So I could be yours."

I smile against his lips, not feeling the need to say anything, and roll my hips up, reminding us both we're tied so closely. He groans and follows my lead, setting the motion, kissing me into an oblivion of Josh. Two people loving each other, feeling the exact same way about each other, should make the path to their happily ever after easy and blissful. But we are not two ordinary people. We have a fight ahead, and our battle plan needs to be set. But for now, we can love each other without the complication and pain of that path tarnishing it.

He really is my king. He rules me. God, I'm so in love with him.

I skate my touch up and down his back, my fingertips delicately tracing each side as he moves inside me. His exploring tongue swirls deeply, not a tiny piece of my mouth not found. My back bows slowly, my pleasure gaining momentum, charging forward unstoppably. "Oh God, Josh."

"My name on your lips is the sexiest thing I've ever heard." His hips buck, hitting hard, and I whimper through a moan. "When you come, I want you to say my name over and over." His pace quickens, like he wants me to get to that point sooner rather than later, and I am fine with that.

I writher and groan, my mind spacing out in a pleasure-induced fog. All my senses heighten, every move is more intense, every feeling more powerful. "I'm coming," I choke, throwing my hands to the headboard and clinging on, as if it can ground me, as if it will save me from being catapulted off the bed from the power of the climax about to attack me. Tingles engulf me, heat surges through me. "Josh."

"Again," he says calmly, pumping on, banging my orgasm out of me. "Say it again."

"Josh!" I scream this time, his name going on and on until my lungs run dry of air. I gasp for breath, my hold of the wood behind me so tight I lose all feeling in my arms.

"Again." He thunders on, moving onto his fists to get more leverage. "Again, Adeline."

"Josh!" The power of my release is almost too much to bear, every nerve ending sparking, cracking, and exploding. "I can't take anymore." It's like he has full control of my orgasm, dictating how long it goes on, making sure I'll not move for a week once he is done with me.

"You can. And you'll be taking a lot more than this, I promise you." His voice is as distorted as his face. "Oh . . . my . . . fuck." His body locks, his chin dropping to his chest, and then he starts

shaking like I would never believe if I weren't lying beneath him, absorbing every vibration with my own. I release one hand from the headboard and reach for his throat, splaying my palm there, feeling every swallow and struggle for air, his skin soaked. "I love you." He strains the words through his exhaustion, and I smile through mine. We are so utterly drunk on pleasure, and it is unquestionably the best feeling in the world. "God, woman, it's never been like this. Never so . . . everything." His face falls into my neck, his breath hot on my skin.

I can feel all the emotion and feelings in his words. Because I feel the same. I've never been an insecure lover, and Josh hasn't really changed that. But now I'm giving him my all, I can't help appreciating his words all the more. I reach for his head and play with his hair. "Thank you for coming to find me tonight."

Lifting from my neck, he smiles, and it is one of my favorite Josh smiles. Genuine. Heartfelt. But it drops a little, and he spends a few quiet moments thinking. "I love you so much, Adeline. I don't know what to do with it all."

I feel myself fold a little, hating his uncertainty, but before I can voice my thoughts, he goes on, blinking his drowsy eyes open. "I just want to take you away from this madness, baby. I want to kiss the ground you walk on for the rest of my life. I want to look at you every day and know that you are mine. Kiss you. Make love to you. Fuck you. Spank you."

"Bring it on," I say clearly, ready for everything he has to throw at me. *Everything*. Belts and all.

On a shake of his beautiful head, he smiles a shy smile and drops to my chest, crowding me completely. But I don't feel suffocated. I don't feel his weight. I feel the freest and lightest I ever have in my entire life. "We need to talk," he breathes.

And just like that, my moment is stained. "Do we have to? Can't you just put me on your private jet and fly me out of the country? Hide me in your mansion in Beverly Hills and worship me day and

night? Because that will suit me, just so you know."

He chuckles. "I would love nothing more. But I also don't want to be on the World's Most Wanted list for kidnapping the Princess of England."

"I won't tell anyone."

"Because you won't be missed?" He laughs and lands me with a chaste kiss, rolling over to his back beside me. I give him roughly two seconds' peace before I crawl up his body, placing myself on his chest. My boobs squish into his pecs and his arms circle my shoulders. "I shouldn't be missed," I say matter-of-factly. "I serve no purpose to this country."

"You are a national treasure, Adeline." Josh smiles, pushing some hair from my face.

"It isn't fair. I want you. You want me. It should be that simple."

"Except it's not."

My lips twist in displeasure. "So what are we going to do?"

"I don't know." He looks defeated all of a sudden. It doesn't suit him—my cocky Hollywood troublemaker.

"You've changed your tune. He who isn't one for playing by the rules," I tease.

"Yeah, well, I feel like I have a lot more to lose now." He moves quickly, flipping me to my back and swathing me, arms pinned on the pillow above my head. "My tactics have changed."

"How so?"

"I plan on wooing your father when he takes me shooting tomorrow."

I can't help it. I laugh, because that is, quite possibly—no, definitely—the funniest thing I have ever heard. "Josh, be real. The King might seem all jolly and friendly, but the moment he gets a whiff of your intentions, I would advise you to be far, *far* away from his shotgun."

"He won't shoot me. And maybe it's a good thing if he does—in the leg or something. He'll be locked up. Problem solved."

"That's an amazing idea." I dazzle him with an excited smile, and quickly let it drop like a rock. "Except the King is the only person in the land immune from prosecution."

His eyes widen. "He is?"

"It's an ancient law. But my point is, he'll get away with it."

"Okay, smart-ass, what do you suggest?"

I land a kiss on his lips and push him back, hopping off the bed and heading for the bathroom. "I already told you." I stop at the door and turn, cocking my eyebrow. "Smuggle me out of the country."

On a roll of his eyes, he props himself up on his elbows. "Sensible ideas, please."

"It's more sensible than yours." I leave Josh with a moody face and head for the toilet. "At least we'll both still be alive," I sit down, smiling when I notice that I didn't even bother to close the door. He's been a spectator while I have relieved myself before, because that was the natural progression of our relationship, apparently. And now he loves me. And I love him.

Josh appears in the doorway, his naked body propped against the frame by his shoulder. I don't get stage fright. I don't even blush. It's liberating. "You're being dramatic," he tells me. "This is the twenty-first century, for Christ's sake. You should be able to date who you please."

His blatant irritation is endearing. I finish up and wash my hands, observing his sulky form in the mirror. He looks like a petulant child. Sounds like one, too. "Like it or not, I require permission to date. If I ever want to marry, I would need the King's permission for that, too." I dry my hands, smiling at his widening eyes.

"Who said anything about marriage?"

I give him a tired look. "I was giving you an idea of how complex and silly protocol is when it comes to dating a royal."

"It's ridiculous."

"I agree."

"So no matter how much your father likes me, it'll be a no?"

I wander over and reach up on my tippy-toes to kiss his bristly chin. My move has him relinquishing the support of the doorframe in favor of me. I look at him, my head tilted far back. "Unless you harbor a secret connection to some blue-blooded, aristocratic family somewhere in Europe, then it's a no."

"That sucks."

"That's my life." I smile sadly at his glum expression, seeing the gravity of this, of *us*, coming to rest on his broad shoulders, forcing them down a fraction. "They'll do everything in their power to rid you from my life."

"And I'll do everything to keep you. I told you, I won't lose."

His gallant gesture is warming. "Neither will I. I know what being with you will cost me, and I'm fine with that. Relieved, actually."

"Your place in succession?"

"And possibly my home. And my family, and definitely my allowances."

"All of it?" He looks horrified, and in this moment I get a pang of worry, stepping back out of his arms. What if my title and position are what's appealing for Josh? What if this is all a big publicity stunt to him? I cock my head, thinking carefully, trying to reason with my runaway thoughts. That's utterly preposterous. He doesn't need the fame, nor does he need my money. Josh's head tilts to the side too, his eyes examining me. "Don't you dare think what I think you're thinking," he says shortly, recoiling a little, offended.

"I wasn't thinking," I lie, guilt quickly eating me up inside. His palm meets my chest and walks me backward until I'm pinned to a wall, his face up close to mine, pure disgust invading it. "I could have nothing left," I murmur, putting it out there. "No title, no money, nothing."

"You will have *me*." His face is so stern, but the words are soft and pleading, and I go lax against the wall.

"I need you to know—" His mouth meeting mine swallows my words and straightens out my tangled mind.

"I know." Josh lifts me from my feet and carries me to the bedroom, placing me on my feet at the end of the bed. "Don't ever question what I want out of this. I want you. Nothing else. Nothing more. Just you."

His phone rings from the side of the bed, and we both turn to face the sound. Josh frowns and moves us toward the bedside, and he solidifies against me when he notes who is calling.

"What?" I question, not liking his wariness. "Who is it?"

"My publicist." He breaks away from me and starts walking across the room, his back to me. "Yeah?" Stopping by the window, I see his muscles roll in waves of aggravation. "What? For fuck's sake. I'll call you back." He hangs up and starts scrolling through his phone, yet I don't ask what has got him agitated. He looks too focused. Too annoyed. So I remain where I am, worrying my lip through my teeth nervously. His attention is unwavering on his screen, and he eventually groans. And I lose my ability to keep quiet.

"What is it?" I ask, nervous, though I still don't know why.

He turns and lifts his phone with a lazy hand, his lips straight. "The Internet has exploded. The one good thing is that no one knows it's you under the hoodie."

I approach him, my eyes set on the screen of his phone, where there is a picture of Josh ushering a bundle into the hotel. Me. "Oh."

"There's a video on YouTube gone viral, too." He swipes his screen, and I suddenly hear Josh yelling at the press to back off. He sighs. "*Who is under that hoodie?* It's the most asked question on the Internet. Apparently, the crowds outside have doubled and the hotel staff are being overrun with calls."

"Oh," I say again, hating the tightness in his jaw.

"We should start thinking about how we're going to get you out of here."

For the first time since I stowed away in Damon's car, I think about the fact that I haven't once considered how I will get back in. "Oh."

"Have you lost the ability to string a sentence together?"

"I can't get back into the palace."

"What?"

I turn and start pacing the room, kicking myself. I was so desperate to escape, I didn't give a moment's thought to getting back in. "I will never get back in without being seen and prompting an investigation as to where I have been and how I managed to get there."

"We'll call Damon," Josh says, all matter-of-factly, like it's problem solved.

"Are you insane?" I gasp, swinging around to face him. "He will string me up alive."

"What else do you suggest? A zip wire from a nearby building? Parachuting in? Or maybe we can dig a tunnel from here." He clasps his chin, contemplating his outlandish ideas as he hums. He's mocking me, and I don't appreciate it. Had I not been blindsided by him, maybe my brain would have been functioning at its fullest when I hatched my escape plan.

Scowling at him, I stomp my way to the bed and drop my arse on the side, flinching when my skin makes contact with the soft sheets. "I hate this." I whine, my fingers fiddling in my lap, resentment building. "When I leave here, I'll leave with my head held high. Let the world see. Let my family see. They can't stop me from being with you."

"Slow down," Josh orders, coming to me and kneeling at my feet, taking my fidgeting hands. "You can't let them find out like that. It won't help."

"Nothing will help. Don't you see?"

"Won't you let me go shooting with your father? Get a feel for how the land lies?"

"The land?" I laugh under my breath. "It will lie under your back when the King orders you dead."

"So dramatic."

"So realistic, Josh."

His phone rings again, and this time he puts it on speakerphone. "Did you see?" a lady asks when he answers.

"Yeah, I saw."

"So who was under that hoodie, Josh? And if you say the Princess of fucking England, I might hunt you down and take you out myself before the royals can get to you."

Josh lips form a perfectly straight line. "Say hello to Adeline, Tammy."

She gasps, a gasp full of horror. "Your Highness."

"Hello." I smile, though it is tinged with despair.

"We have a situation." Josh presses forward.

Tammy scoffs, "You don't say."

"I don't need your jokes, Tammy. I need your help."

"What's the problem?" She all but sighs.

"We need to get Adeline out of here, but the place is heaving with press and fans."

"You need a decoy."

"Something like that." Josh rises to his feet and walks away from me. "What can you do?"

"Give me an hour. I'll call you back."

"Thanks, Tammy."

"Don't mention it." She hangs up and Josh's shoulders rise, a sign of his deep inhale. Then he turns to me, and I can tell by the expression on his face that I am not going to like what he says next. "What's Damon's number?"

I take in air like it could be my last opportunity. "No." I shake my head furiously, flat refusing what he is suggesting.

"Adeline, our options are pretty limited. Tammy can distract the mob, but we hit a brick wall when it comes to the palace gates. We have no choice."

Dread fills me. "But he's having a romantic night in with his wife," I explain, my words coming fast and panicked. "They're

having steak and sex."

Josh's forehead bunches as he pulls his boxers up his legs. "Steak and sex?"

"Yes."

His sweats follow his boxers, his body slowly being covered before my eyes. If I could focus, I'd mourn the loss. But I am too wound up, all for the wrong reasons. "Then let's hope he fucks fast and eats faster."

"Josh!"

"What do you want me to do, Adeline?" He shows the ceiling his palms, and I flop back onto the bed, exasperated and worried. "Give me his number."

"I don't know his number off the top of my head." I lift a limp hand and point to my pile of belongings. "My phone is in my pocket. But it's broken."

"The PIN?"

I look up. "It's working?"

"The screen's fucked. Tell me the PIN."

"Eight-five-nine-three-one-zero-two-two."

He balks at me. It's rather adorable. "What the fuck?"

"Palace security," I grumble, dropping my eyes and watching him blindly navigate the touch screen.

"Bingo." He raises the phone to his ear, and I cringe at the conversation that's about to happen, wishing my phone dead.

"Damon?" Josh says, coming to sit beside my reclined body on the bed. "Yes, Josh Jameson. We have a situation." He flicks his eyes to me, and I scowl. I'm a situation. "You do?" Josh's eyes take on an edge of sympathy. For me. "Bates called you," he says slowly, keeping me abreast of the conversation. I wish he wouldn't. I don't want to know how fuming mad Damon is. "You're on your way," he says quietly, and I cringe, imagining Damon's reaction when Bates put that call in. "Yes, in my suite at The Dorchester." Josh goes on, telling Damon his new room number. "I'll let her explain herself

when you get here." My leg swings of its own volition, booting Josh in the thigh. He smirks at my pursed lips. "There's a circus outside the hotel. We can create a decoy, but we need you to get her back into Kellington." Pause. "Yes. Thanks, bud." Josh chucks my phone on the bed.

"How did he sound?" I don't know why I'm asking.

"Pissed off," Josh confirms bluntly, and I groan, covering my eyes with my palms.

"I'm in so much trouble." The thought of Damon being cross with me isn't thrilling. I hate that I've disappointed him. It's ironic. I couldn't care less about my father or his aides, but Damon is different. I've let him down, and I know I have risked his job.

My hands are suddenly gone from my face, and Josh is suspended over me, grinning. "But I'm worth it, right?"

"I don't know. Are you?"

His sparkly eyes narrow. "You tell me." His hand glides over my hip and under my bum, gripping hard. I jump in his hold, my sore bottom burning, and he laughs. "That's a yes, then." A hard kiss is placed on my mouth. "Come on, time to get dressed and face the music."

18

THE TIME AND effort that went into getting me out of The Dorchester was both brilliant and ridiculous. Poor Josh was forced to endure the crowds, just to keep their attention off the staff entrance so I could escape. Damon's eyes were like steel—hard and formidable. I shied away every time I caught his stare from leaving the suite, to getting back to Kellington. He didn't utter a word for the entire journey, and the silence was agony, full of silent disapproval and fury. I must have shrunk a whole foot in height in the space of an hour, feeling small and inconvenient.

It's the morning after the night before, and I'm sitting at the breakfast table at Kellington. My scrambled eggs haven't been touched, and my eyes haven't moved from the picture dominating the front page of a newspaper. All I can see are my Uggs and my two slim legs sprouting from the tops. Josh's face is perfectly clear, though, and it is etched with infuriation.

"Tell me it isn't you." Eddie's voice startles me, and I quickly flip the newspaper over, like there isn't another million in print available.

"What isn't me?" I force-feed myself some eggs, trying to appear as casual as possible.

Eddie's hand appears and returns the paper upright, his finger landing on the Ugg boots. "You have these, right?"

"As do a million other women in Britain."

"But these ones are yours, yes?"

I drop my fork and look him square in the eye. "If you must know, yes."

Eddie rounds the table, his chest expanding, ready to say some more, but he pulls back his words and sits down when Kim wanders in, her face stony. "New phone," she says, turning on her heels and walking out.

"Thank you," I call, wincing a little at her shortness. She knows she's being kept in the dark, and she doesn't like it.

"Did you feel *free* while you were being hustled through that chaos?" Eddie asks seriously once Kim has gone. "And to think they don't know your identity. Imagine the fuss if they ever find out."

"When," I say curtly. "*When* they find out." Resting my napkin on the table, I stand from my chair, giving up on trying to put something in my tummy, and also giving up on trying to reason with my brother. "Good day to you, Edward." I stroll away, chin held high.

"*When* they find out? So you're going to tell the King?"

"I am." I don't let my steps falter, and I don't let Eddie's surprised tone affect me, either. I'm not enduring the stress of last night again, and I don't mean the hordes of people camping outside the hotel, but more the logistics of getting to the hotel. I'm a grown woman, for pity's sake, and I had to skulk around London like a teenager who had snuck out while her parents were sleeping, just to see her boyfriend. "Don't try to talk me out of it." Will he try to talk me out of it?

"Adeline." Eddie's up and coming after me, his steps hard on the floor.

"I said you shouldn't try to talk me out of it." I turn when I make it into the foyer, aware of the people around us, including Felix, Jenny, and Kim, who all look up from their phones where they're

gathered by the door.

Eddie wisely notes their presence and pulls me to the side, huddling over me. "I don't want to fight with you," he says quietly.

"I don't want to fight with you, either."

"Then listen to what I have to say."

I lean back, cautious. "I've already listened."

"It's impossible. You and him, it can't work."

It takes all my strength and more not to retaliate at his continued efforts to put me off my quest. I cannot, however, halt the tightening of my jaw. "I love him." I practically grind the words out, and Eddie recoils. "Yes, you heard me. I love him. Say what you will, Edward, but it will be a waste of your breath. If I don't get the King's blessing, then I'm willing to walk away from all of this." I motion to the luxury palace interior that surrounds us, the bars of my jail.

"You don't mean that."

"I wholeheartedly mean it." I take in air, gathering strength. "My life has been suppressed for thirty years, and I'm done with it. I'm done with *them*. Done with *this*." I throw my arms up into the air heavily.

"With me?"

My mouth snaps shut, my eyes widening. "Never you." I couldn't be without Eddie. The idea alone hurts my chest.

"And Mother?"

"What?"

"You're talking like it's so simple for you to walk away, but you're forgetting it isn't only the Monarchy you'll be walking away from. Not just the King, but your father. Not just the Queen Consort, but your mother. You're willing to sacrifice your family, a family who loves you, for him? A man you've known a matter of weeks?"

"Our parents' love is conditional," I murmur quietly, as if trying to convince myself of that. "As long as I do as I am told, they are happy. Everyone is happy. Except me. And I wouldn't be walking away just for him. I would be walking away for me, too."

"I don't want you to make a mistake. I don't want you to ostracize yourself."

"And I don't want to drown in this world any longer." I reach up on my toes and kiss his cheek. "I love you." I don't get the chance to walk away, because Eddie takes me in a hug, and though I'm surprised, I'm more relieved. He might not agree, but he will never disown me. I wish I was as confident in my parents.

"I love you, too." Eddie sighs. "I'll try not to shoot him while we're hunting today."

"Wait, what?" I'm out of his arms quicker than a racehorse out of the stalls. "You're going shooting?"

His grin is wicked, and though I really should not be appreciating his sudden easy persona, I'm grateful my brother, as I know and love him, is back. "I'm heading to Claringdon now. We're meeting at the paddocks before we head out." He breezes off, as if he didn't just deliver that bombshell.

I watch him go, my legs stuck in position while my brain tries to comprehend this news, as well as talking my legs into moving. Josh never mentioned where they were meeting. He's at the palace? "Eddie, wait." I rush after him, my mind whizzing. "Josh will be there? At Claringdon?"

Stopping on the steps, he faffs with his collar and then flips a flat cap on his head. "I assume so."

"I'm coming." I backtrack to the foyer where Olive is waiting with my bag and coat, ever the amazing mind reader that she is. "Thank you." I shower her with gratitude as she helps me into my coat, taking off down the steps as I fasten the buttons. Eddie's eyes are alarmed as I fly past him, jumping in the back of the car, offering a small smile to Damon as I land. He is still partially scowling. I deserve it. And more. I could never find what I have with Damon with any other bodyguard, and I truly hope I've not damaged that. I so regret deceiving him, but now is not the time to say sorry, not with an audience. I hope he sees the remorse in my pleading eyes.

Eddie approaches the car and dips down, getting me in his sights. "Get out."

I slam my bag on my lap and focus my attention forward, adamant in my stance. "No."

His exhale is dramatic and long as he falls into the seat. "Don't you think the King will consider it strange that his wayward daughter is *choosing* to visit the palace without a summons?"

"I'm going to have breakfast with Mother." I nod to myself, giving my back a mental pat for being so creative.

"You just had breakfast."

"No, I didn't," I reply coolly, going into my bag for my phone. There's a message from Josh, and I smile like a crazy woman when I open it to find that he has sent me a selfie, only a small white towel wrapped around his trim hips.

"Are you serious?" Eddie snatches my phone from my hand and studies the picture with a sickened expression. I try to grab it back, but with his strength versus mine, it is completely pointless. "*You showed me yours*," he says, reading the text with the picture.

"Stop!" I grapple for his hands, but he holds the phone higher while holding me back with his spare hand. "*So I'll show you mine*? Urghhhhh."

"Eddie, give it back."

"You sent him a picture of your boobs?"

"No, I did not," I gasp, disgusted by his suggestion, swiping my phone from his grip. "We were playing, that's all."

"With fire, Adeline."

I sniff and return to my phone, my smile back, wishing I could blow this image up and paper my suite with it. "There is nothing X-rated about this picture."

"Tell the King that when it falls into the wrong hands." As Eddie goes to close the door, Kim rushes down the stairs, armed with her phone.

"Oh, now what?" I grumble.

"You've gone off schedule," Eddie mutters.

"Ma'am, you have a royal engagement with the founders of Trax. As patron of the charity, I strongly advise you not to cancel."

Bloody hell. I forgot about that. Not surprising when my head is full of an American. "What time?"

"Two-thirty, ma'am. Jenny will be here at midday to help you prepare."

I'm cutting it fine, but Josh is at Claringdon, and I really, *really* want to see him. "I'll be here, Kim."

"Yes, ma'am." She nods—still terse with me—and makes her way back into Kellington.

Damon starts the car, and my stomach does that wonderful flippy-floppy thing it does when I know I'm about to see Josh. I know I won't be able to touch him. I'll hardly be able to talk to him, either. But I will get to *look* at him.

I'll also be offering advice on how to approach this hunting trip *and* my father. His plan is gallant, but we all know it is far-fetched. Yet there's hope inside of me that he can work his magic.

19

I DON'T THINK I have ever been so keen to get inside Claringdon Palace. I'm out of the car as soon as it comes to a halt, and up the steps just as fast. Sid looks in a state of shock when he sees me racing toward him, his mind no doubt searching for the memo that advised him of my visit. "Morning, Sid." I breeze past him and let one of the footmen relieve me of my coat. "Where is the Queen?"

"In the dining room, ma'am."

I'm off across the vast entrance hall before Eddie makes it through the door, my senses alert, keeping a lookout for Josh. As I enter the dining room, Mother is getting up from her chair, delicately patting the corners of her mouth with her luxury napkin. "Adeline," she says softly, unquestionable surprise on her pretty face. "I wasn't aware of a visit."

"Does one need to schedule a visit to see her mother?" I ask in a blasé way that is extremely out of character. *Yes, one does.*

Grasping her hands in front of her, she regards me with a fond smile that is also laced with suspicion. The Queen Consort knows her daughter all too well, and she knows there must be an ulterior motive to me voluntarily visiting Claringdon. It's imperative I uphold

this casual façade. I smile brightly, and Mother's long, slender neck tilts on her head. "One should have called ahead. I'm afraid I'm due to leave the palace shortly to visit The Royal London Hospital." She approaches me and gives my cheek a tender rub. "Accompany me to my suite. Mary-Ann needs to tweak my hair, and I need to change into my outfit."

I return her soft smile and let her link arms with me, leading me on. "Your hair looks rather perfect already, Mother."

Her spare hand comes up to the elegant chignon and pats gently. "A few more pins won't hurt."

My eyes are watchful as we wander through the grand palace, voices coming from all directions, but none of them the smooth American accent I want to hear. When we make it to my parents' private quarters, I look through the huge double doors that lead to the King's sleeping area, which is a massive distance from the area where his wife lays her head. There is no bed sharing for the King and Queen Consort. *Oh no.* Yet another loveless marriage.

Mary-Ann, Mother's long-serving lady in waiting, is by the floor-length mirror, armed with pins and hairspray. I take a seat on the velvet chaise and gaze around the room, using a rare opportunity while I have been invited in here to remind myself of the splendor. High, ornate ceilings, lavish, oversized drapes framing the huge windows, four crystal chandeliers, all grand, but tiny in the massive space. "What do you think?" Mother interrupts me from my observing, pointing to a clothes stand where a two-piece suit hangs, the soft pink almost wishy-washy, the plain court shoes with a one-inch heel bland, but perfect for the Queen Consort.

"It's very nice," I say, feeling a pang of sorrow for my mother. She's a beautiful woman, and her figure at fifty-seven is to die for, not that anyone would know, since she's wrapped up tightly in these formal, stuffy skirt suits every day of her royal life. I would love to cast her stylist aside and let Jenny loose on her. The King wouldn't know whether the flutter of his heart was due to horror

or appreciation. Assuming the King's heart still beats for his queen.

"I think so, too," Mother says, standing as still as a statue while she's groomed. She doesn't think so at all. She tells herself she loves the style forced on her because it is easy. Because it is her duty. When the King met the beautiful Spanish princess in 1977, she probably wasn't aware just how subdued her life would become. She was young and vivacious. She was a fashion icon, a role that died with my grandfather's death and when my father became King. She's like a Barbie doll now. Lifeless. Limited to what her owner demands of her. I'm glad I'll never be in the same boat.

I sit where I am, my eyes constantly flicking to the doors, wracking my brain for a reason to excuse myself, so I can go on a hunt around the palace to find what I really came here for.

"You look distracted, Adeline," Mother says quietly.

"Oh, not at all." I wave her observation off, and my phone starts ringing from my bag. When Matilda's name glows at me, I smile to myself, holding up my mobile so Mother can see. "It's Matilda. Please, excuse me." I'm up and out of there quickly, answering as soon as I am far enough away not to be heard. "Perfect timing," I say in greeting, crossing the huge landing.

"It's you, isn't it? In those pictures spattered in every newspaper."

"It's me," I confirm quietly.

"Christ, Adeline. Do you have a death wish? Where are you?"

"At Claringdon."

"Whatever for? Oh my, does the King know?"

"Not just yet. But enough about me for now." I make it to the window at the far end of the landing and gaze out onto the grounds, seeing a dozen gardeners preening the perfect flowerbeds. "Tell me what happened with the Argentine."

Her soft giggle fills me with all kinds of hope. "We're going to have dinner."

"Oh gosh." My grin is epic. "And your parents, they approve?"

"Why, of course. He descends from Spanish royalty, don't you know?"

"Oh, I know." The intermingling of royal families throughout Europe upsets me greatly. "So do I need to buy a hat?"

Matilda laughs, loud and high, though I sense nerves, too. "Hold your horses, dear cousin."

"I'm very excited for you."

"Me too," she practically squeals. "But I am terrified I'm going to make a complete hash of our date. I get so nervous around him."

"Just be cool. Almost aloof. Make him work hard for your affection." I'm a hypocrite of the worst kind. I dropped to my knees for Josh Jameson in a heartbeat. Not too cool at all. Although I wasn't wanting his affection then. Just his palm on my flesh. My, how things have changed. I smile to myself, warming up inside. "I have to go," I say, glancing around the landing, my eyes homing in on the huge double doors that mark the entrance to the King's office. "I'll call you."

"Okay." Matilda hangs up, and I chew the corner of my mobile, weighing up the chances of being reprimanded for visiting my father's office without an escort or invitation. Is Josh in there? Are they smoking cigars while discussing the plan for their hunting trip? Or is Josh dead already? That thought alone kicks my feet into action, and I head toward my father's private office. I'll think of an excuse for being here. Something believable. Something that won't have the King suspicious. I still don't know what that excuse is as I lift my hand to rap the door, and I don't get a chance to debate it further. His loud voice is easily heard through the door, stalling my balled fist midway through the air.

"I don't care how you do it, just get rid of those letters." The King sounds furious, and I immediately feel terribly sorry for the person in the line of fire. Davenport, no doubt. I'm also wondering with annoying curiosity what letters he is speaking of, my frown deep. "This is unacceptable," my father goes on. "There will be grave consequences should they make it into the cold light of day, I assure you. The Queen Consort will not be thankful. It's been over thirty years. It's history. And while we're discussing problems, get

rid of that blasted banker before I do it myself."

My breath hitches, my steps reversing. Oh, darn. I realize his tirade isn't solely surrounding me, but that last demand has me rethinking my bright idea of a surprise visit. It also confirms that Josh isn't puffing on cigars with him.

"Eavesdropping again, Your Highness?"

I swing around and come chest to chest with Davenport, though he doesn't move away, his stern face glaring at me. "I was doing no such thing," I argue, all in a fluster.

His eyes are tired as he reaches past me, gently knocking the door before entering. My father slams down the phone and Davenport frowns, taking in the angry vibes bouncing around the grand office. "Your Majesty?" he questions tentatively.

My father shoots Davenport down with a scowl of epic proportions, and for the first time in my life, I see the King's private secretary's tall frame shrink somewhat. "Fine," Father barks, sounding less than fine. I look out the corner of my eye to Davenport, who, in turn, is peeking at me. I can see it in his stony eyes. He's wondering what I heard. He's wondering who my father was talking to and what was said on the phone. He can wonder.

"Must dash," I squeak, leaving behind the unbearable awkwardness, glancing over my shoulder as I go.

"The hunting party awaits, sir," Davenport says to the King. His many years of service forbids him from entering without the required invitation.

"I will be down soon."

"Sir." Davenport closes the door, and I return my attention forward, picking up my pace before the major can stop me and wring me for information.

As I'm taking the stairs, I see David Sampson being escorted up them, his body clad in attire suitable only for a hunting trip. My steps falter, surprised to see him. "David, you're back." I kick myself as soon as I have voiced my thoughts.

"Your Highness." He comes to a stop beside me on the stairs, his smile wide. "A few days' getaway was just what I needed."

"That's what I told Haydon," I say on a smile. "It must have been a terrible shock, losing your father."

His hands slip into the pockets of his brown trousers, his eyes definitely glazed. "A terrible shock."

"How is Sabina?"

"Okay. The funeral is expected to be held late next week."

"Of course, I'll be there to pay my respects."

"Very kind of you, ma'am. I know Haydon will appreciate the support."

I hide my flinch and nod my head mildly, looking past him when Davenport appears at the top of the stairs. This flinch, I cannot hide.

"Ah, Davenport, how wonderful to see you, old chap," David gushes, starting back up the stairs. "Will you be joining us this morning?"

Davenport's expression doesn't change from the usual straight-faced one. "I will be accompanying the King, yes."

"Very good." David gives him a firm slap on the shoulder, jolting the major's usually steady frame. Although his expression doesn't crack. "The King is in his office?"

"He doesn't wish to be disturbed," Davenport says flatly, his eyes casting over to me questioning.

I quickly glance away, avoiding his curious stare like the plague. But in avoiding Davenport, I find Sir Don. Oh God, they're all out in force today.

"Ah, Sir Don," David says. "Alfred doesn't wish to be disturbed."

"Your Highness," Sir Don grunts as he passes, being polite and rude all at once.

"I suggest we wait for His Majesty at the paddocks," Davenport calls to his back. "The Land Rovers are ready along with the other members of the party."

"The King wishes to see me." Sir Don doesn't look back, and I

cast a look to Davenport, who looks equally surprised. If the King summons someone, it is Davenport who delivers the summons. But not now. Was it Sir Don on the end of my father's tirade? "Sampson, you as well," Sir Don barks, getting David's feet moving quickly.

David's smile is wide, almost over exaggerated. He looks way too happy for a man who recently lost his father. And why isn't Davenport going? What's going on?

I don't ponder my questions for too long. "Enjoy your day," I say, departing quickly. I don't want to think about why they've been summoned.

The paddocks. Everyone is waiting at the paddocks. I hurry my steps, hoping to make it there before Davenport, even if only to say a quick hello to Josh. And maybe to tell him how sorry I am that he has to spend all day with my father and his army. And not just my father, but my *angry* father.

I take a shortcut and scurry down the pathway at the rear of the estate, passing gardener after gardener, all armed with tiny clippers, primping the perfect box plants that do not need primping.

When I make it to the paddocks, I hear roars of laughter. I spot Senator Jameson, but not Josh. I text him to ask where he is. Perhaps he's jumped ship, deciding that no woman is worth enduring this hardship for. Then I get his response and cast that thought aside.

Putting on my bulletproof vest.

I roll my eyes, but seriously wonder if that is a sensible idea.

I'm at the paddocks and you are not here.

I'm taking a leak.

I laugh to myself, my fingers working fast across the screen of my phone.

Nice. Which loo are you in?

His reply is quick.

Loo? What the fuck is a loo?

I snort unattractively at my phone.

A toilet!

Oh. Just inside the blue door off the small courtyard. I'm alone ;-)

He's taking a *leak*. He's winking at me via text message. "So uncouth," I say around a huge grin, heading for that blue door. I don't get a chance to knock on the wood. The door opens, Josh seizes my wrist, and I am yanked into the bathroom on a startled yelp.

"What took you so long?" he asks before attacking my mouth, not giving me a chance to answer him. And I'm in heaven again. Pure, blissful, beautiful heaven. His tongue is firm but slow, his hands gentle but possessive, as they grip my hair. His body hard, but melding perfectly into mine. He growls, noises that can't be mistaken for anything less than animalistic. We are lost in each other, in the passion, in the chemistry that sizzles so wildly between us. "I'm locked and loaded in more ways than one now." His mumbled words are delivered around his kiss, his hips rolling into my tummy. A wonderful beat drops to between my legs, my veins hot in an instant.

"Aren't you just?" I reach down to his groin and feel his condition, hard and ready. "We should make use of this."

"Like it was ever up for debate." I'm pushed against the door, his hand creeping around the back of my knee and pulling my thigh up to his hip. My dress is around my waist in the blink of an eye, my knickers to the side soon after. My breathing becomes pants, and though I know this is so very risky, there is nothing I can do to stop it. Neither do I want to.

"Hurry," I demand, helping him with the fly of his trousers. My order is fueled only by my desperation for him. *Always desperate.* My hand gets a dash of contact with his arousal, the tip with pre-cum skimming my skin easily.

"Fuckin' clothes," Josh moans, leveling up and sinking into me on one long, smooth thrust.

My breath is gone. My mind is gone. My damn heart is gone. I swallow, my head limp, my body soft against him as my walls mold around the perfection of him. "Can it get any better?" I whisper, held tightly to his body while he breathes into my increasingly sweaty neck, holding still and firm. The feelings Josh evokes in me are mind-twisting. How alive I feel when I'm with him is beyond comprehension. It's crazy how completely and utterly infatuated by him I am. I don't think I've ever felt like I belong, most certainly not in the family. But in Josh's arms, feeling his heartbeats merge with mine, I'm home.

"I wouldn't think so." He kisses my neck, biting between each peck. "But then I do this"—he swivels his hips and grinds deeply—"and it just gets better." Stars jump into my vision, my hands grappling at his back for support.

A groan rumbles up from the deepest part of me, and I'm forced to push my face into his neck to muffle it. Good Lord, where's that pink hanky of his? Meticulous strokes are backed up with expert grinds. His caressing hands are supported by sporadic firm squeezes of my flesh. He works into me at a leisurely, yet constant pace, in no rush to get me to my tipping point, which comes faster than I'd like.

"You're there?" he whispers, and I nod. "Me, too. Kiss me, Your Highness."

Those words, said by Josh, in that gravelly tone and accent, toss me over the edge, and I free-fall through my climax, moaning into his mouth, barely able to maintain our kiss.

I just register the quickening of his tempo, going from easy, smooth strokes, to rapid, ferocious hits, before his body solidifies around me, and a broken, strained sigh pours into my mouth. Then the warmth of his seed fills me, his flesh rolling against my internal walls, as he lets the pleasure take over. The combination of our shaking forces me to grip him harder, our lips touching but

not kissing. "Once again, Princess Adeline, you have bewitched the shit out of me." Biting my bottom lip gently, he pulls back a fraction to find my face. "How do I look?"

"Sweaty." I smile, taking in the glorious mess of his hair. "And like you just screwed someone against a door."

My nose is nipped playfully. "Is it wrong that I don't care?"

"Probably."

"Well, I don't. But I will pretend to care, if only to save my reputation with the King."

I scoff. "I wouldn't waste your time."

"Are you kidding? When I'm done with him, he'll be booking Westminster for our wedding and arranging my bachelor party. No one is immune to my charm." His smirk is conceited and cocky. And gorgeous.

"Who said anything about marriage?"

"I'm speaking hypothetically."

"Your American brain is deluded."

"You wait and see. Ready?" He holds me by the tops of my arms as he slips out of me, both of us wincing a little. Like a gentleman, he grabs some toilet tissue and wipes me up, all the while smiling, before I work to straighten myself out as Josh fastens his zipper.

"Anyway, deluded or not, you should know the King is *not* in a very good mood this morning." Brushing my hair off my face, I continue when Josh gives me a questioning expression. "I heard him shouting on the phone. To Sir Don, I think."

"What about?"

There's only one part of the rant I heard that I am prepared to share. Josh definitely does not need to know about the banker. "Some letters he wants rid of. I don't know, to be honest. All I know is he wasn't very happy about it and Sir Don and David were summoned."

"Are you saying I have my work cut out for me?"

I laugh, thoroughly amused. Has he not been hearing what

I've been saying to him? "Baby, your work isn't cut out for you. It's impossible. Why won't you listen to me?"

"Because you're a pessimist. What is it with you British? Always so reserved and negative."

"Excuse me?" I'm about to have my say on that little matter, by maybe pointing out that his American arse is bolshie and cocky, but a knock on the wood brings my rant to a stop before I've drawn breath. My eyes go like saucers—panicked, worried saucers.

"Someone in there?" David calls, knocking the door again.

"Yeah." Josh looks at me, a little alarmed. "I might be a while." He physically cringes, as do I.

"Ah, the American. Come on, old chap. We're ready to tally-ho." David's voice, all jovial, makes me frown. Why is he so bloody happy? "I'll use the other lavatory."

"Tally-ho?" Josh whispers, his eye-roll spectacular. "What a jerk."

I snigger, covering my mouth to stifle it.

"Did you say something, old boy?" David asks, seeming to be directly behind the wood that I'm leaning against, mere millimeters away.

"No, no." Josh reaches back and flushes the chain. "Just coming, *old chap*." His attempt at a British accent is all the more condescending because it is utterly rubbish.

"Righto. See you in a jiffy."

"Yar, yar." Josh slaps his palm onto his forehead, exasperated, as the sounds of David's steps fade into the distance. He gives me tired eyes. "I *will* win you, if only to save you from that ass-clown and his spawn."

"Have fun today," I chirp, smiling sweetly. I'm eyed with sullenness. It makes me chuckle. "You're regretting this, aren't you?"

"Not at all. I got to fuck you against that door. Death by gunshot is the only thing that'd make me regret today."

"Don't put it past him," I mutter, reaching forward and straightening his collar before popping a light kiss on his parted lips. "I'll

wait until the coast is clear."

Josh backs out, smiling all the way, until the door comes between us and I'm alone. Nothing could wipe the smile from my face.

20

AT JUST PAST four, after spending nearly two hours listening to the charity's CEO tell me all about their fundraising efforts for the remainder of the year and how I can help, I leave the headquarters of Trax. Honestly, I'm exhausted when I drop into the back seat of my car. The effort it has taken to focus on the words being spoken to me instead of how Josh has got on today has been a draining challenge. Damon still hasn't spoken to me beyond anything formal, and while I was bothered earlier, I am far too tired to care now.

As he pulls away from the building, I rest my head on the window, thinking about having a long, hot bath and a relaxing evening. "Back to the palace, ma'am," Damon says, though it isn't a question. And something tells me that he's not referring to Kellington.

I leave my head where it is, but move my eyes to look in the rearview mirror. "Kellington Palace? Yes."

"No," he replies, flat and final, prompting me to find the will to lift my head from the glass.

"Damon?"

"You have been summoned, ma'am." He doesn't even look at me, as if he's avoiding the worry he knows I'll feel.

"What for? I was only there this morning." No sooner has my question passed my lips, I start answering it myself. Oh no. Has Josh said something silly? Has he told the King? Is he *alive*? The stream of questions refuse to stop, and in a flat-out panic, I retrieve my phone and dial Josh. There's no answer.

"Who called you?" I ask Damon, moving forward so I'm wedged between the driver's and passenger seat.

"Davenport, ma'am."

That doesn't really tell me anything. "How did he sound?"

"Grouchy, ma'am." His attention remains on the road, his answers consistently clipped and to the point.

I sigh. "Damon, I realize I was stupid and I put your job in jeopardy, but—"

"My job is of no consequence to me. Your wellbeing, however, is. You are not beyond a dressing down. I don't care who you are. Do *not* do it again. Understand?"

I slowly move back, my proverbial tail between my legs. Well, that told me. "Understand," I murmur, smiling a little on the inside. He was worried. About *me*. Not about the King and his wrath, but me. "Josh went shooting today with the King."

"I am aware, ma'am."

"He's trying to get into his good books. Do you think he can?"

Damon's eyes jump to the mirror, and I can tell he's smiling. "I think he can," he says, surprising me and filling me with a little hope. His eyes return to the road, and he indicates, taking a right. "But as soon as His Majesty finds out that he has a motive, the good book will be snapped shut, probably with Josh's neck in it."

I slump in my seat. "Thanks for the vote of confidence."

"You're welcome."

There's a few beats of silence as I think about everything I heard earlier today. "I overheard the King on the telephone this morning." I try to sound nonchalant, casually toying with my phone, but I can sense Damon's cautious stare. "He mentioned the banker. I

can only assume he's still trying to reach me, as the King told the person he was speaking with to get rid of him."

"I believe he is a problem and does need to be dealt with."

I nod, accepting his reply, concluding that Damon is abreast on all things concerning the banker. "So one can assume that the King really doesn't know about Josh and me, because surely he'd be ordering that *problem* be dealt with, too. Plus, he took Josh shooting."

"One can assume."

"So who vandalized Josh's suite?"

"I believe that's a matter for Mr. Jameson's team, ma'am."

I hum my agreement, though it doesn't stop my mind racing or my fingers strumming the leather armrest. I believe my relationship with Josh is still under wraps. This is good, because, as Josh said, it will be much better for my father to hear it from me. To see how much I want this. To hear the pleading in my voice. Not that I expect it will make much difference, but I am so willing to try. How did Josh get on today? What has the banker been up to now to warrant such fury from the King? No, wait. He was angry before he mentioned Gerry Rush. *The letters.* What letters? Davenport wasn't in on the call, and I could tell he really wanted to be. Neither was he included in the meeting that followed. What if the King hasn't summoned me at all? What if Davenport is being sly, wanting information out of me about that call I overheard? And who the hell trashed Josh's hotel room? I groan, another wave of tiredness coming over me. "Can you put some music on, please?" I ask Damon, hoping to drown out the questions sending my mind into a spin.

"Radio, ma'am?"

"How about a bit of *Take That*?" It's out there before I can stop it, with no hope of being retracted. Damon's eyes, now horrified, find me again. I smile, awkward, and sink into my seat, pushing back my laughter. "Don't give up your day job."

"Didn't plan on it, ma'am. Unless you get me fired, of course."

"Then I guess I should ensure you're never fired." I snicker, he

scowls, and the car picks up speed, whisking me off to somewhere I really don't want to be.

WHY ISN'T HE *answering*? I'm asking myself over and over with each attempt to reach Josh. I need to know how his jolly outing with my father went today.

This time when I arrive at Claringdon, Sid doesn't regard me like a monster with four man-eating heads, because, of course, he is expecting me. He got the memo. But who sent the memo? My suspicions only mount when Davenport appears in the foyer. Since when does he deem my arrival at Claringdon worthy of his escort? He descends on me in long, even strides, his arms poker straight by his sides. "I'll escort Her Royal Highness, thank you, Sid," Davenport says, his voice, as always, leaving no room for argument.

"Sir." Sid wastes no time skulking off, leaving me at the mercy of the King's private secretary. I glare at him, my face low, my expression, I hope, telling him I know of his game. "After you." He gestures toward the stairs.

"No, please, after you." I smile sweetly, neither of us moving. It's a glaring deadlock. I'm not budging. No way.

"Adeline?" Mother's dulcet tone drifts between us, dissolving the tension a little. "Twice in one day? One will start to worry."

"*One* has been summoned," I purr, slowly dragging my hard stare off Davenport, but returning it the moment I catch a mild change in his persona. His always stiff posture seems to soften somewhat, and his cutting eyes grow nervous, fluttering between the Queen Consort and me.

"Whatever for this time?" Mother asks, ever exasperated, breaking my observing of Davenport.

"I guess I'll find out soon." I move toward her and link our arms, gently pulling her away from the listening ears of the major. She looks at me with questions in her tender eyes. "I heard Father

speaking earlier about something," I tell her. Her first reaction is her trained reaction: warning eyes on me, telling me that whatever I have heard, I shouldn't speak of it, no matter what it is. But I ignore her and press on. "He was very mad." I make sure I keep my voice low and quiet. "About some letters that he wants rid of."

Mother stops and turns into me, her warning eyes now questioning. But she doesn't question, just simply maintains her state of duty. "Adeline, you know it is not your place to pry into the King's affairs."

My teeth grind in natural frustration. Her reminder, although accurate, is laughable. No, it's not my place, I learned that from a very early age, yet it is perfectly okay for the King to pry into *my* affairs. And he does. All the flaming time. "He said it was history. Said it would be a disaster if the letters made it into the public domain, that *you* would be very displeased."

Her face is stoic, but there is something else there too, something I cannot quite read. And as infuriating as it is, I know I will get nothing from my mother *if* she knows something. And I have a feeling she does. "Like I said, it is not your place to pry in the King's affairs."

I close my eyes and pray for restraint. She knows something. When I mentioned *letters*, something changed in her. I admit defeat and swallow down my frustration, saying what I'm expected to say. "It's probably nothing."

"I expect so," she agrees, smiling gently, her eyes wandering past my shoulder. I turn to find what has captured her attention, seeing Davenport. He clears his throat and gestures to the stairs. "Yes, yes," I breathe, kissing mother's cheek. I'm halfway up, Davenport on my tail, when my phone rings. I run the rest of the way, leaving the King's private secretary knocked back by the gust of wind that my quick acceleration creates. "Josh," I hiss down the line, moving around the landing to gain some distance from Davenport. "I've been trying to call you."

"I know. I just came out of a meeting and picked up your calls. Everything okay?"

A meeting? He never mentioned a meeting. "Who were you meeting?"

"My publicist. You were right, I was wrong." He sounds a little despondent.

"What do you mean? What happened?"

"What happened? I spent the day with the King of England. *That's* what happened. Like I said, you were right and I was wrong. There's not a fuckin' chance in hell he's going to give us his blessing."

I flick my eyes across the landing, seeing Davenport waiting not so patiently for me at the top of the stairs, his foot tapping. "That bad?"

Josh laughs, but it is not a laugh of joy. It's sarcastic. "Well, I was forced to listen to His Majesty and that David Sampson dick giving me every gory detail of your relationship with Haydon. Fuckin' brilliant. Then I had the pleasure of listening to Haydon I'm-Perfect-For-Adeline Sampson reinforce it, with some added extras. Then I shot a few pretend birds and got an encore of all that torturous information. Did you know you will have two kids? One boy and one girl. The boy will come first, followed quickly by a cute little girl. He doesn't plan on giving you much of a break between the birth of your son and impregnating you again with a daughter." He huffs his displeasure, while my eyes get gradually wider, alarmed. "I swear to God, Adeline, I was so close to turning my gun on that asshole and shooting something with a fuckin' pulse. Pretend fuckin' birds. Who the fuck shoots pretend fuckin' birds?"

I bite my lip, trying to mentally choose my words carefully. I shouldn't be surprised by the onslaught of information, and I'm not, not really, but what I *am* is mad. So mad that they discuss my story like it is already written. "Marvelous day, then," I quip, at a loss for anything else to say. I hate this. My stomach is rolling with frustration and anger, knowing they've subjected Josh to that.

"I've just spoken to my PR team, here and in the States, and enlightened them on . . . well, on us."

"You have?" I say a bit too loudly, causing Davenport's eyebrow to rise, curiosity all over his face. I need to be careful.

"I have. We need to talk."

I hate the fact that my back naturally stiffens and my panic increases. Have they advised him to abandon all hope? Have they convinced him I'm not worth the hassle? "What about?" I push my question out past my diminishing breathing, closing my eyes and turning away from Davenport in an attempt to hide the devastation creeping onto my features.

"Adeline?" Josh say quietly, his voice a little shaky. My dread rockets.

"Yes?" *Please don't say it, please don't say it.*

"I love you."

"Oh, thank God." I place my hand on the window frame before me and sag into it.

"Are you okay?"

"Yes, it's just . . . I thought that . . . I was afraid . . ." I shake my head, trying to toss all that negativity aside. "Never mind."

"Don't even think it."

I half smile. "I'm sorry." My apology is weak but sincere. "So what was discussed?"

"Me and you. About sharing our relationship with the world. Tactics. Strategy. That kind of thing."

I'm in a relationship. It sounds so odd, but equally thrilling. "There's a strategy? Like a plan?"

"It's more preparations," he says, assuring me. I can't argue with that. Above everything, we need to be prepared, not only for the media frenzy, but for the backlash of the monarchy. "We'll talk about it later." Josh sounds determined, and I admire him for it. I think that perhaps spending all day with my kind of people, he's grasped the gravity of our situation. But he is taking the bull by the

horns, so to speak. Leading the way. It is a weight off my shoulders. I would take on my father on my own if I had to, but it makes the path ahead less daunting to know that Josh will be there to hold me up. "Where are you?" he asks.

"I'm at Claringdon. My father wants to see me."

"What about?" The shift in his tone, from level to cautious, is distinct.

"I don't know."

He scoffs. "Probably to restrain you so that jerk can get a ring on your finger."

"He's not a jerk." I feel the need to defend Haydon. He isn't to blame for this mess.

"Or," Josh goes on, his voice low, "it could be about a *banker*."

I still, staring at the summer house nestled under some willow branches in the garden below. "What?"

"Oh, didn't I mention that bit?" If I could see his face right now, it would be twisted in displeasure. "No?"

"No," I squeak. He knows fine well he didn't mention that part.

"Oh, yes. This Gerry Rush. He wants to see you. Or *still* wants to see you." He pauses for a moment while I cringe. "I overheard a hushed conversation between the King and his advisors. Why didn't you tell me about him?"

"I haven't asked about your previous ex-lovers," I retort indignantly, wondering if Gerry Rush is the reason I'm here. "What did you hear?"

"That you had an indiscretion. That he showed up at the polo match. He's stalking you."

"He is not stalking me."

"He *is* stalking you."

I don't argue with him. It will only agitate him further. Looking over my shoulder, I see Davenport still waiting. "I had better go."

"Call me when you're done with King Shoot-a-Lot,' he quips, and I laugh a little. "Oh, and Adeline?"

"Yes?"

"Don't blurt out anything before we've spoken, no matter how tempting it might be to give him the proverbial middle finger. Do you hear me?"

"I've never given anyone the middle finger before," I muse, looking at my hand. "I would love to give the King my first."

"I want your first. Call me." He hangs up, and I rest my shoulder on the frame, gazing out across the grounds, the sky as bright as my secret smile. He's in my corner. He's protecting me.

"Everything okay, ma'am?" Davenport asks. Not once in thirty years has he asked me *that* question.

"It will be," I say, hoping I am right. My smile transforms into a scowl as I turn away from the window and stride across the huge landing to my father's office, conjuring up every ounce of resilience I need.

Davenport taps and opens the door for me. "Her Royal Highness Princess Adeline," he announces.

I immediately hate the scene before me. *Hate* it. The King is puffing away on a cigar, relaxed back in his big chair, and David and Sir Don are looking all cozy on the chesterfield, a tumbler of fine Scotch resting in their palms. Sir Don is twirling his glass casually and slowly, his gaze on that and that alone, regardless of the fact that I have just entered after being announced. And David? He's relaxed back, looking self-important and cocky. What are they doing here?

"Your Majesty." I bow my head with respect that I'm struggling hard to find, my middle finger twitching. I'd love to give David Sampson and Sir Don my second, right after thrusting my first at the King. "How was shooting this morning?"

"You're leaving for Spain this evening."

The bones in my neck crack when my head shoots up. "Pardon?"

"Spain. This evening." His cigar breezes through the air, leaving a wave of swirling, putrid smoke in its wake. "Your mother's family is eagerly awaiting your arrival."

"I don't understand. My trip to Madrid was scheduled for next

month."

"It's been rescheduled. Kim has the details." Turning his attention to David and Sir Don, he points to a document in his hand, shaking his head. "Constitutional nonsense. But it's not like I can object. Imagine that. The King objecting his government's plans." He chuckles. "That would bamboozle the Eton boys, don't you think?"

I ignore his attempt to dismiss me so easily. "What about Sabina's husband's funeral?" I step forward, digging through my scattered mind for more words of semi-reasonable refute. "Shouldn't I be there? Haydon is depending on me." I've just gone below the belt, and I have not a shred of remorse.

"Haydon will be traveling with you. You'll be back in time for the funeral," David pipes up, and my eyes widen.

Oh God, no.

There's a brief silence, a look passing between the men. "It's for your own good, Adeline," my father says. "It's time for you to take stock and think about your future with Haydon."

"What?" Words, words I know I shouldn't say, dance on the end of my tongue. Words about Josh. Words that will expose our relationship. I want to scream, but I quickly rein myself in, reminding myself of Josh's warning. He and his team have a strategy. They've been preparing. Well, I hope that strategy involves keeping me off that plane this evening. "Why are you doing this?"

"I do not need to give you a reason. But you need to learn your place in this world." My father is up from his desk, hands wedged into the wood. "It is to serve your country."

I need to leave before my secrets come pouring out of me. All of them. My jaw tight, aching from the tenseness, I pivot and storm out of his private office before I lose control of my mouth. I am not going to Spain. Not now, not ever.

I rush down the grand staircase and out of the door, desperate to escape the hell that is my life. Damon has the door held open for me when I arrive, as if he was fully expecting me to come running

out. I drop into my seat and wait for him to get in the car. "The King is sending me to Spain," I tell him, gazing out of the window. "With Haydon Sampson."

"I've heard."

I sigh, letting my body sink into the leather behind me, my mind ready to explode. "Home please, Damon."

"Afraid not, ma'am." Damon stops at the gates of Claringdon as they open, and instead of looking at me through the reflection of the mirror, he turns his big body in the seat, swallowing hard. "I have instructions to take you straight to the airport."

"What?" I dive forward, narrowly missing Damon's forehead with my own. "From whom?"

"His Royal Highness King Alfred of England." He delivers my father's full title, as if to serve as a reminder that his hands are tied. My heart sinks. I've been backed into a corner.

"What about my things? I need to pack." When we get to Kellington, I'll disappear. Hide. Scale the walls that are topped with glass shards if I have to. The King can't fire Damon for being given the slip. I breathe out and retract that thought. That's not true. The King can fire whoever he damn well pleases.

"Your luggage has been seen to." Damon's face is full of apologies, and my sinking heart plummets into my feet. "It's in the car."

"I don't want to go."

"Ma'am, I'm afraid you don't have a choice, and neither do I." He turns back in his seat and drives on, and with every precious second that passes, my anxiety grows, my flesh physically hurting from the chills spreading at a ferocious rate. And poor Damon. I can see he's not happy about this unscheduled overseas trip.

"Damon, please, I . . ." My plea dies on my lips when a text drops, and I look down, my struggle for calm breaths getting the better of me.

How'd it go? x

I call Josh straight back, my shaking hand bringing my phone to my ear. "He's sending me to Spain," I breathe when he answers. "He's sending me to Spain, Josh. They're sending me to Spain. They're forcing—"

"Whoa," Josh blurts, alarmed by my high-pitched shouts. "Slow the hell down, Adeline."

"They are sending me to Spain," I whisper softly, my palm on my throat, massaging the swelling down. I can't breathe. Can't think. "With Haydon."

Josh chokes down the line. "Over my dead fuckin' body. Where are you?"

I swallow, pushing out some air. "In my car. Damon has strict orders to take me to the airport immediately."

"What?"

"To the airport, Josh. I'm not even allowed to go home and pack my things. It's been done for me."

"This is fucked up. Where's Damon? Put him on. Now."

My hand shoots forward between the two seats. "He wants to talk to you."

Damon audibly exhales, pulling the car over to the side of the road. His empty eyes meet mine in the mirror as he reaches back and takes my phone. "I'm between a rock and a hard place here." His voice is devoid of emotion, matching his eyes, as he speaks to Josh. He's trying to disconnect himself. He's trying to be professional rather than emotional. Damon knows what's happening here is wrong. "I can't do that," he breathes, and then he laughs. It's a disbelieving laugh, his eyes still stony in the mirror. What's so funny? "You'll give me a job if I lose mine?" he asks, pinching the bridge of his nose. My body moves forward, trying to hear what Josh is saying. He would do that? For me? "Josh, you're American. You live in America. The job would be in America. The commute would be shite. I have a direct order from the King of England. My hands are tied."

I sag, defeated. This is hopeless. Damon's phone starts ringing, and he glances at the screen where it's positioned to the left of the steering wheel. "I have to go." He hangs up without so much as a goodbye, and then proceeds to take the call. "Yes?" He looks left and right a few times, his shoulders rising slowly in the chair. "What the fuck?" He breathes the rhetorical question out, his knuckles going white from the grip he has on the steering wheel. I fly forward in my seat again, trying to hear what has him trembling with anger. "Loud and fucking clear." He slams the ball of his palm into the steering wheel, and I flinch as my phone starts ringing from the seat where Damon threw it.

"Whatever is going on?" I ask as I reach for it.

He barely checks his mirrors before he yanks the steering wheel clockwise and slams his foot down on the accelerator, spinning around in the road and flinging me back in my seat. "Damon!"

"Put your belt on," he shouts, the sounds of screeching tires piercing the air. "Now."

I quickly reach for my belt and clip myself in. "Damon, what is it?"

"There's been an assassination attempt on Prince Edward."

My heart feels like it could break through my chest and land in my lap. "What?" The sound of the roaring engine drowns out my murmured request for confirmation of something I couldn't have heard right. Yet Damon's urgency and intense vigilance, constantly looking around as he drives, tells me I heard him just fine.

Someone tried to kill Eddie?

"Where was he?"

"Riding at the royal stables."

My eyes drop to my lap, where my phone is lying in my limp hand, Josh's name flashing persistently at me. I only just manage to convince my hand to raise it to my ear. "Josh."

"Adeline," he breathes.

"Someone's tried to kill Eddie." The statement comes breezing

out like a pre-programmed robot. And then there is silence down the line. A horrific silence that is filled with the scream of skidding tires as Damon brakes hard in front of the palace gates, smacking his horn.

"Open the fucking gates," he roars.

"Jesus," Josh says, obviously hearing the chaos unfold. I'm stuck to the back of the seat as Damon accelerates through the palace gates, barely waiting for them to open fully. "Where are you now?"

"Back at Claringdon." The car screeches to a stop and Damon is ushering me out soon after, crowding me as he hurries me up the steps. We enter complete and utter chaos, staff racing across the foyer, people on phones, shouting and cursing of the bluest kind saturating the air. I stop, staring at the anarchy, completely bewildered. "I have to go," I tell Josh, my phone limp at my ear. "I'll call you when I know more."

Josh puts the cursing of the palace staff to shame, blurting endless explicit language down the line. "I hate this. I should be there with you."

Hearing his hopelessness, his frustration, has me closing my eyes where I stand. "I'll call you."

I hear him inhale deeply, gathering patience. "Okay." His agreement is strained, but it's all he can do. "I love you."

I smile sadly and cut the call, just as my mother appears across the foyer, virtually being held up by Mary-Ann. Her expression, the visible state of her, haunted and shell-shocked, makes me forget my despondency. I hurry over, quick to comfort her. "Mother." I claim her from Mary-Ann and help her through to the lounge off the foyer, where the chaos continues. "Sit."

For the first time in her existence, my mother follows an instruction from me, lowering to the brocade couch. One of the servants is quick to pour some tea, and I load Mother's with a sugar she never has, stirring it quickly and placing it in her limp hands. Her gaze, empty and vacant, doesn't move from the floor. "How could this

happen?" she asks herself, her hands shaking terribly.

I curl an arm around her shoulder, my only offering, since I don't have the answer to her question. "I'm sure everything is being done to find out."

Davenport marches into the room, his expression lethal. "Are you okay, ma'am?" he asks, coming to a stop before the Queen Consort. Then, shocking me completely, he lowers to his haunches and places a hand over hers, searching out her eyes. "Catherine?"

Never have I heard Major Davenport speak to my mother so informally, and I can only watch as she turns clouded eyes to the major, tears beginning to stream. "How?" she asks, so helpless it breaks my heart.

The lethal edge of Davenport's expression cuts deeper, his hand squeezing Mother's. "I won't rest until I find out." He looks as fierce as a warrior, his stiff upper lip gone. It's an alien sight, but I'm immediately thankful he is with us.

"Where is he? Where is Edward?"

"He should be—" Davenport is cut short by the slam of a door, and all our heads shoot to the entrance of the lounge. Past the madness, I hear a voice.

"It's Eddie." I'm up fast, running to the foyer and fighting through those in my path. Not even the formidable presence of the King deters me. I push my father out of the way and throw myself at a bewildered-looking Eddie. "Thank God," I say into his jacket, clinging to him tightly.

"I'm okay," he says, though he doesn't sound it, his voice broken as he wraps a shaky arm around my waist. "Everyone needs to stop fussing."

"Yes, enough," the King barks, backing Eddie up as he pulls me away. "Let the man breathe, Adeline." Father casts a stern look around the crowded space, and everyone heeds the silent order, dispersing quickly. Except me. I'm going nowhere. "To my office." Father marches on, his relief short-lived. "Now."

He's not even going to give Mother the opportunity to hug her son, to shower him with love and appreciation that he is home. *Safe.* She's standing at the entrance of the lounge, looking on, her place known. Business first, reunions later. That doesn't stop Eddie from going to her, though, giving her a precious moment to feel him, kiss him, and hug him. She looks old all of a sudden, the stress taking its toll on her usual serenity. Holding his face with her palm, she smiles through her tears and pats his cheek lightly, a wordless show of her relief. The light kiss my brother drops on Mother's head before he follows our father leaves the Queen Consort with her eyes closed and Davenport holding her arm to keep her steady, his duties all askew. He should be on the King's heels, not tending to the Queen Consort. There are many other staff to see to her, as well as me, yet I can't help but feel profoundly grateful for his clear concern for her well-being. He even walks her to the couch and helps her down before relieving himself of his duties. As he passes me by the door, I hold my hand out, delaying him.

"Thank you," I say, and he looks at me, definite surprise being masked by his usual harsh blankness.

"Part of the job, ma'am." He heads toward Father's office and I smile, because it most definitely is not part of his job. This horrific news has rocked the palace to the core. An assassination attempt on Prince Eddie? I lean against the doorframe, looking up the stairs. It's crazy. Edward is loved by this country. I watch as Davenport joins Eddie at the top of the staircase, his palm landing on my brother's shoulder and massaging as they walk. And then the doors to the palace swing open again, and John and Helen are hustled in. John goes straight to the King's office, and Helen is shown to the lounge by a footman, not giving me a second's glance as she passes. I stand where I am, the quiet observer, as my mind spins, my problems seeming inconsequential now, and diluted by the madness surrounding me. I nearly lost my beloved Eddie.

21

THE KING HAS been in his office constantly, people coming and going, from MI6, to the Prime Minister, important people on a mission to get to the bottom of what's happened. The incident hasn't been contained from public. Gunshots in the countryside is not unheard of; high society shoot in the area frequently. But on that day, there were no scheduled shooting meetings. The bullet missed my brother, but it took out his horse. The sketchy reports in the newspapers is putting pressure on the Royal Press Office to put out an official statement.

Poor Eddie looks as dazed now as he did on that wretched day. He's here, but not really here. We've talked, but he's not in the conversation, his mind clearly wandering. I can't blame him. The questions are driving everyone around here insane, including me. Not just because it's becoming less likely each day that whoever is responsible will be tracked down and an explanation found, but because until then, no one is going anywhere.

If I ever felt like a prisoner before, now I feel buried alive. Claringdon is on lockdown, no one is permitted to leave. For two weeks, I've been contained within the palace walls, not even allowed

to roam the gardens without Damon in tow. I'm struggling to breathe, and this is only worsened by the fact that I haven't been able to see Josh for the whole time. We have spoken every day and there are constant text messages going back and forth. But no matter how much contact we have, it doesn't ease the growing ache in my heart. He left for New Zealand last week. Now, he's on the other side of the world, and I don't know when I might see him again. The time difference is a nightmare too, our calls limited simply because of that. My only comfort is knowing he is missing me as much as I am missing him. My mobile phone has been glued to my hand wherever I go. When I take a shower, I prop it up on the vanity unit and never take my eyes off the screen until I'm done. When I eat, it's in my lap on vibrate, so I'll know the second Josh calls or texts me and I can excuse myself quickly. I may be naïve, but I am sure Eddie is the only person who has noticed the extreme activity of my phone and my extended time alone so I can talk to Josh. Everyone else is too distracted by the shock of Eddie's incident. It would be a blessing in disguise if I could monopolize on the hypothetical space I'm being given. But I can't, and it is slowly driving me to despair.

As I'm weaving through the maze at the far side of the grounds, my phone clutched in my hand, I smile to myself, looking at the sky for some imaginary sense of freedom. Damon is only a few paces behind me, ever close, though he has detected my need to at least feel like I have some privacy, only speaking to me when he's spoken to.

There's a quick route to the center, where the imposing statue of my grandfather dwells, yet today I take the long route, ambling like I have all the time in the world, which, technically, I have. It's bright today, the sun warming my bare shoulders, the quiet needed. I try to focus on the sounds of birds tweeting, of the hosepipes spraying water upon the beds of flowers, instead of listening to the endless questions circling my mind. To most people, this would be heaven. But for me, it's the farthest away from heaven I could be.

Quite literally.

"It's late in New Zealand," I say to Damon, as I glance at the world clock on my phone.

"Yes. Eleven, ma'am."

I return my attention forward as I near the turning that will have me at the center of the maze.

The day feels like it has gone on forever already, yet it's only midday. As the huge statue of the late king comes into view, I stop at the edge of the clearing, taking him in from top to toe, the white shiny marble perfect in my less than perfect world. And I wonder, is this what I will become? A statue or a portrait on the walls of the palace, perfect in my death. Will people remember me, and if they do, for what? The daughter of the King, the controversial princess who defied the strong arm of the Royal Family? The one person who stood up for herself and refused to bow to the expectations of the throne? The one royal who fought for happiness with the man she loved. I smile, dropping my eyes to the base of the statue, seeing Josh there, champagne in his hand and a cunning smirk on his face. Yes, I will be that princess. Because I refuse to be anything less.

"Ma'am, your phone," Damon says, startling me from my thoughts. I look down and see Josh's name, and life literally surges through my veins at an epic rate.

I answer on a long sigh. "Fifteen days, twelve hours, and sixteen minutes."

"And twenty seconds," he replies. "The longest fuckin' time of my life. Shit, I'm going out of my mind, Adeline."

"Me too." I stroll past the exact point where Josh first got his hands on me, all the feelings and conflict powering forward, reminding me of where my American boy and I began.

"Where are you?" Josh asks as I come to a stop at the foot of the statue, turning and resting my backside on my grandfather's shins.

"I'm in the maze staring at the spot where you ordered me to my knees." My eyes root to the grass and stay there, aware that

Damon is close enough to hear, but I'm way beyond caring. I hope the entire world knows soon.

"Damn you, woman. Why'd you have to tell me that?"

"I miss you," I murmur. Despondency is a vice on my soul, squeezing, the weight pulling me down. "I don't know how much longer I can do this."

"I'm at the airport," he tells me, and I look at Damon, as if searching for confirmation that I heard Josh right. "I'm about to fly to London."

I straighten, and Damon frowns, clearly wondering why I'm tense. "What?"

"Filming is done here. I have a week's grace before we head to South Africa."

"But, Josh, I can't go anywhere. I'm trapped here." Despite the overwhelming happiness that Josh is coming back to London, too much misery is masking it. Knowing he's within a few miles when I'm confined to Claringdon will be torture of the worst kind.

"They can't keep you there forever. Something's gotta give soon, before I do. How's Eddie? Have there been any developments?"

"He's fine. And no, nothing." I hear the sound of an announcement in the background. "What's that?"

"Last boarding call. I've gotta go. I'll call you the moment I land, okay?"

"Okay." I look at Damon as I disconnect, reading his questioning expression. "He's coming back."

Worry. It's written all over his face in an instant at this news. "Don't you be pulling any wild stunts."

"Damon, when will this be over? They can't keep us prisoners here forever."

I see him breathe in his patience, taking his phone from his pocket when it rings. "Yes?" He turns away and starts pacing. "I'm on my way."

"What is it?" I ask, the second he cuts the call, pushing myself

off the legs of my grandfather.

"Meeting in the King's office." He's quick to collect me, tugging me along, his way of telling me I'm not remaining out here without him. "You can have lunch with Queen Catherine while I'm busy."

I take the lead when I note that Damon is going the entirely wrong way through the maze to get us out in the most efficient time. "What is it? Do you think they have found whoever did this?"

"I don't know anything until I get there, Adeline."

"But you'll tell me, won't you?"

Damon looks at me, wary and affectionately. "Yes."

I power on, keen to get Damon to the King's office without delay.

I'M PACING, THE carpet beneath my Uggs close to becoming threadbare. They've been in there for two hours now. The King, the Prime Minister, head of MI6, close protection, Sir Don, Davenport, and David Sampson. The only important person who seems to have slipped the guest list is God himself.

I'm the only one keeping close watch of the doors, the only one who seems to care whether the bars of this godforsaken jail will be opened anytime soon. Of course, I'm desperate to hear news of a satisfactory outcome, first and foremost, but my eagerness is only amplified by the fact that it will signal the end of my captivity.

When the doors to the King's office open, I come to an abrupt halt in my pacing, watching on a held breath to see who will emerge. It's Davenport. He looks at me. The stony face of the man who has served my father so steadfastly for so long is soft, as it has been for these past couple of weeks. This whole messy affair has affected us all, but Davenport, the impenetrable, cold man, seems deeply affected. It's a comfort knowing he's human after all. Nodding, he passes me, making his way down the stairs as the rest of the room empties onto the huge landing of the palace. I spot Damon amid the sea of heads and hurry over to him. "Well?" I ask, falling into

stride next to him. "Have they found whoever is responsible?"

"No."

His straight answer slows my pace, and I deflate, all of my hope wasted. I stare at his suit-covered back as the distance grows between us, until he comes to a stop and looks back, searching me out. His face softens when he sees my utter despair, and he paces back, placing his hand in the customary position on the small of my back to push me on.

"There are no leads. No evidence. No motives. Nothing." I'm escorted down the stairs, Damon scoping the area with keen eyes before moving in close to my ear again. "It seems Eddie got caught in the crossfire of someone out shooting, probably illegally."

"What?"

"No one will come forward and own up to shooting illegally, especially near royal land. I know that, they know that. It's been agreed that the Royal Family can leave Claringdon, but extra security measures will be put in place as a precautionary measure."

My relief is profound, for Eddie and for me, though I'm not sure what *extra measures* means. But I do know the republicans will be up in arms. *Extra measures* is just another reason for them to protest about what a waste of space and money we are. "So I can leave?"

"You can leave." Damon stops us at the bottom of the stairs, taking the tops of my arms. "But, and you hear me well, I am not beyond calling for your detainment here at Claringdon if you so much as put one foot out of place, do you hear me? No silly jaunts across London. No harebrained attempts to escape Kellington. You give me the runaround, young lady, and . . . and . . ." He doesn't know what, but he doesn't need to find a threat.

I place my hand over his mouth. "I swear I won't go anywhere." My promise is solemn, and he nods, thankful. "Without telling you," I add.

I'm scowled at. "You are a pain in the royal arse, ma'am." He releases me and stands back, straightening out his suit. "I'll get the

car ready."

I'm gone in a flash, racing up the stairs as I bash out an excited text to Josh on my way. I don't bother calling Jenny or Kim to help me. It will take too long. I have my things together quickly, everything stuffed into a bag haphazardly with frantic hands before the decision to free everyone is withdrawn. I don't call for assistance from one of the footmen, lugging my bag myself through the palace, my steps rushed, my heartbeats fast.

"Your Highness." Davenport's call from across the gallery landing doesn't slow my stride. If anything, it injects more urgency into it, my bag jumping down the steps behind me as I run down them. "Your Highness."

I stop, closing my eyes, praying I'll be allowed to leave. "Yes, Major?"

"The King would like to see you."

My heart sinks. Everything inside of me sinks. Will he order me to Spain again with Haydon? Looking to Davenport, I try to read him, try to gauge what I'm going to face. He's expressionless, back to the Davenport we all know and *don't* love. "I was just leaving." My declaration carries no impact. His arm sweeps out in gesture toward my father's office, and I follow it with my eyes, staring at the door where the King sits beyond. On a lumpy swallow, I abandon my bag on the stairs and drag myself back up, my heart in my feet as I trudge to the office.

Davenport opens the door and announces me. I'm not in the least bit surprised to find David Sampson and Sir Don relaxed in the chairs opposite my father's desk. Their presence has been a constant for the whole lockdown. The King is immersed in his usual plume of putrid air, chewing on the end of a fat cigar, but he looks tired, his complexion grey, a far cry from the alcohol-induced rosy cheeks he usually sports. Chairs litter the floor space, all brought in to seat the masses of men who have been here for the endless meetings these past two weeks.

"Father." I sound meek, timid, and it is only being fueled by my growing trepidation.

"Sit, Adeline," he orders, sucking tightly on the end of the brown stick hanging from his mouth. Even my moves are apprehensive, my body slow in lowering to the chair, my eyes constantly casting between the men. "You are to return to Kellington," he tells me, firm and blunt. "You will not leave the grounds until clearance has been given."

I nod, though I'm wondering if every other member of this family has received the same warning. So I'm being moved, but only from one prison to another. I still won't be able to see Josh. The King's priorities may have changed since this madness, but I haven't forgotten that I was in the process of being shipped to Spain with Haydon prior to all of this. My mind spirals, questions and worry all blending together, causing a fuzz that is not allowing me to think straight.

"The monarchy has been pulled through the media shredder these past weeks." Father flicks his eyes to David Sampson, who nods mildly, like he is encouraging the King to push on. "We need something to take the limelight off Edward's incident. Some good news."

He doesn't need to go on. I know exactly what will be said next. Some good news. Like an engagement. My ribcage is sustaining some pretty brutal crashes of my heart into it, though I fight not to allow my anger and pain to show. I need to think on my feet. So now I will be used as a distraction from the negativity? Be pushed into a marriage with a man I do not love. Father will be killing two birds with one stone, so to speak. How very resourceful of him. "I understand," I say, my voice calm and straight, though on the inside I am disintegrating. Words form in my head, all sensible words, my survival instinct kicking in. I need to buy myself some time.

I sit forward in my chair, looking directly into my father's eyes. "I would like to go to Evernmore," I say, and his head cocks a little,

interested. The royal estate in the Scottish Highlands is as close as you could get to the wilderness in Britain, nothing within miles and miles. It's where we spend our Christmases, and where the King and Queen Consort holiday. It's where members of the Royal Family escape to when they need space. It's also less of a fortress than any other royal residences. "I realize my role in the good news you speak of." I sound so calm, and I honestly do not know how I'm doing it. "I'm asking for a few days to process this. To process my future."

The King is rarely taken aback. But my lack of retaliation—my seeming compliance—has pushed him back in his chair, his eyes passing between David, Sir Don, and me. David, I notice, is also slightly startled.

"I don't see why not," Father says. I sag in relief, thanking him profusely in my head for giving me this little bit of freedom before he locks me up for my life sentence.

"I'm not sure that would benefit anyone," David says, and I shoot him a look, enraged. "Let us just get on with it."

"Two days," I grate, turning my pleading eyes onto the King. "Just two days, Father. That's all I ask." I can sense David doesn't trust me. I won't let him sway my father's decision, won't allow him to take this gift from me. It feels like a hundred years while I wait for my father to decide whose side he is on, a hundred years of holding my breath and holding back my shakes.

"Two days," Father finally says, making David grunt and me jump up from my chair in elation.

"Thank you so much, Your Majesty." I round his desk and do something so out of the ordinary, dipping and kissing his cheek. "I will relish the fresh air and walk every trail in the loch you showed us as children."

A smile from my father is an exceptional privilege, and so is any display of affection. I get both. He beams at me, tapping my hand where it rests on his shoulder. The easiness, I know, is only because I finally appear to be bowing to his demand, though I cherish it

nevertheless. "Two days," he affirms. "You can leave tomorrow morning. I'll have the royal helicopter take you."

"I'd rather drive." I scold myself for my small protest. I shouldn't be pushing him, but the drive to Scotland will kill more time. "Besides," I rush on, "No need to give the republicans an excuse to criticize our spending habits."

Father waves a dismissive hand as he takes a long draw of his cigar. "The costs will be taken from the duchy. They can't complain about that. By air is safer, and I'll hear no more of it." Smoke billows from his mouth as he speaks, engulfing me in its haze. Coughing under my breath, I move out of the cloud and relent to his wishes, simply grateful for his permission.

"Thank you." I back away, aware of David's sour expression fixed on me, as well as Sir Don's. I'd love nothing more than to toss them a victorious scowl, though I refrain, keeping my head level. They would have a ring on my finger this instant, and Haydon and me on the balcony of the palace soon after, presenting us to the world as a happy couple. David is desperate to be classed as royal by marriage and association, whereas Sir Don is simply an antiquated old fool who's trying to uphold royal traditions.

I have no idea how I play this nightmare once I'm out of this office. For now, I just need to get away from here. I need to find myself, and even more than that, I need to see Josh. He'll know what to do.

22

THE SHADOW OF the helicopter is a mere blip on the plains of barren land beneath us, growing as it glides over the hills, and shrinking when it dips between the valleys. And the noise, a consistent, loud whirring in my ears, has helped drown out my screaming mind. As the walls of Evernmore Estate appear on the horizon, far, far away in the distance, I hope for just a smidgen of ease to dampen the constant fretfulness plaguing me. We pass the Loch, the waters still and eerie, and the scattering of green is sparse. The beauty of this place is almost haunting, the landscape no different to hundreds of years ago.

Our descent is a little hair-raising, the wind whipping through the moors capturing the chopper and swinging it like a pendulum as the pilot brings us in to land. The sensation of the feet meeting the ground kick-starts my breathing again, a voice through my hearing-defenders declaring our landing.

The staff of Evernmore await me, the impromptu visit sure to have sent them into a tailspin. Damon disembarks first, dipping and taking my hand to help me down, and we jog beneath the blades until we're clear of the spinning metal. I nod my hello to the line

of people ready to greet me, one taking my coat, and breach the entrance of the castle, breathing in hundreds of years' worth of history. The echo of my boots hitting the stone floor is only slightly muffled by the tapestries suspended from the brick walls.

I head straight for the stairs that take me to my suite, Damon following, giving orders to the footmen who have my bags. For the thousandth time, I check the time on my phone, and again mentally calculate Josh's flight time and landing. If I'm correct, and I'm sure I am, he should have landed over an hour ago. Why hasn't he called?

"I'll leave you to settle in," Damon says, backing out of the room as I remove my boots.

"Thank you, Damon. I'm sure the cook will fix you something if you are hungry."

"I'm heading straight to the kitchen." He smiles, and I return it. I know he loves it up here, especially the haggis that is served like tea.

Although I'm listening for it, I still startle when my phone rings, and I scramble to answer. "Josh."

"What's going on?" he asks immediately. "I've landed in London, and you've left the fuckin' country."

I smile to myself. He's affronted, and I can't blame him. "We need to talk."

There's silence for a few moments. "Are you breaking up with me?"

"God, no."

"Then explain why you've hauled ass to Scotland."

"Because if I didn't, they would have had me engaged to Haydon Sampson and told the world before I could think to argue. I've bought myself some time."

A growl. Such a deep, hostile growl. "Tell me you're fuckin' with me."

"I'm not fucking with you." I wander to the window and stare out across the Loch. "I thought, what with everything that has happened, my life—and me—would drop down the King's priority

list. I was wrong. I've shot to the top. They're planning on using my engagement to Haydon Sampson as a decoy, as such. A distraction from the negativity surrounding the royals and Eddie's accident." I hear Josh choking down the phone on a cough, my barrage of information obviously hard to swallow.

"You're really not fuckin' with me, are you?"

I sigh, feeling the invisible pressure weighing down on me. "It's now or never, Josh."

"It's now, that's what it is." He's absolutely seething, and while part of me is grateful for his devotion and commitment, the other part is full of dread. I just wonder if he truly appreciates the shit-storm we're about to create. "Where are you?" he demands. "Tell me exactly where you are."

"The Evernmore Estate. It's in the middle of nowhere. I have two days grace from the King before I have to return to London to announce my engagement."

"I'll be there by this evening."

"How?"

"I'll charter a plane. A fuckin' rocket if I need to. Where's the nearest airport?"

"Glasgow."

"I'll call you when I'm there. I'll need directions." Loud, muffled thuds pound in the background, the bustle of the airport getting louder. "I'll call my people. Don't speak to anyone before I'm there, okay?"

"Shouldn't be hard. There's no one here, except Damon, the staff, and me."

"Or calls. Please don't take any calls."

"Why? Who would be calling me?"

"Your father. Davenport. Sir Don. Fuckin' Haydon Sampson or his prick of a dad. I don't want you speaking to any of them until I'm with you. Tell me you understand, Adeline."

He's worried that I'll be brainwashed. Or, worse, followed to Scotland and dragged back to London. That's not going to happen.

At least, not for a few days. Yet I confirm what he wants to hear anyway, imagining he is feeling helpless. And I can understand why. There are so many facets to being royal, so many obligations and protocols to follow. It would be largely unknown to the general British public, let alone an American. He must think this is all far too archaic and nonsensical. Yet it's not. "I understand. Please, just hurry up." Part of me hates needing him so much, yet I don't feel strangled by that need.

But rather . . . soothed.

We say our goodbyes, and I spend endless hours familiarizing myself with Evernmore, roaming the castle corridors alone. Josh texted me not long after our call to tell me he had chartered a plane from Heathrow to Glasgow, and from there he has a helicopter waiting to bring him here. I've never been more grateful that he has more money than God. My ears have been listening for the sound of chopper blades while I've roamed, and I've checked the horizon out of every window I've passed, searching for him. It's been over two weeks since I've seen him. Two weeks of pure misery. Two weeks of constantly reliving every moment we have shared, frightened I might forget. Two weeks of falling asleep with his picture on my phone next to my head on the pillow. I've missed his fun-loving yet cocky presence. Two weeks of Helen's moaning about the stress for the baby. Two weeks of Mother's stoic silence. Two weeks to think about how I nearly lost a brother. What would I have done without Eddie? We'd Skype when he's on tour, naturally, but I haven't feared losing him because after each deployment, he comes home. And two weeks ago, he nearly didn't.

I need to see Josh. Emotionally, my heart has missed its mate. Physically, I'm literally bursting with anticipation to see him. Kiss him. Feel him everywhere.

It's when I'm taking the stone steps of one of the spiral staircases in the west wing tower that I hear it. A helicopter. There is no mistaking it. It's faint, but it's there. With my heart in my mouth, I race down the stairs in search of a south-facing window, skidding

to a stop in front of the first one I find. Gasping for air, I look past the lead-framed glass, having to wipe away the condensation when my hot breath mists the glass. I see it. In the distance, a blob on the horizon. *Josh*.

Throwing myself down the rest of the stairs, I run full pelt through the castle, sailing past many staff who move from my path, no doubt alarmed by my strange behavior. My cheeks are aching with the smile on my face, my skin tingling, as if anticipating his touch. I burst out of the doors, circling round to the helicopter pad, my eyes squinting, seeing he is closer. Waving frantic hands in the air, I jump on the spot. It's pointless. The pilot can't possibly miss the sprawling estate surrounded by nothing, but still.

Unable to contain my excitement, everything feeling a million times better just knowing he is here with me, I send him a text message.

I can see you!

My arms are back in the air again, waving like a loon.

"Ma'am?"

I swing around, my face splitting with my smile, and not even Damon's confusion can wipe it away. He made me promise no runners. I'm not running. He can't possibly chastise me for this.

"Did I miss the memo?" He scratches his head, his muddle clear as he looks past me to the helicopter.

"It's Josh," I say, smiling small and awkward when he darts a shocked stare back to me.

Then his eyes disappear, hidden behind his lids as he gathers patience. "I should have known."

My phone bleeps, and I glance down to read the message from Josh.

You've got good eyesight. I've not even left Glasgow. Technical problem with the chopper.

Ice glides across my skin, and I whirl around, the helicopter now close—close enough to see the royal emblem emblazoned on the side. "Oh my God."

"That's not Josh, Adeline," Damon says gravely. "That's the King."

I'm a statue, watching in horror, numb and muddled, as the chopper comes to land on the pad. My father disembarks, and my dread multiplies when I see David follow closely behind, as well as Sir Don and Dr. Goodridge. "Father?" I question as he strides toward me. I don't like his face. Not at all. It's fixed and determined.

"I'm here to hunt," he declares as he passes, my body turning to follow his path. "And we should discuss the arrangements."

"What happened to my two days?"

He stops and turns, looking me up and down. "Your destiny is written. Two hours, or two days, the end result will be the same. We should plan announcements and press releases. There's a lot to be done." He marches on, disregarding my astonished state.

I feel unwell. "Father!" I run after him, throwing a scowl back at David, unable to let go of the notion that he has something to do with this. And now I come to think of it . . ."Where's Davenport?" I ask.

"Unwell." The King stops at the door for one of the footmen to take his coat.

Unwell? He's never been unwell. Not ever, though I can't deny he has been out of sorts for a few weeks. But more not like himself rather than physically ill. This is all very strange. And hopeless. So hopeless. I turn my glazed eyes onto Damon, maybe searching for some backup. I don't know why. There's no one who can help me.

"John should be here imminently," the King tells one of the staff. "Prepare his room, as well as suites for Sir Don, Sampson, and the doctor."

Great. My eldest brother, too? I don't stand a chance. I just manage to avoid taking my face and burying it in my palms, but I can't stop the swelling in my throat. David and Sir Don follow my

father like the lapdogs they are through the corridors of the castle to his office. The door is slammed before I can join them, and I stare at the wood for an eternity, my head in bedlam. My eyes drift to a window when I hear the sounds of another chopper. It's not Josh. He's still in Glasgow. It's John. More muscle to bully me.

"Your Highness?"

Dragging my heavy head to the other side of me, I find Dr. Goodridge. He's always been old to me, but today he looks exceptionally old. How much longer can he tail the King wherever he goes?

"Are you okay?" he asks me.

I blink and return my eyes to the door of my father's office.

"You need to rein that girl in, sir," David says, his voice clear through the wood.

"She's spirited." There are a few chinks, undeniably glass on glass, the crystal decanter on my father's desk meeting the edge of a tumbler. "If I struggle to keep her in check, how do you suppose your son will?"

My hand is on the doorknob and I've pushed myself into the room before I can think better of it. "I am *not* marrying Haydon," I declare, as stable as I can. "And you cannot make me."

"I knew it," Sampson snarls at me.

"Oh, shut up," I retort. "This has nothing to do with you. Stop clinging to my family. I will not marry your son."

The King points his glass at me, sure and steady. "Make no mistake, my girl, you will do as I say."

"No," I shout, losing my shit. Enough is enough. No more. I will not be held hostage by expectations any longer. I ignore the stunned expressions I'm facing, powering on, to hell with them all. "I refuse to marry Haydon, and it is unfair for you to ask him to marry me, especially when . . . when . . ." I feel like I'm starting to hyperventilate, no air to be found to help me put it out there. "When . . ."

"When, what?" David snaps.

I breathe in and exhale what I've so desperately wanted to tell the world for so long. "When I am in love with someone else."

My confession echoes around the room, bounces off the old stone walls. And then silence. Deafening silence. For ages, there is only silence and three sets of round eyes pointed at me. *Oh shit. Shit, shit, shit.*

"The banker?" Father laughs.

That's it now. I've taken the leap. "No, not Gerry Rush."

"Then who?"

I breathe in more strength to say his name, trying to ignore the feeling that I'm feeding Josh to the wolves. But we can't go on like this. "Josh."

My father looks plain confused, David annoyed, and Sir Don just closes his eyes, probably thinking his work is cut out for him.

"Who the hell is J . . . ?" The King's question wanes, realization dawning. I was right all along. The King and his people aren't responsible for Josh's trashed hotel room. They really had no idea. "The American?" he asks. "Jameson's son?"

I nod sharply. "Correct."

Father bursts into laughter. It's the most insulting reaction to my news. "How preposterous."

"How so?" I ask calmly.

"He's American."

"And?"

"An American in the Royal Family? I won't hear of it. Stop living with your head in the clouds, Adeline. You will marry Haydon Sampson and that will be the last we speak of it."

"Wrong," I say shortly, calmly, and the King recoils at my dismissal. "I love him."

He bears his teeth, a true lion of a king. "I forbid it."

"I don't care."

"You'll be an outcast."

"I don't care."

"You'll lose everything!" he roars.

"Not everything," I say coolly, giving each of the men in the room a moment of my attention. "I'll have him." Josh is the only thing that matters to me in the crazy world I've been born into. The only person I bow to is him. I turn and walk away before I'm dismissed. "Good day, Your Majesty."

"Adeline!"

My pace picks up at the sound of my father yelling, my feet taking me through the castle to the garages at the far end of the East Wing. I grab the first set of keys I can find in the cabinet on the wall and press my thumb into the button on the fob, making the lights of a Land Rover at the back of the garage blink. I don't drive nearly enough to be confident, so I pull away slowly before I find the will to put my foot down, the castle getting smaller and smaller in the rearview mirror as I go. When the gates to the estate come into view, I quickly conclude my current speed will have the Land Rover bouncing back off the iron rails. So I brace myself, closing one eye and pressing my foot into the accelerator, my arms ramrod straight, braced for impact. Call me mad, call me desperate, call it extreme. But it's the only way out of my new prison. I drive at them with nothing but sheer determination, suppressing a yell and closing my eyes when I'm upon them. The metal keeping me contained bursts open, the Land Rover juddering violently, pain shooting up my arms. "Oh my goodness!" I swerve, mounting a grass verge as I fight with the steering wheel to line up the car again, bumping and bouncing all over the place. I'm tossed around, so much so my forehead crashes against the door window. I yelp, but keep my hands where they are, hitting pothole after pothole on the dirt track, none of them helping me pull the car straight. The persistent ringing of my phone doesn't distract me from gaining back control of the Land Rover, and I only find it in my pocket when I am on even ground, driving steadily again. I expect to see Damon calling, mad

and frantic, but it's Josh. Just the sight of his name on my screen sends my emotions off the deep end, all adrenalin draining. "Josh," I blurt down the line, keeping a keen eye on the road, one hand on the wheel. "My father. It was my father in the chopper I could see. He followed me to Scotland. He came to discuss arrangements. Press releases, announcements. I didn't know what to do."

"Fuckin' hell, Adeline," he breathes. "Where are you?"

"I left. I'm driving south."

"On your own?"

"I didn't have time to think, Josh." I need to calm down. Right now, keeping my head is of paramount importance.

"You need to calm down." He mimics my thoughts, but he doesn't sound very calm himself. "How long before you reach any kind of civilization?"

"I don't know. There's a small village thirty miles from here."

"What's it called?"

"Sellington Heights." I hear Josh relaying the name of the village to someone, and then the sound of helicopter blades start, building up, louder and louder, until he's forced to shout down the line. "The pilot says I can be there in thirty minutes. Find a field north of the village. Drive to the middle so we can see you, got it?"

I nod, wondering how on earth it came to this. Me, on the run, and Josh in a damn helicopter trying to find me. It's crazy, yet it's happening.

"Adeline, did you hear me?"

"Yes, I heard you." My phone bleeps and I quickly glance at my screen to see an incoming call from Damon. "Damon is trying to call me."

"Will he be tracking you?"

I look up at my rearview mirror, to the never-ending length of road stretching out behind me. "Undoubtedly."

"Just keep driving. Not too fast. Just make it to that field in one piece, okay?"

My smile is poorly timed, but I can't help it. "Are you regretting this yet?"

"Never. I've already told you. I'm prepared to lose everything I have, except you. Now get your royal ass to that field." He hangs up, and I drop my phone into my lap, returning both hands to the wheel. I ignore the calls from Damon, keeping my attention on the road. My main objective, the most important objective, is making it to Josh safely.

THERE ARE DOZENS of fields. My mind is so messed up, I can't even make the simple decision of which one to put myself in. I pull up to some large wooden gates and jump out of the Land Rover, jogging up the lane a bit and pulling the heavy bolt across. They slowly swing open with little help from me. I turn and run back toward the car, but my pace slows when I hear a familiar, distant sound. Spinning around, I search the sky, the noise growing by the second. He's here. I need to get myself to the middle of the field. Urgency springs into my muscles as I turn . . . and freeze.

Damon reaches inside my Land Rover and shuts off the engine, pulling the keys from the ignition. "Adeline, what on earth?"

My steps back up, my attention split between the sky and Damon. "Don't try to stop me, Damon. Please, you know I can't do what they're demanding."

Damon looks past me, his head tilted back, lines spanning his forehead. I follow his line of sight, seeing a chopper appear over the trees in the distance.

"I have to go," I tell him, reversing my steps.

Damon shakes his head, despair wracking him. He seems to take a timeout, thinking. And he eventually sighs. "Who the hell's going to keep me busy if I don't have you?"

Relief allows me to smile at him. "Thank you, Damon. For everything."

"Just go," he orders, straight and short, his eyes back in the sky.

But I don't. Instead, I run to him, throwing my arms around his big shoulders and cuddling him with all the love and appreciation I feel for him. And he returns it. There are no words. None are needed. Gently breaking away from me, he steps back and nods.

I take his silent order and go, running as fast as my legs will carry me to the center of the field, my arms flailing in the air crazily. The helicopter gradually lowers, hovering, the blades of the grass flapping crazily around me. My phone vibrates in my hand.

"Move back, we're coming down," Josh shouts when I answer.

I back away, my arm held over my head to stop the brutal whip of my hair across my face from the wind, my clothes clinging to my front. The moment the chopper's feet come to rest on the ground, the door is open and Josh is out, running toward me. The sight of him renders me paralyzed, so many emotions holding me where I am. It's all too much, my relief savage in its intensity. A sob rips through me. The only energy left in me lets me lift my arms when he crashes into me. The moment our bodies reunite, my heart explodes, as do my eyes. I grapple at his back, clinging to him with all my strength. "You don't know how happy I am to see you," I cry into his neck, unable to pull myself together.

"I do, baby. Trust me." I'm hushed, kissed, stroked, squeezed, my hair whipping around my head, our clothes flapping, the sound of the helicopter deafening. But I hear him as clear as if we were standing in silence. Reluctantly breaking away from him, I let him feel my face, kiss me over every inch of it. "These past few weeks have been hell. You're not leaving my sight ever again." His palms graze down my cheeks, over my shoulders and down my arms, until he has hold of my hands, his fingers linking with mine, reinforcing his words. "Ever." He looks past me, and I turn to follow his sight, finding Damon has approached behind us.

My head of security raises his phone. "You should go."

He's warning me. "Thank you."

Damon shrugs. "I was thinking of taking early retirement, anyway."

I'm being tugged toward the helicopter, but I keep my eyes on my beloved bodyguard until the final second, my many years with Damon playing through my mind. His presence, his comfort. I'm going to miss him so much. And then he smiles, as if knowing what I'm thinking. Maybe because he's thinking it, too.

Damon slowly raises his hand as I'm forced to turn and climb aboard. Josh places some ear defenders over my head and secures me in the belt before seeing to himself and taking my hand. He looks at me and smiles, small but expressive, as we slowly rise from the ground and soar toward my heaven.

23

I'D HOPED WHEREVER we were going we would have some space so we could catch up on lost time. It wasn't to be. The second we landed at a small airfield on the outskirts of London, we were swarmed by Josh's PR team and protection, and hustled into the back of a car parked a few meters from the chopper. Flurries of rushed, panicked words blended into nothing, and it was obvious each one of his team, mostly Americans, didn't have the foggiest idea how to greet me. All of them curtsied. It was embarrassing, but Josh seemed to find it amusing, as well as Bates and his men. I let them talk tactics on the journey back into London, though I hardly heard a word, most of my time spent cuddled into Josh's side, wondering how it had come to this. Technically, I'm on the run. I'm on the run from my family, and it's only a matter of time before the media catch wind of my whereabouts.

I'm cloaked in one of Josh's security men's jackets as I'm helped from the car, surrounded at every angle, squished in the middle so not to be seen. I don't recognize where we are, though it seems to be residential from what glimpses I have had through the army of people flanking me. I had seen Bates take a call earlier. He watched

me the whole time he was talking. I smiled as he nodded through his conversation, knowing it was Damon on the line giving him instructions. It was reassuring to know that even now, my head of protection is looking out for me.

When Josh's people disperse, we're in the foyer of a plush apartment block, and I look at Josh in question. "A friend's place," he tells me. "He's in LA. Said we could camp out here."

I suddenly feel like such an inconvenience. We're whisked up to the top floor, the lift opening up directly onto a huge open penthouse. "It's not a palace," Josh's publicist says as she exits before us, "but it's off radar for now."

"I hate palaces," I say mindlessly, letting Josh guide me across the open space to the window spanning the far side. The clear view across London is extraordinary. I've never seen it like this. "Oh." I laugh lightly, pointing across the skyline. "And in case I get homesick, I can see Kellington." The royal residence, nestled between one of the smaller royal parks and a row of Georgian terraces, looks so small from here, unimportant and almost bland amid the rest of London's grandeur. "Oh, and there's my parents' house." Claringdon appears anything *but* unimportant; the colossal structure looks like it has grown there over hundreds of years. The lack of a flag tells me the King isn't home yet. No, he's in Scotland, undoubtedly still ranting and raving. Dr. Goodridge has probably been forced to feed him a sedative.

"Why don't you take a shower?" Josh asks, moving in behind me and wrapping his arms around my waist. "One of the guys has gone to collect some things for you to change into, but until then, there's a clean robe on the back of the door."

I turn in his arms. "And what are you going to do?"

His blue eyes look so tired, lacking the brilliant sparkle I love so much. And his dark hair is a wild mess atop his head. His stubble is well overgrown, too. All because of me. "I have a few things to go over with everyone."

I cast my eyes across the room, where a dozen people have set up office, laptops popping up everywhere, people circling the room on their phones, other making notes on pads. It's a little chaotic, all of them talking loudly. I sigh, hating the significance of the scene. Again, all of this because of me. "Shouldn't I know what is happening?"

"No, trust me to deal with it." He turns me by the shoulders and leads me on, persistent and firm.

"When do I get you to myself?" I grumble as we enter a lavish shower room, all black marble and chrome.

"I won't rest until I know exactly how we're moving forward, so you need to be patient."

"I already told you, take me back to America."

"You have your passport?"

I turn my nose up to the mirror before me. "Smuggle me out."

Josh rolls his eyes and flips the shower on, filling the room with steam. "Just do as you're told." A towel is pushed into my front and his lips pushed to mine. "Please, Your Highness."

I smirk through a scowl. "So I have to stay locked in here while you discuss with your people how to deal with me?"

"Oh, I know how to deal with you." He hunkers down, his hands on my arse squeezing hard. "But I'm not sure everyone out there wants to hear the details, darlin'."

"No, but I do," I say, goading him, taking a little nibble of his chin. "I want explicit details."

Josh groans, capturing my lips gently. "We have a lot of catching up to do."

"We do."

"Your ass is gonna be stinging like a bitch."

"Good."

He smiles around our kiss, as do I, and I lock him in my arms. "I may even let you sit on your throne."

I laugh, losing the contact of our lips. "You're terrible."

"And you love it." He turns me and swats my bottom. "In the shower."

"Yes, sir."

He winks and leaves me to sort myself out.

BY THE TIME I'm wrapped in a luxurious robe, my phone is set to explode from the volume of missed calls. I can't look at who has called me though, because at this point, my decision to run is still completely surreal. After the adrenaline rush of racing through the countryside, leaving Damon, *leaving my family*, I feel so flat. So exhausted. Yet I know there is much to be done. Time to rally my royal-arse façade of strength and meet the new people who will manage me. At least, for now.

I walk into the open space of the penthouse, finding everyone sitting around the huge table, and they all fall silent when they detect my presence. "Don't stop on my account," I say, feeling my cheeks heat.

Josh moves back in his chair and pats his lap, and I walk over, placing myself there without question, handing him my phone. "It refuses to stop ringing."

He takes it and passes it over to his publicist. "You should take over this."

She nods sharply. "Your code?"

Josh laughs, and I frown at him. "She'd better write that down for you." He picks up a pen and places it in my hand, pulling a piece of paper forward. I scribble down my code for Tammy and then relax back into the warmth of Josh's body.

"So," I say perkily, "have you figured out how you're going to deal with my delightful family?"

My question prompts a few smiles from around the table, all genuine, one woman looking a little star-struck. "I can't believe I'm sitting at a table with Princess Adeline of England."

Tammy throws her a scornful look, and I smile at her. "I'm not as important as they make out I am, believe me."

"You're third in line to the British throne, ma'am," Tammy reminds me. "That makes you pretty important to us mere mortals."

"Speak for yourself," Josh kids, bumping me on his knee. "To me, she is simply my girlfriend and the woman I love, and I'm tired of keeping that under wraps. So what now?"

I smile on the inside, snuggling deeper into him.

Tammy looks almost grave. "We go public before we go to them," she says, pushing some notes toward me. "A press release. Once it's out there, it's out there. There's nothing the Royals can do. It'll be our words, not those of a journalist. Just a simple statement telling the world you're dating."

"Just dating?" I ask, pressing my lips together cheekily. "Because . . . ouch!" I jump on Josh's lap when he pokes me in a rib, and everyone around the table laughs. It makes me feel somewhat better surrounded by normal people. People who haven't got sticks buried in their arses. "Okay, *dating*," I relent. "If you must insist."

Josh chuckles, burying his nose in my hair. "I love you."

"Stop. You're making everyone blush."

He corrects his position, straight and focused. "When is this statement being released?"

"Tomorrow," Tammy answers promptly.

"Why not now?" I counter immediately, tomorrow feeling like eons away. The royal aides will be hatching a plan as we speak. The less time we give them to do that the better.

Tammy casts her eyes around the table, a Mexican wave-type shrug thing going on. "So we send it out tonight," she agrees.

"You sure?" Josh asks me, encouraging me around on his lap. Looking straight into my eyes, he speaks clearly and concisely. Determinedly. "I'm ready, Adeline. I'd be out on the street this very second shouting it to everyone I see, but I need to know you're ready, too."

Where's this doubt come from? Haven't I proven my commitment? "I've been ready for weeks."

He nods, sharp and final, as he breathes in, keeping his eyes on mine. "Send it out as soon as it's ready," he orders Tammy, standing from his chair and encouraging me with him. "And if we're done, I'd like some privacy, please." He dips and throws me up over his shoulder, and I squeal, shocked.

"Josh!"

"Goodbye, everyone," he calls, slapping my arse as he hauls me to a bedroom. I brace my arms into his lower back and look up through my wet strands, my face flaming. Tammy looks utterly exasperated, and the rest of Josh's team are just laughing to themselves, as if their expression of amusement might be chastised by Josh's publicist. With all eyes on me, I shrug as best I can in my upside-down position and mouth a sorry as I'm carted away. I'm not sorry at all. I've been waiting for this reunion for weeks.

"I don't think Tammy approves," I say to his arse, my feeling palms making the most of their position.

"Fuck Tammy." I'm catapulted onto the bed, the feeling of the luxurious bedding only enhancing the sensation of being back in the clouds. "Fuck the Royals." Josh comes into sight after I've brushed my wet tresses from my face, his T-shirt halfway up his torso. "Fuck the public." It's cast aside, and his stare, weighted with too much longing for me to comprehend, lands on mine. "And now you are going to fuck *me*, Your Highness."

Bang!

That was my heart. And my body. And my mind. Everything, blown. Standing before me is home. The first place in my life where I feel I actually belong. Biting my lip, I watch as Josh slowly strips down until my breath is robbed of me, the unfathomable perfection of him bared. My robe is slowly tugged open, the skin of my stomach delicately stroked.

"Ever wanted something so badly you'd kill for it?" he asks,

helping my arms out of the sleeves. I nod, and Josh smiles, his eyes dragging up my legs to my hips. He kisses the sensitive dip there, smiling through his bite of my flesh. Light pecks journey up my tummy to my boobs, and he strokes my nipples with his tongue in turn. "You have completely derailed me, Adeline. I struggle to think past you."

My body slowly bows, my eyes closing in utter bliss, Josh all over me. It's true. Everything pales when we're together. There are no issues, no problems, nothing to be fixed. It's just us, our feelings, our devotion . . . our love. Fast, solid love. Nothing can break that. It is literally him and me against the world.

I reach for his hair and stroke through his dark strands, pushing my flesh into his mouth. I'm floating on air. As free as I have ever felt. Nothing could rival these feelings. No amount of money and no amount of power. This. This is what life is about. These feelings, the feeling of your soul entwining with another's, melding, blending, coming to together to make one stronger being.

Pushing himself up, Josh rests on his heels, his lips quirked at each corner, a grin being restrained. "Spread 'em, ma'am."

My thighs part in an instant, taking my dignity with them. I couldn't care less, and Josh's suppressed grin breaks, lighting up the room. He drops forward, his palms meeting the soft mattress either side of my head, his face suspended above me. "Good little princess."

Pure contentment makes my heart swell, my smile the widest it's probably ever been. "I've missed you so much." Reaching up to his face, I rest my palm on his cheek, feeling his bristle as he rears back and falls to his forearms, our torsos coming together. His slow sink into me is unimaginably measured. I sigh, sliding my hands over his shoulders, the feeling of completeness overwhelming me. For the first time in my existence, I have a purpose. I have Josh, and I have my dreams that can now be a reality.

Measured movements steal breath after breath, his face so close

to mine that I inhale his exhales. His eyes never waiver from mine, his palms holding my neck as he rocks with painstaking precision into me. "Perfect, huh?" he whispers, bringing our mouths together, our lips resting against each other's.

"Perfect," I say, my hips rolling to meet each plunge. This is slow, purposeful lovemaking, and if there was a word that surpassed perfect, it would be that. Our closeness, our connection, the understanding passing between our locked eyes as he moves above me carefully. Our steady heart rates, our slipping skin, our slow rolling tongues. Everything we are and have in this moment is beyond my wildest imagination. Years of bowing to my father as king has made me somewhat intolerant. Inflexible. I don't need a new lord over me, but I can readily admit that Josh Jameson is my king. Willingly, my king. I can defer to him because I feel secure in his love. His actions speak of adoration and selflessness, and it humbles me to feel I am worthy. I bow to no one except him, and it is easy to do, because I know we will face everything together as equals. He loves me for who I am.

Pressure swirls in my lower tummy, the soft, velvet feel of him stoking me with perfect friction, directing it all south. I hum into his mouth, my fingers curling into the flesh of his shoulders. "Grip harder," he mumbles, moving his hands into my wet hair and fisting, as if demonstrating. I follow his order without question, digging my fingernails into his skin, my kiss beginning to get messy. "That's it." His hips jolt, his control wavering, too. "Jesus, Adeline, how did I survive before you?"

I wonder the same thing, my life seeming so bland before Josh waltzed into it. He bites down harshly on my lip, his control slipping further, and pulls away, bracing his impressive torso on rigid arms. His new position gives him more leverage, and he makes the most of it, abandoning his careful plunges and replacing them with brutal pounds. My hands slap into his forearms to support me, my body absorbing each of his hits on a yell. The twist of gratification on his

face is like nothing else, his mind lost, his need raw. I'm held captive by the sight, forgetting my own need to let the pleasure claim me. Just seeing him so absorbed in the feel of me is pleasurable enough, watching him lose himself so completely. I want to watch him fall apart, see the orgasm rip through him, hear the sounds of him fighting through the intensity. So I focus on Josh alone, forgetting my own physical pleasure and indulging in the exquisite sight of his instead. I marvel at every incredible second of his mission to find the long-overdue release.

His cheeks blow out, his eyes wild as they stare at me. "Go," I order, clawing my nails into his forearms and flexing my hips, taking him to the hilt.

"You," he all but gasps, frantic in his pace.

I shake my head and ensure his temptation to pull back is hindered by moving my hands to his arse and pushing him on. "Go," I demand again.

"Oh, *fuck*, Adeline," he wheezes, clenching his eyes shut, his jaw pulsing.

"Open your eyes, Josh."

They flip open, the blue swimming. "Damn you, woman." His thrusts take on a new level of brutal, and he slams his way home on constant barks, his eyes moving back and forth between my face and my bouncing breasts. I know the moment he tips the edge, the feel of him inside of me thickening and pulsing.

"There it is." I drag my nails over the rise of his glorious arse and his head drops, sweat dripping from his brow, his body slowing. He comes, and it's the most beautiful thing I have ever seen, watching him lose all control of his body, everything limp, his arms buckling so he plummets to my front. Hiding his face in my neck, he fights for breath, his hips involuntarily jerking as he empties himself into me, my internal walls dragging on his twitching cock. I smile and lock him in my arms, not in the least bit unfulfilled. "Welcome home," I whisper, turning my nose into his damp hair and inhaling

him into me completely.

Josh pants, a dead weight spread all over me. My smile widens, my hold tightening. "I love you so much, woman." He tries to kiss my neck. It's feeble. And it only makes me even happier. To know how knocked out he is. To feel him touching me everywhere. To sustain his weight. Just to know how close he is.

"Go to sleep," I say, feeling my own eyes getting heavy.

"I need to see to you." He sounds about ready to do that as I am to release him. Not ready. *Ever*.

I hush him and close my eyes, and it is not long before I hear his soft snoring in my ear.

That's perfect, too.

This is the calm before the storm.

24

WHEN I OPEN my eyes the next morning, it's dusk, a glow from the television illuminating the room. My body is toasty warm, my mind peaceful, and my head is rising and falling in time with Josh's breathing beneath my cheek. The expanse of his chest is before me, my hand resting on his pec, my leg tossed over his thighs. I crane my neck up, finding him looking down at me, his back resting against the headboard. "You comfy down there?" He dips and gives my head a chaste kiss as my limbs start to involuntarily spread, stretching wonderfully.

"Oh, God," I groan, every muscle pulling satisfyingly. "What time is it?"

"Seven." He shuffles down the bed, maneuvering my body as he does until we're on our sides, face to face.

"Why is the television on?"

His lips purse, a grin in hiding. "I heard there's some breaking news on the horizon."

The press release. My tummy flutters, part nerves, part excitement, as my eyes divert from Josh to the television where BBC news is Josh's channel of choice. It's so utterly ridiculous that two

people dating is deemed news worthy. "Do we know when this news might break?"

"I can't imagine it'll be long before the media goes into meltdown." Placing his hand on my naked hip, he flexes his grip, winning back my attention. "You're nervous."

I'm quick to set him straight. "Mostly, I'm excited. Just to know there will be no more sneaking around. I'm not nervous about the reaction of the world, more the retaliation of my family."

Josh smiles, though small and understanding. "We haven't discussed what will happen once the dust settles."

"If it ever settles," I mumble, taking my praying hands and nestling them under my cheek on the pillow.

"It *will* settle." A little squeeze of my hip is a warning to have a little more faith. "And then we need to think about what happens from there."

"What do you mean?"

He rolls his eyes, a little exasperated. "It may have escaped your notice, but I'm not from around these parts."

"Oh," I breathe, feeling a bit silly. The logistics of our relationship haven't cost me a thought, when it really should have cost me plenty. "Well, clearly *you* have thought about it."

"Not stopped," he admits unashamedly.

"And?"

"And I want you in the States with me. Everywhere with me, actually. Wherever I go, I want you by my side."

That sounds just about perfect, even if it is unrealistic. "You realize the logistics of that would be near-on impossible?"

"Why?"

"Because you are you and I am me. Not to mention the fact that I am likely to be stripped of all privileges, and that will include my allowances and security." The consequences of my relationship with Josh don't bother me in the slightest, but it isn't until this moment that I have considered the strain it might have on Josh. The financial

strain especially, because I sure as hell know that protection doesn't come cheap. I roll onto my back, feeling myself deflating.

A low growl rumbles up from his toes, and he's on me quickly, scowling. "Stop that."

"I never—" A firm palm lands over my mouth.

"One more word out of you, you'll regret it." Tilting his head, eyes full of annoyance, he slowly peels his hand away. "Understood?"

"Understood." I'm ready to ask exactly how I might regret it—I need details—but I get distracted by the TV. I hear the mention of the Royals, and Josh must catch it too, because he catapults up, facing the screen. My damn heart is in my throat as I sit up, my hand searching for Josh's to hold. This is it. D-Day, so to speak. The world will know about Josh and me *dating*.

But I frown when the scene on the television registers, the journalist not in a TV studio like I would have expected, but outside instead, in what looks like the English countryside. There are no pictures of me or of Josh. It's the King of England's face displayed in the top right-hand corner of the screen, on the day of his coronation. What's going on?

I sit forward, listening carefully, as the reporter signals behind him. "It's reported that the helicopter experienced a mechanical fault mid-flight and came down in the fields beyond the trees late last night." I frown as the camera zooms in on those trees, panning the far side of the field. "The King was on his way back to London from his royal residence in Scotland." My heart is suddenly a rock in my chest. "He was confirmed dead at the scene."

A violent wail saturates the room, and it takes a few confusing seconds for me to realize where it has come from.

Me.

"Fuckin' hell." Josh grabs me quickly, pushing my shaking body into his chest, shouting above my head. "Tammy!" He gets a robe around me, fastening it loosely before he pulls his boxers on, reclaiming me. "Tammy!"

I can hear the reporter talking still, telling the world that King Alfred is dead. My father is dead. No. No, that can't be. It must be a sick hoax. I wrestle my way out of Josh's hold, my vision hampered by floods of tears. I roughly brush them away, getting to my feet and approaching the television. Josh is behind me quickly, trying to pull my vibrating form back to the bed. I fight him with all I have. "Get off me," I yell, shoving him away.

The camera falls back onto the journalist, his face obviously solemn. "The details are sketchy and the crash site cornered off for a mile in every direction," he goes on. "Not much is clear, only one thing. We've lost our King and the world is in mourning." Shock eats my muscles away, and I drop to my knees before the screen, transfixed by the man who is telling me that my father is dead.

I hear Josh curse from behind me, helpless, and I hear the door fly open. I cast my bleary gaze across the room, where Tammy has a laptop in her arms, a disturbed look on her face. "Prince John was on board, too."

"Oh, Jesus." Josh's hands go to his hair, and my eyes fall to my lap, darting chaotically. "He can't have been," I choke quietly, trying to straighten out my tangled head. Think clearly. "No, it can't be."

Josh joins me on the floor, taking my hands and feeling. "Adeline?"

"John couldn't have been on the flight," I say again, this time clearer, looking across to Tammy. "The Monarch and the Heir Apparent never travel together. For this exact reason." My hand shoots to the television, though I can't bring myself to look. "My father would never have broken age-old rules. He was a stickler for rules." Never would the King have let John travel with him. I just know he wouldn't.

Tammy shakes her head, as if she doesn't know what to say. "I'm just telling you what my source has told me."

"Your source must be wrong." I stand, and it takes me a while, my legs like jelly. "What if everyone is wrong?" This time, I do look

at the TV, and I wish I hadn't. There's an aerial view of a field, the crumpled remains of the royal helicopter scattered over every square meter of it. "Oh my God." I'm pulled back, my face forced away from the TV. "I need my phone," I demand, heading for Tammy. "I need to call Damon."

"I turned it off in case they were tracking you." She pulls it from her pocket quickly, and once I've wrestled with my trembling hands to switch it on, I see the dozens and dozens of missed calls from Damon, Davenport, even my mother. And I know that the nightmare behind me being broadcasted to every country in the world is true. My hands shake as I fight to unlock the screen, and when I eventually dial Damon, he answers with it barely ringing. The tone of his voice is like I have never heard before. Anxious. It adds credence to the reported news. "Adeline, where are you?"

Emotion tightens my throat. "Tell me they're wrong," I sob, feeling Josh close behind me, ready to catch me when my fears are confirmed. "Tell me there's been a massive mistake."

"I can't," Damon breathes, and I fold, agony ripping me in two, my cries wretched and broken. I can't keep hold of the phone, can't keep myself upright. My landing is softened by Josh, and he finds my mobile, taking over the call.

"Damon, it's Josh." He uses his free arm to pull my jerking body onto his lap, and I make myself as small as I can in his chest, my mind muddled, my devastation growing. "And John?" he asks, following it up with a curse.

"No," I cry, pushing my face into Josh's chest, like I can disappear into my heaven and escape this hell. His hand is on the back of my head, holding, stroking, trying to comfort me.

"I'll bring her back now," Josh says, all kinds of unease in his voice. "You need to prepare for her arrival . . . Yes . . . Good." He hangs up, but he doesn't move, keeping us on the floor, holding me. "I need to take you back to Claringdon, baby."

"This is all my fault." Regret and guilt tear through me,

destroying everything in their path. Destroying *me*.

"No," Josh snaps. "Don't you start talking like that, Adeline." He forces me from his body, looking fuming mad, but his hands in contrast stroke my face softly. "You didn't tell him to follow you to Scotland. You didn't tell him to chase you back to London."

My chin trembles uncontrollably. "I need to see my mum. And Eddie. I need to see Eddie."

"I'm taking you back now." He looks past me to Tammy, giving her a sharp nod. "It'll be chaos outside the palace. The Met are controlling the growing crowds and Damon is sending a few more cars to escort us."

"Got it."

"The press release?"

"I stalled." Tammy doesn't sound apologetic. "I . . . I wanted to make sure you were as sure this morning."

Josh breathes out, obviously relieved. "Adeline." He coaxes me out of his lap gently. "You need to dress, baby. I'm taking you home."

I don't have the will or inclination to make myself look half decent. So Josh is forced to dress me himself, while I try to wrap my mind around what is happening.

I can't.

This can't be real.

25

THE BLACKED-OUT WINDOWS are the only thing between Josh and me and the rest of the world. Swarms of people—bystanders, journalists, news networks from across the world—are camping outside Claringdon, the police presence the most prolific I have ever known.

Our convoy is forced to a crawl as we near the gates, a police motorcycle leading the way. Everything is a blur. Sound, movements, sights. I feel like I'm floating on the outside looking in on the carnage. Lights flash, people shout. There are even officers manhandling people out of our path. The palace beyond the gold railings and gates looks gloomy, the usual glittering golden detail dull. The flags are at half-mast, every curtain at the dozens and dozens of windows drawn. My limp hand in Josh's is squeezed tightly, though I am unable to acknowledge his gesture, not with a return flex of my hand, nor by looking at him, when I know he is looking at me. I haven't spoken a word since we were chaperoned from the apartment. All I can hear are the reporter's haunting words. All I can see is the helicopter in a million broken pieces scattered across a field. More tears tumble, more desolation and guilt attacks me.

What have I done?

We're driven through the archways to the rear entrance of the palace to avoid the prying eyes of the crowds out front, and when I'm helped from the car, I look to the sky, seeing helicopters circling the airspace, more cameras giving the world the pictures and footage they're hungry for. We're center stage. The most anticipated production.

An arm is placed around my shoulders, and I'm hurried into the palace. I don't realize it's Josh who has hold of me until I'm through the doors and the buzz of talking dies, my father's advisors falling silent and gawking at my companion like the impostor they believe he is. Looks of judgment, eyes full of shock. It all has me finding Josh's hand and holding it like my life depends on it as Sir Don and David Sampson stare on. They look like they have just arrived back at Claringdon themselves, still in their coats. "You weren't on the flight." I say quietly.

"His Highness left rather abruptly." The spite in David's words cut me in two, and I look away, silence falling.

"Your Highness." Davenport is the first to break the uncomfortable quiet, moving in and bowing his head in respect. "My deepest condolences."

His offer of sympathy is another confirmation that I am not in a horrific dream. "My mother?"

"The Queen Consort is in the Claret Lounge, ma'am. She's awaiting your arrival."

I cast my eyes across to David and Sir Don. They're statues, judging me. It's not intentional, but I again let my gaze drop to the glimmering marble floor, shame getting the better of me. They know this is entirely my fault.

I move toward the lounge in a haze of desolation, bracing myself to face my mother. Josh is by my side, his thumb working circles over my skin where our hands are held. The doors to the lounge are closed, though the grief within the room is so strong it's seeping

through the thick wood and sinking into my skin. I reach for the handle and pull back when another hand finds it first. Flicking my eyes upward, I find Davenport with his signature cold, stoic expression. "I believe Mr. Jameson would like a cup of tea," he tells me as diplomatically as he can, and I look at Josh, knowing he will have caught the Major's not-so subtle hint.

Josh throws a mild scowl toward Davenport before he centers his attention on me, taking both of my hands and turning into me. "You need to be with your family," he says, and I open my mouth to object, needing him with me. Needing him to stay close and catch me when I fall, because I know I will. But he places a soft finger over my lips, hushing me. "I won't go anywhere."

Maybe so, but that won't stop them from making him go. I scope my surroundings for Damon, locating him only a few feet away, behind David and Sir Don. He gives me a mild smile and a thumbs up, his way of telling me Josh will be safe while I am gone. I believe him. I nod and draw breath, as Josh dips and pushes his lips to my cheek. "I love you," he whispers quietly, only for me to hear, and I nod when he leaves me to hold myself up.

Once Josh is gone, Davenport opens the door, and the grief that was being partly contained within the four walls of the Claret Lounge spills out, so potent it could take me from my feet. I hear Helen first, her sobs uncontrolled and loud. And I see my mother sitting on one of the couches, staring ahead at nothing, while Uncle Phillip helps Aunt Victoria pour tea, no maids or footmen in sight. Uncle Stephan is here too, looking grave standing by the fireplace, his wife by his side, and Matilda is in a chair by the window, her face damp and blotchy. She's the first one to notice me, her eyes lifting, her face softening. Then the door shuts behind me and the rest of the room all look up. All eyes on me. I swallow and step forward on unstable legs, as my mother struggles to her feet with the help of Uncle Stephen who rushes to help her. I've never seen the Queen Consort looking anything less than pristine. Now, she

looks washed out. Weak. Vulnerable.

I try to keep my emotions contained, if only to appear strong for my mother, but it all wants out and there is nothing I can do to fight it back. I choke, going to my mother's open arms and burying myself there, hiding, feeling her warmth, our trembling bodies merging and shaking us to our very centers. "I'm so sorry," I sob into her neck, wetting her skin with my relentless flow of tears. She says nothing, no words of comfort and no reassurance, and despite the fact she's holding me, it tears me apart.

I gently break away to find her face, and when I do, she holds my cheek, thoughtful and quiet. I clench her hand, silently begging that she won't hold me responsible. When she finally speaks, it's with the softest tone she is famous for, though I hate what she says. "Where have you been?"

I shake my head, remorse churning my insides. She doesn't know? "I'm here now."

"Lucky us," Uncle Phillip mutters, claiming the attention of everyone in the room, including me. His eyes, full of disdain, are firmly rooted on me. "If you had not scarpered to Scotland, the King would not have either. We wouldn't all be standing here, the family devastated, the country shocked." He flings a deranged arm in the air, snorting his disgust. "I hope you're happy. Your insolence has lost us our King."

I feel my mother's hand squeeze mine, though she doesn't retaliate, and I shrink, knowing I deserve his wrath.

"My husband is dead because of you," Helen wails, and I close my eyes, Mother's hand tightening further still. "All you had to do was marry, you spoilt, self-important little bitch."

"Please." Uncle Stephen jumps to my defense, the only person who I know will. "That's enough."

"Please leave us," Mother demands, casting her watery gaze around the room. "I would like a moment with my daughter." No one argues with the Queen Consort, everyone immediately leaving

the room quietly. "You can stay, Helen."

Helen stops and looks over her shoulder, confusion evident on her face. She waits until everyone is gone before she turns to face my mother. "Catherine?"

My mother's head tilts, thoughtful, and Helen's confusion turns into worry. "I know, Helen," Mother says. "I know your little secret."

What?

Helen rushes across the room to us, noticeably panicked. "Catherine, please." Her hands, full of crumpled tissues, grab my mother and turn her away from me. Instinct has me intervening, not liking the force being used by my sister-in-law, whether she's grieving the loss of her husband or not.

"Helen," I yell, pushing her away, yet she pays no attention to me, muscling me out of the way to get to my mother.

"Catherine, I beg you. Please."

My mother's face gives nothing away, her eyes taking in her frantic daughter-in-law as she begs and pleads.

"What's going on?" I ask, my attention bouncing between the two women, one bordering deranged, one completely impassive.

"Nothing," Helen snaps, shoving me away. "Nothing's going on." Her eyes bore into my mother, something definitely passing between them. What?

I seize my mother, taking her from Helen's clutches to pull her away, staggered when my sister-in-law fights with me. "Helen, get off," I shout, wrestling her off Mother, her motionless form being pulled back and forth between us.

"Enough," Mother yells, startling me into stillness, as well as Helen. She points a fire-filled, angry glare at her son's pregnant wife, who cowers, her head shaking, as if in denial. Then Mother casts her eyes to me, eyes that are usually soft and friendly, but are now hard and determined. She points to Helen's midriff, prompting Helen to cover it with her palms protectively. "That baby is not your brother's."

My mouth falls open in utter disbelief, my eyes flying to Helen's. She crumples, defeated, and starts sobbing again. "What?" I know I heard right, but shock has taken my ability to string a sentence together.

"Catherine." Helen sniffs, backing away. "Please don't."

Mother, stone cold, wanders away and takes a seat on the couch. "What do you think is going to happen, Helen? Your unborn child takes the throne? It's inconceivable." Cold eyes find a wilting Helen, while I stand, motionless, trying to allow this bombshell to sink in. "I remained quiet, but did you think I didn't know? You might have fooled the King, but you most certainly did not fool me. Eight years trying to conceive and nothing. And now by some miracle, you're pregnant?" She laughs coldly. "The only question I have for you now, dear daughter-in-law, is who is the father? Because I sure as hell know it isn't my son."

Hearing my mother say the word *hell* is alarming, a show of her anger, even if she's speaking void of emotion. I watch, rapt, unable to comprehend what I am hearing, as Helen backs away, tears streaming. "Catherine—"

"The throne belongs to my children. You are neither my child, nor is that baby you are carrying my grandchild."

"I was desperate," Helen blurts, her words only just audible through her broken voice. "Our future hung on it. The pressure from the King was getting too much."

"I don't doubt it for a moment." Mother turns away from her daughter-in-law, as I unravel what I'm learning. As far as the world is concerned, with John gone, Helen's unborn child is now the King or Queen of England, and a Regent would be carefully selected to reign in its name until they come of age. But we are not in the sixteenth century anymore. Not that it matters, since Mother has just revealed the shocker news that Helen's baby is illegitimate.

"I'll be banished," Helen whimpers. "I'll have nothing. I'll be hated. Please, Catherine."

"The only people who know of your betrayal are Sir Don, David Sampson, and us in this room." Mother looks to me and then Helen. "I plan on keeping it that way. So we will avoid the scandal by bypassing my unborn *grandchild*. This is the twenty-first century. A child ruler would be ridiculed by the public. Laughed at. The monarchy is already under enough fire without giving the haters ammunition to shoot us down even more."

What my mother's saying suddenly hits home. Bypass the next in line? Bypass Helen's unborn child? "Where's Eddie?" I ask, my hand reaching for my neck, feeling his suffocation as if it is my own. If the crown is bypassing Helen's unborn child, then it will be landing on Eddie's head. "Mother, does he know?"

"He knows," she sighs.

My worry amplifies by a million. My God, he'll be devastated. He wanted the crown as much as me.

Not at all.

"So where is he?" The urgency coursing through me is increasing by the second, my need to get to my brother making me panic. He will hate this. I need to find him. Comfort him. "Mother," I yell, losing my patience. Her reluctance to answer me is positively maddening.

She looks across to me, and I see the sorrow on her face. Sorrow for the burden of the crown now passing over to our beloved Eddie. "Helen, leave us," the Queen Consort demands, and that's all it takes for my sister-in-law to run out, sobbing uncontrollably as she goes. I have no sympathy for her. That's all reserved for Eddie now. As soon as the door closes, Mother is up and across the room to me, but I instinctively back away, not liking her change in persona, from the unfamiliar harshness, back to her soft and pacifying approach. "Adeline." She reaches for my hands, and I pull them back, wary, backing up more.

"Where's Eddie?" I ask, my jaw tight. "Tell me, Mother."

Her shoulders drop, defeated. "I don't know. He ran out."

"This is madness," I yell, heading for the door. I should be grieving the loss of my father and brother, and instead we're dealing with lies and betrayal, fighting our way through the poisonous web that is my family.

"Adeline, wait."

I ignore my mother for the first time in my life, swinging the door open, on a mission to find Eddie. He can't have left the grounds; no one is coming in or out, so he must be here somewhere. I head for the library, catching Davenport's anxious stare as I pick up my pace. Not even Josh stops me when he appears ahead, obviously hearing the commotion, Damon behind him. "Have you seen Eddie?" I ask, not slowing my rushed steps, passing them all and entering the library.

"Not since we returned," Damon confirms, hot on my heels.

"What's going on, Adeline?" Josh joins my side, not attempting to slow or stop me, but demanding in his question.

"I need to find Eddie. John's unborn child is being bypassed, which means Eddie is now King. He doesn't want to be King. I need to find him."

"Oh Jesus," Josh breathes, looking back at Damon. "Any ideas?"

"The maze." It comes to me as I push my way out of the doors into the gardens of Claringdon. It's where he always hid as a child, the place farthest from the stifling palace as we could get as children. Adrenalin pumps through my veins as I race toward the back of the grounds and weave my way into the center of the maze with efficiency.

And when I emerge into the clearing, I see him. On his arse, back against the shins of our grandfather, a bottle of whisky in his hand. His green beret by his thigh, his eyes closed, his head limp and dropped. "Eddie." I rush to him, kneeling by his slumped form. The smell of Scotch hits my nostrils, strong and pure.

His heavy head lifts, his eyes barely open. He's wasted, a sorry state. "Sister," he slurs, a disorientated arm feeling for me. "What

a pleasant surprise."

I sigh, thinking today has been too much for everyone. How much more can we take? But I must prioritize the troubles that have been rained down on us relentlessly. Eddie is my priority right now. I look back when I hear the sound of heavy steps, finding Damon and Josh have found their way to me. I shake my head at them both when they find me on the floor with my wasted brother, telling them to leave us be. Both men back off, and I return my attention to Eddie.

"Have you heard?" He looks at me, one eye closed, struggling to focus. "Have you heard what a fucking joke our family is?"

I sigh, taking the whisky from his hand. "I've heard."

"Give me that back." Eddie reclaims it on a snarl, swiping it from my hand viciously and tipping the bottle back. As he swallows down too much liquor, he looks past me, his snarl taking on a new edge of ominous. It's a look on my brother that I'm not used to at all, not from the famously happy-go-lucky prince. "Oh, goody. Mother's here."

I look over my shoulder, seeing the Queen Consort, breathless, her even olive skin tinged pink. *She ran here?* Giving my brother the benefit of the doubt, I refrain from scorning him for his disrespect, not because the woman to which he's referring is the Queen Consort, but our mother, too. He's angry, and I completely understand. "Eddie, the news is a shock, but how do you think getting yourself mindlessly drunk will help?"

He looks at me, his brow knitted in confusion. Then the line creasing his forehead smooths out, and his head retracts slightly on his neck. "You don't know? Oh, baby sister, there is far more scandal for you to learn."

"Eddie," Mother warns, the volume of her voice telling me she's closer. "Not here."

"If you don't tell her, I will," he slurs, waving his bottle in the air before slugging down another healthy dose.

I look at my mother in question, knowing I'm missing something. Again. But equally worrying is that my mother seems to be in the know of everything. She turns to Damon and Josh. "Leave us."

I can't even wonder what she's thinking about Josh's presence and what she thinks that might mean for me. Josh steps forward to object, but is stopped by Damon. "We should give Her Royal Highness some privacy with her children," Damon says quietly as Josh looks at me for confirmation. I smile when I see his thumb hovering between up and down.

"I'll be fine," I assure him. "Wait in the library."

Eddie starts laughing abruptly, a proper belly laugh. I have no idea what he's finding so funny, putting it down to his inebriated state. "Say goodbye, Mr. Hollywood," he chuckles.

"Edward, stop it," I scorn him, not liking the menacing look ghosting across Josh's face. I'm sure if it wasn't for Damon gently coaxing him out of the maze, Josh would now be on Eddie slapping some sense and respect into him. "What is all this about?" I demand.

Mother's eyes clench shut, and Eddie carries on with his deranged laughter. "Go on, Mother. Tell her."

"The letters," she breathes. "The ones you heard your father speaking of." There was no need for the extra clarification. Just the mention of the letters was all I needed.

"What about them?" I wobble a little on my knees when Eddie gets up, catching my arm to steady himself on the way.

"They were letters between two lovers," Eddie declares, loud and proud.

I'm on my feet far quicker than he is, confused. "Who?"

"Why, our mother, of course," Eddie laughs, staggering back a little, forcing me to catch him before he tumbles into the statue behind him.

My confusion only triples. "Mother?"

"Yes!" Eddie sings, as if it's something to celebrate. "And Major Davenport."

I drop him and whirl around to find my mother. "What?"

Her head is low, ashamed, her usually perfect posture visibly lax. "It is true."

"You had an affair with Major Davenport?" That stoic, cold arsehole? My father's private secretary?

She breathes in, eyes closing. "Yes."

I feel like all air has been beaten out of me. "Father knew," I say, sharing what I know, since I heard him speaking of the letters he didn't want falling into the wrong hands. "He knew, and he kept Davenport here?"

"Punishment." My mother levels a surprisingly steady look on me. "Your father was a cruel man, Adeline."

It all becomes so clear in this moment. The distance my mother kept from Davenport. The softness I saw in him recently with her. The looks being exchanged, his face softening only when he regarded the Queen Consort. "He loves you."

She doesn't answer me, only looks at me, her mask back in place. "Your father put an end to it many years ago."

"Oh my God." I reach for the statue, searching for something to hold me up.

"Oh, you've heard nothing yet, sister." Eddie laughs, wobbling his way over to me. He dips to get his eyes level with mine, swaying terribly. His breath is pure liquor. "This love affair between the major and our mother started in 1981." One eye closes, as if he's trying to figure something out. "The King put a stop to it in 1985." His head cocks a little, waiting for what he has just told me to click.

The possibility hits me like a brick. "You were born in 1986," I whisper, throwing my eyes onto my mother. "No," I breathe, struggling to find oxygen.

"Yes!" Eddie cheers, turning haphazardly on the spot. "That stuck-up arsehole is my father." He laughs hysterically. "So all this time I've been forced to endure this ridiculous fucking family, and I didn't even belong here."

"Edward, please." Mother comes forward, eyes begging. "Don't be like this. You do belong here."

"All these years I could have done what I fucking well liked."

My heart bleeds for him, my struck state struggling to fathom who needs my comfort most. Both my mother and brother look broken. "I'm so sorry, Eddie," I say, at a loss.

He scoffs, slinging his arm around our mother's shoulders. "Don't be sorry. I'm fucking delighted. It's you I feel sorry for."

"Why?" I ask the question before my battered head can think to straighten itself out.

"Well, you understand what this means, don't you?" Eddie asks, performing an over-the-top bow, nearly falling to the ground in the process. "Your Majesty."

I freeze, realization dawning on me through the grief and shock that has been dealt today. The world disappears from under my feet, everything spinning out of control around me. "No." I step back and collide with the statue of my grandfather, jarring my shoulder. But I don't feel any pain. I'm numb. This can't be happening.

My attention is caught when I look up and find Josh. He never left. His face, distorted with pain, tells me he too has grasped what this means.

"I'm Queen," I murmur, so quietly, like if no one hears me, it can't possibly be true. It can't be true. *It can't be, it can't be. It can't be true!*

Yet it is true. Painful as it is, I know it's true.

"I am the Queen of England," I say again, my voice cracking, my eyes welling as I watch Josh backing away, as if he can escape the truth, too.

"No." He shakes his head violently. "No, Adeline, no!" His hands find his hair, gripping hard as my tears tumble.

It's a cruel turn of events, probably the cruelest, and it has nothing to do with the crown I hate so much and what comes with it—the pressure, the commitment, the life-long burden.

It's the one thing that *won't* come with it.
The one thing I can't be without.
My American Boy.

THE END

ACKNOWLEDGMENTS

THIS HAS BEEN a long time coming for me. A book a year, and now two in the space of a few months. Honestly, I still feel like I have not one clue what I'm doing here, but I do know that being a part of this romance gig makes me smile hard every single day.

To my agent, Andrea Barzvi, thank you for joining me on this new venture back into the self-publishing world. It's been scary, but you, as always, make everything so much easier to handle. Your advice and guidance has never failed me. I'm forever grateful.

Nina Grinstead. I still hate tequila, but I'd drink it for you. I feel like us finding each other has been waiting to happen for years. Now, I truly do not know what I would do without you. You have lightened my life a little bit more by being in it. And I love our Facetime calls when I can marvel at your hair each morning.

To my amazing publisher, Grand Central, thank you for your encouragement and support. You'll never know how much it means to have your backing.

Sian Lewis, carry on being wonderful. And thank you for your constant pestering messages.

Marion, thank you for making this process pretty pain free! You know I was nervous. I didn't need to be.

To Bongo, Lisa P, Patty, Lisa S, Nicky, and all the girls who help run the fan pages, I'm forever indebted to you for holding things up for me! You are a truly amazing group of girls, all genuine and real. We miss Sara in the gang, but I know she'd be super proud of all of you for keeping it real. And funny. And sometimes downright filthy.

And to all of my readers, thank you for being a part of my world. I hope you stick around for a long time to come.

JEM x

ABOUT THE AUTHOR

JODI ELLEN MALPAS was born and raised in the Midlands town of Northampton, England, where she lives with her two boys and a beagle. She is a self-professed daydreamer, a Converse and mojito addict, and has a terrible weak spot for alpha males. Writing powerful love stories and creating addictive characters have become her passion—a passion she now shares with her devoted readers. She's a proud #1 New York Times bestselling author, and seven of her published novels were New York Times bestsellers, in addition to being international and Sunday Times bestsellers. Her work is published in more than twenty-three languages across the world.

You can learn more at:
www.jodiellenmalpas.co.uk

Follow Jodi:
Twitter @JodiEllenMalpas
Facebook.com/JodiEllenMalpas
Instagram Jodi_Ellen_Malpas

THIS MAN NOVELS

No other man compares . . .

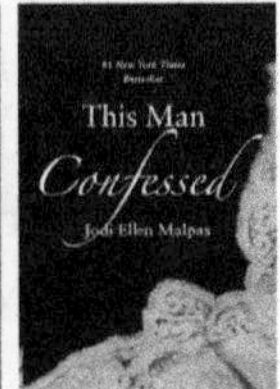

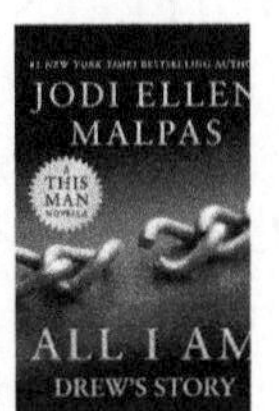

ONE NIGHT SERIES

Meet the mysterious, masterful M . . .

THE SIZZLING STAND-ALONE NOVELS

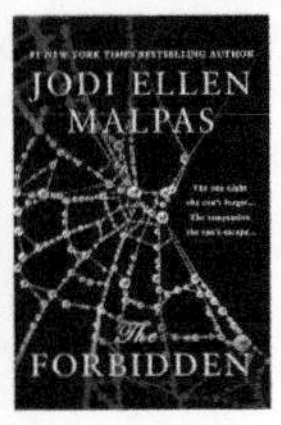

CPSIA information can be obtained
at www.ICGtesting.com
Printed in the USA
BVHW08s2051080618
518343BV00002B/3/P